COLOPHONS OF ARMENIAN MANUSCRIPTS, 1301–1480

A Source for Middle Eastern History

Harvard Armenian Texts and Studies, 2

COLOPHONS OF ARMENIAN MANUSCRIPTS, 1301–1480

A Source for Middle Eastern History

Selected, Translated, and Annotated

by Avedis K. Sanjian

Harvard University Press, Cambridge, Massachusetts

1969

Distributed in Great Britain by Oxford University Press, London
Library of Congress Catalog Card Number 69–18044
SBN 674-14285-3
Made and printed in Great Britain
by William Clowes and Sons,
Limited, London and Beccles

TO MY SON GREGORY

Preface

The authors of the Armenian colophons developed a unique tradition in that they did not confine themselves to brief statements concerning the circumstances of the production of individual manuscripts. In the process of providing these essential data, they also recorded contemporary information on a broad range of subjects which are of great interest to Armenological research. They also provided eyewitness or contemporary accounts of historical events which transpired during the production of the manuscripts. In view of these, the colophons emerge—alongside the Armenian historical works, the chronicles, and the inscriptions—as important primary sources for the history not only of Armenia but also of the entire Middle East. Armenia never emerged as a first-rate power in Middle Eastern history and its territory remained small, but its geographical position afforded Armenian writers a close view of major world events. While narrating the history of their own country, Armenian authors also give us a great deal of information, often otherwise unknown, on the affairs of the oriental world. This is especially true of the Armenian colophons, which were written by scribes in localities extending from Central Asia and Iran on the east to Constantinople and Europe on the west, and from the Crimea and the Caucasus on the north to Egypt on the south. Although the historical information contained in the colophons are for the most part local in nature, many provide data that are broader in scope and therefore of interest to those concerned with major Middle Eastern developments.

The writing of colophons in Armenian manuscripts is a tradition which goes back to the inception of Armenian literature in the beginning of the fifth century after Christ. These colophons were written, as a rule, by the scribes upon the conclusion of the production of a manuscript. Occasionally, they were written at the end of long sections of a text; there are also brief colophons which appear on the margins. There are manuscripts which, in addition to the principal colophon written by the scribe, also contain colophons written by the commissioner or sponsor, by the artist who executed the ornamentation or illumination, and by the craftsman who did the binding.

Finally, we find in many manuscripts a series of other colophons written by their subsequent recipients and rebinders or restorers. All of these provide, in a sense, the "biography" of individual manuscripts. Such colophons continued to be written as late as the seventeenth and eighteenth centuries, or until the manuscripts found their way to a library or museum, thus bringing to an end their centuries-long peregrination.

The utilization of the Armenian colophons as primary sources for historical research is not a recent development. As early as the thirteenth century, the Armenian historian Step'anos Ōrbelean relied, among other sources, upon the colophons for the composition of his *Patmut'iwn Nahangin Sisakan* (History of the Province of Siwnik'). In the seventeenth century, the historian Aṙak'el Davrižec'i used the colophons in compiling his *Patmut'iwn* (History), particularly in the preparation of the first chronology of the catholicoses of the Armenian church. Mik'ayēl Č'amč'ean, an eighteenth-century Mekhitarist monk of Venice, used a large number of colophons in the composition of his three-volume monumental *Patmut'iwn Hayoc'* (History of Armenia), especially the sections that deal with the history of the Armenian church and the struggles among the Muslim rulers of Armenia. The nineteenth century eminent and prolific scholar Łewond M. Ališan drew largely upon the colophons in the preparation of his historical, demographic, and topographical studies. Garegin Zarbhanalean's works on the history of Armenian literature benefited a great deal from the utilization of Armenian colophons. A number of monographs on medieval Armenian feudal families prepared by the late Catholicos Garegin I Yovsēp'ean were based largely upon information which he found in the colophons. However, none of these scholars nor others who used these resources had access to all the colophons to be found in the widely dispersed collections of Armenian manuscripts. Indeed, it was only after the publication of the catalogs of Armenian manuscripts, which began in earnest toward the end of the nineteenth century, that the utilization of the colophons for historical research acquired unprecedented proportions. Since close to half of the extant Armenian manuscripts are now housed in the Matenadaran (Library of Manuscripts) in Erevan, Soviet Armenian scholars have had direct access to the largest fund of documents. This is reflected in the use of colophons in the preparation of the large number of monographs on various Armenological subjects which have appeared in recent years.

The present volume is a collection of historical texts excerpted—and translated for the first time—from the colophons of Armenian manuscripts copied in the years 1301–1480. This work was prompted by the consideration that these hitherto inaccessible and therefore untapped documents have been generally unknown to Western scholars as primary sources for Middle Eastern historical research. For the most part, the texts have been drawn from the three volumes of colophons compiled and published between 1950 and 1958 by Dr. L. S. Xač'ikyan, Director of the Matenadaran in Erevan. I have limited my collection to the period covered by Xač'ikyan's three volumes simply to permit an unbroken chronological sequence. The collection of colophons published by the late Catholicos Garegin I Yovsēp'ean covered the period from the fifth century to the year 1250; Xač'ikyan's three volumes begin with the texts written in the year 1301—thus leaving a gap for the years 1251–1300. It should be noted, parenthetically, that Xač'ikyan and his associates are currently preparing for publication the colophons written prior to 1301, as well as those written subsequent to the year 1480.

In the introduction to his collection, Garegin I Yovsēp'ean asserts that "these brief colophons, with the multifarious bits of information which they contain, are like multicolored mosaic pebbles from which the artist, selecting and utilizing whatever he needs for the accomplishment of his purpose, creates a colorful, vivid, and aesthetic picture." Western historians of the Middle East will find in the present volume a vast amount of information on the ruling dynasties which dotted the map of the area in the fourteenth and fifteenth centuries. These data concern the Seljuks of Asia Minor; the Mamluks of Syria and Egypt; the Mongol Ilkhans of Persia, and the breakdown of their empire following the death of Abū Sa'īd Khān in 1335, as well as the successor dynasties. There is also considerable information on the Golden Horde and the White Horde, and the Tatar kingdom in the Crimea (Girāy) and Kazan; the Djalā'irid dynasty founded by Shaykh Ḥasan Buzurg in Mesopotamia; the Čaghatai of Transoxiana and the Khwārizmī, both in Central Asia; the Shīrwānshāh of Shīrwān, the Ḳaramānids of Ḳaramān; the Ḳara-Ḳoyunlu and the Aḳ-Ḳoyunlu federation of Turkoman tribes, the first in Persia and Mesopotamia and the second in the region of Diyarbakir, as well as their mutual struggles for power; the Dhu'l-Ḳadrid Turkoman dynasty which ruled for nearly two centuries (1337–1522) the region of Marash-Malatya, as clients first of the Mamluk and later of the Ottoman sultans; and the Čūbānid dynasty of Mongol amirs in Asia Minor. There is also a vast amount of information on the conquests of Tīmūr Lang (Tamerlane) and his successors, the Tīmūrids; the Ottoman rulers of Asia Minor; and the Kurdish principalities or amirates of Bitlīs, Khizān, Khilāṭ, Ardjīsh, Wusṭān, and Hakkārī, including data on the Shambo and Rūzagī Kurdish tribes. The colophons also supply ample data on the effects upon Georgia and Caucasian Albania of the various invasions, as well as information on the Armenian Kingdom of Cilicia until its fall at the hands of the Mamluks in 1375, and on the various Armenian princely families and their feudal domains, which had survived under the suzerainty of various Mongol and other Muslim dynasties. Finally, I have incorporated in this volume two contemporary Armenian "Elegies" on the fall of Constantinople at the hands of the Ottomans in 1453, which are rendered into English for the first time from the critical editions published by H. S. Anasyan at Erevan in 1957 under the title: *Haykakan Ałbyurnerə Byuzandiayi Ankman Masin* (The Armenian Sources on the Fall of Byzantium).

The authors of the colophons—like the Armenian historians and chroniclers—employed a large variety of Armenian as well as non-Armenian calendrical systems. The most important among these was the so-called Great Armenian Era, whose starting point was A.D. 552; hence, in order to convert to the current Christian era, the figure 551 must be added to the date given in the Armenian era. This is the system on which Xačʻikyan has based the chronological sequence of the colophons, and the same system has been followed in the preparation of this volume.

The Armenian historians, who in the main represented the ideology and interests of the ruling classes and the ecclesiastical institution, do not generally give a complete picture of the events which occurred during their own time, since they were primarily concerned with political and religious developments. Even within these limits, certain periods of Armenian history have not had their historians, notably the period from the fourteenth to the beginning of the seventeenth century. In contrast to the historical works and the chronicles, the colophons were written either by eyewitnesses or individuals contemporary of the events which they described. Hence, from the standpoint of factual authenticity and chronological accuracy, the colophons are more reliable than the works of the historians who wrote about the same events decades or even centuries later. The colophons frequently complement information contained in the historical sources and the chronicles, and some even provide data not found in other sources. Indeed, the colophons are the most important primary sources for the history of Armenia during the decline of the Mongol Ilkhanid rule, the emergence of the Ḳara-Ḳoyunlu and the Aḳ-Ḳoyunlu Turkoman dynasties, and the rivalry between the Ottoman

Turks and Persia for control of Armenia. Even in the case of periods for which Armenian histories and chronicles exist, the details provided in the colophons frequently elucidate chronological and other problems; they also supply data regarding the internal developments in Armenia, as well as information on the cultural and intellectual activities of the local institutions, about which the historians have generally been silent. Moreover, the colophons are often written with such intimacy and frankness that a great deal can be learned from them about contemporary conditions.

In the main, the scribes of the fourteenth and fifteenth centuries belonged to the lower classes of Armenian society, especially the lower clergy; hence, the colophons which they wrote contain data respecting the conditions of the populace, as well as the prevailing social and economic circumstances, subjects which generally were either ignored by or escaped the attention of the medieval Armenian historians. Besides describing major political events of general or local interest, the scribes give accounts of the frequent epidemics and plagues, the famines and devastation caused by locusts, earthquakes, and other natural calamities. These documents also furnish information on the systems of taxation imposed by various rulers; the effects of the constant invasions, marauding, and banditry upon trade and the economy in general; the monetary currencies that were employed in different parts of the Middle East; the condition of the arts and crafts, and the manufacture of goods. The texts also contain extensive data on the towns, villages, monasteries, and fortresses, as well as on the administration of rural communities and the management of arable lands. As a large proportion of this information is absent from the historical works and chronicles, the colophons assume greater significance as primary sources. It should be pointed out that only a small fraction of the abundant data on these subjects appears in the present volume. The full utilization of these aspects of the documents must, of course, await the preparation of separate monographs.

With rare exceptions, the colophons were written by professional scribes with limited education. They generally tried to emulate the language and style of the classical period of Armenian literature, but few indeed achieved this goal. As a matter of fact, the colophons are replete with dialectal forms, including a considerable number of foreign terms of which only a few have become part of the Armenian literary vocabulary. In view of this, the colophons are of great interest to those concerned with the historical development of the Armenian language, as well as with Middle Eastern linguistics and philology. Although the majority of the colophons were written in prose, a substantial number are in verse; in either event, relatively few are distinguished as works of literary art.

The colophons are also important for the study of Middle Eastern demography and topography. The texts contain data not only on the Mongols, Tatars, Turkomans, and other well-known Muslim ruling dynasties, but also on various smaller tribes, not all of which have been identified. The documents mention place names which are not found in historical works and the chronicles, and which are being made available to students of Middle Eastern topography for the first time. Many of these names appear in the texts in their ancient or medieval Armenian forms; this applies in particular to the large geographical units such as the provinces, districts, and cantons.

As primary sources, the colophons present certain limitations. In their characteristic features, they evidence a general uniformity of style and content; deviations from the stereotyped forms occur only in the recounting of contemporary events and in descriptions of social and economic conditions. With rare exceptions, these accounts are cryptic both in style and content. This can be explained by the fact that the authors of the colophons were not writing histories; rather, they were merely recording the bare facts, as they saw them, concerning significant events which occurred during the course of the production of the manuscripts—facts which they felt must be preserved for the information of future generations. Unlike the Armenian historians, the perspective of the authors of the colophons was very narrow. On the whole, they were interested in only those major political, military, and other developments that affected their immediate environments. The scribes lacked the capacity to relate chains of events to the larger developments that transpired in the Middle East.

Other limitations of the colophons include the general tendency to overdramatize and exaggerate. And, in consonance with the prevailing religious and moral concepts, the scribes, not unlike the historians, ascribed almost every calamity—invasions, plunders, captivity, and natural disasters—to the wrath of God as a punishment for the manifold sins of man, and to the wicked machinations of Satan. This, as well as the milieu in which the scribes lived, explains to a large extent the overabundance of biblical quotations, references, or parallelisms in the colophons. Such references were also employed by the authors of the colophons as a stylistic device to underscore the intensity of calamities.

The above remarks do not, of course, give a complete conspectus of the characteristic features of the Armenian colophons. A fuller examination and evaluation of this literary genre is given in the Introduction, which aims principally at familiarizing the Western reader with the Armenian tradition in this field.

A few words must be said about Xač'ikyan's three volumes of colophons from which the majority of the texts in this volume have been drawn. These collections contain a total of 2164 colophons, of which 1148 are from manuscripts now held in the Matenadaran, and the remainder have been reproduced from published and unpublished catalogs of Armenian manuscripts and from texts published in books and periodicals. Many of the colophons in these volumes were previously unpublished. On the other hand, Xač'ikyan has had no access to some of the largest Armenian manuscript collections, notably in Jerusalem and Venice, which have been only partially cataloged, as well as to certain published catalogs of manuscripts in European museums and libraries. His three collections, therefore, do not contain all the colophons written in the fourteenth and fifteenth centuries.

The colophons published by Xač'ikyan do not contain the customary theological remarks found in the introductory sections and sometimes also in the body of the texts, on the grounds that they are stereotyped formulas and do not supply any information of historical value. These deletions are indicated by three dots (. . .). Manuscripts that have several colophons written in the same year are given one general number, and the colophons are distinguished by letters, such as no. 28 (a, b, c). Since the punctuation employed by the scribes was not based upon any uniform system and each scribe followed his own whim, the editor has almost completely revised the punctuation of the texts to make them more intelligible. The lacunae found in the colophons have been indicated by diagonal lines (/ / /); when these occur at the end it means that the rest of the text is missing. Reconstructed words or suggested readings or marred passages are placed within brackets. Xač'ikyan's three volumes have adequate indexes of personal and geographical names, as well as subject indexes; the glossaries of foreign terminology and the textual annotation are meager.

The present work represents a small fraction of the colophons published by Xač'ikyan, since I have reproduced only those sections of the texts which contain historical information pertaining to the Middle East. In translating these documents I have attempted to render as closely as possible the style and language of the originals. I have retained the poetic lines of colophons written in verse, but my primary objective has been to render the meaning of the text rather than to reproduce its prosody. In transliterating proper names, I have consistently followed the orthography of the texts, even though the author of the colophon may have spelled a certain name in several different ways in the same text. In the case of well-known personal and geographical names, I have provided within brackets their more common forms; the rest are identified in the appropriate appendixes. When necessary to render the meaning of the text more intelligible, I have, more often than did Xač'ikyan, incorporated within brackets supplementary information in the body of the texts. Lengthy explanations, however, have been placed in the footnotes. Although I have, in the main, followed the punctuation of the texts as revised by Xač'ikyan, I have on occasion taken the liberty of reducing the length of sentences for ease in reading.

As for the systems of transliteration employed in this volume, for Armenian I have followed the system currently adopted by the editors of the *Revue des études arméniennes* (Paris, new series); for Muslim names I have used the transliteration adopted by the editors of the *Encyclopaedia of Islam* (both old and new series); for proper names, nomenclature, and terminology with corresponding Turkish forms I have used the modern Turkish orthography.

The appendixes were designed to be more than mere indexes; they also provide, as succinctly as possible, pertinent information regarding individual entries. In Appendix A, the index of personal names, no attempt has been made to supply a complete bibliography; rather, only sufficient bibliographical data, generally from standard reference works, has been provided to identify the individuals mentioned in the texts. The same principle applies to the index of geographical names, Appendix C; in this instance, when applicable, the ancient names as well as the corresponding forms in other languages are also given. The index of biblical quotations and references, Appendix E, was included in the hope that it might be of use to those concerned with biblical philology. Finally, Appendix F gives a complete listing of the foreign terms untranslated in the texts that required discussion of an etymological or philological nature.

I have a distinct and genuine sense of obligation to a number of people who rendered generous assistance and encouragement in the course of this study: to Dr. Omeljan Pritsak, Professor of Turkology at Harvard University, who not only suggested the work but was ever ready to give me the benefit of his wide experience; to Professor Francis W. Cleaves of Harvard University for his assistance in the identification of a number of Mongolian names as well as the etymologies of certain Mongolian terms; to Dr. Andreas Tietze, Professor of Turkish at the University of California, Los Angeles, who kindly read the entire manuscript and made a number of useful suggestions; and to Reverend Arten Ashjian, pastor of the St. James church in Watertown, Massachusetts, for checking with me certain obscure passages in the original texts of the colophons. To all of these individuals I am deeply grateful and appreciative.

Los Angeles, California Avedis K. Sanjian

Contents

Abbreviations Used in Citations

Ačaṙyan, *HAB*	H. Ačaṙyan, *Hayoc' Anjnanunneri Baṙaran*, Erevan, 1942–1962
Ačaṙyan, *HLP*	H. Ačaṙyan, *Hayoc' Lezvi Patmut'yun*, Erevan, 1940–1951
Baṙgirk'	*Baṙgirk' Nor Haykazean Lezui*, Venice, 1836–1837
BSOAS	*Bulletin of the School of African and Oriental Studies, London*
Chèref-Nâmeh	François Bernard Charmoy, trans., *Chèref-Nâmeh ou fastes de la nation Kourde par Chèref-ou'dinne*, St. Petersburg, 1868–1875
Codex Cum.	Kaare Grønbech, *Komanisches Wörterbuch, Türkischer Wortindex zu Codex Cumanicus*, Copenhagen, 1942
Doerfer	Gerhard Doerfer, *Türkische und Mongolische Elemente im Neupersischen*, vol II, Wiesbaden, 1965
EI, OE	*Encyclopaedia of Islam*, Leyden-London, 1913–1934
EI, NE	*Encyclopaedia of Islam, New Edition*, Leyden-London, 1960—.
Eremyan, *Ašx.*	S. T. Eremyan, *Hayastanə əst "Ašxarhac'oyc'i"*, Erevan, 1963
Haïm	S. Haïm, *New Persian-English Dictionary*, Teheran, 1934–1936
Hübschmann, *Arm. Gram.*	Heinrich Hübschmann, *Armenische Grammatik*, Darmstadt, 1962
Hübschmann, *AO*	Heinrich Hübschmann, "Die altarmenische Ortsnamen," in *Indogermanische Forschungen*, Strassbourg, 1904
Inčičean, *Ašx.*	Łukas Inčičean, *Ašxarhagrut'iwn Č'oric' Masanc' Ašxarhi*, Venice, 1806
Malxaseanc', *HBB*	S. Malxaseanc', *Hayerēn Bac'atrakan Baṙaran*, Erevan, 1944–1945
Oskean, *Vank'er*	Hamazasp Oskean, *Vaspurakan-Vani Vank'erə*, Vienna, 1940–1947
Radloff	Wilhelm Radloff, *Versuch Eines Wörterbuches der Türk-Dialecte*, The Hague, 1960
Steingass	F. Steingass, *Persian-English Dictionary*, London, 1947
Wehr	Hans Wehr, *A Dictionary of Modern Written Arabic*, Ithaca, 1961
Zenker	Jules Theodore Zenker, *Dictionnaire Turc-Arabe-Persan*, Leipzig, 1866–1876

Introduction

The Armenian literary genre of colophon writing was an integral part of the art of manuscript production. The principal repository of the colophons is the corpus of extant Armenian manuscripts, now estimated at 25,000. This rich legacy is, of course, only a small fraction of the Armenian manuscripts copied throughout the centuries in the large number of scriptoria which dotted the map of Armenia and the Armenian diaspora. The data concerning the scriptoria and the scribes who labored within their walls are to be found primarily in the colophons. The common designation in Armenian for the scribe is *grič'*; the scribes also referred to themselves as *gragir*, *gcagir*, *gcoł*, *groł*, *mroł*, and so forth. To these unsung heroes we owe the preservation and perpetuation of the rich heritage of Armenian literature.

The Scriptoria and the Armenian Manuscripts

The majority of the scribes acquired their training in the scriptoria under the tutelage of professional instructors, who are frequently referred to by the scribes as their "spiritual parents" (*hogewor cnoł*). Each scriptorium developed its own traditions. As centers of creative writing as well as transcribing, they contributed significantly to the development of Armenian culture. Among the more important scriptoria—a number of which also distinguished themselves as outstanding institutions of higher learning—mention should be made of the following: the school of Siwnik', which flourished during the hegemony of the Bagratuni (or Bagratid) dynasty in the ninth to eleventh centuries; Tat'ew, which was established in the twelfth century; Ani, which functioned in the twelfth and thirteenth centuries; the school of the scholar Vanakan in the twelfth century; Hałbat-Sanahin in the twelfth and thirteenth centuries; Hṙomklay, Skewṙay, Drazark, Akner, and others in Cilicia in the twelfth to fourteenth centuries; Glajor and Mecop' in the fourteenth and fifteenth centuries; Erznkay (Erzincan) and Karin (Erzerum) in the thirteenth to seventeenth centuries; Van in the fifteenth to seventeenth centuries; Kafa in the Crimea in the fourteenth to seventeenth centuries; and Bałēš (Bitlīs), J̌ułay (Djulfa), and Constantinople in the seventeenth and eighteenth centuries. Some of these institutions were so highly developed and their contribution to Armenian learning and literature was so great that contemporaries referred to them as academies or universities, and applied such epithets as "Second Athens" and "capital of wisdom."

Beginning in the eleventh century, the constant invasions, devastation, and plunder by the Seljuk Turks and later by the Mongols compelled large masses of Armenians to abandon their homeland and seek refuge in neighboring and distant lands. The refugees settled in Byzantium, in the Crimea, in territories under the control of the Golden Horde, in Russia, Moldavia, Wallachia, Poland, Hungary, Italy, India, Iran, Syria, Egypt, and other countries. In many of these lands they founded new scriptoria, where the Armenian literary and cultural traditions were continued through original works as well as the reproduction of manuscripts. The activities abroad complemented the cultural and literary life which continued in Armenia despite the dire circumstances resulting from the loss of political independence.

As a rule, the scriptoria were an integral part of monastic institutions which also served as centers of higher learning. Traditionally, education among the Armenians had been confined to the clergy, and was carried on in monastic institutions generally at the feet, as it were, of some learned ecclesiastics, or by traveling pedagogues who on occasion also attracted nonclerical students.[1] The colophons contain abundant information concerning the scriptoria, the medieval institutions of learning, their pedagogical activities, and the backgrounds of the pupils who attended these institutions. Particularly in the second half of the fourteenth century, the military conflagrations and political upheavals in Armenia had the most adverse effect upon the activities of the educational institutions. In consequence, the pedagogues and their pupils were constantly compelled to move from one locality to another; yet they seldom interrupted their intellectual pursuits.[2] The same conditions attended those who were engaged in the production of manuscripts, the scribes, illuminators, and binders.

Many of the medieval Armenian monastic institutions had large libraries of manuscripts, which attracted scholars and scribes alike. A substantial proportion of these libraries was plundered or destroyed by invading or marauding troops. To cite one example out of many, the thirteenth-century historian Step'anos Ōrbelean attests that after

[1] For a general study see Kevork A. Sarafian, *History of Education in Armenia* (Los Angeles, 1930).

[2] See L. S. Xač'ikyan, ed., *XIV Dari Hayeren Jeṙagreri Hišatakaranner* (Erevan, 1950), no. 700, p. 560.

occupying the monastery of Tat'ew in 1170 the Seljuks destroyed more than 10,000 manuscripts found in the institution's library.[3] Despite frequent similar acts of destruction and vandalism, manuscripts continued to be copied and perpetuated. Generally, every effort was made to preserve the Armenian literary legacy, even by hiding manuscripts in the caves and crevices of inaccessible mountains, where they remained until the departure of the invaders. Indeed many an Armenian manuscript bears the scars of blood, fire, plunder, and captivity, like a soldier who has participated in many combats; and a substantial number of extant manuscripts were rescued from captivity at the expense of human lives. Nevertheless, a large number of manuscripts were destroyed as a result of ignorance and carelessness. For instance, toward the end of the eighteenth century a monk at the monastery of Hałbat in charge of clearing up the institution's "worthless objects" made a large pile of its library's dilapidated manuscripts, and set them on fire in the courtyard.[4] Little wonder then that there are only a few insignificant remnants from this monastery's once rich collection of manuscripts, which had filled seven halls. The last severe blow occurred during World War I, when thousands of manuscripts were destroyed or plundered during the Turkish massacres of the Armenians.

The extant Armenian manuscripts are scattered throughout the world in libraries, museums, and private collections. The oldest complete manuscript dates from A.D. 887. The estimate of 25,000 extant manuscripts does not include fragments, the oldest of which are from the fifth and sixth centuries, the folios used in bindings, or those manuscripts which were copied after the eighteenth century.

The Collections of Armenian Colophons

The Armenian term for colophon is *yišatakaran*, which literally means "memorial," "monument"; it is derived from the verb *yišem*, meaning "to remember," "to recollect," "to record." This designation is most appropriate, for the primary purpose of the colophons was to perpetuate the memory of those who had participated in the production of the manuscripts. The study of these manuscripts, as well as the interest which developed in earnest toward the end of the nineteenth century in the related field of Armenian paleography,[5]

[3] See Step'anos Ōrbelean, *Patmut'iwn Nahangin Sisakan* (Tiflis, 1910), p. 336; *Histoire de la Siounie par Stéphannos Orbélian*, trans. from the Armenian by M. Brosset (St. Petersburg, 1864), I, 191.

[4] See *Bazmavēp* (Monthly; Venice), 1956, pp. 109–110.

[5] The more important works on Armenian paleography are Yakovbos Tašean, *Aknark Mə Hay Hnagrut'ean Vray: Usumnasirut'iwn Hayoc' Grč'ut'ean Aruestin* (Vienna, 1898); Garegin

provided the impetus for the greater appreciation of the colophons as primary sources for Armenological studies. The simultaneous interest in and publication of several collections of Armenian inscriptions further enhanced similar endeavors with regard to the colophons.[6]

The oldest colophon preserved in the original is found in the so-called Lazarean Gospel (now in the Matenadaran in Erevan), copied in A.D. 887.[7] Garegin Yovsēp‘ean has published the texts of several colophons presumably written before this text, some as early as the fifth century; but the authenticity of these documents is doubtful.[8] The colophons become quantitatively more abundant beginning in the tenth century; and from the second half of the twelfth on they manifest greater variety in style and content. In consequence, their value as primary sources becomes more and more evident, in direct proportion to their contributions to various fields of Armenological research.

The first attempt at compiling a collection of the colophons from the widely dispersed Armenian manuscripts was made by the nineteenth-century scholar Łewond P‘irłalēmean. Traveling extensively throughout the Ottoman empire, he copied the colophons and other historically important documents from manuscripts which he found in Armenian monasteries and churches as well as with private individuals. In 1878 he augmented his collection with colophons from published sources. The materials which he thus gathered encompassed

---

Yovsēp‘ean, *Grč‘ut‘ean Aruestə Hin Hayoc‘ Mēǰ* (Vagharshapat, 1913); A. G. Abrahamyan, *Hay Gri ev Grč‘ut‘yan Patmut‘yun* (Erevan, 1959).

[6] For collections of Armenian inscriptions, see M. Barxutareanc‘, *Arc‘ax* (Baku, 1895); S. G. Barxudaryan, *Divan Hay Vimagrut‘yan*, vol. II (Erevan, 1960); Karapet Kostaneanc‘, *Vimakan Taregir: C‘uc‘ak Žołovacoy Arjanagrut‘eanc‘ Hayoc‘* (St. Petersburg, 1913); Sargis J̌alalean, *Čanaparhordut‘iwn i Mecn Hayastan* (2 parts, Tiflis, 1858); K. J̌uharyan, *Sovetakan Hayastani Patmakan Hušarjannerə* (Erevan, 1961); M. P‘ap‘azean, *Hnut‘iwnk‘ Vanōrēic‘ Siwneac‘ Ašxarhi* (Vagharshapat, 1895); Mesrovb Smbateanc‘, *Tełekagir Gełark‘uni Covazard Gawaṙi* (Vagharshapat, 1896); Mesrovb Smbateanc‘, *Nkaragir Surb Karapeti Vanic‘ Ernǰakoy ew Šrǰakayic‘ Nora* (Tiflis, 1904); Yovhannēs Šahxat‘unean, *Storagrut‘iwn Kat‘ułikē Ēǰmiacni, ew Hing Gawaṙac‘n Araratay* (2 vols., Etchmiadzin, 1842); M. Tēr Movsisean, *Haykakan Erek‘ Mec Vank‘eri Tat‘ewi, Hałarcni ew Dadi Ekełec‘inerə ew Vanakan Šinut‘iwnnerə* (Jerusalem, 1938). See also the following monographs by Łewond M. Ališan which contain the texts of a considerable number of inscriptions: *Ayrarat, Bnašxarh Hayastaneayc‘* (Venice, 1890); *Hayapatum* (Venice, 1901); *Sisakan, Tełagrut‘iwn Siwneac‘ Ašxarhi* (Venice, 1893); *Sisuan, Hamagrut‘iwn Haykakan Kilikioy ew Lewon Mecagorc* (Venice, 1895). References to European works dealing with specific Armenian inscriptions will be found in Ida A. Pratt, *Armenia and the Armenians; A List of References in the New York Public Library* (New York, 1919), pp. 53–56.

[7] See text of the colophon in Garegin I Kat‘ołikos [Yovsēp‘ean], *Yišatakarank‘ Ješagrac‘* (Antilias, Lebanon), vol. I, cols. 83–86.

[8] See texts in *ibid.*, cols. 1–84. Yovsēp‘ean states that the colophons dated prior to A.D. 887 are not the original texts, but rather reproductions preserved in manuscripts copied in the eleventh and subsequent centuries; hence, their authenticity cannot be substantiated.

texts written between 887 and 1596. However, only a small portion of his collection, the colophons written between 1393 and 1467, has been published;[9] the manuscript of his complete collection, as well as its original draft, are now in the Matenadaran in Erevan.[10]

The second scholar to engage in a similar activity, primarily in the Armenian-inhabited provinces of eastern Turkey, was Bishop Garegin Sruanjteancʻ, the results of whose investigations are to be found in his two-volume *Tʻoros Ałbar: Hayastani Čambord.*[11] The section entitled "Manuscripts and Colophons" in the second volume contains descriptions as well as the colophons of more than 350 manuscripts.

Both Pʻirłalēmean and Sruanjteancʻ, however, frequently merely summarized the contents of the original colophons; they also modernized the more ancient orthography of the texts. Nevertheless, since a substantial number of the manuscripts from which the colophons were reproduced were destroyed or lost during World War I, their compilations constitute the only sources for our knowledge of these manuscripts, as well as of the contents of their colophons.

The publication in the 1890's of Yakobos Tašean's catalogs of the Armenian manuscript holdings in the Imperial Library and the Mekhitarist monastery in Vienna[12] provided the impetus for the concerted effort to catalog, along the scientific lines developed in Europe, the Armenian manuscripts scattered throughout the world. For the most part, the compilers of the scores of catalogs which have since appeared[13] have reproduced the complete texts of the colophons found in the manuscripts which they describe.

Despite these efforts, however, full utilization of the extant colophons is attended by a number of practical difficulties. The first of these stems from the fact that, in addition to the separately published monographs, a substantial number of these catalogs have appeared in widely scattered periodicals. Secondly, some catalogs that have been prepared have as yet not been published.[14] Thirdly, the three largest

[9] See Łewond Pʻirłalēmean, *Nōtarkʻ Hayocʻ* (Constantinople, 1888).

[10] Matenadaran Archives nos. 4515, 6273, 6332.

[11] Published in Constantinople in 1879–1885.

[12] See Yakobos Tašean, *Cʻucʻak Hayerēn Jeṙagracʻ Kayserakan Matenadaranin i Vienna* (*Catalog der armenischen Handschriften in der K. K. Hofbibliothek zu Wien*) (Vienna, 1891); *Cʻucʻak Hayerēn Jeṙagracʻ Matenadaranin Mxitʻareancʻ i Vienna* (*Catalog der armenischen Handschriften in der Mechitharisten-Bibliothek zu Wien*) (Vienna, 1895).

[13] For lists of published and unpublished catalogs of Armenian manuscripts consult H. S. Anasyan, *Haykakan Matenagitutʻyun* (Erevan, 1959), I, lxxvii–xcii; A. G. Abrahamyan, *Hay Gri ev Grčʻutʻyan Patmutʻyun* (Erevan, 1959), pp. 398–402; Ō. Eganyan, et al., *Cʻucʻak Jeṙagracʻ Maštocʻi Anvan Matenadarani* (Erevan, 1965), I, 197–212.

[14] It is to be noted that in recent years the Gulbenkian Foundation in Lisbon has subsidized the publication of a number of catalogs of Armenian manuscripts.

collections of Armenian manuscripts—the holdings of the Matenadaran in Erevan, the Armenian Patriarchate in Jerusalem, and the Mekhitarist monastery in Venice—have not been fully cataloged.[15] This situation, however, has been partially corrected with the publication of a number of collections of colophons since the early 1950's.

Among these, the late Catholicos Garegin I Yovsēp'ean's *Yišatakarank' Jeŕagrac'* (The Colophons of Manuscripts) was the most ambitious endeavor hitherto undertaken. The project envisaged the publication, in four volumes, of all the colophons which this eminent scholar had gathered from the Armenian manuscripts he had studied during his worldwide travels, as well as those which he had found in published sources. This work was to include the colophons written between the fifth and eighteenth centuries, with annotations on the texts, as well as evaluations of the calligraphy and artistic quality of the manuscripts in which the colophons were found, and a bibliography of the sources dealing with individual texts. As a student of Armenian paleography and illuminated art, Yovsēp'ean laid heavy emphasis on these aspects of his work. Regrettably, by the time of his death only the first of the projected four volumes had appeared;[16] and it is not certain whether the manuscripts of the remaining three volumes were readied for publication. The published collection presents in chronological order the complete texts of a total of 472 colophons covering the period from the fifth century to the year 1250.

Finally, the Institute of History of the Armenian SSR Academy of Sciences has already published three large collections of colophons, which were compiled and edited by L. S. Xač'ikyan, Director of the Matenadaran in Erevan.[17] These three volumes contain a total of 2164 colophons, written between 1301 and 1480. A substantial number of these are published for the first time from the manuscripts in the Matenadaran. As in the case of Yovsēp'ean's collection, the orthography of the original texts has been preserved and the archaic punctuation revised; but, unlike Yovsēp'ean's work, Xač'ikyan has deleted certain passages from the texts, notably the introductory sections, as well as repetitive passages in the texts and stereotyped theological statements, on the grounds that they are devoid of historical value.

[15] In 1965 the Matenadaran published the first of its projected two-volume brief catalog of its more than 11,000 manuscripts. The Armenian Patriarchate of Jerusalem has thus far published six volumes of its catalog containing descriptions of 824 manuscripts out of a total of some 4000. The three volumes of the Venice Mekhitarist catalog describe 456 manuscripts out of an estimated total of 3000.

[16] *Yišatakarank' Jeŕagrac'*, published at Antilias, Lebanon, in 1951.

[17] L. S. Xač'ikyan, ed., *XIV Dari Hayeren Jeŕagreri Hišatakaranner* (Erevan, 1950); *XV Dari Hayeren Jeŕagreri Hišatakaranner*, Part I (1401–1450) (Erevan, 1955); Part II (1451–1480) (Erevan, 1958).

The Forms and Basic Content of the Colophons

In their basic features, the colophons evidence a general uniformity of style, expression, and content, which was perpetuated through a constant repetition of stylized forms. Within these general limitations, however, many a scribe or other author of a colophon sought new ways of expressing those concepts that constituted the essential elements of this literary genre.

A typical Armenian colophon would begin with one of several stereotyped introductions, commonly known as the *P'aṙk'* (literally, "Glory be"), which were dedicated to the Holy Trinity. They were often copied verbatim from the colophons of other manuscripts, and there was little effort to deviate from the traditional formulas. As a rule, this section is a statement of the Trinitarian theology of the Armenian church, frequently containing references to the first three Ecumenical Councils—the only ones accepted by the Armenian church—and generally reflecting the church's Christological position along the lines expounded by Cyril of Alexandria. Some of these introductions also contain anathemas against such heretics as Arias, Macedonius, Nestorius, Eutyches. It is not uncommon for the author to repeat the same eulogistic and theological expressions about the Trinity in the body of the colophon, in association with other details concerning the production of the manuscript. Equally repetitious is the scribe's statement that he commenced and concluded the copying of the manuscript through the help which he received from the Holy Trinity.[18] These theological sections are so standardized that they are of little value, even from the standpoint of tracing the historical development of the Armenian theological and Christological position.

The introductory section is followed by remarks eulogizing the contents of the manuscript reproduced, frequently with theological observations. Next is mentioned the name of the commissioner, sponsor, or purchaser of the manuscript, accompanied with words of high praise for him, and followed by the request that he be remembered for this deed, together with his immediate and even distant relatives. Whether the manuscript was commissioned or reproduced at the scribe's own initiative, the colophon as a rule indicates the motivation for the work. After this the author of the colophon identifies himself with a series of deprecatory epithets regarding his scribal qualifications and his unworthy and sinful life.

[18] Typical examples of the introductory sections will be found in Yovsēp'ean, *Yišatakarank'*, I, no. 72, cols. 163–168; no. 86, col. 203; no. 266, col. 593; no. 278, cols. 615–620; no. 391, cols. 849–850.

The author then provides the date for the completion of the work and sometimes even the time of its commencement, as well as the circumstances under which he labored. The chronology is further established by mention of the incumbent catholicos of the Armenian church and other contemporary hierarchs. Frequently, the name of the abbot of the monastery in which the manuscript was copied is also given, and sometimes the name of the prelate of the bishopric within whose jurisdiction the monastery was located. It is in this context that the authors of the colophons usually mention the ruling foreign monarchs or the local chieftains. Next, the author states the place where the manuscript was copied, giving such information as the name of the monastery and its church, the names of the saints with which the institution was associated, including references to their relics; the village or town in which the monastery was located, and the name of the canton or province. As a rule, the historical account of contemporary political and military developments occupies the final part of the colophons; it is in the composition of this section that the author evidences his freedom from the stylized patterns. In the course of providing all these data, the author of the colophon usually embellishes his statements with prayerful supplications for practically all the individuals involved in the production of the manuscript, and with extensive quotations from or references to the Bible and other religio-ecclesiastical works.

Many an author of a colophon merely used standardized forms, simply inserting in appropriate places the name of the sponsor, his own name, the place, date, and the circumstances of the production of the manuscript. What follows is an example of such a colophonic pattern.

> Glory to the singular power and the Trinitarian confession, the consubstantial, equally resplendent, uniform, coequal, sublime, and self-existent essence and union, the Father and the Son and the Holy Ghost, now and forever, amen.
>
> This book emanating from the soul, which is called [title of book], was completed in the year [date], in the canton of [name], during the pontificate of the Lord [name of catholicos], in the celestial, most renowned, angel-inhabited and God-inhabited monastery, which is called [name], and which is like the heavenly Jerusalem, under the protection of [name of saint or saints]; during the abbotcy in our holy congregation of [name of abbot], who is pure in life, humble by nature, affable in speech, generous in heart, judicious like his name-sake, altruistic like Abraham;

at the feet of the prelate [name]; copied by the most sinful and artless scribe [name]. This [manuscript] was received by a certain monk called [name], who is diligent and valorous in virtuous deeds, bred in a monastery, instructed and nurtured at the feet of [name], shining like a lantern in the church, and fragrant like God-pleasing incense, and like a rational swallow perched in a temple, and like a bee yearning for the divine dew-drop. Thus, he longed for this book and had it copied for his own enjoyment and in memory of his parents. I beseech you all, who should encounter this book, to ask God's mercy for him and for me, the unworthy scribe [name], who began to copy this by the grace of God and completed it with His help. For the merciful God heeds those who intercede for others; for what is within your means to do is our most urgent need. And may Christ God have mercy upon you who should remember us, as well as upon us who are hopeful.[19]

The Commissioners and Sponsors of Manuscripts

From the fifth century until the fall of the Bagratuni kingdom in Armenia in 1071 and later under the Armenian kingdom of Cilicia (1080–1375), manuscripts were as a rule commissioned or sponsored by members of the royal family, the nobility or the feudal princely families, and the high-ranking clergy, for only these could afford the expense of their production. With the collapse of political independence in both territories, manuscripts were commissioned or sponsored largely by the members of the clerical institution, by the remnants of the medieval Armenian feudal families, such as the Ōrbeleans, Pṙošeans, Dop'eans, Vač'uteans, and others, and by wealthy householders, middle class merchants, and even affluent peasants. These individuals either received the manuscripts for their own use or donated them to some monastery or church as memorials to themselves. This generosity was generally the subject of high praise in many of the colophons; even when the commissioner or sponsor was not prominent, the scribes attributed to them the most glowing qualities.

Customarily the production of a manuscript depended on the terms agreed upon between the commissioner or sponsor and the scribe. The commissioner asked the scribe to copy and illuminate a work which he was eager to own and promised to compensate in accordance with the terms of their agreement. Upon the completion of the manuscript, the scribe wrote the colophon according to the

[19] Matenadaran MS. no. 2335.

wishes of the commissioner, mentioning the latter's name, as well as those of his wife, parents, children, and other close and even distant relatives, and beseeching the mercy of the Lord for their souls in the life hereafter. Frequently, the names of the commissioner's relatives occupy several pages of the colophon. The colophons written by subsequent recipients of the manuscripts also contain similar records of names.

If the scribe produced the manuscript at his own initiative, he wrote the colophon according to standard patterns, leaving blank spaces for the name of the "commissioner." After locating a purchaser, the scribe inserted his name and gave him the manuscript. A number of extant manuscripts have colophons in which the blanks for the names were never filled.

As a rule, the commissioner or sponsor of a manuscript was a single individual, but there are manuscripts that were sponsored by groups. For instance, the *Čaṙəntir* (Collection of Sermons) copied at Surxatʻ in the Crimea was sponsored by a large group of artisans and one petty merchant residing in that city.[20]

The colophons show that, on occasion, part of the proceeds received by the scribe from the commissioner went to the prelate of the bishopric or the abbot of a monastery or some other ranking clergy under whose jurisdiction the scribe worked. For instance, the colophon of a *Yaysmawurkʻ* (Menology) copied at Khizān in 1407 indicates that the scribe Yovanēs received a total of 2150 *dram* in cash, as well as 6 *kapič* of bread, 1 liter of fat, and 2 liters of honey; in addition, the commissioner paid the bishop the sum of 450 *dram*.[21] In certain instances, the scribe was compensated wholly in cash.[22] Depending on the terms of the agreement, the materials for the manuscript were provided either by the scribe and the craftsmen who worked with him, or by the commissioner himself. The colophon of another *Yaysmawurkʻ* copied in 1427 by Bishop Sargis, for instance, indicates that he offered 2000 *dram* as well as the paper and other materials; because he was unable to come to an agreement with the scribe he himself was compelled to copy the manuscript.[23] In the same year another commissioner, Abraham, paid the scribe Grigor Arckecʻi the sum of 40 *dram* as the price of the paper which the scribe had provided.[24]

The trials and tribulations suffered by certain individuals to secure

[20] *Ibid.*, no. 3797.
[21] See text in Xačʻikyan, *XV Dari, I*, no. 72c, p. 71.
[22] See example in *ibid.*, no. 9a, p. 15.
[23] See text in *ibid.*, no. 385, p. 363.
[24] *Ibid.*, no. 386c, p. 366.

a manuscript are graphically presented in the following translation of the colophon of a Holy Book copied in the year 1332.

> . . . This [Bible] was begun in December [A.D. 1331] and completed in October [1332], at the hands of two expert scribes. I Nersēs, a vardapet in name but the lowliest dust and ash among vardapets in deeds, son of Vahram, from the canton of Sansun [Sasun] in the land of Tarōn, from the monastery of Łazar and from the village of Koṙ, yearned for learning and proceeded to the monastery of Gaylejor in the eastern canton of Vaujor, and spent seven years studying the old and the new scriptures and numerous other holy books. In these times my soul was filled with a great desire for [a manuscript of] the Holy Books; but I was penurious and possessed not even a mite, excepting Christ. Then I made a vow to myself, saying: "If God should give me the means, I will have [a manuscript] copied in the name of the Mother of God." After resolving this, I proceeded to the village of Xantkah in the land of Urnu to seek assistance from my brothers and all my blood relatives. Moved by love and through the compassion of the holy Mother of God, they offered me the cost [of the production] of this Holy Bible, each according to his means: Mleh, 210 *spitak*; his brother Lewon, 90 *dram*; Yovan, 90 *dram*; T'uran, 30 *dram*; Damur, 30 *dram*; my cousin Mxit'ar, 42 *dram*; the carpenter Mxit'ar, 30 *dram*; Vardan, 33 *dram*; Hayrapet, 36 *dram*; Martir / / /; T'adkan, 30 *dram*; the dyer Luser, 30 *dram*; Zak'ar, 18 *dram*; Ṙamanos and his mother, 36 *dram*; Fṙang Xlat'c'i, 100 *dram*; Anton, 20 *dram*; Umek and his sons, 40 *dram*.
>
> Taking this [money] with me I journeyed to the city of T'avrēž [Tabrīz] in Persia in search of paper, and I suffered much fear and trouble on the way, as well as much rancor and anguish at the hands of greedy and vainglorious priests and antagonistic laymen. From there I again, through the mercy of God, returned to [the monastery of] Gaylijor, and I engaged my spiritual brother, Yohannēs Mšec'i, as mediator between me and two scribes, Ep'rem and Dawit', both of whom were celibate priests. And after many days [of negotiation], we were able to agree on the terms, 1500 *dram* including all other expenses. However, Dawit' later broke his promise to me, for he was most greedy and avaricious, and he took an additional 300 *dram* from me—may God forgive his sins. And then I left that place and went to the [monastery of the] Holy Apostle Thaddeus; and the Lord Archbishop Zak'arē offered me 500 *dram*. And many days

later I returned to [the monastery of] Gaylijor with much suffering, for it was winter-time; and I paid the remainder of my debt for the Holy Bible. I then returned to the [monastery of the] Holy Apostle where I remained for some days. But this Holy Bible was still unbound, and I, the wretched one, was ill both spiritually and physically. Then I pleaded with the holy Mother of God Who gave me strength, and I proceeded to see the holy bishop, the Lord Bardołimos, and other Armenian vardapets who were with him at Kṙnay. But the vardapet Margarē, who was a binder of manuscripts, was not there, for he had left for J̌ahuk. And I, through the deed of the evil one [Satan] fell ill for forty-five days; and although I was nearing death Christ brought me back to life. And I journeyed to J̌ahuk, and the vardapet Margarē, who agreed to bind [the manuscript], completed it in forty days and gave it to me. I decided joyously to proceed to the land of Tarun, but I had no means at all to make the journey; hence, I sold [my] priestly mantle and slippers to provide the expenses of [my] journey. Let this also be known, brothers, the aforementioned travels included many places among barbarian places . . . who are called *Mahmetakank*ʻ [Muhammadans], who tyrannically hold sway over Armenia on account of our sins. And the Holy Mother of God helped me wherever I went and I suffered no harm; and whatever need I had She offered and fulfilled. The production of this Holy Bible cost a total of 2200 *dram* . . .[25]

Motives for the Reproduction of Manuscripts

The colophons are also replete with data which give a clear picture of the motives for sponsorship or commissioning of manuscripts. As a rule, the sponsor and the scribe viewed the manuscript as a sacred and venerable object, and therefore explained the act of its production as a morally rewarding endeavor. The author of the colophon, whether he was the commissioner or the scribe, felt himself duty-bound to explain the reasons for his act, and mentioned the rewards he hoped would accrue to him in consequence of his good deed.

The basic motivation common to all who were instrumental in the production of manuscripts, especially if the work was of religious value, was the perpetuation of their memory. The recurrent theme in the colophons is the hope that future readers of the manuscript would not fail to remember and pray for the sponsor, the scribe, the binder, or the restorer. In many a colophon the sponsor says that he acquired

[25] *Ibid.*, *XIV Dari*, no. 307a, pp. 245–246.

the manuscript as an "indelible memorial or monument" to his own soul and to those of his immediate family, as well as his relatives, both living and deceased, many of whom are mentioned by name.[26] The sponsor of a *Maštocʻ* (Ritual Book) expressed the hope that whenever the book was read his name would "be remembered in Christ together with it."[27] A substantial number of manuscripts were commissioned as a token of the sponsor's love for God, or as his "guide to attain the true life," or as a consolation for his soul.[28] To many, the sponsorship of a manuscript was not only a "memorial to the soul," but also the most effective means to attain salvation, to inherit the kingdom of God, or to deliver them from the "inextinguishable fire of hell."[29] One sponsor hoped that the Gospel he commissioned would serve as "an intercessor for my children and for the purification of my soul and that of my wife, in order that we may enjoy mercy on the day of the visitation [of the Lord]. I plead with you, who love Christ, so that when you read this holy Gospel you will without fail beseech the Creator of everything to forgive all my sins; may the Lord Jesus Christ have mercy upon me."[30]

Many manuscripts were copied for the edification and enlightenment of the clergy. A Collection of Commentaries, for instance, was copied not only for the benefit of its sponsor, but also "for the enlightenment of the children of Zion, and for the admonition of the wayward and the ignorant of mind, so that by means of it the mentally blind shall be enlightened."[31] A substantial number of manuscripts were commissioned for the specific purpose of offering them as gifts to monasteries or churches. The donor of a *Yaysmawurkʻ* (Menology) writes: "And I offered this as a gift and indelible monument to the God-inhabited and famous and renowned holy monastery, and the [church of the] Holy Cross at Ałtʻamar, in order that its clergy may enjoy this holy book, always derive enjoyment from it, and also remember [me] without fail in their prayers."[32] Frequently, manuscripts were copied or sponsored because the individual recalled the words, "Blessed is he who has a child in Zion"; and many received a manuscript "as a child in Zion and as an intimate friend in Jerusalem."[33] It was not uncommon for a childless individual to assume

[26] *Ibid.*, no. 1b, p. 1; no. 46a, p. 36; no. 66, p. 52; no. 84, p. 61.
[27] *Ibid.*, no. 129, p. 95.
[28] *Ibid.*, no. 14, p. 13; no. 28, pp. 23–24; no. 47b, p. 37.
[29] *Ibid.*, no. 128b, pp. 94–95; no. 275, p. 219; no. 298, p. 238.
[30] See Yovsēpʻean, *Yišatakarankʻ*, I, no. 32, p. 84.
[31] Xačʻikyan, *XIV Dari*, no. 183a, p. 147.
[32] *Ibid.*, no. 116a, p. 86.
[33] *Ibid.*, no. 291, p. 232; no. 320, p. 259.

the sponsorship of a manuscript as a memorial to himself; in such instances, the book usually remained in the family as an "adopted child" or as a family heirloom. Equally common was the practice of having manuscripts copied to perpetuate the memory of a deceased child or relative.

Frequently, the author of a colophon gave a whole series of reasons for his endeavor, such as Simēon Vardapet who writes: "I traveled in many places in search of books and collected the texts for this holy and resplendent *Maštoc'* (Ritual Book): firstly, to secure an authentic and true copy; secondly, because of its value and benefit to us both in life and in death; thirdly, for the enlightenment and edification of the younger officials of the church; fourthly, so that I may be remembered after my death before the immortal King and so that it may intercede with God [in my behalf]; fifthly, so that through all the graces of this [Ritual Book], by means of which men become worthy, Christ may make us worthy of sharing the hope of His saints."[34] The scribe Yohannēs Eznkayec'i copied his *Žołovacu* (Miscellany) in 1306 "as a consolation for my grief-stricken soul, and for the instruction of the diligent scholar, and as a memorial monument to my soul and to all my ancestors and blood relatives who have passed away in Christ, and to all the clergy and laymen who have left a good name, and so that you [the reader] may be remembered by Christ God our hope, Who is eternally blessed."[35] In the colophon of a Gospel copied in 1310 another sponsor, the princess Mamaxat'un, "recalled the transitory and vain nature of this life, and received this holy Gospel as my guide to the eternal life and as my intercessor before the impartial and incorruptible judgment of Christ, and as a memorial to my soul after my death, as well as to my parents and noble brothers, and for the enlightenment of the young children of the New Zion."[36] And in 1459 a sponsor received a *Čašoc'* (Missal) "as a memorial to his soul, a solace and consolation for his doleful life, and for the cure of the evil thoughts of the soul and flesh, both in life and in death, and as a provision for the irrevocable journey, and in order that he may after death share the life of all the saints mentioned in this [Missal]."[37]

The Scribes and the Art of Manuscript Production

Until the twelfth century the production of manuscripts had been developed in the Armenian scriptoria essentially as a practical art

[34] *Ibid., XV Dari, II*, no. 259, p. 215.
[35] *Ibid., XIV Dari*, no. 58, p. 44.
[36] *Ibid.*, no. 89, p. 65.
[37] *Ibid., XV Dari, II*, no. 157a, p. 120.

transmitted by its practitioners from one generation to another. Beginning in the twelfth century, however, there also developed a theoretical system, based upon the study of linguistic and grammatical features of the Armenian language, which was designed to serve as a guide to future generations of professional scribes. This is substantiated by a number of extant texts which set forth specific rules governing the reproduction of manuscripts.[38]

One of the founders of the science of manuscript production was Aristakēs Grič', a twelfth-century grammarian who is the author of the first dictionary of Armenian spelling. Aristakēs was also a prolific and expert scribe, to whom his contemporaries gave the honorific title of *grič'*. In the introduction to his treatise,[39] Aristakēs set forth his principal objective: to put an end to distortions and errors in the reproduction of manuscripts. His work was written primarily for scribes, who he asserted must gain proficiency in the rules governing the art of manuscript production, understand the principles involved in the writing of poetry, and learn the criteria for the use of paragraphs and for copying complicated sentences and titles. Only by adhering to strict rules could the scribe reproduce an aesthetically satisfying and readable manuscript. Aristakēs asserted that the scribe must understand the contents of the work he is about to copy, rather than reproduce it mechanically. Moreover, he contended that by improving his knowledge of Armenian grammar the scribe would be able to produce a more valuable manuscript. On the basis of his own extensive scribal experiences and intimate knowledge of Armenian literature, Aristakēs set forth specific principles for the art of copying, concentrating primarily on orthographic rules.

The second author to deal with concrete problems of manuscript reproduction was Gēorg Skewṙac'i, a well-known thirteenth-century grammarian who at a young age had devoted himself to the scribal art. His three short treatises contributed to the standardization of Armenian syllabification, spelling, punctuation, and pronunciation.[40] His works, which provided extensive information concerning various aspects of Armenian grammar, were widely reproduced; and many generations of scribes benefited by these important reference sources. Skewṙac'i's treatises not only laid the foundation for the scientific reproduction of manuscripts, but also contributed to the development of creative writing through the formalization of grammatical rules.

[38] For a study of these texts see L. G. Xač'eryan, *Grč'ut'yan Arvesti Lezvakan-K'erakanakan Tesut'yunə Mijnadaryan Hayastanum* (Erevan, 1962). This work also includes the texts of the documents.

[39] See text in *ibid.*, pp. 227–286.

[40] See texts in *ibid.*, pp. 287–320.

Finally, Grigor Tat'ewac'i (1346–1410), philosopher, theologian, educator, and author, contributed three commentaries.[41] Essentially, these treatises are devoted to the elucidation of a number of points made in the works of Aristakēs and Gēorg Skewṙac'i. Since Tat'ewac'i was deeply versed in the medieval tradition of scholasticism, many of the questions he tackled are explained from the philosophical and theological standpoints.

The great impact of Aristakēs, Skewṙac'i, and Tat'ewac'i on the development of the Armenian art of manuscript production cannot be overemphasized. Their wide dissemination attests to the fact that, throughout the Middle Ages, the scribes had to acquire a theoretical as well as a practical knowledge of their craft. A competent scribe was not one endowed only with the gift of penmanship; he had to be well versed in the intricacies of the Armenian language and its grammar. Numerous colophons written by the scribes attest to the fact that, in the Middle Ages, the production of manuscripts was a highly specialized art, and that its practitioners viewed this art with veneration. Even as late as the seventeenth century the well-known author and pedagogue Vardan Bałišec'i, whose monastic institution in Bitlīs was vigorously engaged in educational and scribal activities, suggested that the reproduction and even the restoration of manuscripts was more important than construction of churches.[42]

In the colophon of a *K'erakanut'iwn* (Grammar) copied in 1357 by the scribe Step'anos at Surxat' in the Crimea we read the following appraisal of the scribal art.

> As it is impossible for the birds to pull a yoke and make a furrow, and for the oxen to fly, so also no one can attain mastery in the great art of manuscript production without studying it. And should anyone be audacious enough to engage [in this art without studying it], he will fail, and he will corrupt the art and adulterate the text, like the stupid . . . butcher who cannot distinguish the joints [of the animal] and unskillfully cuts the meat from the limbs . . . For in the hands of a foolish and stupid man this [art] is like a pearl on the nose of a pig or like a golden necklace around the neck of a donkey; but he who is intoxicated with its love, he alone appreciates its sweetness.[43]

The majority of the scribes were, of course, professionals who devoted their lifetime to the production of manuscripts. While for the

[41] See texts in *ibid.*, pp. 321–365.
[42] See G. V. Abgaryan, *Matenadaran* (Erevan, 1962), p. 9.
[43] Xač'ikyan, *XIV Dari*, no. 510, pp. 426–427.

most part the scribes were adults, there is evidence that some began their career at a very young age. It is known, for instance, that the scribe of a beautiful manuscript copied in the city of Tokat was only twelve years old.[44] Women dedicated themselves to the art of copying manuscripts beginning in the thirteenth century, and there were some in the profession as late as the eighteenth century.[45]

Among those who devoted their lifetime to this art mention should be made of Yovannēs Mangasarenc' from the town of Ardjīsh who was born about 1417–1419, and who by the time of his death at the age of eighty-six years had copied more than 132 manuscripts. His last work, a Gospel, was completed by his pupil Zak'ara, who in a colophon written in 1505 at the city of Van writes: this Gospel of John "was copied by my vardapet, the Lord Yohanēs Mangasarenc', the expert scribe, who labored as a copyist for seventy-two years, in the summer and in the winter, at night and during the day. He copied forty menologies and chronicles; and of the smaller books he copied fifty to sixty and even more, such as prayer books, hymnaries, psalm books, ritual books, and hymnals, as well as thirty-two Gospels. And he copied this book of Yohan [John] at an old age, when his eyes could no longer see and when his hand trembled; and he barely completed it with much suffering, and thereafter he could not hold a pen until his death, and he passed away in Christ at the age of eighty-six years."[46]

Bishop Sargis Partawec'i also spent his life as a scribe. In one of the last colophons he wrote he states: "This book was completed . . . in much and infinite bitterness and grief. The finger with which I write is dried up; that is why this script is so crooked; I beg your forgiveness. I have been doing this for forty-two years."[47] In the colophon of another manuscript which he copied he remarks that it "contains many and countless errors . . . my hand was trembling and my eyes could not see at all; the finger with which I write was dried up, so I wrote with my middle finger . . . Oh, my Lord, it has been forty-two years, and this is the best I could do; [my script] had never been so clumsy, and I am ashamed of myself; I beg your forgiveness." Another colophon in the same manuscript indicates that, because of the scribe's death, the work was completed by his pupil Yunan.[48] Another scribe gives the following succinct account of his thirty-year career: "I was fifteen years old when I learned the scribal art. I have reached

[44] Matenadaran MS. no. 843, cited in Abrahamyan, *Patmut'yun*, p. 371.
[45] See Abrahamyan, *Patmut'yun*, p. 371; Abgaryan, *Matenadaran*, p. 8.
[46] Xač'ikyan, *XV Dari*, I, 587, note 1.
[47] *Ibid.*, no. 310a, p. 297.
[48] *Ibid.*, no. 273a, p. 245; no. 273b, p. 246.

the age of forty-five years; for thirty whole years I have been engaged in copying numerous books, twenty hymnals, three menologies, and countless other books."[49] In his old age, the well-known chronicler and prolific scribe Mxit'ar Anec'i complains in a colophon written in verse about his physical ailments, his trembling hands, as well as the thickness of the ink, the abundance of the flies, and other nuisances.[50] The above quotations, as well as similar data in scores of other colophons, give ample evidence of the degree of devotion which motivated the scribes.

It was the fervent hope of every scribe that he would be remembered by future generations for his labors. He always beseeched the readers to pray for the forgiveness of his manifold sins so that he might inherit the Kingdom of God. He regarded the fruits of his labor as an "indelible memorial" to himself on earth. The colophons are replete with such expressions as: "My hand shall turn into dust, but this book shall remain as a memorial to me"; or, "Remember me when you read this manuscript." In the course of copying a *Žołovacu* (Miscellany) at the monastery of Xorin in 1280, the scribe Basil K'ahanay began to have doubts about the usefulness of his work because he was mortal and upon his death someone else would obtain the manuscript. But he comforted himself with the thought that future generations would derive enjoyment from it; and he concluded his colophon with the request that those who benefited by it should remember him.[51]

Customarily, after identifying the commissioner or sponsor of the manuscript with appropriate characterizations, the writer of the colophon would refer to himself by name—and in many instances to his parents and near and distant relatives as well. He then would proceed to describe his social status, pass moral judgments upon himself, and apologize for the inadequacies of his artistic endeavors—in all these instances generally employing stereotyped expressions. Whereas the scribes are lavish in extolling the virtues of the commissioners or sponsors, even the much sought-after master craftsmen are equally lavish in deprecating themselves and their handiwork. Indeed, there is not a single colophon in which one would find even the slightest indication of self-adulation; on the contrary, the expressions of humility and self-depreciation are so pronounced that they frequently become highly exaggerated. The majority of the scribes merely repeat

[49] See text in Babgēn Kiwlēsērean, *C'uc'ak Hayerēn Jeṙagrac' Karmir Vanuc'n Ankiwrioy* (Antilias, 1957), p. 221.

[50] Xač'ikyan, *XIV Dari*, no. 38ob, pp. 311–312.

[51] Abrahamyan, *Patmut'yun*, pp. 390–391.

the common phrases or epithets; only a few depart from the standard forms, both stylistically and in content.

A few quotations from the colophons will illustrate the point. The scribe Vardan writes: remember "the miserable petty scribe, the deacon Vardan, wavering in good acts and vigilant in evil deeds, lacking in the light of rationality and full of darkness." Another scribe claims to be a "suffering sinner, shipwrecked and sinful, the false Lord Avagerēcʻ, for I am called a priest, but I have never recalled the terrible day of judgment, I have never said 'I have sinned, oh Lord,' [and] like a pig I have tumbled into the mire." The scribe Yakob refers to himself as "a much sinful soul Yakob, falsely named a monk, who holds the rank of a priest in name only but am removed so far from it in deeds, like the east from the west, who am half alive, spiritually dead and physically alive, like a corpse upon the earth, who copied and completed this [manuscript] with the help of Jesus, with crude fingers and infirm hands." The scribe Yovsēpʻ, after referring to himself as a foolish scribe who bears the name of a priest but is lacking in deeds, says that "I appear to be graceful in the eyes of men, but indeed I am a rapacious wolf." Some scribes go to great lengths in drawing parallels, such as "the fruitless in good deeds, the sinful among the righteous, the imperfect among the perfect, the sinful among the unsinful, the inordinate among the ordained, the immemorable among the scribes and the artless among the artists, the ignorant among the learned, the most sinful and unworthy, curdled in sin and priest in name only, Atom, who has the appearance of a priest but is wanting and void in deeds." And, finally, the scribe Mattʻēos writes: "I, the unworthy copyist of this most glorious Lectionary, who has become like the ashes and charcoal-powder of the bath-houses, sooty, and stained with dirty colors of filth like the officials of the heathen temples. For I have become devoid of the means to engage in good deeds and to repent, because although I perceive the light I proceed toward darkness, on account of which I have become woeful and wretched and am condemned to death."[52]

The Conditions Under Which Manuscripts Were Copied

The adverse conditions under which the scribes, illuminators, and binders worked are vividly reflected in the colophons. The authors of these colophons frequently complain about the "bitter, most grievous, and anxious times" as well as their "manifold difficulties." Even a

[52] Xačʻikyan, *XIV Dari*, no. 733, p. 585; no. 22, p. 26; no. 700, p. 558. *XV Dari*, I, no. 82b, p. 84. *XV Dari*, II, no. 271, p. 224; no. 90, pp. 65–66.

cursory perusal of the texts reveals that the authors had nothing pleasant to record regarding their personal experiences. Their personal adversities never shook their resolve to carry on their noble professions, however, and in the process of describing their plight they provide a clear picture of the times in which they lived and labored.

Natural disasters, the political upheavals which resulted from constant wars, the invasions and marauding expeditions, and continual devastations created conditions hardly conducive to the pursuit of uninterrupted intellectual and educational activities in the institutions of Armenia. Many of the colophons in the present volume reflect the impact of massacres, captivity, and looting upon the scribes, who were compelled to carry on their labors under conditions of insecurity or even terror, sometimes while wandering from place to place. For instance, in 1352 the scribe Kirakos Ałbakec'i pleads with the reader not to blame him for the quality of his calligraphy because when he was copying the manuscript his "heart trembled with fear . . . for I was engulfed with consternation and was trembling, and my hand was shivering on the paper." He left five empty folios because "there was terror and fear," he was unable to find additional writing paper, and there was death all around him.[53] The scribe Yovhannēs was so terrified by the atrocities that Tīmūrtash committed at Erzincan in 1338 that he was forced to suspend the copying of the manuscript.[54] Fear caused by invaders frequently compelled the scribes to continue their labors in hiding or in secret. The scribe Mxit'ar, for example, informs us that he copied his manuscript "at night and during the day, in hiding and in fear."[55]

A considerable number of colophons indicate that, because of the prevailing political and military upheavals, the scribes were wandering about from place to place, carrying with them their writing materials. The scribe Mxit'ar began his manuscript at the monastery of Mecop' in 1305, but was forced "to move to another place, and then again moved somewhere else carrying it [the manuscript] with me; and then . . . I returned here [Mecop'] where I completed it."[56] The scribe Xač'atur complains in 1319 that he did "not have a permanent place; rather, I wandered about from place to place";[57] and the scribe Yovannēs informs us that in the course of copying his Gospel he was compelled to move to five different places.[58] When invaders

[53] *Ibid.*, *XIV Dari*, no. 476a, p. 395; no. 476b, p. 395.
[54] *Ibid.*, no. 378a, pp. 304–305.
[55] See Abrahamyan, *Patmut'yun*, p. 383.
[56] Xač'ikyan, *XIV Dari*, no. 52, p. 38.
[57] *Ibid.*, no. 193, p. 156.
[58] *Ibid.*, no. 378a, p. 304.

attacked the region of Orotan, the scholar and pedagogue Yovhannēs Orotnec'i and his sixty pupils fled and wandered about for two years without interrupting their activities. And the scribe Yakob states that he accompanied them carrying with him "the paper and the exemplar, the writing pen and ink. I went with them and continued my studies; and wherever we went I copied this holy book, with much anguish and suffering, for I did not complete it where I began [to copy it]."[59]

Natural disasters like earthquakes and famines and such calamities as epidemics and plagues, invasions by locusts and caterpillars, frequently interfered with the labors of the scribes, and the colophons are replete with vivid descriptions of the havoc they wrought.[60] The scribe Grigor, for instance, provides a touching description of the plague that occurred at Āmid in the year 1431, which resulted in the death of 75,000.[61] And the scribe Sargis gives a moving account of the intensity of the locusts that arrived at Erzerum in 1314 and devastated the region for forty-one days.[62]

Political, economic, and personal reasons also frequently compelled the scribes to abandon their homes; wandering about in other lands, they continued their labors as strangers. The common Armenian terms for such individuals are *łarip* and *panduxt*. The colophons contain ample data regarding the difficulties they encountered, including the psychological effects of separation from family and familiar environs. In a colophon written in 1318 the scribe Nersēs describes the circumstances in his native region which compelled him to leave.[63] In another colophon the scribe Grigor informs the reader that he "was not a native of this place, but a stranger to these regions and a shelterless wanderer; I could not stay in any single place, and never had a day's rest."[64] Another scribe, Grigor, remarks in a marginal note that "I copied this page in one country and the other page in another land."[65] The scribe Grigor Axalc'xec'i regards himself most unfortunate because he was a *łarip*, and warns: "For God's sake, he who has not gone to a strange land as a *łarip*, let him not go."[66] And the scribe Mxit'ar expresses his grief: "I was delirious and my heart was tormented, because I was a *łarip* at the doors of strangers, where the food is bitter

59 *Ibid.*, no. 700, p. 560.

60 For colophons describing or referring to these calamities see *ibid.*, index, pp. 663, 664; *XV Dari*, I, index, p. 811; II, 596, 597.

61 *Ibid.*, *XV Dari*, I, no. 433a, pp. 403–405.

62 *Ibid.*, *XIV Dari*, no. 135a, p. 102.

63 *Ibid.*, no. 179, p. 143.

64 *Ibid.*, no. 332, p. 269.

65 *Ibid.*, *XV Dari*, I, no. 220d, p. 206.

66 *Ibid.*, no. 739a, p. 658.

and the water is like blood."[67] The most vivid description of the state of being a *ƚarip* is provided by Mkrtič' Lehac'i: "being indigent, a stranger, and a *ƚarip* caused me anguish. Hence, I copied this in a hurry and wrote in large letters, for my mind had become delirious on account of my anguish, poverty, and yearning for my parents, relatives, and country. My dear fathers and brothers, you know full well that emigration produces intense and insufferable pain, even as it is said, 'It is better to fall into the hands of barbarians than to spend the life of a stranger and an émigré.' And the wise Xikar said, 'I carried a load of bricks and it was not as heavy as poverty and indigence'; and, likewise, 'I carried a load of lead on my shoulder and found it to be lighter and more bearable than being a *ƚarip* and a stranger'."[68]

The colophons also supply substantial data concerning the physical conditions of the scribe's place of work. Many complain of the cold winter and lack of heating, leaky roofs and walls, and so forth. The scribe T'uma remarks: "I was in great anguish . . . because of the severity of the winter weather, the darkness during the daytime, and from the lighting at night . . . do not blame me, for this is the best I could do, because this place was dark and it was wintertime."[69] And another scribe complains: "Woe! Woe! My shelter is naught; that which leaks from the roof drops on the script and ruins it."[70] Most of the scribes worked in small cells with inadequate facilities, and these conditions are described in the colophons with vivid and intimate details. Writing in 1428, the scribe Melk'iset' states that he could not work during the day "because the day was too short, the distractions were many, and my heart is wounded by brothers"; hence, he was compelled to work primarily at night and under a very dim light. In view of this he pleads with the reader to forgive him for the largeness of his calligraphy, "because I wrote this at night under a lamp; every night I copied eight folios, but during the day only two or three folios."[71]

The colophons also provide accounts of the scribes' physical ailments. In 1439, for instance, Simēon relates that "one of my eyes was sore, I covered it and wrote with one eye." In the course of copying the manuscript he occasionally complains, with remarks written in the margins, about the severe pain in his eye; but upon completing the work he was so overwhelmed with joy that he could not resist writing: "At last you are delivered, oh you dazed eyes, hunched neck, and

[67] See text in E. Lalayean, *C'uc'ak Hayerēn Jeṙagrac' Vaspurakani*, I (Tiflis, 1915), 674.
[68] Siwrmēean, *Mayr C'uc'ak*, I, 122.
[69] Xač'ikyan, *XV Dari*, I, no. 69a, pp. 63–64.
[70] See text in *Ējmiacin* (monthly; Etchmiadzin), Nov.–Dec. 1950, p. 85.
[71] Xač'ikyan, *XV Dari*, I, no. 411, p. 387.

broken legs."[72] Another scribe, Ezekiēl Orotnecʻi, complains: "Today I had a severe headache, but no one sympathized with me; I hope that Christ will show them no mercy."[73] The scribe Grigor, working in the monastery of Xaṙabast, suffered from a severe headache, but he informs us that the book which he was copying was so interesting that he became unmindful of his discomfort.[74] The scribe Nersēs Krakcʻi relates that he copied his manuscript in grievous circumstances, that is "when the light in my eye had diminished, and when my stomach ached at all times, and when there was neither monk nor friend to comfort me, save God of all."[75] The scribe Movsēs, who labored in the monastery of Tatʻew in 1411, writes that he "suffered an intense and incurable pain in my belly, and since I could obtain no medicine from anyone, I appealed in my prayers to the Holy Mother of God and to the Holy Fathers, and I was cured."[76] In 1464 the scribe Stepʻannos lamented: "Woe, my loins and teeth ache, indeed my whole body; and my only hope rests in God."[77] And, finally, the scribe Zakʻēos begs for the forgiveness of his readers for the poor quality of his work, because "I cut my finger with a sickle . . . I lost as much blood as that of a sheep!"[78]

The fact that many of the scribes worked under conditions of extreme poverty is underscored by such Armenian expressions as "they labored with a wafer and a draught of water." In the margin of a manuscript, for instance, we find the following scribal comment: "Oh Lord, remember the poor Vardan . . . today I ate moldy bread and I drank lime-water from a well, and I copied this with much grief at Jerusalem."[79] In 1414 the scribe Yovsēpʻ writes: "Woe! I beg you not to reproach me for the largeness of my calligraphy, because I ate a loaf of bread made of plain millet and copied this; do not blame me."[80] Another scribe records the following comment on poverty: "I ate *daṙnič* [a wild bitter plant] and it was less bitter than poverty; I carried a load of salt on my back and it was lighter than poverty."[81] The scribe Simēon complains bitterly against the commissioner of the manuscript who "not a single day remembered me with a loaf of

[72] *Ibid.*, no. 553, p. 497.
[73] *Ibid.*, no. 110d, p. 110.
[74] *Ibid.*, no. 149e, p. 145.
[75] *Ibid.*, *XIV Dari*, no. 338a, p. 274.
[76] *Ibid.*, *XV Dari*, I, no. 125e, p. 124.
[77] *Ibid.*, *XV Dari*, II, no. 256f, p. 212.
[78] *Ibid.*, no. 454, p. 359.
[79] See Kiwlēsērean, *Cʻucʻak Ankiwrioy*, p. 291.
[80] Xačʻikyan, *XV Dari*, I, no. 735c, p. 652.
[81] Kiwlēsērean, *Cʻucʻak Ankiwrioy*, p. 426.

bread."[82] And another scribe, Yovanēs, claims: "I have received neither an apple nor a cucumber from anyone, because charity among the Armenians, particularly the ecclesiastics, has vanished."[83] In contrast, the grateful Zak'ēos requests that the newly ordained priest T'uma be remembered in the prayers of the readers because "he arrived today and brought me two loaves of unleavened bread made with olive oil, which I ate; also [remember] his mother, who had baked these large loaves of bread."[84]

A number of scribes even mentioned being inconvenienced by animals and insects. For instance, in 1338 Mxit'ar Anec'i writes in verse:

And from these accursed flies,
From these animals who labor in vain,
They constantly rest on my pen,
And also suck the ink of my script.[85]

Another scribe, Yovhannēs, describes his cell as being "most grievous, because of the mosquitoes and the flies and such others that are like them."[86] The scribe Yovhannēs of Bałēš writes: "The fleas in my cell caused me intense annoyance, for they were numerous; and since there was no one else here besides me, they ate me up in place of them all."[87] And yet another, Zak'ēos, informs us that while he was writing "a mouse urinated on the margin" of the manuscript.[88]

The animals and insects were not the only creatures that broke the monotony of the scribes' labors. There are frequent complaints about interference from the noise made by human beings. The scribe Movsēs states that he copied a Gospel in 1455 in the steward's chamber, which was shared by thirteen other monastics, and he adds: "And there was so much talking and reading and prayer that I cannot describe everything." Another scribe, Łazar, complains that in the monastery where he copied a hymnal "there was so much traffic to and fro and so much worthless conversation by men which caused me much tedium." Even a single individual's garrulity was irksome to some scribes, as in the case of Alek'sianos, who asks forgiveness for his scribal errors because his friend was a "babbling chatterbox."[89]

No less frequent are the scribes' protestations about the poor

[82] Tašean, *C'uc'ak Mxit'. Vienna*, pp. 49–50; Xač'ikyan, *XV Dari*, I, no. 553b, p. 496.
[83] Xač'ikyan, *XV Dari*, I, no. 621a, p. 547.
[84] *Ibid.*, *XV Dari*, II, no. 454g, p. 359.
[85] *Ibid.*, *XIV Dari*, no. 380b, pp. 311–312.
[86] *Ibid.*, no. 554, p. 459.
[87] *Ējmiacin*, Oct. 1951, p. 83; Xač'ikyan, *XV Dari*, I, no. 621b, p. 548.
[88] Xač'ikyan, *XV Dari*, II, no. 454b, p. 358.
[89] *Ibid.*, no. 68a, p. 53. *XV Dari*, I, no. 338, p. 322; no. 101, p. 99.

quality of their materials and writing instruments. The well-known author and scribe T'ovma Mecop'ec'i states that the parchment was so old that he could not smooth it out, "because it was dry and large, and the times were wicked, and it was wintertime."[90] The scribe Yohanēs, writing in 1458, also deplores the poor quality of the paper: "This and the other papers are unstarched; what use is there in writing on them! Some are saying, in ignorance, that the ink is of poor quality; I say no, it is the paper."[91] In other instances, however, the scribes admit that "the ink was bad and it spread"; that the ink was constantly thickening; and that "the ink always became viscid from the wind, on account of which I suffered much grief."[92]

In rare cases only was the entire production of a manuscript the work of a single individual; rather, as a rule, the operation was a collective enterprise. Generally, one person was in charge of securing the writing paper; others were responsible for the polishing of the paper and preparation of the ink; a scribe copied the manuscript; another individual compared the new copy of the manuscript with the exemplar and corrected the scribal errors; an artist did the ornamentation, illustration, or illumination; a binder bound the manuscript; a blacksmith made the fasteners for the cover; and so forth.

The colophons provide considerable data concerning these specialized functions. This information is usually provided in an indirect manner—as part of the scribe's acknowledgment of the services rendered by others in the production of the manuscript. Customarily, the scribe mentioned the names of all who participated, in many instances mentioning the specific nature of the service as well. Even the names of people who were remotely or indirectly involved in the work, such as those who may have shown a special favor to the scribe, were deemed worthy of mention in the colophon. All such individuals were singled out, usually by name, and commended to future generations of readers of the manuscript, and the scribe beseeched that prayers be said for them.

On the other hand, the scribes occasionally record bitter experiences and severe indignities which frustrated their endeavors. A case in point is the manner in which the scribe Grigor Axalc'xec'i was treated by the monks of the monastery of Hermon. In the colophon of a manuscript which he completed in 1419 he writes:

> When I arrived in this monastery two years ago, the locusts devoured the produce and intense anguish befell our eastern

[90] *Ibid.*, no. 588a, p. 523.
[91] *Ibid.*, *XV Dari*, II, no. 151d, p. 114.
[92] *Ibid.*, I, no. 66d, p. 62. *XIV Dari*, no. 380b, p. 311; no. 8, p. 7.

lands, because for three years in succession they devoured the produce and devastated our country. Up until the time I copied half of this book, there was a refectory, but afterwards the steward of the monastery left and its refectory ceased to exist. Discord reigned among the monastics, slander and grumbling increased, and the monks took care of themselves on their own. They all had their own cells but not I; they all had food to eat but not I; and they divided the monastery's food amongst themselves but they gave me none, saying, "he is a *łarip*, do not give him a share." They all had their own novices and servants but not I. They all had loved ones who brought them food and things to drink but none for me. They all had access to the vardapet's cell, where they ate and drank but not I. The vardapet sympathized with the hunger of everyone but not mine; he took the monastics individually to his cell and fed them but not me; and he inquired the pleasure and complaint of everyone but not mine. He consoled everyone but not me, even though I labored to copy this book for his holiness, famished, hungry, and without wine. On one occasion after the departure of the steward I ate no food for three days and asked for none. On another occasion I remained hungry for two days, and although I asked for food they gave me none. And one day I remained hungry until evening and they gave me a cucumber only, but I did not eat it and continued to write until the night and in solitude. When I went to the church services the monks bore a grudge against me and they would not speak to me. And whereas they spend time with the vardapet from early morning until the evening, I never went near him. And once a week the vardapet would ask me to return the exemplar [of the manuscript which he had lent me], but I could not keep pace with my labor. The vardapet's senior pupil was exceedingly solicitous to me, for he used to complain to the vardapet saying, "You are giving the exemplar to [Grigor] Axalc'xec'i and not to me." This was the extent of the monks' assistance to me, and this was the extent of the worldly joy which was meted out to me during the course of the copying of this book. And the vardapet divided the exemplars among his pupils giving them two and three sections, and to me not even one. For God's sake, he who has not left his home for the life of a *łarip* let him not do so. I cannot express with words the intensity of the spiritual wound I suffered at the hands of Satan. I had occasion to leave here but my mind was not tranquil. I suffered all this grief while copying this book and no one knew of it. The senior pupil beat the junior

> *abeła* [monk] saying, "Why are you smoothing out the paper for Grigor and are not doing the same for me?" Then God the Creator, Who dispels man's anguish and feeds the hungry, dispatched a good man who became a father to me and his spouse a mother to me. Up to the time I completed this book, they sent me food every day on the back of their son; may the Lord God grant them the food that they might eat and never grow hungry again, and may He let the novice Jamaladin reach a ripe old age. And thus I, wretched and solitary, who had no one to bring me even a pitcher of water and had only God as my protector, began this by the will of God and completed it within seventy-four days with the strength which He gave me.[93]

A number of scribes have left us some glimpses of their emotional states. For instance, one of them begs his readers not to condemn him for the errors in his manuscript, "because I copied it with a bitter heart, for I was aggrieved by false monks and false friends, and I was in a state of bewilderment both spiritually and bodily, and I have only Christ as my recourse, as well as His help and the prayers of all His saints." Another scribe writes: "Alas! I am in grief and am poor of mind . . . for my mind is intensely delirious, and the script of my exemplar is tiny, and my mind wanders more often than it concentrates." Yet another scribe bemoans that his "mind was distracted by worldly preoccupations, and I was in grave anguish, for when I wrote a single letter a thousand other thoughts occurred to me, and the pen remained idle."[94]

There were instances when a scribe went to considerable pains to secure exemplars of manuscripts, or when circumstances compelled him to copy several manuscripts at once. This is illustrated in a colophon written by the scribe Zak'ariay in 1304: "do not criticize me for the errors, because an exemplar could not be found, and I suffered much grief on account of an exemplar which did not exist. And I, taking my copy book, wandered hither and thither and copied with much labor. I was copying other manuscripts as well, a music book and a hymn book. I used to write a page of the music book and put it aside to dry, and then do likewise with the hymn book, and then go on to copy the Gospel. Later, I would observe that all my pens were unhealthy, rather they were broken and shattered; and this was because I did not have a private and permanent place."[95]

93 *Ibid., XV Dari*, I, no. 739a, pp. 657–658.

94 *Ibid., XV Dari*, II, no. 220, p. 171; *XV Dari*, I, no. 220e, p. 206; *XIV Dari*, no. 637, p. 517.

95 *Ibid.*, no. 27, p. 23.

Among the difficulties which the scribes encountered occasional reference is also made to the poor quality of the exemplars or to the errors they contained. In the Middle Ages the texts which were tampered with were generally the historical works and commentaries. There was a strict injunction against editing religious and canonical works; and committing errors in their reproduction was regarded as an unpardonable sin. Indeed the Armenian synod held at Sis in 1243 passed a resolution which enjoined that the reproduction of religious works should be entrusted only to "competent, learned, and orthodox" scribes, these qualifications to be attested by experts.[96] In view of this, the scribes took greater pains in copying these works and compared completed manuscripts with the exemplars.[97] There is evidence that such texts were often checked two or three times. For instance, in a colophon written by the scribe Karapet future scribes are warned not to pervert or distort the text by ignorance; rather, they should follow his example and check their work "twice and even three times."[98] Another scribe, who copied "Sargis Šnorhali's Commentary on the Encyclical Letters," remarks: "not everyone has the authority to add or delete [from the texts], but only the learned scholars, who are versed in the Old and New Testaments and those who are recognized for their learning in the art."[99]

Scribal ignorance was of course responsible for many errors in the manuscripts. Such errors were frequently detected by competent and learned scribes. In the colophon of a commentary on the Gospel by John copied in 1117, for instance, the scribe Step'anos complains that the text was "corrupted and distorted by a foolish and ignorant scribe immersed in darkness."[100] Another scribe, alluding to errors found in the texts, reproaches ignorant scribes for "defiling" the originals; he also criticizes them for attempting to exonerate themselves by putting the blame on the authors or the previous reproducers of the text.[101] Hence, with a view to reassuring the sponsors and future readers, the scribes in their colophons frequently assert that they have copied the manuscripts from "authentic, excellent, and choice exemplars."

On the other hand, some scribes, mindful of the errors they might have committed, request future scribes to make the necessary correc-

[96] See Małak'ia Ōrmanean, *Azgapatum* (3 vols., Constantinople and Jerusalem, 1913–1927), col. 1120; Garegin Yovsēp'ean, *Niwt'er ew Usumnasirut'iwnner Hay Aruesti ew Mšakoyt'i Patmut'ean*, II (New York, 1943), 12.

[97] Xač'ikyan, *XV Dari*, I, no. 156, p. 155.

[98] Matenadaran MS. no. 2072, cited in Abrahamyan, *Patmut'yun*, p. 365.

[99] Xač'ikyan, *XIV Dari*, no. 503a, p. 420.

[100] Matenadaran MS. no. 6273, cited in Abrahamyan, *Patmut'yun*, pp. 362–363.

[101] Matenadaran MS. no. 1465, cited in Abrahamyan, *Patmut'yun*, p. 363.

tions. For example, the scribe Łazar, who in 1416 copied "The Commentaries by Grigor Tat'ewac'i," writes: "Moreover, I plead with you not to reproach me for my errors and the largeness of my calligraphy, for this was the extent of my experience in the art of copying manuscripts, and this is the best I could do. Erase whatever is superfluous and insert whatever is lacking." [102] Other scribes relied on the charitableness of future copyists: "And do not criticize me for the poor quality and artlessness of my calligraphy, for this was the limit of my ability and no more. Do not be angry if you find errors, but make the corrections with a sweet disposition, insert what is missing and erase what is superfluous, and deliver me from accusations." [103] The scribe Step'anos, who copied a Gospel in 1467, resorts to a strategem which is quite unique in the field of colophon writing. Conscious of possible deficiencies in his work, and eager to avoid condemnation, he seeks a mutual concession: "you ignore my errors and God will ignore yours." [104]

Injunctions Regarding Use of Manuscripts and Anathemas Against Violators

The great cost of the production of manuscripts, the relative scarcity of books in contrast to the great demand for them, and the deep sense of veneration with which manuscripts were regarded account for the abundance of various kinds of warnings with respect to the proper handling of manuscripts, as well as anathemas against those who violated these injunctions.

The scribes beseech the owners of the manuscripts, whether individuals or ecclesiastical institutions, not to regard manuscripts as salable merchandize or an object that can be mortgaged. A corollary of this is the frequent refrain that the manuscript in question is "free and clear" from any monetary obligation, or that it was acquired by its commissioner or sponsor with his *halal* (honestly earned) assets. For instance, a scribe writes:

No one has the authority
To mortgage this for silver,
Or to sell it for money,
For it is free in all respects.[105]

[102] Xač'ikyan, *XV Dari*, I, no. 208, p. 192.
[103] Xač'eryan, *Grč'ut'yan Arvest*, p. 214.
[104] Xač'ikyan, *XV Dari*, II, no. 337a, p. 264.
[105] Matenadaran MS. no. 7446, cited in Abrahamyan, *Patmut'yun*, p. 387.

Secondly, the scribes placed a moral obligation on future generations to recover manuscripts carried off as booty, by ransom or other means. Many colophons attest to the fact that this injunction was carried out most diligently, sometimes even at the expense of human lives; such colophons were generally written by the purchasers or the rescuers themselves, who wished to be remembered for their deed. These texts also confirm that, in the Middle Ages, captured manuscripts were never referred to as booty, but rather, like human beings, they were either "carried off into captivity," or they were "rescued or purchased from captivity." An example of this kind of injunction is found in a Gospel manuscript then in the cathedral of the Holy Sepulcher at Jerusalem; the scribe Kostandin Vahkacʻi writes in 1413:

> Let no one remove it from this place,
> Let no one hand it over to an infidel.
> Should there be any fear from the Muslims,
> Let them put it in safekeeping in the fort,
> Or take it to the island of Cyprus;
> And when the danger has passed
> Bring it back to this place,
> And receive their fitting reward.[106]

Thirdly, the scribes frequently pleaded with the owners of the manuscripts not to create obstacles in the event someone wished to reproduce a copy of the text. Indeed, in the opinion of the scribes, "a locked manuscript is like an idol." The scribe Vardan, who copied Ełišē Vardapet's historical work on the Battle of Awarayr, writes: "And if they should ask for this for purposes of reading or copying it, let this [request] not be denied, for the reason for my copying it was that everyone might benefit by it."[107]

Fourthly, the colophons are replete with injunctions and warnings concerning the proper handling of manuscripts. For example, they warn against the delivery of manuscripts into the hands of ignorant people lest they cut off folios, ruin the margins by scribbling, remove the illuminations, or damage the bindings by various means. In the colophon written by the prince Yovhannēs in Cilicia in 1286 children were strictly forbidden to handle manuscripts because they damaged them.[108] The scribes plead that manuscripts be kept away from fire, water, dampness, mice, moths, and other insects; they caution the

[106] Xačʻikyan, *XV Dari*, I, no. 159b, p. 158.
[107] *Ibid.*, *XIV Dari*, no. 94, p. 70.
[108] Lalayean, *Vaspurakan*, p. 108.

users to handle them with clean and dry hands and with a cloth, and not to drop candlewax or oil on them, and so forth. A few quotations will illustrate the forms of the customary warnings. The scribe Łazar, who copied a hymnal in 1424, writes in a colophon which contains a lacuna: "I plead with you who may encounter this [hymnal] to take good care of this book and [not to handle it] without a cloth / / / not to wet the fingers at all and not to turn the pages in vain; and he who tears off any folios from this may God cut off his life, and he who takes good care of it may God adorn his soul and make him worthy of paradise." Another scribe, Matt'ēos, pleads: "For God's sake, keep it away from candle and oil and hold it with a white cloth, I beg you." Garianē, the recipient of a missal in 1412, requests "the priests, and the deacons, and the servants of the church to take good care of this book; not to keep it without a cover, or lay it on the stone without a cover."[109] Another scribe, Daniēl, asks that the clergy of the Church of the Holy Cross at Ałt'amar handle the missal which he copied "with compassion and to use it with circumspection, and not to turn its weak folios in vain but to read it with care, because I accomplished this with much and great labor; the learned and the clergy will fully understand the labor it involved, just as the apostle said, 'For in that he himself hath suffered being tempted, he is able to succour them that are tempted,' and you should do likewise so that you may be worthy of Christ's blessings, amen!"[110] The sponsor of a manuscript containing excerpts from the Old Testament warned its users "to be cautious of water, fire, and all other destructive elements"; and yet another scribe, Step'annos, asked that the manuscript which he copied be protected against all elements that might cause its destruction, that is, "from moths, pilferers, moisture, and from everything that would waste away its beauty; moreover, you should take care of it with a cloth cover even as a wise merchant does with his precious pearls."[111]

The various violations of injunctions concerning the proper treatment of manuscripts compelled many scribes or commissioners to record strict rules and to pronounce anathemas against violators. As early as the year 989, we read in the colophon of a Gospel: "And let no one dare to remove for any reason this Word of God from this holy church at Noravank'; and should anyone dare to remove this Gospel from the holy altar, may the usurper like Satan be denied the grace bestowed by the Son of God, and may his soul and flesh be anathema

[109] Xač'ikyan, *XV Dari*, I, no. 338, pp. 322–323; *XV Dari*, II, no. 157a, p. 120; *XV Dari*, I, no. 145, p. 140.

[110] Xač'ikyan, *XIV Dari*, no. 116a, p. 86. Daniēl quotes from the Epistle to the Hebrews, 2:18.

[111] *Ibid.*, no. 140, p. 108; no. 461a, p. 383.

and may he, like the infidels who commit sacrilege, be condemned by the Son of God." The scribe Awag writes in a colophon dated 1337: "and should anyone dare to steal this holy Gospel, or tear off pages from it, or remove it from the great church of the holy and most immaculate monastery of Tat'ew, may he share the fate of Cain, Judas, and the crucifiers and inherit the doleful maledictions, amen!" The donor of a ritual book to the church on the island of Ałt'amar wished that similar offenders "share the fate of Judas and the crucifiers and of the heretics Arius and Nestorius; and may he receive no forgiveness or salvation, neither in this life nor in the hereafter, amen!" The donor of a Gospel to an Armenian church in Moldavia wished that those who removed it from its place would receive the same reward that befell Korah and Dathan. And in the event the menology offered to the church of St. Peter and Paul at Van were stolen or mortgaged, the scribe Vardan hoped that the perpetrator would "share the fate of Judas and the crucifiers, as well as of Korah, Dathan, Abiron, Anēs, Amrēs, and Cain."[112]

The colophons also contain injunctions against the theft, sale, and mortgaging of manuscripts, and the usual damnatory expressions were addressed against those who committed these acts. For example the scribe Xač'er writes in 1307 with regard to a Gospel: "if anyone should dare to steal, sell, or mortgage this, or if he should for any reason remove it from the church of St. Mary at Ałt'amar, may he be denied the mercy of Christ and may he share the fate of Judas and the crucifiers, whether he is a priest or layman, man or woman."[113] On the other hand, manuscripts could be removed from the churches under rare circumstances, as illustrated in the colophon written by the scribe Step'an at Jerusalem in 1321: "And if anyone should remove it because of attacks by horsemen or any other turbulence, but returns it to its place after the peace is restored, may he be blessed by God." In the year 1452 a certain Sargis Vardapet purchased a number of items which had been mortgaged, including a Gospel, which he donated to the monastery of St. James at Jerusalem. In his colophon he states: "And whoever dares to mortgage or sell it or remove it from our dominical see, may his memory be erased by Christ God; and the foolish buyer who buys it because of greed or removes it from our holy see, may his memory be erased from the book of life; but if he should buy it and not remove it may he receive the diadem of life, for he who

[112] Yovsēp'ean, *Yišatakarank'*, I, no. 70, p. 156; Xač'ikyan, *XIV Dari*, no. 360, p. 293; *ibid.*, *XV Dari*, I, no. 48c, p. 47; *ibid.*, *XV Dari*, II, no. 14, p. 13; *ibid.*, no. 286a, pp. 234–235.

[113] *Ibid.*, *XIV Dari*, no. 63a, p. 49. For other examples see *ibid.*, no. 202b, p. 163, and no. 274a, p. 218; *XV Dari*, I, no. 156, pp. 155–156.

receives it for the purpose of taking it away takes to his home God's fire, which burns and is incendiary."[114]

Extant manuscripts attest to the prevalence in the Middle Ages of two types of falsification of data in colophons. The first involved the alteration of the original date of the manuscript's completion to make it appear to be considerably older than it actually was; secondly, the name of the real scribe on occasion was replaced by that of another, who thus claimed someone else's fine work as his own. To guard against such falsification, the scribes inserted anathemas in their colophons against those who altered the names of the scribes or tore off the colophon in its entirety. In a Collection of Homilies copied in 1553 and now in the British Museum we read: "Whoever dares to mutilate or efface this colophon, let his name be effaced from the book of life." The scribe Yohanēs writes in 1319: "do not erase names, for it is an evil habit; and if you are a worthy individual write your name in a different place." A group of individuals who bought a Gospel and donated it to the priest T'uma in 1306 hoped that he who tears off the colophon would be "put in chains and condemned by God, and Christ would erase him from the book of life." The priest Sargis, who purchased a Gospel in 1325, warns those who might inherit it: "do not erase the names or even any letter of the original and do not write your name in its place; rather, write your name somewhere else. And if anyone, big or small, should erase the original name may he be erased from the book of life; do not, do not do it, for it is evil, a great evil." There were also injunctions against tearing off folios from the manuscripts, as in the following colophon written in 1410 by the scribe Step'anos: "and whoever approaches this holy book with a sword or a knife and cuts off folios from this book, may the flaming sword cut off his loins."[115]

It was also customary for the scribes or the donors, in order to perpetuate their memory, to request that on a specified day their colophons be read in public, as illustrated in the colophon of a Gospel written by its donor Awetik' at Kafa in the Crimea in 1456: "Let this colophon be read every year on Palm Sunday; and may the individual, whether he be a priest or layman, who acts contrary to this, be anathematized by the power on high, and may he be denied participation in the divine liturgy in this church, and may he be accursed by all the saints, amen!"[116]

[114] *Ibid.*, *XIV Dari*, no. 210a, p. 169; *XV Dari*, II, no. 35, p. 28.

[115] F. C. Conybeare, *A Catalogue of the Armenian Manuscripts in the British Museum* (London 1913), p. 193. Xač'ikyan, *XIV Dari*, no. 199b, p. 159; no. 57b, p. 43; no. 245b, p. 197. Xač'ikyan, *XV Dari*, I, no. 115, p. 114.

[116] Xač'ikyan, *XV Dari*, II, no. 108, p. 78.

The Calendrical Systems Used in the Colophons

The chronological data supplied by the scribes is one of the most important aspects of the colophons. In the first place, the scribes as a rule indicated when individual manuscripts were completed; occasionally, they also mentioned the year and even the month in which the work was started. Moreover, many colophons are written in the form of short chronicles, and the historical information they contain are usually presented in chronological sequence. In addition, colophons frequently provide evidence on the basis of which historical events can be dated. On the other hand, there are a considerable number of manuscripts which do not supply any of this information. In such cases, the scribe may have failed to record the dates; the colophon may have been tampered with; or this information may have been lost because of lacunae in the text or the removal of the colophon from the manuscript, either deliberately or inadvertently in the course of its rebinding and restoration. In the absence of chronological data, catalogers of Armenian manuscripts have usually determined the date on the basis of paleography.

Armenian historians and chroniclers, as well as the authors of the colophons, employed various calendrical systems. In the early Middle Ages, the chronology employed in Armenian historical and other literary works, as well as in the inscriptions, was based upon the reigns of monarchs or historically prominent figures. Subsequently, the chronology was provided by means of various Armenian and foreign calendars. The oldest of these was the calendrical system associated with the Creation, which appears in Armenian sources under several names, such as *T'uarkut'iwn Adamay* (Era of Adam), *T'uakan Yelaneloy Adamay i Draxtēn* (Era of Adam's Expulsion from Paradise), *Žamanak Skzbanc' Ararč'ut'ean* (Era Since the Beginning of the Creation), and so forth. Of the many calendars computed on the basis of the Creation, the Armenians generally employed the following four systems.[117]

1) The Imperial Era of the Creation (also known as the Constantinopolitan or Byzantine Era) was used principally in the Byzantine empire and in those countries which had close cultural contacts with it. The beginning of this era was reckoned from the year 5508 B.C. For instance, the scribe Step'anos states that he copied a portion of the manuscript of a Holy Bible "in the year 6821 of Adam [6821 − 5508 = A.D. 1313], and in the year 762 of the Haykazean Era [762 + 551 = A.D. 1313]."[118]

[117] See Abrahamyan, *Patmut'yun*, pp. 250–255.

[118] Xač'ikyan, *XIV Dari*, no. 130b, p. 96. For other examples of the use of the Imperial Era of the Creation in the colophons see Yovsēp'ean, *Yišatakarank'*, I, nos. 18–20, pp. 53–56.

2) The Septuagint (*Eōt'anasnic'*) Era of the Creation began in 5200 B.C.; the Armenians generally reckoned as its starting point the year 5198 B.C. For instance, the scribe Grigor completed a Gospel "6430 years after the expulsion of Adam from Paradise [that is, 6430 − 5200 = A.D. 1230]; . . . and in the year 679 of the Haykazean Era [679 + 551 = A.D. 1230]."[119] Similarly, Grigoris C'ałmanec'i received a manuscript "when 5198 [years] had passed since the expulsion of Adam until [the birth of] Christ; . . . and in the year 763 of the Great Armenian Era [763 + 551 = A.D. 1314]."[120]

3) The Alexandrine Era of the Creation was reckoned from 5423 B.C.; Armenian sources usually used the year 5425 as a starting point. For example, the scribe Sargis completed a manuscript "in the year 763 of the Haykazean Era [763 + 551 = A.D. 1314] . . . and when 6739 years [6739 − 5425 = A.D. 1314] had passed since the expulsion of the first-created from the magnificent abode." To cite another example, the scribe Step'anos completed a *Čašoc'* (Missal) at Surxat' in the Crimea "in the year 820 of the Askanazean and Japhetic Era [820 + 551 = A.D. 1371] . . . and [in the year] 6796 [− 5425 = A.D. 1371] since the expulsion of Adam from Paradise."[121]

4) The Armenian Era of the Creation, named after its originator, the seventh-century mathematician Anania Širakac'i, used as its starting point 5281 B.C. For instance, the scribe T'adēos completed the manuscript of "The Lives of the Church Fathers" at Kafa "in the year 6711 of Adam [6711 − 5281 = A.D. 1430] according to the [calculations of] vardapet Anania Širakac'i . . . and in the year 879 of the Japhetic Armenian Era [879 + 551 = A.D. 1430]."[122]

It is obvious that there was no agreement in these calendars on the exact date of the Creation. As the above examples illustrate, the Armenian authors seldom mentioned by name which of the Creation eras they actually used. Nevertheless, this can as a rule be determined by the corresponding dates in other calendars which they generally provided, primarily the dates given according to the "Great Armenian Era."

Prior to the adoption of the Christian calendar in the first quarter of the fourth century, the Armenians used two calendars simultaneously, the one immovable and the other movable or civil. In the civil calendar, the year consisted of 365 days, and therefore once in every four years the Armenian New Year (the first of Nawasard) occurred

[119] See Sargisean, *Venetik*, I, 572.
[120] Xač'ikyan, *XIV Dari*, no. 136a, pp. 102–103.
[121] *Ibid.*, no. 135, p. 101; no. 608, p. 496.
[122] *Ibid.*, *XV Dari*, I, no. 430, p. 401.

one day in advance of the New Year in the Julian calendar. They also had a second New Year, computed according to the immovable calendar, which fell on March 21.[123]

The controversy among the eastern and western churches, which resulted from the various systems for computing the Easter festival, was eventually resolved by the Council of Nicaea in 325. The Council ordained that the celebration of Easter—which governed all the other movable feasts—should thenceforth always take place on the Sunday which immediately followed the full moon that happened upon, or next after, the day of the vernal equinox, which was fixed invariably in the calendar on March 21. On the basis of this and other conditions laid down by the Council, Easter could not happen earlier than March 22 nor later than April 25.[124]

For two hundred years (353–552), the eastern churches, including the Armenian, celebrated Easter according to the luni-solar calendar prepared by Andrew of Byzantium on the basis of the decisions of the Council of Nicaea. In 562 a conclave of mathematicians meeting in Alexandria agreed on a new calendar—known under the name of Aeas—based upon a cycle of 532 years. In the same year, the Patriarchate of Byzantium, accepting the basic formula of the Calendar of Aeas, accepted another—known as the Calendar of Irion—which included some slight modifications from the former in the computations of the full moon. Because of the difference between the epacts of these two otherwise identical calendars, four times in a cycle of 532 years the two Easters occurred with a week's interval between them.

The first discrepancy in the Easter celebration, which occurred in 570, necessitated the regulation of the Armenian ecclesiastical calendar. The Armenian church synod, held at Dwin in 584, adopted in principle the Alexandrine calendar of Aeas with its cycle of 532 years,[125] and adapted it to the Armenian movable or civil calendar.[126] Since the year in the civil calendar consisted of 365 days, the additional day was intercalated in the leap years in accordance with the Julian calendar.[127] In this new calendar, commonly known as the Great Armenian Era, the year was divided into twelve months of thirty days

[123] See Edouard Dulaurier, *Recherches sur la Chronologie Arménienne* (Paris, 1859), I, 1–17.

[124] See article "Calendar: Christian" by James G. Carleton, in *Encyclopaedia of Religion and Ethics*, III (New York), 88–90.

[125] For the reasons that led the Armenians to follow the calendar of Aeas rather than that of Irion, and for the effects of the discrepancy in the dates of the Easter celebrations upon the relations of the Greek and Armenian churches, see Avedis K. Sanjian, "Cṙazatik 'Erroneous Easter'—A Source of Greco-Armenian Religious Controversy," in *Studia Caucasica* (The Hague), 2: 26–47.

[126] See Dulaurier, *Recherches*, I, 18–110.

[127] See Ōrmanean, *Azgapatum*, col. 506.

each, with five additional days (Aweleac‘) intercalated after the twelfth month. The names of the months were as follows: (1) Nawasard; (2) Hoṙi; (3) Sahmi; (4) Trē; (5) K‘ałoc‘; (6) Arac‘; (7) Meheki; (8) Aregi; (9) Aheki; (10) Mareri; (11) Margac‘; and (12) Hrotic‘.

The Great Armenian Era was the most important among the various eras created by the Armenian chronologists. It is also referred to in Armenian sources by other names, such as Haykazean, T‘orgomean, Ask‘anazean, Aramean, Yabet‘ean, Xosrovayin, and so forth. The starting point of this era is still a matter of debate. The proponents of the preponderant view argue that when the Armenians adopted the quincentenary cycle of Aeas they reckoned 562—the date on which the latter calendar was devised—the tenth year of their own cycle; thus 552 became the first year of the Great Armenian Era.[128] On this basis, the difference between the Armenian Era and the modern calendar is 551 years, a figure which is still employed in calendrical conversions. The opponents of this view contend that the Great Armenian Era began in 553, on the grounds that the 200-year cycle of Andrew of Byzantium previously followed by the Armenians was completed in 552, and that the following year was the starting point of Aeas' quincentenary cycle.[129] It is noteworthy that this minority group continues to use the figure 551 in converting the Great Armenian Era into the modern calendar.

The vast majority of the colophons use only the Great Armenian Era when supplying dates. Sometimes corresponding dates according to other Armenian and non-Armenian calendars are given; in such cases, however, the date according to the Great Armenian Era should be considered more reliable. This explains why the catalogers of Armenian manuscripts are guided principally by this calendar; and this is the criterion used by Yovsēp‘ean and Xač‘ikyan in their compilations of the colophons.

Aeas' quincentenary cycle terminated on two different dates in the Julian and Armenian calendars—July 11, 1084, and February 28 of the same year. The discrepancy of 133 days between the two calendars resulted from the fact that the Armenians had failed to account for the bissextile day in the leap years. Because of this difference, the Armenians were unable to restore the 532-year cycle of Aeas as a guide for computing their Easter and other feasts. This difficulty was resolved by Yovhannēs Sarkawag (John the Deacon), who devised the

[128] See the article "Calendar: Armenian" by Frédéric Macler, in *Encyclopaedia of Religion and Ethics*, III, 70; Dulaurier, *Recherches*, I, 52; Ōrmanean, *Azgapatum*, col. 385.
[129] See Abrahamyan, *Patmut‘yun*, p. 263.

so-called Lesser Armenian Era or the Sarkawagadir Era. The starting point of this calendar, which substituted the Julian calendar for the old "vague" Armenian system,[130] was the year 1084. Besides making the fixed year begin, as in the Julian calendar, on August 11, Sarkawag fixed absolutely the correspondence between the Armenian and the Roman months. He also intercalated the bissextile day of the Julian calendar after the fifth additional day, in imitation of the Alexandrians, and counted six instead of five additional days every fourth year. Thus, with the establishment of a fixed year, the Armenian menology received a regular, definite, and fixed form.[131] On the basis of these important reforms, Sarkawag constructed a new quincentenary (532-year) cycle, which could be repeated without difficulty upon its termination in 1616.[132] For the conversion from the Lesser Armenian Era to the modern calendar, the figure 1083 or 1084 should be added to the former—1083 if the event occurred between August 11 and December 31, and 1084 if it occurred between January 1 and August 10.

Despite the marked improvement of Sarkawag's calendar over the system employed in the Great Armenian Era, the latter remained the basic calendrical system for a long time. Even when dates were given in the colophons in accordance with the new calendar, the older era was still mentioned. For instance, the scribe Step'an states that the Gospel he copied at Surxat' was completed "in the year 801 of the Ask'anazean and Abet'akan Era [the Great Armenian Era; 801 + 551 = A.D. 1352], and in the year 269 of the new era [the Lesser Armenian Era; 269 + 1083 = A.D. 1352]." Another Gospel copied at Surxat' by the scribe Step'an Sewaglxonc' was completed "in the year 824 of the Ask'anazean and Yabedakan Era [Great Armenian Era; 824 + 551 = A.D. 1375], and in the year 291 of the new era [Lesser Armenian Era; 291 + 1084 = A.D. 1375]."[133]

In addition to the Great or Lesser Armenian eras, the authors of the colophons also provide the chronology in accordance with the Armenian as well as non-Armenian Christian ecclesiastical calendars.

130 For a discussion of the ancient Armenian calendar and the "vague" year see Dulaurier, *Recherches*, I, 1–17.

131 For discussions of Sarkawag's reforms of the Armenian calendar consult: A. G. Abrahamyan, *Hovhannes Imastaseri Matenagrut'yunə* (Erevan, 1956), pp. 65–100; Dulaurier, *Recherches*, I, 111–115; F. K. Ginzel, *Handbuch der mathematischen und technischen Chronologie* (Leipzig, 1914), IIIB, pp. 314–321; Macler, "Calendar: Armenian," p. 71; Abrahamyan. *Patmut'yun*, pp. 268–271.

132 Upon the conclusion of Sarkawag's 532-year cycle in 1616, Azaria J̌ułayec'i prepared a new table; but this calendar failed to gain widespread use in Armenia. See Dulaurier, *Recherches*, I, 115–117.

133 Xač'ikyan, *XIV Dari*, no. 479, p. 399; no. 639, p. 518.

The Armenian chronologists calculated that Christ was born two years before the beginning of the Christian era. For instance, the scribe Grigor T'orosanc' indicates the date of the Bible which he copied as follows: "in the year 1373 since the incarnation of the Savior, and in the year 820 of the Great Armenian Era [820 + 551 = A.D. 1371]." The difference of two years between the two calendars indicates that the first is the Armenian Christian era.[134] The scribe Markos, on the other hand, provides the chronology in his colophon according to several Christian calendars based upon the birth of Christ: "1390 according to the Armenian calculation, and 1396 according to the Greeks, and 1388 according to the Franks, and 1381 [?] according to the Syrians, and 837 [837 + 551 = A.D. 1388] according to the Japhetic calendar of the Armenians."[135] Since there are discrepancies among these calendars because of their disagreement on the actual date of Christ's birth, and since Markos also provides the date according to the Japhetic or Great Armenian Era, the last must be taken as the basis of the chronology.

Even as late as the fifteenth century, the authors of the colophons continued to provide the chronology according to both the movable and the immovable Armenian calendars. The months of the year were given according to either the Julian calendar or Sarkawag's immovable calendar; sometimes the corresponding months and days according to both calendars were supplied. It is to be noted that the New Year (the first of Nawasard) in the calendar of Sarkawag always corresponded to August 11 in the Julian calendar—a fact which must be taken into account in conversion from one system to the other.

The following examples illustrate the use of the Armenian movable and immovable calendars in the colophons. The manuscript of a "Collection of Philo the Hebrew's Writings" received by Kirakos and Yovhannēs was completed "in the year 791 [of the Great Armenian Era; 791 + 551 = A.D. 1342], on the seventh of March, on the twelfth of Sahmi." Since the first of Nawasard in 1342 corresponded to December 26 in the Armenian movable calendar, calculations show that the twelfth of Sahmi actually corresponded to March 7. The manuscript of a "Calendar," which was edited and copied by Yohannēs, was completed "in the year 833 of the Great Armenian Era [833 + 551 = A.D. 1384], and in the year 300 of Sarkawag's Era [300 + 1084 = A.D. 1384] . . . on the sixteenth of Aheki of the Great Armenian Era . . . and on the seventeenth of Nawasard of Sarkawag's

[134] *Ibid.*, no. 586b, p. 481; for another example of the use of the Armenian Christian calendar together with the Great Armenian Era see *XV Dari*, I, no. 16, p. 19.
[135] Xač'ikyan, *XIV Dari*, no. 722a, p. 575.

Era." In this text, the sixteenth of Aheki is according to the movable calendar, and the seventeenth of Nawasard according to Sarkawag's immovable era.[136]

In addition to the calendrical systems described thus far, the colophons attest to the use of several other non-Armenian calendars. Among these was the Roman ecclesiastical calendar, the current era, which was used largely by Armenian clergy who belonged to the Fratres Unitores. For instance, the manuscript of an *Oskep'orik*, now in the library of the Mekhitarists in Venice, was copied by the scribe Israyēl "in the year 776 [of the Great Armenian Era = A.D. 1327], and in the year 1327 of Christ."[137] The date given according to the birth of Christ is definitely the Roman, which corresponds to that given in the Armenian Era. A substantial number of scribes also used the Indiction, the fiscal period of fifteen years instituted by the Emperor Constantine in A.D. 313, and reckoned from September 1, 312, which became a usual means of dating events. In employing the Cycle or Era of Indiction, the Armenian scribes frequently mention the number of the Indiction from its inception as well as the year within the cycle.[138] For instance, Manuscript number 906 of the Matenadaran was copied "in the year 495 of the Armenian Era [A.D. 1046], and in the thirteenth year of the Indiction of the Romans, during the reign of the Emperor Monomachus."[139]

Finally, the authors of the colophons occasionally supply the chronology according to the Jubilee Calendar, consisting of a cycle of fifty years; the Olympiad, with a cycle of four years; the Ides, with eight years; and the Nones, with five years.

Not a few authors of the colophons supplied dates according to several eras. Two examples will illustrate the point. The scribe Step'anos Sewaglxonc' states that the Gospel he copied was completed "in the year 824 of the Ask'anazean and Yabedakan Era [the Great Armenian Era; 824 + 551 = A.D. 1375]; and in the year 291 according to the new era [Sarkawag's Era; 291 + 1084 = A.D. 1375]; and in the year 1377 since the birth of the Savior [Armenian Christian Era; 1377 − 2 = A.D. 1375]; and in the year 6800 since the expulsion of Adam from Paradise [the Armenian-Alexandrine; 6800 − 5425 = A.D. 1375]." The scribe T'adēos Avramenc' records the chronology of

[136] *Ibid.*, no. 412, p. 332; no. 687, p. 551. For other examples of the simultaneous use of the movable and immovable calendars, with corresponding months according to the Julian and Armenian calendars, see no. 723c, p. 576; no. 724, p. 576; no. 738a, p. 594; no. 738b, p. 594.

[137] *Ibid.*, no. 260c, p. 206.

[138] See Dulaurier, *Recherches*, I, 187–191.

[139] Yovsēp'ean, *Yišatakarank'*, I, 230. For other examples of the use of the Indiction see nos. 18–20, pp. 53–56.

the "Lives of the Holy Fathers" which he copied as follows: "in the year 6630 since the expulsion of Adam from Paradise [the Septuagint; 6630 – 5200 = A.D. 1430] . . . and again in the year 6855 since Adam [Armenian-Alexandrine; 6855 – 5425 = A.D. 1430] according to the quincentenary of the philosopher Aeas [devised] at the meeting in Alexandria . . . and again since Adam in the year 6711 [6711 – 5281 = A.D. 1430] according to the vardapet Anania Širakac'i; and in the year 1432 [Armenian Christian Era; 1432 – 2 = A.D. 1430] since the birth of our Savior Jesus Christ; and in the year 1430 of the Romans; and in the year 879 according to the Japhetic calendar of the Armenians [Great Armenian Era; 879 + 551 = A.D. 1430], on the twenty-fifth of the month of August, on Tuesday."[140]

The preceding discussion is by no means an exhaustive study of all aspects of Armenian colophonic writing, for there are many other facets that still require special examination. Moreover, since the texts that follow are merely historical excerpts, they do not give a complete picture of all the characteristic features of the colophons. Nevertheless, the foregoing discussion and the texts herewith published are sufficient to underscore the unique literary art developed by the Armenian scribes, the unsung heroes of Armenian literature.

[140] Xač'ikyan, *XIV Dari*, no. 639, p. 518; *XV Dari*, I, no. 430, p. 401.

The Colophons

1301

1. Place: city of Berkri; scribe and author of col.: Yovhannēs; MS. title: Gospel.
Source: Xač'ikyan, *XIV Dari*, no. 2, p. 2

. . . [copied in 1301] during the reign of Łazan Łan [Ghāzān Khān], [and] the pontificate [*hayrapetut'iwn*] of the Lord Zak'aria [I of Ałt'amar] . . .

1302

1. Place: begun at monastery of Glajor in canton of Vayoyjor, and completed at monastery of T'ełeneac' in province of Ayrarat; scribe and author of col.: Mkrtič'; MS. title: Commentary on the Psalms by Nersēs of Lambron.
Source: Xač'ikyan, *XIV Dari*, no. 8, p. 6

. . . [copied in 1302] when the pontifical see of the Armenians was occupied by the Lord Grigoris [Grigor VII], surnamed Anawarzec'i . . . [and] during the tyrannical rule of the savage and barbaric nation of archers [azgn netołac'], the name of whose chief is Łazan [Ghāzān Khān], in the eastern regions of Asia. Many nations vanquished by them lived in servitude and under the heavy yoke of exorbitant taxes levied by them, especially in our country of Armenia, as in Israēł [Israel] at one time, [that is] during the period of anarchy. At this time the kingdom of Kilikia [Cilicia] was held by Het'um [II], son of Lewon [Leon II] . . .

2. Scribe and author of col.: Serob; MS. title: Gospel.
Source: Xač'ikyan, *XIV Dari*, no. 11, p. 10

. . . [copied] in the year 751 of our Haykazean Era [A.D. 1302], during the pontificate of the Lord Grigor [VII, Anawarzec'i], overseer [*veraditoł*] and catholicos [*kat'ułikos*] of the Armenians, [and] during the reign of Łazan Łan [Ghāzān Khān], son of Arłun [Arghūn Khān] . . .

1303

1. Place: Ałt'amar; scribe and author of col.: Daniēl; MS. title: History by T'ovma Arcruni.
Source: Xač'ikyan, *XIV Dari*, no. 14, p. 13

... this history was written in the year 752 of the Armenian Era [A.D. 1303], and during the imperial reign of Łazan [Ghāzān Khān] ...

2. Place: [monastery of Glajor]; author of MS. and of col.: Esayi Nč'ec'i; MS. title: Collection of Commentaries on the Prophecy of Ezekiel by Esayi Nč'ec'i.
Source: Xač'ikyan, *XIV Dari*, no. 15, p. 14

... I compiled this ... in the year 752 of our Haykazean Era [A.D. 1303], in bitter and wicked times, when we were afflicted with multifarious perils, both from within and without ...

3. Place: monastery of Nṙnawnic' in canton of Ayrarat; scribe and author of col.: T'adēos; MS. title: Commentary on the Twelve Prophets by Nersēs of Lambron, and Commentary on Daniel by Vardan Arewelc'i.
Source: Xač'ikyan, *XIV Dari*, no. 16a, p. 15

[When this manuscript was completed] ... the emperor was the imperial conqueror Xazan Łan [Ghāzān Khān], of the nation of archers [azgn netołac'], who ruled over the Armenians and Syrians [Asoroc'], the Georgians [Vrac'] and [Caucasian] Albanians [Ałuanic'], the Mars [Marac'] and Persians [Parsic'], the Turks [T'urk'ac'] and Hagars [Hagarac'oc'] ... Moreover, this was written in bitter and grievous times, in the winter season, with much suffering and tribulation. Sometimes I suffered from the cold weather and from the severity of the winter; sometimes we took to flight on account of the marauding Tatars [T'at'ar] and the destruction of our places [of habitation], but nowhere did we find solace ...

4. Place: monastery of Gṙner, near Barjr-Berd [in Cilicia]; scribe and author of col.: Martiros; MS. title: Bible.
Source: Xač'ikyan, *XIV Dari*, no. 17b, pp. 16–17

... I wrote this ... in the year 752 of the Great Armenian Era [A.D. 1303], in the month of May according to the Roman [Hṙomayec'woc'] names of the months, and on the seventeenth day of this month, on the same day that we received the bad news that the lord of our country marched forth, together with troops known as Mułal [Mongol], against the land known as Šambn [Syria]; and, because of our sins, he was defeated by the infidels [and] fled to the land of the Babylonians [Babelac'woc' ašxarh], near Xazan Xan [Ghāzān Khān]; hence, our country is in a grave tartarean [*tartaros*] state.

5. Place: Eznkay (?); MS. title: Law Book by Mxit'ar Goš.
Source: Xač'ikyan, *XIV Dari*, no. 20, p. 18

... This was copied in the capital city of [Eznkay?] ... in the year 752 of the Armenian Era [A.D. 1303], during the pontificate of the [Lord] Grigorios [Grigor VII, Anawarzec'i] and the prelacy of the Lord Nersēs at Eznkay; during the reign of the pious and devout King Het'um [II of Cilicia]; and during the reign of the imperial conqueror and great Łazan Łan [Ghāzān Khān] ...

6. Place: monastery of Akner; scribe and author of col.: Vardan; MS. title: Gospel.
Source: Xač'ikyan, *XIV Dari*, no. 231, p. 186

... This [Gospel] was completed in the year 772 of the Armenian Era [A.D. 1323].[1] In this year Xazan Xan [Ghāzān Khān] invaded, with numerous and countless troops, the country called Šamb [Syria]. With these [troops] God wished to punish and avenge the evil deeds of the Ismaelites [Ismayelac'oc'n] ...

1304

1. Place: monastery of Xač'atur, near Barjr-Bert [in Cilicia]; scribe and author of col.: Martiros; MS. title: Bible.
Source: Xač'ikyan, *XIV Dari*, no. 17d, p. 17

... This was written in the year 753 of our [Armenian] Era [A.D. 1304], in the month of July, at the monastery of Xač'atur, near Barjr-Bert, in the country of Kilikia [Cilicia], by the river Šlrkay, in a grotto, and in bitter times. In this month [July] Muhammadan [Mahmetakan] troops arrived from Šamb [Syria] and by peaceful means occupied the fortress of T'il; but, betraying their promise, they

[1] Xač'ikyan has included this text among the colophons of A.D. 1323, but this date is obviously erroneous. In view of the fact that Ghāzān Khān died in A.D. 1304 and the episode mentioned in the colophon refers to his invasion of Syria in A.D. 1303, the text is included here under 1303.

slaughtered whomever they found in it; and many who escaped from their hands were drowned in the great J̌ahan [Djayḥān] river; and all of this [came to pass] on account of my sins.

2. Place: [province of Vaspurakan]; scribe and author of col.: Zak'ariay; MS. title: Gospel.
Source: Xač'ikyan, *XIV Dari*, no. 27, pp. 22–23

. . . this holy Gospel was copied [in 1304] during the reign of Łazan Łan [Ghāzān Khān], who is a wise and beneficent king, and who is an uplifter of the downtrodden; may whom the Lord God grant a long life; during the reign of King Het'um [II of Cilicia] of the Armenians; [and] during the overseership of the Lord Catholicos Zak'aria [I of Ałt'amar] . . .

3. Place: city of Naxiǰawan; scribe and author of col.: Yakovb; MS. title: Gospel.
Source: Xač'ikyan, *XIV Dari*, no. 28, pp. 24–25

. . . In this year [1304] the monarch Łazan [Ghāzān Khān] departed this life and great grief befell all the peoples of the east, especially among our suffering Christian nations. May his memory be blessed and may he occupy the throne with the holy kings, because during his reign there was peace on earth as in God's paradise, [and] everywhere all taxes were removed. The Lord God gave him, as the Psalmist said, "the justice of a king" [cf. Psalms 72:1], for he was the son of Arłun Łan [Arghūn Khān], the just king, and "the king's strength loves justice" [cf. Psalms 99:4].

In these times, the arrogant, haughty, and imperious Ismaelites [azgn Ismayili] were subdued, and the glory of the holy church was uplifted, the singing of the psalms and the songs of hallelujahs increased, [and] the faith of the Christians flourished. The words of Esayi [Isaiah], born of Amoz [*amovsacin*], that "Wolves and lambs shall graze together" [cf. Isaiah 11:6], were fulfilled in this place. He rendered justice to the widows; he removed the interests charged on debts, and he returned to those who had been despoiled that which had been confiscated from them. He put an end to the traffic of the *despak*, *elč'i*, and *arłuč'i*,[2] and he appointed couriers everywhere, who are called *šk'rikk'*. And, because of his acts of justice, the Lord God delivered his enemies into his hands.

[2] See Appendix F for all untranslated terms.

He set forth with a large force and thunderous fury, with numerous spears, motley multitudes, and countless divisions, and he vanquished all of Syria [Tunn Šamay]. In a big and fierce battle he slaughtered the forces of Msr [Egypt] and caused not a little bloodshed, so much so that the bodies of men and the corpses of the fallen floated in the blood like the leaves of a fig tree; and, pursuing them until the sunset, they insatiably put them to the sword. And he returned with great rejoicing to the royal city of Dahavrēž [Tabrīz]. He accomplished numerous similar deeds of valor, which we cannot recount one by one . . .

4. Place: town of Karp'i in canton of Ayrarat; scribe and author of col.: Mkrtič'; MS. title: Catechism of Cyril of Jerusalem.
Source: Xač'ikyan, *XIV Dari*, no. 29, p. 25

. . . In this year [1304], the *p'ašah łan* named Xarpanday [Kharbanda] ascended the throne; may Christ the King guide him to protect the Christians with piety and affability . . .

5. Place: village of Awans in canton of Van; scribe and author of col: Yovannēs; MS. title: The Writings of Epiphanius the Cypriot.
Source: Xač'ikyan, *XIV Dari*, no. 30, p. 26

. . . This was written during the pontificate of the Lord Zak'arē [Zak'aria I] of Ałt'amar . . . and during the imperial conquest of the nation of archers [azgi netawłi] . . . in this year [1304] the benevolent and just Łazan Łan [Ghāzān Khān], who was the guardian of our Armenian nation, departed this life, causing much grief among the Christians. He was succeeded on the imperial throne by his brother, who is called Xarpandawłəl [Kharbanda]; he, too, exhibits goodwill toward everyone . . .

6. Place: city of Tp'xis; scribe and author of col.: Xač'atur; MS. title: Gospel.
Source: Xač'ikyan, *XIV Dari*, no. 33, p. 28

. . . This was written in the year 753 of the Armenian Era [A.D. 1304], on August 9, during the reign of King Het'um [II of Cilicia] of the Armenians and King Dawit' [David VII] of the Georgians [Vrac'];

during the pontificate of the Lord Grigor [VII, Anawarzec'i], catholicos of the Armenians; [and] during the imperial conquest of Xarpand [Kharbanda], brother of Łazan [Ghāzān Khān] [and] son of the great monarch Arławn [Arghūn Khān] . . .

1305

1. Place: monastery of Xorin in Kiłikē [Cilicia]; scribe and author of col.: Tirac'u; MS. title: Miscellany [*Žołovacu*].
Source: Xač'ikyan, *XIV Dari*, no. 42, p. 34

. . . [completed] in the year 754 of the Haykazean Era [A.D. 1305], and during the pontificate of the Lord Grigor [VII, Anawarzec'i] and the reign of King Het'um [II of Cilicia], in bitter and wicked times, when we were suffering at the hands of the nation of Ismael [azgn Ismayeli], for in this year the forces of Egiptos [Egypt] penetrated our country of Kilikē [Cilicia], on account of my evil deeds, [and] inflicted a cruel scourge in many localities, carried off the youth and children into captivity. Those of us who were left here are in anguish, [and] are terrified during the day and at night . . .

2. Recipient of MS.: Yovhannēs; author of col.: Yovhannēs (?); MS. title: Ritual Book [*Maštoc'*].
Source: Xač'ikyan, *XIV Dari*, no. 45, p. 35

In the year 754 of the Armenian Era [A.D. 1305], during the reign of Xarpand [Kharbanda], of the nation of archers [azgn netołac'] . . .

1306

1. Place: Ałt'amar; scribe and author of col.: Daniēl; MS. title: Commentary on the Epistles by Sargis Šnorhali.
Source: Xač'ikyan, *XIV Dari*, no. 54, p. 41

. . . [completed] during the pontificate of the Lord Zak'aria [I of Ałt'amar], and in the year 755 of our Armenian Era [A.D. 1306], and the reign of Het'um [II] in the Armenian kingdom of Kilikia [Cilicia], and during the imperial conquest by the nation of archers [netołakan azg], when they marched en masse in company with naught and shall find naught. They converted to the false faith of Mahmed [the

Prophet Muhammad], which will lead them directly into perdition. And they coerce everyone into converting to their vain and false hope. They persecute, they molest, and they torment, some by confiscating their possessions, some by tormenting them, some by slandering, [and] by insulting the cross and the church; and all of this [came to pass] on account of our sins . . .

2. Place: island of Lim; scribe and author of col.: Abraham; MS. title: Gospel.
Source: Xač'ikyan, *XIV Dari*, no. 55, p. 41

. . . Remember [the Lord pontiff] Zak'aria [I of Ałt'amar], who recently secured the faith of the Armenians from the wicked masters, and thus, through the intercession of God, freed the churches . . . [Written] in the year 755 of the Haykazean Era [A.D. 1306], in bitter and grievous times, in which year and because of our sins all these levies were imposed upon us . . .

3. Place: city of Ełegis; scribe and author of col.: Sargis; MS. title: Gospel.
Source: Xač'ikyan, *XIV Dari*, no. 56, p. 42

. . . [copied in 1306] during the imperial conquest of Xarpant Łan [Kharbanda Khān], whom the Ismaelites [azgn Ismayēli] call Sultan, during the reign of King Het'um [II] of the Armenians [of Cilicia], and during the princedom in this province of the devout and most blessed prince of princes Burt'ēl and Bułda, sons of the pious and illustrious prince of princes Ēlikum, son of the great Tarsaič . . . During the pontificate of the God-honored Lord Grigor [VII] Anawarzec'i, catholicos of the Armenians . . .

4. Place: village of Berdak in Tarberuni; scribe and author of col.: Yovsian; MS. title: Gospel.[3]
Source: Xač'ikyan, *XIV Dari*, no. 57a, p. 42

. . . this holy Gospel was copied during the reign of Sultan Awljat'u [Öldjaytü], who is a wise and merciful king, and an uplifter of the

[3] Xač'ikyan points out that the reading of the date in this colophon is uncertain. The last number of the date given in the Armenian Era may also be read 7, in which case the colophon should be included under A.D. 1308. See *XIV Dari*, p. 42, n. 1.

downtrodden, may whom the Lord God grant a long life; [and] during the catholicosate and overseership of the Lord Zak'aria [I of Ałt'amar] . . .

1307

1. MS. title: History by Vardan Arewelc'i.
Source: Xač'ikyan, *XIV Dari*, no. 61, p. 46

In the year 756 of our [Armenian] Era [A.D. 1307] when, because our righteousness had diminished and our impiety had increased, the wrath and wickedness of the nation of archers [azgn netołac'] increased and intensified against us, the Christian nations, and there came from Xorasan [Khurāsān] a young and one-eyed man, who looked like the Antichrist [*Neṙn*] who is to arrive some day, by the name of Xarbanda [Kharbanda Khān], which means the slave of a donkey, son of Arłun [Arghūn Khān], son of Hulayun [Hūlāgū Khān]. He sought to efface Christianity from Armenia and Georgia [Vrac' ašxarh], but the Lord prevented him and his evil design was not achieved. The servant of Satan then contemplated another thing; he issued orders that Christians throughout his domains should wear a symbol of opprobrium, and he decreed that taxes should be collected from them ranging from ten to forty silver per individual, each according to his means. It was in such bitter times that this [manuscript] was completed . . .

2. Place: Ałt'amar; scribe and author of col.: Daniēl; MS. title: Cyril's Catechism.
Source: Xač'ikyan, *XIV Dari*, no. 62, p. 47

. . . [written] in bitter and tartarean [*tartaros*] times, when the Ismaelites [azgn Ismayēli] became so powerful that they succeeded in converting to their vain hope the entire nation of archers [azgn netołac'], so that none among them remained who did not confess their fallacious and false faith, which will lead them directly into perdition.[4] They harass all the Christians to convert to their false hope;

[4] The reference is to the Mongols' adoption of the Muslim religion. Ghāzān Khān (1295–1304) was the first Mongol ruler who definitely adopted Islam with a large number of his subjects. This development had a profound effect upon Armeno-Mongol relations. Prior to this, the Armenian feudal lords had recovered their ancestral domains under Mongol vassalage, and the Armenian church institution had enjoyed extensive privileges. The religious intolerance and persecution that followed the Islamization of the Mongols,

some they molest, some they torture, some they kill, and they confiscate the possessions of others. Not contented with all these, they also levied taxes upon all the Christians and made them wear symbols of opprobrium, a black linen over the shoulders, so that whoever saw them would recognize that they are Christians and would curse them; and they make every effort to efface Christianity from the earth. And all of this [came to pass] on account of our sins . . .

3. Place: city of Berkri; scribe and author of col.: Xačʻer; MS. title: Gospel.
Source: Xačʻikyan, *XIV Dari*, no. 63a, p. 48

. . . [completed] during the rule of the nation of archers [*azgn netołacʻ*], at a time when they compelled the Christian flock to wear symbols; [and] during the pontificate of the Lord Zakʻaria [I of Ałtʻamar] . . .

4. Place: village of Šinamēǰ in canton of Arčēš or Kʻaǰberunikʻ; scribe and author of col.: Mkrtičʻ; MS. title: Gospel.
Source: Xačʻikyan, *XIV Dari*, no. 64a, p. 50

. . . [copied] during the reign of Xarpanday [Kharbanda Khān], of the nation of archers [netołakan azg], whom the Ismaelites [Ismaēlacʻocʻ] called Sultan / / /

5. MS. title: Gospel.
Source: Xačʻikyan, *XIV Dari*, no. 65, p. 51

. . . Thus, in diminishing days and waning times, that is in recent days, when, on account of multitudinous sins, the world trembled and wavered, as though in a tempestuous storm, from the tyrannical sword of the nation of archers [azinn netołacʻ], which for a long time intensified its sway in all lands, beginning from where the sun rises, from the Caspian Sea [Kasbicʻ Cov], and encompassing the northern regions up to the Pontus Sea [Pontosi Cov], and then stretching to the south and encircling the land of Babylonia [Babilacʻwocʻ ašxarh] and all of Asoris [northern Syria] and Kulikeay [Cilicia] and up to the same sea in the land of Pontus [Pontacʻwocʻ ašxarh]. All of Mēǰerkray [Asia Minor], and numerous peoples speaking various languages,

---

coupled with the levying of exorbitant taxes, compelled large masses of Armenians to abandon their native land and to seek refuge elsewhere.

were held under their evil yoke and servitude, as predicted by the great pontiff Nersēs, [Catholicos] of the Armenians.[5] Moreover, the pontifical line of Grigor Lusaworič‘ [St. Gregory the Illuminator] and of the Aršakuni [Arsacid] royal dynasty had waned and weakened, just as St. Isahak had foreseen in his vision.[6] And because of our impenitence, His [God's] wrath has not abated; rather, His hand is still raised to punish and chastise us. Yet we are still unrepentant; we have become feeble and lean, emaciated and languished, and we are nearing death and hell. For the savage, strange-looking and dark-countenanced nation of archers [azgn netołac‘] abandoned their native faith and followed the evil sect of the forerunner Antichrist [*Karapet Neṙn*] Mahmet [the Prophet Muhammad], and they subjected the Christians to more intense anguish and persecution . . .

Thus, in these bitter and evil times, when we were disconsolate and when darkness had spread and engulfed everyone . . .[7]

6. Place: [Cilicia]; MS. title: Psalm Book.
Source: Xač‘ikyan, *XIV Dari*, no. 72, p. 55

In the year 756 of the Armenian Era [A.D. 1307], on November 17, the Armenian Grand Baron Het‘um and his nephew, the handsome and all-bountiful youth Lēon [King Leon III of Cilicia], son of Baron T‘oros [III, King of Cilicia], were slain by the wicked Pelarłoy [Būlārgī] at the foot of Anarzab,[8] which caused great grief among the Armenian nation. Thus, we beseech you all, to heartily remember the aforementioned Baron Het‘um of the Armenians and the pious King Lēon [Leon III of Cilicia], who were martyred for our Armenian nation, so that Christ God, Who is eternally blessed, would seat them to His right, amen! Also, their fellow martyrs, Awšin [Oshin], the *asparapet* of the Armenians, and Baron Vasak, their [paternal] uncle.

[5] The prophecy attributed to Catholicos Nersēs I the Great (353–373) is preserved in the form of a vision, and is alleged to have been made shortly prior to his death. It predicts such events as the Crusades, the arrival of Antichrist, the end of the world, and the last judgment. See text in Mesrob Erēc‘, *Patmut‘iwn S. Nersisi Hayoc‘ Hayrapeti* (*Sop‘erk‘ Haykakank‘*, vol. VI; Venice, 1853), pp. 89–104.

[6] The apocryphal text concerning the vision of Catholicos Sahak I (387–436) will be found in "Lazare de Pharbe, Histoire d'Arménie," in Victor Langlois, *Collection des historiens anciens et modernes de l'Arménie* (Paris, 1869), II, 274–277.

[7] This incomplete colophon has been preserved through a seventeenth-century copy. See Xač‘ikyan, *XIV Dari*, p. 51 note.

[8] Būlārgī entered the city of Anarzab purportedly to discuss matters with the Armenian king; instead, he and his Mongols set upon the king and a score of Armenian nobles and massacred them. It is claimed that this crime was committed at the instigation of other members of the Armenian nobility who resented the pro-Latin concessions made by the king.

1308

1. Place: city of Sis; scribe and author of col.: Grigor; MS. title: Hymnary [*Šaraknoc'*]
Source: Xač'ikyan, *XIV Dari*, no. 73, p. 56

. . . This hymnary was copied in the year 757 of our Armenian Era [A.D. 1308], during the barony of the Armenians of Awšin and his brother Alinax; and during the pontificate of the Lord Kostandin [III] Kesarac'i . . .

. . . this was copied in bitter and difficult times, for in this year the wicked chief Pularłu [Būlārgī], of the nation of archers [azgn netołac'], treacherously slew the young and newly anointed King Lewon [Leon III of Cilicia], as well as the Grand Baron Het'um, and other princes . . .

2. Place: village of Awans in canton of Van; scribe and author of col.: Yovanēs; MS. title: Commentary on the Epistles by Sargis Šnorhali.
Source: Xač'ikyan, *XIV Dari*, no. 74, p. 57

This was copied and bound in the year 757 of the Haykazean Era [A.D. 1308] . . . during the imperial conquest of Xarpandawłəl Łan [Kharbanda Khān], of the nation of archers [azgn netołac'], and during the pontificate of the Lord Zak'arē [Zak'aria I] of Ałt'amar, catholicos of the Armenians . . .

1310

1. Place: Yohanavank' in canton of Anberd in Ayrarat; scribe and author of col.: Sarkawag; MS. title: Gospel.
Source: Xač'ikyan, *XIV Dari*, no. 89, pp. 65–66

. . . [copied] during the imperial conquest of Łarpanta Łan [Kharbanda Khān] of the nation of archers [azgn netołac'], and the reign of King [*sic*] Alinax of the Armenians . . . and when the prince of our canton was K'urd, son of Tayir and grandson of the great and pious K'urd.

But who can recount the tragedy and the lamentation of anguish, because sons and daughters in our land are being sold to pay excessive and intolerable levies, and numerous villages and monasteries are in ruins and in anguish, and ecclesiastics are seeking refuge abroad; and all of this [came to pass] on account of our sins . . .

2. Place: monastery of Yarates; scribe and author of col.: Pawłos; MS. title: Gospel.
Source: Xač'ikyan, *XIV Dari*, no. 90a, pp. 66–67

. . . I completed this [Gospel] . . . during the khanate of the Tatar [T'at'ar] Xarvand [Kharbanda Khān], and during the reign of King Awšin [Oshin] of the Armenians, and during the pontificate of Kostandin [III, Kesarac'i], who renounced the rules and traditions of our holy fathers and followed the Franks [P'rangac'] and Greeks [Hoṙomoc']—may the Lord Jesus be his guide; and during the overseership in our province of Siwnik' of the Lord Yovanēs, surnamed Urpel, archbishop and true and holy philosopher—may whom Christ God keep holy and immaculate for a long time for the prosperity and enlightenment of the holy catholic church; and during the principality in this canton of the brothers Baron Burt'el, Baron Pułtay and Baron Č'aysar—may whom Christ God maintain for many long years valorous and victorious over the enemies of Christ's cross . . .

3. Place: island of Lim; scribe and author of col.: Abraham; MS. title: Ritual Book [*Maštoc'*].
Source: Xač'ikyan, *XIV Dari*, no. 91, pp. 67–68

. . . This [manuscript] was completed . . . in the island called Lim . . . during the pontificate of the Lord Zak'aria [I of Ałt'amar], who is wholly indulgent, guileless, and affable. In humility and tolerance, he is like Surb Grigor [St. Gregory], who occupied the same throne, for, just as he [St. Gregory] endured the poisonous snakes for fifteen years,[9] so also he [Zak'aria] endured, in bitter and grievous times, the lawless and bloodthirsty beasts, the nation of archers [azgn netołac'], who constantly stab and wound [his] soul and body. May the Lord God drive away and humiliate all of his enemies, the visible and the invisible, and may He grant him a long life for His glory and for our own glory, amen! . . .

[9] The reference is to the incarceration, for about fifteen years, of St. Gregory the Illuminator in the pits at Artashat by order of the pagan King Tiridates III of Armenia. This occurred after it was revealed that St. Gregory was a Christian and that he was also the son of the assassin of the king's father. According to tradition, St. Gregory survived his long ordeal thanks to a pious widow who secretly provided his subsistence. For the biography of St. Gregory see Langlois, *Collection*, I, 97–174.

1312

1. Place: P'ok'r Siwnik'; MS. title: Gospel.
Source: Xač'ikyan, *XIV Dari*, no. 114, p. 84

During the universal dominion and rule in all lands of the nation of archers [azgin netołac'], who controlled [the territories] extending from the Pontus Sea [Pontosi Cov] to the Caspian Sea [Kaspic' Cov], and from the Ep'rat [Euphrates River] to beyond the Kovkas [Caucasus Mountains], [and] whose chief and monarch is the conqueror named Xarbanday Xan [Kharbanda Khān]; in the year 761 of the Armenian Era [A.D. 1312] . . .

1313

1. Place: monastery of Glajor in canton of Vayojor; scribe and author of col.: Pawłos; MS. title: Gospel.
Source: Xač'ikyan, *XIV Dari*, no. 125, p. 92

. . . I, Pawłos vardapet, copied this holy Gospel with much effort and great suffering . . . in the year 762 of our Haykazean Era [A.D. 1313], under the tutorship of our great [master] Esayi, during the princedom in our canton of Papak' and Ēač'i, during the pontificate of Kostandin [III] Katukec'i, during the reign of King Awšin [Oshin of Cilicia], and during the khanate of Xarband [Kharbanda Khān], who rightly was called the slave of a donkey, for / / / and he [Kharbanda] had no respect for the precepts of Christ and who, through various means, deprived our nation of all its riches, for he collected levies both from the *azats* and from the others . . .

2. Place: monastery of Mecop'; scribe and author of col.: Mxit'ar; MS. title: Gospel.
Source: Xač'ikyan, *XIV Dari*, no. 126, p. 93

. . . [copied] In bitter and grievous times, when the infidel nations, which had betrayed the glory of the Son of God,[10] caused extreme dangers and miseries of anguish to our Christian faith by coercion, by torment, by the imposition of levies, and by derisive scorn . . .

[10] See note 4 above.

3. Place: Sebastia; scribe and author of col.: Step'annos; MS. title: Bible.
Source: Xač'ikyan, *XIV Dari*, no. 130a, p. 96

. . . And this [Bible] was completed . . . during the pontificate of the Lord Kostandin [III, Kesarac'i], and the reign of the devout King Awšin [Oshin of Cilicia], and the episcopacy of the Lord Step'anos in our canton. Thus, this was copied in bitter, difficult, and wicked times, when we suffer much anguish at the hands of the lawless ones, and when not a little anguish is caused by external evil beasts . . .

1314

1. Place: T'ēawdoypawlis; scribe and author of col.: Sargis; MS. title: The Acts of the Apostles.
Source: Xač'ikyan, *XIV Dari*, no. 135, pp. 101–102

. . . And this [manuscript] was completed during the reign of King Awšin [Oshin of Cilicia] of the Armenians and during the khanate of Xarpanda [Kharbanda Khān] of the nation of the Ismaelites [azgn Ismaelac'oc']; in grievous and bitter times, when our Armenian nation fell under the yoke of levies, and there is neither hope for refuge nor a place for shelter; and the whole country is in suffering and subjected to taxation; and our Armenian nation was substantially reduced in number. And in this city [Theodosiopolis = Erzerum] they demolished many churches; and some individuals, abandoning their faith in Christ, joined the wicked nation of the Ismaelites [Ismayelac'oc' azg], and others sold their children and fled to various places, but they found refuge nowhere; and there were numerous other afflictions and sufferings everywhere on account of our sins . . .

2. Place: monastery of Glajor; scribe: Mxit'ar Eznkayec'i; MS. title: *Patčaṙ Sahmanac' Groc'*.
Source: Xač'ikyan, *XIV Dari*, no. 136f, p. 104

In the year 763 of the Armenian Era [A.D. 1314], the [Mongol] census-takers and tax-collectors arrived in Vayujor, and they registered even those children who were a month old.

1315

1. Place: island of Lim; scribe and author of col.: Abraham; MS. title: Excerpts from Bible.

Source: Xač'ikyan, *XIV Dari*, no. 150, p. 113

... Thus, in diminishing days and waning times, that is in recent days, when, on account of multitudinous sins, the world trembled and wavered, as though in a tempestuous storm, from the tyrannical sword of the nation of archers [azinn netołac'], which for a long time intensified its sway in all lands, beginning from where the sun rises, [that is] from the Caspian Sea [Kasbic' Cov] and encompassing the northern regions up to the Pontus Sea [Pontosi Cov], and then stretching to the south and encircling the land of Babylonia [Babelac'woc' ašxarh] and all of Asoris [northern Syria] and Kiwlikeay [Cilicia] and up to the same sea in the land of Pontus [Pontac'woc' ašxarh]. All of Mijerkray [Asia Minor], and numerous peoples speaking various languages, were held under their evil yoke and servitude, as predicted by the great pontiff Nersēs of the Armenians. And the pontificate of Grigor Lusaworič' [St. Gregory the Illuminator] and the kingdom of the Aršakuni [Arsacid] dynasty had waned and weakened, just as St. Isahak had foreseen in his vision. And because of our impenitence, His [God's] wrath has not abated; rather, His hand is still raised to punish and chastise us. Yet we are still unrepentant, we have become feeble and lean, emaciated and languished; we are nearing death and hell, and our loins have been lowered to the ground. For the savage, strange-looking, and dark-countenanced nation of archers [azgn netołac'] abandoned their native faith and followed the evil sect of the forerunner Antichrist [*Karapet Neřn*] Mahmet [the Prophet Muhammad] and subjected the Christians to more intense anguish and persecution. Who, indeed, can recount or put into writing their tragic suffering? ...

2. Place: monastery of St. T'adēos in canton of Artaz; scribe and author of col.: Ṙstakēs; MS. title: Commentary on the Psalms by Nersēs Šnorhali.
   Source: Xač'ikyan, *XIV Dari*, no. 151, pp. 114–115

... [this manuscript was begun] during the reign of King Awšin [Oshin of Cilicia] of the Armenians, and during the pontificate of the Lord Kostandin [III, Kesarac'i] ...

Moreover, at the end of the year 764 of the Armenian Era [A.D. 1315], on the 1st of the month of Nawasard, in bitter, grievous and waning times, when by the will of the Lord charity withered away among many and falsehood and hatred reigned, and when the death-exhaling lyre of Satan fecundly rejoices everywhere with boastful pride, especially among the nation of Aram [azgs Arameni], the race of Hayk [seṙs Haykay], and the stock of T'orgom [zarms T'ork'o-mean]. Because of our unworthy behavior and destructive falsehood we angered the imperturbable God. We provoked the most compassionate and all-merciful to rebuke and chastise us, for as an admonition and as a [sign of His] indignation God raised his wrath from slumber by setting against the Christians the Ismaelites [azgn Ismayēli], born of a female slave [Hagar], who by fraudulent magic deceived the nation of archers [azgn netołac'] [and] who for many years had tyrannically occupied the eastern lands, stretching from north to south up to the Mediterranean Sea [Arewmtakan Cov], and [under whom] the Christian churches enjoyed little peace . . .

1316

1. Place: village of Hazarakn; scribe and author of col.: Yovsian; MS. title: Gospel.
Source: Xač'ikyan, *XIV Dari*, no. 158a, p. 122

. . . This was copied in the year 765 of the Armenian Era [A.D. 1316] . . . during the reign of the Sultan Xarpandawłul [Kharbanda Khān], during the pontificate of the Lord Zak'aria [I of Ałt'amar] . . .

1318

1. Place: monastery of Varag; scribe and author of col.: Yakob; MS. title: The Epistle of Paul, and the Prophet Isaiah.
Source: Xač'ikyan, *XIV Dari*, no. 178, pp. 138–139

. . . in the year 767 of our Haykazean Era [A.D. 1318], in which year all the Christian flocks were at the mercy of Łarbandałul Łan [Kharbanda Khān], of the nation of archers [netołakan azg]. Instigated by Satan, he issued orders that levies should be collected from all Christians on account of their faith in Christ, and that a blue sign should be sewn on the shoulders of the believers. They collect more levies from us ecclesiastics without the specific instructions of the *xan* [khan]. Hence, the thrice-blessed pontiff Zak'aria [I of Ałt'amar] went to see the khan in Babelon [Babylon = Baghdad] and spent a whole year there, and, obtaining an *aṙlex* from him, secured for the monks and priests exemption from taxation. Nevertheless, levies were still collected from the laymen and children . . . In the spring of this year, they collected the levies, and the khan died in the autumn. But there came others, such as Ałlału, Sint'amur, and Hasant'amur, with 1300 men, and again collected exorbitant taxes, and no one could resist them. Although the monastics were tax-exempt, they persecuted with terrible torture those whom they seized and collected an enormous amount of *tukat* [ducat] from them. In particular, our holy institution [the monastery of Varag] fell into their hands. They arrived suddenly and stealthily at night and we all took to flight; and those of us whom they seized they subjected to severe torture, the details of which we cannot relate. And the Tačiks of the city gave much riches and thus were scarcely able to free themselves from their hands. And those of us who fled dared not return to our monastery, because every day, during the day and at night, they came out in search of us, and we, terrified by them, remained in fear and in trembling by night and day in the holy mountain, in the niches and in the caverns of rocks; but they continued to come back every day. They opened all the gates of the churches and they opened all the cells, and they looted whatever they found. Only the gate of [the church of] St. Yovhannēs remained intact, because the monk Łazar, our recluse gatekeeper, casting aside all fear, remained in the church for many days, and the Holy Cross saved him and the church and stupefied the hearts of the aliens, who did not attempt [to break] the iron gate. And we suffered much grief, tribulation, and suffering from all sides, during the summer and in the winter, by fleeing and living without shelter in the holy mountain, and [suffered] other severe tribulations, which we cannot relate . . . Although we suffered all this and more for a long time, yet because of our love of the Holy Cross and resting our hopes in it we did not abandon our holy monastery and remained firmly in our place. Those who lived in the city and in the country fled hither and thither . . . but we remained in our place for the love of the Holy Cross.

2. Place: city of Berkri; scribe and author of col.: Yakob; MS. title: Gospel.
Source: Xač'ikyan, *XIV Dari*, no. 180, p. 144

. . . [copied] during the reign of Abusait Łan [Abū Sa'īd Khān], and the pontificate of the Lord Zak'aria [I of Ałt'amar] . . . in grievous, bitter and wicked times, when there was extreme persecution of the Christians, all of whom were captives in their hands, as though they were bound in chains, as Israel in the past under the Pharaohs, and there is no hope for salvation from anywhere, except from our Savior Christ, Who will soon annihilate the persecutors of the Christians and will crush their heads by hurling them down into the abyss of perdition for their wickedness and [evil deeds], and He will also restore us the believers in our unshakeable faith until the day of reckoning, and keep us steadfast and unshakeable upon the foundation of our mother, the New Zion . . .

3. Purchaser of MS. and author of col.: Mxit'ar; MS. title: Gospel.
Source: Xač'ikyan, *XIV Dari*, no. 187b, p. 151

. . . I, the humble priest Mxit'ar, who received this as my spiritual child in grievous and bitter times, when the iniquitous ones had become stronger, when they were torturing us Christians with whips; but Christ is mighty and will deliver us from all perils . . .

4. Place: monastery of Uṙnkar; scribe and author of col.: Yovannēs; MS. title: Gospel.
Source: Xač'ikyan, *XIV Dari*, no. 190a, p. 152

. . . [copied] during the imperial conquest of Busayit Łan [Abū Sa'īd Khān], the pontificate of the Lord Zak'aria [I of Ałt'amar] . . .

1319

1. Place: monastery of Arjkēoy; scribe and author of col.: Vardan; MS. title: Gospel.
Source: Xač'ikyan, *XIV Dari*, no. 191, p. 154

. . . This holy manuscript was copied . . . in the year 768 of our Haykazean Era [A.D. 1319] . . . in bitter and grievous times, when the infidels, who had renounced the glory of the Son of God,[11] subjected the ranks of the Christian peoples to manifold misery and anguish through coercion, torment, imposition of levies, and scorn and derision. May the mighty King Christ recompense them seven-fold for their deeds . . .

2. Place: monastery of Gełark'uni in village of Xorvaget; scribe and author of col.: Yovanēs; MS. title: Gospel.

[11] See note 4 above.

Source: Xač'ikyan, *XIV Dari*, no. 195, p. 157

... [copied] during the khanate of Busayit [Abū Sa'īd Khān] and of Č'ōpan [Amīr Čūbān], who was in his service; during the reign of King Ošin [Oshin in Cilicia], and the pontificate of the Lord Kostandin [III, Kesarac'i] ...

3. Place: monastery of Uṙnkar; scribe and author of col.: Ovannēs; MS. title: Gospel.
Source: Xač'ikyan, *XIV Dari*, no. 198, p. 158

... [copied] during the imperial conquest of Busayit Łan [Abū Sa'īd Khān] [and] the pontificate of the Lord Zak'aria [I of Ałt'amar] ...

1320

1. Place: monastery of Aṙak'eloc' in Tarōn: scribe and author of col.: Yovannēs; MS. title: Missal [*Čašoc'*].
Source: Xač'ikyan, *XIV Dari*, no. 204, p. 164

... [copied] in bitter and grievous times, when taxes were imposed upon the Christians, and when they were suffering at the hands of the aliens, and when law and order had diminished everywhere ...

2. Scribe and author of col.: Sargis; MS. title: Gospel.
Source: Xač'ikyan, *XIV Dari*, no. 205, p. 165

... [completed] during the pontificate of the Lord Zak'aria [I of Ałt'amar], [and] during the reign of Busait [Abū Sa'īd Khān], in bitter and grievous times ...

1321

1. Place: monastery of Glajor; scribe and author of col.: Kiwrion; MS. title: Gospel.
Source: Xač'ikyan, *XIV Dari*, no. 207a, p. 166

This was copied in the year 770 of our Haykazean Era [A.D. 1321], in bitter and evil times, when the nation of archers [azgn netołac'] held under tyrannical sway all of Armenia and Georgia [Vrac' ašxarh];

during the reign of King Gorgēn [Giorgi V] of the Georgians [Vrac‘], and of our heir-apparent King Lewon [IV of Cilicia] of Armenia Major [Hayoc‘ Mecac‘]; and during the pontificate of the Lord Kostandin [III, Kesarac‘i], and the overseership of the Lord Yovhanēs and the Lord Step‘anos in our province of Siwnik‘; and during the generalship and principality of Burt‘el and Amir Hasan in our cantons . . .

2. Place: monastery of Tat‘ew; scribe and author of col.: Matt‘ē; MS. title: Ritual Book [*Maštoc‘*].
Source: Xač‘ikyan, *XIV Dari*, no. 208, p. 167

. . . This was completed in the year 770 of the Armenian Era [A.D. 1321], during the imperial conquest of Busaid [Abū Sa‘īd Khān], and when the commander-in-chief was Č‘opan [Amīr Čūbān]; and during the principality of our pious and devout, great and Christ-loving prince, Baron Boyrt‘el; and during the catholicosate of the Lord Kostandin [III, Kesarac‘i] . . .

3. Scribe and author of col.: Mxit‘ar Anec‘i; MS. title: Miscellany [*Žołovacu*].
Source: Xač‘ikyan, *XIV Dari*, no. 213b, p. 171

. . . I copied this in anxious and horrid, bitter and grievous times, when there was severe famine, and pestilence, and trembling, and manifold and multifarious calamity, on account of my sins.

1322

1. Place: village of Vahraway in Kapan; scribe and author of col.: Yakob; MS. title: Gospel.
Source: Xač‘ikyan, *XIV Dari*, no. 221a, p. 176

. . . [copied] during the khanate of the youth named Busait [Abū Sa‘īd Khān], in the year 771 [of the Armenian Era = A.D. 1322] . . .

2. Place: monastery of Akner in Cilicia; scribe and author of col.: Minas; MS. title: Miscellany [*Žołovacu*].
Source: Xač‘ikyan, *XIV Dari*, no. 224, p. 178

... [copied] in turbulent times, during the pontificate of Kostandin [III, Kesarac'i] and the reign of the youthful King Lewon [Leon IV of Cilicia], who ... marauded the entire country, and plundered the glorious maritime city of Egeay, that is Ayan [Ayas], and all the Christians ...[12]

1323

1. Place: monastery of Glajor in canton of Siwnik'; recipient of MS. and author of col.: Esayi Nč'ec'i; MS. title: Gospel.
Source: Xač'ikyan, *XIV Dari*, no. 228a, p. 182

... [written] during the conquest of the great monarch called Pusait Xan [Abū Sa'īd Khān]; during the reign of Łewon [Leon IV] who occupied the Armenian throne in Cilicia [Kilikec'oc']; and during the reign of King Gawrgi [Giorgi V] in Georgia [tann Vrac'] and Armenia Major [Mecac' Hayoc'] ...

2. Place: village of Gumbayt' in canton of Apahunik'; scribe and author of col.: Nersēs; MS. title: Missal [*Čašoc'*].
Source: Xač'ikyan, *XIV Dari*, no. 229a, p. 184

... [completed] in the year 772 of the Haykazean Era [A.D. 1323], during the pontificate of the Lord Kostandin [III, Kesarac'i] of the Armenians, during the reign of the pious and devout King Lewon [Leon IV] of the Armenians, [and] during the imperial conquest of the great Pusayit Łan [Abū Sa'īd Khān] ...

1325

1. Place: monastery of Xařabasta or Suhara in canton of K'aǰberunik'; scribe and author of col.: Sargis; MS. title: The Twelve Prophets and Job.
Source: Xač'ikyan, *XIV Dari*, no. 239, p. 192

... Thus, in diminishing days and waning times, that is in recent days, when, on account of multitudinous sins, the world trembled and wavered, as though in a tempestuous storm, from the tyrannical

[12] This text is not the original but a summary previously published by G. Sruanjteanc'. See Xač'ikyan, *XIV Dari*, p. 178, note 2.

sword of the [nation of] archers [netołac‘], which for a long time intensified its sway in all lands, beginning from where the sun rises, [that is] from the Caspian Sea [Kasbic‘ Cov] and encompassing the north up to the Pontus Sea [Pondosi Cov], and then stretching to the south and encircling the land of Babylonia [Babelac‘woc‘ ašxarh] and all of Asoris [northern Syria] and Kiwlikia [Cilicia], and up to the same sea in the land of Pontus [Pontac‘woc‘ ašxarh]. All of Mijerkray [Asia Minor], and numerous peoples speaking various languages, were held under their yoke of servitude, as predicted by the great pontiff Nersēs of the Armenians. And the pontificate of Grigor Lusaworič‘ [St. Gregory the Illuminator] and the kingdom of the Aršakuni [Arsacid] dynasty had waned and weakened, as foreseen in the vision of St. Sahak. And because of our impenitence, His [God's] wrath has not abated; rather, His hand is still raised to punish and chastise us. And yet we are still unrepentant; we have become feeble, lean and languished; we are nearing death and hell, and our loins have been lowered to the ground. For [the savage, strange-looking and dark-countenanced nation of archers abandoned their native faith and followed the evil sect of the forerunner Antichrist Mahmet],[13] and they subjected the Christians to more intense anguish and persecution. Who, indeed, can recount or put into writing their tragic anguish? . . .

2. Place: monastery of Maškuor; author of MS. and of col.: Barseł Vardapet; MS. title: Commentary on the Gospel of Mark by Barseł Vardapet.
   Source: Xač‘ikyan, *XIV Dari*, no. 240, pp. 193–194

. . . This commentary was completed during the reign of King Lewon [Leon IV of Cilicia], son of Awšin [King Oshin], the minor, newly anointed and most pious and devout child. Because of his minority, the throne is administered by the three principal and illustrious princes, [namely] the two brothers, Baron Awšin [Oshin] and Baron Kostandin, who hold the ranks of Grand Baron and *Gundustapl* respectively, and the third Baron Het‘um Nłrc‘i . . .

This [manuscript] was copied in the monastery called Maškuor, during the pontificate of the Lord Catholicos Kostandin Drazarkec‘i, who toils and strives much to bring peace to this country [Cilicia]. Although he was old and frail, he ignored the strenuousness of the trip and personally journeyed to Msr [Egypt] to see the sultan [Al-Malik

[13] This bracketed passage has been completed from colophons number 5 for 1307 and number 1 for 1315.

al-Nāṣir Muḥammad]; and he succeeded in softening and allaying his harsh and bitter disposition.[14] May Christ grant him a long life for [the glory of] His church . . . In the year 774 of the Armenian Era [A.D. 1325].

3. Place: Julay; scribe and author of col.: Xač'atur; MS. title: Missal [*Čašoc'*].
Source: Xač'ikyan, *XIV Dari*, no. 249, p. 199

. . . [completed] in the year 774 of the Haykazean Era [A.D. 1325], during the khanate of Pusait[15] [Abū Sa'īd Khān], son of Xarband [Kharbanda Khān]; during the reign of King Lewon [Leon IV] of the Cilicians [Kilikec'oc']; and during the pontificate of our Lord Kostandin [IV, Drazarkc'i] . . .

1327

1. Place: village of Ałēt' in canton of Bznunik'; scribe and author of col.: Yovannēs; MS. title: Gospel.
Source: Xač'ikyan, *XIV Dari*, no. 254, p. 202

. . . [copied] in the year 776 of the Armenian Era [A.D. 1327] . . . during the pontificate in Cilicia [Kilikec'woc'] of the Lord Yakovb [II], and during our pontificate at Ałt'amar of the Lord Zak'aria [I]; and during the reign of the Christ-crowned and devout King Łewon [Leon IV] in Cilicia [Kilikec'woc']; and during the imperial tyranny of the nation of archers [azgn netołac'] under Pusayit Xan [Abū Sa'īd Khān], in wretched and evil times, when justice was diminished and lawlessness was intensified everywhere. And the prophecy that "There shall come a time when they will say to the mountains fall upon us and to the hills cover us" [cf. Luke 23:30; Revelation 6:16; Hosea 10:8] was fulfilled . . .

[14] This cryptic remark refers to the peace treaty which Catholicos Kostandin IV Drazarkc'i or Lambronac'i concluded, in behalf of the Armenian kingdom of Cilicia, with the Mamluk Sultan al-Malik al-Nāṣir Muḥammad of Egypt. The treaty was to last for fifteen years in consideration of an annual tribute of 50,000 gold florins to be paid by the Cilician kingdom, plus one half of the customs revenues of the port of Ayas and one half of the proceeds from the sale of salt to foreigners. On these terms the Sultan of Egypt withdrew his troops from Cilicia. See details in *Samuēl K'ahanayi Anec'woy Hawak'munk' i Groc' Patmagrac'*, p. 158; Ōrmanean, *Azgapatum*, col. 1269.

[15] In the original manuscript the spelling of this name is "Musait"; Xač'ikyan has corrected it. See *XIV Dari*, p. 199, n. 1.

2. Place: [Cilicia]; scribe and author of col.: Yohannēs; MS. title: Gospel.
Source: Xač'ikyan, *XIV Dari*, no. 255, p. 203

... [copied] in the year 776 of the Armenian Era [A.D. 1327], during the pontificate of the Lord Yakovb [II], and the reign of the devout and pious King Lewon the Fourth of the Armenians, son of King Awšin [Oshin] of the Armenians [in Cilicia] ...

In this notable year, when this [Gospel] was completed, the pious old man and devout prince, Baron Het'um Nłrc'i, journeyed to Egiptos [Egypt] for the purpose of alleviating the condition of the Christians. May the Lord Jesus have mercy upon him! ...

1329

1. Place: Tarōn (?); scribe and author of col.: T'oros; MS. title: Gospel.
Source: Xač'ikyan, *XIV Dari*, no. 272, pp. 215–216

... [copied] during the imperial conquest of the great monarch named Busayid Łan [Abū Sa'īd Khān], who ruled over numerous nations, from the Pontus Sea [Pontosi Cov] to the Caspian Sea [Kasbic' Cov] and up to the river called J̌ahun [Djayḥān] ...

Who indeed can recount—we surely cannot recount—the disaster, the lamentation, the mourning, the pestilence, the famine, the slavery, and the quailing, and other multifarious scourges which befell us on account of our sins, in the city and in the country of Tarōn, and in all the surrounding cantons, at the hands of the wicked nation of the Kurds [azgn K'rdstanac'], the Christians were exterminated in the whole country.

2. Place: Ōrtubazar; scribe and author of col.: Grigor; MS title: Gospel.
Source: Xač'ikyan, *XIV Dari*, no. 274a, p. 218

... [completed in A.D. 1329] during the reign of Busayit Bahatur Łan [Abū Sa'īd Bahādur Khān]; and during the reign of the pious and devout King Lewon [Leon] the Fourth of the Armenians [in Cilicia] ... and during the pontificate of the Lord Yakovb [II] ...

1330

1. Place: monastery of J̌ławna; scribe and author of col.: Kirakos Eznkayecʻi; MS. title: Gospel.
Source: Xačʻikyan, *XIV Dari*, no. 283a, p. 225

... This [Gospel] was copied in the year 779 of our Haykazean Era [A.D. 1330], during the pontificate of the Lord Yakob [II]; and during the reign of King Lewon [Leon IV] of the Armenians and of Gēorg [Giorgi V] of the Georgians [Vracʻ]; and during the khanate of Pawsayit [Abū Saʻīd Khān] . . .

2. Place: village of Lōngšēn; scribe and author of col.: Xačʻatur; MS. title: Gospel.
Source: Xačʻikyan, *XIV Dari*, no. 284, p. 226

. . . copied in the year 779 of the Armenian Era [A.D. 1330] . . . during the pontificate of the Lord Zakʻaria [I of Ałtʻamar], and during the imperial conquest of Busait [Abū Saʻīd Khān], in bitter and grievous times, when we paid taxes on account of our faith in Jesus. However, when the Lord sits in judgment, He will recompense the tributaries . . .

1331

1. Place: monastery of Xumitʻ in canton of Cařutijor; scribe and author of col.: Mkrtičʻ; MS. title: *Hayr Maštocʻ*.
Source: Xačʻikyan, *XIV Dari*, no. 291, p. 232

. . . [copied] in the year 780 of the Armenian Era [A.D. 1331], during the khanate of Busait[16] [Abū Saʻīd Khān]; and during the reign of King Lewon [Leon IV] of the Armenians [in Cilicia]; and during the reign of King Gawrgē [Giorgi V] of the Georgians [Vracʻ] . . . [and] the principality of the baron of barons, Šex Hasan [Shaykh Ḥasan Buzurg] . . .

2. Place: village of Ałētʻ in canton of Bznunikʻ; scribe and author of col.: Yovanēs; MS. title: Gospel.
Source: Xačʻikyan, *XIV Dari*, no. 292, p. 234

. . . [copied] during the imperial conquest of the great monarch

[16] In the original manuscript the spelling of this name is "Musait"; Xačʻikyan has corrected it. See *XIV Dari*, p. 232, note 1.

Busayit Xan [Abū Sa'īd Khān], who rules over numerous nations, stretching from the Sea of Pontus [Pontosi Cov] to the Caspian Sea [Kasbic' Cov] and up to the river called J̌ahun [Djayḥān]; during the catholicosate of the Lord Yakovb [II] of the Haykazean race, and the reign of King Lewon [Leon IV] who occupied the Cilician [Kilikec'-woc'] throne. May the Lord God maintain unshakeable the [Armenian] pontifical and royal thrones, so that upon the mention of their names the enemies of the truth will tremble and hide themselves . . .

3. Place: monastery of Argelan; scribe and author of col.: Yovannēs; MS. title: Ritual Book [*Maštoc'*].
Source: Xač'ikyan, *XIV Dari*, no. 293a, p. 235

. . . [copied in A.D. 1331], during the reign of Sultan Abusayit [Abū Sa'īd Khān] of the nation of archers [azgi netołac'], and of our Armenian King Lewon [Leon IV], and the prince of princes Burt'el, [and] during the pontificate of the Lord Zak'aria [I of Ałt'amar] . . .

1332

1. Place: monasteries of Glajor and K'ṙnay; recipient of MS. and author of col.: Nersēs Taronac'i; MS. title: Bible.
Source: Xač'ikyan, *XIV Dari*, no. 307a, p. 245

. . . [completed] during the imperial conquest of Pusait Łan [Abū Sa'īd Khān], and the reign of King Lewon [Leon IV], son of Awšin [King Oshin], of the Armenians [of Cilicia] . . .

2. Place: monastery of Kuk'i; MS. title: Commentary on the Divine Liturgy by Nersēs Lambronac'i.
Source: Xač'ikyan, *XIV Dari*, no. 308, p. 247

. . . This was copied during the pontificate of the Armenians of the Lord Yakovb [II], and the reign of King Lewon [Leon IV], and under the tutelage of the *rabunapet* Yesayi, and during the principality in our province of Vasak, grandson of Pṙoš . . . During the khanate of Pusait [Abū Sa'īd Khān], whose khanate lasted for eighteen years . . .

3. Place: Lori in Xałteac' Jor; scribe and author of col.: Melk'isedek; MS. title: Gospel.
Source: Xač'ikyan, *XIV Dari*, no. 310a, p. 249

. . . completed in wicked times and in a dark place, when the times were altogether grievous and bitter, especially for the Christians, for our town [Lori] was completely ruined at the hands of cruel and multifarious exactors [tax-collectors] . . .

1333

1. Scribe and author of col.: Yovannēs; MS. title: Gospel.
Source: Xač'ikyan, *XIV Dari*, no. 315, p. 255

In the beginning of the year
Seven hundred and eighty-two [A.D. 1333]
Of the era of the nation of Hayk [Haykan azgi],
And of the race of T'orgom the Great [T'orgoma meci];
In grievous times,
When the aliens were harassing,
When the Christians they were insulting,
When the churches they were demolishing
And shaking them from their foundations;
When the priests were lamenting
And regrouping their flock.
Why did all this befall them?
Because of the sins they committed,
Which multiplied in number
Like the waters of a torrent . . .

2. Place: near Sebastia; scribe and author of col.: Hayrapet; MS. title: Missal [*Čašoc'*].
Source: Xač'ikyan, *XIV Dari*, no. 316, p. 256

. . . [I copied this manuscript] in bitter and difficult times when, on account of my multitudinous sins, the Christians were severely anguished because of the illegitimate levies, deprivations, and also on account of the clandestine perfidy of the aliens, who, like wicked beasts mercilessly slaughter the rational flock of Christ . . .

3. Place: monastery of Veri Noravank' in canton of Vayoc'jor; scribe and author of col.: Kiwrion; MS. title: Gospel.
Source: Xač'ikyan, *XIV Dari*, no. 317, p. 257

. . . [completed] in the year 782 of the Armenian Era [A.D. 1333], during the tyrannical rule of Busayit [Abū Saʻīd Khān] of the nation of archers [azgin netołacʻ]; [and] during the reign of King Lewon [Leon IV] of the Armenians [in Cilicia], [and] the catholicosate of the Lord Yakob [II] . . .

4. Place: Ałtʻamar; scribe and author of col.: Karapet; MS. title: Commentary on the Epistles by Sargis Šnorhali.
Source: Xačʻikyan, *XIV Dari*, no. 320, p. 259

. . . [copied in A.D. 1333] during the pontificate of the Lord Zakʻaria [I of Aghtamar], and during the imperial conquest by the nation of archers [netołakan azg], in bitter and grievous times . . .

1334

1. Place: canton of Eznkay; recipient of MS. and author of col.: Kirakos Agrkcʻi; MS. title: Commentary on the Fourteen Epistles of the Apostle Paul, and of Ephraim and John Chrysostom.
Source: Xačʻikyan, *XIV Dari*, no. 326a, p. 263 (verse)

> . . . [completed] during the khanate of Bawsait [Abū Saʻīd Khān],
> [And] King Lewon [Leon IV] of the Armenians . . .

1335

1. Scribe and author of col.: Grigor Erēcʻ; MS. title: Miscellany [*Žołovacu*].
Source: Xačʻikyan, *XIV Dari*, no. 332, p. 268

> . . . when the nation of Hagar [azgn Hagarean] grew in strength,
> [That is] the Ismayēleankʻ [Ismaelites] and Mogakankʻ [Magians], who are in league with one another.
> In this year Busayit Łan [Abū Saʻīd Khān] became dominant,
> And held all the lands under his sway.
> Xorasan [Khurāsān] he held by force, up to the river named Amu [Amū-daryā],
> All of Asorestan [Assyria], Mijaget [Mesopotamia] and Babylonia [Babel ašxarhn],

Kilikia [Cilicia] and Hoṙomk‘ [Rūm] and Parthia [Palhawean
ašxarh],
As well as the seat of the Psalmist and the canton of Georgia
[Vrac‘akan gawaṙn].
A wicked monster he became to our Christian nation of Hayk
[Haykean azg];
Like a bloodthirsty scorpion he thirsts for our blood;
He made war against our churches and transgressed all bounds,
And with an evil intent he made [the Christians] wear a blue
cloth sign . . .

2. Place: city of Karin; MS. title: Gospel.
Source: Xač‘ikyan, *XIV Dari*, no. 333, p. 270

. . . This was copied in grievous and bitter times, during the khanate of the Muslim [*aylazgi*] Busait [Abū Sa‘īd Khān], the pontificate of our Lord Yakob [II], and the reign of King Lewon [Leon IV], of the Armenians [in Cilicia] . . .

3. Place: monastery of Uṙnkar; MS. title: Gospel.
Source: Xač‘ikyan, *XIV Dari*, no. 334, p. 270

. . . [copied] during the imperial conquest of Busayid Łan [Abū Sa‘īd Khān], [and] the pontificate of the Lord Zak‘aria [I of Ałt‘amar] . . .

4. MS. title: Gospel.
Source: Xač‘ikyan, *XIV Dari*, no. 335, pp. 270–271

. . . At this time there arose, from the family of Vač‘ē, the brave and mighty, the victorious and valiant prince of princes named K‘urd, son of Tayir, son of the pious and devout K‘urd. Thanks to his fame and valor, our cantons and monasteries remained unshaken and unharmed in these times of calamity and bitter turbulence; for in these waning and bitter days, which were due to our sins, there emerged the glorious and God-pleasing great general and outstanding champion, the most-blessed K‘urd, the pride and ornamental son of the Armenians. The sound of the trotting of his horses, and the swinging of his lances, and the flashing of his saber, and the crackling of his bows, and his solid and shielded armor, and other awesome protective apparatus [which he wore], all these terrified his enemies. Besides his triumphs and deeds of valor, his repulsion of many in numerous wars, and the great number of his regiments, he was as beautiful as the heavenly host and he was as brave as a lion or a mighty eagle in all of his wars. He was deemed worthy of respect and honor by the alien Kings Łazan [Ghāzān Khān] and Łarapand [Kharbanda Khān] and Pusayid [Abū Sa'īd Khān], as well as by the great *noyins*. He received from them all manner of respect and honor and *xilay*. Moreover, through the protection of the merciful God, he brought peace not only to his own domains and its monasteries, but rendered much assistance to his compatriots in the neighboring cantons. May the right hand of the uncreated and the arm of the mighty God be his shield and guardian by day and by night, as well as to his pious and benevolent wife, Xoyan Xat'un, and to all his horsemen. May the eyes of the tyrants and of the notables look gently upon him; and may his enemies blush and be humbled before him, and like Korx [Korah] and Dadan [Dathan] fall into the abyss; and may he always vanquish his enemies, amen!

5. Place: monastery of Glajor in canton of Vayoyjor in province of Siwnik'; scribe and author of col.: Sargis; MS. title: Commentaries by Nersēs of Lambron on the Book of Proverbs and by Vardan and Grigor Narekac'i on the Song of Songs.
   Source: Xač'ikyan, *XIV Dari*, no. 336a, p. 271

... [copied] In the year 784 of the Haykazean Era [A.D. 1335], and during the imperial conquest of Pusait Xan [Abū Sa'īd Khān], of the nation of the archers [azgn netołac']. When this divine manuscript was completed, the tragic news was reported that Pusait [Abū Sa'īd Khān] had joined his forefathers [that is, he had died] ...

6. Place: Erusałēm; scribe and author of col.: Nersēs Krakc'i; MS. title: Collection of Homilies [*Čaṙəntir*].
   Source: Xač'ikyan, *XIV Dari*, nos. 338a, 338b, 338c, 338d, pp. 273–275

... This is an evil time, for the dominical holy places [in Jerusalem] are in captivity and are completely destroyed, and it is doubtful that they will be restored. The Christians are being insulted and trodden under the feet of the infidels. Yet, we received the good tiding that the Franks [Fṙang azgn] are on the move to save the dominical sanctuaries in the Holy City of Jerusalem. May this come true, so that our despondent hearts may be restored, so that our heads which have fallen to the ground may rise as high up as heaven, so that the Cross may shine, and the church may be adorned.

But, because of my [sinful] deeds which persist, I am doubtful that these shall come to pass. Yet, everything is possible with my Lord God, Jesus.

In these venomous times, when the Armenians were languishing, the lawless Ismaelites [azgn Ismayēli] marched upon the country of Kilikē [Cilicia]; they slaughtered everyone, carried off some into captivity to Msər [Egypt] and others to the country of Xaraman [Ḳaramān] . . .

Oh, brothers, there are so many *xapr* [reports] that I know not what I am writing; it is said that the inhabitants of Ayas have killed a Tačik *xati* [ḳāḍi].

A thousand woes unto me and unto all of us Christians at Jerusalem, for like the Ninuec'ik' [Ninevans] we are scorched by the terror caused by the infidels. We are told that we will be herded like sheep by the evil ones, [and] that they will assemble all the Armenian Christians in one place and slaughter us; for they are barking at us and charging that the Armenians have killed the *xati* [ḳāḍi] and *danušman* [dānishūmand] at Ayas, and that for all these they will take their revenge from us. We are all trembling; and some have fled to the Hoṙom [Greek] villages; and only God knows what is forthcoming . . .

Woe, brothers, for the evil *xapr* [report], for it is said that the sultan's son is advancing upon Sis with numerous forces . . .

7. Place: fortress of Ganjē and village of Mawšrēfi; scribe and author of col.: Simēon; MS. title: Missal [*Čašoc'*].
Source: Xač'ikyan, *XIV Dari*, no. 342a, pp. 277–278

. . . Because of the bitterness of our time and on account of my multitudinous sins, in this year the nation known as Xaraman [Ḳaramānoghlu] penetrated our country of Kilikia [Cilicia], and caused much devastation in a number of places . . .

1336

1. Place: monastery of Kopatap', near village of Bstoy, in canton of Gołt'an; scribe and author of col.: T'umay Arčišec'i; MS. title: Gospel.

Source: Xač'ikyan, *XIV Dari*, no. 347a, pp. 281–282

. . . In this year [1336], when the eastern lands were without a king for a year, because three kings were replaced, and none of them remained in power for any length of time. The first among these was exceedingly kind toward the Christians and he believed in Christ God; but the second, named Ali P'ašax ['Alī Pādshāh], was abominable and accursed, and he was like the erstwhile idol worshipers. He committed much persecutions of the Christians; he shut down the churches; he destroyed the crucifixes; and he committed much evil against the believers in Christ; but in the end God had him fall victim to the sword and had him slain.

Now, brothers, all these that came to pass at this time were on account of our sins.

This was written in the year 785 of the Armenian Era [A.D. 1336]. . . . Those of you who should benefit by this [Gospel] . . . do not blame me for the coarseness [of the calligraphy] and the despicable errors, for only the Lord is *anxalat'*. Moreover, so bitter were the times, at the hands of the lawless ones, that it was impossible to write for an hour, [and] we all took to flight and remained in hiding . . .

2. Place: city of T'avrēž; scribe and author of col.: T'uma; MS. title: Gospel.
Source: Xač'ikyan, *XIV Dari*, no. 348, p. 283

. . . [copied] when all the worshipers of the Cross suffered persecution and anguish. Much bitterness befell us because of our sins, for our invisible and wicked enemy [Satan] rose against us, and incited the hearts of the wicked aliens against the Christians, and he meted out to us afflictions and persecutions of every kind at the hands of the lawless and *t'axsup* archers [*netołakank'*] . . . Moreover, they persecuted the Christians in many different ways; they forced them to wear a blue *tawlpand*, and in a number of places the lawless evildoers destroyed several churches from their foundations . . .

3. Place: city of Sis; scribe and author of col.: Sargis; MS. title: Gospel.
Source: Xač'ikyan, *XIV Dari*, no. 349a, pp. 283–284

... In this bitter and evil time, the lawless nation of the Ismaelites [azgn Ismayēlac‘], from the land of the Pharaohs, subjected Cilicia [Kilikec‘woc‘ ašxarh] to great suffering and danger. They invaded with troops and captured the magnificent and God-protected fortress of Nłir; they held it for a long time and destroyed it. They, then, penetrated our country [Cilicia]; and there was not a city or fortress or village, monastery or hermitage, in the mountains and in the plains, which these wicked people did not penetrate in the entire country. With their swords they killed numerous people, including many churchmen, [that is] priests and monks, vardapets and bishops, deacons and scribes. And they carried off countless Christians, men and women, boys and maidens, into captivity. May the Lord God punish them as befits their deeds; and this will suffice.

This [Gospel] was completed in the capital city of Sis ... in the year 785 of the Armenian Era [A.D. 1336], on Sunday the twenty-ninth day of the month of December ... during the reign of King Lewon [Leon], the Fourth, son of the Armenian King Awšin [Oshin], and during the pontificate of the Lord Yakovb [II] ...

4. Place: town of Mənžənkert in canton of Basen; scribe and author of col.: Barseł; MS. title: Gospel.
Source: Xač‘ikyan, *XIV Dari*, no. 350a, p. 285

... [completed] in the year 785 of the Armenian Era [A.D. 1336] in bitter and grievous times, when the Ismaelites [azgn Ismayēli], led by T‘amur [Ṭugha Tīmūr], tyrannized the Christian nations. They destroyed numerous churches and monasteries; and the fear caused by the infidels compelled the holy monks to seek refuge abroad ...

5. Place: monastery of Awag; scribe and author of col.: T‘oros; MS. title: Hymnary [*Šaraknoc‘*].
Source: Xač‘ikyan, *XIV Dari*, no. 356, p. 290

... [copied] in the year 785 of the Armenian Era [A.D. 1336], during the reign of King Lēovn [Leon IV] of the Armenians and the pontificate of the Lord Yakovb [II], in bitter times, when the Christians were being persecuted by the lawless nation of the Turks [azgn T‘urk‘ac‘], may whom the Lord destroy ...

1337

1. Place: Sult'aniay and T'avrēž; scribe and author of col.: Awag; MS. title: Gospel.
Source: Xač'ikyan, *XIV Dari*, no. 360, p. 292

... [copied] in the year 786 [of the Armenian Era = A.D. 1337], during the tyranny of the short-lived Arp'ay [Arpa Khān], of the nation of archers [*azgn netołac'*] ...

2. Place: Ayas (?), Cilicia; scribe: Step'annos; author of col.: Vasil; MS. title: Gospel.
Source: Xač'ikyan, *XIV Dari*, no. 363, pp. 294–296

... Because of our increasing impiety and on account of our numerous sins, Alt'un Pułay [Altūn Bugha], the iniquitous *nayip* [nā'ib] of Halap [Aleppo], like the erstwhile Ṙap'sak [Rab-shakeh], deceived King Lewon [Leon IV] of the Armenians [of Cilicia] with many soothing words. Hence, the King remained unconcerned at Atanay [Adana], and [like him] the whole country [of Cilicia] remained unconcerned. Everyone [remained] in his home and [attended] his business, placing their trust in the *amanat'* of the sultan [of Egypt]. Moreover, our emissaries had gone to see the sultan and the infidel *amirays* [amirs].

But, claiming that he was proceeding toward Ep'rat [Euphrates river], he [Altūn Bugha] surreptitiously moved the cavalry from Halap [Aleppo] and entered our country on Thursday May 26, on the feast of the Ascension of our Savior. He marched directly toward Mlun and Atanay [Adana], and proceeded as far as Tarsus; and he carried off numerous *lułak* and men and animals. He committed much slaughter and looting, and he set many places on fire. The King [Leon IV] barely escaped from Atanay [Adana]; while he [Altūn Bugha] went to Mulewon. He [Altūn Bugha] remained in our country for nine days and then departed. This holy Gospel, together with other ecclesiastical vessels, were taken to Halap [Aleppo] as captive. The bless-worthy and honorable prince and baron Petros Xpaeanc', who had been dispatched as an emissary to the amir, found this [Gospel], and because of his love for God and realizing that it belonged to our church, he purchased it and brought it back to our country. He gave it to me, the unworthy servant of God, who am the King's [Leon IV] clerk, and I reimbursed him the money he had paid for its acquisition from the wicked ones. And I acquired it most gladly and eagerly for your enjoyment, for the enjoyment of the holy churches, and for the church of St. Mary, the Mother of God.

After the devastation of our country by the infidels, he [Altūn Bugha] again uttered deceitful words saying that what was done was done and that the sultan was in peace with us; and he asked us to give him the *mal*. And he took from us a *xasat* of *mal*, that is 600,000 *dram*; and for a whole year, that is, until the following April, he subjected our country to torture and *haram*. After taking the *mal*, the sultan demanded the fortresses, which were located on the other side of the river, and which had been given to others. King Lewon [Leon IV], then, dispatched the *marajaxt* [marshal] and baron Paltin and me, the unworthy Vasil, to Sultan Nasr [Al-Malik al-Nāṣir Muḥammad] of Egiptos [Egypt], to seek an *amanat*ʻ so that the King might journey in person [to Egypt] to secure the deliverance of our country. But the iniquitous Altʻun Pułay [Altūn Bugha] imprisoned us in the citadel of Halap [Aleppo]. And taking his cavalry, he invaded our country and occupied Nłir. After seven months of much torture in the prison, the *marajaxt* [marshal] died—may the Lord Jesus have mercy upon him and grant him the diadem of a martyr—and his body was brought to Haykʻ [Cilicia]. The iniquitous amir held me in prison for a whole year. The Sultan wanted to cross [the river] J̌ahan [Djayḥān]; and the King [Leon IV] labored much to protect the country, but to no avail. In the following year, the same amir penetrated other parts of our land, with numerous Arab [*reading uncertain*] horsemen, and they devastated our country, the mountains and the plains. They committed much slaughter, carried off numerous captives and infinite booty, and they devastated the country. The helpless King [Leon IV] succumbed to the Sultan's will, and allowed him to cross [the river] J̌ahan [Djayḥān] and occupy the fortresses and their lands, including this magnificent [city of] Ayas, which he [Leon IV] had built with much expense.

Thanks to the mercy of God in the highest and through the intercession of the Virgin Mary, I, the unworthy, was released from prison and returned to my country.

There was great anxiety in our country of Kilikia [Cilicia] this year, because of the terror caused by the infidels, and also on account of the plague, captivity, and the famine. Except for the fortresses, everything was demolished; those places that were not devastated were deserted by their inhabitants; and those who lived in the fortresses fled, resting their hopes in the mercy of God . . .[17]

[17] The text of this colophon, as published by Xačʻikyan, contains a number of obscure passages, which in the present translation were clarified after comparison with excerpts from the same text published in Ališan's *Sisuan*, pp. 142b, 413, and 559.

3. Place: village of Ałēt‘ in canton of Bznunik‘; scribe and author of col.: Yovhannēs; MS. title: Gospel.
Source: Xač‘ikyan, *XIV Dari*, no. 364, p. 296

... [copied] with much suffering and prolonged emigration ... During the prelature [pontificate] of the Lord Zak‘aria [I of Ałt‘amar], and the imperial conquest of the great monarch Mahmut Łan [Muḥammad Khān], who rules over numerous nations extending from the Sea of Pontus [Pontosi Cov] to the Caspian Sea [Kazbic‘ Cov] and up to the river called J̌ahun [Djayḥān]. During the catholicosate of the Haykazean nation of the Lord Yakob [II], and the reign of King Lewon [Leon IV] who occupied the Cilician [Kilikec‘woc‘] throne. May the Lord God maintain unshakable the pontifical and royal thrones, so that upon the mention of their names the enemies of the truth will tremble and hide themselves ...

1338

1. Place: completed at Člimon; scribe and author of col.: Yovannēs; MS. title: Gospel.
Source: Xač‘ikyan, *XIV Dari*, no. 378a, pp. 304–305

... [copied] In the year 787 of the Armenian Era [A.D. 1338], during the reign of King Lewon [Leon IV] of the Armenians, son of Awšin [King Oshin], and during the pontificate of the Lord Yakovb [II] ...

This was written at Eznkay [Erzindjān] in the canton of Ekełec‘; and, because of the bitterness of our times, I moved to five different places during the writing of this [manuscript].

Oh brothers, do not blame me for the coarseness of the calligraphy and for the errors, because this was copied in bitter and grievous times. For in this year there appeared Tamurtaš [Tīmūrtash] and attacked our God-protected city of Eznkay [Erzindjān], and, after assembling all the K‘urt‘ [Kurds] and T‘at‘ar [Tatars] in the vicinity, he laid our city to siege. And he remained here for four months and caused bitter anguish; but he failed to cause any damage to the city, for /// then the country he bitterly /// put them to the sword. He confiscated the possessions and properties of some; and during their flight some died in the snow and in the ice, for it was wintertime. Those who remained in their homes were delivered into their hands, and those who fled were devoured by the cold weather; and our land came to its last breath. And hearing and seeing all this, and grieving much, I could not write ...

2. Scribe and author of col.: Melk'isēdek; MS. title: Gospel.
Source: Xač'ikyan, *XIV Dari*, nos. 379a, 379b, pp. 306–307

... [copied in 1338], at a time when there was neither a *łan* [khan] nor a sultan, and when our country was like a wavering ship, and when Christians were being persecuted and were in flight.

For there arose one by the name of Damurtaš
[Tīmūrtash],
He caused much affliction to our nation;
But Christ gave him the food of death,
And before our eyes a miracle came to pass;
Hail unto the immortal Christ,
Who made him a *laš*.

... Written in bitter times, in the year 787 [of the Armenian Era = A.D. 1338]. At this time there arose a wicked man whose name was Damurtaš [Tīmūrtash], and who plundered the Christian nations; but Christ destroyed him afterwards, together with Alitaš [or Alibaš].

3. Place: monastery of Arckoy; scribe and author of col.: Yovan; MS. title: Gospel.
Source: Xač'ikyan, *XIV Dari*, no. 384a, p. 314

... [written] in bitter and grievous times, when the nation of the infidels caused extreme dangers and miseries of anguish to our Christian faith by torment and torture, by the imposition of levies, and by derisive scorn ...

1339

1. Scribe and author of col.: Nater; MS. title: Gospel.
Source: Xač'ikyan, *XIV Dari*, no. 392a, p. 320

... it was an exceedingly anxious and acute time for the Christians, and this was on account of all manners of sins of the flesh, and because of the inclemency of the people a hypocritical man now reigns. It would have been fine if there were only one man as king and abomination; rather, they are all princes and *aparas*, which cannot be described in writing ...

1340

1. Place: monastery of Aławnic‘; scribe and author of col.: Sargis; MS. title: Missal [*Čašoc‘*].
Source: Xač‘ikyan, *XIV Dari*, no. 399, p. 324

. . . [copied] during the pontificate of Step‘annos [III of Ałt‘amar], who freed all the clergy from the levies imposed by the persecutors. He also secured his own freedom within the kingdom, which in fact did not exist; rather, there is anarchy, because the princes are mutineers and agitators, and they have risen against one another. No tongue can relate the misery caused by the horsemen which our eyes have witnessed this year, for thirty thousand of these human-figured beasts came into our land. And who can relate the wicked deeds which they committed? They captured and destroyed numerous cantons, and they plundered all the fruits of labor; they looted all the Christians, left them naked and barefooted, and they denuded the Christians of all their garments. They separated the cattle according to their kind—the sheep and the oxen, the cows and the bulls, the donkeys and the horses—and carried them away. They disrobed the people and made them naked and exposed them to the ridicule of onlookers. What eyes can behold this grievous misery, or who can bear this suffering after having witnessed it? Yesterday the house had its master and was filled with all kinds of goods; but today he [the master] sits on ashes with a broken heart, in grief and naked. So abundant was our land with all kinds of provisions; but they committed these acts with such suddenness, and they emptied out the granaries to such an extent that dogs died of the famine; and they let themselves loose in all our land with such fury and rage that one hundred souls were slaughtered by sword and were martyred, including this scribe's mother, who, stricken with an arrow, died in Christ.

2. Place: city of Eznkay in canton of Ekełeac‘; scribe and author of col.: Grigoris; MS. title: Collection of Homilies [*Čaṙəntir*].
Source: Xač‘ikyan, *XIV Dari*, no. 400, p. 325

. . . I plead with you not to blame me for the errors and the artlessness of my calligraphy, because this was copied in bitter and turbulent times. For, on account of our multitudinous sins, the nation of archers [azgn netołac‘] are attacking the Christians. They are slaughtering and plundering them; they are carrying off captives from numerous cantons; and they are imposing multifarious and illegitimate levies upon everyone. And countless other atrocities are being committed in these days, and it is not possible to relate them in detail or to put them in writing . . .

1341

1. Place: village of Vardnšēn in canton of Tayk'; scribe and author of col.: Nater; MS. title: Gospel.
Source: Xač'ikyan, *XIV Dari*, no. 403, p. 327

. . . And I arrived from the impregnable fortress in the canton of Baberd [Bayburt] and lived in the village called Kan, [where] I began to copy part [of this Gospel]. But there was a general flight from the canton, as well as from the city [of Bayburt], that is of the Christians, the Ismaelites [Ismayelac'oc'], and of all the inhabitants, on account of two princes, whose names need not be mentioned. Everyone fled and took refuge in foreign lands. And there occurred a snowstorm in Mount Vtvak, and some people and many animals perished there; also in the other mountain, called Teṙewanc', countless men and animals [perished]. And who can recount the tragedy of anguish which occurred on the fortieth day of Lent, on the feast of K'aṙasnic' [the Forty Martyrs]? And all of this came to pass on account of the sins and the countless errors of man . . .

2. Place: city of Sultaniay; scribe and author of col.: Karapet; MS. title: Gospel.
Source: Xač'ikyan, *XIV Dari*, no. 404b, p. 328

. . . in the year 790 of the Armenian Era [A.D. 1341], during the imperial conquest of the younger Šex Hasan [Ḥasan Küčük] . . .

3. Place: city of Azax; scribe and author of col.: Tērtēr Erewanc'i; MS. title: Vardan Aygekc'i's Book of Sermons.
Source: Xač'ikyan, *XIV Dari*, no. 405, p. 329

. . . [copied] in the year 790 of the Armenian Era [A.D. 1341], during the reign of King Levon [Leon IV] of the Armenians, son of Awšəntr [King Oshin], and the catholicosate of the Lord Mxit'ar [I, Gṙnerc'i]. This book was copied in the land of the most blessed Awzpēk Xan [Özbek Khān] and of his renowned son Dinipēk [Tinibeg Khān] . . .

1342

1. Place: T'avrēž; scribe and author of col.: Sargis; MS. title: Gospel.
Source: Xač'ikyan, *XIV Dari*, no. 409, p. 331

. . . [completed] in the year 791 of the Armenian Era [A.D. 1342], during the reign of Sulayiman Bahadur Xan [Sulaymān Bahādur Khān], of the nation of archers [netołakan azg], and of the great *noyin* Šex Hasan [Shaykh Ḥasan Küčük], son of T'amurt'aš [Tīmūrtash], may whom the Lord God grant a long life, amen! . . .

1343

1. Scribe and author of col.: Nersēs; MS. title: Hymnary [*Šaraknoc'*].
Source: Xač'ikyan, *XIV Dari*, no. 414a, p. 334

. . . We lived in bitter times, for Sulayiman Łan [Sulaymān Khān] attacked Yarat'in [Eretna] at Sebastia, and with the help of God he defeated Yarat'in [Eretna] and compelled them to flee; in the year 792 [of the Armenian Era = A.D. 1343] . . .

2. Place: Xlat' (?); MS. title: Gospel.
Source: Xač'ikyan, *XIV Dari*, no. 415, p. 334

In the year 792 [of the Armenian Era = A.D. 1343], when Łaray Hasan [Ḳara Ḥasan] marauded [*t'axt'aneac'*] Xlat' [Khilāṭ] . . .

1344

1. Place: Kafay; recipient of MS. and author of col.: Mkrtič'; MS. title: Gospel.
Source: Xač'ikyan, *XIV Dari*, no. 425, p. 341

. . . [completed] in the year 793 of the Armenian Era [A.D. 1344], in bitter times, [and] during the siege of Kafay [Kafa] . . .

1346

1. Place: fortress of Baberd in canton of Xałteac'; restorer of MS. and author of col.: Yovhannēs Nałaš; MS. title: Gospel.

Source: Xač'ikyan, *XIV Dari*, no. 433, p. 346

... [this Gospel was restored] In grievous and bitter times, when the great capital city of T'ēodupawlis [Erzerum] was deserted by its inhabitants and animals on account of the nation of Hagar [azgn Hagaru] and the Ismaelites [Ismayelac'oc'n]. Also, all the inhabitants in the east, that is in the land of the Georgians [tun Vrac'], where many were slaughtered, while others died of the famine. No one can relate the tragedies that befell us the Christians, which came to pass because of the multiplication of our sins. Many householders and priests wandered about begging in their native cantons ... Eremiay [Jeremiah] would have wept for the incomprehensible grief of the Christians, especially of the Armenians ...

The last time this holy Gospel was restored was in the year 795 of the Armenian Era [A.D. 1346], in the canton of Xałteac', in the impregnable fortress called Baberd [Bayburt] ... during the overseership of the Lord Mxit'ar [I, Gṙnerc'i] ... and the reign of King Kostandin [Constanine IV] of the Armenians, and during the princedom of Yorat'nay [Eretna] in the land of Rūm [Hoṙmac' ašxarh], who was a pious man, for many who were tormented by hunger found food in his land; may the Lord God keep him at the helm of his state for a long time, amen! ...

2. Place: city of Surxat' in Xrim; scribe and author of col.: Nater; MS. title: Gospel.
   Source: Xač'ikyan, *XIV Dari*, no. 435a, p. 348

... This was copied in the northern country known as Xrim [Crimea], in the city called Surxat' [Solghat], during the imperial conquest of Čanipēk Xan [Djānībeg Khān] ...

3. Place: city of Surxat' in Łrim; scribe and author of col.: Nater; MS. title: Bible.
   Source: Xač'ikyan, *XIV Dari*, no. 436, p. 349

... This Bible was completed in the year 795 of the Armenian Era [A.D. 1346] ... in our northern country, in the capital of Łrim [Crimea], in the magnificent, renowned, and populous place called Surxat' [Solghat] ... during the imperial conquest of Čanipēk Łan [Djānībeg Khān] and during the governorship of Ṙamatan [Ramaḍān], who is deserving of mention here for his mission of arbitration of the boundary in accordance with the political demands ...

1348

1. Recipient of MS. and author of col.: Step'anos; MS. title: Gospel.
Source: Xač'ikyan, *XIV Dari*, no. 447, p. 368

... In these bitter and tartarean [*tartaros*] times, in the year 797 of the Armenian Era [A.D. 1348], our whole country was destroyed and laid to ruins by the bloodthirsty nation of archers [azgn netołac']. It was deserted by men and animals, and the famine spread ... and the gates of many magnificent churches were closed, and prayers and the divine liturgy were discontinued, and vessels and holy gospels were taken as "captives" ...

2. Place: monastery of Hermon, in canton of Vayoc' Jor, in province of Siwnik'; scribe and author of col.: Sion; MS. title: Gospel.
Source: Xač'ikyan, *XIV Dari*, no. 448, p. 369

... [begun] in the year 797 of the Haykazean Era [A.D. 1348] ... in the bitter and wicked time of the warlike and mischievous tyrant, whose name should be erased from the register of names. During the lordship and princedom, in the province of Siwnik' ... of the prince of princes Bēšk'ēn and of his brother Ivanē, sons of the late ... Baron Birt'ēl ...

3. Place: monastery of Awt'mna in canton of Tivrik; scribe and author of col.: Nersēs; MS. title: Ritual Book [*Maštoc'*].
Source: Xač'ikyan, *XIV Dari*, no. 449, p. 369

... [written] in the year 797 of the Armenian Era [A.D. 1348], on September 10. I plead with you not to blame me for my errors ... for we witnessed the corpses of numerous men who died before our eyes, and I was distraught like a wild beast and could barely maintain my wits for fear of death; otherwise, I could have completed the copying of this [manuscript] sooner; moreover, we too were afflicted by the plague, but through the mercy of God I was spared ...

1349

1. Place: monastery of Ereran; scribe and author of col.: Vahan; recipient of MS.: Princess T'uxt'ani; MS. title: Gospel.

Source: Xač'ikyan, *XIV Dari*, no. 456a, p. 375

. . . This [Gospel] was purchased [by Princess T'uxt'ani] in bitter and grievous times, during the tyranny of the Tačik Melik' Ašrap' [Malik Ashraf] and Aštar (?); and during the khanate of Ēdil Šrwan [Nūshīr-wān al-'Ādil], whose judgments were mere shadows and unjust; and during the princedom of the brave Armenian generals and the devout and pious prince of princes Bešk'en and Iwanē, who succeeded the pious, devout and king-like Baron Biwrdel and Vaxax, who died in Christ. Following their deaths, there occurred a severe famine and one third of the inhabitants of Armenia fell victim to it; and after the famine was lifted, God's wrath again fell upon us, and there occurred a plague in all the land which took away half of the people; and this came to pass on account of our multitudinous sins. Despite this, we do not repent; rather, like the infidels, we continue to compound our sinful acts . . .

2. Place: village of Ałēt' in canton of Bznunik'; scribe Yovhannēs; author of col.: Sargis; MS. title: Gospel.
Source: Xač'ikyan, *XIV Dari*, no. 458, p. 379

. . . In the year 798 of the Armenian Era [A.D. 1349], in bitter and grievous times, when the Ismaelites [azgn Ismayēli] have grown stronger, and when they torture and persecute the Christians with much ignominy and contempt. They confiscate the possessions and properties of some; they impose fines on some; and they seek to destroy the homes of some by *buxtank'*, by acts [designed to] create cleavage, and by false accusations. They did this on many occasions to my host Daniēl; they subjected him to false and unjust accusations and collected 1000 *dahekan* from him, which he, for the love of Christ, paid voluntarily and willingly and without sorrow, for in its stead he will receive hundred-fold and thousand-fold and ten-thousand-fold at the time of the holy judgment, amen! . . .

1350

1. Place: city of Surxat'; MS. title: Bible.
Source: Xač'ikyan, *XIV Dari*, no. 464, p. 385

. . . Written in the year 799 [of the Armenian Era = A.D. 1350], during the pontificate of the orthodox pontiff Lord Mxit'ar [I, Gṙnerc'i];

during the reign of King Kostandianos [Constantine IV of Cilicia] . . . and during the imperial conquest of J̌anipēk Łan [Djānībeg Khān], and when the prince of the city [of Surxat‘ = Solghat] was Ṙamatan [Ramaḍān], the wise judge.

1351

1. Place: monastery of Hermon in Vayoc‘ Jor; scribe Sion; author of col.: Grigor; MS. title: Gospel.
Source: Xač‘ikyan, *XIV Dari*, no. 466, p. 388

> . . . In bitter and grievous times,
> When many in the land were persecuted,
> Some dwelt among bushes,
> Some fell prey to the wolves,
> Many became victims of the famine,
> Fathers disavowed their children . . .

2. Place: Erkir Lewonoy [Cilicia]; scribe and author of col.: Kirakos; MS. title: Gospel.
Source: Xač‘ikyan, *XIV Dari*, no. 467a, p. 389

. . . this colophon was written in the year 800 [of the Armenian Era = A.D. 1351], in wicked and bitter times, for we had fled from the region of Axbak, on account of the war waged by the Muslims [*aylazgi*] / / / the prince, Ašraf [Malik Ashraf] . . .

3. Place: completed in Mount Bt‘ni in canton of Ekełeac‘; scribes: Simēon and Azaria; author of col.: Azaria; MS. title: Gospel.
Source: Xač‘ikyan, *XIV Dari*, no. 468, p. 390

. . . in view of the evil and bitter times, resulting from our multitudinous sins, and also because many villages were destroyed and deserted by numerous men and animals, he [Simēon] left the canton of Ekełeac‘ and went to distant cantons, and this holy Gospel was not completed for a long time . . .

Written in the canton of Ekełeac‘, in the monastery of St. Kirakos, near the foot of Mount Bt‘ni, which is our place of refuge, in the year 800 of the Armenian Era [A.D. 1351] . . .

1354

1. Place: Ałt'amar; scribe and author of col.: Grigor; MS. title: Commentary on the Book of Job by Vanakan Vardapet and Commentary on St. John's Revelations by N. Lambronac'i.
Source: Xač'ikyan, *XIV Dari*, nos. 485a, c, pp. 405–406

... [copied] in the year 803 of the Armenian Era [A.D. 1354], in bitter, grievous, and acute times, the like of which has not happened since the beginning of the world, and which will never happen again ...

... [completed] in this year [A.D. 1353], when all the enemies of the churches and of the Christians multiplied, when order and faith disappeared from amongst the believers and the ecclesiastics, and when only their name, form, and number remained, and when the good life totally disappeared. Alas! Alas! Blessed are those who have not come to this hour ...

2. Place: city of Sultaniay; recipient of MS. and author of col.: Ep'rem; MS. title: Bible.
Source: Xač'ikyan, *XIV Dari*, no. 486, p. 406

... [received in A.D. 1341] during the imperial conquest of the younger Šex Hasan [Ḥasan Küčük] ...

... in this year [A.D. 1354], and on the 25th of September ... [Ep'rem received this Bible], during the tyrannical rule of the great Šex Hasan [Shaykh Ḥasan Buzurg] in the capital of Bałtat [Baghdad], and during the pontificate of All Armenians of the Lord Mxit'ar [I, Gr̈nerc'i] ...

3. Place: city of Surxat'; scribe: Step'annos; recipient of MS. and author of col.: Minas Derǰanec'i; MS. title: Commentaries by Cyril of Alexandria.
Source: Xač'ikyan, *XIV Dari*, no. 491b, p. 410

> ... [completed] In the city of Sulxat' [Solghat],
> During the reign of Čanipek [Djānībeg Khān],
> Son of the great Ōzpēk Xan [Özbek Khān] ...

1355

1. Place: city of Eznkay; scribe and author of col.: Step'annos; MS. title: Book of Canons [*Kanonagirk'*].
Source: Xač'ikyan, *XIV Dari*, no. 493, p. 411

. . . This book of canons was completed in bitter and grievous times, when there was no king among the nation of archers [azgn netołac']; rather, malevolent men held the whole country in tyranny, and entrenched themselves in the fortresses and in the cities and rose against one another . . . [this was completed] when Yaxiayna Bēk controlled our city [Eznkay = Erzindjān], and when someone named Xočay Yali attacked it with numerous troops . . .

2. Place: Ałt'amar; scribe and author of col.: Grigor; MS. title: Gospel.
Source: Xač'ikyan, *XIV Dari*, no. 496, p. 414

. . . This was written in the year 804 of the Armenian Era [A.D. 1355] . . . in time of anarchy, when the spiritual and temporal authority of our Haykazean nation had disappeared, because the forerunner Antichrist [*karapet Neṙn*] nation held all the people of Mijerkreay [Asia Minor] in bondage. They persecute the Christians most severely, until their souls are departed from them. It was in such bitter, grievous, and anxious times that I undertook and completed the task of copying this . . .

1356

1. Place: city of Surłat' in canton of Łrim; scribe and author of col.: Xosrov; MS. title: Missal [*Čašoc'*].
Source: Xač'ikyan, *XIV Dari*, no. 502, pp. 418–419

. . . This was completed in the year 805 of the Armenian Era [A.D. 1356], on January 22, during the pontificate of the Lord Mxit'ar [I, Gṙnerc'i] . . . during the reign of King Kostandianos [Constantine IV of Cilicia], [and] the imperial conquest of Čanipēk Łan [Djānībeg Khān], in the renowned city of Surłat' [Solghat], in the canton of Łrim [Crimea] . . .

1357

1. Scribe and author of col.: Karapet; MS. title: Gospel.
Source: Xač'ikyan, *XIV Dari*, no. 508, p. 425

... Oh, brothers, in this year [A.D. 1357], when I was copying this holy Gospel, the *łan* [Djānībeg Khān] arrived from the east and seized Ašraf [Malik Ashraf]. We do not know what will happen next; surely, whatever God wills! ...

2. Place: Łrim (?); scribe and author of col.: Grigor (son of Nater); MS. title: Gospel.
Source: Xač'ikyan, *XIV Dari*, no. 509, p. 426

... In the year 806 [of the Armenian Era = A.D. 1357], the Great Xan [Djānībeg Khān of the Golden Horde] marched upon T'awrēz [Tabriz].

1358

1. Scribe and author of col.: Yovanēs; MS. title: Book of Lamentations by Grigor Narekac'i.
Source: Xač'ikyan, *XIV Dari*, no. 519, p. 433

... This book of prayers was copied in the year 807 of the Armenian Era [A.D. 1358], when the king in the north named J̌anibēk [Djānībeg Khān] attacked the wicked prince, the destroyer of countries, and the servant of satan, whose name was Ašraw [Malik Ashraf]. He slew this forerunner [*Karapet*] Antichrist [*Neṙn*], and thus put an end to his evil deeds.

1361

1. Place: village of Anapatik in Hayk'aray Jor; scribe and author of col.: Zak'arē; MS. title: Commentary on the Divine Liturgy.
Source: Xač'ikyan, *XIV Dari*, no. 544a, p. 450

... [copied] during the khanate of Yois [Sulṭān Uwais Djalā'ir], in bitter times, when the Christians were being persecuted; pray to God. [This was] written in the year 810 [of the Armenian Era = A.D. 1361] ...

2. MS. title: Excerpts from Bible.
Source: Xač‘ikyan, *XIV Dari*, no. 545, p. 451

In the year 810 of the Armenian Era [A.D. 1361], the iniquitous Tačik judge, Pak‘il [or, Pakiš], carried off captives from the regions of Šik‘ar and Xardberd [Kharput]; and they were sold like sheep . . .

3. Place: city of Sis; scribe and author of col.: T‘oros; MS. title: The Life of Nersēs the Great.
Source: Xač‘ikyan, *XIV Dari*, no. 546, p. 451

. . . In the year 809 [of the Armenian Era = A.D. 1360], in the month of May, Paytamur, the *amiray* [amir] of Halap [Aleppo], invaded Hayk‘ [Cilicia] with the forces of Msr [Egypt], and he captured Atanay [Adana] and Tarson [Tarsus] and Bari-K‘aruk, and also seized the son of Lewon [King Leon V of Cilicia] . . .

1362

1. Place: village of Soranc‘ Orc‘eanc‘ in the plain of Gawaṙuc‘; scribe and author of col.: Andrēas; MS. title: Gospel.
Source: Xač‘ikyan, *XIV Dari*, no. 550, p. 455

Written in the year 811 [of the Armenian Era = A.D. 1362], during the barony of Amir Diatin [Amīr Diādīn], [and] during the khanate of Oyis [Sulṭān Uwais Djalā'ir] . . .

1363

1. Place: Hayk‘ar; scribe and author of col.: Petros; MS. title: Gospel.
Source: Xač‘ikyan, *XIV Dari*, no. 553, p. 458

. . . This was copied in the year 812 of our [Armenian] Era [A.D. 1363], during the time of / / / of the nation of archers [netołac‘ azg], who held Armenia and numerous countries under his tyrannical rule. I cannot adequately describe the bitterness in, and the destruction of, our country, for it was like an agitated, tempestuous, and stormy sea. No territory, no city, no village, no town, and no magnificent monastery enjoyed peace; rather, they were all reduced to ruins and were demolished. Troubled by these torments, I, the wretched one, escaped and came to the land of Hayk‘ar. I came and sojourned here, in much suffering and as a stranger, among a few Christians who had taken shelter here out of fear of their tormentors, like grains of wheat in the midst of thorns . . .

2. Place: monastery of Gamałiēl, near city of Xizan; scribe and author of col.: Yovhannēs; MS. title: Commentary on the Gospel by Matthew.
Source: Xač'ikyan, *XIV Dari*, no. 554, p. 459

. . . this was copied in difficult and grievous times, when all the Christians were being enslaved and plundered on account of my multitudinous sins, and when we all lived in suffering and in anguish . . .

3. Place: Sulxat'; scribe and author of col.: Step'anos, son of Nater; MS. title: Miscellany [*Žołovacu*].
Source: Xač'ikyan, *XIV Dari*, no. 556, p. 460

. . . In this time there was much confusion and agitation at the hands of temporal conquerors, because there was neither leader nor king who could restore the peace, for, as the Lord said, "a divided kingdom cannot stand" [cf. Luke 11:17; Mark 3:24]. Because of this, the governor of this city [Surxat' = Solghat] is digging trenches; he is digging a pit around this city, and he is destroying numerous houses from their foundations. And there is much destruction, and everyone is stricken with fear . . .

1365

1. Place: city of Łrim; scribe and author of col.: Awetis, son of Nater; MS. title: Missal [*Čašoc'*].
Source: Xač'ikyan, *XIV Dari*, nos. 568b, c, pp. 467–468

. . . This [manuscript] was completed . . . in the year 814 [of the Armenian Era = A.D. 1365], on the twenty-third of the month of August, in times of tumultuous anxiety, for men and animals from the whole country extending from Kec' [Kerch] to Saruk'arman [Sarî-Kerman] have assembled here [that is, at Łrim]; and Mamay is at Łarasu [Ḳara-su] with numerous T'at'ar [Tatars]; and our city is trembling and shaking; only He knows the future, He Who is the lord and protector of all, Who is eternally holy.

The war brought mourning to the entire city of Łrim, because its chief prince was unable to offer resistance and fled in defeat; and [the invaders] killed some 2000 of his men, and they took the riches as well as the arms and carried them off to Mōl.

2. Place: city of Kafa; scribe and author of col.: Karapet; MS. title: Missal [*Čašoc'*].
Source: Xač'ikyan, *XIV Dari*, no. 569, pp. 468–469

. . . This was completed in the year 814 of the Armenian Era [A.D. 1365], on August 15, during the pontificate of the Lord Mesrovp [Mesrop I, Artazec'i] . . . [and] the reign of King Kostandianos [Constantine V of Cilicia]; in the renowned city of Kafa . . . in bitter and grievous times. In this year, there arrived the Antichrist [*Neṙn*] and contagion, who is named Č'alibēg, of the Ismaelite nation [Ismayēlean azg], who slaughtered the Christians, and who held the entire neighboring country in terror and in trembling by day and by night. But, as predicted by the Lord Nersēs,[18] there arrived this year, through divine Providence, from among the courageous Hṙomayakan nation [that is, the Genoese] . . . a *ganjawlaws* [consul] in our city as [military] commander. As instructed by the Hṙomayec'ik' [the Genoese], and with the help of God, he captured the city of Sułda [Sughdāḳ] and seized whatever he found therein. And he slaughtered all the Ismaelites [Ismayēlean azg] and Hebrews [Ebrayec'ik'], who are the enemies of Christ's Cross and of the Christians, and also confiscated their possessions . . .

1366

1. Place: Erusałēm [Jerusalem]; scribe and author of col.: Vardan Łrimec'i; MS. title: Book of Lamentations by Grigor Narekac'i.
Source: Xač'ikyan, *XIV Dari*, no. 577a, p. 473

. . . This was copied in the year 815 of the Armenian Era [A.D. 1366]. In this year the Franks [P'ṙankn] carried off captives from Ałek'sandr [Alexandria]; hence, whatever Christians there were in this country they [the Mamluks of Egypt] seized and carried off; and whatever bishop and *abełay* [monk] and priest there were they cast them in prison; and whatever churches there were they shut them all down. They killed our *əṙayis* [*ra'īs*]; they also killed numerous other priests

[18] See note 5 above.

and churchmen. And many became T'urk' [Turks] because of their bitter suffering. And those of us who were in Erusałēm [Jerusalem] spent the greater part of the year in prison, and, for the sake of Christ, we suffered much grief and torture, which I cannot describe in writing . . . I copied this under much anguish and fear; and day in and day out we expected to be tortured or killed . . .

1367

1. Scribe and author of col.: Sargis; MS. title: Collection of Commentaries on the Holy Prophet Isaiah by Gēorg Vardapet Lambronac'i.
   Source: Xač'ikyan, *XIV Dari*, no. 582, p. 477

In the year 816 of the Armenian Era [A.D. 1367], on the sixth day of the month of May, Minč'ak', the *amiray* [amir] of Tarsoy [Ṭarsūs], incited by satan, recruited soldiers. He enlisted as many horsemen as he could from Šamb [Syria], as well as all of his T'urk'man [Turkmens] and numerous other Xaramnc'ik' [Ḳaraman-oghlus]. And he marched upon the citadel of the capital city of Sis, during the pontificate of the Lord Mesrop [I, Artazec'i] and the reign of King Kostandin II of the Armenians, son of the deceased in Christ, the most praiseworthy and the great and mighty Grand *Jambl* [Chamberlain] of the Armenians, Baron Het'um, and during the *guntustaplut'iwn* [constablecy] of the Armenians of Baron Bazun, son of Baron Lewon Bazunenc', and during the Grand *marajaxtut'iwn* [marshalcy] of the Armenians of Liparit, son of the *Awag Marajaxt* [Grand Marshal] Baron T'oros.

In the aforementioned year [1367], on May 6, [Minč'ak' invaded] Anc'mnc'ik with numerous horsemen as well as many footsoldiers, who numbered 12,000 men, and even more. With the help of Jesus Christ, the Armenian King Kostandin came out to resist him, and they joined in battle, in fierce battle. But, fearful of the Sultan, they [the troops] did not carry out the King's orders to continue the fighting; instead, the multitudes in the city transported, on horses and on foot, all their belongings into the citadel. And, on the following day, he [the Sultan] sent an emissary to the King requesting permission to approach the city merely to *fruč*, [that is] to see the city. But after his arrival he deceitfully entered the city and set it on fire; and by such deceit and treachery he wanted to subdue the city. On the following day, which was the eighth day of the month, on the sabbath, he camped by the river Maxt'lša. He left his *mažařostun* [?] and other effects in his tent, and taking his troops with him he arrived at Šaplxeroy K'ar, and then proceeded toward Krtunaki K'arkit' and Pslenc'acvuk' [?] / / /

2. Place: Erusałēm [Jerusalem] (?); scribe and author of col.: Grigor Aknerc'i; MS. title: Gospel.
Source: Xač'ikyan, *XIV Dari*, no. 583, p. 478

. . . we were afflicted with manifold grief; we were imprisoned and put in chains; we were dragged before the judges every day, by reason of the fact that the Franks [Fřankn] had occupied Skandər [Alexandria] and had killed numerous and countless Tačiks and had carried off men and women as captives to the island of Kipros [Cyprus] . . .

1368

1. Place: city of Muš; author of col.: Dawit' Mšec'i; MS. title: Gospel.
Source: Xač'ikyan, *XIV Dari*, no. 590, p. 483

. . . in bitter times, when the Muslims [*aylazgik'*] were persecuting the Christians, especially the renowned monastery of St. Karapet in Tarōn, whose [monks], because of their poverty, wagered [their manuscripts] to the Muslims [*aylazgik'*] . . . I paid 200 *dekan* from my own *halal* assets and recovered this holy Gospel, and gave it back to the monastery of St. Karapet in memory of myself and my ancestors . . .

It was in the year 817 of the Armenian Era [A.D. 1368] that I recovered it.

2. Place: city of Sultaniay; scribe and author of col.: Barseł; MS. title: Gospel.
Source: Xač'ikyan, *XIV Dari*, no. 591, p. 483

In the year 817 of the Armenian Era [A.D. 1368] everything was in abundance; but the *ǰabřən* troops do not permit us to rest in peace . . .

3. Place: city of Kazaria; scribe and author of col.: Step'anos, son of Nater; MS. title: Bible.
Source: Xač'ikyan, *XIV Dari*, no. 594, p. 487

... [The Old Testament was completed] in the year 817 of our [Armenian] Era [A.D. 1368], three years after the occupation of the city [that is, Kazaria], followed by a terrible famine which exterminated numerous and countless people, which cannot be described in writing.

1369

1. Place: village of Artamēt; scribe and author of col.: Step'annos; MS. title: Book of Lamentations by Grigor Narekac'i.
   Source: Xač'ikyan, *XIV Dari*, no. 598a, p. 489

... We first began to copy this book at Varag; [but] the accursed scorpion and evil enemy [Satan], who from the beginning has been opposed to God, rose up against us. And we suffered much from the tyranny of the lawless ones, and for a whole year we were in flight, and we wandered about because of the persecution, and because of the attacks upon the country by the horsemen. We left / / / .

1370

1. Place: town of T'lak in canton of Ekełeac'; scribe and author of col.: Yovannēs-Alinax; MS. title: Gospel.
   Source: Xač'ikyan, *XIV Dari*, no. 601, p. 491

This was completed on November 17 of the year 819 of the Armenian Era [A.D. 1370]. This holy Gospel was copied ... in bitter and anxious times, when the Christians were persecuted by the Ismaelites [azgn Ismayēli] ...

1371

1. Place: city of Surxat' in Honac' ašxarh or Xrim; scribe and author of col.: Step'anos; MS. title: Missal [*Čašoc'*].
   Source: Xač'ikyan, *XIV Dari*, no. 608, p. 496

... [completed in A.D. 1371] in most wicked times because, on account of my multitudinous sins and the instigation of the evil one [Satan], the princes and military commanders assembled in the north are killing one another. We hope that the forgiving and unrevengeful

[God] will have mercy upon us all, so that those of us who have become enslaved and have taken refuge in various places shall not, because of our sins, be plundered again . . .

. . . [This manuscript was completed] during the pontificate of the Lord Mesrovb [I, Artazec'i] . . . during the reign of King Kostandin [Constantine V of Cilicia]; and during the imperial conquest of the Tačik Mamay; [copied] in our land of Honac', and in the country of Xrim [Crimea], in the magnificent and renowned city which is called Surxat' [Solghat] . . .

2. Scribe and author of col.: Mkrtič'; MS. title: Miscellany [*Žołovacu*].
Source: Xač'ikyan, *XIV Dari*, no. 611, p. 498

. . . This was copied in the year 820 of the Armenian Era [A.D. 1371], during the khanate of Ois [Sulṭān Uwais Djalā'ir].

3. Recipient of MS. and author of col.: Simēon; MS. title: Gospel.
Source: Xač'ikyan, *XIV Dari*, no. 612, p. 499

In the year 820 of the Armenian Era [A.D. 1371], the Persians [azgn Parsic'] came to Berkri and carried off captives. They plundered Bandumahi, and captured the holy Gospel called "Karmir." [The Gospel] flew off from the arms of the individual who captured it and fell into the river, and for four years no one could find it. Later its location was revealed to the sacristan in a dream, and the sacristan informed me, the sinful Simēon, about it. Then I went to the sanctuary of the Lord Yusik's son [Uxtn Tēr Yuskan Ordin]. I took with me the vardapet Step'anos, the vardapet Martiros, the priest T'umay, the priest Yōvsēp', the priest Xač'aytur, the *ṙayēs* Grigor, the *ṙayēs* P'anos, the *ṙayēs* Karaypet, and others old and young. We entered the church; we prayed until the morning. After the divine liturgy we all went to the bank of the river; we witnessed a new miracle, for when [the water?] pulled to one side, the holy Gospel was revealed in the cavern of a rock, and we pulled out the holy Gospel. It healed all the sick and the blind and the demoniacs who were among those assembled there. Three years later, I left my home, took the Karmir Gospel with me, and fled to the province of K'aǰberunik'. The son of the Kurd Ibrahim Ała [Ibrāhīm Agha], who had been blind from birth, gained his sight. We arrived in the village of Maǰar, where there was a Christian by the name of Martiros, whose son had been in fetters for five years, his knees had been tied to his abdomen and his hands to his heart. He was brought before the holy Karmir Gospel; he was healed and released from his fetters. Then we arrived in the province of Arcrunik', in the village called Aṙēn. There were two T'urk' [Turkish] boys, one blind who gained his sight, and one demoniac who was healed. And all the blind and the demoniacs and the feeble who were in the region came to the "feet" of the holy Karmir Gospel and were healed.

1374

1. Place: monastery of Gamałiēl; scribe and author of col.: Nahapet; MS. title: The Prophecies of Jeremiah.
   Source: Xač'ikyan, *XIV Dari*, no. 631, p. 514

. . . [copied] in bitter and grievous times, when the country was afflicted with much suffering on account of the drought, captivity, caterpillars, locusts, abundant rains, plagues, high prices, and other tribulations, in the year 823 [of the Armenian Era = A.D. 1374].

1375

1. Place: Sis; scribe: Sargis; author of col.: Zak'arē; MS. title: The Assizes of Antioch and the Law Book of Smbat.
   Source: Xač'ikyan, *XIV Dari*, no. 635, p. 516

In the year 824 of the Great Armenian Era [A.D. 1375], in bitter and grievous times, in the year when the city of Sis was captured. And I, the humble and false bishop Zak'arē, chanced to be there. Who can recount in writing the tragedy which my eyes witnessed, for I saw the bright sun, the stars, and the moon fall down.

2. Place: Kilikia (?); scribe: Nersēs; MS. title: Ritual Book [*Maštoc'*].
   Source: Xač'ikyan, *XIV Dari*, no. 636, p. 516

In the year 824 [of the Armenian Era = A.D. 1375], Yašēx T'amur [Ašiq Temür al-Māridānī] captured the royal city of Sis, and there was great mourning. In this year there occurred a severe famine in the entire country, and the price of one measure of wheat was 100 *tahiri dram*.

1376

1. Place: Ayas; purchaser of MS. and author of col.: Fimi; MS. title: Gospel.
Source: Xač'ikyan, *XIV Dari*, no. 647, p. 521

The last recipient of this holy Gospel, I, Fimi, wife of Vahram. In bitter times the castle of Lambron was plundered, and this holy Gospel was brought to the city of Ayas as captive, and I, Fimi, bought this holy Gospel in memory of my soul and the souls of my parents . . .

1377

1. Place: city of Łrim; scribe and author of col.: Yovannēs; MS. title: Commentary on the Epistles by Sargis Šnorhali.
Source: Xač'ikyan, *XIV Dari*, no. 651, p. 524

. . . [copied] in the year 826 of the Armenian Era [A.D. 1377], during the imperial conquest of the baron of barons, Mamay . . .

1378

1. Place: Tarōn; restorer of MS. and author of col.: Yovanēs; MS. title: Bible.
Source: Xač'ikyan, *XIV Dari*, no. 652a, p. 525

. . . In the year 820 of the Armenian Era [A.D. 1371], instigated by the evil one [Satan] and on account of our multitudinous sins, the levies imposed by the aliens ruined our land of Tarōn, as well as the holy monastery of Łazar, whose monks . . . crossed over into other cantons and became refugees . . .

1383

1. Place: Trapizon; recipient of MS. and author of col.: Sargis; MS. title: Gospel.
Source: Xač'ikyan, *XIV Dari*, no. 679a, p. 544

. . . in the year 832 [of the Armenian Era = A.D. 1383], when P'awlat Łan [Pulad Khān of the Golden Horde] attacked Kafa . . .

1384

1. Place: city of Kafay in Honac' Ašxarh or Xrim; scribes and authors of col.: Yovhannēs and Markos; MS. title: Missal [*Čašoc'*]. Source: Xač'ikyan, *XIV Dari*, no. 684, pp. 548–549

... This was completed, with the help of the Divine Providence, in most wicked times because, on account of our multitudinous sins and the instigation of the evil one [Satan], the princes and military commanders assembled in the north are killing one another. We hope that the forgiving and unrevengeful [God] will have mercy upon us all, so that those of us who have become enslaved and have taken refuge in various places shall not, because of our sins, be plundered again ...

... [This manuscript was completed] during the imperial conquest of the Tačik T'awxt'amiš Łan [Toḳtamīsh Khān of the Golden Horde], of the Apu tribe; [copied] in our land of the Huns [Honac' Ašxarh] and in the country of Xrim [Crimea] in the magnificent and renowned capital city which is called Kafay [Kafa], by the seashore, under the rule of the Latins [Ladinac'woc'] ...

2. Place: Naxiǰewan (?); MS. title: Book on the Mystery of the Incarnation of Christ by Thomas Aquinus. Source: Xač'ikyan, *XIV Dari*, nos. 686b, d, p. 550

The commotion is intense and turbulent,
The land is evil and uproarious,
May God bring immediate peace,
That I may be saved from this deep sea.

I worried much this year,
The plague came to our country,
It is passing through Naxiǰewan,
Many *łaripni* are dying.

1386

1. Place: Ernǰak; scribe and author of col.: Yakob; MS. title: Collection of the Works of Grigor Narekac'i, Grigor Tłay and Others. Source: Xač'ikyan, *XIV Dari*, no. 700, pp. 559–560

... This divine manuscript was copied in the year 835 of the Armenian Era [A.D. 1386], in bitter and tearful times, for everyone, old and young, is tired of life, just as Christ said that there will come a time when they will say to the hills fall upon us and to the mountains hide us [cf. Luke 23:30; Revelation 6:16; Hosea 10:8], which we have witnessed with our own eyes . . .

. . . because of my multitudinous sins, contingents of infidels [rose] upon the Christians, especially upon the territory of Burdel. They came and occupied the fortress of Orotan, and deprived the Baron Smbat, son of Nanik, of his ancestral lands. They also sought to arrest our holy master [that is, Yovhannēs Orotnec‘i] in order to appropriate his ancestral domain. But he, by the will of God, escaped from their hands, and wandered about in different places for two full years, together with his pupils, and [continued] to instruct them. And I [accompanied him wherever he went] and continued to copy this holy book, with much anguish and suffering, for I did not finish it where I started.

Then God softened the hearts of the infidels toward our holy vardapet, who came back in peace and [recovered] the monasteries in the canton of Ernǰak which had been under his jurisdiction; and he built magnificent and splendid holy churches amidst infidel princes and masters of fortresses; and we lived in greater joy and cheer than heretofore.

2. Place: city of Arcrunis; scribe and author of col.: Xač‘atur; MS. title: Gospel.
Source: Xač‘ikyan, *XIV Dari*, nos. 702a, b, pp. 561–562

. . . [copied] in the year 835 of the Haykazean Era [A.D. 1386] . . . during the pontificate of the Cilicians [Kilikec‘woc‘] of the Lord T‘ēodoros [II, Kilikec‘i], and the pontificate in our [see of] Axt‘amar of the Lord Zak‘aria [II], and during the imperial tyranny of Ahmat Łan [Sulṭān Aḥmad Djalā'ir] of the nation of archers [azgn netołac‘], in wretched and evil times, when justice had diminished and injustice had increased everywhere. In this year the churches and their servants suffered much tribulation and persecution at the hands of the infidel Łaray Mahmat [Ḳara Muḥammad Tūrmush], for as in ancient times God made Nabugotonosor [Nebuchadnezzar] rise upon Erusałēm [Jerusalem], so also recently the evil and haughty tyrant Łara Mahmat [Ḳara Muḥammad Tūrmush] rose upon us . . .

In the beginning of the year
Eight hundred and thirty-five

Of the Haykazean Era [A.D. 1386],
In times of anguish,
When the Muslims [*aylazgik‘*] were harassing,
The Christians they were insulting,
The churches they were destroying.
I, the sinful one, counted seventy churches,
Which were in the province of Arcruni;
They crushed their gates,
They demolished their altars,
They shook their foundations,
They carried off the holy books.
The clergy sat and wept
And regrouped their people.
Behold, oh brother, the grief
Which they meted out to the churches.
And why did all this come to pass?
Because of the sins which they committed.

3. Place: Ostan; restorer of MS. and author of col.: Arłun; MS. title: Gospel.[19]
Source: Xač‘ikyan, *XIV Dari*, no. 703, p. 563

In recent times, in the year 835 of the Armenian Era [A.D. 1386], I Arłun, who was in the palace of the Amir Mēlik‘ Asad [Amīr Asad al-Dīn Zarrīn Čang] of the city of Ostan [Wusṭān], had this Gospel restored as a memorial for myself and my parents . . .

1387

1. Place: fortress of Šahapōnk‘; author of MS. and of col.: Grigor Tat‘ewac‘i; MS. title: Questions by Gēorg Vardapet and Responses by Grigor Tat‘ewac‘i.
Source: Xač‘ikyan, *XIV Dari*, no. 709, pp. 567–568

. . . [this was written] in times of anguish and in an unsafe place, when we were again besieged by the marauding archers [*netołac‘*], [that is] the nation called Xorazm [Khwārizmī], who with an innumerable multitude marauded and devastated the lands of Armenia, Persia [Parsic‘ ašxarh], Georgia [Vrac‘ ašxarh], and all the eastern

[19] The MS. was copied in 1294; the date of the colophon is 1386. See Xač‘ikyan, *XIV Dari*, p. 563, n. 2.

countries. They carried off some men and women into captivity; others, both clergy and laymen, were trampled underfoot and slain with swords. Corpses were thrown upon corpses and were left unburied; and others were afflicted with various and sundry means of torture. Some, half-burned by fire, were devoured; others, on account of the famine, were left in danger of being torn apart by wild beasts. Some were subjected to various kinds of torture, and others were chilled with horror. As for us, we remained like voluntary prisoners in the fortress of Šahapōnk‘, always mindful of the great and awesome [last] judgment. As yonder where they greet one another in peace and tranquility but disaster strikes unexpectedly, so also happened here on the Sunday of the Octave of Easter [*krknoy zatik*], when the awesome-looking forces of the archers [*netołac‘*] suddenly poured forth, with a violent hue and cry and with naked swords, and, inundating us like a turbulent torrent, they beseiged us. The aforementioned occurred not only in far off places but also here. They lingered around for a little while by the gate of our *klay*; and some they set free and others they carried off into captivity. Only with tearful countenances and voluntarily emitted sighs could one behold the tragic sight, when loved ones, parents and brothers, were helplessly carried off into captivity, as on the day [of judgment] when [the sinners] will be doomed to perish. It is useless to cry here as it is yonder; as no one can return from yonder, so also those who were traded away, for like the foolish maidens they cannot be redeemed and cannot be saved by compassion.[20] Those who had provisions enjoyed a prosperous life, but those who had not suffered the death of starvation, they were deprived of all charity and hope; for blasphemy abounded and impenitence reigned . . . And this lasted not days and weeks but three months, and the perpetrators were not avenged in a manner befitting their deeds.

And this tragedy of inextricable anguish engulfed us in the year 836 of the Haykazean Era [A.D. 1387] . . .

2. Place: K‘aǰberunik‘; scribe and author of col.: Petros; MS. title: Gospel.
Source: Xač‘ikyan, *XIV Dari*, no. 710, p. 569

. . . The copying of this holy Gospel was begun in the year 836 of the Haykazean Era [A.D. 1387], in bitter times, when many places were destroyed because of our sins. Emerging from the east with innumer-

[20] For the parable of the ten virgins see Matthew 25:1–13.

able forces, the wicked Mahmetakan [Muḥammadan] tyrant, whose name was Lank-T'amur [Tīmūr Lang], vanquished all the territories extending from Persia [Parsic'] up to the country of Rūm [Hṙomac' erkir]. And arriving in Armenia he devastated it and carried off everyone into captivity, and he brutally put to the sword those Armenians and Tačiks whom he found. And who can describe the wickedness and destruction which he committed in several places? . . . this [Gospel] was completed in K'ajberunik' . . . during the pontificate of the Lord Zak'aria [II of Aghtamar], and during the tyranny in our land of Łaray Iwsiwf [Ḳara Yūsuf], who is wicked, acrimonious, abominable, and a ravager of lands. I . . . Petros Abełay, consented and, with much suffering and in wandering, copied this at a time when all provisions and foodstuffs became scarce, and when there was peace nowhere in the land. Only this plea we make to God that He spare us from witnessing again that which we have seen.

3. Place: city of Eznkay; scribe and author of col.: Gēorg; MS. title: Missal [*Čašoc'*].
Source: Xač'ikyan, *XIV Dari*, no. 711, p. 570

. . . At this time, in the year 836 of the Armenian Era [A.D. 1387], there emerged from among the savage nation in the east, from the northern region, one who was named Lank-T'amur [Tīmūr Lang]. He reached as far as Arzrum [Erzerum], and committed numerous crimes / / / but then God turned him away, and the prayers of St. [Gregory] the Illuminator saved our city of Erznkay [Erzindjān] and its cantons . . .

1388

1. Place: canton of Spatkert; scribe and author of col: son of Alek'san; MS. title: Commentary on the Book of Proverbs by Nersēs Lambronac'i.
Source: Xač'ikyan, *XIV Dari*, no. 717, p. 573

. . . In this year [A.D. 1388] the wicked *łan* [khan] named T'amur-Lank [Tīmūr Lang] arrived in the city of Vaspurakan, and he captured the fortress and demolished it. He carried off some into captivity; he hurled down some from the precipice, and he put others to the sword; and he burned the country by fire.

2. Place: monastery of Łazar in canton of Tarōn; scribe: Step'anos; recipient of MS. and author of col.: Tirac'u; MS. title: Gospel.
Source: Xač'ikyan, *XIV Dari*, no. 719, p. 574

In these past days . . . there arose from among the nation of archers [azgn netołac'] one named T'amur [Tīmūr Lang], [who was] of a different aspect, who spoke an alien tongue, [and who] looked like the second Antichrist [*Neřn*]. He came out of the east and, traversing the whole world, he slaughtered everyone, and carried off the rest into captivity. Who can recount in writing the grief, affliction, and bitterness of our time? . . .

3. Place: town of T'ilkuran; scribe and author of col.: Step'annos; MS. title: Book of Questions by Vardan Vardapet.
Source: Xač'ikyan, *XIV Dari*, no. 720, pp. 574–575

. . . [copied in 1388] in bitter and grievous times, when T'amur-Lank [Tīmūr Lang] marched forth and arrived with a countless multitude of barbarians, and devastated the eastern lands stretching from the city of Smrłand [Samarkand] to Ep'rat [Euphrates river] in Tarōn, and then he went away . . .

1389

1. Place: Ałt'amar; scribe and author of col: Karapet; MS. title: Collection of Homilies [*Čařəntir*].
Source: Xač'ikyan, *XIV Dari*, no. 725a, pp. 577–579

Now, oh brothers and believers in Christ, hark unto the tragedy which befell us on account of our sins . . .

Some were hurled down into the precipice and were torn to pieces; and some were tortured with scourges of one kind or another. This is what happened in recent days and in waning times, in the year 836 of the Haykazean Era [A.D. 1387], when there appeared the wicked man called Lank-T'amur [Tīmūr Lang], who had the likeness of Gołiat' [Goliath], and whom God held in his hands like a large bowl filled sevenfold with bitterness and from which He poured upon wicked men, as He did in olden times through Asur [Ashurbanipal], Nabupałsar [Nabopolassar], and other brutes. Thus leaving his capital of Sməřłənd [Samarkand] in the east, he [Tīmūr Lang] uttered a horrible roar and marched into numerous regions ruled by others, and many from fear of external threat / / / a multitude of one hundred thousand soldiers with naked swords and with iron-clad armor. He first contemplated invading this place in the year 830 [of the Armenian Era = A.D. 1381], and six years later we heard the frightful rumors. In the month of Mehekan the impending death knell was broadcast throughout Armenia. It was a sight to behold the terror caused upon sighting these awesome and beastly men, for those who heard their arrival were struck with consternation; and those who chanced to see them from afar were amazed by the uncustomary sight, because the dust caused by the hooves of their fiery and fast-running horses was like a dark cloud. If anyone took refuge on the peaks of high mountains and looked down upon the many legions which were amassed like a turbulent sea, the soul in his body trembled. And although he was alive, yet he felt weaker than the one who had been dead for many days, when he beheld the glittering of the swords, the swinging of the bombs[?], the stamping of the hooves of the horses, the clatter of the chariots, the neighing of the proud horses, the shrill of the sounds, [and] the sight of the immense horsemen, who crawled, crept, swarmed the fields, encircled the mountains, fixed their arrows, fenced in the broad expanses, uttered noises that were heard far and wide. And stretching for a distance of eight days, they filled the country with star-studded and red-painted tents, and carefully spun their ropes and masts. And if anyone in impregnable fortresses resisted them, they forthwith came upon them like a multitude of locusts; they surrounded them and squalled, bellowed, howled, lowed, barked, groaned, neighed, [and] roared. They *damdam* the *dhawls*, they thumped the *nałarays*, they drew the *č'arxs*, they showered arrows / / / they whirled the catapults, they flung the *blgihons* / / /; they destroyed, they demolished, they dug ditches, they trampled, they hammered, and in a single day they wiped out completely that which had been built in thousands of years. And those who remained within the fortresses were scorched and tormented, they grew weaker and trembled, they became thirsty and starved to death, they languished and they were terrified with fear.

It was a sight to behold the weeping of the parents, the misery of the children, the contraction of the intestines, the disfigurement of the countenances, the yellowing of the faces, the fading away of the voices, the prostration of the feet, the inaction of the hands, the growing dumbness of the tongues, and the paralysis of the brains. Some entreated, some screamed, some pleaded, some implored, some prayed, and some shed tears. But God heeded none of this because of our sins and perverse behavior; rather, He delivered us into the hands of the infidels. And when they tyrannized and then occupied any fortress /// they uttered a loud roar. And those who were in the mountains came down and assembled before the cities and fortresses. They instantly assaulted and demolished the iron gates, and they scaled them from all sides, and they engulfed them like the foaming billows of the sea. Woe unto these times! The corpses of some floated in a sea of blood; some, whose heads were half cut off from their bodies, pleaded for water and soon died of thirst; [and] fountains of blood gushed out of the mouths of those whose heads were dangling. Oh, the cries! Oh, the laments! Oh, the tearful and heart-rending anguish! They piled up the corpses in clusters, and kicked them around! There were woeful cries hither and thither! Now, the sea of the horsemen calmed down; now, they went about in search of the Christians, and when they found them they mercilessly slaughtered them /// they numbered in thousands. They put the wondrous bishops to the sword; they ground the heads of the pious priests between stones; they cast the flock of Christ as food for the dogs; they trampled the children with their horses; they debauched the women, and carried off their infants into captivity. Like the threshing-floor of flails, they thrashed the children with their horses; and, in place of grain, rivers of blood began to spring forth, and in place of straw the bones flowed forth like dust. The beasts were satiated; the birds grew weary of eating; the wolves wondered whose flesh they should eat—the flesh of the patriarchs, the priests, the deacons, the servants of the church, the anchorites, or the hermits? Moreover, they attacked the churches; they demolished the altars; they set their gates on fire; they desecrated the temples; they smashed the incense boxes and chalices; they forced them to renounce their faith and then slaughtered them. They made them starve, so much so that they began to feed on dogs, cats, donkeys, horses, corpses, and *murtaṙ*; and they even roasted their tenderly nursed infants, and then ate them up. There was neither bread nor water.

Verily, I say in Christ, I have singled out only a few out of a thousand and ten thousand, in order not to cause tedium to the readers. And all of this came to pass on account of our multitudinous sins . . .

1391

1. Place: Van; scribe and author of col.: T'uma; MS. title: Book of Lamentations by Grigor Narekac'i.
Source: Xač'ikyan, *XIV Dari*, nos. 734a, b, pp. 587, 589–590

. . . [completed] in bitter and grievous times, in the year 840 of the Armenian Era [A.D. 1391] . . . So evil were the times that I copied [this] manuscript in the course of four hazardous years, [for] we all took to flight and lived at the summit of the mountains in hunger and wandering, and all of us were like living dead from fear of T'amur [Tīmūr Lang]. Who can recount or write about this evil? . . .

Oh, brothers, I suffered much anguish because we were shelterless and it was wintertime,
And the aliens had risen upon the Christians.
In grievous times and when the Tačiks had increased in number,
The Christians were condemned at the instigation of satan;
There came from Xorasan [Khurāsān] a dog and cripple named T'amur [Tīmūr Lang];
He was filled with wrath like a viper and an aspic serpent.
The evil which he wrought what tongue can recount?
Let no earth-born man behold what we witnessed in these times.
Refugees everywhere, naked, shelterless and resourceless;
Our entire land is quavering like a wrecked ship at sea.
Great grief befell the Armenians when he [Tīmūr Lang], who was from the *muxanat'* nation,
Dispatched a *ǰalat'* from Łzuin [Qazwīn] and offered much bribe in gold,
Saying that whoever mentioned the name of Christ the Lord should be severely punished;
Not only should they be tortured but be beheaded forthwith,
And that those who offered bribes their heads should be brought to him,
And all those who bore the name of a Christian should be put to the sword.
Carrying their two-edged swords they went about the land like mad dogs;
They mercilessly slew the Armenians and Georgians [Vrac'i]
Who professed the Father and the Son, the infinite God, and living Lord.
Many pious priests and humble deacons,
And hermits in seclusion, all these they made victims of their sword.
Many churches, monasteries, and sanctuaries they demolished;
Above all our land of Vaspurakan they laid to utter ruin;

He [Tīmūr Lang] captured the citadel of Van; he had no pity
for the old and the young;
He hurled them all down from the citadel and carried off the
rest as captives.
Who among the earth-born can recount the wickedness of
T'amur [Tīmūr Lang]?
No father had mercy for his child, no mother nursed her
child . . .

2. Author of MS. and of col.: Grigor Tat'ewac'i; MS. title: Explication of the Commentaries by Cyril and by Grigor Tat'ewac'i. Source: Xač'ikyan, *XIV Dari*, no. 735, p. 591

. . . [completed] in the year 840 of the Haykazean Era [A.D. 1391], in grievous and waning times, when a short time ago alien, marauding forces vanquished, enslaved, and devastated our country, and when many other punishments engulfed us; but now the merciful Lord in heaven, witnessing our suffering, has permitted us to breathe a little, although His hand is still raised and ready to smite us . . .

1392

1. Place: Ałt'amar; purchaser of MS. and author of col.: Simēon; MS. title: Book of Lamentations by Grigor Narekac'i. Source: Xač'ikyan, *XIV Dari*, no. 743, p. 597

In the year 841 of the Armenian Era [A.D. 1392], in the month of Nawasard, on Tuesday during the fast of Epiphany, Amir Ēzdin [Amīr 'Izz al-Dīn Shīr] captured the city of Ostan [Wusṭān], from his own brother, and substantially reduced the number of the Christians . . . They devastated our land of Ostan [Wusṭān]. This [manuscript], which was at Ałt'amar, was brought by the vardapet Yakob to Van. When the T'urk' [Turkish] troops were slaughtered, the vardapet fled from Van but, arriving at Narek, he was martyred by the horsemen. This manuscript was kept at Van with a secular priest, who took it to Ałt'amar . . . and I [Simēon] paid 30 *t'ankay* and secured it.

2. Place: village of Nvəndi in K'ajberunik'; scribe and author of col.: Petros; MS. title: Gospel.

Source: Xačʻikyan, *XIV Dari*, no. 744, p. 597

... [completed] In the year 841 of the Haykazean Era [A.D. 1392], during the pontificate of the Lord Zakʻaria [II of Aghtamar], and during the conquest of the region of Kʻajberunikʻ by Łara Yusuf [Ḳara Yūsuf] ...

3. Place: Erusałēm [Jerusalem]; scribe: Karapet; recipient of MS. and author of col.: Yohanēs; MS. title: Excerpts from the Bible.
Source: Xačʻikyan, *XIV Dari*, no. 745, p. 598

... In the year 841 [of the Armenian Era = A.D. 1392], the Catholicos of Sis, Lord Tʻēodoros [II, Kilikecʻi], died in the good faith of Christ; and after him, in the following year, the Lord Zakʻaria [II], incumbent of the see of Axtʻamar and the reverend Catholicos, was assassinated by the aliens ...

1393

1. Place: begun at the monastery of Suharay or Xaṙabastay and completed at monastery of Cʻipnay; scribe and author of col.: Grigor [Xlatʻecʻi]; MS. title: Gospel.
Source: Xačʻikyan, *XIV Dari*, nos. 746a, b, pp. 599–601

... And, now, who can recount or put into writing the anguish of our time, the carnage and enslavement, the famine and quailing, which we Christians suffered at the hands of the wicked and alien infidels? For the Xorazm [Khwārizmī] race, that is the Tʻatʻar [Tatars] in general, marched forth and devastated and desecrated our entire country. We tremble from fear of them, and day in and day out we seek death, and with faith we beseech God to save us from their terrible threats. Moreover, the bitter grief which we suffer at the hands of our own princes, be they Tʻurkʻ [Turks] or Kʻurd [Kurds], natives or strangers, from within or from without, is ineffable and inexpressible.

Moreover, they killed our two catholicoses within one year. Last year they killed the Lord Tʻēodoros [II, Kilikecʻi] at Sis, and before the year was over they stoned and killed the Lord Zakʻaria [II of Aghtamar] at Ostan [Wusṭān], not to mention other tribulations to which they continue to subject us.

Come, brothers, let us lament the wickedness of the nation of
archers [azgn netołac‘]!
Armenian flocks tormented by the infidels, [who are]
Like harmful *gałjn* growing in the fields of Armenia;
They stifle us by depriving us of our lands.
As Aram and Ep‘rem [Ephraim] persecuted Judaea [tunn
Yudayanc‘],
In like manner the T‘orgomeank‘ and the Mars [azgn Marac‘]
Torment us severely with anguish from all sides.
We Armenians are without a leader and plagued on all sides;
Masters of our people shed tears for us who are at the mercy
of the aliens.
In the year 842 of the Armenian Era [A.D. 1393],
They made our pontiff [Zak‘aria II of Aghtamar] a witness to
the Lamb of God;
The children of Hagar wounded us severely,
And took away from us the head of our Armenian flock,
On Wednesday the fifteenth day of the month of Mehekan,
They seized our Lord and sentenced him to death;
They killed him for Christ. Their chiefs seized this Christian
And took him to the bathhouse, before the impure *amiray*
[amir];
They accused him bitterly saying, "He smote our *ładi* [kadi]."
The impure *amiray* [amir] demanded that he "betray the
living Christ,
The immortal crucified King, the binder of the arch of
heaven."
But our holy pontiff professed the Only-begotten Son:
"Christ is the God of my flock, the creator of eternity,
I believe in the true Spirit, who shares His glory."
When the orders were issued, the *molnay* and *ładi* [kadi]
Stabbed the Lord forthwith and made him cry out like a
leopard.
They brought him out of the bathhouse and smote his head
with stones,
They tied a rope around his neck and dragged him off with it;
They smote him with swords and stones until he was finished;
They hurled our patriarch's body in the street,
They removed his brain and then cut off his head.
They wished to light a torch by burning the remains of our Lord;
But the *amirapet* ordered that his body be taken to his ancestral
home.

The loud laments of the flock, who fled and hid while he was being stoned,
Now resounded throughout the land.
Their laments, mourning, and woes over their Lord were intense,
Like those of the daughters of Jerusalem on the dominical day.[21]
Like the Naxavkay [Protomartyr], our Lord became a witness at Ostan [Wusṭān].
Woe unto us I say, brothers, who came upon these terrible days!
We received deep and severe wounds at the hands of the alien race;
Let the light of the moon and the rays of the sun darken for us today!
Let us, brothers, also lament the terrible tragedy
That befell the glorious see of Sis, our Lord's domain,
And its pontiff, the vicar of [St. Gregory] the Illuminator.
The Lord T'oros [T'ēodoros II, Kilikec'i], head of all the Armenian flock, they killed there,
During the past year and on the anniversary of our Lord;
We were smitten with bitter wounds by this terrible grief.
The Lord Zak'aria became a noble martyr for Christ,
The Lord Zak'aria valiantly shared the Cross of Christ;
The Lord Zak'aria, chosen a brave shepherd like Christ . . .

2. Place: monastery of C'ipnay; editor of MS. and author of col.: Grigor [Xlat'ec'i]; MS. title: Hymnal [*Ganjaran*].
Source: Xač'ikyan, *XIV Dari*, no. 747, p. 602

. . . [copied] During the reign of Łaray Usuf [Ḳara Yūsuf] and his sons, of the nation of archers [azgn netołac'] . . .

1394

1. Place: island of Lim; MS. title: Hymnal [*Ganjaran*].
Source: Xač'ikyan, *XIV Dari*, no. 756, p. 607

. . . [copied] in the year 843 [of the Armenian Era = A.D. 1394], in which year the wrath of God came upon the earth, [that is] the bloodthirsty T'at'ar [Tatar] forces, whose chief was named Lank-T'amur [Tīmūr Lang] . . .

[21] See Luke 23:28.

1395

1. Place: city of Xizan; scribe and author of col.: Step'anos; MS. title: Ritual-Book [*Maštoc'*].
Source: Xač'ikyan, *XIV Dari*, no. 762, p. 611

... [copied] in the year 844 of the Haykazean Era [A.D. 1395] ... during the pontificate of the Cilicians [Kilikec'woc'] of the Lord Karapet [I, Kełec'i], who is surnamed Bokik, and in our pontifical see [of Aghtamar] of the Lord Dawit' [III] Ałt'amarec'i, and during the rule of the aliens under Lank-T'amur [Tīmūr Lang], whose hegemony extended from the land of Səmərłənd [Samarkand] to Babelon [Babylon = Baghdad], and from there up to Urxa [Urfa] in Syrian Mesopotamia [Mijaget Asoroc'], and from there up to the source of Ep'rat [Euphrates river]. Who can recount the atrocities which he committed against the churches, the clergy and the [Christian] believers; for many were killed by the sword, and many died of hunger, and others died with cruel torture after being trampled by the horses. May the Lord God efface his [Tīmūr Lang's] kingdom and hurl him into the abyss, and may He give us a peace-loving king ...

2. Place: monastery of Ewstat'ē; author of MS. and of col.: Matt'ēos; MS. title: On the Creation of Man by Matt'ēos Vardapet.
Source: Xač'ikyan, *XIV Dari*, no. 765, p. 613

... [completed] in the year 844 of the Haykazean Era [A.D. 1395], in grievous times, when the southern fire named T'amur [Tīmūr Lang] devastated our entire country ...

1396

1. Place: Axalc'ixē; donor of MS. and author of col.: Amir-Sargis; MS. title: Gospel.[22]
Source: Xač'ikyan, *XIV Dari*, no. 767, p. 614

... I donated this [Gospel] to the church of the Forty Martyrs at Axalc'ixē [Akhal Tsikhe], during the reign of King Gēorgi [Giorgi VII of Georgia]; during the barony of the *at'apak* [atabeg] Iwanē; [and]

[22] The MS. was copied in A.D. 1237; 1396 is the date of the colophon, which is only partially preserved. See Xač'ikyan, *XIV Dari*, p. 614, n. 1.

during the catholicosate of the Lord Karapet [I, Kełec'i] . . . in the year 845 of the Armenian Era [A.D. 1396] . . .

1397

1. Place: city of Hizan; scribe and author of col.: Ṙstakēs; MS. title: Gospel.
   Source: Xač'ikyan, *XIV Dari*, no. 772, p. 618

. . . [copied in A.D. 1397] in wretched and evil times, during the conquest of T'amur Xan [Tīmūr Lang Khān] of the nation of archers [azgn netołac'], who captured Babelon [Babylon = Baghdad], [D]klat, Edesia [Edessa], Ṙa[. . .]łēn, Merdin [Mārdīn], Amit' [Āmid], and the fortress of Awənka. He put them all to the sword and set them on fire; and he also carried off some into captivity. This came to pass when justice had diminished and when injustice had increased everywhere, as a result of which the churches and their servants suffered much grief and torture at the hands of the insidious aliens . . .

2. Place: monastery of Gamałiēl; scribe and author of col.: Nersēs; MS. title: Collection of Discourses [*Žołavacu Čaṙic'*].
   Source: Xač'ikyan, *XIV Dari*, no. 773, p. 619

. . . [copied] in the year 846 of the Armenian Era [A.D. 1397] . . . during the pontificate of the Cilicians [Kilikec'oc'] of the Lord Karapet [I, Kełec'i], and our pontificate at Ałt'amar of the Lord Dawit' [III], and during the reign of the alien T'amur-Lang [Tīmūr Lang]. May the Lord God efface his [Tīmūr Lang's] kingdom and hurl him into the abyss, and . . . deliver us from our tormentors, as [He delivered the children of Israel] from the hands of the Pharaoh. And may the right hand of the immortal [God] and the arm of the mighty King maintain unshakeable the [Armenian] royal and pontifical thrones, so that at the mention of their names the enemies of the truth will tremble and hide themselves and disappear forever . . .

1398

1. Place: canton of Barmn or Axbak; scribe and author of col.: Petros; MS. title: Commentary on the Pentateuch by Vardan Arewelc'i.

Source: Xač'ikyan, *XIV Dari*, no. 778, pp. 621–622

. . . [copied in 1398] in bitter and grievous times because, on account of our multitudinous and numerous sins, our country is in much anguish . . . In this year, they seized the baron of Hayk'ar [Hakkārī], who protected the Christians more staunchly than his ancestors. They seized him and cast him in a dungeon at sea. With a large force, they arrived in Diza Jor and plundered the country up to J̌ulamērk and Gawaṙ. They burned the dwellings of some; they consumed the [fruits of] labor and the provisions of some. And they captured the impregnable fortress of Ani; and those whom they spared they later plundered through taxation. God is our only hope and refuge . . .

This book was copied . . . during the principality of Mir Aladin [Mīr 'Alā'al-Dīn] and Amir Zēndin [Amir 'Izz al-Dīn Shīr], who is still held [as prisoner] on the island of Ałt'amar . . .

2. Place: city of Xalatan, opposite Kostandinupawlis; scribe and author of col.: Pawłos; MS. title: Commentary on the Epistles by Sargis Šnorhali.
Source: Xač'ikyan, *XIV Dari*, nos. 779a–b, pp. 622–623

. . . [copied] in grievous and anxious times when, on account of our multitudinous sins, the T'urk' [Turks] had besieged [*xsar*] us, as well as Stəmbawl [Istanbul]. Our hope and salvation rest with the merciful Lord in heaven, for this is the fourth year that many of us, who are in prison, seek death . . .

This was written in the year 847 of our Armenian Era [A.D. 1398].

. . . I plead with you holy priests, who may read or copy [this manuscript], not to blame [me] for the largeness [of the calligraphy] or for the errors . . . because this was copied in grievous and bitter times, for the wicked T'urk' [Turks] arrived in Łalat'an [Galata] with numerous troops and horsemen. They committed much destruction on the outskirts of our city, and we remained in anguish and in suffering by night and by day, and we yearned for a spoon of victual. This was copied in such times of anguish and bitterness . . .

1399

1. Place: monastery of Sanahin; scribe and author of col.: Yovannēs; MS. title: The poetic works of Nersēs Šnorhali.[23]

[23] This colophon does not mention the date. As the author refers to King Giorgi VII's peaceful reign, and since Tīmūr Lang's invasion of Georgia took place in A.D. 1399,

Source: Xačʻikyan, *XIV Dari*, no. 783, p. 626

... This was copied during the reign of King Gēorgi [Giorgi VII of Georgia], son of the victorious and mighty King Bagrat [V], under whom there was much peace in Georgia [kołmann Vracʻ] ...

1400

1. Place: monastery of Suxaray or Xaṙabastay in canton of Kʻaǰberunikʻ; scribe and author of col.: Grigor [Xlatʻecʻi]; MS. title: Commentary on the Epistles by Sargis Šnorhali.
   Source: Xačʻikyan, *XIV Dari*, no. 784a, pp. 627–629

... [completed] in bitter and evil times, when the forerunner Antichrist [*karapet Neṙn*] and Satan's servant, the man of wickedness, the son of damnation and the inheritor of the abysmal hell, the perfidious and impure creature and the bloodthirsty Lanka-Tʻamur [Tīmūr Lang] attacked our land. Because of our multitudinous sins, the imperturbable God became angered, and His beneficence toward us was changed into anger, [His] sweetness became bitter, and [His] goodness was transformed. And this is the third time that this evil creature and the staff of God's admonishing wrath came to punish our country. The first time the evil creature arrived was in the year 834 of the Armenian Era [A.D. 1385], when he invaded Persia [Parsicʻ ašxarh]. He devastated and carried off captives from Parskastan [Persia] and Armenia for two years, [that is,] until the end of the year 836 [of the Armenian Era = A.D. 1387], at which time there was much destruction, much shedding of blood, and famine, and much turmoil.

And again he came in the year 842 [of the Armenian Era = A.D. 1393] and attacked Babelon [Babylon = Baghdad]. After destroying all of Asorestan [Assyria], he invaded Armenia and devastated it for the second time; and after carrying off captives he passed through the Gate of the Huns [Pahakn Honacʻ], and with a fury went upon the king of the Huns [Honacʻ], and there, too, he committed much destruction and took captives, and vanquished them. But, on account of the famine, his forces were reduced in number; and this haughty creature lost many of his troops. From there he proceeded toward the Gate of the Alans [Duṙn Alanacʻ] and returned to his own country.

Xačʻikyan suggests that the colophon must have been written at the latest in that year, that is, prior to the invasion. See *XIV Dari*, p. 626, note.

Then again he reinforced himself with warriors and cavalrymen, and marched upon Hndustan [Afghanistan], whence he returned, after a great victory [and] with much booty and many elephants, to his capital of Samarłand [Samarkand].

And while the country was enjoying some peace and the people began to breathe a little from the severe punishment meted out by the evil one, the king of the Georgians [Vrac'], Gōrgi [Giorgi VII], scored a great victory . . . He came to the citadel of Erənǰak, in the canton of Naxǰawan, whence he rescued Sultan Tahir [Sulṭān Ṭāhir Djalā' ir], son of Ahmat Łan [Sulṭān Aḥmad Djalā'ir], who had been besieged [*hsar*] by the forces of T'amur-Lank [Tīmūr Lang] for thirteen years, that is from the year 835 until the year 848 [of the Armenian Era = A.D. 1386–1399].

In view of this, Lank-T'amur [Tīmūr Lang] roared like a ferocious beast, and again marched forth for the third time with a multitude of troops, more numerous than those during the first and second [invasions].

He camped on the soil of Georgia [Vrac' ašxarh] from the autumn until the summer seasons, for seven months, even more but not less. He captured numerous fortresses, and he killed many of their inhabitants. And while he slaughtered almost all the men, he carried off innumerable and countless women and children into captivity. These calamitous tragedies were witnessed not only by the Christians but also by the non-Christians. They witnessed how the innocent lambs fell into the hands of bloodthirsty and human-faced beasts, who had no mercy for the women, no pity for the children, no compassion for the sick, who did not cast their eyes upon those who were afflicted, who did not help the aged, and who did not spare the tender children. Rather, they mercilessly took them away on foot, naked, with bare feet, and uncovered heads. And they stoned and killed those who were unable to walk, and thus proceeded on their march. And those who witnessed these miseries asked the mountains to fall upon them and the hills to cover them up [cf. Luke 23:30; Revelation 6:16; Hosea 10:8].

Thus, this was completed in such bitter days and terrible times, in the year 849 of our [Armenian] Era [A.D. 1400], during the pontificate of the Lord Dawit' [III] in our province of Axt'amar . . .

. . . In these turbulent days, the forces of Lank-T'amur [Tīmūr Lang] marched into the land of Gamirk' [tunn Gamrac'] to wage war and to commit destruction. And I, frightened by this, left my abode and went to Aṙənǰik, where I remained for a while [and completed this manuscript] . . .

2. Place: city of Hizan in canton of Hizan; scribe and author of col.: Yovanēs; MS. title: Gospel.
Source: Xačʻikyan, *XIV Dari*, nos. 785a, c, pp. 630, 631

. . . [copied] in the year 849 of the Great Haykazean Era [A.D. 1400], in the canton and in the city of Hizan . . . during the pontificate of the Cilicians [Kilikecʻwocʻ] of the Lord Karapet [I, Kełecʻi], and during the pontificate in our province of Ṙštunikʻ, with its seat on the island of Ałtʻamar, of the Lord Dawitʻ [III], brother of the Lord Zakʻaria [II of Aghtamar] who, like the prophet of old, was martyred at the hands of the infidels.

He [Zakʻaria II] was caught in a trap unawares,
There was none like him in our midst,
Yet without cause he was slain by stoning,
The fire was inflamed in Ostan [Wusṭān],
The Lord of Israyel [Israel] was angered anew.
Yet, may the Lord God of all
Keep the Lord Dawitʻ [III] steadfast.
No king had we when I copied this;
Tʻamur-Lang [Tīmūr Lang] of Səmərłənd [Samarkand]
Hardened against the world
And set himself against one and all.
The Gate of the Alans [Duṙn Alanacʻ] was opened wide,
Which had been shut for so long;
Tʻamur [Tīmūr Lang] arrived with intense evil
And afflicted every one.
He arrived in the land of Georgia [Vrastan],
Booty much and slaves many he took.
The whole country is quavering
Like a sparrow on a branch . . .

Woe unto these days, I say, [for we are] floundering in the tempest brought on by the invincible and merciless Tʻamur-Lang [Tīmūr Lang].

3. Place: monastery of Ewstatʻē; scribe and author of sol.: Simēon; MS. title: Ritual Book [*Maštocʻ*].
Source: Xačʻikyan, *XIV Dari*, no. 786, p. 632

. . . [copied] in bitter and grievous times and when anarchy reigned in Armenia, [and] when the Christians were in grave danger at the hands of the Muslims [*aylazgacʻ*] called J̌ładaykʻ [Čaghatai] . . .

4. Scribe and author of col.: Yohanēs Aparanerec'i; MS. title: Bible.
Source: Xač'ikyan, *XIV Dari*, no. 787a, p. 633

... [completed in A.D. 1400] during the reign of T'amur [Tīmūr Lang] and of his son Miranša [Mīrānshāh]. In this year the forces of Šam, son of Ildrum [Yildirim, Ottoman Sultan Bāyezīd I], marched against T'amur [Tīmūr Lang].

5. Date of col.: A.D. 1400; date of MS.: A.D. 1205; place: city of Xarberd; scribe: Kozma; author of col.: T'awak'al (?); MS. title: Gospel.
Source: Xač'ikyan, *XV Dari*, I, p. 3, n. 1; Sargisean, *Venetik*, I, 401–402

When the barbarian king of the Persians [Parsic'], T'amur Łan [Tīmūr Lang Khān], who possessed a different aspect and countenance, a large forehead and narrow eyes, and who was *k'awsa* and pestilential, marched forth from the east with numerous forces. And with an exceedingly large number of troops he attacked Šam [Syria], and proceeded toward Erusałēm [Jerusalem]. He remained in this land for a whole year and he committed such acts of cruelty that I cannot describe in writing. He killed so many people; some he carried off into captivity; and many died of starvation, so much so that the father abandoned his son and the son his father. At this time T'awak'al, who was a *tanutēr* [householder] from Halap [Aleppo], had left for the city of Ant'ap' [Ayntab] to buy provisions. Finding this holy Gospel in the hands of the infidels he wept exceedingly, because they were deprecating the Gospel as well as Christ ... Desirous of securing this holy Gospel, he offered the money with which he [planned] to purchase the provisions, and acquiring this holy Gospel he delivered it from the hands of the infidels; and he brought it to his home, and they all rejoiced ... The year in which we acquired this holy Gospel was 849 of the Armenian Era [A.D. 1400].

1401

1. MS. title: Miscellany [*Žołovacu*].
Source: Xač'ikyan, *XV Dari*, I, no. 1, pp. 3–4

In the year 850 [of the Armenian Era = A.D. 1401], in the spring season and at the time of the feast of the Ascension [of the Lord], there came from Šamb [Syria] a terrible and dense [wave of] yellow and four-winged locusts. But the divine mercy of God killed them all in the sea of Ṙštōnik‘ [Lake Van], and the waves of the sea piled them up, like heaps of sand, on the seashore; and their stench kept the people away.

In this year, T‘amur Bēk [Tīmūr Lang Beg] captured the city of Sewast [Sebastia = Sivas], and demolished and devastated it. He slaughtered everyone; and he carried off numerous women and children into captivity; and, digging a ditch in the earth, he buried alive 3000 men who had shot arrows at him. Having done this, he left with numerous troops for Halap [Aleppo] and Damaskos [Damascus] in Šamb [Syria]. God delivered them into his hands. He captured the city of Halap [Aleppo] and committed so much slaughter that he built a three-tiered *mnira* with [the skulls of] the Tačiks. He then proceeded toward Damaskos [Damascus] and captured it, and for thirty days he looted its gold, silver, and pearls, and also took 12,000 camels as *hasay*.

Afterwards, he issued orders to set the whole city afire, and they burned it to ashes. He had the great *msk‘it‘*, which contained the grave of the apostle Ananiay [Ananias], demolished. And whatever *mniray* and *mzkit‘* there were in the two cities, he had them all destroyed and demolished. No one can estimate the number of those whom he carried off into captivity, or those whom he slaughtered. And, with great force, he set upon Mērdin [Mārdīn], destroyed the city from its foundations, and made it [as flat as] an arable land. But he was unable to capture the citadel; instead, he carried off many Christians from the country as captives. The T‘amurc‘ik‘ [Tīmur's forces] and the locusts arrived successively in our country, that is in Ostan [Wusṭān] and its canton.

2. Place: monastery of Ewstat‘ē; scribe and author of col.: Sargis; MS. title: Book of Questions by Grigor Tat‘ewac‘i.
Source: Xač‘ikyan, *XV Dari*, I, no. 2, p. 5

. . . [completed] in the year 850 of the Haykazean Era [A.D. 1401] . . . during the principality in our province of Siwnik‘ of Baron Smbat and his brother Baron Biwrt‘ēl, sons of Iwanē, son of the great Biwrt‘ēl of the Ōrpelean family . . .

. . . In the past year [A.D. 1400], on account of our manifold sins, there was grave anguish and destruction, for the iniquitous prince and son of damnation, from the nation of Xorazm [Khwārizmī], named

T'amur Lank [Tīmūr Lang], who had thrice before devastated Armenia, arrived again with numerous and countless troops and occupied Georgia [Vrac' ašxarh], with the connivance and assistance of the wicked and accursed Georgian [Vrac'] princes and *azats*. He conducted a general slaughter and carried off captives, totaling some 100,000 victims, and he demolished the churches. We cannot relate by word of mouth nor can we commit into writing the extent of the disastrous tragedy; rather, we can only lament and pray, at the sight of the misery of the parents who sob with sighs, and say, "Blessed are the barren who did not give birth and the breasts that did not give suck" [cf. Luke 23:29] . . .

3. Place: monastery of Varag; scribe and author of col.: Awetis; MS. title: Lectionary [*Tōnakan*].
Source: Xač'ikyan, *XV Dari*, I, no. 3, p. 6

. . . [completed] in bitter and grievous times, when our entire country was enslaved and was in a tartarean [*tartaros*] state at the hands of the iniquitous Lank T'amur Łan [Tīmūr Lang Khān]; in the year 850 of the Armenian Era [A.D. 1401] . . .

4. Place: city of Ostan; scribe and author of col.: Cerun; MS. title: Lectionary [*Tōnakan*].
Source: Xač'ikyan, *XV Dari*, I, no. 4a, p. 7

. . . [copied] in the year 850 of the Armenian Era [A.D. 1401], during the pontificate of the Lord Dawit' [III] at Ałt'amar and of the Lord Karapet [I, Kełec'i] of the Cilicians [Kilikec'oc'], in bitter and grievous times, during the imperial conquest of Amir T'amur [Amīr Tīmūr Lang], who in this year devastated Halap [Aleppo] and D[mšx] [Damascus] and Bałdat [Baghdad], and caused much and inconsolable grief to the Tačiks . . .

5. Place: city of Hizan; scribe and author of col.: Zak'aria; MS. title: Gospel.
Source: Xač'ikyan, *XV Dari*, I, no. 5, p. 8

. . . [copied] with much suffering and wandering and inquietude. Because of my multitudinous sins, the locusts came into our country and there was a severe famine throughout the land; and a *kapič* of bread was worth 200 *dram*; and all of this came to pass on account of our sins . . . [copied in A.D. 1401], during the catholicosate of our Haykazean nation of the Lord Dawit‘ [III] Ałt‘amarc‘i, brother of the Lord Zak‘aria [II of Aghtamar] who was slain as a martyr by the wicked *amiray* Ēzdin [Amīr ‘Izz al-Dīn Shīr], and there was great mourning in Armenia; but later, through the guidance of the Holy Spirit, he was succeeded on the [pontifical] throne by his brother, Lord Dawit‘ [III], and thus our intolerable sadness was transformed into gladness. And during the reign of the alien T‘amur Lank [Tīmūr Lang], who is victorious and invincible . . .

6. Scribe and author of col.: Yohanēs Aparanerec‘i; MS. title: Bible.
   Source: Xač‘ikyan, *XV Dari*, I, no. 9b, p. 15

. . . [copied in the year A.D. 1400] during the reign of T‘amur [Tīmūr Lang] and of his son Miranša [Mīrānshāh].

In this year, the forces of Šam, son of Ildrum [Yı̊ldı̊rı̊m, Ottoman Sultan Bāyezīd I], marched against T‘amur [Tīmūr Lang].

7. Place: monastery of Nkar in Ṙštunik‘; MS. title: Hymnal [*Ganjaran*].
   Source: Xač‘ikyan, *XV Dari*, I, no. 12, p. 17

. . . [copied] during the pontificate of the Lord Dawit‘ [III of Aghtamar], and during the imperial conquest of T‘amur Łan [Tīmūr Lang Khān] . . .

8. Place: fortress of Tašk‘awbru in Łrim; scribe and author of col.: Markos; MS. title: *Abba Yovhannu Sanduxk‘ Astuacayin Elic‘*.
   Source: Xač‘ikyan, *XV Dari*, I, no. 16, p. 19

. . . [copied in A.D. 1401] during the catholicosate of the Armenians of the Lord Karapet [I, Kełec‘i] . . . and in anxious times, when the prices were very high, and a *kapič* of bread was worth 30 *dram* . . .

1402

1. Place: city of Hizan: scribe and author of col.: Yovanēs; MS. title Gospel.

Source: Xač'ikyan, *XV Dari*, I, no. 19a, p. 22

. . . [copied] with suffering and much wandering, and in turbulent, difficult and uncertain times, in the year 851 of our Great Armenian Era [A.D. 1402], during the catholicosate of our Haykazean nation of the Lord Dawit' [III] Ałt'amarec'i, brother of the Lord Pontiff Zak'aria [II of Aghtamar] who shed the blood of a martyr for Christ at the hands of the *amiray* [amir] of Ostan [Wusṭān]. And during the reign of the alien T'amur Lank [Tīmūr Lang], the victorious and invincible, who in this year [1402] penetrated the land of Rūm [tunn Hoṙomoc'] and subdued everyone. He also captured and bound Ildrum [Yïldïrïm, Ottoman Sultan Bāyezīd I], the *amirapet* of the country, as well as his son . . .

2. Scribe and author of col.: Yov[hannēs]; MS. title: Gospel.
Source: Xač'ikyan, *XV Dari*, I, no. 22a, p. 25

. . . [copied in A.D. 1402] in these bitter times, when our unprotected Armenian nation was subjected to manifold afflictions, because they demand a price for our faith; may the protection of God and of our Lord Jesus Christ sustain our nation until His second coming . . .

3. Place: monastery of Matnevan, near Xlat', in canton of Bznunik'; scribe and author of col.: [Grigor Xlat'ec'i]; MS. title: Gospel.
Source: Xač'ikyan, *XV Dari*, I, no. 23, p. 26

. . . [copied] during the imperial conquest of the nation of archers [netołac azg], under Mir T'amur [Tīmūr Lang] and of his family and children . . .

1403

1. Place: village of Matrasay in Šrvan; scribe and author of col.: T'umay T'avrizec'i; MS. title: Commentaries and Sermons by Matt'ēos Vardapet, Pupil of Grigor Tat'ewac'i.
Source: Xač'ikyan, *XV Dari*, I, no. 31a, p. 31

. . . [copied] with much pain and labor . . . [and] in anxious, bitter and anguished times, for we were plundered, held in terror and trembling at the hands of the wretched and forerunner Antichrist

[*Neṙn*] T'amur [Tīmūr Lang], which means *da mur* [he is soot],[24] for wherever he goes he darkens and blackens, some by robbing, some by torture, some by slaying, some by carrying off into captivity, and also by separating the father from his child and the child from its father, and so forth. Those who escaped and [took refuge] in caves and crevices, in fortresses and castles did not enjoy freedom, because some died from famine and others from the heat and of thirst, some, who were struck by fear, threw themselves down into the precipice. And there were numerous other evils, which I hesitate to relate in order not to cause tedium to you readers . . .

2. MS. title: Gospel.
   Source: Xač'ikyan, *XV Dari*, I, no. 32, p. 33

T'amur [Tīmūr Lang] arrived in this country, and carried off captives, and committed much atrocities. He also carried off as captive and slew the King [Ottoman Sultan Bāyezīd I, Yildirim] of Rūm [Hoṙmac']. Many died and were lost; and many fled to other lands and died. In the year 852 of the Armenian Era [A.D. 1403].

3. Author of MS. and of col.: Aṙak'el Siwnec'i; MS. title: Adam-Book by Aṙak'el Siwnec'i (A).
   Source: Xač'ikyan, *XV Dari*, I, no. 35, pp. 35–36

> . . . [Written] During the khanate of T'amur [Tīmūr Lang],
> Who held sway over many lands,
> [He was like a] golden cup in the Lord's hand,
> [Who] gave to drink whom He wished.
> He [Tīmūr Lang] was paralytic and frail;
> Eight hundred thousand troops he had;
> Mightily he conquered the world,
> And no one dared to resist him.
> Numerous countries he plundered;
> Carried off captives to Səmərłant [Samarkand];
> Many remained in distant lands,
> And never again saw their ancestral home . . .

[24] This is an attempt on the part of the author of the colophon to give an Armenian etymology for the name of T'amur. Armenian *da* is the third person singular pronoun; and *mur* means "lamp-black, pine-soot, soot, blacking; ink."

4. Author of MS. and of col.: Aṙak'el Siwnec'i; MS. title: Adam-Book by Aṙak'el Siwnec'i (B).
Source: Xač'ikyan, *XV Dari*, I, no. 36, p. 38

... At this time the sultan was T'amur [Tīmūr Lang];
The year was eight hundred and fifty-two [of the Armenian Era = A.D. 1403] ...

5. Place: village of Xayik'; author of col.: Sēt'; MS. title: Gospel.
Source: Xač'ikyan, *XV Dari*, I, no. 37a, p. 39

... In the year 852 [of the Armenian Era = A.D. 1403], they demolished the churches at Eznkay [Erzindjān] and [the village of] Xayik' ...

6. Place: Łrim; recipient of MS. and author of col.: Grigor; MS. title: Gospel.
Source: Xač'ikyan, *XV Dari*, I, no. 38, p. 40

... In the year 851 of the Armenian Era [A.D. 1402], on the 19th of May, Č'ekir [Bistām Djāgīr] invaded Łrim [Crimea].

This was written in the year 852 [of the Armenian Era = A.D. 1403], on June 30.

7. Place: village of Mgunk'; MS. title: Gospel.
Source: Xač'ikyan, *XV Dari*, I, no. 41, p. 41

In the year 852 [of the Armenian Era = A.D. 1403], during the barony of Amir Abdal ...

1404

1. Author of MS. and of col.: Aṙak'el [Orotnec'i]; MS. title: Ode on the Annunciation by the Lord Aṙak'el Orotnec'i.
Source: Xač'ikyan, *XV Dari*, I, no. 43, p. 42

... This was written
In the year eight hundred and fifty-three
Of the Armenian Era [A.D. 1404],
In the days of T'amur Łan [Tīmūr Lang Khān].

2. Place: village of Tšoł; scribe and author of col.: Step'annos; MS. title: Lectionary [*Tōnakan*].
Source: Xač'ikyan, *XV Dari*, I, no. 44, p. 43

. . . [copied] in the year 853 of the Armenian Era [A.D. 1404], during the pontificate of the Lord Dawit' [III of Aghtamar], and during the tyrannical rule in our country of T'amur Łan [Tīmūr Lang Khān] . . .

1405

1. Place: Ērewan; scribe and author of col.: Manuēl; MS. title: Gospel.
Source: Xač'ikyan, *XV Dari*, I, no. 51a, p. 50

. . . [received] in bitter and anxious times, during the tyrannical rule of God's wrath T'ēmur-Lank [Tīmūr Lang] and his son Mirzay Miranša [Mīrza Mīrānshāh] in numerous countries and in our eastern lands of Armenia and Persia [tunn Parskac']. Because of our sins, he left the city of Sməłan [Samarkand] in the east with numerous and countless horsemen to mete out God's punishment and, by multifarious witchcraft, caused havoc in numerous countries and in Armenia, the details of which we cannot commit to writing . . .

2. Author of MS. and of col.: Grigor [Tat'ewac'i]; MS. title: Commentary on the Psalms by Grigor Tat'ewac'i.
Source: Xač'ikyan, *XV Dari*, I, no. 52, p. 52

. . . [compiled] in anxious and calamitous times, when the tyrant T'amur [Tīmūr Lang], by divine Providence, vanquished and devastated numerous lands; and he himself was extirpated [that is, died] in this year of 854 [of the Armenian Era = A.D. 1405] . . .

3. Place: monastery of Vardpatrik; authors of col.: Yovanēs, T'umas, Mkrtič', and Kirakos; MS. title: Book of Lamentations by Grigor Narekac'i.
Source: Xač'ikyan, *XV Dari*, I, no. 53, p. 53

. . . we offered this [manuscript] as a memorial . . . when the abominable T'amur [Tīmūr Lang] was extirpated, in the year 854 [of the Armenian Era = A.D. 1405] . . .

4. Place: monastery of Ancłnapat; MS. title: Menology [*Yaysmawurk*ʿ].
Source: Xačʿikyan, *XV Dari*, I, no. 54, p. 53

Written in the year 854 of the Armenian Era [A.D. 1405], in the monastery of Ancłnapat, during the pontificate of the Lord Dawitʿ [III of Aghtamar] and the reign of Ēzdinšer [Amīr ʿIzz al-Dīn Shīr] of the Mars [azgin Maracʿ]. In this year died Tʿamur Łan [Tīmūr Lang Khān], whom God for twenty-one years held in His hands like a cup of wrath and from which He caused to drink whomever He wished, for he [Tīmūr Lang] enslaved and slaughtered everyone, the believers and the nonbelievers, extending from the east up to where the sun sets; and he did at Dəmšx [Damascus] what the pontiff Nersēs wrote in his "Lament on Edessa" [*Ołbn Uřhayoy*].

In this year the earthquake destroyed ten villages in the region of Hēšat. In this year there was so much scarcity of water that numerous river-mills were shut down.

1406

1. Place: monastery of Ewstatʿē; scribe and author of col.: Grigor Gōrecʿi; MS. title: Book of Questions by Grigor Tatʿewacʿi.
Source: Xačʿikyan, *XV Dari*, I, no. 61, pp. 57–58

. . . [copied] during the principality in our region of the devout princes Smbat and Burtʿel, in the year 855 of the Armenian Era [A.D. 1406], in wretched and evil times, both spiritually and temporally; when the sword and enslavement always threatened the Christians as well as the Muslims [*aylazgik*ʿ] . . .

2. Place: village of Maku in canton of Artaz; scribe and author of col.: Mxitʿaričʿ; MS. title: Commentary on the Psalms by Vardan Arewelcʿi.
Source: Xačʿikyan, *XV Dari*, I, no. 65, p. 61

. . . [written] in the canton of Artaz, in the village called Maku [Mākū], during the barony of Baron Nuradin . . .

1407

1. Place: city of Xizan; scribe and author of col.: Yovannēs; MS. title: Menology [*Yaysmawurk*ʿ].

Source: Xač'ikyan, *XV Dari*, I, no. 72a, pp. 66–70

. . . [copied] in the year 856 of the Armenian Era [A.D. 1407], during the pontificate of the Lord Dawit' [III] Ałt'amarec'i, and during the khanate of the T'urk' [Turk] Łara Yusuf [Ḳara Yūsuf] . . .

We must relate the tragedy,
The bitterness of our time,
That which occurred in recent times,
When these holy words were copied.
Behold! Darkness befell our land
At the evil news of Łara Yusuf [Ḳara Yūsuf],
Who is the baron of T'urk'əstan [Turkestan],
Haughty and undefeated in this world.
He shrivels and shatters everyone's heart,
Beginning from the citadel of Mērdin [Mārdīn],
Up to the city of T'avrēž [Tabrīz].
He filled our spleen with bitter grief,
He went to the land of the Georgians [tun Vrac'],
Like a scorpion he filled it with poison,
And brought death to the Christians.
Whence he took numerous captives,
Numbering fifteen thousand,
And slew five thousand yonder,
With tortures of many kind.
He unsheathed his sword,
And pierced it through all our hearts,
They spilled abundantly the blood
Of the holy children of new Zion.
In the magnificent houses of the Lord,
In the mystical churches,
Raging fires crackled,
And burned them piece by piece.
Impregnable forts replete with statues,
And glorious Christians within them,
Together fell prey to the flames
And burned like dry lumber.
Likewise, like a lamp,
The whole country was ablaze;
Like lambs they were lost
Amongst rapacious wolves.
The new Antichrist [*Neṙn*] issued orders,
His words gushed forth like those of a leper,

That he who kills earns commendation
And attains his glorious destiny.
People united in holy faith,
Many ennobled by good deeds
Dispersed in far off lands
In search of captives deeply wounded.
No heart can comprehend
The horrible deeds thus committed;
We cannot recount all the details,
The lamentable anguish and tragedy.
Alas, from the land of Xizan [Hizan]
Grievous news came anew,
That the Ismaelites [azgn Ismayelay]
Intensified [their] thirst for blood.
They spare no one's blood,
Be they women or children,
They mercilessly pierce them through
To ensure their pain will not abate,
To ensure that the woes and laments
Of the Christians will not cease,
And their bread will taste like ashes,
And they will drink water with tears . . .

2. Place: monastery of Ewstat'ē; scribes Matt'ēos, Grigor, and Ełia; author of col.: Matt'ēos; MS. title: Gospel.
Source: Xač'ikyan, *XV Dari*, I, no. 75, p. 76

. . . copied in the year 856 of the Armenian Era [A.D. 1407], in bitter and anxious times, when the nation of archers [azgn netołac'] was completely crushed, and in its place ruled, on the throne of Atrpatakan [Ādharbaydjān], a T'orgomacin named Łara Usuf [Ḳara Yūsuf], who twice waged battle against and defeated the malevolent, awesome-looking and evil-hearted Ab[u-B]ak'r [the Tīmūrid Abū Bakr], one of the grandsons of the wicked beast T'amur [Tīmūr Lang]. Moreover, through the Providence of the Almighty God, he freed our country from the iniquitous [tax] collectors, who had subdued and enslaved many nations speaking various languages, and who now were delivered by our Saviour Jesus Christ . . .

3. Place: monasteries of Tat'ew and Mecop'; scribe and author of col.: T'ovmay [Mecop'ec'i]; MS. title: Book of Questions by Grigor Tat'ewac'i.

Source: Xač'ikyan, *XV Dari*, I, no. 77b, p. 79

... In this year was completed, with the help of the Almighty God, the construction of the holy altar [of the church of] St. Mary, Mother of God, [in the monastery of Mecop']; but the iniquitous and wicked sect of the abominable Muslims [*aylazgik'*] was disconcerted, because they had opposed the construction of this holy temple ...

4. Place: province of Siwnik'; scribe and author of col.: Yohanēs; MS. title: Book of Sermons by Grigor Tat'ewac'i.
Source: Xač'ikyan, *XV Dari*, I, no. 79, pp. 82–83

... /// our country was ruled by a T'urk'man [Turkmen] named Yusup' [Ḳara Yūsuf], who in this year /// [defeated?] the Čałat' [Čaghatai], who [Ḳara Yūsuf] attacked the grandson of T'amur [Tīmūr Lang] named /// Abu-Bak'r [Abū Bakr]; and this Yusup' [Ḳara Yūsuf] now reigns /// in the year 856 of the Armenian Era [A.D. 1407], on the twenty-fifth of the month of Mareri, on the ninth of the month of May.

1408

1. Place: monastery of Stat'ew in province of Siwnik'; scribe and author of col.: Yakob Aspisənkc'i; MS. title: Book of Sermons by Grigor Tat'ewac'i.
Source: Xač'ikyan, *XV Dari*, I, no. 85a, p. 87

... In the year 857 [of the Armenian Era = A.D. 1408], Łara Yusuf [Ḳara Yūsuf] occupied T'avrēz [Tabrīz] in Atrpaičan [Ādharbaydjān].

2. Place: city of Muš; author of col.: Dawit' Mšec'i; MS. title: Gospel.
Source: Xač'ikyan, *XV Dari*, I, no. 87, p. 89

... in bitter times, when the Muslims [*aylazgik'*] were persecuting the Christians, especially [those at] the famous monastery of St. Karapet in Tarōn. Their [the monastics'] poverty compelled them to mortgage [their manuscripts] to the Muslims [*aylazgik'*] ... I paid 200 *dekan* from my *halal* [honestly earned] assets and recovered this holy Gospel, and gave it back to [the monastery of] St. Karapet ... I recovered it in the year 856 of the Armenian Era [A.D. 1408].

3. Place: monastery of C'ipnay; editor of MS. and author of col.: Grigor Cerenc' Xlat'ec'i; MS. title: Hymnal [*Ganjaran*].
Source: Xač'ikyan, *XV Dari*, I, no. 88, p. 91

... [written] during the reign of Łara Usuf [Ḳara Yūsuf] and his sons, of the nation of archers [azgin netołoc'] ...

1409

1. Place: monastery of Mecop'; scribe and author of col.: Sargis; MS. title: Book of Questions by Grigor Tat'ewac'i.
Source: Xač'ikyan, *XV Dari*, I, no. 91a, p. 94

... [copied] during the khanate of the baron Usf [Ḳara Yūsuf] ...

2. MS. title: Book of Sermons by Grigor Tat'ewac'i.
Source: Xač'ikyan, *XV Dari*, I, no. 93, p. 95

Oh, oh, oh! I heard sounds of lament and sounds of grief and mourning. They made a martyr of the Lord Awetik' on the eleventh of the month of December. He was the sun of our nation, and today he passed into darkness. And this came to pass in the year 858 [of the Armenian Era = A.D. 1409], on Wednesday of the week ...

3. Place: village of Kagt'anc' in canton of Moks or T'raka; scribe and author of col.: Yohanēs: MS. title: Gospel.
Source: Xač'ikyan, *XV Dari*, I, no. 94, p. 95

... witnessing the bitterness of our time caused by the intensification of the exactions imposed upon the Christians by the lawless ones; and because the entire country was in perennial effusion and was wasting away, and there was no cessation [of these exactions]; and seeing that the provisions had depleted and the [infidels] were confiscating the goods, he [T'adēos the priest] received this God-embracing Gospel in memory of his soul and [the souls] of his parents ...

4. Place: Ałt'amar; scribe and author of col.: Daniēl; MS. title: Lectionary [*Tōnakan*].
Source: Xač'ikyan, *XV Dari*, I, no. 96a, p. 97

... In these times, when our country was tyrannized by the Ismaelites [azgn Ismayēlean] who unjustly and unlawfully persecute the Christians . . .

1410

1. Place: monastery of Mecop' in K'ajberunik'; scribe and author of col.: T'ovmay Mecop'ec'i; MS. title: Book of Sermons by Grigor Tat'ewac'i.
Source: Xač'ikyan, *XV Dari*, I, no. 103a, pp. 103–104

. . . [copied] in bitter and wicked times, for the sword of the Ismaelites [Ismayelac'oc'] has become sharper and they persecute us, as foreseen in the vision of St. Sahak. Hence, we are quavering and are afloat because of the manifold perils, both from within and without, all of which have stupefied our minds as well as our deeds . . .

2. Author of col.: T'uma; MS. title: Treatise on Feast Days [*Tōnapatčaṙ*].
Source: Xač'ikyan, *XV Dari*, I, no. 111, p. 111

. . . This [manuscript] remained for fifteen years in bondage at Bawlli, since the time when the *amirzay* [*mīrzā*] / / / son of T'amur [Tīmūr Lang] attacked Bałēš [Bitlīs], and they carried it [the manuscript] off to T'awrēž [Tabrīz]. And I was always in tears and in anguish on account of this [manuscript], but I found no means to rescue it, because it had fallen into the hands of merciless clergymen. But later . . . they themselves voluntarily returned this book to me . . .

3. Place: village of Tšoł; scribe and author of col.: Step'annos; MS. title: Menology [*Yaysmawurk'*].
Source: Xač'ikyan, *XV Dari*, I, no. 115, p. 114

. . . [copied] in bitter and grievous times / / / during [the tyranny] of Łaray Yusuf [Ḳara Yūsuf] in our country, and also of Amir Ēztin [Amīr 'Izz al-Dīn Shīr] in our region . . .

1411

1. Author of MS. and of col.: Matt'ēos; MS. title: Commentary on the Acts of the Apostles by Matt'ēos Vardapet.
Source: Xač'ikyan, *XV Dari*, I, no. 121b, p. 119

... [written] in the year 860 [of the Armenian Era = A.D. 1411], during the tyranny [of Ḳara Yūsuf] of the T'orgomean nation [azgin T'orgomean], who was like the meanest beast described in [the book of] Daniel, who devoured and minced his own [men] as well as the aliens, whether they were chieftains or subjects. Indeed, he equally slew and cruelly tortured them, reminding us of the atrocities previously committed by the cripple named T'amur [Tīmūr Lang], for [we are] subject to the same calamities. He [Ḳara Yūsuf] then totally devastated the plain of Vatniar and captured its ruler; and he slew King Kostandin [Constantine I] of Georgia [Vrac'], and he carried off numerous captives ...

2. Place: monastery of Getamēǰ in region of Car; scribe and author of col.: T'ovma Siwnec'i; MS. title: Missal [*Čašoc'*].
Source: Xač'ikyan, *XV Dari*, I, no. 124, p. 122

... [completed] in the year 860 of the Haykazean Era [A.D. 1411], during the reign of Yusuf [Ḳara Yūsuf] ...

3. Place: Ałčałalay or Tikrana-Berd in canton of Bagaran; scribe and author of col.: Yohannēs Sebastac'i; MS. title: Gospel.
Source: Xač'ikyan, *XV Dari*, I, no. 126, p. 124

... [copied] with suffering and in much wandering ... during the imperial tyranny of the nation of archers [azgin netołac'] under Usup' Xan [Ḳara Yūsuf Khān], and under the barony of P'ir Husen [Pīr Ḥusayn]; and when levies were imposed upon the Christians, who suffered at the hands of the aliens; and when law and order had diminished and when injustice had intensified everywhere. And the prophetic words that "There shall come a time when they will say to the mountains fall upon us and to the hills cover us up" [cf. Luke 23:30; Revelation 6:16; Hosea 10:8] were fulfilled. May the Lord God visit upon our nation and deliver us from the hands of our persecutors ...

4. Place: monastery of Mecop' in K'aǰberunik'; scribe and author of col.: Yovanēs; MS. title: Book of Sermons by Grigor Tat'ewac'i.
Source: Xač'ikyan, *XV Dari*, I, no. 128, p. 128

... [copied] in bitter and wicked times, when our persecution by the Ismaelites [Ismayelac'woc'] had intensified, as foreseen in the vision of St. Sahak. Hence, we are quavering and are afloat because of the manifold perils, both from within and without, all of which have stupefied our minds as well as our deeds . . .

5. Place: city of Ostan; MS. title: Gospel.
Source: Xač'ikyan, *XV Dari*, I, no. 129, p. 129

. . . Copied in the year 860 [of the Armenian Era = A.D. 1411]. In this year Łara Usuf [Ḳara Yūsuf] burned our vicarage; but the Christians of the city [Ostan = Wusṭān] built a new one . . .

1412

1. Place: town of Aflisc'ixē; scribe and author of col.: Melk'isedek; MS. title: Hymnal [*Šaraknoc'*].
Source: Xač'ikyan, *XV Dari*, I, no. 135, p. 133

. . . completed in Georgia [Vrac' ašxarhn], during the reign of King Kostandil [Constantine I] . . . and during the principality in our region of Baron Smbat and his son Baron Bēšk'en, who, by instigation of the evil one [Satan], were expelled from their ancestral domain . . .

2. Place: city of Karuc' [Kars]; MS. title: Gospel.
Source: Xač'ikyan, *XV Dari*, I, no. 136, p. 134

. . . In the year 861 of the Haykazean Era [= A.D. 1412], our famous city of Karuc' [Kars] was built [that is, rebuilt] and restored by the just baron P'ir Hiwsēn [Pīr Ḥusayn] . . .

1413

1. Place: city of Van; scribe and author of col.: Zak'aria; MS. title: Gospel.
Source: Xač'ikyan, *XV Dari*, I, no. 153, p. 147

. . . [copied] during the catholicosate of the Haykazean nation of the Lord Dawit' [III] Ałt'amarec'i, and during the reign of the alien Łara Eusuf [Ḳara Yūsuf] . . .

2. Place: monastery of Cpat in Mokk‘; scribe and author of col.: Karapet; MS. title: Collection of Sermons and Lectionary [*Čaṙəntir-Tōnakan*].
Source: Xač‘ikyan, *XV Dari*, I, no. 154a, p. 149

... [copied] during the pontificate of the Armenians of the Lord Dawit‘ [III of Aghtamar], in bitter and grievous times, when our nation was being ruined by the levies imposed by the wicked nation of archers [azgn netołakan]; in the year 862 of the Armenian Era [A.D. 1413] ...

1414

1. Place: town of Awšakan; scribe and author of col.: Sargis T‘mok‘ec‘i; MS. title: Missal [*Čašoc‘*].
Source: Xač‘ikyan, *XV Dari*, I, no. 163a, p. 162

... [completed] during the reign of Usup‘ [Ḳara Yūsuf], and of P‘iwr Husin [Pīr Ḥusayn], son of Sahat‘ ...

2. Place: monastery of Ktuc‘; scribe and author of col.: Yovsēp‘; MS. title: Gospel.
Source: Xač‘ikyan, *XV Dari*, I, no. 169, p. 166

... This holy Gospel was copied in bitter and anxious times, when our nation was being ruined on account of the levies /// for we have grown exceedingly weary of the tyranny of the infidels—the K‘urt‘ [Kurds], T‘at‘ar [Tatars], and all other [tax collectors?] ///.

3. Place: monastery of Yuskay Ordi in canton of Tarberuni; scribe and author of col.: Mkrtič‘; MS. title: Collection of Treatises on the Psalms by Grigor Tat‘ewac‘i.
Source: Xač‘ikyan, *XV Dari*, I, no. 174, p. 170

... [copied] during the pontificate of the Lord Yakob [II, Ssec‘i], and during the tyrannical rule of the baron Usuf [Ḳara Yūsuf] ...

4. Scribe and author of col.: Yovsēp‘; MS. title: Missal [*Čašoc‘*].
Source: Xač‘ikyan, *XV Dari*, I, no. 735a, p. 652

. . . [completed] in the year 863 of the Haykazean Era [A.D. 1414], during the pontificate of the Lord Yakob [II, Ssecʻi], [and] during the reign of Armenian kings who no longer exist, in bitter and anxious times, when they ruined the Armenians through taxation and when we were being persecuted / / /

5. Scribe and author of col.: Łazar; MS. title: Hymnal [*Šaraknocʻ*].
Source: Xačʻikyan, *XV Dari*, I, no. 175, p. 170

. . . [completed] in the year 863 [of the Armenian Era = A.D. 1414], during the pontificate of [the Lord] Dawitʻ [III of Aghtamar], and during the tyrannical rule in Armenia of Amir Ezdin [Amīr ʻIzz al-Dīn Shīr] . . .

1415

1. Place: village of Narek; scribe and author of col.: Stepʻannos; MS. title: Gospel.
Source: Xačʻikyan, *XV Dari*, I, no. 185, p. 177

. . . [copied] in the year 864 of the Armenian Era [A.D. 1415], during the pontificate of the Lord Dawitʻ [III of Aghtamar], and during the rule in our canton of the prince Bēlēkʻ Bēk . . .

2. Place: village of Iloyvankʻ; scribe and author of col.: Łazar; MS. title: Menology [*Yaysmawurkʻ*].
Source: Xačʻikyan, *XV Dari*, I, no. 187, p. 177

. . . [copied] during the pontificate of the Lord Dawitʻ [III of Aghtamar] . . . in the year 864 of the Armenian Era [A.D. 1415], during the khanate of Łaray Usuf [Ḳara Yūsuf], and the amirate of Ezdinšēr [Amīr ʻIzz al-Dīn Shīr] and of his son Melik [Malik Muḥammad] . . .

1416

1. Scribe and author of col.: Vardan; MS. title: Gospel.
Source: Xačʻikyan, *XV Dari*, I, no. 195, pp. 183–184

. . . copied in the year 865 [of the Armenian Era = A.D. 1416] . . . / / /

when there was severe persecution /// against /// the Christians at the hands of the Ismaelites [azgn Ismaēlean], who never ceased to demand the levies from the Christians, all of whom were held in their hands as though they were bound in chains, even as Israyēl [Israel] in olden times at the hands of the Pharaoh. They [the Christians] had no hope for salvation from any quarter, but only from Christ our Saviour, Who we hope will soon destroy the persecutors of the Christians and hurl them down into the precipice.

2. Place: monastery of Kap'os; scribe and author of col.: Grigor; MS. title: Book of Sermons by Grigor Tat'ewac'i.
Source: Xač'ikyan, *XV Dari*, I, no. 199, pp. 186–187

... [copied in A.D. 1416] in bitter and evil times, at the end of my transient life. The word of God was fulfilled in our time, namely, that "In that day nation will rise against nation and there will be pestilence and plague" [cf. Mark 13:8]. We became an eyewitness of the first and we heard of the second. For there was exceedingly much death in our canton of Ekełeac'; and who, indeed, can describe these tragedies in writing? Moreover, the lawless tyrant named Xara Usuf [Ḳara Yūsuf], inflamed by evil, invaded Georgia [Tunn Vrac'], and captured the city of Yałlcxa [Akhal Tsikhe]; and he massacred all the men, and carried off the women and children into captivity. And we have seen many more such deeds in recent times ...

1417

1. Place: monastery of Ganjasar in Arc'ax or Xač'en; scribe and author of col.: Matt'ēos Monozon; MS. title: Panegyrical Poems on the Saints, and Miscellany.
Source: Xač'ikyan, *XV Dari*, I, nos. 211a, b, pp. 194–195, 197

... This was completed in [Caucasian] Albania [tunn Ałuanic'], in the year 866 of the Armenian Era [A.D. 1417] ... In this year there occurred a severe famine, and all the plants withered away and the waters dried up; during the pontificate of Catholicos Karapet of the [Caucasian] Albanians [tann Ałuanic'], and at a time of anarchy among the Christians. This came about because Smbat, the scion of the Biwrt'elean family, fled to Georgia [tunn Vrac'] and died there in a foreign land. His two surviving sons returned to their ancestral domain, but they are not the masters of their own principality; rather, they are the subordinates of the lawless ones. In our region of Xač'en, there was a pious man by the name of Zazay, who departed this life. And the survivors of his family, J̌alal and his sons, and the sons of Zazay, namely Arłut'ay and J̌alaladawli, and his [Zazay's] brothers Ēlēgum and Ēlēgan—all are the subjects of the lawless ones. And, thus, the authority in our Haykazean land [Armenia] has diminished.

This was a bitter time, for the ruler was a T'urk'man [Turkmen] named Usuf [Ḳara Yūsuf]. He was chosen by God to be an exorciser, through whom evil would be punished by evil [cf. Matthew 21:41]. For, after the death of the fourth beast [cf. Daniel 7:7, 19, 23], namely T'amur the Lame [Tīmūr Lang], the tyrant Usuf [Ḳara Yusuf] thrice waged war against his [Tīmūr Lang's] sons and slew them, while the others fled to their own country. The actual *xan* [khan], named Ahmat [Sulṭān Aḥmad Djalā'ir], left Babelon [Babylon = Baghdad] and voluntarily came to the city of T'awrēz [Tabrīz]; but Usuf [Ḳara Yūsuf] attacked him, as well, and killed him. And there remained only the *amiray* [amir] of Šruan [Shīrwān] who, having rebelled, Usuf [Ḳara Yūsuf] attacked him thrice. During his last attack [Ḳara Yūsuf] captured him, as well as many of his men. He also slew Kostandin [Constantine I], the unfortunate king of the Georgians [Vrac'], who had come to the aid of the prince of Šruan [Shīrwān]; and after plundering the country he departed. Usuf [Ḳara Yūsuf] committed so many atrocities against the chiefs of our country, not to mention what he did to the lowly ones. Wherever his brutal soldiers went, they did not distinguish between the natives and the aliens. They plundered and trampled underfoot all those who fell into their hands, whether they were on the highways, or at home, or in seclusion, or in the city. Thus, there was no accounting for the intensity of our lamentation.

All of this befell us on account of our sins. And we are still groping in doubt, not knowing what the future holds for us nor how we shall be delivered from these bitter afflictions. All tearful eyes are looking up to God, hoping that He might show mercy for us.

In such bitter and anxious times was this book completed . . . [and] before this manuscript was completed, we were once again plundered by the same wicked T'urk'man [Turkmens]. We met them while we were traveling to Shīrwān [Šruan]; they first looted us, and then they cast our manuscripts in the abode of the vipers. Moreover, they set the iniquitous Tatars [azgn T'at'arac'] upon us. They again plundered our holy monastery; nothing was left of our worldly possessions, only our own selves and the sacred effects . . .[25]

[25] This colophon has been preserved through a seventeenth-century copy. See Xač'ikyan, *XV Dari*, I, pp. 195–196, n. 2.

. . . Three years before this [manuscript] was copied [that is,
A.D. 1415],
Kostandin [Constantine I], King of Georgia [Vrac'tun],
Was slain and deprived of his life,
At the hands of the evil Turkmen [T'urk'men],
Whose name was Usuf [Ḳara Yūsuf].
He caused intense grief
On both sides and to both people,
For he [Constantine] was also the vicar of our
Great [Armenian] nation, whom we lost;
In a place of impurity
The wolves and birds ate him up.
The forerunner of our great grief
Was the destruction of our monastery.
At first the wicked P'irumar [Pīr 'Umar],
The commander of his [Ḳara Yūsuf's] forces,
Invaded the plain of Vatneac'.
He first looted our monastery,
And on the morrow he went away;
He ransacked the plain lamentably,
And despoiled a part of it.
The prince of that plain
Enlisted troops from Shīrwān [Šrvan];
He crossed the river Kura [Kur]
First trampled underfoot our monastery
And then the mountain nearby,
Where with divine help we took refuge,
Forsaken, empty-handed, and in tears.

2. Place: [city of Xizan]; scribe and author of col.: Zak'aray; MS. title: Lexicon [*Bařgirk'*].
Source: Xač'ikyan, *XV Dari*, I, no. 212a, p. 198

. . [copied] in this year [A.D. 1417], when fathers rose against their children and /// the city and joined Łara Yusuf [Ḳara Yūsuf] /// 1000 or 1100, and harassed the Christians /// beating up the T'urk' [Turks], and many took to flight and escaped from their hands; may the Lord God visit /// upon the Armenians, amen! In the year 866 [of the Armenian Era = A.D. 1417].

This came to pass with the help of the Holy Cross,
Which was avenged through Amir Dayut' [Amīr Davud];

For last year, when they captured the Holy Cross,[26]
They broke their *ławl* and oath,
And imposed a penalty on the Holy Cross.
They first obtained 50,000 [*dram*],
Then 20,000 more they demanded.
Likewise Amir Dayut'’s [Amīr Davud] father [Amīr Malik?]
Gave his own *huk'm* to his son,
But when he failed to heed his command,
He took it back and banished his son,
And this came to pass with the power of the Cross.

3. Place: city of Hizan; scribe and author of col.: Yovanēs; MS. title: Gospel.
Source: Xač'ikyan, *XV Dari*, I, no. 213a, p. 200

. . . The name of their wicked chief,
The haughty *łan* [khan] of T'urk'stan [Turkestan],
Łara Yusuf [Ḳara Yūsuf], inscribed in black,
Who darkness caused to our nation and race.
He now controls the citadel of Merdin [Mārdīn],
As well as the great *t'ałt'* of T'avrēž [Tabrīz];
He has vanquished the K'urd [Kurds] and Persians [Parsiks],
And demands levies as well as interest . . .

4. Place: monastery of C'ipnay; MS. title: *Oskep'orik*.
Source: Xač'ikyan, *XV Dari*, I, no. 216, p. 203

. . . [completed] in the year 866 of the Armenian Era [A.D. 1417], during the khanate of Usuf [Ḳara Yūsuf], and during the catholicosate of Grigor [VIII, Xanjołat] at Sis and the catholicosate of the Lord Dawit' [III] at Ałt'amar, in wicked and bitter times . . .

5. Place: monastery of Narek; scribe and author of col.: Astuacatur; MS. title: Book of Sermons by Grigor Tat'ewac'i.
Source: Xač'ikyan, *XV Dari*, I, no. 217, p. 204

[26] This is probably a reference to the Church of the Holy Cross on the island of Aghtamar, the seat of the Armenian regional catholicosate.

... In the year 866 [of the Armenian Era = A.D. 1417], during the pontificate of the Lord Dawit' [III of Aghtamar], [and] during the reign of ... Łaray Yusuf [Ḳara Yūsuf] ... Also, during the principality in our canton of the prince Melik' Mahmat [Malik Muḥammad], [who] protects us well ...

1418

1. Place: village of Poṙ in canton of Bałēš; scribe and author of col.: Mkrtič'; MS. title: Menology [*Yaysmawurk'*].
Source: Xač'ikyan, *XV Dari*, I, no. 231, p. 215

... I was in great anguish because of the bitterness of our time and the destruction of our country. Who can put into writing the sufferings of our nation? For, due to the multiplication of our sins, the door of God's mercy was shut down and the windows of [His] wrath were opened in our times ...

2. Place: city of Van; scribe and author of col.: Karapet; MS. title: Gospel.
Source: Xač'ikyan, *XV Dari*, I, no. 235a, p. 218

... In the year 867 of the Haykazean Era [A.D. 1418], during the pontificate of the Lord Pawłos [II, Gaṙnec'i], and during the imperial conquest of Łaray Usuf [Ḳara Yūsuf] ...

3. Place: monastery of St. Vardan near Gawaš in province of Ṙštunik'; scribe and author of col.: Astuacatur; MS. title: Ritual-Book [*Maštoc'*].
Source: Xač'ikyan, *XV Dari*, I, no. 238a, p. 220

... [completed] in bitter and anxious times ... during the khanate of the baron Yusuf [Ḳara Yūsuf], and the tyrannical rule in our province of Amir Ēzdin [Amīr 'Izz al-Dīn Shīr] and of his son Melik' Mahmad [Malik Muḥammad]. May the Lord God help and protect them, for they are most beneficent protectors of our Armenian nation ...

4. Scribe and author of col.: Sargis; MS. title: Gospel.
Source: Xač'ikyan, *XV Dari*, I, no. 244a, p. 223

. . . In the year 867 [of the Armenian Era = A.D. 1418], during the imperial conquest of Usuf [Ḳara Yūsuf].

1419

1. Place: monastery of C‘ipnay; scribe and author of col.: Grigor; MS. title: Gospel.
Source: Xač‘ikyan, *XV Dari*, I, no. 246, p. 225

. . . [copied] in the year 868 [of the Armenian Era = A.D. 1419], during the pontificate of the Lord Pawłos [II, Gaṙnec‘i], and during the imperial conquest of Łaray Usuf [Ḳara Yūsuf]. In this year, there arrived locusts from the east and covered with great density all the fields and mountains, the summits and valleys, stretching from Salmast to Arzəṙum [Erzerum]. They ate up much products of labor in numerous places, as a result of which the people were terrified, and the prices went up . . .

2. Place: monastery of Hermon in canton of Ełegeac‘; scribe and author of col.: Grigor Axalc‘xec‘i; MS. title: Book of Questions by Grigor Tat‘ewac‘i.
Source: Xač‘ikyan, *XV Dari*, I, no. 739a, p. 656

. . . [copied] in the year 868 of the Armenian Era [A.D. 1419], during the imperial conquest of the T‘urk‘man [Turkmen] baron Usuf [Ḳara Yūsuf], and the catholicosate of the Lord Pawłos [II, Gaṙnec‘i] . . . Also during the reign of King Ałēk‘sandr [Alexander I, the Great] of Georgia [Vrac‘], son of Kostandianos [King Constantine I] who was slain at the hands of the baron Usuf [Ḳara Yūsuf]. This Kostandianos [Constantine I] was the son of King Bagrat [V]; and when the *at‘abag* [atabeg] was Ivanē, son of Ałbuła [Aghbugha].

. . . [copied also] during the pontificate [*sic*] in our holy monastery [of Hermon] and in our canton of Baron Tarsayič, son of Gugun, son of Inanik, son of Burt‘el. In this year he [Tarsayič] suffered much anguish, tribulation and penury, for he, who once controlled the entire canton, now controls not a single farm or village, because they confiscated and wrested all of [his] villages and towns, monasteries and sanctuaries; and he took to flight and hid himself in the crevices of rocks and in the woods, until such time that the Lord God would restore to him his former glory and authority. And also [copied] during the pontificate [prelacy] in this province of the Lord Step‘anos, surnamed Iwanē, son of Baron Smbat and brother of Baron Bēšk'ēn. May the Lord God protect them and their family for a long time . . .

3. Place: village of Tayšoł in province of Ṙštunik'; scribe and author of col.: Step'annos; MS. title: Collection of Sermons [*Čaṙəntir*]. Source: Xač'ikyan, *XV Dari*, I, no. 247, p. 226

. . . [completed] in bitter times when, because of our multitudinous sins and evil deeds, the country suffered multifarious punishments—famine, pestilence, [and] plague. And in this year, also, there arrived numerous locusts in our country, and ate up all the fresh plants, and there was great anxiety. This occurred in the year 868 of the Armenian Era [A.D. 1419], on the twentieth of the month of Nawasard, during the pontificate of the Lord Dawit' [III of Aghtamar] and of the younger Zak'aria [III of Aghtamar], and during the tyrannical rule in our country of Łara Yusuf [Ḳara Yūsuf] and Amir Ēzdin [Amīr 'Izz al-Dīn Shīr] . . .

4. Place: village of Narek; scribe and author of col.: Step'annos; MS. title: Gospel. Source: Xač'ikyan, *XV Dari*, I, no. 252, p. 231

. . . [copied] in the year 868 of the Armenian Era [A.D. 1419], during the pontificate of the Lord Dawit' [III of Aghtamar], and during the principality in our province of Melik' [Malik Muḥammad], son of the *melik'* Amir Ēzdin [Amīr 'Izz al-Dīn Shīr] . . .

5. Place: Erusałēm; scribes: Manuēl and Yohanēs Ezənkec'i; author of col.: Manuēl; MS. title: Collection of Sermons [*Čaṙəntir*]. Source: Xač'ikyan, *XV Dari*, I, no. 255a, p. 233

. . . [completed] in the year 868 of the Armenian Era [A.D. 1419], during the rule of the aliens and the sultanate of Šex [Al-Mu'ayyad Shaykh]; and during the pontificate of the Lord Pōłos [II, Gaṙnec'i], who had this manuscript copied . . .

1420

1. Place: Ałt'amar; scribe and author of col.: T'umay Minasenc'; MS. title: Gospel.

Source: Xač'ikyan, *XV Dari*, I, no. 263, pp. 238–239

. . . [completed] during the pontificate of the Lord Dawit' [III of Aghtamar], and in the year 869 of our Haykazean Era [A.D. 1420], on the fifteenth of the month of Sahmi, in bitter and anxious times, when the entire country trembled and quivered at the hands of the lawless nation of archers [azgin netołac'] . . .

In the year 868 of the Haykazean Era [A.D. 1419], on the twenty-fourth of the month of Areg [August 10], God's cup of wrath overflowed, that is, the contaminating locusts arrived in our country, and wherever they found semi-ripened products of labor they ate them up; they dropped their seeds in the land, and everyone was terrified . . .

2. Place: Ałuank'; MS. title: Book of Questions by Grigor Tat'ewac'i.
Source: Xač'ikyan, *XV Dari*, I, no. 264, p. 240

. . . [copied in A.D. 1420] during the reign of the great Iwsuf [Ḳara Yūsuf], the brave and valiant godless one. Although he is a Muslim [*aylazgi*], he is kind toward the Christians, the priests, and the churches. Nevertheless, on account of our sins, the locusts have, for the past seven years, devastated the whole country, and we still are anxious . . .

3. Place: monastery of Sanahin in canton of Joroc' in province of Gugark'; scribe and author of col.: Martiros; MS. title: Gospel.
Source: Xač'ikyan, *XV Dari*, I, no. 265, p. 240

. . . This was copied at the time of the tyrant Yusov [Ḳara-Yūsuf], [and] during the reign of King Alek'sandr [Alexander I, the Great] of Georgia [Vrac']; [copied] in the province of Gugark', in the canton of Joroc', and in the most renowned and celestial holy monastery of Sanahin . . .

4. Place: village of Narek; scribe and author of col.: Izit; MS. title: Gospel.
Source: Xač'ikyan, *XV Dari*, I, no. 269a, p. 243

. . . [copied] in the year 869 of the Armenian Era [A.D. 1420], during the pontificate of the Lord Dawit' [III of Aghtamar], and during the tyrannical rule in our province of the notorious Mēlēk' [Malik Muḥammad] . . .

5. Place: city of Xzan; scribe and author of col.: Step'annos; MS. title: Gospel.
Source: Xač'ikyan, *XV Dari*, I, no. 274, p. 247

. . . [copied] in the year 869 of the Great Armenian Era [A.D. 1420], during the catholicosate of the Haykazean nation of the Lord Grigor [VIII, Xanjołat], and of our catholicosate at Ałt'amar of the Lord Dawit' [III], and during the reign of the alien Łaray Yusuf [Ḳara Yūsuf] . . . in bitter and grievous times . . .

1421

1. Place: Ałēt'; scribe and author of col.: Karapet; MS. title: Missal [*Čašoc'*].
Source: Xač'ikyan, *XV Dari*, I, no. 277a, p. 250

. . . I consented to copy this with much labor and suffering, in fear and in refuge, in terror and trembling. For the Čałat'ay [Čaghatai] Šahṙux [Shāhrukh], the benevolent and just king, came to Xlat' [Khilāṭ] and put the T'urk'man [Turkmens] to flight. Nevertheless, we and others suffered much want, because the T'urk'man [Turkmens] first fled to the interior of the country, and then returned with numerous forces, [that is] with 150,000 horsemen; but they were ignominiously slaughtered by the Č'ałat' [Čaghatai] forces in the canton of Vałaškert, near Bagwan. But because Šahṙux [Shāhrukh] was compassionate and gentle-hearted, he permitted them to flee and he also freed those whom he had taken as captive.

. . . It was a troubled year when I copied this book, because of the invasion, the high cost of food, and the scarcity of all kinds of goods . . .

2. Place: Ałt'amar; scribe and author of col.: T'umay; MS. title: Missal [*Čašoc'*].
Source: Xač'ikyan, *XV Dari*, I, no. 278, p. 251

. . . [copied] in the year 870 of the Armenian Era [A.D. 1421], in bitter and grievous times, when we were living in anxiety and were suffering at the hands of the alien nations, because they are torturing and harassing everyone, they are imposing fines and they are penalizing, tormenting, and plundering, and they are torturing with afflictions of every kind. . .

3. Place: monastery of Lim; scribe and author of col.: Yovanēs; MS. title: Gospel.
Source: Xač'ikyan, *XV Dari*, I, no. 279b, p. 254

In the year 870 of the Armenian Era [A.D. 1421], after the death of Łara Yusuf [Ḳara Yūsuf], there was intense agitation and confusion throughout Armenia, because the cavalry troops were in disarray and they were slaying and plundering one another. A detachment of marauding troops,[27] numbering five thousand households, broke off, and arriving in the province of K'aǰberunik' they carried off much booty and many captives. One of the sons of Yusuf [Ḳara Yūsuf], who was mischievous, perfidious, and most cruel, was in the citadel of Arckē. He went forth to greet them and made peace with them, and he made them go back and, together with their familes and children, scattered them about in the country. And who can recount the persecution and tragic grief which, for seven months, they meted out to our suffering Christian nations! . . .

4. Scribe and author of col.: Yovhannēs; MS. title: Collection of Writings by Grigor Tat'ewac'i.
Source: Xač'ikyan, *XV Dari*, I, no. 280, p. 255

. . . [completed] in the caves of mountain rocks, where we had taken shelter [out of fear of] the awesome-looking J̌ałat'ay [Čaghatai] and T'urk' [Turkish] troops, who both tormented us . . .

5. Scribe and author of col.: Mkrtič' Ełegec'i; MS. title: *Lucmunk' Parapmanc' Grigori Tat'ewac'woy.*
Source: Xač'ikyan, *XV Dari*, I, no. 281, p. 255

. . . In the year 870 [of the Armenian Era = A.D. 1421] we remained in our holy monastery of Varag, out of fear of the king of the east called Šaxruh [Shāhrukh] . . . And in this year the Č'ałat' [Čaghatai] defeated the sons of the T'urk'man [Turkmen] Yusuf [Ḳara Yūsuf] at Vałaršakert, and carried off numerous captives.

[27] The term used in the text is *p'awřnak*, which is rendered here as "marauding troops." However, with reference to this passage Xač'ikyan states: "This information is of great interest for the study of the internal organization of the Ḳara-Ḳoyunlu army. It is clear from this that each regiment within this army represented one of the elements of the Ḳara-Ḳoyunlu federation of Turkmen tribes. Like the other tribes, the *p'ořnak* (variant of *p'awřnak*) nomadic tribe, consisting of 5000 families, was among Ḳara Yūsuf's active army with its families and possessions." See *XV Dari*, I, p. xvii.

6. Place: Berkri (?); recipient of MS. and author of col.: Grigor; MS. title: Lexicon [*Bařgirk'*].
Source: Xač'ikyan, *XV Dari*, I, no. 282, p. 256

... This [manuscript] was acquired in the year 870 [of the Armenian Era = A.D. 1421], when the nation of archers [azgn netołac'] invaded and devastated all of Armenia, alas!

7. Place: monastery of Suxaray or Xařabastay in K'ajberunik'; recipeint of MS. and author of col.: Karapet; MS. title: Gospel.
Source: Xač'ikyan, *XV Dari*, I, no. 283a, p. 256

... I was desirous [of making a pilgrimage] to the God-inhabited city of Erusałēm [Jerusalem]; and many times I tried to make the journey but I could not ... for the levies imposed upon us by Łaray Usuf Xan [Ḳara Yūsuf Khān] were most exorbitant ... In the following year, longing for my parents and for my native country, I beseeched God to help me reach safely the monastery of Suxaray, which now is called the monastery of Xařabastay, in the region of K'ajberunik' ... Having seen this holy Gospel in Erusałem [Jerusalem] ... I bought it with my *halal* [honestly earned] assets ...

Upon my return I could not see my brother Yohannēs, for he had died in Christ in wicked and bitter times, and when Łaray Usuf [Ḳara Yūsuf] had expired ...

8. Place: monastery of Sanahin; scribe and author of col.: Yohanēs; MS. title: Menology [*Yaysmawurk'*].
Source: Xač'ikyan, *XV Dari*, I, no. 284a, p. 257

... in this year [A.D. 1421], *p'at'šah* Šahrux [Shāhrukh] of Persia [Parsic'], who was from the Xorazm [Khwārizmī] race of the nation of archers [azgin netołac'], and who crushed the T'urk'man [Turkmen] race, came to maraud [our country] for the fourth time during our life ...

9. Scribe and author of col.: Sargis; MS. title: Gospel.[28]
Source: Xač'ikyan, *XV Dari*, I, no. 288b, p. 260

... I fled from place to place, lived as a refugee, without any rest, famished and thirsty, so much so that who can put [the details] into

[28] Xač'ikyan points out that the colophon is badly damaged, and that the date is barely legible and therefore uncertain. (See *XV Dari*, I, p. 260, n. 2.)

writing, on account of Šałṙux [Shāhrukh] of the nation of archers [netołac' azg] . . .

10. Place: Ałt'amar; scribe: T'umay; author of col. (written at monastery of Varag): Sałat'ēl; MS. title: Bible.
Source: Xač'ikyan, *XV Dari*, I, no. 291d, p. 265

This was completed in the year 871 of the Armenian Era [A.D. 1422] during the barony of Ēzdinšer [Amīr 'Izz al-Dīn Shīr] and of his son Melek' [Malik Muḥammad] . . .

11. Place: village of Marmet in Vaspurakan; scribe and author of col.: Simēon; MS. title: Gospel.
Source: Xač'ikyan, *XV Dari*, I, no. 292, p. 266

. . . This holy Gospel was copied in the year 870 of the Armenian Era [A.D. 1421], during the pontificate of the Armenians at Sis of the Lord Catholicos Pōłos [II, Gaṙnec'i], and of the Lord Dawit' [III] at Ałt'amar, and during the imperial conquest of Sk'antar Łan [Iskandar Khān] . . .

12. Place: city of Xizan; MS. title: Gospel.
Source: Xač'ikyan, *XV Dari*, I, no. 293, p. 267

. . . Copied in the year 870 of the Great Armenian Era [A.D. 1421], during the catholicosate of the Haykazean nation of the Lord Pōłos [II, Gaṙnec'i], and during the amirate of Amir Dayut [Amīr Davud] in the city of Xizan [Hizan].

13. Place: monastery of Cpat; scribe and author of col.: Vardan; MS. title: Gospel.
Source: Xač'ikyan, *XV Dari*, I, no. 295, p. 268

. . . [copied] in bitter times, when good reports were not to be found, and when the Armenians were without leaders, [and] when we were exceedingly tormented by the aliens . . . In the year [A.D. 1421] . . . during the catholicosate of the Haykazean nation of the Lord Dawit' [III of Aghtamar], brother of the Lord Zak'aria [II of Aghtamar], who gave his blood and died as a martyr . . .

In appearance he [Zak'aria II] was like a holy angel,
As well as like the light of a sacrifice;

His countenance was like that of Jesus,
His heart was filled with compassion.
He was most wise and valiant,
In all things / / /
Immense and vigorous in person,
Young in his thirty-five years.
He was crowned with the blood of goodness;
He refused to betray the Lord of all;
He gave his valorous and mighty self,
A victim to the sword for Jesus . . .

14. Place: Kafay; scribe and author of col.: Yōvasab Aparanec'i; MS. title: *Girk' Kaycakanc' Bēda K'ahanayi.*
Source: Xač'ikyan, *XV Dari*, I, no. 296, p. 270

. . . In this year [A.D. 1421] there was a fire at Samison [Samsun] / / / and it burned practically everyone / / / and of all ages. In this year / / / the T'urk'n [Turks] were slaughtered / / / some 70,000 individuals.

1422

1. Author of col.: Grigor Cerenc' Xlat'ec'i: MS. title: Hymnal [*Ganjaran*].
Source: Xač'ikyan, *XV Dari*, I, nos. 300, 300b, pp. 272–288

Text A[29]

In the year eight hundred and thirty-five
Of the Armenian Era [A.D. 1386],
On January 1, at the hour of the sun's unveiling,
There was an eclipse of the sun . . .
In these days of bitterness,
On the eve of the feast of Epiphany,
The tribe of the barbarians

[29] The title of this text is: "Yišatakaran Ałētic' i Žamanakis Merum, Zor Asac'eal ē Grigor Vardapeti, or Makanun Cerenc' Koč'i, Xlat'ec'i" (Memorial of the Tragedies Which Occurred in Our Time, by Grigor Vardapet Xlat'ec'i, surnamed Cerenc'). The text has been preserved in two versions, the original and its abridgement. The complete version was first published by Grigor Xalat'eanc', *Yišatakaran Ałētic' Grigori Xlat'ec'woy* (Vagharshapat, 1897). The second edition can be found in Ališan, *Hayapatum*, II, 563–568. Both texts were published on the basis of a single manuscript copied by the scribe Karapet at Van in 1462. In contrast, the present critical text prepared by Xač'ikyan is based upon four manuscripts. For details see *XV Dari*, I, pp. 272–275, note.

Caused great harm in *šahastan.*
T'uxt'amiš Xan [Toḳtamish Khān], king of the Huns [Honac'],
Dispatched troops to Parskastan [Persia];
They came, looted, and committed *t'axt'an*
As far as the land of Hayastan [Armenia].
On the fifth of January they entered T'arvēz [Tabrīz];
And on the twenty-ninth Naxč'əwan [Nakhijewan]
From there they went toward Mułan [Mūghān];
And then returned to their native land.
They carried off loot and booty,
And returned to the land of the Huns [ašxarhn Honakan].
They committed much destruction
From the time they arrived until they departed.
The blood of many was shed on the ground
And many grew frigid in the snow,
Many fearing them took to flight
And died in the *nłmuns*;
Mothers no more pitied their children,
Parents became their infants' executioners;
Many died by their swords
And numerous others were tortured.
On top of all these evil deeds
And besides Armenia's demise,
There came another blow
More bitter than the first,
For while we still were in grief
We heard the grievous news
That the tribe of Xorazm [Khwārizm] was on the march,
That is the T'at'ar [Tatar] race in general,
The heirs of Səmərłand [Samarkand];
The alien children of Abraham
Entered en masse our land
As well as the seat of Atrpatakan [Ādharbaydjān].
They took booty from and enslaved
The Persian [Parsic'] and Armenian races;
They demolished and razed to the ground,
Mercilessly covered with wounds,
They put the men to the sword,
And the women they carried off;

They flayed the heads of some
And pulled them apart by the hair;
They prevented others from breathing
And made them die by suffocation;
Some they skinned like sheep,
Removed the flesh from the shoulder-bones;
Some they roasted in the fire
And rejoiced in the odor of the burning flesh;
Many renounced [their faith in] Christ
And professed [the faith of] Mahmet [Prophet
Muhammad].
They entered the canton of Ayrarat'
As well as the land of the Ałwan [Caucasian Albania];
They captured the royal city
Which was called Təp'xis [Tiflis];
They forced the Georgian [Vrac'] King Bagrat [V]
His faith to renounce.
Whence they returned
And wintered in Mułan [Mūghān];
But in the days of spring
To Siwnik' Major [Siwnis Mecn] they returned,
Captured the fortress of Orotayn,
Marched up to [the city of] Kars,
They turned the whole country into *č'awl*
With their traffic to and fro;
For they went away and then returned
For the third and even the fourth time,
The chief of their wicked cohorts
Was Lank-T'amur [Tīmūr Lang] by name.
This was in the year eight hundred
And thirty and six [A.D. 1387];
They plundered impregnable places
And atrocities much they committed;
One such place was Bǰni,
Which was the seat of two chiefs [bishops?].
They captured and demolished it,
And its bishop they slew.
They also slew Hasan Carec'i
Together with his three sons;
They captured their fortress
And carried off many into captivity.
They captured the fortress of Kaputic',

And slew four hundred therein;
And in the great town of Erewan
They slaughtered five hundred men.
I cannot say more of what
The Christian Armenians endured.
My bones tremble and quiver,
My life is consuming, my heart grows faint;
For with my own eyes I witnessed
The tragic grief which befell them.
Many princes abandoned their homes
And of their goods they were deprived;
Their horses were taken away
And on foot they went away.
Children died on the highway
For they could walk no more;
And the monastic clergy
Wandered about and shelter found not;
Some unprotected women
Were compelled to join them,
They yearned for bread and went about naked,
And with bare feet they went along.
No more honors for the noble
And no banners for the wealthy;
No bread was there for the bread-distributor
And no wine for the drunkard,
No horse for the horseman
And no *səlex* [arms] for the foot-soldier.
Strangers wandered about in strange places
And begged for food to eat;
Ladies who had owned opulent homes
And paraded in silken dresses
Were in dire need of bread,
And begged for dresses to cover themselves;
Princes who were called chieftains,
And glutted themselves with their silver,
Had become penurious
And longed for food to eat;
And those who offered bread to many
Now yearned for a morsel,
And though they were much chagrined
Their need compelled them to beg,
Although they were leery about begging

Yet they ventured for they were famished,
Those weakened by pain grew more ill
And died hither and thither.
Infants looked up to their mothers
To seek a panacea for their plight,
Mothers anguished in their remorse
And sought immediate death.
Fathers cried for their children,
They lamented in anguish
At seeing those whom they had nurtured
In bitter and painful need;
Upon the death of their infants
Their own souls they took away.
Some had no mourners at all,
Their graves were unknown,
And so tragic they appeared
To those who witnessed them.
This befell not the Christians alone,
But all the Tačiks as well,
For the anguish was common to all
The Persians [Parsicʻ], Armenians, and Tʻurkʻ [Turks].
All this occurred on the other side
Of the river called Erasx [Araxes].
After crossing to this side of the river,
And invading with the Tʻurkʻ [Turks],
They reached the waters of Amitʻ [Āmid],
And committed many atrocities.
From there they came up to Haykʻ [Armenia],
And marched upon [the city of] Van,
They surrounded and besieged it,
They plundered the impregnable fortress,
They bound the Armenians and Tačiks
And hurled them down from the rocks;
They smote and slew so many
That they made a pile out of flesh.
I should also mention what transpired
At the fortress of Ernǰak,
For from the time of the feast of Easter
Until the feast of the Holy Cross
They besieged it with numerous troops,
But harm it they could not;
Afterwards they returned

To the country whence they came.
And again they marched forth
In the year [eight hundred and] forty-two [A.D. 1393];
They invaded Babelon [Babylon = Baghdad],
And Mijaget [Mesopotamia] they trampled;
The magnificent city of Urha [Urfa]
And Amit‘ [Āmid] the renowned,
The fortress of Mērdin [Mārdīn] and Nəsebin
[Naṣībīn],
All these they totally enslaved;
Also numerous other cities
They demolished and enslaved.
Whence they turned toward the north
And marched up to Awnik,
Which they captured after much effort
And carried off captives to Msr [Egypt].
From there they proceeded again
And left troops at Ernǰak;
Before capturing the citadel of Ernǰak
They held it under siege [*xsar*] for fifteen years.
I should mention the valorous deeds,
The great feats of Georgia's [Vrac‘] king,
Who scored many victories
And put the Č‘ałat‘ [Čaghatai] forces to flight,
Those who had surrounded and laid siege [*xsar*]
To the impregnable citadel of Ernǰak.
From it he rescued the khan's [*xan*] son,
Namely Sultan Tahir [Ṭāhir Djalā'ir] of Ernǰak.
He took him away and gave him troops,
And sent him away to Ahmat Xan [Sultan Aḥmad
Djalā'ir].
But after the wicked son departed,
He rebelled against the *xan* [khan],
Namely the king called Sultan Ahmat [Aḥmad
Djalā'ir],
Who was the son of Oyis Xan [Uwais Khān].
But failed the luckless
Sultan Tahir, the khan's [*xan*] son,
For the river of Bałtat [Baghdad] carried away
The wicked one who betrayed his father.
And when Lank-T‘amur [Tīmūr Lang] learned
What the king of Georgia [Vrac‘] had done,

He was again consumed with wrath
And mustered his horsemen.
With troops more numerous than heretofore,
T'amur Bēk [Tīmūr Lang Beg] marched forth again;
He captured the forts of Vrac'tun [Georgia]
And enslaved all their inhabitants.
Whence he went all the way to Zmiwṙ [Smyrna],
The city on the Lycian [Likeac'] shore.
He crushed the forces of Ildrum [Yi̊ldi̊ri̊m],
The mighty, valorous, and great sultan.
Among others, he carried off
All the Łaray-T'at'ar [Ḳara Tatar] as well;
Countless was the number of those
Who were slain and enslaved
In the land of Gamirk' in Kapadovk [Cappadocia],
Which are called Mējerkreay [Asia Minor] and
    Hoṙomk' [Rūm].
Oh, the *łazay* which they meted out
To the men, women, and children;
They buried the men alive,
Choked them to death in the soil and water;
And the tender children and infants
They cast under the horses' hoofs.
And when Mir T'amur [Tīmūr Lang] marched upon
The city of Damaskos [Damascus] in Šamatun [Syria],
The sea and the land quivered
From the reports of this evil news.
They put some to the sword;
Others they burned in flames of fire;
And with the heads that they cut off
They built many a *mniray*.
And everyone quivered
Upon hearing of such evil news.
Having done all this, Mir T'amur [Tīmūr Lang]
Returned to his throne at Səmərłənd [Samarkand],
And there he reached the end of his days.
He perished on his throne.
And his son Miranšay [Mīrānshāh]
Came to occupy the *t'axt'* of T'avrēz [Tabrīz];
But against him there arose
Łara Usuf Bahaduṙ [Ḳara Yūsuf Bahādur],
Who smote the Č'ałat' [Čaghatai] forces,

And cut off the head of Miranšay [Mīrānshāh].
He ruled from the same *t'axt'*
Of the *šahastan* city of T'awrēz [Tabrīz];
He brought peace to many places
And prosperity to mankind;
There was *ēmnut'iwn* and prices were low,
And no robbery at all.
But when the sins multiplied
Among the Christian nations,
The Xan Usuf [Ḳara Yūsuf Khān] marched upon
The Georgian [Vrac'] city of Axəlcəxē [Akhal
Tsikhe];
He waged *łazay* and took captives,
Committed much damage and wickedness.
This came to pass in the year eight hundred
And sixty and five [A.D. 1416].
The captives which they took
They removed to foreign lands,
Took them to Bałdat [Baghdad] and Məsər [Egypt],
To Xorasan [Khurāsān] in Parskac'tan [Persia];
Not one or five or six thousand,
But more than a *biwr* [ten thousand];
Those who were slain were multitudes
And countless, their numbers unknown.
And in the year eight hundred
And seventy [A.D. 1421]
Łaray Usuf [Ḳara Yūsuf], the master of the *t'axt'*,
Perished in a manner deserving;
They mocked and disgraced him when they saw
This abominable man's body fallen on the ground,
The impure corpse swollen with stench,
And the crows removed his eyes.
Confusion set in among this evil one's troops,
They dispersed and took to flight.
Three days later they came back,
And carried off the corpse to Arčēš [Ardjīsh].
But the forces of the wicked Mir Usuf [Ḳara Yūsuf]
Caused devastation wherever they went;
They were the children of the evil, wicked,
And *anasax* T'urk'man [Turkmen] race.
After the death of Usuf Bēk [Ḳara Yūsuf Beg],
There came the Č'ałat' [Čaghatai] troops,

Whose chief and leader was
One by the name of Šaxṙuh [Shāhrukh].
He was the son of Mir T'amur [Tīmūr Lang],
And the younger brother of Miranšay [Mīrānshāh].
His forces were more numerous than T'amur's
[Tīmūr Lang];
Five *biwr*, that is, fifty thousand,
Was the total number of his troops;
For T'amur [Tīmūr Lang] had thirty [*biwr*];
And more than these Šahṙuh [Shāhrukh] had
Thirty-five *biwr* all in all.
Yet wickedness he possessed not;
Rather, he was benevolent and serene;
Because of the evils which they wrought,
The T'urk'man [Turkmen] feared him very much.
For they were cruel and unjust,
They were *anmərwat'* and *anšaławat'*,
They were lawless and infidel,
Impure, even wicked and inhuman,
Impudent and shameless,
Vessels of sin, receptacles of evil.
Glory to God for what He did
To the T'urk'man [Turkmens], befitting their evil
deeds;
For they first were frightened and fled,
They were slaughtered when they came back,
And deservedly they fell
Into the hands of Šahṙux [Shāhrukh].
Many of them died by the sword
And others fled and fell captive;
They were trampled by horses and died,
They were utterly disgraced and plundered,
And fled to the mountains and the vales.
Those who took to flight were pursued,
And executioners they became to one another.
They carried off countless *əṙzak*,
Handsome horses, and many camels;
No count was made of women and children
Who were enslaved and trampled upon.
But Šahṙux [Shāhrukh] had a heart which was
Both merciful and compassionate;
He issued an *asax*, a *huk'm*, and an order

Not to slaughter everyone;
Rather, he permitted them to disperse
And flee to foreign lands.
And this great Sultan Šahṙux [Shāhrukh]
Left and returned to Xorasan [Khurāsān];
He returned to his own seat
In his ancestral Səmərłənd [Samarkand];
He left the *t'axt'* unoccupied
At the *šahastan* city of T'awrēz [Tabrīz].
Then the sons of Usuf Bēk [Ḳara Yūsuf Beg]
Came and occupied that *t'axt'*;
But in harmony they were not,
And one the other put to flight.
As for the wholly accursed
Younger son of Mir Usuf [Ḳara Yūsuf],
Spandiar, the vessel of evil,
The shameless, wicked, and insane soul,
He was pernicious and the destroyer
Of many splendid and prosperous cantons.
He destroyed Arčēš [Ardjīsh] and Arckē,
He demolished Basen and Awnık;
But the city of Karin, [that is] Aṙzəṙum [Erzerum],
He destroyed worst of all.
And Sk'andar [Iskandar], the eldest son
Of Łara Usuf Bahaduṙ [Ḳara Yūsuf Bahādur],
Occupied the *t'axt'* at T'awrēz [Tabrīz],
He established *asax* and did much good;
But he plundered us and caused anguish,
As well as wicked deeds, harsh and bitter.
A year after his flight
From the hands of the Č'ałat' [Čaghatai],
He assembled a multitude of horsemen
And attacked the citadel of Xlat' [Khilāṭ];
They could do no harm to the citadel,
But they set the city on fire.
They invaded [the village of] Ałuvank'
And evil atrocities they wrought;
They captured the citadel, and slaughtered,
Many Christians they slew there,
Two hundred and even more.
Some they slew by the sword,
Others were drowned in the sea,

And still others were hurled down from rocks.
Oh, the beautiful shape and *surat'*
Of the infants who were lost;
Noble, honorable *tanutērs* [householders],
Modest, pretty, and noble ladies,
Tall in stature and handsome
Young men, rich in color and mien.
All these were put to the sword;
Deprived they were of their own graves;
Women, with their children, were carried off,
More than five hundred in number.
From one village alone they were not,
But from many different parts,
From Xizan [Hizan] and from Bałēš [Bitlīs],
Who had come to reap the crop;
From Cłak' and Ałał altogether,
Many were from Ałēt' and beyond,
Some of whom were slain by the sword,
While women and children were carried off.
All this transpired on account of
The *amiray* Šaməzdin [Amīr Shams al-Dīn],
The servant of the evil satan,
And the forerunner Antichrist [*Neřn*],
Who became haughty and proud,
And refused to submit to Sk'andar [Iskandar].
Many who died were left unburied,
Neither food for the soul nor *dram* for the soil;[30]
And those who were carried off
Were dispersed in foreign lands;
They intermingled with Muslims [*aylazgi*],
And learned their wicked ways;
They were estranged and became degenerate,
Their native country they forgot;
Not willingly but involuntarily
This became their lot.
Will God show them compassion
And save them from yonder? . . .
When I wrote this lamentation . . .
We were afflicted with anguish

30 The reference is to the Armenian tradition of offering a requiem meal to the mourners after the funeral services. Since the bereaved were despoiled of their possessions and assets they could not observe the tradition. Because of their poverty, they could not even afford to pay for the grave site, and therefore left their dead unburied.

Which befell our land
And our nation, in particular,
Our suffering Armenian race . . .
Our churches are in darkness,
Our nation dispersed everywhere.
Yet we thank the benevolent [God],
For we survived this grief,
For He left us not in anguish,
But soon brought comfort to us . . .

Text B

". . . In the year [A.D. 1387], with great fury,
The forces of T'amur [Tīmūr Lang] marched forth;
They wrought many atrocities
And spilled much blood on the ground.
He trampled the land of Parskastan [Persia],
And Armenia he brought under his feet;
He was like the beast
Whom the holy [Prophet] Daniel described.[31]
He reached the borders of Amit' [Āmid],
The whole country he made *č'awl*;
He then returned and came to Van,
He besieged the impregnable citadel;
Twenty-six days he kept it under siege [*hsar*],
Before it fell into his hands.
Many reached their hour of destiny;
They were hurled down from the precipice and died,
Not one or two thousand,
But more than three.
The heaps of flesh were piled up high;
Some, though smitten, were not dead.
The number of captives was without count;
Those who were captured and sent away
Reached the city of Səmərłand [Samarkand].
Seven years later [A.D. 1394] they again
Marched forth with a great multitude,
They invaded Chaldaea [K'ałdēac'woc' ašxarhn],
And captured the city of Babelon [Babylon = Baghdad].
They marched into Mijaget [Mesopotamia]
And wrought much devastation there;
And in the magnificent city of Amit' [Āmid]

[31] See Book of Daniel 7:1–8.

They slaughtered indiscriminately.
Then they marched against the northern lands,
They captured the fortress of Awnik,
As well as the citadel of Bagran,
An impossible feat to accomplish.
They brought many to their last hour,
Many they hurled down the precipice;
And with the heads which they cut off
They erected a *mənara.*
This occurred in the year
Eight hundred and forty-three [A.D. 1394].
All the lands trembled
With the terror which they brought.
And from the day they laid siege [*hsar*]
To the impregnable fortress of Erənǰak,
They surrounded and encircled it,
And erected strong barricades.
Five years later [A.D. 1399], moreover,
The king of the Georgians [Vrac‘] marched forth . . .
He came to the fortress of Erinǰak
With many awesome-looking troops,
And rescued the son of Ahmat Łan [Aḥmad Djalā'ir Khān];
He put the Č‘ałat‘ [Čaghatai] forces to flight,
And placed other garrisons in the fortress.
When T‘amur Bēk [Tīmūr Lang Beg] heard of this,
With a fury he again marched forth
From the city of Samarłand [Samarkand].
He returned with troops many and awesome,
With numerous elephants of colossal size,
And other machines of war.
In the year eight hundred and forty-eight
Of the Armenian Era [A.D. 1399],
In the days of autumn he arrived,
And remained until the summer season.
The Georgians [Vrac‘] he devastated and slew
For seven whole months;
The number of those slain was found
To be more than one hundred thousand;
But the number of those carried off
Was numerous and beyond count,
Excluding those who were trampled by horses,

And those who were hurled down from rocks.
It was like what befell the Israelites [Israyeleanc‘n]
In the days of the Maccabees [Makabayeanc‘n],
Which the prophet had foretold
And had divinely prophesied.
The arrow of God drunk with blood,
His sword soaked in blood;
All these were the fruits of our sins
And our wicked and evil deeds,
Which satan meted out to us,
And destroyed us, false Christians.
And deservedly we drank
From the bitter cup of the aliens.
Thereafter the wicked one marched forth,
And with his countless forces he departed.
With threats he entered the Greek land [tunn Yunac‘],
The metropolis of Sebastia
Within the bounds of Gamirk‘ in Mējerkreay [Asia
Minor].
It [Sebastia] received most severe blows;
They besieged it in a novel fashion
Before they finally captured it.
They made all the men of the city,
The prominent ones in particular,
Dig a ditch and *xandak*
And cast them in it alive;
They hurled stones at them all,
Filled up the ditch while they were still breathing.
Oh, the terrible, unheard of and
Indescribable scourge!
For even on the fourth day
The moans could be heard from the abyss,
For not a hundred or a thousand,
But eight thousand their number was.

2. Place: city of Eznka in canton of Ekełeac‘; scribe and author of col.: Simēon; MS. title: Ritual-Book [*Maštoc‘*].
Source: Xač‘ikyan, *XV Dari*, I, no. 301, pp. 289–290

. . . Do not blame me for the inadequacy of my calligraphy and for my errors, because this was copied in most bitter times, for Awt‘man

[Ḳara Yoluḳ 'Uthmān] attacked us and committed grave plunder. He besieged our city for thirteen weeks and [his troops] consumed all the products of labor. From among those who fell into his hands, he killed some and he enslaved some; and the siege [*xsar*] was intense . . . and those who were captured were brought here and sold [as slaves]. The siege [*xsar*] was so intense that a *mot'* of bread was worth 800 *dram* and a *mot'* of salt 1200 *dram*. And the same befell those who were at Ani. But then God took pity on them; and the baron of the city [Ani] said to them [the invaders], "Permit those of us who have no *azex* to leave the city," and they permitted us all to leave. The compassion of God was inexhaustible, for He softened Awt'man's [Ḳara Yoluḳ 'Uthmān] heart, so much so that he assigned a man to accompany everyone who left here until they arrived in a prosperous land . . .

3. Place: city of Xlat'; scribe and author of col.: Karapet; MS. title: Bible.
Source: Xač'ikyan, *XV Dari*, I, no. 302a, p. 291

. . . [copied] in anxious and wretched times, for we have taken refuge in the caverns and in the caves of rocks, because of our fear of the lawless ones [that is, Iskandar's troops] . . .

1423

1. Place: monastery of Hermon; scribe and author of col.: Yovhannēs; MS. title: Gospel.
Source: Xač'ikyan, *XV Dari*, I, no. 317, p. 304

. . . When Sk'andar [Iskandar] ruled in the country of T'awrēz [Tabrīz] and slaughtered numerous Christians . . .

2. Place: monastery of Cpat in province of Mokk'; scribe and author of col.: Karapet; MS. title: Missal [*Čašoc'*].
Source: Xač'ikyan, *XV Dari*, I, no. 319, p. 306

. . . [completed] in the year 872 of the Haykazean Era [A.D. 1423], during the pontificate of the Lord Dawit' [III of Aghtamar] . . . [and] during the khanate of the T'iwrk'mēn [Turkmen] Isk'antar Bēk [Iskandar Beg] . . .

3. Scribe and author of col.: T'umay; MS. title: Gospel.
Source: Xač'ikyan, *XV Dari*, I, no. 323, p. 308

[Copied] In the year eight hundred and seventy-two [1423] . . .
In times of anguish,
When the Muslims [*aylazgik'*] were harassing,
The Christians they were insulting,
The churches they were demolishing,
Their foundations they were shaking,
The priests were sitting and lamenting
And their flock they were assembling.
And why did all this come to pass?
Because of the sins they committed,
Which had become as abundant
As the waters of a torrent . . .

1424

1. Recipient of MS. and author of col.: Xoǰa Gorg; MS. title: Gospel.
Source: Xač'ikyan, *XV Dari*, I, no. 330, p. 314

. . . In this year [A.D. 1424] . . . on account of our multitudinous sins, Sk'andar [Iskandar] invaded the province of Ṙštunik' with numerous horsemen, and besieged [*xsar*] the citadel of Van. And he committed much destruction; he slew some, he carried off some into captivity, and he burned some. They demolished the churches, and they carried off the manuscripts and brought them to the city of Słerd [Si'irt]; and . . . *xoǰa* Gorg . . . rescued this holy Gospel from bondage . . . by paying 1500 *mertin dram* for it . . .

2. Recipient of MS. and author of col.: Kirakos; MS. title: Commentary on the Gospel of Matthew by Grigor Tat'ewac'i.
Source: Xač'ikyan, *XV Dari*, I, no. 331a, p. 314

In the year 873 of the Armenian Era [A.D. 1424] Skandar Łan [Iskandar Khān] captured the citadel of Van . . . and numerous Christians were persecuted and dispersed abroad . . .

3. Place: monastery of Sanahin; scribes and authors of col.: Łazar and Yohanēs; MS. title: Gospel.
Source: Xač'ikyan, *XV Dari*, I, no. 332, p. 315

... This was completed in the year 873 of the Haykazean Era [A.D. 1424], in which year there occurred a terrible plague, as an admonition for our sins. During the reign of King Alēk'sandr [Alexander I, the Great] of Georgia [Vrac'], and during the tyrannical rule in Armenia of the T'urk'man [Turkmen] Sk'andar [Iskandar] ...

1425

1. Place: Ałt'amar; scribe and author of col.: T'umay Minasenc'; MS. title: Gospel.
Source: Xač'ikyan, *XV Dari*, I, nos. 345a, b, pp. 326–327

... [copied] during the pontificate of the Lord Dawit' [III of Aghtamar], and in the year 874 of the Haykazean Era [A.D. 1425], in exceedingly evil and bitter and anxious times, when all of Armenia was subjected to devastation and plunder, to slaughter and captivity, on account of my multitudinous sins, at the hands of the lawless and accursed nation of archers [azgin netołac']. Because for a whole year the wicked tyrant *amirza* Sk'andar [Iskandar Mīrzā], the master of T'avrēz [Tabrīz] and a T'urk' [Turk] by race, has seized the *amirapet* of the city of Ostan [Wusṭān], Sultan Ahmat [Sulṭān Aḥmad], and has imprisoned him with iron fetters in the citadel of Alənǰa, and he claims the impregnable fortresses which he held. He also made uninhabitable the regions of Ałbak [Albāq], K'arpah and Ostan [Wusṭān] in Armenia, as far as Bałēš [Bitlīs]. The inhabitants of these regions took refuge abroad, naked, barefooted, and famished. And some, who had escaped to this God-protected island [of Aghtamar] and placed their trust in God and the power of the almighty Holy Cross, escaped from the evil captivity of the wicked tyrant.

We should also relate the tragedy and grief, deserving of tearful lament, which befell the Christians. For Awt'man Bēk [Ḳara Yoluḳ 'Uthmān], the master of Amit' [Āmid], in response to the pleas of our princes, arrived with numerous forces. He carried off into captivity everyone in the regions of Arčēš [Ardjīsh] and Arckē and put them to the sword ... Alas! ... the bitterness of our time which befell us, because our country is in ruins; the altars and gates of our churches are demolished; our sacred vessels have been captured and carried off; and the divine hymns have been silenced throughout our country; only our magnificent [church] of the Holy Cross has remained like a mighty king, unshakeable and invincible ...
Alas! Alas! A thousand times, alas, for our bitter condition, because

at this time our country was plundered and subjected to captivity by the T'urk' [Turkish] forces, on the twentieth of the month of Trē . . .

2. Place: monastery of Sxgay, near Van; MS. title: Ritual Book [*Maštoc'*].
Source: Xač'ikyan, *XV Dari*, I, no. 346, pp. 327–328

. . . the pious *tanutēr* [householder] Yovanēs . . . who recovered this holy book from the infidels, when Iskandar *amirzay* [mīrzā] captured Van, and he returned it to the church of St. Mary in the monastery of Sxgay . . . in the year 874 [of the Armenian Era = A.D. 1425].

3. Purchaser of MS. and author of col.: Xōǰay Astuacatur; MS. title: Book of Lamentations by Grigor Narekac'i.
Source: Xač'ikyan, *XV Dari*, I, no. 347, p. 328

I, Xōǰay Astuacatur . . . bought this book [of Lamentations by Grigor] Narekac'i, which was held in bondage by the T'urk'man [Turkmens], in the year when Sk'andar *amirza* [Iskandar Mīrzā] captured the citadel of Van from the K'urd [Kurds], in the year 874 [of the Armenian Era = A.D. 1425]. And they committed much destruction, and they carried off all the sacred effects. And I saw this book by Narekac'i when they brought it to Veri Varag; and I purchased it with my *halal* [honestly earned] assets and offered it to the holy monastery of Veri Varag, where it had been before, in memory of myself and of my parents . . .

4. Place: city of Hizan; scribe and author of col.: Karapet; MS. title: Gospel.
Source: Xač'ikyan, *XV Dari*, I, no. 348, p. 328

. . . This holy Gospel was copied . . . in bitter and grievous times when, on account of our multitudinous sins, the iniquitous Isk'andar [Iskandar] seized our *amiray* Sultan Ahmat [Kurdish Amīr Sulṭān Aḥmad], and arriving with numerous troops he besieged [*xsar*] our impregnable fortress of Van for fifty days, but he failed to capture it. After making a false vow, he left for Dawrēž [Tabrīz]; but in the spring he dispatched troops to the province of Ṙštunik', and they carried off captives and destroyed it. And we fled and came to Hizan, where this [Gospel] was completed . . . in the year 874 of the Armenian Era [A.D. 1425] . . .

5. Place: monastery of Xaṙabasta; scribe and author of col.: Yakob; MS. title: Menology [*Yaysmawurk'*].[32]
Source: Xač'ikyan, *XV Dari*, I, no. 350, pp. 329, 331, 332, 333

And in the year 874 of the Armenian Era [A.D. 1425]. And the bloodthirsty beasts, the troops of Ōt'man [Ḳara Yoluḳ 'Uthmān] and the Ǝṙoškan [Rūzagī] horsemen invaded the country. They plundered, and they carried off into captivity as many as they could, and they spilled the blood of many in our country. Among these, they killed and made a martyr of our *rabunapet* [Grigor Xlat'ec'i] and the illuminator of our souls and flesh in the monastery of C'ipna, on Sunday the day of the feast of Pentecost, and thus subjected the entire country to irremediable grief . . .

. . . The wondrous *rabunapet* [Grigor Xlat'ec'i],
Slain at the hands of infidels.
. . . They suddenly arrived,
The Mars [azgn Marac'] who are called K'urt' [Kurds];
They slew [our] dear father
In the renowned monastery of C'ipna . . .[33]

6. Place: Jagavank'; scribe and author of col.: Step'anos; MS. title: Commentary on the Calendar by Yakob Łrimec'i and Miscellany.
Source: Xač'ikyan, *XV Dari*, I, no. 352a, p. 335

. . . [copied in A.D. 1425] During the tyranny of Sk'andar [Iskandar], son of Usuf [Ḳara Yūsuf] the T'orgomean, the second Ašrap' [Čūbānid Malik Ashraf] to us Armenians and the destroyer of churches; and during the barony in our land of P'ir Łaip and Awdul, grandsons of Sahat' . . .

[32] The MS. in which this colophon is found was copied by the scribes Yovsēp' and Grigor in A.D. 1477. It appears that the colophon written by Yakob in 1425 was reproduced from the MS. which these two scribes used as exemplar, for their text of the Menology. See Xač'ikyan, *XV Dari*, I, p. 329, n. 1.

[33] This is an elegy dedicated to the martyrdom of Grigor Cerenc' Xlat'ec'i (see App. A), written by Aṙak'el Bałišec'i (see App. A). It consists of forty stanzas with four lines each. Only the few lines that contain historical information are excerpted and translated here.

7. Place: village of Agulis; scribe and author of col.: Matt'ēos; MS. title: Book of Questions by Grigor Tat'ewac'i.
Source: Xač'ikyan, *XV Dari*, I, no. 354, p. 337

... [Iskandar] was most beneficent toward our Armenian nation, especially toward our village of Agulis, [which] he made his own *xas* and made *t'arxan* for a whole year ...[34]

8. Place: village of Xarhoc'; scribe and author of col.: Yohannēs; MS. title: Gospel.
Source: Xač'ikyan, *XV Dari*, I, no. 361, p. 342

In the year eight hundred and seventy-four
Of the Armenian Era [A.D. 1425],
In bitter and grievous times,
During the pontificate of the Lord Dawit' [III of Aghtamar] of the Armenians,
During the khanate of Sk'andar [Iskandar] at T'avrēz [Tabrīz],
Who plundered the region of Hek'ar [Hakkārī] ...

9. Place: monastery of Kapos, in canton of Daranałeac': author of col.: Awetik'; MS. title: Bible.
Source: Xač'ikyan, *XV Dari*, I, no. 362, p. 344

... I received this most blessed Bible in the year 874 of the Armenian Era [A.D. 1425], in bitter and anxious times, because a grave calamity befell our canton of Ekełeac'. For in the same year that our renowned *rabunapet* Gēorg passed away in Christ, the master of Amit' [Āmid] attacked Eznkay [Erzindjān], and ... set on fire practically all the towns and the monasteries, including our famous monastery of Kapos which was burned and destroyed. He held the city under siege [*xsar*] for three years before he captured it. Afterwards he restored the peace, and with the help of God our canton began to prosper. And we, with the benevolent help of God, restored our holy monastery more resplendently than before, and also built a vicarage, cells, a building for the steward, as well as other structures ...

[34] Xač'ikyan has reproduced the text of this colophon from Ališan's *Sisuan*, p. 326. Ališan's text, however, is partially a verbatim reproduction from the original MS. and partially a paraphrase of the text. See *XV Dari*, I, p. 337, note.

10. Place: Eznkay; scribe and author of col.: Yovanēs Selaenc'i; MS. title: Missal [*Čašoc'*].
Source: Xač'ikyan, *XV Dari*, I, no. 363, p. 344

... [copied] during the time of Ōt'man Pak [Ḳara Yoluḳ 'Uthmān Beg] ... in the year 874 of the Armenian Era [A.D. 1425].

11. Place: monastery of K'oštenc' in canton of Hamšen; MS. title: Miscellany [*Žołovacu*].
Source: Xač'ikyan, *XV Dari*, I, no. 364, pp. 344–345

[copied in A.D. 1425] at the behest of the baron of barons Dawit' ... during the pontificate of the Lord Pōłos [II, Gaṙnec'i], and the reign of Sk'antar Pak [Iskandar Beg], and the barony of the baron Dawit'.

1426

1. Place: monastery of Hermon in canton of Ełegeac'; scribe and author of col.: Yakob; MS. title: Hymnal [*Šaraknoc'*].
Source: Xač'ikyan, *XV Dari*, I, no. 368, p. 349

... [completed] in bitter and grievous times, when the Hagar [azgn Hagaru] T'urk'man [Turkmens] held sway over Armenia, and when they subjected the entire country to slaughter, famine and enslavement, and when we received consolation from no quarter ...

2. Scribe and author of col.: Step'anos; MS. title: Gospel.
Source: Xač'ikyan, *XV Dari*, I, no. 369a, pp. 349–350

In bitter and grievous times,
During the khanate of the T'at'ar [Tatar] Sk'andar
[Iskandar];
The wicked one who roared at us
And warned us of the impending evil;
As foretold by the prophet,
He brought grief to us all.
He enslaved many imperious kings,
[As well as] lords of great cities,
He made our Armenian homeland like a desert,
And he carried off captives.
Only this place he did not penetrate,

But he made everyone tremble,
And wherever his evil foot reached
He made them victims of his sword.
Some died of starvation,
Others were slain by the sword.
All this cannot by the pen be told
Nor be related by word of mouth . . .

3. Place: monastery of Yełevank' in canton of Berkri; scribe and author of col.: Petros; MS. title: Ritual Book [*Maštoc'*].
Source: Xač'ikyan, *XV Dari*, I, no. 370, p. 353

. . . [copied] during the khanate of Sk'andar *amirza* [Iskandar Mīrzā], son of Usuf [Ḳara Yūsuf]. This is his third annual arrival; each time he plundered and carried off captives from our regions of Van and Ostan [Wusṭān]. He then captured the citadel of Van, and all of us generally, bishops and vardapets, monks and priests, *tanutērs* [householders] and ladies, took to flight and wandered about in foreign lands and became strangers; and all of this befell us on account of our multitudinous sins . . .

4. Place: begun at Davrēž and completed at the monastery of the Apostle Thaddeus; scribe and author of col.: Grigor; MS. title: Miscellany [*Žołovacu*].
Source: Xač'ikyan, *XV Dari*, I, no. 371, p. 353

. . . [completed in A.D. 1426], when a tyrant named Ǝsk'andar [Iskandar], son of Łara Usuf [Ḳara Yūsuf], captured the impregnable citadel of Maku [Mākū] and dispersed and deported to other lands the [Armenian] dyophysite *axt'armay* sect, and thus the words of the Lord, "he destroyed evil by evil and he gave the vineyards to other cultivators" [cf. Matthew 21:41], were fulfilled.

And I [Grigor] . . . yearned for a long time to restore our holy church of the Apostle [Thaddeus], but the aforementioned adversaries, [namely] the inhabitants of Maku [Mākū], would not permit us. Hence, doubly more intense grief was meted out to them from the canton of Artaz, when [Iskandar] gave [the citadel] to a Muslim [*aylazgi*] named Šex Bayazit' [Shaykh Bāyezīd]. And those [items] which the aforementioned wicked ones had removed from our holy monastery of the Apostle [Thaddeus] and had carried them off with *t'asup* and rancor, he [Bāyezīd] brought them back most willingly and gladly to our church, [that is] the gate of our church, the large bell, the beam of our vicarage, and all other /// and the charity he manifested toward us we never received from that selfish and accursed sect; may he be rewarded in equal measure with good health and *dawlat*ʻ in this worldly life.

5. Place: city of Mertin; scribe and author of col.: Kirakos; MS. title: Gospel.
Source: Xačʻikyan, *XV Dari*, I, no. 372, p. 354

... [copied] in bitter and anxious times ... during the pontificate of the Lord Pōłos [II, Gaṙnecʻi] ... during the reign of *amirzay* Skʻantar [Iskandar Mīrzā] of the nation of archers [azgin netołacʻ], and when Mertin [Mārdīn] was ruled by amir Nasr [Amīr Nāṣir al-Dīn Muḥammad]; in the year 875 of the Armenian Era [A.D. 1426].

6. Place: Cyprus (?); scribe and author of col.: Gaspar Hamtʻecʻi; MS. title: Commentary on the Epistles by Sargis Šnorhali.
Source: Xačʻikyan, *XV Dari*, I, no. 373, p. 354

... At this time, in the year 874 [of the Armenian Era = A.D. 1426], on the Sunday of the Transfiguration of our Lord [*Vardavaṙ*], the Sultan of Msr [Egypt] occupied Kipros [Cyprus] and carried off numerous Christians into captivity, that is, 5000 individuals; and who knows the number of those who were slain? Oh, woe unto me!

1427

1. Place: monastery of Mecopʻ; author of col.: Tʻovma Mecopʻecʻi; MS. title: Collection of Commentaries.
Source: Xačʻikyan, *XV Dari*, I, no. 383a, p. 361

... in bitter and evil times, when divine charity was diminished among the people and the clergy, who bear the name only, as a result of which our entire country was devastated by the iniquitous Tʻurkʻman [Turkmens]; and this is the sixth year that the divine liturgy has not been performed ...

2. Place: monastery of Małard in canton of Šambi-Jor; scribe and author of col.: Grigor Arckecʻi; MS. title: Gospel.
Source: Xačʻikyan, *XV Dari*, I, no. 386a, p. 365

... [copied] During the reign of Isk'andar [Iskandar], son of Usuf [Ḳara Yūsuf], and during the incumbency of the Lord [Catholicos] Pōłos [II, Gaṙnec'i] in Cilicia [Kilikec'woc'], and in the year 876 of the Armenian Era [A.D. 1427] ...

3. Place: monastery of Gamałiēl in Hizan; scribe and author of col.: Yohannēs; MS. title: Gospel.
Source: Xač'ikyan, *XV Dari*, I, no. 388, p. 367

... This holy Gospel was completed in the year 876 of the Armenian Era [A.D. 1427], during the khanate ... of Sk'antar [Iskandar], and when the amir of our [district] was the K'urd [Kurd] amir Dawut [Amīr Davud].

1428

1. Place: Ałt'amar; scribe and author of col.: T'uma [Minasenc']; MS. title: Gospel.
Source: Xač'ikyan, *XV Dari*, I, no. 400a, pp. 374–376

... [copied] During the pontificate of the Lord Dawit' [III of Aghtamar], and during the khanate of *amirza* Sk'andar [Iskandar Mīrzā] of the nation of archers [azgin netołac'], a T'urk' [Turk] by race, who captured our land and occupied by force the impregnable fortresses of our country, that is, our inaccessible island of Ałt'amar, which has not been trodden by enemy feet and which is a refuge amidst our land, as well as the impregnable fortress and the metropolis of our region, the city of Ostan [Wusṭān], and the massive Amuk. He held all these and the territories extending to Hēšat and Nəwan under his tyrannical sway and control. And he committed numerous and countless atrocities and he caused ineffable and unrecountable bitterness throughout our land, and I cannot describe in writing the destruction of our country and the decimation of its population. For this is the tenth year that the tempest of God's wrath has visited our country on account of my multitudinous sins.

I shall relate briefly the principal events which we have witnessed with our own eyes, so that those of you who come after us, after learning of our tragedies and in fear of God, shall cease to sin.

In the year 868 [of the Armenian Era = A.D. 1419] numerous locusts, as many as the sands of the sea, arrived during the time of harvest. They ate up some of the produce, and some they left untouched; but they left their seeds in the land, and in the following year the young [of the locusts] were born and caused severe destruction. But the prince of our land Amir Ēzdin [Amīr ʻIzz al-Dīn Shīr], moved by the compassion of God, dispatched some men to bring water; after the water was brought, the birds arrived and killed the locusts, and our country was saved.[35]

In the year 870 [of the Armenian Era = A.D. 1421] *amirza* Šałṙux [Shāhrukh Mīrzā] marched forth from the east with countless horsemen. Łaray Usuf [Ḳara Yūsuf], the master of T'avrēz [Tabrīz], died of natural causes, and his son, *amirza* Sk'andar [Iskandar Mīrzā], waged war against the J̌alat'ay [Čaghatai]. But he was defeated, and many of his troops were killed by them, and he barely escaped from their hands. But the king of the east took all the booty and countless goods from the T'urk [Turkish] troops, returned to his country, and the *t'ałt'* [at Tabrīz] remained without a master. Afterwards Sk'andar [Iskandar] again returned to T'avrēz [Tabrīz] and occupied it. And he assembled numerous troops, and in the following year, he marched against Xlat' [Khilāṭ] with numerous forces, and many Christians were carried off by them into captivity, and many were put to the sword /// Sk'andar [Iskandar] came /// to our country and went peacefully to T'avrēz [Tabrīz], carrying off the captives with him.

In the year 872 [of the Armenian Era = A.D. 1423] the self-same Sk'andar [Iskandar] marched against Avrel with numerous forces and occupied it. And the prince of our land set forth with countless gifts to side with him in battle; but he [Iskandar] made our prince Mēlik' Mahmad [Malik Muḥammad] drink poison and thus killed him, causing great mourning and inconsolable sadness throughout our land.

And in this year there occurred a severe plague in our land, which lingered on for two years all around our sea [Lake Van], and numerous families were decimated and many parents were left without children.

In the year 873 [of the Armenian Era = A.D. 1424] the self-same Sk'andar [Iskandar] treacherously invited before him the Sultan Ahmad [Sulṭān Aḥmad], the master of Ostan [Wusṭān], and Šəməzdin [Shams al-Dīn], the master of Bałēš [Bitlīs], and he seized both of them. He killed Šmzdin [Shams al-Dīn] at Xlat' [Khilāṭ]; and he himself proceeded toward the impregnable citadel of Van in a daring attack, filled with bitterness, and with countless troops; and he

[35] The reference here is to the prevailing belief that there were certain birds that could be lured by holy water and would eat the locusts. See Jean Deny, "La Légende de 'l'eau des sauterelles' et de l'oiseau qui détruit ces insectes," *Journal Asiatique*, 222 (1933): 323–340.

brought with him the Sultan Ahmat [Sulṭān Aḥmad] bound in iron fetters. And for two years, he ransacked and plundered our country and carried off captives. We have not sufficient paper to put in writing all the devastation that he committed in our land, all the physical torture and the grief in our souls which we suffered on the island of Ałt'amar.

In the year 874 [of the Armenian Era = A.D. 1425] *amirza* Sk'andar [Iskandar Mīrzā] captured Van and other fortresses, and he made our country his *mulk'*. And in the following year, he marched against Bałēš [Bitlīs]. This is the third year that Bałēš [Bitlīs] has been under siege [*xsar*]; and only God knows the outcome.

In the year 876 [of the Armenian Era = A.D. 1427] the self-same Sk'andar [Iskandar] captured the impregnable citadel of Maku [Mākū] from the hands of the Christians / / / and caused inconsolable grief among all the Christians, because in this entire country this was the only fortress that had remained in the hands of Christians; and this, too, he took away from us . . .

2. Place: Bałēš and Arčēš; scribe and author of col.: Melk'isēt' Bałišec'i; MS. title: Gospel.
Source: Xač'ikyan, *XV Dari*, I, no. 401a, p. 378

. . . Half of this holy Gospel was copied in the city of Bałēš [Bitlīs]. And when our sins multiplied, God was angered and dispatched upon us the baron Sk'andar [Iskandar], who arrived and besieged our city, and committed many atrocities in our city and country. He demolished many God-inhabited monasteries and shut down numerous places of worship. Hence, we took to flight and wandered about in numerous places, and we suffered much grief on account of our numerous sins, and we found no refuge. In the end God the Creator took pity upon us and through His guidance we reached the province of K'ajberunik'. We came and sojourned in the city of Arčēš [Ardjīsh], where this [Gospel] was completed . . .

3. Place: monastery of Mecop'; scribe and author of col.: Yohannēs; MS. title: Menology [*Yaysmawurk'*].
Source: Xač'ikyan, *XV Dari*, I, no. 402, p. 380

. . . [copied in A.D. 1428] during the pontificate of the Lord Pōłos [II, Gaṙnec'i], and during the imperial conquest of Šah Isk'antar [Shāh Iskandar], who occupied the *t'ałt'* and controlled numerous lands from Sōlt'aniay [Sulṭānīya] up to Mērtin [Mārdīn], and he held all of these territories in his hands. And since he was young and hard-headed, he committed much destruction in K'rdastan [Kurdistān]; he slew the barons, and he carried off much booty and many captives, on account of our multitudinous sins . . .

4. Place: monastery of Kołuc'; scribe and author of col.: Karapet; MS. title: Collection of Sermons and Lectionary [*Čaṙəntir-Tōnakan*].
Source: Xač'ikyan, *XV Dari*, I, no. 403a, b, pp. 380–381

. . . [copied] in the year 877 of our [Armenian] Era [A.D. 1428]. During the imperial conquest and the reign of *imirza* Isk'andar [Iskandar Mīrzā], who held the *t'axt*, and who ruled over Persia [Parsic'] and Babylonia [Babelac'woc'], Armenia and Syrian Mesopotamia [Mijagetac' Asorwoc'], from the Armenian province of Ararat up to Eznkay [Erzindjān], Merdin [Mārdīn], Bałdat [Baghdad] Sawlt'aniay [Sulṭānīya], and the *šahastan* of T'awrēz [Tabrīz] in Ganjak, and up to the great river K'uṙ [Kura]. All of these Isk'andar *imirza* [Iskandar Mīrzā] held in tyranny . . .

Among others, say "May God have mercy" upon Yohanēs, Ełi, and his grandmother Iktiš, for this book was completed at Arckē, since we had fled from [the hands of] the K'urd [Kurds], and we had taken shelter in their home; may Christ offer refuge to their souls, amen!

5. Place: [Ostan?]; scribe and author of col.: Step'anos; MS. title: Abstract of Commentary on the Gospel.
Source: Xač'ikyan, *XV Dari*, I, no. 404, p. 381

. . . [copied] during the pontificate of the Lord Pawłos [II, Gaṙnec'i, in Cilicia] and of [the Lord] Dawit' [III] at Ałt'amar; during the khanate of Sk'andar [Iskandar], in grievous and evil times, when the cost [of goods] was extremely high, so that a bale [*beṙ*] of bread was worth 1000 *dram*.

6. Place: village of Ankełakut'; scribe and author of col.: Movsēs Ankełakut'ec'i; MS. title: Gospel.
Source: Xač'ikyan, *XV Dari*, I, no. 405, p. 382

... [copied in A.D. 1428] during the khanate of Sk'andar *mirza* [Iskandar Mīrzā], and the principality of Bēšken, and when Šapan was the *tanutēr* [householder] ...

7. Place: village of Šušu, bishopric of Amarasay, in Ałuank'; scribe and author of col.: Manawēl; MS. title: Gospel.
Source: Xač'ikyan, *XV Dari*, I, no. 408a, p. 384

... [copied] in the year 877 of the Armenian Era [A.D. 1428], in the land of Ałuank' [Caucasian Albania], in the bishopric of Amarasay, in the village named Šušu ... during the catholicosate of the Lord Yohanēs, may whom the Lord Jesus protect for many years; and during the tyrannical rule of Ǝsk'andar [Iskandar], who is a T'orgomacin and a persecutor of Christians; and God is [our] only hope ...

8. Place: monastery of K't'isoy in bishopric of Amarasay; scribe and author of col.: Manawēl; MS. title: Gospel.
Source: Xač'ikyan, *XV Dari*, I, no. 409a, p. 385

... This Gospel was copied in the year 877 of the Armenian Era [A.D. 1428] ... in the bishopric of Amarasay, in the monastery of K't'isoy, in bitter and evil times, when the T'orgomac'i people ruled the country, and when everyone was in great grief, and when [our] salvation depended on the will of the Lord ...

1429

1. Place: monastery of Manuēli, near Ayrivank', in canton of Gaṙni; scribe and author of col.: Grigor; MS. title: *Manrusmunk'*.
Source: Xač'ikyan, *XV Dari*, I, no. 417, p. 391

... In this year [1429] the Č'ałat'ay [Čaghatai] Šahṙux [Shāhrukh], son of Lang-T'amur [Tīmūr Lang], came from Samarłand [Samarkand] in the east, with numerous troops and countless horsemen, and captured the city of Dawrēž [Tabrīz]; and he plundered the T'urk'man [Turkmens] and carried off numerous captives. The only consolation was that he did not kill and shed blood; [rather], he dispersed the T'urk'man [Turkmens] on the face of the earth. After abandoning their own dwellings, the Christians took to flight and sought refuge in caves and holes. After routing the T'urk'man [Turkmens], he plundered Armenia; they [his troops] appropriated the foodstuff and the wine, and committed much destruction in our country. And our nation is in grave danger; terror and fear have engulfed us; and we are fearful that in the spring he will carry off our entire people into captivity; but He, Who delivered mankind from the servitude of Satan, will deliver [us].

This was copied in the year 878 of the Armenian Era [A.D. 1429] ... in bitter and evil times, when we fled and came to this monastery [of Manuēli], and remained here for two months ...

2. Place: monastery of J̌orehangist in canton of Ekełeac'; scribe and author of col.: Grigor Tiwrikec'i; MS. title: Ritual Book [*Maštoc'*].
Source: Xač'ikyan, *XV Dari*, I, no. 422, p. 394

... [copied] In the year 878 of the Armenian Era [A.D. 1429], during the rule of Awt'man Pak [Ḳara Yoluḳ 'Uthmān] ...

1430

1. Place: monastery of Małard; scribe and author of col.: Mxit'ar; MS. title: Hymnal [*Ganjaran*].
Source: Xač'ikyan, *XV Dari*, I, no. 426a, p. 396

... this was completed in the year 879 of our [Armenian] Era [A.D. 1430] ... in bitter and anxious times, for Šahṙuł Łan [Shāhrukh Khān] arrived in our country and committed much destruction. He carried off captives from Armenia and subjected us to misfortunes, on account of my manifold sins. A thousand woes unto me, for with my own eyes I saw how my own people, who were delivered by the blood of Christ, were carried off into captivity, and how they became denuded, how they famished, and how they came under the servitude of the iniquitous ones ...

2. Restorer and binder of MS. and author of col.: Step'anos; MS. title: Gospel.
Source: Xač'ikyan, *XV Dari*, I, no. 427, p. 397

> ... And out of fear of the wicked Šahəṙux [Shāhrukh],
> Who plundered our Haykaznean [Armenian] land,
> This [Gospel] was hidden in a rock,
> And there gushed a stream of water,
> And upset the ever flowing living spring ...

1431

1. Place: city of Amit‘ in canton of Mijaget; scribe and author of col.: Grigor; MS. title: Gospel.
Source: Xač‘ikyan, *XV Dari*, I, no. 433a, p. 403

. . . [copied] During the pontificate of the Lord Kostandin [VI] Vahkec‘i . . . and during the reign in all of Mijaget [Mesopotamia] of the baron of barons named Šah Awt‘man Pahatur [Shāh ‘Uthmān Bahādur]; in the year 880 of the Haykazean Era [A.D. 1431] . . .

2. Place: city of Erznkay; scribe and author of col.: Łazar; MS. title: Gospel.
Source: Xač‘ikyan, *XV Dari*, I, no. 434, p. 407

. . . In these bitter, grievous, and anxious times, when the Hagarac‘ik‘ [Hagarians], who are called T‘urk‘iman [Turkmen], were harassing the Christians, and when the faithful Christians upon the face of the earth were suffering grave anguish . . .

3. Place: Hizan (?); restorer and binder of MS. and author of col.: Nersēs; MS. title: Gospel.
Source: Xač‘ikyan, *XV Dari*, I, no. 441, p. 412

. . . The monk Hayrapet . . . bought this [Gospel] in memory of his soul and for his personal enjoyment . . . in the year 880 of the Great Armenian Era [A.D. 1431], during the catholicosate of the Haykazean nation of the Lord Kostandin [VI, Vahkac‘i], and of our catholicosate at Ałt‘amar of the Lord Dawit‘ [III], and during the reign in our region of Amir Dayut [Amīr Davud], and during the khanate in our country of Sk‘antar [Iskandar] . . .

1432

1. Place: monastery of Ereran in canton of Ekełeac‘; scribe and author of col.: Dawit‘; MS. title: Ritual Book [*Maštoc‘*].
Source: Xač‘ikyan, *XV Dari*, I, no. 448a, p. 419

. . . [completed] in the year 881 of the Great Armenian Era [A.D. 1432] /// during [the pontificate of the Lord] Kostandin [VI, Vahkac‘i], and during the imperial conquest, by the consent of God, of Sk‘andar [Iskandar] . . . in bitter times, when there occurred a severe famine, so much so that many people ate impure animals. Moreover, they also ate human flesh at Dawrēž [Tabrīz], and they also sold to one another the fat of humans as though it was [the fat] of animals. This punishment befell us when, on account of our multitudinous sins, King Šahṙuh [Shāhrukh], of the wicked Persian [Parsic‘] nation called Č‘ałat‘ay [Čaghatai], invaded Armenia for the second time. He devastated and demolished numerous places, and he carried off numerous captives. Moreover, there remained neither women nor children in the provinces of Vaspurakan and K‘aǰberunik‘, for he carried them all off to Samərłand [Samarkand]. And after his departure, there occurred the aforementioned famine, and for four years the tempest of agitation did not cease in our country; rather, it is still with us . . .

2. Place: Bǰni; donor of MS. and author of col.: Catur; MS. title: Gospel.
Source: Xač‘ikyan, *XV Dari*, I, no. 450, p. 421

. . . in evil and wicked times, in the year 881 of the Haykazean Era [A.D. 1432], at a time of anarchy in our canton of Ararat, when we were dispersed as foreigners among . . . the Georgians [Vrac‘]. Thus, at this same time . . . I, Catur, servant of the servants of God, master, prefect and overseer of our city of Bǰni, and my wife, Saribēk, having reached a ripe old age . . . devoutly acquired this holy Gospel . . . and offered it most gladly to our archepiscopal see of Bǰni . . .

3. Place: monastery of Agulis in canton of Gołt‘n; scribe and author of col.: T‘umay; MS. title: Histories by Michael the Syrian, Vardan, and Kirakos.
Source: Xač‘ikyan, *XV Dari*, I, no. 453, p. 423

. . . [copied] during the reign of the abominable, wicked, and alien Sk‘antar [Iskandar], and the catholicosate of the Lord Kostandin [VI, Vahkac‘i] . . .

4. Place: city of Arčēš in province of K‘aǰberunik‘; scribe: Karapet; recipient of MS. and author of col.: Mkrtič‘; MS. title: Ritual Book [*Maštoc‘*].
Source: Xač‘ikyan, *XV Dari*, I, no. 455, pp. 424–425

. . . This was written in the year 881 of the Armenian Era [A.D. 1432], in wicked and bitter times, when the Christians suffered, by God's consent, multifarious afflictions at the hands of the iniquitous ones, on account of our manifold sins. During the reign of the destroyer of the world and foolish Sk'antar [Iskandar], and the pontificate of the Lord Kostandin [VI, Vahkac'i] . . .

5. Place: begun in city of Amit' and completed at the monastery of Erkēn-Ǝnkuzec' in canton of C'ałman in province of Č'mškacak; scribe and author of col.: Grigor Kuzec'i; MS. title: Gospel.
Source: Xač'ikyan, *XV Dari*, I, no. 458, p. 426

. . . [completed] during the catholicosate in Kilikia [Cilicia] of the Lord Kostandin [VI, Vahkac'i], and during the imperial conquest of Ōt'man Bēk [Ḳara Yoluḳ 'Uthmān Beg]; in the year 881 of the Armenian Era [A.D. 1432].[36]

1433

1. Place: village of Uranc'; scribe and author of col.: T'umay; MS. title: Gospel.
Source: Xač'ikyan, *XV Dari*, I, no. 471, p. 433

. . . [copied] through tribulations and in much wandering, in bitter and grievous times. For the wicked P'iri Bēk [Pīr Beg] arrived stealthily and besieged and captured the island of Ałt'amar, and we, fleeing from that place naked and deprived of our ancestral possessions, came to live in the Christ-protected village of Uranc', where I copied this holy Gospel . . .

2. Place: village of Surbkanc' in province of Mokk'; MS. title: Gospel.
Source: Xač'ikyan, *XV Dari*, I, no. 472b, pp. 434–435

> . . . The horsemen marched forth from the east,
> They attacked the metropolis,
> Carried off booty and captives.
> P'ir Bek [Pīr Beg] brought darkness to us,
> He landed on the island of Ałt'amar,
> Carried off crucifixes and gospels . . .

[36] This text is a summary, done by M. Tēr-Movsisean, of the original colophon. See Xač'ikyan, *XV Dari*, I, p. 426, note.

3. Place: village of Mokunk'; MS. title: Gospel.
Source: Xač'ikyan, *XV Dari*, I, no. 478, p. 438

... [copied in 1433], during the barony of Amir Abtal, and the pontificate of the Lord Kostandin [VI, Vahkac'i] ...[37]

1435

1. Place: monastery of Karmir [in Č'mškacag]; scribe and author of col.: Grigor; MS. title: Ritual Book [*Maštoc'*].
Source: Xač'ikyan, *XV Dari*, I, no 493a, p. 448

... [copied in A.D. 1435], during the pontificate of the Lord Kostandin [VI, Vahkac'i], and during the tyrannical rule of Awt'man Bēk [Ḳara Yoluḳ 'Uthmān Beg] ...

2. Place: monastery of Erkayn-Ənkuzeac' [in Č'mškacag]; scribe and author of col.: Minas; MS. title: Menology [*Yaysmawurk'*].
Source: Xač'ikyan, *XV Dari*, I, no. 494, p. 449

... [copied in 1435] during the pontificate of [the Lord] Kostandin [VI, Vahkac'i] ... during the barony of Ōt'man Bēk Xan [Ḳara Yoluḳ 'Uthman Bēg Khān], and when the *nayip* of the canton was Xošladam, for whom this book was copied and in whose name was built this monastery at Arzn ...

3. Place: monastery of Mecop' in K'aǰberunik'; editor of MS. and author of col.: T'ovma Mecop'ec'i; MS. title: Commentary on the Fourteen Epistles of Paul.
Source: Xač'ikyan, *XV Dari*, I, no. 495a, p. 452

... before this holy book was completed, the iniquitous King Šahruh [Shāhrukh] arrived in our country with numerous troops, and besieged the citadel of Ernǰak, and the T'urk'man [Turkmens] left for the interior of Armenia. Their king, named Sk'andar [Iskandar], killed the King of Amit' [Āmid] and of all of Diarbak [Diyarbakir], named Ōt'man [Ḳara Yoluḳ 'Uthmān], who had shown great love

[37] This text is a summary, done by Łewond P'irłalēmean, of the original colophon. See Xač'ikyan, *XV Dari*, I, p. 438, note.

for the Christians and the ecclesiastics. As for us, we fled [from the monastery of Mecop'] and arrived in the city of Xlat' [Khilāṭ], where we witnessed the bitterness caused by the self-same Antichrist [*Neṙn*]. For the multitudes of the Kurdish [Marac'] forces cried out to one another from the mountains and the hills, and they assembled in the demon-inhabited city, and they planned to slaughter our suffering nation. And who can recount the tragic laments and the sounds of crying and the clamor which the Christians and the infidels uttered, for they left behind neither animals, nor wearing apparel, nor foodstuffs. We barely escaped from their hands, and by night arrived in the mountains of Bałēš [Bitlīs]. When the news reached the reverend archbishop Lord Step'anos as well as the multitude of Christ-loving priests and God-loving population, both the old and the young in unison lamented for us. They flocked together and left their city and villages, and with tearful eyes and with sighs they came and found us in the mount of Urtab, and they rejoiced with indescribable joy. As for the God-honored and Christ-loving man of God, the Lord Step'anos, he led on foot all the priests and people, like David walking before the ark of God, and came to meet us. He gave thanks to God and made all the people do likewise, in great rejoicing, for having found us all in good health; and he, like a true apostle and prophet, made us, the unworthy ones, the object of their love. Besides, he also offered us his God-inhabited religious institution, together with its priests, its provisions, its animals, and all other material effects . . .

4. Place: city of Van; scribe and author of col.: Karapet; MS. title: Gospel.
Source: Xač'ikyan, *XV Dari*, I, no. 497, pp. 456–457

. . . [copied] in the year 884 of the Armenian Era [A.D. 1435], during the pontificate of [the Lord] Kostandin [VI, Vahkac'i] . . . in bitter and most grievous times, when, on account of our multitudinous sins, the gates of Xorasan [Khurāsān] were opened, and Šahṙux [Shāhrukh], son of T'amur [Tīmūr Lang], came to Armenia, and when Isk'andar [Iskandar], son of Łara Usuf [Ḳara Yūsuf], fled into the interior of the country and killed Łara Ōt'man [Ḳara Yoluḳ 'Uthmān] and his son, as well as many of his men. And his [Iskandar's] other brother, J̌xanšay [Djihānshāh], went and submitted to Šaxṙux [Shāhrukh] in person, and by the latter's order he [Djihānshāh] occupied [the throne] at T'awrēz [Tabrīz]. The two brothers became adversaries, and we do not know what our lot will be . . .

5. Place: city of Amit‘; scribe and author of col.: Grigor; MS. title: Hymnal [*Ganjaran*].
Source: Xač‘ikyan, *XV Dari*, I, no. 499, p. 458

... [copied] during the pontificate of the Lord Kostandin [VI, Vahkac‘i], and during the reign of Awt‘man Bēk's [Ḳara Yoluḳ ‘Uthmān] son, King Ali Bēk [‘Alī Bayāndur Beg]; may the Lord God grant him victory over his enemies ...

1436

1. Place: village of Krcanis near Tp‘xis in Vrac‘tan; scribe and author of col.: Yohanēs; MS. title: Hymnal [*Ganjaran*].
Source: Xač‘ikyan, *XV Dari*, I, no. 505, p. 461

... [copied in A.D. 1436] during the pontificate of the Lord Kostandin [VI, Vahkac‘i] ... [and] during the reign of King Alēk‘sandr [Alexander I, the Great] of the Georgians [Vrac‘], in anxious and bitter times, when, on account of my multitudinous sins, the wicked and iniquitous Šalṙux [Shāhrukh] arrived and committed great destruction in the country. I then journeyed to the blessed places in Erusałēm [Jerusalem], and kissed the Holy Sepulcher as well as all the other dominical holy places. Upon my return I secured at Dməšx [Damascus] the paper and other writing materiel for this manuscript, and brought them with me to Vrac‘tun [Georgia]. I left the paper there and went to Ganjak, because I longed to see my brother and relatives. But the atrocities of the wicked J̌ałat‘ [Čaghatai] caused us anguish; hence, we took all our ecclesiastical vestments, the chasubles, the Gospels, the holy books and the censers, in fact all the spiritual and physical effects which we had, and with a large caravan proceeded to Vrac‘tun. We journeyed as far as Ałestew, where we encountered the *illar* of the J̌ałat‘ [Čaghatai], that is, numerous horsemen. And they looted us as well as all the Christians; and they denuded us, save our footwear, despite the wintry weather and the cold. When we arrived at the fortress of Gavazan, the Christians came out to meet us and covered our naked bodies. And I went with tearful eyes and took the [writing] paper ...

2. Place: Ałt‘amar; scribe and author of col.: Daniēl; MS. title: Gospel.
Source: Xač‘ikyan, *XV Dari*, I, no. 506, p. 463

. . . [copied] during the pontificate of the Lord Zak'aria [III of Aghtamar], and in the year 885 of the Armenian Era [A.D. 1436] . . . in bitter and grievous times, when the iniquitous tyrant P'iri Bēk [Pīr Beg] arrived and captured our island of Alt'amar, and completely ransacked and plundered it. We fled and, deprived of all our ancestral possessions, took refuge for two years in the God-protected village of Uranc', until the great Lord sent men after us and brought us back. But he is now dead, and we live in doubt and are downcast. And all of this came to pass because of our multitudinous sins . . .

3. Place: Bałēš; scribe and author of col.: Step'anos; MS. title: Menology [*Yaysmawurk'*].
Source: Xač'ikyan, *XV Dari*, I, no. 508, p. 465

. . . [copied] during the pontificate of the Lord Kostandin [VI, Vahkac'i] . . . [and] during the tyrannical rule in our country of Armenia of Łaray Usuf's [Ḳara Yūsuf] son, Sk'andar [Iskandar], the destroyer and devastator of all the cantons from Darband [Derbend] to Sewast [Sebastia = Sivas], who became the second Ašraf [Čūbānid Malik Ashraf] to our nation; and during the rule [in our region] of our *amiray* Šex Mahmut [Amīr Shaykh Maḥmūd] . . .

4. Place: monastery of Sałmosavank' in canton of Ayrarat; scribe and author of col.: Karapet; MS. title: Ritual Book [*Maštoc'*].
Source: Xač'ikyan, *XV Dari*, I, no. 509, p. 466

. . . [copied] in the year 885 [of the Armenian Era = A.D. 1436] during the tyrannical rule of Sk'andar [Iskandar] . . .

5. Place: monastery of Aguleac'; scribe and author of col.: Yovhannēs; MS. title: History of the General Theodorus.
Source: Xač'ikyan, *XV Dari*, I, no. 510, p. 466

This history was copied in the year 885 of the Armenian Era [A.D. 1436], during the reign of the T'orgoma Askantar [Iskandar], son of Usep' [Ḳara Yūsuf], and during the pontificate of the Lord Kostandin [VI, Vahkac'i] . . .

6. Place: monastery of Karmir in canton of Erapōlis or Č'mškacak; scribe and author of col.: Mkrtič'; MS. title: Hymnal [*Ganjaran*].
Source: Xač'ikyan, *XV Dari*, I, no. 511, p. 466

. . . This holy book was copied in the year 885 of our [Armenian] Era [A.D. 1436], during the pontificate in Cilicia [Kiwlikec'woc'] of the Lord Kostandin [VI, Vahkac'i], and during the imperial conquest of Ali Pēk ['Alī Bayāndur Beg] . . .

1437

1. Place: monastery of Sanahin; scribe and author of col.: Šmawon; MS. title: Hymnal [*Šaraknoc'*].
Source: Xač'ikyan, *XV Dari*, I, no. 514a, pp. 468–470

. . . [completed] in the year 886 of the Haykazean Era [A.D. 1437], and during the reign of the pious King Alek'sandr [Alexander I, the Great] of Georgia [Vrac'], and the principality in our region of the prince of princes, Baron Bēšk'en, of the Ōrbelean family, and of his son, Baron Ǝṙəstam, who is my spiritual son . . .

/ / / in personal anguish, on account of the bitterness of our time, and numerous afflictions, and the destruction of Armenia. For the accursed and wicked tyrant and forerunner Antichrist [*Neṙn*], the son of Satan, Šahəṙux [Shāhrukh], son of T'amur [Tīmūr Lang] from the Persian [Parsic'] nation, marched forth from the south with numerous forces and countless horsemen. He came and devastated and looted our country, and he enslaved everyone; and he also forced our conqueror Askandar [Iskandar], son of Yusuf [Ḳara Yūsuf], from the nation of T'orgom [azgn T'orgoma], to flee. Who can describe in writing the tragedy and lamentation and manifold grief and bitterness of our time? For this was the third time that he [Shāhrukh] arrived and devastated and caused darkness to fall upon our churches. And because they completely destroyed our angel-inhabited see of the Holy Apostles at the monastery of Ewstat'ē, and because they set all the dwellings on fire and looted all its possessions, we the monastics fled in unison and scattered about in the land of the Georgians [Vrac' ašxarh], together with our God-given prince and all-blessed baron of barons, Bēšk'en, as well as with the nobles and the people. For this reason, we lived in the holy monastery at Sanahin . . . but we suffered great grief and anguish, by day and night, on account of the devastation of our country and the gloomy state of our churches. Bēšk'en, the baron of barons and the prince of princes . . . again brought relief to our suffering nation; he appealed in person to the tyrant and freed all the captives from the hands of his troops . . .

2. Place: Sewerak‘; scribe and author of col.: Mxit‘ar; MS. title: Gospel.
Source: Xač‘ikyan, *XV Dari*, I, no. 515, p. 471

. . . the accursed dog [from the nation of] archers [*netołakan*], Šahṙux *imirzē* [Shāhrukh Mīrzā], arrived with numerous and countless troops. He devastated Armenia, carried off many into captivity and slaughtered them, he demolished and burned, and forced many to renounce their faith. And I witnessed all this and uttered woes for myself and for those who could hear me. And with tearful eyes and anguished heart I left my parents, brothers, sisters, and mother and came to this city of Hamit‘ [Āmid] and, at the behest of the Christians at Sewerak‘, I remained here and copied this holy Gospel . . .

3. Place: city of Xłat‘; scribe and author of col.: Astuacatur; MS. title: Gospel.
Source: Xač‘ikyan, *XV Dari*, I, no. 516, p. 472

. . . [copied] during the universal pontificate of the Lord Kostandin [VI, Vahkac‘i], and of the Lord Catholicos Zak‘ar [Zak‘aria III] in our province of Ałt‘amar, and during the imperial conquest of J̌xanšay *amirza* [Djihānshāh Mīrzā], who forced his own brother Sk‘andar [Iskandar] to flee. He also marched upon Aləнjay and besieged [*xsar*] it with numerous troops . . .

4. Place: monastery of C‘awłac‘k‘ar in canton of Ełegeac‘; scribe and author of col.: Matt‘ēos; MS. title: Hymnal [*Šaraknoc‘*].
Source: Xač‘ikyan, *XV Dari*, I, no. 517, p. 472

. . . Completed in bitter and anxious times, when Armenia was controlled by the T‘urk‘man [Turkmens], who subjected our entire country to the sword and to famine, and carried off captives, and there was no consolation for us from any quarter . . .

5. Place: city of Van; scribe and author of col.: Karapet; MS. title: Gospel.
Source: Xač‘ikyan, *XV Dari*, I, no. 518a, p. 473

. . . [copied] in the year 886 of the Armenian Era [A.D. 1437], during the pontificate of the Lord Kostandin [VI, Vahkac‘i], and during the reign of J̌xanšay *amirza* [Djihānshāh Mīrzā] . . . in bitter and most grievous times when, on account of our multitudinous sins, the plague spread from Asorik' [northern Syria] to Hayk' [Armenia], and mercilessly killed countless children and infants . . .

6. Place: monastery of Betłahem in Tip'xis; scribe and author of col.: Karapet; MS. title: Hymnal [*Ganjaran*].
Source: Xač'ikyan, *XV Dari*, I, no. 520, p. 475

In the year 886 of the Armenian Era [A.D. 1437] . . . during the reign of King Ałēk'sandr [Alexander I, the Great] of the Georgians [Vrac'] . . .

7. Place: monastery of St. Gēorg Zawravar in canton of Balu; scribe and author of col.: Awetik'; MS. title: Gospel.
Source: Xač'ikyan, *XV Dari*, I, no. 522, p. 476

. . . [completed] in bitter and in anxious times, when the plague ordained by God prevented the priests from eating food.[38]

. . . [copied] during the catholicosate of the Lord Kostandin [VI, Vahkac'i] in Kilikia [Cilicia], and during the imperial conquest in Mijaget [Mesopotamia] by Sultan Hamzay [Sulṭān Ḥamza Bayūndur]; in the year 886 of the Armenian Era [A.D. 1437] . . .

8. Place: village of T'ac'u; scribe and author of col.: Yusēp'; MS. title: Gospel.
Source: Xač'ikyan, *XV Dari*, I, no. 523, p. 477

. . . [copied] in the year 886 of the Armenian Era [A.D. 1437], during the pontificate of the Lord Catholicos Step'anos of the see of Ałt'amar, and during the barony of Awdal Bēk, in bitter and grievous times . . .[39]

9. Purchaser of MS. and author of col.: Yōsēp'; MS. title: Philosophical Works.
Source: Xač'ikyan, *XV Dari*, I, no. 527, p. 479

[38] This passage suggests that the plague was so intense and the priests were so busy officiating at the burial of the numerous dead that they had no time to eat.

[39] Originally, Xač'ikyan included this text among the colophons of A.D. 1357, although he expressed certain reservations concerning the accuracy of the date. (See *XIV Dari*, no. 518, p. 432, and n. 2.) The text published under the year 1437 is identical with that under 1357, except that it contains sections not found in the first. An examination of the two texts convinces us that the colophon was written in A.D. 1437.

In the name of God; in the year 1437 of our Lord, on the nineteenth of June, I, Fra Yōsēpʻ, vardapet and overseer, bought [this collection of] philosophical works for eleven *tʻankay* from the Lord Bishop Yohanēs, with my *halal* [honestly earned] assets . . . In this year I became forty-nine years old; and the king was J̌hanša [Djihānshāh].

1438

1. Place: city of Arckē; scribe and author of col.: Yovhanēs; MS. title: Missal [*Čašocʻ*].
Source: Xačʻikyan, *XV Dari*, I, no. 535, pp. 484–485

. . . This was copied during the pontificate of the great Armenian see of the Lord and universal Catholicos Kostandin [VI, Vakhacʻi], and under the spiritual leadership in our region of the valiant and *rabuni* hermitical vardapet Tʻovma Mecopʻecʻi, in bitter and wicked times, when Šahṙux [Shāhrukh], of the Čʻałatʻay [Čaghatai] people, arrived and put Skʻandar [Iskandar] to flight /// and the horsemen of Šahṙux [Shāhrukh] attacked the fortress of Šamiram [Semiramis], which is the citadel of Van, because /// Skʻandar's [Iskandar] brother, J̌hanšah [Djihānshāh] [was there?]; and he came out of the citadel and went to Šahṙux [Shāhrukh] in person, and [the latter] pardoned him and gave him the *tʻaxt* with its *tʻaman*, and then departed. Later, Skʻandar [Iskandar] returned and, putting his brother [Djihānshāh] to flight, he occupied the *tʻaxt*. There remained only one from among the barons of J̌hanšah [Djihānshāh] at the citadel of Amuk, namely, the accursed Pʻir Ali [Pīr ʻAlī], who every day came out of the citadel and attacked the regions of Arčēš [Ardjīsh] and Arckē. He harassed, he killed some, and he took as captives the children of some, and their parents burned with heart-rending grief and could not help their innocent lambs.

And we witnessed more grief when the iniquitous one [Pīr ʻAlī], after failing to bring out of their house the *tanutēr* [householder], three children and two men, burned the house, including these individuals [who died] as brave martyrs . . .

2. Place: monastery of Hałbat [in Georgia]; scribe Yohanēs; author of col.: Astuacatur; MS. title: Missal [*Čašocʻ*].
Source: Xačʻikyan, *XV Dari*, I, no. 536, pp. 485–486

. . . I, the sinful priest Astuacatur, yearned for this sacred book in bitter and grievous times, when Šahṙux [Shāhrukh], son of the great

Xorazm [Khwārizmī] T'amur [Tīmūr Lang], four times invaded our region of T'avrēz [Tabrīz] with numerous merciless, perfidious, and cruel horsemen who were thirsty for the blood of the Christians, and also committed much and indescribable destruction in Armenia. He killed some by the sword; he mercilessly carried off some into captivity and annihilated them; some died of starvation; some died of the plague; some were devoured by the wolves and wild beasts; and the rest fled hither and thither and took refuge in Georgia [Vrac' ašxarh]. Our country was completely depopulated and demolished; the gates of the heavenly temples were shut down, and their candles and lanterns were extinguished and were darkened; the incense and the pious contributions diminished, and the prayers and the singing of the psalms decreased and ceased; and the oblations of the mass and all the sacred ecclesiastical effects, the crucifixes and Gospels, and all the vestments, the church vessels, were captured by the Muslims [*aylazgi*]. And great grief, lamentation, sadness, and anguish befell the Armenian churches; and we became like Israyēl [Israel] of old, trampled underfoot and the object of ridicule to all nations. And all of this was meted out to us because of our multitudinous, prodigal, irrevocable, and impenitent sins.

. . . [copied] during the reign of King Alek'sandr [Alexander I, the Great] of Georgia [Vrac'], and during the barony in our province of Loṙi of the illustrious and pious prince of princes, Baron Bēšk'en Ōrbēlean, grandson of the great Baron Biwrt'ēl; in the year 887 of the Haykazean Era [A.D. 1438].

3. Place: Axalc'xay in Georgia; scribe and author of col.: Sargis; MS. title: Gospel.
   Source: Xač'ikyan, *XV Dari*, I, no. 537, p. 486

. . . [copied] in the year 887 of the Great Armenian Era [A.D. 1438] . . . when Šahṙuh [Shāhrukh] marched against Sk'andar [Iskandar], who fled as far as Sewast [Sebastia = Sivas], and devastated numerous cantons, and he carried off many captives from among the Armenians, many of whom perished in the mountain from nakedness and the cold, and many died of starvation. He [Iskandar] then marched against [his brother] J̌hanša [Djihānshāh]; however, because of the [latter's] superior forces all of his [Iskandar's] horsemen went over to his brother; and he, escaping from his brother J̌hanšah [Djihānshāh], took refuge in the fortress of Ernjak, where he received the reward of eternal torture [that is, he was killed by his son Shāh-Ḳubād] . . .

4. Place: Bałēš; scribe and author of col.: Kirakos; MS. title: Menology [*Yaysmawurk*‘].
Source: Xač‘ikyan, *XV Dari*, I, no. 538, pp. 486–487

... [copied] during the pontificate of the Lord Kostandin [VI, Vahkac‘i] and during the amirate of Šex Mahmat [Shaykh Maḥmūd] in our city [of Bitlīs], and the khanate of J̌hanšay *mirza* [Djihānshāh Mīrzā], in which year [A.D. 1437] his brother, Sk‘andar [Iskandar], was slain by his son [Shāh-Ḳubād], and J̌hanšay [Djihānshāh] occupied the *t‘alt‘* ...

5. Place: Təp‘xis; MS. title: Hymnal [*Ganjaran*].
Source: Xač‘ikyan, *XV Dari*, I, no. 540a, pp. 487–488

... [copied in A.D. 1438] during the pontificate of the Lord Kostandin [VI, Vahkac‘i], and during the reign in Georgia [Vrac‘] of the pious and devout King Ałēk‘sandrē [Alexander I, the Great], may whom the Lord God preserve in chaste life for many years, together with his troops and children, so that he may expel and repulse the infidel cohorts and also protect the holy church ...

6. Place: Gori; scribe and author of col.: Yohannēs; MS. title: Gospel.
Source: Xač‘ikyan, *XV Dari*, I, no. 541, p. 489

... [copied] during the reign of King Ałek‘sandr [Alexander I, the Great] in Georgia [Vrac‘] ... in the year 887 [of the Armenian Era = A.D. 1438] ...

1439

1. Place: monastery of Awak‘ in canton of Ekełeac‘ or Daranałeac‘; scribe and author of col.: Simēon; MS. title: Menology [*Yaysmawurk*‘].
Source: Xač‘ikyan, *XV Dari*, I, no. 553a, p. 496

... [completed] in bitter times, when Xul invaded with 100,000 troops, but he committed no destruction. After him, there arrived Ayxanənlu and committed much destruction ...

2. Place: monastery of Cnanaṙič in canton of Daranałeac'; MS. title: Missal [*Čašoc'*].
Source: Xač'ikyan, *XV Dari*, I, no. 555, p. 498

... This was copied in the year 888 of the Armenian Era [A.D. 1439] ... during the principality of Iału Bak [Ya'ḳūb Beg], who was a protector of the Christians. Moreover, he was not avaricious; rather, he cared for, and permitted the construction of, churches, and performed numerous other good deeds ...

1440

1. Place: monastery of Małardē; binder of MS. and author of col.: Mxit'ar; MS. title: Catechism of Cyril of Jerusalem.
Source: Xač'ikyan, *XV Dari*, I, no. 566, p. 504

... This was bound in the year 889 [of the Armenian Era = A.D. 1440] ... when the wicked, accursed, and impure J̌ihanšay *imirzay* [Djihānshāh Mīrzā] occupied Vrac'tun [Georgia], and put numerous Christians to the sword. And who can describe [the mourning] ... of the Christians and the slaughter of many of them? No tongue can describe the countless multitude of men and women, of infants and children, who were slaughtered on account of their Christian faith, for their love of Christ and hope for the holy kingdom. They preferred to die and sought from Christ the diadem of martyrs; they were slain by the sword and by stoning, and they were rewarded with eternal life. They brought to us the pretty infants whom they [the invaders] had carried off as captives, and we found them in the hands of the lawless ones, tormented and choleric, naked and famished, beaten and maltreated / / /.

2. Place: Ałt'amar; author of col.: T'umay [Minasenc']; MS. title: Gospel.
Source: Xač'ikyan, *XV Dari*, I, no. 567b, p. 505

In the year 880 of the Haykazean Era [A.D. 1431] there occurred a grave tragedy and great anguish in our land, because the amir P'iri Bēk [Amīr Pīr Beg], a K'urd [Kurd] by race [and] grandson of the amir Ēzdin [Amīr 'Izz al-Dīn Shīr], occupied the God-protected and impregnable island of Ałt'amar, which was a refuge in all our land. He plundered and carried off the vessels and ornaments of the heaven-like temple, as well as the holy books and other sacred vessels from all the monasteries and villages around the sea [Lake Van], and dispersed them far and wide . . .

3. MS. title: John Chrysostom's Commentary on the Epistle to the Ephesians.
Source: Xač'ikyan, *XV Dari*, I, no. 568, pp. 506–507

In the year 870 [of the Armenian Era = A.D. 1421] Sk'andar [Iskandar] occupied [the throne] / / /; in the year 871 [A.D. 1422] Šahṙux's [Shāhrukh] first invasion; 878 [A.D. 1429] his second invasion, and Busait [Abū Sa'īd] / / /; 885 [A.D. 1436] his [Shāhrukh] last invasion . . . In 889 [A.D. 1440] J̌anhanšay [Djihānshāh] captured Šamšuldē [Shamshwildé], slew more than three thousand [souls], carried off more than nine thousand into captivity, and caused great mourning among the Christians, and many abandoned Christ . . .

1441

1. Place: monastery of Haxbat; MS. title: Gospel.
Source: Xač'ikyan, *XV Dari*, I, no. 579, pp. 514–515

. . . [completed] in the year 890 of the Haykazean Era [A.D. 1441], in bitter and evil times, when the persecuting sword of the Ismaelites [Ismayelac'oc'] had intensified against us, as St. Sahak had foreseen in his vision, when we were afloat in all kinds of calamities from within and without . . . For in this year the *łan* [khan] of Dayvrēz [Tabrīz], J̌ahanšay *imirza* [Djihānshāh Mīrzā], son of the T'urk'man [Turkmen] Usuf [Ḳara Yūsuf], son of Łara Mahmat [Ḳara Muḥammad Tūrmush], marched forth with numerous troops and countless Mahmetakan [Muhammadan] horsemen and arrived in Verastun [Georgia] and attacked the Georgians [Vrac'], because the Georgians [azgn Vrac'] refused to submit to the Łan [Khan] of T'avrēž [Tabrīz]. When the Tačiks arrived, the Georgians [azgn Vrac'] fled and went into [the land of the] Ap'xaz [Abkhāzia]. Only the Armenians, who had come and sojourned in Vrac'tun [Georgia], were left at the mercy of the infidels. But, like ferocious beasts, they attacked the Armenians and mercilessly slew some five thousand of them. They smote with their swords and stoned and slew more than sixty monks and priests. They demolished numerous churches from their foundations. They wrested numerous children from their mothers and beat them to death with stones before the eyes of their mothers. They disrobed numerous innocent infants and pierced them with their swords; and while the children screamed, cried, and wailed the lawless ones laughed and said, "There's a sound that comes out of their *bēhēšt*"; and seeing this the mothers were pitiably and deeply grieved and wept, and no one offered them succor. Numerous women, holding their children in their bosoms, hurled themselves down into the precipice. They laid siege to the fortress of Samšultē [Shamshwildé] for three months; and after they deceitfully captured the citadel, how they ravished the goods, or how they separated the men from the women, or how they grabbed the children / / /.

2. Purchasers of MS. and authors of col.: Grigor and Barseł; MS. title: Gospel.
   Source: Xačʻikyan, *XV Dari*, I, no. 580, p. 515

In the year 979 of the Armenian Era [A.D. 1530], when J̌ahanša [Djihānshāh] besieged [*hesar*] the fortress of Loṙi, this holy Gospel fell "captive."[40]

I the Lord [priest] Grigor and the *abełay* Barseł offered 1000 *dekan*, and delivered it from bondage in memory of ourselves and of our parents, amen!

3. Place: city of Van in province of Vaspurakan; scribe and author of col.: Vardan; MS. title: Menology [*Yaysmawurkʻ*].
   Source: Xačʻikyan, *XV Dari*, I, no. 581, pp. 515–516

This was copied in the year 890 of the Great Armenian Era [A.D. 1441] . . . in bitter and evil times, during the barony of J̌hanšay [Djihānshāh], who filled with wickedness invaded Vracʻtun [Georgia] . . . and captured the fortress of Šamšultay [Shamshwildé]. They put to the sword more than nine thousand Christians, including priests; and they carried off the women and children into captivity. Who can recount or put into writing their tragic grief? And all of this came to pass in our land on account of [our] sins . . .

[40] Xačʻikyan states that the date mentioned in the colophon is A.D. 1530, which of course is erroneous. It is known that Djihānshāh invaded Georgia in 1440; hence, the editor has put the colophon under the year 1441, assuming that the MS. was recovered some time after its capture in 1440. See *XV Dari*, I, p. 515, n. 2.

4. Place: city of Arčēš in K'ajberunik'; scribe and author of col.: Yovhannēs; MS. title: Missal [*Čašoc'*].
Source: Xač'ikyan, *XV Dari*, I, no. 582a, p. 516

... [copied] during the reign of Sultan Čihanšay [Djihānshāh], of the nation of archers [azgin netołac'] ...

5. Place: city of Arckē; MS. title: Missal [*Čašoc'*].
Source: Xač'ikyan, *XV Dari*, I, no. 583, p. 517

... [copied] in bitter and wicked times, when the abominable J̌ihanša [Djihānshāh] invaded; in the year 890 of the Armenian Era [A.D. 1441], when all of these things transpired.

6. MS. title: Commentary on the Gospel by Matthew.
Source: Xač'ikyan, *XV Dari*, I, no. 584, p. 517

... [written] in the year 890 of the Great Armenian Era [A.D. 1441], on Wednesday the fifteenth of the month of March ... during the pontificate of the Lord Catholicos Grigor [X, J̌alalbēkeanc'] of All Armenians; [and] during the sultanate of Egypt [Egiptac'woc'] and the imperial conquest of Melik' Tahar [Al-Malik al-Ẓāhir Sayf al-Dīn] surnamed Č'axmax [Čaḳmaḳ]; in bitter and anxious times ... when they drove some of us from this land to other cantons, and when they separated some from their brothers and mothers ...

7. Purchaser of MS. and author of col.: Amir P'ašay; MS. title: Missal [*Čašoc'*].
Source: Xač'ikyan, *XV Dari*, I, no. 585a, p. 518

... A *mahdasi* nobleman named Amir-P'ašay, from the famous canton and from the renowned and outstanding city of Axəlc'xay [Akhal Tsikhé] ... journeyed to Erusałēm [Jerusalem] to worship at the dominical holy places. From there he returned to the east, and on his way he encountered the army of the tyrant named Šahṙux [Shāhrukh], son of Lank-T'amur [Tīmūr Lang], which had camped around the fortress of Erənčak. They had brought this book with them, which they had captured in the province of Siwnik'. The devout *mahdasi* Amir-P'ašay found this and paid for it from his own *halal* [honestly earned] assets. And he bought this book and delivered it from the Muslims' [*aylazgeac'*] bondage ...

8. Place: canton of Mawṙkay; scribe and author of col.: Sargis; MS. title: Ritual Book [*Maštocʻ*].
Source: Xačʻikyan, *XV Dari*, I, no. 586a, pp. 519–520

. . . And because of the wicked and bitter times in which we live, it is difficult to recount or put into writing the tragic calamities, the imposition of taxes, and the manifold grief and anxiety which we Christians suffered, and which was brought about by the increasing number of the infidels. Woe unto us, and again woe unto us, for the prophecy of the divinely inspired man of God, St. Nersēs, concerning the Christians came to pass, that "They shall be persecuted from all sides, and they shall be transplanted from place to place, and they shall find no comfort, at the hands of the human-faced and venomous beasts, the nation of archers." Behold, all of this came to pass, for "We say to the mountains to cover us up and to the hills to fall upon us" [cf. Luke 23:30; Revelation 6:16; Hosea 10:8], because of our intense anguish and because of these most wicked times . . .

9. Place: monastery of Gēorgay Zoravar in Kʻaǰberunikʻ; scribe and author of col.: Tʻovma Mecepʻcʻi; MS. title: Gospel.
Source: Xačʻikyan, *XV Dari*, I, no. 587, p. 522

. . . [copied] in the year 890 of our [Armenian] Era [A.D. 1441], during the pontificate of the Lord Grigor [X, J̌alalbēkeancʻ] at Holy Ēǰmiacin, and during the reign of J̌əhanša [Djihānshāh] . . .

10. Place: Erusałēm; scribe and author of col.: Grigor Arckecʻi; MS. title: Gospel.
Source: Xačʻikyan, *XV Dari*, I, no. 598, p. 529

. . . [copied] during the catholicosate of the Lord Grigor [IX, Musabēgeancʻ] in Cilicia [Kilikecʻwocʻ], and during the tyrannical rule of the Egyptians [Egiptacʻwocʻ] under Čʻaxmax [Čaḳmaḳ].

1442

1. Place: village of Serkewili in province of Ararat; scribe and author of col.: Ohannē Tʻmokʻuecʻi; MS. title: Lectionary [*Tōnakan*].

Source: Xač'ikyan, *XV Dari*, I, no. 603a, pp. 532–534

... At this time there occurred a massacre of innocent Christians at Samšuildē [Shamshwildé], who died for Christ and became martyrs. For, instigated by Satan, J̌ahanšah *mirzē* [Djihānshāh Mīrzā], of the Scythian [Skiwt'ac'woc'] race, assembled many legions of troops, besieged the citadel for four months, and caused them much anguish, for many died of grief. The iniquitous ones swore by the living God that they would inflict no harm upon them. And they, trusting their false oath, opened the gate of the citadel, and the infidels poured in and mercilessly slew more than 3000 of them. I cannot describe in writing the lamentation and the bitter anguish and grief, for they slew some by the sword, they killed some by stoning, they crushed some with cudgels, they cut off the heads of some and built three *mniras*. It was a sight to behold the awesome moaning and lamenting over the dear ones, for the mother wept over her son, the sister over the brother, the bride over the bridegroom; and they received no consolation from any quarter, neither from God nor from man.

The number of those who were carried off into captivity exceeded 9000, whom they divided amongst themselves. It was a sight to behold the calamity meted out to the parents and the children, for they separated the mother from her child and the child from its mother, and brother from brother, and bride from bridegroom, and bridegroom from bride. They cruelly wrested the tender children from the bosoms of their mothers and cast them into the river, and the mournful mothers went into captivity. They carried off some of them to Xorasan [Khurāsān] in the east, some to Hoṙmastan [Rūm] in the west, some to Arabstan [Khuzistān] in the south, [and] some to Lakstan [Daghestān] in the north, just as Israēł [the Israelites] in olden times were scattered to the four corners of the world. The father was separated from his son, the daughter from her mother, loved one from loved ones, and friends from friends, and they went to the Tačik lands never to return again. And the churches of Armenia wept even as Eremia Ełkesac'i [Jeremiah the Elkoshite] said: "Go, go, for I have become desolate; verily, verily I say unto you passers by, behold my tragic grief and wail for me, because I have become desolate and deserted by my children" [cf. Lamentations 1:12].

Yet, we need not lose faith in God, but beseech Him, with faith and through the intercession of all the saints, to return the captives, as He did in olden times to Israēl [Israel], amen!

... [copied] during the khanate of J̌ahanšah [Djihānshāh], and the reign of King Vaxt'ank [Wakhtang IV] in Georgia [Vrac'], and the principality in our region of the baron Alibēk ['Alī Beg] ...

2. Place: city of Van; scribe and author of col.: Karapet; MS. title: Menology [*Yaysmawurk'*].
Source: Xač'ikyan, *XV Dari*, I, no. 604, p. 536

... [copied] during the reign of J̌hanšah [Djihānshāh], who in this year [A.D. 1442] captured the impregnable citadels of Zəṙel and Julamerk.

3. Place: monastery of Ałǰoc' in K'ełoy-Jor in canton of Ararat; scribe and author of col.: Galust; MS. title: Missal [*Čašoc'*].
Source: Xač'ikyan, *XV Dari*, I, no. 605, pp. 536–537

... [completed] in the year 891 of the Haykazean Era [A.D. 1442], during the pontificate of the Armenians of the Lord Kirakos, and during the imperial conquest, by the will of God, of the bloodthirsty beast J̌hanšah [Djihānshāh], who, upon assuming power and upon occupying the throne of the erstwhile constructive and beneficent khans, began to devastate and destroy numerous cities and cantons, and turned them into arid and uninhabitable lands. No one can put into writing the evil which he wrought, especially in the city of Šamšuldē [Shamshwildé] in Georgia [ašxarhn Vrac'], for he captured it deceitfully and put everyone to the sword. And, as the prophet said, "There was no one to bury them" [cf. Psalms 79:3], and such was the case with them. They dispersed countless and numerous priests and laymen, as well as their wives and children, into all countries. Whose tongue can relate the tragic calamity which befell our Armenian nation this year? And it was in such bitter and anxious times that this manuscript was copied ...

4. Place: monastery of Gamałiēl [in Xizan]; scribe and author of col.: Yohannēs; MS. title: Missal [*Čašoc'*].
Source: Xač'ikyan, *XV Dari*, I, no. 607, p. 538

... [completed] in the year 891 of the Armenian Era [A.D. 1442], during the pontificate of the Lord Kirakos ... and when the amir [of our region] was the K'urd [Kurd] Amir Dayud [Amīr Davud] ...

1443

1. Place: city of Bałēš in canton of Ałjn; scribe and author of col.: Mkrtič'; MS. title: Gospel.

Source: Xač'ikyan, *XV Dari*, I, no. 620, p. 545

. . . [copied in A.D. 1443] During the imperial tyranny of the baron J̌hanšah [Djihānshāh], son of Usuf [Ḳara Yūsuf], of the nation of archers [azgin netołac']; in anxious and evil times, when justice was diminished and injustice was intensified everywhere . . .

2. Place: city of Bałēš; scribe and author of col.: Yovanēs; MS. title: Menology [*Yaysmawurk'*].
Source: Xač'ikyan, *XV Dari*, I, no. 621a, p. 546

. . . [copied] in bitter times, when we suffered grief at the hands of the infidels and Satan.

. . . [copied] in the year 891 of the Armenian Era [A.D. 1442] . . . when the amir of our city [Bitlīs] was Šix Mahmat *amirza* [Shaykh Maḥmūd Mīrzā], and during the reign of Šah J̌hanšay *amirza* [Shāh Djihānshāh Mīrzā], who slew his brother [Iskandar] at the hands of his son [Shāh-Ḳubād], and J̌hanšay *amirzē* [Djihānshāh Mīrzā] occupied the *t'alt'*. He marched into Vrac'tun [Georgia] and committed much destruction; for he captured the citadel of Šamšuldē [Shamshwildé] and slew many; for he had the priests bound together with a rope and had them stoned; and he had others cruelly beheaded. He also had 2000 women and children carried off into captivity. And all of this came to pass on account of our sins . . .

3. Place: city of Arckē; MS. title: Missal [*Čašoc'*].
Source: Xač'ikyan, *XV Dari*, I, no. 622, p. 548

. . . [completed] in the year 892 [of the Armenian Era = A.D. 1443], during the reign of J̌hanšah [Djihānshāh], son of Łaray Iwsuf [Ḳara Yūsuf] . . .

4. Restorer of MS. and author of col.: Karapet; MS. title: Gospel.
Source: Xač'ikyan, *XV Dari*, I, no. 624, p. 549

. . . In the year 892 of the Haykazean Era [A.D. 1443], in bitter and anxious and evil times, for the Christians are tottering and are dispersed at the hands of the Ismaelites [Ismayēlakan azgac'] . . . during the reign over the Christians of Vaxtang [Wakhtang IV], son of Ałēksandr [Alexander I, the Great], and the khanate of J̌ahanšah [Djihānshāh], son of Usuf [Ḳara Yūsuf], and when the prince of our region was / / / -kin, son of J̌aǰuṙ . . .

5. Place: monastery of Aɫǰoc‘ in K‘eɫoy-Jor in canton of Ararat; scribe and author of col.: Galust; MS. title: Gospel.
Source: Xač‘ikyan, *XV Dari*, I, no. 626a, p. 551

. . . This holy Gospel was copied in the year 892 of the Armenian Era [A.D. 1443], during the pontificate of the Lord Grigor [X, J̌alalbēkeanc‘], and during the reign of King Vaɫt‘ank [Wakhtang IV] in Georgia [Vrac‘], and the khanate of the bloodthirsty beast J̌ahanšah [Djihānshāh], son of Yusup‘ [Ḳara Yūsuf] . . .

6. Place: monastery of Aɫǰoc‘ in K‘eɫoy-Jor in canton of Ararat; scribe and author of col.: Galust; MS. title: Gospel.
Source: Xač‘ikyan, *XV Dari*, I, no. 628, p. 553

. . . This holy Gospel was copied in the year 892 of the Armenian Era [A.D. 1443], during the pontificate of the Lord Kirakos, and during the reign of King Vaɫt‘ank [Wakhtang IV] in Georgia [Vrac‘], and the khanate of J̌ahanšah [Djihānshāh], son of Yusup‘ [Ḳara Yūsuf] . . .

7. Scribe and author of col.: Yovhannēs; MS. title: Missal [*Čašoc‘*].
Source: Xač‘ikyan, *XV Dari*, I, no. 633, p. 558

. . . [copied] in bitter and dark times, for in this year [A.D. 1443] the Christians suffered intense grief and affliction at the hands of the iniquitous nations and the tax-collectors . . .

1444

1. Place: monastery of Ayrivank‘; MS. title: Menology [*Yaysmawurk‘*].
Source: Xač‘ikyan, *XV Dari*, I, no. 636, pp. 560–561

. . . [copied] in the year 893 of the Haykazean Era [A.D. 1444], during the pontificate of [the Lord] Grigor [X, J̌alalbēkeanc‘], incumbent of the newly restored see of Holy Ēǰmiacin, and during the imperial conquest of the valiant and victorious J̌hanšah *imirza* [Djihānshāh Mīrzā], son of the great Yusuf [Ḳara Yūsuf] . . .

2. Place: Aɫt‘amar; scribe: Hayrapet; illuminator and author of col.: T‘umay Minasenc‘; MS. title: Gospel.

Source: Xač'ikyan, *XV Dari*, I, no. 637a, pp. 563–566

... [copied] during the pontificate of the Lord Zak'aria [III] of Aghtamar], and in the year 893 of the Haykazean Era [A.D. 1444], in bitter and evil times, when the lawless nation of archers [azgn netołac'] who are the lords and kings and princes of our lands and who are T'urk' [Turks] by race, torment and cause anguish to the Christians by manifold plundering and merciless imposition of taxes, and by expelling them with their families like slaves from country to country.

... the vaulted and magnificent church of St. Vardan Zawravar was constructed during ... the khanate of Łara Yusuf [Ḳara Yūsuf], and the chief amirate in the city of Ostan [Wusṭān] of Amir Ēzdin [Amīr 'Izz al-Dīn Shīr] and of his son Mēlik' Mahamad [Malik Muḥammad] ...

... [The construction was done] During the chief amirate in our region of Mēlik' Mahmad [Malik Muḥammad], and of his father and mother ...

Moreover, this holy Gospel was illuminated during the reign of J̌əhanšay *amirza* [Djihānshāh Mīrzā], and when the *kołmnapet* of our region was the baron Łəlič-Aslan [Ḳilidj Arslan b. Pīr 'Alī] ...

3. Place: monastery of Mecop' in Arčēš in K'aǰberunik'; scribe and author of col.: T'uma; MS. title: Missal [*Čašoc'*].
Source. Xač'ikyan, *XV Dari*, I, no. 639, p. 567

[Copied] In the year 893 of the Armenian Era [A.D. 1444], during the pontificate of the Lord Grigor [X, J̌alalbēkeanc'] at Ēǰmiacin in Vałaršapat, and during the reign of J̌hanšah [Djihānshāh], who occupied two *t'axt's*, one of Armenia and the other of northern Syria [Asoroc'], and who brought about not a little peace; but the levies that he imposed upon us priests were excessive and heavy ...

4. Place: monastery of Varag; MS. title: Gospel.
Source: Xač'ikyan, *XV Dari*, I, no. 640, p. 568

... copied in the year 893 [of the Armenian Era = A.D. 1444] ... during the pontificate of the Lord Grigor [X, J̌alalbēkeanc'], who recently assumed the [office of] catholicos at Holy Ēǰmiacin, and when the catholicos at Ałt'amar was the Lord Zak'aria [III], and during the reign of J̌xanša *mirza* [Djihānshāh Mīrzā], who devastated Vrac'tun [Georgia] and carried off captives.

May God destroy him, for he demanded excessive taxes from the Christians.

5. Place: Ałt'amar; scribe and author of col.: Grigor; MS. title: Menology [*Yaysmawurk'*].
Source: Xač'ikyan, *XV Dari*, I, no. 642, p. 570

... [completed] during the pontificate of the Lord Zak'aria [III of Aghtamar], in the year 893 of the Armenian Era [A.D. 1444], in bitter and grievous times, when we suffer under the weight of levies and are in servitude of the nation of archers [azgin netołac'] ...

6. Place: Ałt'amar; scribe and author of col.: Grigor; MS. title: Ritual Book [*Maštoc'*].
Source: Xač'ikyan, *XV Dari*, I, no. 643, p. 571

... [completed] during the pontificate of the Lord Zak'aria [III of Aghtamar], in the year 893 of the Armenian Era [A.D. 1444], in bitter and grievous times, when we suffered anguish at the hands of the infidels ...

7. Place: fortress of Arłni; scribe and author of col.: Awetik'; MS. title: Gospel.
Source: Xač'ikyan, *XV Dari*, I, no. 647, p. 576

... [completed] in bitter and anxious times ... during the imperial conquest of Sultan Hamzay [Ḥamza Bayāndur], in the year 893 of the Armenian Era [A.D. 1444] ...

8. Place: fortress of Sinamut in city of Xarberd; scribe: Minas; author of col.: Grigor; MS. title: Menology [*Yaysmawurk'*].
Source: Xač'ikyan, *XV Dari*, I, no. 648, p. 576

... [illustrated] in the year 893 of the Armenian Era [A.D. 1444], during the pontificate of the Lord Grigor [IX, Musabēgeanc'] in Cilicia [Kilikec'oc'] and of the Lord Kirakos in Vałaršapat, and during the imperial conquest of Sultan Hamzay [Ḥamza Bayāndur] ...

1445

1. Place: Ałt'amar; scribe and author of col.: T'umay Minasenc'; MS. title: Ritual Book [*Maštoc'*].

Source: Xač'ikyan, *XV Dari*, I, no. 653, pp. 579–581

. . . [completed] during the imperial conquest of J̌hanšay *amirzay* [Djihānshāh Mīrzā], and when the *kołmnapet* of our region was the baron Łlič-Aslan [Kilidj Arslan b. Pīr 'Alī] who controls Van and Ostan [Wusṭān], both of whom are T'urk' [Turks] by race, and they both impose exorbitant levies on and plunder the Christians . . . during the pontificate in our province of the Lord Zak'aria [III of Aghtamar], and in the year 894 of the Haykazean Era [A.D. 1445] . . .

. . . And in the year 861 of the Haykazean Era [A.D. 1412], when the *t'ałt'* was occupied by Łaray Yusuf [Ḳara Yūsuf] and when the *kołmnapets* of our region were Ēmir Ezdin [Amīr 'Izz al-Dīn Shīr] and his son Melik' [Malik Muḥammad], who was most beneficent and friendly toward the Christians, and during the pontificate in our see of the Lord Dawit' [III of Aghtamar], a certain renowned and beneficent vardapet, endowed with God-given qualities, called Step'annos and surnamed P'ir, from the village of Baxvanic' in the province of Ṙštunik', who had been the pupil of Yohan Orotnec'i surnamed Kaxik, wandered about in many lands on a preaching mission. He spent many years in the land of Rūm [Hṙomoc']; he journeyed twice to Erusałēm [Jerusalem]; and then he returned to his native country of Armenia with many gifts to all the churches, and he brought chasubles and chalices and Gospels for the monasteries and for the churches of the villages. In response to his exhortations and under his leadership, the Christians constructed more than ten domed and lime-plastered churches in the province of Ṙštunik', during the chief amirate of Melik' [Malik Muḥammad] and of his father [Amīr 'Izz al-Dīn Shīr]. He then . . . came to the renowned monastery of St. Yakob [James] built by the [Armenian] royal family, which for a long time had been in ruins and had been deserted. And they [that is, Step'annos and several other collaborators] began to restore the structure and, with the help of God, other monks and laymen, [that is] servants of the monastery, congregated here . . . and restored the monastery altogether; they restored the brick and lime-plastered dome of St. James . . . And the vardapet Step'annos for some years remained at the newly constructed [monastery of] St. James and, entrusting his pupil [Simēon] and the residents of this place to the mercy of God, he again went to the holy city of Erusałēm [Jerusalem], where he passed away . . .

During his [Simēon's] and our time, much anguish befell our country. The accursed Sk'andar [Iskandar] occupied our country, as well as the impregnable fortresses of Van and Ostan [Wusṭān], and others in K'rdstan [Kurdistān] from the hands of our native barons;

and he destroyed the Shambo [Šamōan] dynasty; and our country remained in much ruin.

He [Iskandar] captured Van in the year 874 [of the Armenian Era = A.D. 1425]. And in 880 [A.D. 1431] P'ir Bēk [Pīr Beg] captured the island of Ałt'amar, and brought indescribable grief to our land and Armenian nation; and for two years our country remained in ruins. And in 884 [A.D. 1435] Šahṙuh [Shāhrukh] marched forth, and Sk'andar [Iskandar] took to flight; and our country was in terror. But later Šahṙuh [Shāhrukh] installed J̌hanšay [Djihānshāh] as baron and our country was pacified . . .

2. Place: city of Van in Vaspurakan; scribe and author of col.: Karapet; MS. title: Menology [*Yaysmawurk'*].
Source: Xač'ikyan, *XV Dari*, I, no. 655, p. 584

. . . [completed] during the pontificate of the Lord Grigor [X, J̌alalbēkeanc'] . . . in the year 894 of the Armenian Era [A.D. 1445], in bitter times, during the reign of J̌hanšay [Djihānshāh], who in this year invaded Axlc'xay [Akhal Tsikhé] with numerous troops and carried off numerous Christians into captivity, and we witnessed with our own eyes their sorrow and anguish . . .

3. Place: Bałēš; MS. title: Gospel.
Source: Xač'ikyan, *XV Dari*, I, no. 657, p. 585

. . . [copied] during the khanate of J̌hanšah *amirza* [Djihānshāh Mīrzā] and the amirate in our city [Bitlīs] of Šex Mahmud [Shaykh Maḥmūd], who became insane, and all the notables assembled and appointed in his place his nephew, Amir Šamšadin [Shams al-Dīn Dushevār].

4. Place: city of Xlat'; scribe and author of col.: Astuacatur; MS. title: Menology [*Yaysmawurk'*].
Source: Xač'ikyan, *XV Dari*, I, no. 658, p. 586

. . . [copied] in the year 894 [of the Armenian Era = A.D. 1445], during the imperial conquest of the nation of archers [netołac' azg], under J̌ənxanšah *amirza* [Djihānshāh Mīrzā], the T'urk'man [Turkmen] . . .

5. Place: city of Arčēš in canton of K'aǰberunik'; scribe and author of col.: Yohannēs [Mangasarenc']; MS. title: Gospel.

Source: Xač'ikyan, *XV Dari*, I, no. 659, p. 587

... [copied] during the imperial conquest of J̌hanšay Łan [Djihānshāh Khān] of T'avrēz [Tabrīz] ...

6. Place: fortress of Arłni; scribe and author of col.: Grigor; MS. title: Psalms.
Source: Xač'ikyan, *XV Dari*, I, no. 662a, p. 590

... [copied] during the reign of the Msulim [*aylazgi*] ruler of our province, J̌hangir *amirzay* [Djihāngīr Bayāndur Mīrzā], grandson of Awt'man Bahaduṙ [Ḳara Yoluḳ 'Uthmān Bahādur], who built our holy church on the summit of the impregnable *klay* of Arłni ...

1446

1. Place: city of Bałēš; scribe and author of col.: Step'anos; MS. title: Menology [*Yaysmawurk'*].
Source: Xač'ikyan, *XV Dari*, I, nos. 666a, b, pp. 592–593

... I [Step'anos] undertook to copy this holy book in bitter times, when we were suffering grief at the hands of the infidels and Satan.

This was copied ... during the amirate of Šex Mahmat [Shaykh Maḥmūd], whom they banished from the throne and replaced him with his nephew, the younger amir Šməzdin [Amīr Shams al Dīn Dushevār]; and during the khanate of J̌əhanša *amirza* [Djihānshāh Mīrzā].

And in this year the prices [of goods] were very high, so that one load [*beřn*] of wheat was worth 60 *t'ankay*. But the Creator God looked after his faithful Christians.

This was written in the year 895 of the Armenian Era [A.D. 1446] ...

... And during our time, in the year 850 of the Haykazean Era [A.D. 1401], the blessed vardapet Grigor Xlat'ec'i, descended from the Cerenc' family ... supplemented this [martyrology], which had been compiled in the past by others, with many worthwhile and useful writings from historical and martyrological works concerning those who became holy martyrs in recent times and in our own day, and thus he enriched this book. And later he himself was slain by the sword at the hands of the iniquitous ones, [namely] the accursed Ǝṙōškan [Rūzagī] tribe, at the monastery of C'ipnay in the year 874 [of the Armenian Era = A.D. 1425]; may his memory be blessed! ...

2. Place: Ałt'amar; scribe and author of col.: T'umay Minasenc'; MS. title: Gospel.
Source: Xač'ikyan, *XV Dari*, I, no. 668, p. 595

... In this year J̌əhanša *amirza* [Djihānshāh Mīrzā] occupied Bałdat [Baghdad], which is Babelon [Babylon]; and the year was 895 [of the Armenian Era = A.D. 1446].

3. Scribe and author of col.: Yovsēp'; MS. title: Missal [*Čašoc'*].
Source: Xač'ikyan, *XV Dari*, I, no. 669, p. 595

... This was copied in the year 895 [of the Armenian Era = A.D. 1446], in grievous times ... [Djihānshāh Khān] issued orders and assembled all the T'orgomac'is from the east, and with numerous troops invaded Bałdat [Baghdad] and he took to battle. But he failed to capture anything; rather, 2000 of his men and 300 of his barons were slain. And we knew that this was the work of God ... as the Lord said, "He who takes the sword will perish by the sword." [cf. Matthew 26:52] ...

4. Place: city of Van; scribe and author of col.: Vardan; MS. title: Menology [*Yaysmawurk'*].
Source: Xač'ikyan, *XV Dari*, I, no. 671, p. 596

... [copied] during the reign of J̌hanšay [Djihānshāh], who in this year [A.D. 1446] captured the impregnable city of Bałdat [Baghdad] ...

5. Place: Eznkay; scribes: Sargis, et al.; author of col.: Sargis; MS. title: Menology [*Yaysmawurk'*].
Source: Xač'ikyan, *XV Dari*, I, nos. 678 a, b, c, pp. 601–603

... This was written in the year 895 of our Abet'akan [Japhetic] Era [A.D. 1446], in bitter and evil times, for on account of our multitudinous sins the heart of the prince of our city of Eznka [Erzindjān] was hardened ... and in league with the *danušmans* he resolved to demolish the churches and monasteries in our city and its villages. He himself took numerous troops and attacked the citadel of Kamax [Kemakh], and he had promised the *mōlnays* that after he captured the citadel they should demolish all the churches in the two regions ... But the Only-Begotten Son of God did not abandon us—whom

He had redeemed with His precious and sacred blood—and taking mercy upon us He saved the Christian churches. The prince [of Erzindjān] clearly saw mounted on white horses St. Sargis and other saints, who urged him to proceed immediately and capture the citadel. He arrived at the citadel by night, and he himself bound a rope around his neck, and they pulled him up and cast him in prison. His troops, fleeing to our city, acknowledged his son as their baron. They also reaffirmed their erstwhile design to demolish the churches.

And in these days, about a month later, the brother of Šex Hasan [Shaykh Ḥasan] arrived from a foreign land and entered our city with twenty men. And, seeing the blue symbols on the heads of the Christians and their anguish, he proceeded with his twenty men to the gates of the palace, and, after arresting the prince's son, he himself occupied the city. And he issued orders that the Christians should remove the blue symbols from their heads and should freely practice their religion.

Some days later, the baron of the citadel of Kamax [Kemakh] released Šex Hasan [Shaykh Ḥasan]. The *mōlnays* of this city again sent a secret letter to him urging him to return to the city, and they [promised] to break the gate and let him enter [the citadel] in order to kill his brother and to carry out their original plan. But his brother, the baron Mahmut [Maḥmūd], being apprised of this, seized them all, hanged the chief *mōlnay*, severely tortured many others, confiscated their goods and possessions, and banished them to another country.

After a few days, Šex Hasan [Shaykh Ḥasan] left Kamax [Kemakh] and returned to his land in Derǰan; and his brother, learning of this, dispatched troops, seized him, and cast him in prison in iron fetters. Thus, their wicked design was frustrated . . . and the words of David that "They dug out and opened up a pit, and they fell into the abyss which they made" [cf. Psalms 7:15], were fulfilled.

. . . All of the above transpired from the autumn season until the spring season. But when the summer season arrived, Čihankir [Djihāngīr Bayāndur], nephew of the baron Mahmut [Maḥmūd], attacked our city [Erzindjān] . . . with numerous troops, and besieged [*xsar*] our city from the twenty-seventh of the month until the tenth of August. He completely demolished our region of Ekełeac', set all the villages on fire, and leaving our region he went to the neighboring cantons with the purpose of destroying them. The males in our region were banished to foreign countries, and thus our country was made uninhabitable. And we are still amidst these waves like a wrecked ship, and only God knows what would happen in the future . . .

Woe unto these bitter times, for numerous troops have besieged the city of Eznkay [Erzindjān].

Oh brother, do not blame me for the largeness of my calligraphy and my errors, because, first, I was inexperienced and, secondly, we were besieged [*xsar*] and were in anguish, for they burned with fire all the villages of Eznkay [Erzindjān] and the monasteries, and they also burned the monastics. As for the produce and the vineyards and everything else, some they captured and ate up, [and] some they trampled underfoot; and we are in anguish.

Oh brothers, do not blame me for the largeness of my calligraphy and my errors, for we were in terror and took to flight . . . and all the males in our country were banished to foreign lands, and our land became desolate . . .

6. Place: monastery of P'rkič' in Arapkir; scribe: Minas; author of col.: Grigor; MS. title: Missal [*Čašoc'*].
Source: Xač'ikyan, *XV Dari*, I, no. 679a, p. 603

. . . This holy book was completed . . . in the year 895 of the Armenian Era [A.D. 1446], during the pontificate of the Lord Karapet [Ewdokiac'i] in Cilicia [Kiwlikec'woc'], and during the reign in Egiptos [Egypt] of Sultan Tahir [Al-Malik al-Ẓāhir Sayf al-Dīn, Čaḳmaḳ], the Mahmedakan [Muhammadan] . . .

1447

1. Place: monastery of Ayrivank'; scribe and author of col.: Mat'ēos; MS. title: Hymnal [*Šaraknoc'*].
Source: Xač'ikyan, *XV Dari*, I, no. 680, p. 604

. . . [copied] in the year 896 of the Armenian Era [A.D. 1447], in bitter and evil times when we were suffering at the hands of the infidels and the unjust tax-collectors; during the pontificate of the Lord Grigor [X, J̌alalbēkeanc'] at the see of Holy Ēǰmiacin in Vałaršapat in the province of Ararat, [and] during the khanate of J̌ahanšah [Djihānshāh] . . .

2. Place: monastery of Ałǰoc' in K'ełoy-Jor in canton of Ararat; scribe and author of col.: Galust; MS. title: Gospel.

Source: Xač‘ikyan, *XV Dari*, I, no. 682, p. 606

. . . [copied] in bitter and wicked times.
. . . This holy Gospel was copied in the year 896 of the Armenian Era [A.D. 1447], during the pontificate of the Lord Grigor [X, J̌alalbēkeanc‘], and the reign of King Gawrgē [Giorgi VIII] of the Georgians [Vrac‘], and the khanate of J̌ahanšah [Djihānshāh], son of Usup‘ [Ḳara Yūsuf] . . .

3. Place: city of Arckē; MS. title: Gospel.
Source: Xač‘ikyan, *XV Dari*, I, no. 685, p. 608

. . [copied] during the reign of J̌hanšah [Djihānshāh], son of Łara Eusuf [Ḳara Yūsuf], in the year 896 of our [Armenian] Era [A.D. 1447], at a time when the Armenians were suffering on account of the imposition of exorbitant taxes . . .

1449

1. Place: Amit‘ (?); author of col.: Astuacatur; MS. title: Menology [*Yaysmawurk‘*].
Source: Xač‘ikyan, *XV Dari*, I, no. 704, pp. 622–629

. . . In this manner, at the end of time and at the nadir, when all the flowers had withered and all the leaves had dried, God revealed to us an incorruptible flower whose fragrance filled the entire universe, namely the Lord Mkrtič‘ surnamed Nałaš, of whom was heard throughout the universe and who became the second illuminator in all of Miǰaget [Mesopotamia], as well as the pride of all the Christians.

He was a native of the province of Bałēš [Bitlīs], from the village Poṙ, the son of the noble and holy priest Aṙak‘el and of a pious mother. He had two brothers [Yovannēs K‘ahanay and Abgar] . . . Since his boyhood, the blessed Lord Mkrtič‘ had been fond of clerical life. He loved the ecclesiastics and the monastics. And, being a devotee of the arts and of learning, he daily pursued their study . . . When he was fifteen years old, he was already accomplished in learning and in the arts, in philosophy and in theology; he was a distinguished writer, an unequaled painter and a master of many trades . . . and his gifts and wisdom became known in all countries.

And since he had no love for worldly life [and after his wife, whom he married at the insistence of his parents, died at childbirth] . . . he left his native canton, and came to sojourn in the renowned monastery in the metropolis of Amit' [Āmid] . . . From the day he arrived in Mijaget [Mesopotamia], God made everyone love him and the tongues of everyone to praise and to bless him, and to spread around his good fame.

And God opened before him the gates of charity, for whoever saw him wished to give him even his soul, voluntarily, gladly, and plentifully; not only the Christian, but also the T'urk' [Turk], the T'at' [Tat], the T'at'ar [Tatar], the K'urt' [Kurd], the Arap [Arab], the J̌hut [Jew], and all other races. When they saw him, they prepared honors and gifts for him, [such as] horses and mules, and precious *xlays*, all ineffable and indescribable. They came to him not only from his own theme and bishopric, but from all countries, from the east and from the west. And they brought with them gold, silver, precious gems, and magnificent cloths as gifts; and many brought to him 1000 and 2000 *t'ankays* as gifts. His fame spread throughout all lands; it even reached the king of Persia [Parsic'] and the master of Egiptos [Egypt], and also beyond the Great Sea [the Mediterranean], the Pope at Hṙom [Rome], Kostandnupawlis [Constantinople], all of whom sent him linens, interlaced with gold and precious gifts.

He was especially beloved in the eyes of the baron of barons, Šah Awt'man Bēk [Shāh Ḳara Yoluḳ 'Uthmān], whose rule stretched from Xaṙan [Ḥarrān] up to the Sea of Pontus [Pontosi Covn], which is Trapizon [Trebizond]. For God so sweetened the tyrant's heart toward him that he ['Uthmān] placed all his Christian subjects under his [Mkrtič''s] jurisdiction. And he honored him by offering large gifts and imposts to him, and bestowed on him regal vestments and royal horses, so much so that the king made him wear his own garments. The love which he had for him and the gifts which he offered him cannot be described in writing by anyone, for no Christian king honored any of the holy fathers with such gifts. The extent of his love can be gauged by his munificence, for he always offered him 1000 and 2000 *t'ankays* as gifts. And when he [Mkrtič'] went to see him, he came out in person to greet and kiss him. He even made him sit on his own royal *xalič'ay*; and he listened to his words as the words of the servant of God, for he was fond of hearing the word [of God]. He sent for his own chieftains, and made him speak to them all night from the Holy Bible. And he, with his God-given charm and God-instructed preachment, put them all to shame; and he was so convincing that the king offered him presents . . .

And after [the death of] Awt'man Bēk [Ḳara Yoluḳ 'Uthmān Beg], his son, Sultan Hamza [Sulṭān Ḥamza Bayandur], received him with greater honor than he had seen his father bestow upon him, and he even looked upon him as a father. He bestowed greater honors upon him than upon his own notables, so much so that many said that he [Ḥamza], too, was a Christian, for he so loved and honored the bishop.

And he was consecrated a bishop by the Lord Catholicos Kostandin [VI] Vahkec'i in the year 879 of the Great Armenian Era [A.D. 1430]. The Catholicos also honored him with various honors and gifts, and invested him as archbishop over twenty-four *gawazans*. And they all gladly obeyed him and received him as an apostle of God, and his preachments bore fruit throughout the country. In his time the Armenian churches flourished; the authority of the priests increased; the Christian faith flourished; and all the believers rejoiced. For there was elevated a brave shepherd and a worthy heir to the [episcopal] office . . .

It is customary among historians to exaggerate their laudatory remarks; but we have written what we have witnessed and what is known everywhere. Yet, to write of every detail would cause tedium to the readers . . .

He was the only one who could despoil the money-changers, and with the help of God he accomplished manifold good deeds. First, no one could affix a stone onto the churches that were in ruins; yet he restored with new arches and vaults all the churches that were in ruins, that were old and made of dirt. He also built many new ones, such as the great church of St. Mary on the summit of the great citadel of Arłni.

Second, he furnished the churches with numerous precious chasubles, books, gospels, and exquisite and admirable chalices, and always looked after their [the churches'] needs.

Third, no one could freely perform services in the churches; but during his time they worshiped more freely than in the hermitages and in the monasteries.

Fourth, the priests had been persecuted more severely than the laity, and they had suffered more on account of the levies; yet he, with the help of God, freed them all from the crown levy.

Fifth, the churches in Mijaget [Mesopotamia] were subjected to the *dimosakan* tax, and the bishops, [who acted as] customs chiefs, gave away as taxes what they received from the Christians, and they could not offer even [a loaf of] bread to God or to the poor; but he, with the help of Christ, had the tax imposed on the churches removed, and he even obtained ten and twenty thousand from the barons and distributed them among the churches, the poor, and the needy.

Sixth, thanks to him the clerical class enjoyed greater respect from the barons than did their own chieftains.

Seventh, no one dared to walk around with *p'ilons* [priestly mantles] and *vełars* [hoods]; but, during his time, they dressed freely everywhere and walked around, with palpable pomp, in their priestly habits.

Eighth, the mention of his name freed many from trial, from fines, and from the hands of the tyrants; and when people were seized on the highways they were released when they said that they were the men of Lord Nałaš.

Ninth, he delivered numerous captives from the hands of the infidels, some by paying ransom for them, some by interceding with the barons, and some he rescued on the highways. He used to dispatch strong and courageous men from among his servants, who wrested the captives from the infidels and brought them to his newly constructed monastery of St. Mary. He kept them there for a while, until their masters arrived, and gave them garments and *nafałays*, and dispatched them to their own localities.

Tenth, he regarded as his own the penury, anguish, and grief of others; and he helped everyone by giving them food and gifts, by sympathizing with them and by comforting them both with words and deeds.

Eleventh, the gates of the churches had always been closed and there was no dining hall in the episcopal residence; but he, with the help of Christ, built such a dining hall that people from all nations came there and ate, drank, and carried away plentiful victuals without any restriction, so much so that the barons wondered how he could have enough food not only to feed them, but also to give more to carry away with them. Some said that he possessed a *k'ēmiay*, and many said that he had found a treasure. But he had no money; rather, through the grace of God he received an inexhaustible treasure, [that is] 100 *t'ankay* and 200 *musx* every day . . . for he gave away horses, mules, garments, gold, silver, and wheat as gifts more plentifully than even the great kings could. And the more he gave away the more was given to him by Christ . . .

Twelfth, he was the only one in these times who carried out the commandment of the Lord who said, "Do good unto those who hate you" [cf. Matthew 5:44]; and, throughout his entire life, he loved his enemies and did good unto those who hated him . . .

Thirteenth . . . the Armenians, Asorik' [Syrians], the Nestorakank' [Nestorians], and J̌hutk' [Jews] were forced to drag off the bodies of the Christian dead, and if they paid even as much as 100,000 *dekan* there could be no change in this custom. After arriving here he appeared before the Sultan, and, among numerous other privileges which he received from him, he sought and secured permission to remove the Christian dead by uplifting them, and this became customary.

Moreover, in the year 880 [of the Armenian Era = A.D. 1431] he ascended the episcopal seat at the *šahastan* of Amit' [Āmid]; and in the year 882 [of the Armenian Era = A.D. 1433] he built the great church of St. Mary in the citadel of Arłni; [and] in the year 888 [of the Armenian Era = A.D. 1439] he began to restore the most praiseworthy and magnificent cathedral of St. T'eōdoros [Theodorus] at the *šahastan* of Amit' [Āmid] . . . and for four years he shed a living martyr's blood to construct the holy church, and he completed the vaulted edifice with ineffable and indescribable beauty. The summit of its dome was taller than the *mnarays*; it had eighteen corners, and eighteen windows on the dome . . .

When the Christ-hating Mahmetakank' [Muhammadans] saw it they were intensely aroused. The children of Hagar exhorted one another; they spread rumors and protested to the Sultan of Egiptos [Egypt], to the King of Persia [Parsic'], and to the Sultan of Rūm [Horomac' tun], concerning the beautiful construction of the Christian church. When they learned of it, they were filled with wicked jealousy and dispatched forthwith emissaries and edicts to Sultan Hamza [Sulṭān Ḥamza Bayāndur], to demolish the most praiseworthy holy cathedral. This caused insufferable grief to the Armenians, and all were deeply smitten, and woeful tears flowed from every eye. They offered large amounts of money as bribe, but they could not save it, because they demolished and leveled with the ground the magnificent and glorious dome, and all the Christians mourned. Oh, oh, oh, who can describe the unbearable grief and pitiful anguish, the sighs and the tragic lamentation, the loud moaning and the heart-rending grief, for all hearts were sad and all eyes in tears and all mouths were crying and all tongues bewailing. Most of all, the brave bishop and valiant shepherd, Lord Mkrtič', the builder of the holy cathedral. Because of his intense grief and bitter anguish, he went abroad, crossed the Sea of Pontus [Pontosi Covn], and arrived in Kafay [Kafa] and Stampōl [Istanbul], and by day and night and with a smitten heart he pleaded with God to visit the holy cathedral before his death, so that he would not go to his grave in grief.

The merciful God . . . heard his supplication and fulfilled his request. God caused those who demolished the dome to perish, and installed another king in Mijaget [Mesopotamia], [namely] J̌hangir *imirzay* [Djihāngīr Mīrzā]. J̌hangir . . . dispatched letters and emissaries; and all the notables, the *łatēstan*, the masters of the Christian households, and all the priests and people, as well as the barons, wrote two and three letters and dispatched them to Kafay [Kafa], and brought back, with great honors, the most-beloved leader, the Lord Mkrtič‘. They all went in unison to meet him at a distance of two days, and they received him with great honors and rejoicing, for since the time he left Mijaget [Mesopotamia] all the churches had been in mourning, they were in anguish like a mother whose child had died, and all the Christians were in affliction. For this reason, the Christians rejoiced over his arrival, all the churches were ecstatic, and the children of Zion rejoiced. And he, strengthened by the Holy Spirit, obtained a permit from the baron, offered 3000 *t‘ankay* to the barons and chieftains, and restored [the dome] . . .

And the inhabitants of the city, the priests and the people, joined their hands together in labor, in offering money, in supplying food, and in toiling. With single-minded valor and abundant faith, the poor and the rich labored, and in ten days completed the construction of the *łupay* [dome].

. . . The [restoration of the] holy cathedral was completed in the year 896 [of the Armenian Era = A.D. 1447], on the sixth of the month of August, on Monday, by the master builder Nek‘amat . . .

2. Place: Ałt‘amar; scribe and author of col.: Grigor; MS. title: Gospel.
Source: Xač‘ikyan, *XV Dari*, I, no. 708, p. 634

. . . [copied] during the pontificate of the Lord Zak‘aria [III of Aghtamar], and in the year 898 of the Armenian Era [A.D. 1449] . . . in bitter and grievous times, when we were subjected to taxation by the infidels, [namely] the nation of archers [azgin netołac‘] . . .

3. Place: monastery of Arjonic‘ in province of K‘ajberunik‘; scribe and author of col.: T‘umay Mecop‘ac‘i; MS. title: Gospel.
Source: Xač‘ikyan, *XV Dari*, I, no. 710, p. 637

. . . [copied] during the pontificate of the Lord Grigor [X, Jalalbēkeanc‘] at Holy Ējmiacin, and during the reign of Jhanšay [Djihānshāh], son of Usuf [Ḳara Yūsuf], who ruled in Armenia and Asorik‘ [northern Syria]; he was peace-loving, [but] the levies were exorbitant . . . on account of our sins; and in the year 898 of our [Armenian] Era [A.D. 1449] . . .

4. Place: monastery of Joroyvank‘ in canton of K‘aǰberunik‘; scribe and author of col.: T‘uma; MS. title: Gospel.
Source: Xač‘ikyan, *XV Dari*, I, no. 711, p. 637

... [copied] during the pontificate of the Lord Grigor [X, J̌alalbēkeanc‘] at Holy Ēǰmiacin, and in the year 898 of our [Armenian] Era [A.D. 1449], and during the reign of J̌hanšay [Djihānshāh], son of Usuf [Ḳara Yūsuf], and brother of Sk‘antar [Iskandar], who ruled in two kingdoms, in Armenia and in Asorik‘ [northern Syria]. He was peace-loving; but the levies he imposed on the Christians were exorbitant ...

5. Place: monastery of Hermon in province of Ełegeac‘; scribe and author of col.: Alēk‘sanos; MS. title: Selected Commentary on the Gospel by Matthew by Grigor Tat‘ewac‘i.
Source: Xač‘ikyan, *XV Dari*, I, no. 712, p. 638

... [copied] in the year 898 of the Armenian Era [A.D. 1449], in bitter and anxious days, in prostrate and anxious times, when charity had diminished and when evil reigned in abundance everywhere. For the infidels are depriving the Armenians and their priests of their possessions, and are condemning us mercilessly ...

6. Place: Argelan; author of col.: Yohanēs; MS. title: Hymnal [*Šaraknoc‘*].
Source: Xač‘ikyan, *XV Dari*, I, no. 714, p. 639

I [bought this manuscript] for four *T‘amuri t‘ankay* from the Č‘ałat‘ [Čaghatai], in memory of myself and of my parents, [and] for the enjoyment of my children ...

This was written at Argelan ... in the year [A.D.] 1449, during the pontificate of the Catholicos Grigor [X, J̌alalbēkeanc‘], [and] during the reign of J̌hanša [Djihānshāh], who left for Hrē [Herāt] and for Xorasan [Khurāsān].

7. Place: city of Eznkay; scribe and author of col.: Sargis; MS. title: Ritual Book [*Maštoc‘*].
Source: Xač‘ikyan, *XV Dari*, I, no. 715, p. 640

... [copied] During the rule of the barbarians, and the catholicosate of the Armenians of the Lord Grigor [X, J̌alalbēkeanc‘] ...

8. Place: monastery of St. Lusaworič‘ in Mount Sepuh in canton of Daranałeac‘; scribe and author of col.: Eremia; MS. title: Gospel.
Source: Xač‘ikyan, *XV Dari*, I, no. 716, p. 640

. . . [copied] during the pontificate of the Lord Grigor [X, J̌alalbēkeanc‘] in the city of Vałaršapat, and during the tyrannical rule of Čawar Bēk in our canton of Daranałeac‘ . . .

1450

1. Place: monastery of C‘ipna; scribe and author of col.: Yovanēs; MS. title: Gospel.
Source: Xač‘ikyan, *XV Dari*, I, nos. 721a, b, pp. 644–645

. . . This holy Gospel was copied in the year 899 of the Haykazean Era [A.D. 1450] . . . during the khanate at the city of T‘awrēz [Tabrīz] of the peace-loving baron J̌hanša [Djihānshāh]; and during the catholicosate of the Lord Grigor [X, J̌alalbēkeanc‘] at Holy Ēǰmiacin in the city of Vałaršapat . . .

In the year 889 [of the Armenian Era = A.D. 1440] J̌əhanša *amirzay* [Djihānshāh Mīrzā] invaded Vrac‘tun [Georgia]; he committed much destruction, demolished the churches, and he slew and carried off into captivity more than 12,000 Armenians. And in the year 895 [of the Armenian Era = A.D. 1446] he captured Bałdat [Baghdad].

In the year 899 [of the Armenian Era = A.D. 1450] J̌əhanša *amirzay* [Djihānshāh Mīrzā] captured Eznkay [Erzindjān], and seized countless Christian women and children as captives. And in the year 900 [of the Armenian Era = A.D. 1451] he enslaved and devastated the regions of Łəlat‘ [Khilāṭ] and Bałēš [Bitlīs]. Woe a thousand times, for we witnessed this tragedy with our own eyes and in our own times . . .

2. Place: Tiwrik; author of col.: Mkrtič‘; MS. title: Missal [*Čašoc‘*].
Source: Xač‘ikyan, *XV Dari*, I, no. 722a, p. 645.

. . . Nur-Alwand attacked Arčēš [Ardjīsh] and looted all of us . . .

3. Place: Tiwrik; purchaser of MS. and author of col.: Łazar; MS. title: Missal [*Čašoc‘*].

Source: Xač'ikyan, *XV Dari*, I, no. 722b, pp. 645–646

... marching forth from his *t'ałt'* at T'awrēz [Tabrīz], Sultan Čihanšah [Djihānshāh] attacked the city of Ezənkay [Erzindjān] and captured Ezənkay [Erzindjān] and subjected the Christians to much tribulation. But the baron Xut'lupak [Ḳutlu Beg] did not submit to Čihanšah [Djihānshāh], [whereupon] Čihanšah [Djihānshāh] issued orders to his troops and generals, who attacked him and took much booty and carried off numerous captives. Who can recount the tragic grief and lamentation of the Christians? Returning from there, they marched toward Kamax [Kemakh]; and they took much booty and numerous captives. Misery and misfortune befell the Christians at Kamax [Kemakh], and the command of the Lord, that "Let not your flight be in the winter and on the sabbath day" [cf. Matthew 24:20], was fulfilled at Kamax [Kemakh] ...

4. Place: monastery of T'ort'anay; scribe and author of col.: Martiros; MS. title: Book of Sermons by Grigor Tat'ewac'i.
Source: Xač'ikyan, *XV Dari*, I, no. 723, p. 646

Alas, the terrible tragedy, which occurred in our canton [of Darana-łeac'] and its environs, for the Ismaelite [Ismaeli] troops overran and mercilessly plundered them; they slew some and carried off others into captivity. We had no help from any quarter, [and] we seek visitation from on high ...

5. Place: village of Harhoc'; scribe and author of col.: Yohannēs; MS. title: Gospel.
Source: Xač'ikyan, *XV Dari*, I, no. 726, p. 648

... This holy Gospel was copied in the year 899 of the Armenian Era [A.D. 1450], in bitter and anxious times, during the pontificate of the Lord Grigor [X, J̌alalbēkeanc'] of the Armenians, [and] during the khanate at T'avrēz [Tabrīz] of J̌əhanša [Djihānshāh] ...

1451

1. Place: city of Eznkay; scribe and author of col.: Grigor; MS. title: Gospel.
Source: Xač'ikyan, *XV Dari*, II, no. 1, p. 3

This holy Gospel was copied in the year 900 of the Armenian Era [A.D. 1451] . . . during the pontificate of the Lord Grigor [X, J̌alalbēkeanc‘] . . . and during the khanate, by the grace of God, of the bloodthirsty beast J̌ihanša [Djihānshāh]; for, on account of our numerous and countless sins, he marched forth from the eastern regions with numerous troops and attacked us. He carried off captives from and devastated numerous cantons and cities. And who can relate the other countless atrocities [which he committed], for innocent children, male and female, were devoured by the wicked turbulence which he caused . . .

2. MS. title: Menology [*Yaysmawurk‘*].
Source: Xač‘ikyan, *XV Dari*, II, no. 2, p. 3

This Menology was copied in the year 900 of the Armenian Era [A.D. 1451], during the pontificate of the Lord Catholicos Grigor [X, J̌alalbēkeanc‘], and the reign of J̌ihanšah [Djihānshāh] of the Persians [Parsic‘], in bitter times and wicked days[41] . . . He held our entire country under his *hiwk‘m*; but, alas, for he persecuted all the Christians bitterly and caused them much agitation and oppressed them by the levies which he imposed.

3. Place: monastery of P‘ok‘r Akoṙ in region of J̌ermajor; scribe and author of col.: Step‘annos; MS. title: Gospel.
Source: Xač‘ikyan, *XV Dari*, II, no. 3, p. 4

. . . [copied in A.D. 1451] at the behest of the honorable and judicious *mahdasi* Pōłos, who most eagerly had this holy Gospel copied in memory of his own soul and [the souls] of his parents, his father Step‘annos, who was slain by the infidels, and his mother J̌uhar, and his brothers T‘umay K‘ahanay and Astuacatur, who was slain with the sword by the infidels, and the daughter of Grigor, [namely] Guhar, who was hurled down from the citadel of Zṙayl . . .

This was written during the pontificate of [the Lord] Zak‘aria [III] Ałt‘amarc‘i, and the reign of J̌hanšay Łan [Djihānshāh Khān] . . .

[41] Up to this point, the text is a summary of the contents of the original colophon, done by its publisher Yovhannēs Vałaršakertc‘i (see Xač‘ikyan, *XV Dari*, II, p. 3, note). The rest represents the original words of the colophon.

4. Place: island of Sevan in region of Gełam; scribe and author of col.: Daniēl; MS. title: Grigor Tat'ewac'i's Commentary on the Holy Gospel by Matthew.
Source: Xač'ikyan, *XV Dari*, II, no. 4a, p. 5

... [copied] During the catholicosate of the Lord Grigor [X, J̌alalbēkeanc'], incumbent of the great and holy see of Ējmiaycin, [and] the khanate of J̌ahanšah [Djihānshāh], son of Usup' [Ḳara Yūsuf], in the year 900 of the Armenian Era [A.D. 1451] ...

5. Place: city of Van; scribe and author of col.: Karapet; MS. title: Gospel.
Source: Xač'ikyan, *XV Dari*, II, no. 5, pp. 5–6

... This holy Gospel was copied in the year 900 of the Armenian Era [A.D. 1451] ... during the pontificates of the Lord Grigor [X, J̌alalbēkeanc'] and the Lord Zak'aria [III of Aghtamar], during the reign of J̌xanšay [Djihānshāh], in evil times, for, on account of our multitudinous sins, numerous Christians were carried off as captives by the wicked T'urk' [Turks], which I cannot describe in writing.

In these bitter times, the loyal, devout and pious lady P'ašay expressed desire for this ... book ... in memory of her good soul and ... [the soul] of her son J̌anibēk, who became a martyr at the hands of the infidels, which caused inconsolable grief to his parents, and of her husband, Hawkit' Atom, who out of grief for his son became *xasrat'amah* ...

... And again remember in your chaste prayers the pious lady P'ašay, the recipient of this holy Gospel, and her husband Atom, who passed away in God, and her brother, the *xoǰa* Faruxšah ... and her other brother Sultanšay, who went on a journey and no one knew what became of him. Also remember in your prayers the pious *tanutēr* [householder] Hawkit' Atom, who died in Christ, and his spouse P'ašay, and his son J̌anibēk, whom the infidels slew stealthily at Hizan and made him a martyr and whose body his father could not find, and went to his grave in grief and lamentation ...

1452

1. Place: monastery of Ayrivank'; scribe and author of col.: Mat'ēos; MS. title: Hymnal [*Šaraknoc'*].
Source: Xač'ikyan, *XV Dari*, II, no. 19, p. 15

. . . [completed] in the year 901 of the Haykazean Era [A.D. 1452], in bitter and evil times, when we were suffering from the tyranny of the infidels . . .

2. Place: city of P'aytakaran or Tp'xis; scribe and author of col.: Yovanēs; MS. title: Book of Sermons by Grigor Tat'ewac'i.
Source: Xač'ikyan, *XV Dari*, II, no. 22, p. 17

. . . [completed] during the pontificate of the Lord Grigor [X, J̌alalbēkeanc'], patriarch at Vałaršapat . . . and during the reign of King Gēorgi Bagratuni [Giorgi VIII, Bagrationi] of the Georgians [Vrac']; may the Lord God, for many long years, make him victorious over the enemies of the Cross of Christ . . .

3. Place: monastery of Ałǰoc' in K'ełoyjor in canton of Ararat; scribe and author of col.: Galust; MS. title: Gospel.
Source: Xač'ikyan, *XV Dari*, II, no. 23a, p. 18

. . . This holy Gospel was copied in the year 901 of the Armenian Era [A.D. 1452], during the pontificate of the Lord Grigor [X, J̌alalbēkeanc'] at Vałaršapat, and during the khanate of J̌ahanšah [Djihānshāh], son of Usuf [Ḳara Yūsuf] . . . in bitter and evil times . . .

4. Place: Ałt'amar; scribe and author of col.: Grigor; MS. title: Gospel.
Source: Xač'ikyan, *XV Dari*, II, nos. 25a, b, pp. 20–22

. . . [completed] during the pontificate of the Lord Zak'aria [III of Aghtamar], in the year 901 of the Armenian Era [A.D. 1452] . . . copied with much labor . . . [and] with suffering and much sorrow, in bitter and grievous times, when the *p'at'šah* J̌əhanšay [Pādishāh Djihānshāh] arrived with numerous troops and besieged Ostan [Wusṭān] for the whole winter; may the Lord grant him a serene life, amen!

. . . I, *ust'ay* Atom, recovered this Gospel from the infidels, which had been captured by the abominable tyrant Ēztinšēr ['Izz al-Dīn Shīr]. And I returned it to the monastery of the Protomartyr [*naxavkay*] St. Stephen in the city of Ostan [Wusṭān] . . .

5. Place: city of Merdin; scribe and author of col.: Dawit‘ [Merdinc‘i]; MS. title: Chronicle by Samuēl Anec‘i and Book of Questions by Grigor Tat‘ewac‘i.
Source: Xač‘ikyan, *XV Dari*, II, no. 37, p. 29; Hakobyan, *Manr Žam.*, II, 210–212

. . . This was written in the year 901 of the Armenian Era [A.D. 1452], on the twenty-ninth of the month of December, on Wednesday, the feast of the Epiphany, in bitter and anxious times.

(*Chronicle*)[42]

In the year 899 [of the Armenian Era = A.D. 1450], *mirza* Čhanšay [Djihānshāh Mīrzā] marched forth from the land of T‘avrēz [Tabrīz] and captured Eznkay [Erzindjān]; and from there he dispatched a certain general, by the name of T‘rxan Awłli [Rustam Turkhān-oghlu] to Mijaget [Mesopotamia]; and he arrived at T‘ilguran, took captives, devastated it, and tortured numerous Christians and made them martyrs; and from there he came to Ṙasəlēn [Ra's al-‘Ayn], within the boundaries of Mertin [Mārdīn]. The inhabitants of Mertin [Mārdīn] were terrified, and many of them entrenched themselves in the fortress of Merdin [Mārdīn].

In the year 900 [of the Armenian Era = A.D. 1451], on Sunday in the month of Nawasard [November 29, 1450], T‘rxan Awłli [Turkhān-oghlu] waged battle against the inhabitants of Mertin [Mārdīn], and the head of Azap was cut off at Tnisay. And six days later, on Friday [December 4, 1450], the city-dwellers rebelled against Čhangir *amirzay* [Djihāngīr Mīrzā] and delivered the city to T‘arxan-Awłli [Turkhān-oghlu]; and he, as befitting each one, imposed fines on some and looted some. He also began to open the *daran*, where the inhabitants of Mertin [Mārdīn] had stored away their possessions, and he confiscated whatever was pleasing to him, and he took one-fifth of whatever was left. He also put a blue symbol upon the Christians, and committed numerous atrocities which, if I were to mention one by one, would make a book, like the Book of Isaiah and many others. And the city-dwellers and the Łara-Łoyunlu [Ḳara Ḳoyunlu] took refuge in the citadel from the sixth of Nawasard [December 4, 1450] on, in the year 900 [of the Armenian Era = A.D. 1451]. And twenty-eight days after Easter, on Sunday the [feast of the] Revelation

[42] The original text of this chronicle, which was written by the eyewitness priest Dawit‘, is found in MS. no. 1198 in the library of the Armenian Patriarchate in Jerusalem. The present text, as published by Hakobyan, is based upon a copy made by M. Tēr-Movsisean. See Hakobyan, *Manr Žam.*, II, 209.

of the Cross [May 23, 1451], Čhangir [Djihāngīr] arrived at Mertin [Mārdīn] from Yamit‘ [Āmid]; but the inhabitants of Mertin [Mārdīn] did not submit to him. He returned to Yamit‘ [Āmid], after which there was a fierce battle at the gate of Amit‘ [Āmid] and a large number from both sides were slain . . . This battle took place on Tuesday [June 1, 1451], two days after which was Thursday, the [feast of the] Ascension [June 3, 1451].

In the year 901 [of the Armenian Era = A.D. 1452], on Monday [May 17], they released the ailing *ṙaṫiat‘* from the citadel . . . the *ṙaṫiat‘* remained under siege [*xsar*] for a year, less five days. And in these days there arrived Mhamat *amirzay* [Muḥammad Mīrzā], son of Čhanša [Djihānshāh], to join Ṙustam T‘rxan Awłli [Rustam Turkhān-oghlu]; and they both defeated Čhankir [Djihāngīr] at Amit‘ [Āmid], when this manuscript was concluded, and only God knows the future.

On Easter day of this year [April 9, 1452] peace was concluded. Čhanšah [Djihānshāh] and Čhankir [Djihāngīr] reconciled, and Mertin [Mārdīn] was given back to Čhankir [Djihāngīr]. And, during the great Lent [February 20–April 8] Ṙustam [Rustam] went to J̌ermuk to wage battle against Hasan Pēk [Uzun Ḥasan Beg], and Ṙustam [Rustam] was slain.

During the same period the mosque [*mzkit‘*] in the citadel of Mertin [Mārdīn] fell down, but not by an earthquake or the rain.

Again, during the same Lent, lightning struck at Mertin [Mārdīn] and burned it, including the citadel of Mertin [Mārdīn].

In the same year [A.D. 1452], Čhankir [Djihāngīr] left Amit‘ [Āmid] and went away to plunder the K‘urt‘ [Kurds]. Hasan Pēk [Uzun Ḥasan Beg] arrived and captured Amit‘ [Āmid], and Čhankir [Djihāngīr] took to flight, and on the twentieth of September he took refuge in the citadel of Mertin [Mārdīn].

In the year 902 [of the Armenian Era = A.D. 1453] Hasan Pēk [Uzun Ḥasan Beg] arrived and besieged [*xsar*] Mertin [Mārdīn] for fifteen days; but later the two brothers, Čhankir [Djihāngīr] and Hasan Pēk [Uzun Ḥasan Beg] reconciled . . .

In the year 905 [of the Armenian Era = A.D. 1456], Hasan Pēk [Uzun Ḥasan Beg] left Amit‘ [Āmid] and went to Čziray [Djazīra] to capture it; and the inhabitants submitted to him and became his tributaries. From there he came to Mertin [Mārdīn], and he asked that Sultan Hamzay [Sulṭān Ḥamza], son of Čhankir [Djihāngīr], and sixty other individuals, be given to him as hostages, but Čhankir [Djihāngīr] refused to comply. Thereupon he [Uzun Ḥasan] demolished the entrance of Mertin [Mārdīn] and destroyed the vineyards. As for Čhankir [Djihāngīr], he went to Čhanšah [Djihānshāh] and asked him to provide him with horsemen, so that he could return and fight against his brother, Hasan Pēk [Uzun Ḥasan Beg]. He gave him the city of Eznkay [Erzindjān]; and he told him to go to Eznkay [Erzindjān] and to take with him Arapšah Pak ['Arab-Shāh Beg], who was at Eznkay [Erzindjān], and proceed together to fight against Hasan Pak [Uzun Ḥasan Beg]. But Arapšah ['Arab-Shāh] did not dare to join him in battle against Hasan Pak [Uzun Ḥasan Beg]; instead, he abandoned Eznkay [Erzindjān] to Čhankir [Djihāngīr] and he himself went by Čhanšah [Djihānshāh], who then was in Č'ałat'ay [Čaghatai]. As for Hasan Pēk [Uzan Ḥasan Beg], he pursued him for a distance of eight days, and when he failed to find him returned to his city of Yamit' [Āmid]. When Hasan Pēk [Uzun Ḥasan Beg] went after Arapšah ['Arab-Shāh] and became *žłul* there, Čhankir [Djihāngīr] fled from Eznkay [Erzindjān] and, leaving his son Murat Bēk [Murād Beg] there, he came to Mertin [Mārdīn].

In the year 906 [of the Armenian Era = A.D. 1457], Čhankir [Djihāngīr] dispatched his brother, Uayis Pēk [Uwais Beg], to Čhanšah [Djihānshāh] in Č'ałat'ay [Čaghatai] to protest against Arapšah ['Arab-Shāh]; and Čhanšah [Djihānshāh] despoiled and imprisoned Arapšah ['Arab-Shāh]. In place of Arapšah ['Arab-Shāh], other horsemen came to join Čhankir [Djihāngīr]. The principal horsemen were Ṙustam Pak [Rustam Beg], son of T'rxan [Turkhān], Ališak'ar Pak ['Alī Sheker Beg] and his son, Sawalan Pak [Beg], and P'ir Bak [Pīr Beg]. These were dispatched, together with their own horsemen, by Čhanšah [Djihānshāh] to assist Čhankir [Djihāngīr] in his battle against Hasan Pēk [Uzun Ḥasan Beg]. Čhankir [Djihāngīr] joined them with his own horsemen, and, together with the baron of Sawray, they proceeded to Yamit' [Āmid] to wage battle. The two sides readied themselves for combat; Hasan Pak [Uzun Ḥasan Beg] triumphed and Čhankir [Djihāngīr] was defeated, because the troops of Čhankir [Djihāngīr] were crushed, and Čhankir [Djihāngīr] himself took to flight and his troops dispersed. Ṙust'am [Rustam], T'rxan's [Turkhān's] son, was captured and was taken to Hasan Pēk [Uzun Ḥasan Beg], who killed him three days later. Ṙustam's [Rustam's] wife fled to their own city of Awrēl, and, at her request Ṙust'am's [Rustam's] *laš* [corpse] having been sent to her, she took it to Ōrēl. Ališak'ar ['Alī Sheker] and his son Ali Mirzay ['Alī Mīrzā], and Sawalan Pak [Beg] were also captured, and Hasan Pēk [Uzun Ḥasan Beg] cast them in a dungeon; but P'iri Pak [Pīr Beg] narrowly escaped. The slaughter of these horsemen resulted from Čhankir's [Djihāngīr's] own fear, as well as from the panic within the ranks of his forces. Uyanis [Uwais] also took to flight; but the master of Suray was captured and Hasan Pēk [Uzun Ḥasan Beg] occupied his two impregnable fortresses and gave him, instead, the district of Ōšin. When the inhabitants of Mertin [Mārdīn] witnessed all of this they, the old and the young, united and said to Čhankir [Djihāngīr]: "Obey your brother and give him your son as hostage, otherwise we no longer can offer resistance to Hasan Pēk [Uzun Ḥasan Beg] if he were to wage war against us." And Čhankir [Djihāngīr] dispatched his son, together with thirty men, as hostages, and they made peace. Behold, brothers, the imprudence of Čhankir [Djihāngīr], for not before all this consternation and devastation came to pass did he give up his son; if he had given up his son a year earlier, all of this devastation would not have taken place.

In this year there was an earthquake and half of the citadel of Keṫi collapsed; and the city of Eznkay [Erzindjān] was demolished and was inundated.

1453

1. Place: Xarberd; scribe and author of col.: Dawit‘ Episkopos; MS. title: Menology [*Yaysmawurk‘*].
   Source: Xač‘ikyan, *XV Dari*, II, no. 38, pp. 30–31

Written during the rule of the Egyptians [Egiptac‘woc‘] and the reign of Sulēyman Pak [Sulaymān Beg], who is a Dulłatarc‘i [Dhu'l-Ḳadrid] by race. This is the third year that our citadel and city [Kharput] have been in the hands of the Dulłarac‘i [Dhu'l-Ḳadrid], who is under the suzerainty of the sultans of Egiptos [Egypt] and is also their tributary, and they are allies both in evil and in good [deeds].

In this year the city of Stambul [Istanbul] was captured from the Greeks [Hoṙomoc‘]. It was attacked by the king, who is called Xondk‘ar, with 500,000 horsemen and footsoldiers, as well as with ships; and for three whole years he waged war for Ǝstambul [Istanbul]. The leader of the Franks [Fṙankac‘], namely the sovereign Pap [Pope], invited the patriarch and king of the Greeks [Hoṙomoc‘] of Stambul [Istanbul] to the city of Hṙovm [Rome] to reaffirm their faith [in Roman Catholicism]; and the patriarch and the king remained there for a whole year with the sovereign Pap [Pope].

When the patriarch and the king returned to Stambawl [Istanbul], the princes of the Greeks [Hoṙomoc‘] suspected that they had adhered to the Frankish faith [*Frangut'iwn*]. Although they swore many times [to the contrary], the princes of the Greeks [Hoŕomoc'] did not believe them; and the princes of the Greeks [Hoŕomoc'] harbored resentment against their king and patriarch, and never reconciled with them. Hence, a certain Greek [Hoŕom] prince, by the name of Kiwŕlikē [Lucas Notaras], dispatched a secret message, through couriers and intermediaries to the Xondk'ar king, saying, "I will deliver you the city of Stambul [Istanbul], do not go away." And, one day, when they had joined battle, and 5000 out of 100,000 Tačiks and 10,000 Greeks [Hoŕom] died, the self-same prince Kiwŕlikē [Lucas Notaras] opened one of the gates of the city . . . and the Tačiks, together with their king, entered the city. On the other hand, the patriarch and the king . . . boarded a large ship and, together with numerous people, numbering some 20,000 men, fled to Hŕovm [Rome]; and they took with them all the sacred effects, because they had a month earlier already made preparations to flee . . . Thus, as at the time of the [battle of the] holy Vardaneans [Vardananc'] the wicked prince of Siwnik', the traitor Vasak, caused the destruction of Armenia, so also the abominable Greek [Hoŕom], Kiwŕlikē [Lucas Notaras] . . . the wanting in faith and the accursed by God . . .

We will record here briefly the tragic events which befell the Christians. In the year 899 of the Armenian Era [A.D. 1450] the Sultan of T'awrēz [Tabrīz] named J̌ihanšah [Djihānshāh], who belonged to the Payəntur [Bayandur] tribe, marched forth with numerous and countless forces, [that is] 60,000, and captured Eznkay [Erzindjān] from the T'urk'man [Turkmens]. He captured the prince of the city of Eznka [Erzindjān], as well as forty well-known *amiray* [amirs]; and he carried them off to the east and killed them. He also carried off into captivity many of the inhabitants of the divinely built land of Kamax [Kemakh], that is some 10,000 individuals, both men and women, not to mention those who perished. He also carried off captives from Nerk'in-Derjan and Verin-Derjan, Baberd, Keli, Kočak, Gayl Get, Šiŕean, and Satał . . . Then they proceeded to and besieged Amit' [Āmid], Arłni, and Mērtin [Mārdīn] for five whole years. They waged daily battle to capture them. But the inhabitants of the fortresses descended upon the enemies and slew them . . . and then returned and entrenched themselves in their fortresses. On Saturday of the week of *Barekendan* [Shrovetide], on the feast-day of the Holy Fathers, the cavalry which had besieged Amit' [Āmid] left secretly and encircled the region of Arłni before dawn. They subdued [the inhabitants of] four villages, numbering some 500 individuals; they slew 40 souls; and then returned to their own dwellings. Moreover, on Palm Sunday they made peace with one another; and, through the grace and mercy of Christ, the captives at Arłni were released. He thus failed to capture Arłni, Amit' [Āmid], and Mērtin [Mārdīn], and returned to his own country . . .

. . . Written in the year 902 [of the Armenian Era = A.D. 1453] at Xarberd [Kharput].

2. Place: Constantinople; author of MS. and of col.: Aṙak'el Bałišec'i; MS. title: Aṙak'el Bałišec'i's Elegy on the Capital City of Stəmpol [Istanbul].
Source: Anasyan, *Haykakan Ałbyurnerə*, pp. 64–77[43]

All nations and peoples
Lament you, city of Stəmpol [Istanbul],
For to all creatures
You were the glory and honor, Stəmpol.

You were the habitat of divinity,
And the resting place, city of Stəmpol;
Today you've become the heathens'
Dwelling place, city of Stəmpol.

Heaven and earth in unison
Compose a lament for you, Stəmpol;
By the celestial and terrestrial
You were protected, city of Stəmpol.

Heavenly angels spread your fame,
Peerless city of Stəmpol;
You were protected by celestial powers,
Magnificent city of Stəmpol.

The resting place of evil-doers
You became today, Stəmpol;
And all your glory and honor
Vanished, city of Stəmpol.

[43] The critical edition of the Armenian text of this elegy, prepared by H. S. Anasyan, is based on fifteen manuscripts; for these, see Anasyan, *Haykakan Ałbyurnerə*, pp. 60–63. The Russian translation of this text, done by S. S. Arevšatyan, will be found in *ibid.*, pp. 129–140; the same translation is in *Vizantiiskii Vremennik*, vol. VII (1953, Moscow), pp. 460–466. A French translation was done by A. Tchobanian, "Lamentation sur la prise de Constantinople," in *La Roseraie d'Arménie*, vol. III (Paris, 1929), pp. 109–118.

You were a second Erusałēm [Jerusalem],
Renowned city of Stəmpol;
To you all were drawn
To see your glory, Stəmpol.

Imperial city of Stəmpol,
Called mother of cities, Stəmpol,
You're the glory of sea and land,
Harbor city of Stəmpol.

The mighty King Kostandianos [Constantine I the
Great]
Made you famous, great Stəmpol;
And he named you after himself
Polis of Kostandin [Constantine], Stəmpol.

Today he mourns and laments,
For they enslaved you, Stəmpol;
For the body adorned by God
Was preserved within you, Stəmpol.

Gratianos [Gratian] and T'ēodos [Theodosius],
Compose a lament for Stəmpol;
Onorios [Honorius] and Ustianos [Justinian],
Shed tears over Stəmpol.

Holy patriarchs and theologians
Who bestowed blessings upon Stəmpol,
Today turn over to malediction
The holy and great city of Stəmpol.

Holy Yovhannēs Oskeberan [John Chrysostom],
Come and behold Stəmpol;
And utter woes over your throne
In the great city of Stəmpol.

You were brilliant, Stəmpol,
Like the sun, Stəmpol;
At noontime you became dark
At the hands of infidels, Stəmpol.

You were the spring of life, Stəmpol,
For the thirsty, you Stəmpol;
Your water of life was dried out
Because of the infidels, Stəmpol.

Like the paradise of Edem [Eden], Stəmpol,
By the Lord's hands planted, Stəmpol;
Abundant fruits of immortality
Were gathered within you, Stəmpol.

You were destroyed by the infidels,
You were trampled underfoot, Stəmpol;
And all your glory and honor
Vanished, Stəmpol.

The treasure trove of the Lord's
Spiritual gifts [cf. Nehemiah 12:44], Stəmpol,
You were suddenly plundered
By the infidels, Stəmpol.

You pearl, the herald of the Lord's
Kingdom on earth, Stəmpol;
Which all the believers
Yearned to behold, Stəmpol.

They came to you with yearning,
City of holy vows, Stəmpol;
Just as they went to Holy Erusałēm [Jerusalem]
So also to you, city of Stəmpol.

You were the abode of blessings
And the subject of praises, Stəmpol;
Today you've become detestable,
A place of shame, Stəmpol.

Woe and alas unto that moment
When we learned the news, Stəmpol,
That "The Turks [azgn T'urk'ac'] captured
And enslaved the great Stəmpol."[44]

[44] This stanza indicates that Aṙak'el, the author of the elegy, was not at Constantinople during its capture by the Ottomans.

When the bells tolled
In your churches, Stəmpol,
The heavenly host descended
And danced within you, Stəmpol.

In place of the services and bells
The *mułrik‘* utter cries within you, Stəmpol;
In all your churches now
They recite the *namaz*, Stəmpol.

The heavenly host mourned
When they captured you, Stəmpol;
And the whole universe bewailed
When they heard of it, Stəmpol.

Because for all the Christians
You were a joy, Stəmpol;
And the infidels were enraged
When we spoke of you, Stəmpol.

Today you're the object of ridicule
To all the heathens, Stəmpol;
And you have caused grief
To all the Christians, Stəmpol.

. . .

I call you by your real name,
Chosen city, Biwzandia [Byzantium],
The infidels surrounded you
And declared *łaza* against you.

Divinely wrought Biwzandia,
Miraculous Biwzandia,
By God you were chosen
As the city of saints, Biwzandia.

Magnificent Biwzandia,
And marvelous Biwzandia,
The jewel of the world, Biwzandia,
Renowned Biwzandia.

Strong city, Biwzandia,
Built on seven hills, Biwzandia,
All the saints came to you
And assembled here, Biwzandia.

Elegant abode, Biwzandia,
A strong rampart, Biwzandia,
The joy of the celestial
And of the terrestrial, Biwzandia.

Eulogized in all tongues
And a victorious name, Biwzandia;
And all nations and peoples
Always respected you, Biwzandia.

Today you are lamentable
And deserving of tears, Biwzandia;
The woe that befell you
Was heard everywhere, Biwzandia.

Your rejoicing was transformed
Into sadness, Biwzandia;
And throughout the world you became
The subject of discourse, Biwzandia.

You were surrounded and defiled
By the infidels, Biwzandia;
You became an object of ridicule
To your heathen neighbors [cf. Psalms 79:1,4],
Biwzandia.

Like a gorgeous vineyard,
You flourished with vines, Biwzandia;
Today your fruit is changed to thorn,
It has become worthless, Biwzandia.

Biwzandia! Biwzandia!
City of Stəmpol, Biwzandia!
Called the Polis of Kostandin [Constantine],
Filled with blood, Biwzandia.

The abode of angels and also
Of the celestial host, Biwzandia;
Today you are the abode of demons,
Because of [your] sins, Biwzandia.

The gathering place of the clergy
And of hymns of praise, Biwzandia;
Today you're the assembling place
For the Tačik nation, Biwzandia.

The healer of wounds, Biwzandia;
The remitter of sins, Biwzandia;
And the giver of health
To all the weak, Biwzandia.

I'm hopeful that before the end
You'll be revived and will shed
The tyrannical yoke of the infidels,
Biwzandia! Biwzandia!

. . .

For the Franks [Frankac' azgn] will set forth
By the will of the immortal King,
As foretold in days gone by
By the holy and pious fathers.[45]

They spoke by the Holy Spirit
And told of things to come—
The arrival of the Franks [Frankac' azgn]
In subsequent times and days.

In unison and one and all,
The valiant nation shall move forth,
United unto one another
Burning with divine love.

[45] Beginning with this stanza, the author describes the future Crusade by the Franks against the Muslim east. It is based on the apocryphal prophecies attributed to St. Nersēs I the Great (see note 5 above) and to the philosopher Agatron. For discussions of the text of Agatron see Anasyan, *Haykakan Ałbyurnerə*, pp. 7, 9–10; Ačaṙyan, *HAB*, I, 45–46; Anasyan, *Matenagitut'yun*, I, cols. 144–149.

By sea and land they shall come,
Countless like the stars,
Urging one and all
To the war ordained by God.

First they shall take the city of Stəmpol
By the will of the Almighty Savior;
Then they shall venture further
And spread throughout the world.

They shall proceed to the eastern land
And cut everyone to pieces,
And roaring like lions,
They shall triumph over the infidels.

They shall capture the city of Erusałēm [Jerusalem],
And the holy dominical places;
They shall adorn with gold
The gate of the Holy Sepulcher.

For their time has now come [cf. Romans 11:25],
According to the command of Christ,
As foretold long ago
In the Gospel by the Son of God.

The Christians shall rejoice
In the Holy City of Erusałēm [Jerusalem];
And the heathens shall perish,
And vanish like dust.

Blessed are those who shall see
That day of infinite glory,
Like the old man Simēon
Who yearned to see the Savior.

The power of the Cross shall increase
Through the glory of the crucified King;
And all the heathen nations
Shall be destined to perish.

Countless shall be the Frank [Frankish] troops,
Like the sands of the seashore;
And no one shall be able to defeat
The valiant Frankish nation [Frank azgn].

Like a lightning bolt among the reeds [cf. Isaiah 5:24],
They shall descend upon the Muslims [*aylazgik'*];
They shall drive out the Tačiks,
The adversaries of the Holy Cross.

They shall vanquish all of Rūm [Hoṙmoc' ašxarh],
And reach as far as Məsər [Egypt];
They shall demolish the demons' abode,
The sanctuary of the infidels.

They shall reach as far as *šahastan*,
And advance as far as Dawrēz [Tabrīz];
They shall penetrate Xorasan [Khurāsān]
And carry off all into captivity.

The whole world shall be illumined
By the Christian faith,
And all the heathen nations shall be
Driven from the face of the earth.

Demolished churches everywhere
Shall be restored again,
And the whole world shall be glorified
By hymns of praise of Christ.

Our Armenian nation shall flourish,
For it shall be delivered from the Muslims [*aylazgik'*];
And everyone shall rejoice
As in the days of the Lusaworič' [St. Gregory the
Illuminator].

For when Trdat [Tiridates III] and St. Grigor
[Gregory]
Made their journey to Hṙom [Rome],
There were seventy thousand
Who entered Hṙom [Rome] with them.

The Lusaworič' [Illuminator] and Trdat
[Tiridates III]
Remained there for a whole year;
And Kostandianos [Constantine I the Great], every
day,
Presented their horsemen with *xilat'*.

Then they concluded an agreement
And they signed a treaty;
The Armenians and the Frank [Franks]
Concluded a pact of mutual love.[46]

They left four hundred men yonder,
From the Aršakuni [Arsacid] and Pahlawuni
[Parthian] clans,
To remain there and to multiply,
Thus to unite the Frank [Franks] and Armenians.

They shall now serve as guides
To the brave Franks [Frank azgn];
They shall come by sea and land
And render us assistance.

They shall take the canton of Ayrarat,
Where the Lusaworič' [Illuminator] had his seat;
They shall reign at Ējmiacin,
In the holy city of Vałaršapat.

. . .

Glory to God the Father on high
And to His Only-Begotten, His Word,
To the Holy Ghost, giver of life
And the bestower of peace.

[46] This assertion is based upon the apocryphal document known in Armenian as *Dašanc' T'ult'*, which was fabricated by Latinophile Armenians at the time of the Crusades. According to this document, the Armenian church hierarchy, originally connected with that of Caesarea in Cappadocia, was subsequently instituted as an autocephalic see through the license of Pope Sylvester I (314–335); this was agreed upon when St. Gregory the Illuminator and King Tiridates III of Armenia journeyed to Rome. There is, however, no historical evidence that St. Gregory ever made a trip to Rome; moreover, it was not Tiridates III but Tiridates I who actually journeyed to Rome in the first century after Christ to receive his royal crown from the Emperor. The first printing of the Armenian text, with a translation in Italian, will be found in *Lettera dell'Amicitia e dell'Vnione di Costantino gran Cesare*, Venice, 1683. The unauthenticity of the document was first established by Karapet Šahnazarean, *Dašanc' T'lt'oy K'nnut'iwnn u Herk'umə*, Paris, 1862.

In the year nine hundred and two
Of the Great Armenian calendar [A.D. 1453],
When they captured the city of Stəmpol
And the Christians they slaughtered.[47]

I, Aṙak'el, abundant with sin,
Filled with calamitous evils,
Wrote these words of lamentation
On the great city of Biwzandia.

Called the Polis of Kostandin [Constantine],
Named after the great king [Constantine I the Great],
Before which the angels hovered
And always steadfastly served.[48]

I, the totally unworthy,
Who am called a vardapet,
But wanting in deeds so much,
Brainless, foolish, and worthless.

These words I arranged
As a memorial to me on earth;
That whoe'er may encounter my ode,
With goodwill shall remember me.[49]

That they may say, "Lord have mercy"
Upon the most sinful Aṙak'el,
Who put these words together,
A lament on the Polis of Kostandin [Constantine].

Also for my worthy parents,
Łut'lumelik' and Nersēs,
Who gave birth to this wretched child,
Captive of manifold sins.

[47] This and the following ten stanzas have been reproduced by Xač'ikyan (see *XV Dari*, II, pp. 31–32).

[48] Compare this stanza with *Agat'angełeay Patmut'iwn Hayoc'*, publ. by G. Tēr-Mkrtč'ean and S. Kanayeanc', Tiflis, 1909, pp. 458–459.

[49] The Russian translation by Arevšatyan, referred to in note 43 above, terminates at this point.

And for my *rabuni* [mentor], Grigor,
Who is surnamed Cerencʻ,
A blessed martyr he was,
And an eloquent vardapet.[50]

And for my own beloved son,
Tēr Yovhannēs the priest,
Who at a tender age
Passed away into the living world.

And for Yakob the monk,
The scribe who with gold embroidered,
Who wrote on paper
The song which I composed.

And for him who sings with fervent love,
And for the sympathetic listener,
And for him who renders this lament,
And for him who recalls what I've written.

May the Lord have mercy upon all,
For He is magnanimous toward all;
Moreover, He encourages everyone
Who repents [*pʻošiman*] his sins.

For the Son of God promised
To His servant in the Gospel,
"I have come for the sinful,
For I am the healer of the sick" [cf. Mark 2:17].

Glory to the Creator of everything,
To the Father and His Only-Begotten Son,
To the Holy Ghost, giver of all grace,
In the past, present, and future.

3. Author of MS. and of col.: Abraham Ankiwracʻi; MS. title: Abraham Ankiwracʻi's Lament on the Fall of Constantinople. Source: Anasyan, *Haykakan Ałbyurnerə*, pp. 35–55[51]

[50] Aṙakʻel Bałišecʻi is also the author of an elegy on the martyrdom of Grigor Cerencʻ Xlatʻecʻi (see App. A), who was his paternal uncle and mentor.

[51] The critical edition of the Armenian text of this elegy, prepared by H. S. Anasyan,

In the year nine hundred and two [A.D. 1453],
In bitter and in wicked times,
The Lord was angered much again
By the Yunakan [Greek] and Rūm [Hoṙmocʻ] nation.

There arose a terrible sultan,
Whom they called Mahamat [Mehmet II, Fatih];
He was a descendant of Ōtʻman [ʻUthmān I],
And son of Murat [Murād II] the great *xondkʻar*.

He first conceived a small plan,
Which he accomplished at great expense;
A fort he began to build on the seashore,
At the Połaz of Ałekʻsandr [Strait of Alexander].[52]

What he began he soon completed,
In one summer, in three months;[53]
Five miles it was distant
From the Frank [Frankish] city of Łalatʻia [Galata].

He then returned to whence he came,
To his *tʻaxtʻ* at Atrana [Edirne],
And conceived a plan of perfidy
Against the great city of Biwzandia [Byzantium].

---

is based on seventeen manuscripts (for these, see Anasyan, *Haykakan Ałbyurnerə*, pp. 29–34). There are three translations of the text in French: E. Boré, "Touchante élégie sur la prise de Constantinople, arrivée l'an 902 de notre ère, époque fatale et douloureuse, où le Seigneur fit encore éclater violemment sa colère contre la nation des Latins et des Grecs," in *Nouveau Journal Asiatique*, Paris, 15 (1835): 271–298; M. Brosset, "Mélodie élégiaque sur la prise de Stamboul, traduite de l'arménien," in C. Lebeau, *Histoire du Bas-Empire* (ed. J. Saint-Martin), vol. XXI (Paris, 1836), pp. 307–314; and A. Dethier, "Abraham prêtre arménien. Mélodie élégiaque sur la prise de Stamboul," in *Monumenta Hungariae Historica*, vol. XXII, pt. 2 (Buda-Pest, 1872), pp. 225–248. A Russian translation of the text will be found in S. S. Arevshatian, "Abraam Ankirskii: Plach na vzatie Konstantinopolia," published by A. S. Anasian, in *Vizantiiskii Vremennik*, vol. VII (Moscow, 1953), pp. 452–460. The same text is in Anasyan, *Haykakan Ałbyurnerə*, pp. 113–128.

[52] The reference is to Mehmet II Fatih's construction of the fortress on the European shore of the Bosphorus at its narrowest point and opposite to Anadolu Hisar. The fortress, then known to the Turks as Boğaz-kesen and now called Rumeli Hisar, was completed on August 31, 1452. (See Runciman, *Fall of Constantinople*, p. 66; Vasiliev, *History*, II, 646–647.) It is not known how widely the name "Strait of Alexander," with an obvious reference to Alexander the Great, was used in the mid-fifteenth century.

[53] The work on the fortress was begun on April 15, 1452, and completed on August 31, 1452. See Runciman, *Fall of Constantinople*, p. 66.

He planned all through the winter,
Made preparations for war;
He issued orders everywhere,
"Come you all to wage *łaza*."

In the second week of Lent,[54]
He set forth and came upon the city;
He assembled countless horsemen,
Seven hundred thousand in number.

They laid siege [*xsar*] to it from all sides;
By sea and land they pressed;
The number of T'urk' [Turkish] troops swelled,
Those of the Christians diminished.

But the King [Constantine XI] of Stampol [Istanbul]
Was altogether powerless;
He cast his eyes upon the Franks [Frank azgn],
Expecting them to come to his aid.

But the cruel Latin nation
Laid down an improper condition:
"Convert to our own faith,
And to us your city relinquish."

And King Kostandin [Constantine XI]
Acquiesced in their demand;
The city was split into two,
Half Greek [Hoŕom] and half Latin.[55]

And misfortune befell
The Greek [Yunac'] and Frank [Frankish] nations;
The northern wind blew intensely,
And cut off the *lotos* wind.

The *łatərła* and ships
That came to render help,

[54] This line can also be rendered: "On the second Saturday of Lent." According to the Armenian church calendar, the second Saturday of Lent in the year 1453 fell on February 24.

[55] The reference is to the two Greek factions: the one which favored union with Rome, and the other which was opposed to it.

Floundered and rocked back and forth,
Remained where they were.[56]

And the evil Sultan Mahamat [Mehmet II, Fatih]
Placed a great and huge *t'op'*,[57]
Causing wonderment to those who saw it,
And amazement to those who heard it.

He demolished the city's five *purčes*,
And leveled them with the ground;
He built a road on the sea,
And they marched on it as on land.

A speech he made before his large army,
Words of encouragement he uttered to them,
Saying, "Hearken, *məsəlmank'* [musulmans],
You shall hear great and good tidings."

That "The Great city of Stampol [Istanbul]
Shall be your *t'axtan* and share;
Men, animals, and all *əṙzak*
Whoe'er takes shall be his own."[58]

And in the month of May,
On the twenty-eighth day,
And on the day that was Monday,
When the feast of Hṙip'simeanc' was held,

Toward the evening they arrived,
And reached the bank of the *xantak;*
They brought together the *santaluns*,
And ladders they erected.[59]

They took to battle and fought
Until the hour of daybreak;

[56] For the details regarding these developments see Runciman, *Fall of Constantinople*, pp. 100–103.

[57] Regarding this cannon see *ibid.*, pp. 66, 77–78, 79, 97, 116, 135, 136; Vasiliev, *History*, II, 650; G. Schlumberger, *Le Siège, la prise et le sac de Constantinople en 1453* (Paris, 1926), pp. 57–62.

[58] Regarding Mehmet's speech to his generals and troops see Runciman, *Fall of Constantinople*, pp. 126, 128.

[59] Regarding the scaling ladders used by the Turks see *ibid.*, pp. 119, 134–137 *passim.*

Half of them boarded the ships
And surrounded [the city] from the sea.

And at the breaking of the sun,
On Tuesday of the week,
On the third of the Armenian month of *Mehek*,
On the feast of the holy Gayianeanc‘,[60]

The Lord arose in great wrath
Upon the city of Kostandinupolis [Constantinople],
Delivered it into the hands of the hated,
Wicked enemies surrounded it [cf. Psalms 106:40–41].

The King [Constantine XI] and his troops
Joined in battle with all their might;
But they failed in their resistance,
For the Lord denied them His aid.

For they were split into two,
They failed to achieve unity;
Some were loyal to the King,
Some said we'll surrender [the city] to the T‘urk‘
[Turks].

Like the torrents of a flood,
The Tačiks broke through the city;
Many scrambled up the ramparts,
Others pulled each other up by rope.

When the King [Constantine XI] saw this,
And powerless in the combat,
He decided to take to flight,
For smitten was he by affliction.

Someone from among the Franks [yazgac‘ən Fərankin],
Whom they called *łap‘utan*,
Took the King [Constantine XI] and the notables,
On a ship they fled by sea.

[60] In 1453 the third of Mehek, according to the Armenian calendar, corresponded to May 29 of the Christian calendar; on this day, a Tuesday, according to the Armenian church calendar, was held the feast of St. Gayianeanc‘.

And when the *məsəlmans* [musulmans] came in,
They poured in upon the city;
They first captured the palace,[61]
Which was the *darpas* of the King [Constantine XI].

Then they left there and proceeded
To the cathedral church,
Which was called Sop'ia [Sophia]
And where the patriarch had his seat.

The numerous male Christians
There assembled joined in battle;
They were inflamed with intense fervor,
Like children for their parents.

They gave up their lives,
They went like sheep to the slaughter,
Countless fell victim to the sword,
And blood flowed like a brook.

And the wicked Sultan Mahamat [Mehmet II, Fatih],
Having entered the great cathedral,
Rejoiced exceedingly
For having attained his desired goal.

And the countless troops who entered with him
Scattered about in the streets;
They roared like wild beasts
Who are thirsty for blood.

The warriors whom they found
They slaughtered one and all;
But the other men and women
Into captivity they led away.

The young children they tore away
From the bosoms of their mothers,
And crushed them against the rocks,
The aged they pierced with their swords.

[61] The reference is probably to the palace of Blachernae. See account in Vasiliev, *History*, II.

Their cries and laments,
Their wailing and moaning,
No one can describe by mouth,
No one can relate with words.

As many monks as there were,
Whom they called *Kalogerosk*',
And many of the female sex,
Who were called *Kalokriayk*',

They seized and dragged them cruelly,
To tie them up and to carry them off;
And those who by force resisted them
Were smitten to the ground and rolled over.

Many prostrated on their knees
And willingly offered their necks to the sword,
With a martyr's voluntary death
They breathed their last and died.

The divinely ornamented churches
They mercilessly plundered;
They denuded them of their
Precious vessels and ornaments.

The sacred relics of the martyrs,
Which had been guarded with reverence,
They dispersed them everywhere,
They trampled them underfoot.

The graves of the kings
Covered with marble sarcophagi,
They opened and plundered,
And crushed all the bones.

Yet none of these sacred relics
Wrought any miracles;
Because of our multitudinous sins,
They all remained intensely mute.

They hurled the church bells down,
The bell-ringers they slew,
They annihilated the Cross,
The holy communion they scattered about.

They removed out of the city
The booty and captives which they took;
From the hour of three until nine,
They left nothing in the city.

As for the great prince of the Greeks,
Whom they called Kir Luka [Lucas Notaras]
They found him and seized him,
And brought him before the wicked Sultan [Mehmet II,
Fatih].

And he honored him exceedingly
Until he found out his secret;
Then he had him beheaded,
Together with his two sons.[62]

All the *məsəlman* [musulmans] who were there
Reveled with great rejoicing,
They rejoiced with great satisfaction,
They told one another the great tidings.

They said, "Stampol the eternal,
Which the Tačiks had never captured,
Now in these latter times
God gave to us to be our own."

But all the Christian nations
Were grieved with deep sadness;
Because the city of refuge was delivered
Into the hands of the Muslims [*aylazgi*].

They carried off much booty,
Silver, gold, and pearls,
Exquisite and precious gems,
Ne'er before seen by the nation earth-born.

[62] The references here are to Emperor Constantine's senior minister, Lucas Notaras, the Megadux and Greek Admiral of the Fleet. For the circumstances regarding his death see Runciman, *Fall of Constantinople*, p. 151.

The choice, pearl-studded and precious
Vessels found in the churches,
Gospels bound with silver and replete
With exquisite illuminations.

All these they took to the city of Atrana [Edirne],
With them they made Pursa [Bursa] abundant,
They took much goods to Ankiwria [Ankara],
They scattered them all over the world.

They carried off countless books;[63]
The Tačiks who saw them were wonder-struck;
The Christians recovered [books] without number,
Yet the majority remained with the Tačiks.

As for the people whom they took captive,
The notables and the commoners,
And so many from the clerical class,
No accounting of the common folk.

The old and the young, the youth,
Numerous women and their daughters,
They dispersed them like the dust
To all the corners of the world.

In the small city of Łalat'ia [Galata],
Which was under Frankish [Frankac'] rule,
The notables boarded a ship
And fled across the sea.

The remainder of its residents,
And the leaders who were left behind,
In terror and trembling they came
And prostrated at the feet of the Sultan [Mehmet II,
Fatih].

And he demanded from them,
"Submit to my command,
Demolish the city's ramparts,
And the strong *purč* of the *sahat'*."

[63] Regarding the capture of the books and their disposition see *ibid.*, p. 148; Vasiliev, *History*, II, 653.

And they acquiesced,
They carried out his command;
They demolished [the walls] by the sea coast,
And leveled them with the ground.

He changed the name of Stampol,
Which meant "to the city."
He said, "It shall be called Islampol,"
Which means "multitude of Tačiks."

The renowned Sop'ia [Sophia],
Which means "wisdom,"
He converted it into the main *məzkit* [mosque]
And retained its name Sop'ia [Sophia].

A prince he appointed for the city,
Sulēyman [Sulaymān] was his name;
He gave him numerous troops,
And [appointed] Łara-Łati [Ḳara-Ḳāḍī] as judge.

He also issued a stern order—
Causing anguish to all who heard it,
To all the cities in Rūm [Hoṙmoc' tun]
Which were under his dominion.

He said to remove men with their families,
To bring and settle them in this city;
This brought great grief to the T'urk' [Turkish] nation,
Who are lamenting with bitter tears.

For they separated fathers from sons,
They separated daughters from mothers,
They separated brothers from one another,
They deprived many of their ancestral homes.

Not only Tačiks but also
Christians they brought here;
On the twenty-eighth day of October
They brought four Armenians from Ankiwria [Ankara].

Astuacatur Sat'əlmiš,
And Simēon Barip'aš,
And Ayvat son of Papa,
And baron Gorg, the *hēšim hači*.

We must now bring our narrative to a close,
For the more we write the more we pain;
In the year nine hundred and two [A.D. 1453],
The Tačiks captured Biwzandia.

And we cry out with intense laments,
And we sigh tearfully,
We groan and mourn grievously,
And anguish for the great city.

Come, believer brothers,
Fathers and dear chosen ones,
Compose this tearful lament
On these events that have transpired.

Kostandinupolis [Constantinople] the exalted,
The former throne for kings,
How could you be overthrown
And be trampled by infidels?

You, chosen Kostandinupolis [Constantinople],
Mother of cities you were called,
To the enemies you were delivered,
Your tormentors now dominate you.

Kostandianos [Constantine I], the great king,
Who reigned in the city of Hṙom [Rome],
And together with the pontiff Sełbestros [Pope Sylvester]
He believed in Christ.

He encountered you during his travels,
He beheld you and loved you much,
He erected a place for his throne,
And named you the Nor Hṙom [New Rome].

T'ēodos [Theodosius] the Great sat on your throne,
With his two sons he sojourned within you,
You were chosen by Argatios [Arcadius] and Onorios
[Honorius],
As well as by T'ēodos P'ok'r [Theodosius the Younger].

Yustinianos [Justinian] reigned here,
A most renowned emperor he was,
Your stature he elevated
And erected the Sop'ia [Sophia].

Across from the church's gate
He erected a colossal statue,
He set up a replica in copper
Of himself mounted on a horse.

The heathens have come into you,
They have defiled your holy temple,
They turned you into a cell of gardeners,
And threw the corpses to the birds [cf. Psalms 79:1–2].

Their blood flowed all around you,
And no one buried them;
They made you a taunt to your neighbors,
You were mocked by those round about you [cf.
Psalms 79:3–4].

The fire devoured your young men,
Your virgins no one mourned,
Your priests fell by the sword,
No one wept for your widows [cf. Psalms 78:63–64].

The sound of psalms is no longer heard in you,
The clerics have been reduced in number,
Sweet melodies have been silenced,
The sound of the bells no longer resound.

The divine liturgy has been silenced in you,
The Lord's body and blood are no longer dispensed,
The sweet songs of hallelujahs
Were reduced much and have expired.

Oh, were that the Lord had awakened,
Like a strong man shouting because of wine,
And put your adversaries to rout,
And restored you eternally [cf. Psalms 78:65–66, 69].

Brothers, and this we must remember,
Why did this happen to them?
Because the pious ones were much diminished,
And the truth had pined away.

And their leaders went astray,
Far removed they were from sanctity,
The services and prayers
They performed without chastity.

Their princes adjudged unjustly,
They caused grief to the orphan and widow,
And the people in general
Committed acts of great wantonness.

Because of this, God was intensely angered
And punished them most severely,
He smote them with bitter blows,
And scattered them like dust.

Remembering all of this,
Let us have done with sins,
Abandon the familiar evils,
Tenaciously persevere in good deeds.

Let us turn to the church with hope,
Say prayers more frequently,
Observe the fasts with chastity,
And give alms incessantly.

Confess our sins more properly,
And do penance with tears;
And witnessing them, spare ourselves,
And avoid being like them.

Perhaps the Lord will have mercy
And deliver us from evil,
Spare us and take pity,
And prevent calamity.

Protect us hence from temptation,
Deliver us from the wicked Satan,
Save us from the infidels' evils,
And deliver us from oppressors.

Give us succor on the hour of death
By sending a good angel,
And communing with the Lord's body and blood
Be buried in blessed soil.

On the day of the great judgment,
To hear His holy voice saying, "Come to me"
[cf. Matthew 11:28];
To be seated among those on His right
And eternally praise the Lord.

I, Abraham, abundant with sin,
Composed this lament with great grief,
Because Kostandinupolis [Constantinople] I've seen
In its days of prosperity.[64]

For three months I sojourned there,
And before the sacred relics prayed;
The garment of Christ I saw yonder
Many times with mine own eyes.

I plead with you most tearfully,
Who might read my elegy,
That should you find errors therein
Be forgiving and not reproving.

4. Place: village of Avan; scribe and author of col.: Melk'iset'; MS. title: Hymnal [*Ganjaran*].
Source: Xač'ikyan, *XV Dari*, II, no. 42, p. 33

[64] Xač'ikyan reproduced this and the following stanzas. (See *XV Dari*, II, pp. 32–33.)

. . . [copied] in the year 902 of the Armenian Era [A.D. 1453], during the pontificate of the Lord Grigor [X, J̌alalbēkeanc‘], and the khanate of the Tačik J̌hanšah [Djihānshāh]. In this year there arrived locusts and caused much destruction in several places; and we hope that the Lord God of all will have mercy for His creatures and remove all the scourges from the earth . . .

5. Place: town of Akanc‘ in canton of K‘aǰberunik‘; scribe and author of col.: Yovsēp‘; MS. title: Gospel.
Source: Xač‘ikyan, *XV Dari*, II, no. 43, p. 34

. . . [completed in A.D. 1453] during the pontificate of the Lord Grigor [X, J̌alalbēkeanc‘] [and] the reign of J̌əhanšah *ēmirza* [Djihānshāh Mīrzā], who holds our whole country in his hands . . .

6. Place: city of Van; scribe and author of col.: Vardan; MS. title: Gospel.
Source: Xač‘ikyan, *XV Dari*, II, no. 44b, p. 35

. . . [copied] in the year 902 [of the Armenian Era = A.D. 1453], during the pontificate of the Lord Grigor [X, J̌alalbēkeanc‘], and the reign of J̌hanšay *imirza* [Djihānshāh Mīrzā], who in this year went to wage war against Pars [Fārs], and captured Xorasan [Khurāsān]; may the Lord God grant him victory, amen!

7. Place: monastery of Varag; scribe and author of col.: Yovanēs; MS. title: Ritual Book [*Maštoc‘*].
Source: Xač‘ikyan, *XV Dari*, II, no. 45, p. 35

This was copied in the year 902 of the Armenian Era [A.D. 1453] . . . during the imperial conquest of J̌xanšay Łan [Djihānshāh Khān], in a noteworthy year, when he captured the territories of the Č‘ałat‘ [Čaghatai], namely Širaz [Shīrāz] and Aspahan [Iṣfahān], and other cities . . .

8. Place: city of Van; scribe and author of col.: Vardan; MS. title: Gospel.
Source: Xač‘ikyan, *XV Dari*, II, no. 46, pp. 35–36

... [copied] in the year 902 of the Armenian Era [A.D. 1453], during the pontificate of the Lord Grigor [X, Ĵalalbēkeanc'], Catholicos of the Armenians ... and during the reign of Ĵhanšay *imirza* [Djihān-shāh Mīrzā] ...

1454

1. Place: monastery of Suxaray or Xaṙabastay in canton of K'ajberunik'; scribe and author of col.: Ignatios; MS. title: Commentary on the Epistles.
   Source: Xač'ikyan, *XV Dari*, II, no. 51, p. 39

... this was completed in the year 903 of the Armenian Era [A.D. 1454], during the pontificate of the Lord Grigor [X, Ĵalalbēkeanc'], Catholicos of All Armenians and vicar of Grigor Lusaworič' [St. Gregory the Illuminator], and in our province of the Lord Zak'aria [III], overseer [*veraditoł*] of Ałt'amar ... in times of bitter anguish, when many who feared the enemy took to flight. Some took refuge on the impregnable island of Lim, and many dispersed in the region of Amuk; and, on account of our multitudinous sins, they fell into the hands of the horsemen, they were looted and plundered, [and] many were slain ... and who can recount or put into writing the intense lamentation, the mourning, and the penetrating and heart-rending weeping? And those of us who came to Lim suffered from starvation and much wandering ...

2. Place: city of Arčēš and island of Lim; scribe and author of col.: Yovanēs Mankasarenc'; MS. title: Gospel.
   Source: Xač'ikyan, *XV Dari*, II, nos. 52a, b, pp. 40–41

... completed in the year 903 of the Armenian Era [A.D. 1454] ... during the pontificate of the Lord Grigor [X, Ĵalalbēkeanc') at the great see of Holy Ējmiacin, and during the khanate of the bloodthirsty tyrant Ĵhanšay [Djihānshāh], who captured by force Širaz [Shīrāz] and Ispahan [Iṣfahān] and numerous other cities and fortresses in the lands of the Č'ałat'ay [Čaghatai]. As for us, we are in fear and in flight, for the troops of Uzun Hasan are carrying off captives and plundering us every day ...

Alas for the bitterness of these days, and woe unto our lives, for I am dying ten times a day from fear of being killed, and I am writing this while I am trembling.

3. Place: monastery of Bazenic‘; scribe and author of col.: Yovanēs; MS. title: Gospel.
Source: Xač‘ikyan, *XV Dari*, II, no. 53a, p. 42

. . . [copied] during the pontificate of the Lord Zak‘aria [III of Aghtamar], and the reign of J̌hanšay [Djihānshāh], son of Łara Usuf [Ḳara Yūsuf]. In the year 903 of our [Armenian] Era [A.D. 1454], when our Armenian nation was suffering from the most rigorous levies imposed by the wicked T‘urk‘ [Turkish] tyrants . . .

4. Place: city of Van; scribe and author of col.: Karapet; MS. title: Ritual Book [*Maštoc‘*].
Source: Xač‘ikyan, *XV Dari*, II, no. 55, p. 44

. . . Copied in the year 903 of the Armenian Era [A.D. 1454] . . . during the pontificate of the Lord Grigor [X, J̌alalbēkeanc‘], and the reign of J̌xanšay [Djihānshāh], who, marching forth with numerous troops, penetrated Parskastan [Persia]; and we were in constant flight . . .

5. Place: city of Bałēš; scribe and author of col.: Kirakos; MS. title: Gospel.
Source: Xač‘ikyan, *XV Dari*, II, no. 57, pp. 45–46

. . . I copied this in bitter and anxious times . . . in the year 903 of the Armenian Era [A.D. 1454], during the khanate of J̌hanša [Djihānshāh], and the barony of *mir* Šamsadin [Mīr Shams al-Dīn Dushevār] in our region, [and] during the pontificate of the Lord Grigor [X, J̌alalbēkeanc‘] . . .

6. Place: city of Bałēš; scribe and author of col.: Step‘anos; MS. title: Gospel.
Source: Xač‘ikyan, *XV Dari*, II, no. 58, p. 46

. . . [copied] in the year 903 of the Armenian Era [A.D. 1454] . . . during the pontificate of the Lord Grigor [X, J̌alalbēkeanc‘], and the pontificate of the Lord Zak‘aria [III] at Ałat‘amar, and the imperial rule of amir J̌hanšah [Amīr Djihānshāh] of the nation of archers [azgin netołac‘] . . .

1455

1. Place: monastery of Hałbat; scribe and author of col.: Grigor; MS. title: Gospel.
Source: Xač'ikyan, *XV Dari*, II, no. 66, p. 51

... [copied] in the year 904 of the Armenian Era [A.D. 1455], during the catholicosate of the Lord Grigor [X, J̌alalbēkeanc'] ... [and] during the khanate of the Tačiks under J̌ihanšah [Djihānshāh], in bitter and anxious times, [and] under the rule of people who belong to a different religion. On account of the fear and terror which they have caused, we are languished and persecuted, we are in flight and in confusion, we have been enslaved and are quivering; [and] particularly because of the most excessive levies and of the large number of those who have been carried off into captivity, and of the scarcity of goods, no brother could help his brother and no one had mercy for the other ...

2. Place: city of Arčēš in province of K'aǰberunik'; scribe and author of col.: Yovhannēs; MS. title: Gospel.
Source: Xač'ikyan, *XV Dari*, II, no. 72, p. 55

This holy Gospel was copied [in A.D. 1455], during the pontificate of the Lord Grigor [X, J̌alalbēkeanc'] ... [and] during the reign of the T'urk' [Turk] J̌hanšah [Djihānshāh] and the Kurd amir Šamšadin [Amīr Shams al-Dīn Dushevār].[65]

3. Place: monastery of Bazēnic'; MS. title: Gospel.
Source: Xač'ikyan, *XV Dari*, II, no. 76, p. 57

... [copied] during the pontificate of the Lord Grigor [X, J̌alalbēkeanc'], supreme catholicos of the Armenians, and the incumbency of the Lord Catholicos Zak'aria [III] in our see of Ałt'amar; [and] during the reign of J̌hanšah [Djihānshāh], son of Łara-Eusuf [Ḳara Yūsuf]; in the year 904 of our [Armenian] Era [A.D. 1455], when our Armenian nation was suffering on account of the imposition of the most rigorous levies.

[65] This text is a summary of the original colophon. (See Xač'ikyan, *XV Dari*, II, p. 55, note.)

4. Place: Ałt'amar; scribe and author of col.: Hayrapet; MS. title: Excerpts from Missal [*Masn Čašoc'i*].
Source: Xač'ikyan, *XV Dari*, II, no. 77, p. 57

. . . [completed in A.D. 1455], during the pontificate of the Lord Zak'aria [III of Aghtamar], in bitter and most grievous times, when we were in great anguish and were in the servitude of the wicked nation of archers [azgin netołac'], for they loot and plunder the Christians most severely . . .

5. Place: village of P'asayvank' in canton of Mokk'; scribe and author of col.: Israyēl; MS. title: Gospel.
Source: Xač'ikyan, *XV Dari*, II, no. 79, p. 59

. . . [copied in A.D. 1455] during the pontificate of the Lord Zak'aria [III] Ałt'amarec'i, and during the reign of J̌əxanšay Łan [Djihānshāh Khān] . . .

6. Place: monastery of Gamałiēl; scribe and author of col.: Yohannēs; MS. title: Gospel.
Source: Xač'ikyan, *XV Dari*, II, no. 80, p. 59

. . . This holy Gospel was copied in the year 904 of the Armenian Era [A.D. 1455], in bitter and anxious times, during the khanate of J̌ihanša *amirzay* [Djihānshāh Mīrzā], and the amirate in our region of Łasəm *amirzay* [Amīr Ḳāsim], may whom the Lord God keep invincible and soften his heart toward us Christians, amen!

7. Place: monastery of Paṙuagrak; scribe and author of col.: Sargis; MS. title: Ritual Book [*Maštoc'*] and Hymnal [*Ganjaran*].
Source: Xač'ikyan, *XV Dari*, II, no. 82a, p. 60

. . . And because of the wickedness and bitterness of the times in which we live, it is not possible to recount or put into writing . . .

8. Place: Kafay; scribe and author of col.: Xač'atur; MS. title: Hymnal [*Ganjaran*].
Source: Xač'ikyan, *XV Dari*, II, no. 85, p. 62

Alas, a hundred thousand times!
Č'it'ax captured the great Kafay [Kafa]
In the year nine hundred and four
Of the Armenian Era [A.D. 1455] / / /

1456

1. Place: monastery of Getamēj in Ałuank'; scribe: T'ovma; author of col.: Vrt'anēs; MS. title: Gospel.
Source: Xač'ikyan, *XV Dari*, II, no. 92, p. 66

... [copied] in the year 905 of the Haykazean Era [A.D. 1456] ... during the imperial conquest of the bloodthirsty tyrant J̌hanšay [Djihānshāh] ...

2. Place: Salmast (?); binder of MS. and author of col.: Sar̄ačenc'; MS. title: Gospel.
Source: Xač'ikyan, *XV Dari*, II, no. 94, pp. 67–68

This holy Gospel had fallen captive in the hands of Muslims [*aylazgi*] at T'avrēz [Tabrīz], and I, Tēr Łazar, and my brother Blēl, and our father Isaz, and our mother Xamuš, found and bought this in our memory and in memory of our sons ...

... Moreover, oh brother, this holy Gospel was bound when they brought the population of the city of Salmast from Ahar to their own place. I, Sar̄ačenc', bound this Gospel in the year 905 of the Armenian Era [A.D. 1456], to the glory of our Christ God.

3. Place: city of Bałēš; scribe and author of col.: Step'anos; MS. title: Gospel.
Source: Xač'ikyan, *XV Dari*, II, no. 96a, p. 68

... [copied in A.D. 1456] during the pontificate of the Lord Grigor [X, J̌alalbēkeanc'] at Ējmiacin in Vałaršapat, and during the khanate of J̌əhanšay *amirza* [Djihānshāh Mīrzā], in wicked times when justice had diminished and injustice had intensified everywhere. And the words of the prophet that "There shall come a time, when they will tell the mountains fall upon us" [cf. Luke 23:30; Revelation 6:16; Hosea 10:8], were fulfilled ...

4. Place: city of Bałēš; scribe and author of col.: Step'anos; MS. title: Gospel.
Source: Xač'ikyan, *XV Dari*, II, no. 97, p. 71

... [copied in A.D. 1456] during the pontificate of the Lord Grigor [X, J̌alalbēkeanc'], and during the khanate of J̌hanšay *amirza* [Djihānshāh Mīrzā], in anxious and evil times ...

5. Place: city of Xizan; scribe and author of col.: Mkrtič'; MS. title: Gospel.
Source: Xač'ikyan, *XV Dari*, II, no. 104, p. 76

... [copied] with suffering and much wandering, in most bitter and most anxious times ... In the year 905 [of the Armenian Era = A.D. 1456], during the catholicosate of the Haykazean nation of the Lord Grigor [X, J̌alalbēkeanc'] at the holy see of Ējmiacin, and of the Lord Zak'aria [III] Ałt'amarec'i; and during the reign of the alien J̌hanša [Djihānshāh], and the barony in our city [Xizan] of amir Sulēyman [Amīr Sulaymān] ...

6. Place: city of Hizan; scribe and author of col.: Mkrtič'; MS. title: Gospel.
Source: Xač'ikyan, *XV Dari*, II, no. 105, p. 76

... this holy Gospel was completed [in A.D. 1456] during the catholicosate of the Lord Grigor [X, J̌alalbēkeanc'], and the khanate of J̌hanšay [Djihānshāh].

7. Place: city of Kafay; recipient of MS. and author of col.: Awetik'; MS. title: Gospel.
Source: Xač'ikyan, *XV Dari*, II, no. 108, p. 78

... In this year [A.D. 1456] Sultan Mahmut'ag [Maḥmūdek] arrived and put Hači-Kire Xan [Ḥadjdjī Giray Khān] to flight; and our city [Kafa] is exceedingly happy ...

1457

1. Place: Lim, monasteries of Suxaray and Argelan; scribe and author of col.: Łazar; MS. title: Menology [*Yaysmawurk'*].

Source: Xač'ikyan, *XV Dari*, II, nos. 111a, b, pp. 79–80

... [copied in three different places] on account of the agitations in Armenia, because J̌hanša [Djihānshāh], son of Łara Usuf [Ḳara Yūsuf], had gone to the land of the [nation of] archers [*netołac'*] and had captured all their fortresses, [that is] Hamadan [Hamadhān], Saway, Aspahan [Iṣfahān], Ṙē [Raiy], Łazwin [Ḳazwīn], Gelan [Gīlān], K'ašan [Kāshān], Širaz [Shīrāz], K'rman [Kirmān], and Xorasan [Khurāsān], as well as countless cities; and he also plans to proceed to Hrē [Herāt]. Insofar as our own situation is concerned, Hasan Bak [Uzun Ḥasan Beg], grandson of Łaray Ot'man [Ḳara Yoluḳ 'Uthmān], is holding our country of Armenia in terror ...

And it should be known that I began to copy this in the year 901 of the Armenian Era [A.D. 1452] and completed it in the year 906 [of the Armenian Era = A.D. 1457], because of the bitterness and the agitations of our times ...

... Let no one blame me, for I [Yovanēs] copied [part of] this in bitter days, in great fear and trembling, for Hasan [Uzun Ḥasan] carried off innocent Christians from the plain of Muš [Mush]; hence, we are despondent for ourselves and for the children, and we are fearful that the calamity may any day reach us as well. I diligently copied this [manuscript] in these bitter days, because of my love for the *mahdasi* [Step'anos], who is loved and respected by all for his good deeds and the firmness of his faith, and because in our presence he expended all his assets to save the captives from the hands of the infidels, and also provided the money [to recover] the precious books and other ecclesiastical vessels [from the infidels]; may he be rewarded with plentiful blessings from God, amen!

2. Place: monastery of C'ipnay; scribe and author of col.: Yohanēs; MS. title: Ritual Book [*Maštoc'*].
Source: Xač'ikyan, *XV Dari*, II, no. 112, p. 81

... [copied] during the barony of Adibek, [and] the khanate of J̌xanšay Łan [Djihānshāh Khān].

In this year [A.D. 1457] J̌əxanšay Łan [Djihānshāh Khān] captured Bałdat [Baghdad] and vanquished 60 baronies. They slew 60,000 souls, and they carried off 30,000 mule-loads of *mal* to Łap'an [Ghapan].

And again, on account of our sins, the wicked Murat Bēk [Murād Beg] captured Əstənbawl-Kostandnupawlis [Istanbul-Constantinople], and they carried off 40 loads [*beṙn*] of crucifixes and Gospels, relics and paintings of patriarchs.

And again, J̌xanšay Łan [Djihānshāh Khān], the servant of Satan, attacked Bałēš [Bitlīs], Muš [Mush], and Łlat‘ [Khilāt]. He captured and plundered them, and carried off 1,500 women, children, and deacons into captivity; and they are selling each captive for 500 *t‘amuri* . . .

3. Place: village of Urc in canton of Ararat; scribe and author of col.: Xač‘atur; MS. title: Missal [*Čašoc‘*].
Source: Xač‘ikyan, *XV Dari*, II, no. 113a, p. 82

. . . [completed] in the year 906 [of the Armenian Era = A.D. 1457], during the pontificate of the Lord Grigor [X, J̌alalbēkeanc‘] . . . and during the imperial conquest of the great and victorious hero J̌ihanša [Djihānshāh], in bitter and anxious times; we suffer the anguish of grief and tragedy at the hands of the infidels and unjust tax-collectors, and may the Lord recompense their evil deeds sevenfold . . .

4. Place: monastery of Hermon; scribe and author of col.: Yakob; MS. title: Gospel.
Source: Xač‘ikyan, *XV Dari*, II, no. 117, p. 85

. . . [completed in A.D. 1457] during the reign of J̌hanšay [Djihānshāh], son of Usuf [Ḳara Yūsuf] . . . [and] during the pontificate of the Lord Grigor [X, J̌alalbēkeanc‘] Makuec‘i . . .

5. Place: city of Arčēš, in province of K‘aǰberunik‘; scribe and author of col.: Yovanēs [Mangasarenc‘]; MS. title: Missal [*Čašoc‘*].
Source: Xač‘ikyan, *XV Dari*, II, no. 118a, p. 86

. . . [copied] during the pontificate of the Lord Catholicos Grigor [X, J̌alalbēkeanc‘] at the great see of Ēǰmiacin . . . during the reign of the wicked prince J̌hanšay [Djihānshāh], who held the eastern lands of Aspahan [Iṣfahān] and Hamadan [Hamadhān], Širaz [Shīrāz] and K‘rman [Kirmān], Ēzd [Yazd] and Dałman [Dāmghān], and the entire country of Irał [Iraq]; and he fears no one and is frightened by no one . . .

6. Place: Axt'amar; scribe and author of col.: Nersēs; MS. title: Gospel.
Source: Xač'ikyan, *XV Dari*, II, no. 123, p. 92

. . . [completed] in the year 906 of the Haykazean Era [A.D. 1457], in bitter and anxious times, when we were suffering gravely on account of levies imposed by the infidels . . .

1458

1. Scribe and author of col.: Yovhannēs; MS. title: Menology [*Yaysmawurk'*].
Source: Xač'ikyan, *XV Dari*, I, pp. 507–508, n. 1

The wicked and abominable tyrant of T'avrēz [Tabrīz] named J̌hanšay [Djihānshāh], son of Usuf Bēk [Ḳara Yūsuf Beg], slew his brother Sk'andar Bahadur̄ [Iskandar Bahadur], at the hands of his [Iskandar's] son named Łan [Shāh-Ḳubād], at the fortress of Ernčak, by order and command of the wicked king of the east named Šahr̄ux [Shāhrukh]. And he himself nurtured a grudge against King Alēk'sianos [Alexander I, the Great] of Georgia [Vrac'] because he had not come to him in submission and had not paid the prescribed royal tribute. Hence, the abominable, Christian-hating, and fore-runner Antichrist [*karapet Ner̄n*] J̌hanšah [Djihānshāh] became as furious as a bloodthirsty wild beast. He assembled troops, he formed contingents, and, recruiting more than 20,000 men, he marched into Vrac'tun [Georgia] . . .

Arriving at the city of Təp'xis [Tiflis], they demolished, destroyed, and burned the city; and they demolished all the churches from their foundations; and then returned from there. He arrived at and be-sieged the city of Šamšultē [Shamshwildé] for forty days, from the feast of Palm Sunday until the [feast of the] Ascension of our Christ God. On the miraculous Sunday, the accursed and wicked J̌hanša [Djihānshāh] besieged them. And the Christians rested their hopes in their own accursed king to come to their aid and to deliver them from the affliction caused by the infidels. But he showed no concern for them; he preferred to save himself, rather than concern himself about the annihilation of the Christians, who [in turn] were found to be lacking in courage and were cowardly, and who were unable to harm even a single individual.

Hence, the inhabitants of the city, tormented by starvation and thirst, neglected the protection of the citadel. And they [Djihānshāh's troops] secretly opened a hole in the walls of the city and entered it. And they were awe-struck, and trembled, and pleaded with the tyrant, who was at the gate of the city, to take pity on them. And he [Djihānshāh] swore falsely and deceitfully by God the Creator that he intended to commit no harm against them or to put them to death. And they believed his oath, and they opened the gate of the city, and surrendered it to him. But they removed everyone outside [of the city]; and he issued orders to torture them for three days, and to confiscate their concealed and visible possessions. And three days later he issued an order to assemble all the believers in a solemn tribunal. Then the multitude of infidels, with swords in their hands, surrounded them on all sides, and entrapped the believers . . .

And at that moment, two strong youths and valiant martyrs, putting aside all fear, cried out in a loud voice so that everyone could hear them: "Your law-giver Mahmet [the Prophet Muhammad] is anathema; we are the pupils of Christ and the twelve apostles, and the spiritual children of Surb Grigor Lusaworičʻ [St. Gregory the Illuminator] . . ."

And then the infidels raised a cry and growled like ferocious dogs at them, and instantly pierced the two martyrs with many arrows. And the wicked tyrant said: "Behold, why are you waiting? They cursed our master; kill them all with your swords, cut off their heads, and crush their heads with stones." And they carried out his wicked orders; they slew more than one thousand, forty of whom were monks, priests, and deacons. The clamor of their cry caused the earth to tremble and astonished the angels in heaven, and their innocent blood, like that of Abel, cried out to the Lord to avenge their innocence.

And the wicked tyrant issued orders to carry off all the women and their children into captivity, more than 10,000 souls, and dispersed them all over Tačkastan [Tačikistān], [that is] to Msr [Egypt] and to Xorasan [Khurāsān].

What a sight it was to behold the tragic grief of the entire Christian cohort, for the mother wept for her child and the child for its mother with lamentable grief and bitter tears: "My fondling child, I shall see you no more; woe unto my womb that gave birth to you, and woe unto my eyes that beheld you, woe unto my ears that heard your voice." And, again, the child cried out to its mother: "Oh divinely merciful and beloved begettor of mine, woe and alas unto me on this earth, and woe unto my day of judgment, for I have lost my chaste faith and I have lost [favor] in the eyes of God."

And no one can put into writing the indescribable bitterness which befell the Armenians. And all of this was meted out to us because of our sins. Through the intercession [of these martyrs] and their bitter suffering, Christ God deliver all our Christian captives from the infidels!

All of the above took place in the year 889 of the Armenian Era [A.D. 1440] . . .

2. Place: city of Van; scribe and author of col.: Karapet; MS. title: Ritual Book [*Maštoc'*].
Source: Xač'ikyan, *XV Dari*, II, Addenda (a), p. 600

. . . [copied in A.D. 1458] during the reign of J̌ianšay [Djihānshāh], who marched forth with numerous forces and captured Širaz [Shīrāz] and K'rman [Kirmān], Hrē [Herāt] and Xorasan [Khurāsān], as well as all of Persia [Parskac' tun].

And his son left Maku [Mākū] and installed himself at T'avrēz [Tabrīz] as a rival of his father; and we do not know what will happen to us. And in this year there was a severe plague, and thirty to forty individuals died every day in our city [Van] alone . . .

3. Place: monastery of Haxbat in canton of Lawṙi; scribe and author of col.: Yohanēs; MS. title: Missal [*Čašoc'*].
Source: Xač'ikyan, *XV Dari*, II, no. 132a, p. 98

. . . completed in the year 907 of the Haykazean Era [A.D. 1458], during the pontificate of the Lord Grigor [X, J̌alalbēkeanc'] at Vałaršapat . . . and during the imperial conquest of Armenia by J̌hanšah [Djihānshāh], the T'urk'man [Turkmen] and bloodthirsty beast . . .

4. Place: monastery of Xaṙabastay in province of K'aǰberunik'; scribe and author of col.: Ignatios; MS. title: Psalm Book, Liturgy, and Prayer Book.
Source: Xač'ikyan, *XV Dari*, II, no. 135a, b, p. 100

. . . [copied] In the year 907 of our [Armenian] Era [A.D. 1458], during the khanate of J̌hanšay [Djihānshāh], and during the pontificate of the Lord Grigor [X, J̌alalbēkeanc'] at Holy Ēǰmiacin . . .

. . . [copied] in most grievous and bitter times, when we were in the servitude of the Muslims [*aylazgi*]; in the year 907 of our [Armenian]

Era [A.D. 1458], during the khanate of J̌hanšay *imirza* [Djihānshāh Mīrzā], who came to Armenia and Xorasan [Khurāsān] in great victory; [and] during the catholicosate of the Lord Grigor [X, J̌alalbēkeanc‘] at Holy Ēǰmiacin in Vałaršapat . . .

5. Place: city of Bałēš; MS. title: Menology [*Yaysmawurk‘*].
Source: Xač‘ikyan, *XV Dari*, II, no. 136, p. 101

. . . [copied] during the amirate of Melik‘ Šaraf [Malik Sharaf] in our city [Bitlīs], and the khanate of Melik‘ J̌hanšay [Malik Djihānshāh]. In this year [A.D. 1458] Hasan Ali *amirza* [Ḥasan ‘Alī Mīrzā] escaped from the prison [in the fortress of Mākū] and captured T‘avrēz [Tabrīz]. And, on account of our multitudinous sins, there came a plague in this year and killed numerous people; in the year 907 of our [Armenian] Era [A.D. 1458].

6. Place: village of Soravank‘ in Kec‘anay-Jor; scribe and author of col.: Yovannēs; MS. title: Gospel.
Source: Xač‘ikyan, *XV Dari*, II, no. 142a, p. 106

. . . [copied] In the year 907 of the Great Armenian Era [A.D. 1458], during the catholicosate of the Haykazean nation of the Lord Zak‘aria [III] Axt‘amarec‘i, and during the reign of the T‘urk‘man [Turkmen] J̌hanša [Djihānshāh], who went to Pars [Fārs] and remained there . . .

7. Scribe: Yakob; recipient of MS. and author of col.: Zak‘ar; MS. title: Hymnal [*Šaraknoc‘*].
Source: Xač‘ikyan, *XV Dari*, II, no. 149, p. 113

. . . the *šah* [shāh] is J̌hanša [Djihānshāh], who went to Xorasan [Khurāsān] and left the *t‘ałt‘* unattended.

1459

1. Place: Kostantinoypawl; author of MS. and of col.: Amirdovlat‘ Amasiac‘i; MS. title: Medical Science by Amirdovlat‘ Amasiac‘i.
Source: Xač‘ikyan, *XV Dari*, II, no. 153a, p. 115

. . . [copied] in the year 908 of the Armenian Era [A.D. 1459] . . . during the catholicosate of the Armenians of the Lord Grigor [X,

J̌alalbēkeanc‘], and the prelacy of the Lord Martiros in the bishopric of Kostantinoypawl [Constantinople], and the barony of Muhamat Xan [Sultan Mehmet II, Fatih] . . .

2. Place: city of Ostan; recipient of MS. and author of col.: Abdəl-Aziz; MS. title: Missal [*Čašoc‘*].
Source: Xač‘ikyan, *XV Dari*, II, no. 154, pp. 117–118

. . . the judicious, pious and devout *tanutēr* [householder], Xōǰay Abdəl-Aziz, of the city of Ostan [Wusṭān], wished to own this book and acquired it through his *halal* [honestly earned] assets in memory of his own soul and [the souls] of his parents . . . request God's plentiful mercy upon Abdəl-Aziz, who built a church and offered much munificence to the holy churches; he is merciful and magnanimous toward the poor and the clergy, and he rescued this holy book from the infidels.

Moreover, I should inform you of the destruction of our country, which came to pass, on account of our sins / / / Maku [Mākū]. And, at the instigation of the evil one [Satan] and because of our multitudinous sins, [Ḥasan 'Alī, son of Djihānshāh] freed himself from his iron fetters, and committed much destruction in the cities. He also freed those whom his father had held in chains, [namely] Łlič-Aslan [Ḳilīdj Arslan b. Pīr 'Alī] and his son, as well as Arapšah ['Arab-Shāh] and his son. He had these men join his forces, and also recruited numerous horsemen. He then dispatched Łlič-Aslan [Ḳilīdj Arslan b. Pīr 'Alī] to attack and capture the citadel of Van, but he failed. He then conceived an evil plan against our country, and he committed much destruction and plunder, and he shamelessly went back and left our country in ruins. Only the region of Gawaš remained somewhat unharmed, but later there arrived on the day of *Tearṙəndaṙaǰ* [Penthesis], Sētali, the accursed by God who belonged to the impure and accursed Ǝṙoškan [Rūzagī] tribe. He plundered the region of Gawaš and despoiled the Christians of their possessions. He remained for twelve days in the village of Axavanc‘, and, after sending for two rafts from the village of Ałunay, he made preparations to land on the impregnable [island of] Ałt‘amar. He also threatened to put everyone there to the sword, to spill their blood in the sea, to demolish the holy churches, and to carry off the sacred objects. But he was overcome by the power of the Holy Cross, and the abominable and accursed Sētali went away in shame, and his designs were frustrated by the will of God. Having witnessed this, the venerable and most virtuous Catholicos, the Lord Zak‘aria [III of Aghtamar], marched forth like a valiant general strengthened by the grace of God and the power of the Holy Cross to wage battle against the infidels. He seized the two rafts and brought them to Ałt‘amar, and thus the Christians were delivered from the [hands of the] infidels, who returned to their own places in shame. And Ałt‘amar remained in peace thanks to the power of the Holy Cross and the valor of the Lord Catholicos Zak‘aria [III].

In these days, he [Catholicos Zak‘aria III] journeyed to plead with J̌hanša *mrzay* [Djihānshāh Mīrzā], and [informed him] of the destruction of our country; and [Djihānshāh] left the city of Xōy [Khoi] with numerous troops and arrived in our country to avenge its destruction and the suffering of the Christians. We hope that God will grant J̌hanša *mrzay* [Djihānshāh Mīrzā] a long life and cast his enemies into the abyss, for if he had not arrived here the Christians would have been annihilated . . . May the Lord God help him in all his wars, and may his enemies be driven away by the power of our God, amen!

And this came to pass in the year 908 of our Armenian Era [A.D. 1459], [in the year] when this book was brought to our city of Ostan [Wusṭān] . . .

3. Place: city of Hizan; scribe and author of col.: Mkrtič‘; MS. title: Gospel.
   Source: Xač‘ikyan, *XV Dari*, II, no. 155, p. 118

. . . This holy Gospel was copied in the year 908 of the Armenian Era [A.D. 1459], in bitter and anxious times, during the khanate of the T‘urk‘ [Turk] J̌hanša [Djihānshāh], and during the time of our *amiray* Sulēyman [Amīr Sulaymān] . . .

4. Place: Kikēt‘; scribe and author of col.: Grigor Angełakoydec‘i; MS. title: Gospel.
   Source: Xač‘ikyan, *XV Dari*, II, no. 156a, p. 119

. . . the wicked J̌ahanša [Djihānshāh] attacked the country, and carried off numerous captives and slaughtered many. And . . . they cut off my mother's two hands, and they cast her head in the blood, and I buried her severed body in a grave on the day of the feast of Surb Gēorg [St. George] . . .

5. Place: monastery of Ayrivank‘; scribe and author of col.: Mat‘ēos; MS. title: Missal [*Čašoc‘*].

Source: Xač'ikyan, *XV Dari*, II, no. 157a, p. 120

. . . [completed] in the year 908 of the Haykazean Era [A.D. 1459], in most grievous times, when we were suffering at the hands of the infidels and unjust tax-collectors; during the reign of King Gawrki [Giorgi VIII] of the Georgians [Vrac'], son of Alek'sandr [Alexander I, the Great]; and the pontificate of the Armenians of the Lord Grigor [X, J̌alalbēkeanc'] at the Holy see of Ēǰmiacin; [and] the khanate of J̌ahanšah [Djihānshāh], son of Łara Usuf [Ḳara Yūsuf] . . .

6. Place: village of Srkłunk'; scribe and author of col.: Dawit'; MS. title: Gospel.
Source: Xač'ikyan, *XV Dari*, II, no. 158, p. 122

. . . this was completed in the year 908 of the Armenian Era [A.D. 1459], during the khanate of J̌hanša [Djihānshāh].

7. Place: city of Arckē; scribe and author of col.: Yovhannēs; MS. title: Gospel.
Source: Xač'ikyan, *XV Dari*, II, no. 163, p. 124

. . . [copied] during the imperial conquest of J̌hanšay [Djihānshāh], son of Łaray Usuf [Ḳara Yūsuf], in the year 908 of our [Armenian] Era [A.D. 1459] . . .

8. Place: city of Bałēš (?); scribe and author of col.: Yovanēs; MS. title: Menology [*Yaysmawurk'*].
Source: Xač'ikyan, *XV Dari*, II, no. 165a, p. 126

. . . [copied] when the *t'alt'* was occupied by J̌hanšay [Djihānshāh]; and during the rule of the amir Šaraf [Amīr Sharaf] in our city of Bałēš [Bitlīs] . . .

9. Place: Ałt'amar; scribe and author of col.: Hayrapet; MS. title: Gospel.
Source: Xač'ikyan, *XV Dari*, II, no. 166a, p. 127

. . . [completed] during the pontificate of the Lord Zak'aria [III of Aghtamar], in the year 908 of the Haykazean Era [A.D. 1459], in bitter and anxious times, when the whole country was quivering at the hands of the lawless nation of archers [azgin netołac'] . . .

1460

1. Place: Bǰni; recipient of MS. and author of col.: Simēon; MS. title: Hymnal [*Ganjaran*].
Source: Xač'ikyan, *XV Dari*, II, no. 172, p. 131

... [written] in the year 909 of the Armenian Era [A.D. 1460], during the pontificate of the Lord Grigor [X, J̌alalbēkeanc'] in the city of Vałaršapat ... and during the khanate of J̌hanšah [Djihānshāh], son of Usuf [Ḳara Yūsuf], who controlled numerous cantons ...

2. Place: monastery of Ałǰoc'; scribe and author of col.: Vardan; MS. title: Gospel.
Source: Xač'ikyan, *XV Dari*, II, no. 173, p. 131

... This holy Gospel was copied in the year 909 of the Armenian Era [A.D. 1460], during the pontificate of the Lord Grigor [X, J̌alalbēkeanc'] at the holy see of Ēǰmiacin, and during the khanate of J̌ahanšah [Djihānshāh], son of Usuf [Ḳara Yūsuf], who went to Hrē [Herāt] with two hundred thousand horsemen. And he remained there for seven years, and returned with much booty. Copied ... in bitter and in anxious times, when our Armenian nation was tottering and quavering at the hands of the infidel Muslims [*aylazgi*] and unjust tax-collectors ...

3. Place: village of Urc in canton of Ararat; scribe and author of col.: Xač'atur; MS. title: Menology [*Yaysmawurk'*].
Source: Xač'ikyan, *XV Dari*, II, no. 174a, p. 132

... [copied] in the year 909 of the Haykazean Era [A.D. 1460] ... during the pontificate of the Lord Grigor [X, J̌alalbēkeanc'] ... and the imperial conquest of J̌ahanšah [Djihānshāh], who controlled with tyranny and despotism numerous lands and cantons extending as far as Xorasan [Khurāsān]; [and] he subjected many to plunder, persecution, slaughter, and captivity ...

4. Place: monastery of Hermon; scribe and author of col.: Zak'ar; MS. title: Gospel.
Source: Xač'ikyan, *XV Dari*, II, no. 175, pp. 133–134

... this was copied in the year 909 of the Armenian Era [A.D. 1460] ... during the reign of J̌hanšay [Djihānshāh] ...

5. Place: village of Ełujor in province of Ełegeac'; scribe and author of col.: Mat'ēos; MS. title: Gospel.
Source: Xač'ikyan, *XV Dari*, II, no. 176a, p. 134

... [completed] in the year 909 of the Armenian Era [A.D. 1460], during the pontificate of the Lord Grigor [X, J̌alalbēkeanc'], [and] during the khanate of J̌hanša [Djihānshāh] ...

6. Place: city of Arckē; scribe and author of col.: Yovanēs; MS. title: Missal [*Čašoc'*].
Source: Xač'ikyan, *XV Dari*, II, no. 177, p. 135

... [copied] in the year 909 of our [Armenian] Era [A.D. 1460], during the reign of J̌hanšay [Djihānshāh], son of Łaray Usuf [Ḳara Yūsuf] ... in most grievous times, when the Christians were suffering incalculable grief and anguish on account of the exorbitant levies imposed by the infidels ...

7. Place: city of Arckē; scribe and author of col.: Atom; MS. title: *Oskep'orik.*
Source: Xač'ikyan, *XV Dari*, II, no. 178a, p. 138

... [completed] during the imperial conquest of and the occupancy of the *t'ałt'* by J̌hanša *imirza* [Djihānshāh Mīrzā] ...

8. Place: city of Arckē; scribe and author of col.: Daniēl; MS. title: Gospel.
Source: Xač'ikyan, *XV Dari*, II, no. 179, p. 139

... [copied] In the year 909 [of the Armenian Era = A.D. 1460] ... and during the khanate of J̌hanšah [Djihānshāh], son of Łara Usuf [Ḳara Yūsuf] ...

9. Place: city of Bałēš; scribe and author of col.: Step'anos; MS. title: Gospel.
Source: Xač'ikyan, *XV Dari*, II, no. 181, pp. 141–142

... [completed] in bitter and evil times, when the iniquitous Ismaelites [azgn Ismayēli] persecute us because of our multitudinous sins, and when they cause anguish to the suffering Christians by manifold tortures and indignities . . . This holy Gospel was completed during the khanate of J̌hanša *amirza* [Djihānshāh Mīrzā] . . .

This was written in the year 909 of our Armenian Era [A.D. 1460], during the khanate of J̌hanša [Djihānshāh], and the pontificate of the Lord Zak'aria [III] Ałt'amarc'i, in harsh times, when they were persecuting the Christians most exceedingly . . .

10. Place: Ałt'amar; scribe and author of col.: Nersēs; MS. title: Gospel.
Source: Xač'ikyan, *XV Dari*, II, no. 182a, p. 142

. . . I copied this [in A.D. 1460] . . . under much suffering and great affliction, in bitter and grievous times, when we were subjected to levies by the infidels . . .

11. Place: city of Xizan; scribe and author of col.: Yovanēs; MS. title: Gospel.
Source: Xač'ikyan, *XV Dari*, II, no. 187, p. 148

. . . [copied in A.D. 1460] during the reign of the alien baron J̌hanša [Djihānshāh] . . .

12. Place: monastery of Ełrdut, near Muš; MS. title: Menology [*Yaysmawurk'*].
Source: Xač'ikyan, *XV Dari*, II, no. 188, pp. 148–149

. . . This menology was copied in the year 909 of the Armenian Era [A.D. 1460] . . . during the tyrannical rule in our country of Armenia of the wicked J̌hanšah [Djihānshāh], the destroyer and devastator of all the cantons, and during the amirate in our region of the Amir Šaraf [Amīr Sharaf].

I suffered much grief and anguish while copying this [manuscript], [and] I was sick for a whole year. After that, Hasan Pēk [Uzun Ḥasan] arrived and devastated and burned our plains. Two months later, more or less, there came a plague, which separated many children from their fathers, daughters from their mothers, sisters from their brothers, and wives from their husbands. Who can describe their tragic grief? . . .

13. Scribe and author of col.: Step'anos; MS. title: Gospel.
Source: Xač'ikyan, *XV Dari*, II, no. 192, p. 153

... this was copied in the year 909 of the Armenian Era [A.D. 1460], during the khanate of J̌hanša [Djihānshāh], and the pontificate of the Lord Zak'aria [III] Ałt'amarec'i ...

1461

1. Place: Ējmiacin; scribe and author of col.: Step'anos; MS. title: Ritual Book [*Maštoc'*] for the Ordination of Bishops and Catholicoses and for the Anointment of Kings.
Source: Xač'ikyan, *XV Dari*, II, no. 194, p. 156

... [completed] during the khanate of J̌ahanšah *p'at'šah* [Djihānshāh Pādishāh], in the year 910 [of the Armenian Era = A.D. 1461] ...

2. Place: town of Urc; scribe and author of col.: Xač'atur; MS. title: Gospel.
Source: Xač'ikyan, *XV Dari*, II, no. 197a, p. 158

... [copied] in the year 910 of the Haykazean Era [A.D. 1461], during the pontificate of the Lord Grigor [X, J̌alalbēkeanc']. Also during the imperial conquest of J̌ahanša [Djihānshāh], who controlled with tyranny and despotism numerous lands and cantons extending as far as Xorasan [Khurāsān] ...

3. Place: city of Arčēš in K'aǰberunik'; scribe and author of col.: Yovhannēs; MS. title: Missal [*Čašoc'*].
Source: Xač'ikyan, *XV Dari*, II, no. 200, p. 160

... [copied] during the pontificate of [the Lord] Zak'aria [III of Aghtamar], and during the reign of the *p'at'šah* J̌hanšah [Djihānshāh].

4. Place: monastery of Kołuc'; scribe and author of col.: Vardan; MS. title: Gospel.
Source: Xač'ikyan, *XV Dari*, II, no. 202, p. 161

... [completed in A.D. 1461], during the pontificate of the Lord Grigor [X, J̌alalbēkeanc'], [and] during the reign of J̌hanša [Djihānshāh], when the Christians were persecuted by the infidels.

5. Place: Aƚt'amar; scribe and author of col.: Nersēs; MS. title: Gospel.
Source: Xač'ikyan, *XV Dari*, II, no. 205, p. 163

... [completed] during the pontificate of the Lord Zak'aria [III of Aghtamar], and during the khanate of the baron J̌ihanšay [Djihānshāh], in the year 910 [of the Armenian Era = A.D. 1461] ...

6. Place: city of Ostan; scribe and author of col.: Karapet; MS. title: Gospel.
Source: Xač'ikyan, *XV Dari*, II, no. 206, p. 164

... [copied in A.D. 1461], in bitter and most grievous times, when the Christians were in grave anguish and under evil servitude ...

7. Place: monastery of Palaxoru in canton of Xaƚteac'; scribe and author of col.: Karapet; MS. title: Gospel.
Source: Xač'ikyan, *XV Dari*, II, no. 209, p. 166

... And because of the evil and bitter times in which we live, it is impossible to recount or put into writing the extreme misery suffered by the Christians on account of the famine ... as well as by the manifold grief and anguish. Woe unto us, and woe again! For the prophecy of St. Nersēs, the divinely inspired man of God, concerning the Christians came to pass, [that is] that they shall be persecuted on all sides and they shall be transplanted from place to place, and they shall find no comfort ... Behold, all of this came to pass, for on account of our intense anguish and because of the most wicked times we are asking the mountains to fall upon us and the hills to cover us [cf. Luke 23:30; Revelation 6:16; Hosea 10:8]. Let this suffice, brothers!

8. Recipient of MS. and author of col.: Step'anos; MS. title: Concordance to the Gospel.
Source: Xač'ikyan, *XV Dari*, II, no. 215, p. 168

... I wrote this much in the year 910 of the Armenian Era [A.D. 1461], during the barony of J̌ahanšay [Djihānshāh], and the catholicosate of the Lord Grigor [X, J̌alalbēkeanc'] ...

1462

1. Place: city of Tup'xis; scribe and author of col.: Dawit'; MS. title: Gospel.
   Source: Xač'ikyan, *XV Dari*, II, no. 216b, p. 169

... during the reign of King Giawrgi [Giorgi VIII] of the Georgians [Vrac'], in the year 911 of the Armenian Era [A.D. 1462] ... on April 22 during the week of Easter, when we celebrated a black Easter. On Thursday, 1000 T'urk' [Turks] came to Lawčin to water [their animals]; and twenty horsemen came ... and carried off the cattle from Hawčalay [Avčala]. And rumors spread in the city [Tiflis] that the horsemen were few in number; [hence], 200 brave men from our city went after them as far as Lawčin. They crossed [the river] on foot; they were exhausted, their arrows spent ... and they were unarmed [*ansleh*] ... The multitude of horsemen came out, surrounded them on both sides, slew them all with their swords, and carried off their heads. Woe unto these days of mourning! Who can describe the lamentation, when they brought these headless and naked men in groups, so much so that no one could recognize his own dead. The weeping and the lamentation of that day no one can recount; woe unto me a thousand times! ...

... in bitter and anxious times when this pestilence and slaughter occurred on Easter Thursday. Woe, woe, what can this slave do!

2. Place: village of Tepur; scribe and author of col.: Tiratur; MS. title: Gospel.
   Source: Xač'ikyan, *XV Dari*, II, nos. 218b, c, d, pp. 170–171

... This holy Gospel was copied in the year 911 of the Great Armenian Era [A.D. 1462] ... during the khanate of J̌ahanša [Djihānshāh], and the pontificate of the Armenians of the Lord Grigor [X, J̌alalbēkeanc'] ...

... This holy Gospel was copied during the khanate of J̌ahaynšay [Djihānshāh] ...

May the Lord God have mercy upon the baron *dēp'al* T'amar and King Alēk'sandr [Alexander I the Great, of Georgia], amen!

3. Place: city of Arčēš in K'aǰberunik'; recipient of MS. and author of col.: T'umašay; MS. title: Menology [*Yaysmawurk'*].

Source: Xač'ikyan, *XV Dari*, II, no. 221, pp. 172–177

. . . [copied] during the pontificate of the Lord Zak'aria [III of Aghtamar], Catholicos of All Armenians, and the tyrannical rule of the nation of archers [azgin netołac'] under the *p'at'šah* J̌ahanšah [Pādishāh Djihānshāh], who left with numerous marauders and countless troops and, marching into the land of Irał [Iraq], occupied the whole country. He then arrived at the great city of Aspahan [Iṣfahān]—which is the city of Šōš [Shūsh], which the prophet Daniel saw in his vision—which was well-fortified and inhabited by a large population. They took to battle to resist him, but he defeated them and captured the city. He put all the warriors to the sword, and demolished and devastated the city. And he diverted the waters of the river in the direction of the city so that those who had taken refuge or hidden in the caverns, cellars, and subterranean dwellings [*daran*] drowned, suffocated, and died. Moreover, the whole city crumbled upon them, because it was built of dirt. From there, he proceeded to Hrē [Herāt] and Xorasan [Khurāsān]; and he vanquished the whole country of the T'at'ar [Tatars]; and then he returned to his *t'axt'* at the *šahastan* capital city of T'awrēz [Tabrīz].

The great pontiff Lord Zak'aria [III], incumbent of the see at the [cathedral] of the Holy Cross at Ałt'amar, who was of royal descent and was one of the grandchildren and a scion of King Gagik, went to meet him [Djihānshāh] with many gifts and presents. The king of kings J̌əhanšah *p'at'šah* [Djihānshāh Pādishāh] and the *dšxoy* [queen] [Bēkum-Xat'un] received him most respectfully. They honored him and offered him a *xlay*; [and] they also granted him the [relic of the] right hand of our Surb Grigor Lusaworič' [St. Gregory the Illuminator], as well as the title of patriarch. By the governance of God, by the will of the Surb Lusaworič' [Holy Illuminator], and by order of the *p'at'šah* [padishah], he [Zak'aria] arrived at the divine and magnificent cathedral of Holy Ēǰmiacin, founded by, and the apostolic see of, St. Gregory, and he began to reign as absolute patriarch of all the [Armenian] Christians, [that is] of all those who were scattered throughout the world [cf. John 11:52]; and he, as the Lord said, united them all into one fold with one shepherd [cf. John 10:16]; and he guided them all in the orthodox faith of the holy Nicaean doctrine.

In those days, the *p'at'šah* [padishah] was greatly incensed at the *amiray* of Bałēš [Amīr Sharaf of Bitlīs], and, filled with fury, he dispatched four generals, with 12,000 horsemen, against the city of Xlat' [Khilāṭ]. They arrived there and devastated and demolished it, and, after amassing a large booty, they laid siege to the citadel and made attempts to capture it. They also made preparations to do likewise at Bałēš [Bitlīs] and Muš [Mush], at Xut‘ and Sasunk‘ [Sasun], and all of their cantons.

The newly consecrated patriarch, Lord Zak‘aria [III], witnessed the anguish in these regions, the enslavement of the people at the hands of the infidels, the devastation and demolition, the ruination of the churches and the destruction of the holy altars, the capture of the sacred objects, the cessation of the glorification of God, and the dispersion of the multitudes of people and their enslavement and anguish. Witnessing all of this, the great pontiff, Lord Zak‘aria [III], recalled the words of the Lord, saying, "I am the good shepherd; the good shepherd lays down his life for the sheep" [cf. John 10:11]. And, putting these words into action, he laid down his life for the rational flock of Christ, [that is] for the entire population of Bałēš [Bitlīs]. Strengthened by the Holy Spirit and with a heart as hard as a rock, he appeared before the king [Djihānshāh] and he offered himself as ransom for all the people. He gave his signature and offered his own *daman* to collect the levies from the *amiray* [amir] of Bałēš [Bitlīs] and to give them unto Caesar, so that the country would enjoy peace. He also offered to pray for the continued health of the king and of his sons. The king and the queen gave their consent, and accordingly gave him an official letter and permission to do whatever he wished.

Leaving their presence, he immediately hurried forth on a fast-running horse and arrived at the city of Bałēš [Bitlīs]. The *amiray* [Amīr Sharaf], together with his chieftains, came out to greet him, and with great ceremony took him to the summit of the citadel. They promised to carry out his wishes and to give him whatever he wanted, on condition that all the horsemen would be sent away from the citadel of Xlat‘ [Khilāṭ].

After receiving their verbal assurances, he went to Xlat‘ [Khilāṭ], and again offered the generals his signature. He also showed them the padishah's official letter and persuaded them to return peacefully to their own places. And he returned to Bałēš [Bitlīs], where he remained for three months. He collected the imperial levies that they had promised, and turned them over to the padishah, and thus he brought peace among them, and saved all the motley population, Armenians and Tačiks, from the hands of the infidels and from bitter enslavement. May the Lord God protect him from all spiritual and physical temptations, amen!

Leaving the padishah, he returned to his seat at Holy Ējmiacin. He was honored with *xlays* by the two alien tyrants, the T‘urk‘man

[Turkmen] padishah and the Kurd *amiray* [Amīr Sharaf], even as Zōrababēl [Zerubbabel] by Dareh [Darius I], and continued to guide his faithful people.

The padishah J̌hanšay [Djihānshāh] again invaded Irał [Iraq], Širaz [Shīrāz], and K'rman [Kirmān]. He had a son named Hasan Ali [Ḥasan 'Alī], who wandered about in the northern regions of the canton of Ararat. Incited by the perfidious accusations of some individuals, he [Ḥasan 'Alī] decided to seize the great patriarch Lord Zak'aria [III], and to demand from him treasures and other riches. When the great pontiff learned of his perfidy, he took [the relic] of Surb Lusaworič''s [the Holy Illuminator's] right hand and other ecclesiastical effects and, in wintertime, he went as far as Bagu [Bagarvan], and from there he arrived at the citadel of Bayazit [Beyazid], and from there he went down to the holy monastery of Argilan, where rest the venerable relics of the holy vardapet Step'annos, son of the priest Yusik. And arriving there, he revealed the divine treasure, [the relic] of the right hand of our Surb Grigor Lusaworič' [St. Gregory the Illuminator], as well as the *xač'alam* [ecclesiastical banner], on one side of which was painted the picture of the Lord [Jesus Christ] and on the other the [pictures of] our Surb Grigor Lusaworič' [St. Gregory the Illuminator], of King Trdat [Tiridates III], and of the very graceful virgin St. Hṙip'simē, as well as the gold-laced and multicolored holy veil, which astonished the beholders. He then set forth to proceed to his ancestral seat in the beautifully vaulted [church of the] Holy Cross [on the island of] Ałt'amar.

The news of his arrival, together with the holy right hand and the ecclesiastical banner, which was raised upon a pole with a golden crucifix on it summit, spread around. When the pontiff arrived in any canton, its entire population thronged to him. They all came out to greet him with incense and candles and the sacrifice of rams and oxen. They prostrated themselves before the holy right hand and before the pontiff, and kissed him most reverently. This went on until his arrival in the canton of Tosp. He entered the city of Van with numerous bishops, vardapets, and priests and multitudes of people with horses and horsemen. The priests, who walked both in front of and behind the banner, sang sweet melodies. And, thus, with great pomp and ceremony, he entered the city of Van.

But the baron who occupied the fortress of Šamiram [Semiramis], that is, the citadel of Van, namely Mahmut Bēk [Maḥmūd Beg], who was padishah J̌hanšah's [Pādishāh Djihānshāh] foster brother, witnessing the prosperity of the Christians, wished to see the holy right hand, and he sent for it. When the great pontiff, with the holy right hand, entered the gate of the uppermost part of the citadel, the tyrant Mahmut Bēk [Maḥmūd Beg] came out to greet him with all his chieftains and their families and with his *amirzay* [mīrzā] sons. They fell down before the holy right hand and kissed it; and they offered supplications. He [Maḥmūd Beg] also honored the pontiff with a *xlay*, and [then] sent him to his lodging. The multitudes of the city and of the canton arrived every day with numerous gifts and offerings, and prostrated themselves before the holy right hand and greeted the great pontiff. Some days later, he obtained the baron's permission to proceed to his ancestral seat at Ałt'amar. When he left the city, multitudes of bishops, vardapets, and priests and all the corps of noble *xoǰas* of Van accompanied him, with their horses and armed horsemen. They arrived near the coastal city of Ostan [Wusṭān]. All of its inhabitants, priests and multitudes of people of all ranks, came out to greet them with incense and candles and resounding melodies; so much so that there were more than one thousand men in front of and behind the great pontiff. The ecclesiastical banner was carried in front, and the golden crucifix affixed on the top shone like a light; and with such pomp and ceremony he entered the city of Ostan [Wusṭān]. When the alien inhabitants of Ostan [Wusṭān] witnessed this rejoicing, they were deeply aggrieved by the splendor and by the forwardness of the pontiff, who had traveled from the canton of Tarberunik' to the city of Ostan [Wusṭān] with the banner and with bishops, vardapets, and numerous clergymen and people. Hence, they met with the city's prince, who was a Kurd by race, and who was wicked and perfidious, and wholly inimical to the Christians. And they conceived an evil plan, [namely] to plot secretly against the pontiff. When the brave overseer [*ditapet*] learned of their wicked intent, he took the holy right hand and at dawn went to the harbor on the seashore. Those who learned of his arrival came from Van and other cantons, and they accompanied him until they arrived at the great fortress of Manačihr, that is Karatash, opposite the God-protected island of Ałt'amar.

He stopped there and blessed everyone with the grace-bestowing holy right hand, and kissing everyone with a sanctifying kiss he dismissed them and sent them back to their homes in peace and blessing. And he took the holy right hand of the Lusaworič' [Illuminator] and, boarding the boat, went to his ancestral domain, the God-inhabited island of Ałt'amar. When he landed, the entire population [of the island] came to greet him on the shores of the sea, with incense and candles, and the priests sang melodious songs. They carried the holy right hand and placed it in the magnificent church of the Holy Cross of Ałt'amar; and they knelt before the holy right hand and the pontiff, and they chanted songs of praise and exaltations to the miraculous God, for making them worthy of witnessing the grace-bestowing holy right hand of the Lusaworič‘ [Illuminator]. The holy right hand thus arrived at the impregnable island of Ałt‘amar and found there its original resting place in the year 911 of our [Armenian] Era [A.D. 1462], in the beginning of this year, that is, on Friday the sixteenth of the month of Nawasard, on the fast day of St. James [December 11, 1461]. It was placed in the [church of the] Holy Cross at Ałt‘amar to protect all of us believers, and everyone rejoiced not a little.

The inhabitants of those cantons who learned of this arrived everyday to prostrate themselves before the holy right hand and to greet the great pontiff, with numerous gifts, offerings, and blessings, and returned to their homes with great rejoicing, and they glorified the Holy Trinity, the Father, the Son, and the Holy Ghost, now and always and forever and ever, amen! . . .

4. Place: monastery of Tērpet in province of Vaspurakan; MS. title: Collection of Sermons [*Čaṙəntir*].
Source: Xač‘ikyan, *XV Dari*, II, no. 222, pp. 177–178

. . . [copied] during the pontificate of the Lord Zak‘aria [III of Aghtamar] of All Armenians . . . An evil report arrived that [someone from among] the nation of archers [azgn netołac‘] was approaching the province of Ṙštunik‘ and he forthwith sent an emissary to the pontiff Zak‘aria. And he [Zak‘aria] voluntarily went to see a certain well-disposed individual, who was second in command among his generals, and he informed him of the impending threat, for they had said: "Seize the pontiff and slaughter the Christians and destroy the churches." A certain benevolent /// appeared before the chief general and secured his acquiescence in their plea, [namely] that no one should set hands upon the Christians . . .

5. Place: city of Arčēš in K‘ajberunik‘; scribe and author of col.: Yovan; MS. title: Gospel.
Source: Xač‘ikyan, *XV Dari*, II, no. 224a, pp. 179–180

. . . [completed] in the year 911 of the Armenian Era [A.D. 1462] . . . during the imperial conquest of the great padishah J̌hanša Łan [Pādishāh Djihānshāh Khān], who most valiantly controlled the land of Irał [Iraq]; and during the catholicosate of the great philosopher and brave and valiant pontiff, Lord Zak‘aria [III], who, by the power granted by God, occupied the two [pontifical] seats at Ējmiacin and Ałt'amar; may the Lord God protect him, amen! . . .

6. Place: monastery of Ktuc'; scribe and author of col.: Xač'atur; MS. title: Menology [*Yaysmawurk'*].
Source: Xač'ikyan, *XV Dari*, II, no. 225a, p. 181

. . . [completed in A.D. 1462] During the catholicosate of the Armenians of the Lord Zak'aria [III], who occupied both [pontifical] seats, not by *łabal*, but by the dispensation and grace of J̌ahanšay Łan [Djihānshāh Khān]. The Lord Catholicos Zak'aria proceeded to and occupied the seat at Ējmiacin. He voluntarily brought [the relic of] the right hand of the Lusaworič' [Illuminator] to the province of Vaspurakan. And [on his way] he visited the villages and the cities so that the Christians might see it, and they rejoiced because of the God-given blessings and grace which the right hand of the Lusaworič' [Illuminator] bestowed upon them. And everyone gave thanks to God the Creator and to the Lord Catholicos Zak'aria [III], who made them worthy of witnessing the holy right hand of the Lusaworič' [Illuminator]. He then took it to the God-protected island of Ałt'amar, which resounded when its inhabitants came out to greet the holy right hand and also the royal scion, the Lord Catholicos Zak'aria [III], who descended from the family of King Gagik. And, with adoration and rejoicing, they carried it to the heaven-like, illumined, and vaulted [church of the] Holy Cross. And it was a sight to behold the rejoicing and exultation of the vardapets and bishops, the priests and monks; for the priests and people arrived in droves from all places to see the holy right hand of the Lusaworič' [Illuminator], which was placed in the holy church beside the other sacred relics. And he [Zak'aria] returned to his seat at Ējmiacin, where he remained for a long time and occupied the two [pontifical] seats. In the year 910 [of the Armenian Era = A.D. 1461], during the reign of J̌ahanšay Łan [Djihānshāh Khān], who marched forth from T'awrēz [Tabrīz] and proceeded to Hrē [Herāt], and captured all of Xorasan [Khurāsān]. He ruled in Parskastan [Persia] for fifteen years, and made all the Č'ałat'ay [Čaghatai] his tributaries. He then returned to T'awrēz [Tabrīz]; and his sons ruled as kings in Širaz [Shīrāz], Aspahan [Iṣfahān], and K'rman [Kirmān], and all the countries enjoyed peace . . .

7. Place: Ałt'amar; scribe and author of col.: Grigor; MS. title: Gospel.

Source: Xač'ikyan, *XV Dari*, II, no. 226, pp. 184–185

... [completed] during the pontificate of the Lord Catholicos Zak'aria [III], Catholicos of All Armenians and patriarch of the most blessed seats at Vałaršapat and Ałt'amar, when the Lord Catholicos Zak'aria [III] brought the holy right hand of the Lusaworič' [Illuminator] to Ałt'amar, in the year 911 of our Armenian Era [A.D. 1462] ... I copied this with much labor and suffering, in bitter and most grievous times, when we were subjected to levies by the infidels ...

8. Place: city of Van; scribe and author of col.: Karapet; MS. title: Gospel.
Source: Xač'ikyan, *XV Dari*, II, no. 229, p. 187

... Copied in the year 911 of the Armenian Era [A.D. 1462] ... during the pontificate of the Lord Zak'aria [III of Aghtamar] ... and during the reign of J̌hanšay [Djihānshāh], son of Łara Usuf [Ḳara Yūsuf] ...

9. Place: city of Tiwrik; scribe and author of col.: Zawrvar Erēc'; MS. title: Gospel.
Source: Xač'ikyan, *XV Dari*, II, no. 230, p. 188

When Čihanšah [Djihānshāh] arrived and devastated our cantons of Kamax [Kemakh]; and he plundered much and carried off many captives, but through the protection of God we escaped from that calamity and came to this city of Tiwrik.

10. Place: city of Tiwrik; scribe and author of col.: Zak'aria; MS. title: Gospel.
Source: Xač'ikyan, *XV Dari*, II, no. 231, p. 188

... [copied] during the reign of J̌ihanšah [Djihānshāh], in the year 911 [of the Armenian Era = A.D. 1462].

11. Scribe and author of col.: Melk'isēt'; MS. title: Gospel.
Source: Xač'ikyan, *XV Dari*, II, no. 234, p. 189

... This holy Gospel was copied in the year 911 of the Armenian Era [A.D. 1462] ... during the catholicosate of the Lord Grigor [X, J̌alalbēkeanc'] at holy Ējmiacin, and when the *p'at'šah* [padishah] was J̌ahanša [Djihānshāh].

1463

1. Place: monastery of Ełrdot in canton of Tarōn; scribe and author of col.: Step'annos; MS. title: Gospel.
Source: Xač'ikyan, *XV Dari*, II, nos. 236a, b, pp. 193–194

. . . [copied in A.D. 1463] during the catholicosate of the Lord Zak'aria [III of Aghtamar] . . . in bitter and evil times, when justice was diminished and injustice was intensified everywhere . . .

On this day unbearable grief befell us in the region of Muš [Mush], for they seized the Lord Bishop Yohannēs, abbot of the holy monastery of St. Karapet. They carried him off to Bałēš [Bitlīs] where, after being severely tortured, he became a martyr;[66] may his memory be blessed! This came to pass in the year 912 [of the Armenian Era = A.D. 1463], on the second Wednesday of Yinanc', on the twenty-sixth of the month of K'ałoc'. All of this came about because of our sins. Who can recount the tragedy and affliction which took place?

In this year locusts arrived and defiled our country.

2. Place: city of Bałēš; scribe and author of col.: Yovsēp'; MS. title: Commentary on the Calendar by Yakob Łrimec'i.
Source: Xač'ikyan, *XV Dari*, II, no. 237, p. 194

. . . [copied] during the khanate of Amir Šaraf [Amīr Sharaf], in the year 912 of the Armenian Era [A.D. 1463], when, angered by our sins, God sent harmful locusts upon us, which devoured the produce in certain places; but again, through the mercy of God, they vanished and drowned in the sea . . .

3. Place: city of Bałēš (?); scribe and author of col.: Kirakos; MS. title: Gospel.
Source: Xač'ikyan, *XV Dari*, II, no. 238, pp. 194–195

. . . [completed] in this bitter and evil time, when the lawless Ismaelites [azgn Ismayēli] are tyrannizing us on account of our sins;

[66] The story of Bishop Yohannēs' martyrdom has been written by a number of contemporary authors. According to certain sources, some of the monks in his own monastery betrayed him to the amir of Bitlīs, Malik Sharaf, alleging that he had demolished a building belonging to the Muslims and had used its stones for the restoration of the monastery of St. Karapet at Mush. (See Xač'ikyan, *XV Dari*, II, p. 194, note.)

and, with manifold torture and indignities, they persecute the tarnished Christian nations; may the Lord God punish them befitting their deeds.

This was written in bitter times, in the year 912 of our Armenian Era [A.D. 1463] . . . during the pontificate of the Lord Zak'aria [III of Aghtamar] . . . during the khanate of J̌hanšay *mirza* [Djihānshāh Mīrzā], and the amirate of Mēlēk' Šaraf [Malik Sharaf] in our region . . . when we were persecuted at the hands of the Muslims [*aylazgi*]; may the Lord God punish them for their deeds . . .

4. Place: city of Tp'xis; scribe and author of col.: Mkrtič'; MS. title: Gospel.
Source: Xač'ikyan, *XV Dari*, II, no. 239, p. 195

. . . Copied during the reign of the pious king of kings Gorgi [Giorgi VIII of Georgia]; may the Lord God make him always victorious over the enemies of Christ's Cross; [and] during the pontificate of the Lord Zak'aria [III of Aghtamar] . . .

5. Place: monastery of C'awłeac'-K'ar in canton of Vayoc'-Jor; MS. title: Gospel.
Source: Xač'ikyan, *XV Dari*, II, no. 240, p. 196

. . . [copied] in the year 912 of the Haykazean Era [A.D. 1463], in the second year of the catholicosate of the Lord Zak'aria [III], [and] in the twenty-fourth year of the khanate of J̌hanšah [Djihānshāh].

6. Place: city of Arckē; scribe and author of col.: Yovanēs; MS. title: Gospel.
Source: Xač'ikyan, *XV Dari*, II, no. 241, p. 196

. . . In the year 912 of our [Armenian] Era [A.D. 1463], during the pontificate of the Lord Zak'aria [III], Catholicos of All Armenians, and during the imperial conquest of J̌hanšay [Djihānshāh] . . .

7. Place: city of Arčēš in K'aǰberunik'; scribe and author of col.: Yovhannēs Mangasarenc'; MS. title: Gospel.
Source: Xač'ikyan, *XV Dari*, II, no. 242, p. 197

. . . [completed in A.D. 1463], at a time when the *p'at'šah* J̌hanša

[Pādishāh Djihānshāh] was in Irał [Iraq], and when his son Hasan Ali [Ḥasan 'Alī] was the prince of our region . . .

8. Place: monastery of Ktuc' in province of Vaspurakan; scribe and author of col.: Xač'atur; MS. title: Gospel.
Source: Xač'ikyan, *XV Dari*, II, no. 243, p. 197

. . . [completed] in the year 912 of the Armenian Era [A.D. 1463], during the pontificate of the Lord Catholicos Zak'aria [III of Aghtamar], and the imperial conquest of the *p'at'šah* J̌hanšah [Pādishāh Djihānshāh], in bitter times, when I know not what will happen / / /

9. Place: city of Van; scribe and author of col.: Azariay; MS. title: Gospel.
Source: Xač'ikyan, *XV Dari*, II, no. 244, p. 198

. . . I copied this . . . [in memory of] my parents and also of my mentor, the priest Karapet, who, at the instigation of the evil one [Satan], was martyred in the city of Arčēš [Ardjīsh] at the hands of the infidels . . . This was written . . . in the year 912 of the Armenian Era [A.D. 1463] . . . during the pontificate of the Lord Grigor [X, J̌alalbēkeanc'] and the reign of J̌hanšay [Djihānshāh] . . .

10. Place: city of Van; scribe and author of col.: Nikolayos; MS. title: Gospel.
Source: Xač'ikyan, *XV Dari*, II, no. 245, p. 198

. . . [copied] in the year 912 of the Armenian Era [A.D. 1463], during the pontificate of the Lord Zak'aria [III of Aghtamar], Catholicos of the Armenians . . . and the reign of J̌hanšah *imirza* [Djihānshāh Mīrzā].

11. Place: Ałt'amar; scribe and author of col.: Grigor; MS. title: Ritual Book [*Maštoc'*].
Source: Xač'ikyan, *XV Dari*, II, no. 246, p. 198

. . . [completed] in the year 912 of the Armenian Era [A.D. 1463], in bitter and most grievous times, when we were tributaries of the nation of archers [azgin netołac'] . . .

12. Place: Ałt'amar; scribe and author of col.: T'umay; MS. title: Grand Ritual Book [*Mayr Maštoc'*].
Source: Xač'ikyan, *XV Dari*, II, no. 248, p. 200

... [completed] during the patriarchate of the Lord Zak'aria [III of Aghtamar], overseer [*veraditoł*] of the Armenians; in the year 912 of the Armenian Era [A.D. 1463], in bitter and most grievous times ...

13. Place: monastery of Ereran; scribe and author of col.: Małagiay; MS. title: Gospel.
Source: Xač'ikyan, *XV Dari*, II, no. 251, p. 202

... [copied in A.D. 1463] during the reign of J̌ahanšah [Djihānshāh], [and] the pontificate of the Lord Grigor [X, J̌alalbēkeanc'] ...

14. Place: village of Armizawnk'; scribe and author of col.: Sargis; MS. title: Hymnal [*Šaraknoc'*].
Source: Xač'ikyan, *XV Dari*, II, no. 252, p. 202

... [copied in A.D. 1463] during the reign of J̌hanšay [Djihānshāh] ...

1464

1. Place: monastery of Awak' in canton of Daranałeac'; scribe and author of col.: Step'anos; MS. title: The Works of Dionysius the Areopagite.
Source: Xač'ikyan, *XV Dari*, II, no. 256a, p. 211

... This was completed ... in the year 913 [of the Armenian Era = A.D. 1464], on Thursday the fourteenth of June, in bitter and anxious times, when the lawless Tačiks were tyrannizing and persecuting the Christians. They have become more wicked than the wild beasts; they are thirsty for the blood of the Christians, and they are revealing anew their evil intent toward the Christians. They have raised the *xarač* to 4 *flori*; they forced the Christians to wear a blue symbol on their heads; they are compelling [the Christians] to drag their dead [on the ground]; and they are contemplating numerous other evils, and they are scornful of the Christians. May the Lord God bring this to a happy conclusion!

Many other calamities came to pass in our time, for the city of Stəmpawl [Istanbul] was captured and its population was put to the sword; countless people were carried off into captivity; innumerable relics of saints were trampled underfoot by the infidels; the churches became dwelling places of the infidels; and there came to pass many other calamities; and who can put them all into writing? And ten years later, more or less, Pontos [Pontus], that is, Trapizon [Trebizond], was captured; and so much damage was done there, for they separated sons and daughters from their mothers and fathers, and brothers from brothers. The weeping and lamentation were so heart-rending that I cannot describe them in writing. And who can estimate the damage done to the churches and the sacred effects!

Ten years before this, they carried off captives from our canton of Daranałeac‘, that is, Kamax [Kemakh]; and who can recount the destruction and deprivation suffered by the Christians and the monasteries, as well as the loss of their sacred effects! Five years after this, there was a terrible earthquake which destroyed the entire metropolis of Ezənkay [Erzindjān], and twelve thousand men and women were buried underground.

There were numerous other destructions and damages in Vrac‘tun [Georgia], in the eastern [regions] and in all the cantons; [and] who can recount them or put them into writing! All of this was recorded as an admonition to you and for your benefit, for all of this came to pass on account of [our] sins, and so that the Lord God shall deliver you from all temptations, amen!

2. Place: monastery of Hayoc‘-T‘aṙ; scribe and author of col.: Step‘anos; MS. title: Missal [*Čašoc‘*].
Source: Xač‘ikyan, *XV Dari*, II, no. 258, p. 214

. . . [copied] in bitter and anxious times which befell us, on account of [our] sins, at the hands of the infidels, who belonged to an alien religion, and the wicked tyrants; during the khanate of J̌ahanšah [Djihānshāh], son of Usuf [Ḳara Yūsuf], who marched into Xorasan [Khurāsān]. And for seven years he kept our country in bondage and in trembling by imposing levies, by torment and torture, so much so that fathers disavowed their children . . .

3. MS. title: Miscellany [*Žołovacu*].
Source: Xač‘ikyan, *XV Dari*, II, no. 260, p. 261

On the twenty-second of the month of April in the year 913 of our Armenian Era [A.D. 1464], the Lord Nersēs, bishop of Ankuria

[Ankara], passed away. He was from the land of Łrim [Crimea], pupil of the vardapet Sargis, who shone like a sun in the land of Rūm [Hṙomanc‘ erkir], [and] many called him the second Lord Nersēs. He was charitable, ascetic, and, as the Lord said, he freely received and freely gave away [cf. Matthew 10:8]. He never entered a bathhouse; he never set his eyes on women; and he incessantly preached, with the grace of the Holy Spirit, to the Armenians and Franks [Fṙank] and Greeks [Hoṙom]; and many Tačik notables listened to the word of God and believed in Christ.

But the wicked king of the Tačiks [Mehmet II, Fatih] gathered Christian children and brought them to Ǝstəmpōl [Istanbul]; and the bishop, who arrived with the children, brought with him a letter guaranteeing the freedom of the Armenians, but the wicked king considered the letter worthless. Nevertheless, he granted to him [jurisdiction over] the Christians of Ankuria [Ankara]. Six years later, they took the parents of the children to Ǝstəmpōl [Istanbul] and the holy man [Nersēs] went with them to Łalat‘an [Galata]. The holy Lord Nersēs was the bishop not only of those who were in his own diocese, but of all the [Armenian] Christians. He passed away as a good man of Christ at the age of forty-five years and he was buried at Łalat‘an [Galata].

4. Place: city of Arckē; scribe and author of col.: Yakob; MS. title: Gospel.
Source: Xač‘ikyan, *XV Dari*, II, no. 261, pp. 216–217

. . . [copied] during the pontificate of the Lord Zak‘aria [III] Ałt‘amarc‘i, [and] the khanate of J̌hanšay [Djihānshāh], [son of] Łaray Usuf [Ḳara Yūsuf], in the year 913 of our Armenian Era [A.D. 1464] . . .

5. Place: city of Arckē; MS. title: Gospel.
Source: Xač‘ikyan, *XV Dari*, II, no. 262, p. 217

. . . [copied] during the catholicosate of the Lord Ǝṙəstakēs at Vałaršaypat and the imperial conquest of J̌ahanšah [Djihānshāh], who invaded Bałdat [Baghdad] and roared like a lion . . .

6. Place: city of Arckē; scribe and author of col.: Yohannēs; MS. title: Gospel.

Source: Xač'ikyan, *XV Dari*, II, no. 263, p. 217

... [copied] during the pontificate of the Lord Zak'aria [III of Aghtamar], and when the *t'ałt'* was occupied by J̌hanšay [Djihānshāh], in the year 913 of our Armenian Era [A.D. 1464] ...

7. Place: monastery of Argelan in Tarberunik'; scribe and author of col.: Azaria; MS. title: Hymnal [*Šaraknoc'*].
Source: Xač'ikyan, *XV Dari*, II, no. 264b, p. 218

... [copied] during the catholicosate of the Lord Zak'aria [III of Aghtamar], who resides in the city of Vałaršapat, and during the reign of J̌hanšay [Djihānshāh], who besieged the city of Babelon [Babylon = Baghdad] with numerous troops ...

8. Place: monastery of Malēzker in Ałuank'; scribe and author of col.: Anton; MS. title: Ritual Book [*Maštoc'*].
Source: Xač'ikyan, *XV Dari*, II, no. 265, p. 219

... [copied in A.D. 1464], in bitter and evil and most grievous times, when we were suffering at the hands of the infidels and unjust tax-collectors; during the pontificate of the Lord Ohanēs, Catholicos of Ałuank' ...

9. Place: village of Xortt'anc' in region of Aylax; scribe and author of col.: Mat'ēos Šrvanec'i; MS. title: Gospel.
Source: Xač'ikyan, *XV Dari*, II, no. 266a, p. 220

... [copied] during the khanate of J̌hanšay [Djihānshāh]. This holy Gospel was completed on the fifth of the month of Areg, in the year 913 [of the Armenian Era = A.D. 1464] ...

10. Place: village of Konkŕay; purchaser of MS. and author of col.: Grigor; MS. title: Hymnal [*Ganjaran*].
Source: Xač'ikyan, *XV Dari*, II, no. 267, p. 221

... In this year [A.D. 1464], Sultan Hasan [Uzun Ḥasan] of Amit' [Āmid] arrived with 20,000 horsemen and devastated the region of Kesaria [Kayseri], and the T'urk'man [Turkmens] severely plundered it. May Christ God save our [village of] Konkŕay from him and from his wicked designs.

11. Scribe and author of col.: Step'anos; MS. title: Gospel.
Source: Xač'ikyan, *XV Dari*, II, no. 269, p. 222

. . . This was copied during the pontificate of the Lord Zak'aria [III] Ałt'amarec'i, and the reign of J̌əhanša Łan [Djihānshāh Khān] . . .

12. Purchaser of MS. and author of col.: Yovanēs; MS. title: Gospel.
Source: Xač'ikyan, *XV Dari*, II, no. 270, p. 223

In the year 913 of our Armenian Era [A.D. 1464]. The Lord Catholicos Zak'aria [III of Aghtamar] occupied [the see of] Ēǰmiacin. He sojourned there for two years and then was poisoned by them [his Armenian rivals]. And the holy crucifixes and the Gospels and other books fell into the hands of the infidels. And I, *małt'asi* Yovanēs, delivered this holy Gospel . . .

13. Place: village of Šatwan in Ṙštunik'; scribe and author of col.: Atom; MS. title: Menology [*Yaysmawurk'*].
Source: Xač'ikyan, *XV Dari*, II, no. 271, p. 224

. . . [completed] during the pontificate of the Lord Zak'aria [III of Aghtamar], who in this year passed away in Christ, and during [the pontificate of] our newly ordained pontiff Lord Step'anos [IV of Aghtamar], and in the year 913 of the Armenian Era [A.D. 1464], in bitter and most grievous times, when we were subjected to levies and were in the servitude of the nation of archers [azgin netołac'] . . .

14. Place: city of Keli; scribe and author of col.: Eremia; MS. title: Ritual Book [*Maštoc'*] and Hymnal [*Ganjaran*].
Source: Xač'ikyan, *XV Dari*, II, no. 272a, p. 225

. . . [completed in A.D. 1464], during the pontificate of the Lord Step'anos [IV of Aghtamar]; [and] the barony of Sk'antar [Iskandar] . . .

15. Place: monastery of Ēreran; scribe and author of col.: Małagiay; MS. title: Gospel.
Source: Xač'ikyan, *XV Dari*, II, no. 275, pp. 227–228

. . . [copied in A.D. 1464] during the reign of J̌ahanšay [Djihānshāh], [and] the pontificate of the Lord Grigor [X, J̌alalbēkeanc'] . . .

16. Place: village of Xalifi near Hřovmklay; scribe and author of col.: Anania; MS. title: Gospel.
Source: Xač'ikyan, *XV Dari*, II, no. 277, p. 229

... [copied in A.D. 1464] during the pontificate of the Lord Karapet [Ewdokiac'i of Cilicia], and the reign of ... baron Č'ak'am Pak ...

1465

1. MS. title: Excerpts from the Bible.
Source: Xač'ikyan, *XV Dari*, II, no. 281, p. 230

... In this year [A.D. 1465] Gorgi [Giorgi VIII], king of the Georgians [Vrac'], was seized by the wicked prince Ławrławrē [Qwarqwaré II], [and they kept him bound]. After him, the [Georgian] royal throne was occupied by his nephew Kostandin [Constantine II]. A year later, Kostandin was succeeded by Bagrat [VI].

2. Place: village of Kac in canton of Gełark'unik'; scribe and author of col.: Yovanēs; MS. title: Missal [*Čašoc'*].
Source: Xač'ikyan, *XV Dari*, II, no. 282a, p. 231

... [copied] in bitter times, when we were suffering from the tyranny of the infidels, especially from the double taxation; during the pontificate of the Lord Grigor [X, J̌alalbēkeanc'], Catholicos of All Armenians and patriarch of Ējmiacin at Vałaršapat, [and] during the conquest of J̌hanšay *imirza* [Djihānshāh Mīrzā], son of Łaray Usuf [Ḳara Yūsuf] ...

3. Place: monastery of Ełivard in canton of Ararat; scribe and author of col.: Matt'ēos; MS. title: Gospel.
Source: Xač'ikyan, *XV Dari*, II, no. 284, p. 232

... [copied] during the reign of J̌hanša [Djihānshāh], son of Usuf [Ḳara Yūsuf], [and] under the baron Višel, overseer of our region; in the year 914 of the Great Armenian Era [A.D. 1465] ...

4. Place: town of Ełivard in canton of Ararat; MS. title: Commentary on the Epistles by Sargis Šnorhali.

Source: Xač'ikyan, *XV Dari*, II, no. 285, p. 232

During the pontificate at Ējmiacin of the Lord Ṙstakēs, and the reign of J̌hanša [Djihānshāh] ...

5. Place: city of Van; scribe and author of col.: Vardan; MS. title: Menology [*Ɣaysmawurk'*].
Source: Xač'ikyan, *XV Dari*, II, no. 286a, p. 234

... [copied] during the reign of J̌hanšay [Djihānshāh]. This is the second year that he has camped near the city of Bałdat [Baghdad], and has besieged [*xsar*] his son P'ir Putax [Pīr Budaḳ]. May Christ God grant him [Djihānshāh] a long life and bless his kingdom, amen! ...

6. Place: city of Arčēš; scribe and author of col.: Yovanēs Mangasarenc'; MS. title: Gospel.
Source: Xač'ikyan, *XV Dari*, II, no. 287, pp. 235–236

... the unhappy and aggrieved lady Xalim-Xat'un ... received this holy Gospel in her own memory and also of her good son, the handsome and graceful youth Karapet, who cheerfully journeyed to the city of Sult'ania [Sulṭānīya], but when he returned home he was delivered into the hands of the bloodthirsty Tačik *ǰalats*, who killed him with a sword and a *xanǰal*, and made a martyr of this innocent one. Whose tongue can relate the innocent slaying of Karapet? He was a new bridegroom, and he became a *hasrat'amah* martyr. Likewise his brother, *xoǰay* Yōhanēs; he too was slain at a youthful age by the sword at the hands of wicked *haramiks* in Ispahan [Iṣfahān] ...

Also [in memory of] her younger son, Ēzdanbaxš, who at a youthful age went to trade in the east, and when he cheerfully returned and reached T'avrēz [Tabrīz] he suffered an acute fatal pain and passed away in God.

And their unfortunate father, Grigor, journeyed with a stricken heart and in grief to far off Ispahan [Iṣfahān] in search of his son Yōhanēs, and returning to Sōlt'ania [Sulṭānīya] he died sobbing and in anguish ...

In this year [A.D. 1465] the *p'atšah* J̌hanšah [Pādishāh Djihānshāh] cruelly slew his own son P'ir Putax Xan [Pīr Budaḳ Khān] at Bałdat [Baghdād], and then returned to his *t'axt'* at T'avrēz [Tabrīz] ...

7. Place: Ałt'amar; scribe and author of col.: Hayrapet; MS. title: Gospel.
Source: Xač'ikyan, *XV Dari*, II, no. 291, p. 239

... During the pontificate of the Lord Catholicos Step'anos [IV of Aghtamar], in bitter and grievous times, when we were in extreme anguish and in the servitude of the nation of archers [azgin netołac'], for they are looting and plundering exceedingly the Christians.

1466

1. Place: town of Ełivard; MS. title: Gospel.
Source: Xač'ikyan, *XV Dari*, II, no. 304a, p. 244

... [completed] during the catholicosate of the Lord Grigor [X, J̌alalbēkeanc'], in the year 915 of the Armenian Era [A.D. 1466], [and] during the khanate of J̌hanšay [Djihānshāh] ...

2. Place: monastery of Gaṙnaker in canton of Ganjak; illuminator of MS. and author of col.: Azariay; MS. title: Gospel.
Source: Xač'ikyan, *XV Dari*, II, no. 304b, p. 244

... /// the baron of Ganjak; and in this year [A.D. 1466] Kawrki [Giorgi VIII], King of the Georgians [Vrac'], at the hands of /// Ławrławrē [Qwarqwaré II] the brave, and the throne was occupied by Bak'rat [Bagrat VI]; may the Lord God increase his strength, and grant him victory over his enemies and may he reign; blessed be the name of the Lord, and may the Lord guide him who is virtuous.

3. Place: monastery of Lełan in canton of Ganjak; scribe and author of col.: Step'annos; MS. title: Gospel.
Source: Xač'ikyan, *XV Dari*, II, no. 305a, p. 245

... [begun] during the catholicosate of the Lord Yohanēs [of the Caucasian Albanians], and the reign of King Gawrki [Giorgi VIII] of the Georgians [Vrac'], and the khanate of J̌ahanšah [Djihānshāh] ...

4. Place: town of Akanc' in province of K'aǰberunik'; scribe and author of col.: Yovsēp'; MS. title: Gospel.
Source: Xač'ikyan, *XV Dari*, II, no. 307, p. 246

... [copied] in the year 915 of the Armenian Era [A.D. 1466], and during the khanate of J̌hanšay [Djihānshāh]. This is the second year that [the rulers of] Babelon [Babylon = Baghdad] have risen against the *xan* [khan], but they have failed to do him any harm.

5. Place: city of Arckē; scribe and author of col.: Atom; MS. title: Gospel.
Source: Xač'ikyan, *XV Dari*, II, no. 309, p. 247

... [copied] during the imperial conquest of J̌hanšay [Djihānshāh], son of Łaray Usuf [Ḳara Yūsuf], in the year 915 of the [Armenian] Era [A.D. 1466].

6. Place: monastery of Aṙberd in village of P'asavank' in province of Mokk'; scribe and author of col.: Israyēl; MS. title: Menology [*Yaysmawurk'*].
Source: Xač'ikyan, *XV Dari*, II, no. 311, p. 248

... [copied in A.D. 1466] during the khanate of J̌hanša [Djihānshāh], and during the pontificate at Ałt'amar of the newly ordained Lord Step'annos [IV] ...

7. Place: monastery of Ełrdot; scribe and author of col.: Step'annos; MS. title: Hymnal [*Ganjaran*].
Source: Xač'ikyan, *XV Dari*, II, no. 315, p. 250

... All of this befell us on account of our multitudinous sins, for in this year [A.D. 1466] they demolished the citadel of Muš [Mush] and committed many atrocities. And J̌hanša [Djihānshāh] captured Pałdat [Baghdad] and held it under siege [*xsar*] for two years.

8. Place: city of Xarberd; scribes and authors of col.: Yakob and Pawłos; MS. title: Missal [*Čašoc'*].
Source: Xač'ikyan, *XV Dari*, II, no. 316, p. 251

... [copied in A.D. 1466] during the amirate of Hasan Xan [Ḥasan Khān, amīr of Kharput] ...

1467

1. Place: C'łnay in canton of Gołt'an; author of col.: Umid; MS. title: Gospel.

Source: Xač'ikyan, *XV Dari*, II, no. 327, p. 256

... [MS. restored in A.D. 1467] during the reign of the baron J̌anhanša *mirza* [Djihānshāh Mīrzā] ...

2. Place: begun at Bałēš and completed at Ałt'amar; scribe and author of col.: Kirakos [J̌ōškanc']; MS. title: Collection of Sermons [*Čarəntir*].
Source: Xač'ikyan, *XV Dari*, II, no. 328a, p. 257

... [completed in A.D. 1467] during the khanate of J̌hanšay [Djihānshāh], and the amirate of Mēlik' Šaraf [Malik Sharaf] in the city of Bałēš [Bitlīs] ...

3. Place: Ałt'amar; scribe and author of col.: Hayrapet; MS. title: Collection of Sermons [*Čarəntir*].
Source: Xač'ikyan, *XV Dari*, II, no. 327, p. 257

... [copied in A.D. 1467] at a time when we were the tributaries [and] in servitude of the nation of archers [azgin netołac'] ...

4. Place: city of Van; scribe and author of col.: Vardan; MS. title: Menology [*Yaysmawurk'*].
Source: Xač'ikyan, *XV Dari*, II, no. 328, p. 258

... [copied] during the catholicosate of the Lord Aristakēs ... [and] during the reign of J̌hanšay *imirza* [Djihānshāh Mīrzā], who in this year [A.D. 1467] marched against Uzun Hasan ...

5. Place: city of Van; scribe and author of col.: Karapet; MS. title: Ritual Book [*Maštoc'*].
Source: Xač'ikyan, *XV Dari*, II, no. 329, p. 258

... Hasan / / / and many barons with him, and with the help of God Hasan / / / occupied the *t'axt'* ...

6. Place: monastery of Varag in Van; scribe and author of col.: Karapet; MS. title: Hymnal [*Ganjaran*].
Source: Xač'ikyan, *XV Dari*, II, no. 330, p. 259

. . . [copied] during the reign of *p'at'šah* J̌hanšay [Pādishāh Djihānshāh], who arrived this year [A.D. 1467] with numerous troops to wage war against Hasan Bēk [Uzun Ḥasan Beg]; may the Lord God grant him victory, for he is [like] a strong rampart for the Christians . . .

7. Place: city of Arckē; scribe and author of col.: Yakob; MS. title: Gospel.
Source: Xač'ikyan, *XV Dari*, II, no. 331, p. 260

. . . [copied in A.D. 1467] during the reign of J̌hanšay's [Djihānshāh] son, Hasan Ali *imirza* [Ḥasan 'Alī Mīrzā]. In this year, Uzun Hasan slew J̌hanša [Djihānshāh], and we are frightened and in flight, and living in bitter times . . .

8. Place: city of Ostan; scribe and author of col.: Karapet; MS. title: Gospel.
Source: Xač'ikyan, *XV Dari*, II, no. 332a, p. 260

. . . [copied in A.D. 1467] in bitter and grievous times, when we were under the servitude of the Muslims [*aylazgi*] . . .

1468

1. Place: city of Hizan; scribe and author of col.: Mkrtič'; MS. title: Gospel.
Source: Xač'ikyan, *XV Dari*, II, no. 345, pp. 270–271

. . . [copied in A.D. 1468] in bitter and anxious times, for in this year[67] J̌hanšay Łan [Djihānshāh Khān] marched forth from Šahastan, that is, T'awvrēz [Tabrīz], with numerous marauders and troops, and planned to attack the city of Amit' [Āmid] and further south up to Damaskos [Damascus]. As he marched forth, many trembled by the fear that he caused, for J̌hanšay [Djihānshāh] controlled numerous cantons and cities. Moreover, he held sway over Persia [Parsic' ašxarh] up to Hrē [Herāt] and all of Xorasan [Khurāsān]. His sword caused trembling in the east and in the west, and the [countries] in the north and in the south were his tributaries. Yet, he was beneficent toward the Christians; and many churches were built and restored

[67] According to Xač'ikyan, Djihānshāh began his invasion in May of 1467. (See *XV Dari*, II, p. 271, note.)

during his reign; and there was peace in Armenia, and the number of priests and monks and monasteries increased; and there was prosperity throughout all his domains.

During his march, numerous cantons were destroyed, and the inhabitants of these cantons fled and took refuge in caves and in the crevices of rocks, and they died of starvation. He arrived in the canton of Tarawn [Ṭarūn] in the plain of Muš [Mush]; and his troops committed much destruction there, for they were numerous and countless. And they did not recognize God, and they asked, "What is a Christian?" and "Does the Christian have eyes and mouth?" They went into the monastery of Łazar, and roasted the sacristan in the fire and made him a martyr, and then they went away. And they camped on the road; and he [Djihānshāh] disbanded his troops, and, without fearing or suspecting his enemies, he said, "There is no one on earth who can confront me and who can draw his sword upon me."

Learning of this, his enemies attacked him, looted his possessions, and slew him as well as his sons. As a result of his slaying, there was large-scale destruction in all places, especially in Armenia. Numerous churches were destroyed, and numerous Christians died by the sword and starvation, and no one can describe in writing or recount that which took place in the country. The prices went up everywhere, and we bought a *kapič* of bread for 120 *t'ankays* . . .

This was written during the catholicosate of the Lord Step'annos [IV] Ałt'amarec'i, and the khanate of the alien Hasan Ali [Ḥasan 'Alī], son of J̌hanša [Djihānshāh] . . .

2. Place: monastery of Gaṙnaker in canton of Ganjak; illuminator of MS. and author of col.: Azariay; MS. title: Gospel.
Source: Xač'ikyan, *XV Dari*, II, no. 346, p. 272

. . . This was completed in the town of Ełivard, during the catholicosate of the Lord Grigor [X, J̌alalbēkeanc'], in the year 917 of the Armenian Era [A.D. 1468], during the khanate of Čhanšah [Djihānshāh] . . .

. . . The illuminations were done in the region of Ganjak, in the monastery of Gaṙnaker . . . In this year [A.D. 1468] Gawrgi [Giorgi VIII], king of the Georgians [Vrac'] / / /.

3. Place: monastery of Sirunk'ar in canton of Menckert; scribe and author of col.: Margarē; MS. title: Menology [*Yaysmawurk'*].

Source: Xač'ikyan, *XV Dari*, II, no. 348, pp. 272–273

... [copied in A.D. 1468] during the imperial conquest of Hasan Bēk [Uzun Ḥasan Beg] ... And because of our multitudinous sins, the *xan* [khan] of T'avrēz [Tabrīz; that is, Djihānshāh] arrived in our country, and the old and the young trembled from fear of the *šah* [shah] and took to flight. But the merciful God made him go back, for He gave Hasan Bak [Uzun Ḥasan Beg] the power and strength to make him [Djihānshāh] and his sons and horsemen victims of the sword, worse than the Pharaoh and Ṙap'sak [Rab-shakeh]; and thus he saved the Christians from captivity. Glory be unto the Providence of God. This came to pass during the pontificate of the Lord Ṙstakēs who occupied the divinely established holy seat of Ējmiacin at Vałaršapat ...

4. MS. title: unknown.
Source: Xač'ikyan, *XV Dari*, II, no. 349, pp. 273–274

In the year 916 of the Great Armenian Era [A.D. 1467], when the sins of man increased and by the instigation of the evil one [Satan], a certain Tułłarc'i [Dhu'l-Ḳadrid] by the name of Šah-Suar [Shāhsuwār] rose against the Sultan of Msr [Egypt]. He committed much destruction in his land; he slew many T'urk'man [Turkmens] who were called Apaneri; and he committed many atrocities. He also captured Vahkay. After all this, he conceived an evil plan against the city of Sis and its citadel. Hence, on the second day of June, he advanced upon it with numerous horsemen; and after setting it on fire, he departed and captured Atana [Adana] and Tarson [Ṭarsūs] and the coastal city of Yayas [Ayas]. He also captured Anarzaba ['Ayn Zarba], Kovaṙa [Kawarrā] and the entire plain. He also captured the citadel of Pałras, Ant'ap [Antep], Nayipenc', Lewon Berd, and Kopitaṙ [Gubidara], and then Barjraberd; and he vanquished the entire mountainous region.

Then the sultan's horsemen came forth; and Šah-Suar [Shāhsuwār] marched against the ruler of Šam [Syria]. He slaughtered [the sultan's troops] and made them flee as far as Halap [Aleppo], and he plundered numerous places. He then returned, with a growl, to attack the citadel of Sis, and he set it on fire. The baron Č'agam was in the citadel. And the Christians in the citadel took to battle and killed many Tačiks. Nevertheless, because of the great pressure, we surrendered the citadel on the third of December.

And in the year 917 [of the Armenian Era = A.D. 1468], Šah-Suar [Shāhsuwār] again invaded the land of Šam [Syria]; and capturing one thousand Tačik families from Šam [Syria], he transplanted them to the city of Sis. Again, larger forces marched forth from Šam [Syria], and Šah-Suar [Shāhsuwār] proceeded against them. The T'urk' [Turks] of Sis and Šamc'ik' [Syrians] joined forces, and on the fourteenth of the month of May they took to battle; and they captured the horses and mules of the baron of the citadel. And the baron, in turn, seized the Christians and cast them in the well. And all of us inhabitants abandoned our homes and *ərzak*; and the *farsah* [Varsaq] T'urk'man [Turkmens] looted the city, carried off much *ərzak*, and plundered the vessels of the churches. I cannot put into writing all the destruction that they wrought. And we came to the citadel of Kopitař [Gubidara].

5. Place: monastery of Gamaliēl in Xizan; scribe and author of col.: Łazar; MS. title: Gospel.
Source: Xač'ikyan, *XV Dari*, II, no. 350, p. 274

... [copied in A.D. 1468] during the khanate of Hasan Ali [Ḥasan 'Alī], and the amirate of the Kurd Amir Melek' [Amīr Malik] in our district ...

6. Place: Ankuria; author of col.: Yovanēs; MS. title: Gospel.
Source: Xač'ikyan, *XV Dari*, II, no. 357, p. 278

... This holy Gospel was a "captive" in the hands of infidels. They brought it to Ankuria [Ankara] and sold it; and it was sold by Murvat', who was from the village of Č'uk'i in Gankřay.

1469

1. Place: city of Arčēš; scribe and author of col.: Yovhannēs Mangasarenc'; MS. title: Hymnal [*Šaraknoc'*].
Source: Xač'ikyan, *XV Dari*, II, no. 363, p. 281

... [copied] in the year 918 of the Great Armenian Era [A.D. 1469], during the khanate of Uzun Hasan, who within one year slew three *p'at'šahs*, [namely] J̌hanšah [Djihānshāh], Hasan Ali [Ḥasan 'Alī], and Sultan Busait [Tīmūrid Sulṭān Abū Sa'īd], as well as their troops and children. And he ruled from the Syrian Gate [Šamay Duřn] to Xorasan [Khurāsān] ...

2. Place: village of P'asavank' in Mokk'; scribe and author of col.: Israyēl; MS. title: Menology [*Yaysmawurk'*].
Source: Xač'ikyan, *XV Dari*, II, no. 364, p. 281

. . . [completed] in the year 918 of the Armenian Era [A.D. 1469], during the catholicosate of the Lord Step'annos [IV] Ałt'amarc'i, and the reign of Hasan Bēk [Uzun Ḥasan Beg], who slaughtered the innumerable troops of J̌anšay *mirza* [Djihānshāh Mīrzā]. He occupied [the territories] extending from Halap [Aleppo] up to Səmrłand [Samarkand], and made them his tributaries. Woe unto the infinite bitterness which he brought to the Christians . . .

3. Place: village of Tayšoł; illuminator, binder of MS., and author of col.: Grigor; MS. title: Gospel.
Source: Xač'ikyan, *XV Dari*, II, no. 365, p. 282

. . . [illuminated and bound] in bitter and grievous times, when J̌hanšay [Djihānshāh] invaded Amid [Āmid] and was slain, and when the accursed Ēstinšēr ['Izz al-Dīn Shīr] arrived and plundered our canton of Ṙštunik', on the feast of the birth of Christ. It is stated in the Gospel, "Watch and pray at all times [cf. Mark 14:38] that your flight be not in the winter and on the sabbath day" [cf. Matthew 24:20], which indeed came to pass on account of our multitudinous sins. For, with bitter hearts and tearful eyes, covered with snow and tormented, we fled and took refuge in various foreign places. Such anguish befell us Armenians; and the prayers and divine liturgy ceased in the churches and monasteries . . .

4. Place: town of Ełivard in canton of Ararat; scribe and author of col.: Matt'ēos; MS. title: Commentary on the Epistles by Sargis Šnorhali.
Source: Xač'ikyan, *XV Dari*, II, no. 366, p. 283

. . . this manuscript was commenced during the khanate of J̌hanša [Djihānshāh], who was slain at the hands of Hasan Bēk [Uzun Ḥasan Beg]. He [Uzun Ḥasan] arrived and conquered our country, and also put to flight Hasan Ali [Ḥasan 'Alī], son of J̌hanša [Djihānshāh]. And I carried this manuscript and fled from place to place, and I was constantly in flight and trembling. But I ignored all this and put everything aside; and for one year and six months I remained in uncertainty at the town of Ełivard, which is at the foot of [Mount] Ara, in the canton of Ararat . . .

5. Author: Mkrtičʻ Nałaš; MS. title: Elegy by Mkrtičʻ Nałaš.
Source: Xačʻikyan, *XV Dari*, II, no. 367, p. 284

I, bishop Nałaš, servant of the Virgin,
With mine own eyes saw the bitter, heart-rending grief,
I wept and tearfully lamented,
With bitter tears I composed this elegy on the newly dead.
In the year nine hundred and eighteen
Of the Great Armenian Era [A.D. 1469],
With mine own eyes I saw the heart-rending lament and anguish,
Which brought tears to everyone in the city of Mērtin [Mārdīn].[68]

6. Place: Cilicia (?)[69]
Source: Xačʻikyan, *XV Dari*, II, no. 368, p. 285

. . . our blessed pontiff, the Lord Catholicos Karapet [Ewdokiacʻi of Cilicia], arrived from Tʻōxatʻ [Tokat] and restored the holy see of our Lusaworičʻ [St. Gregory the Illuminator] in the capital city [Sis] in Kiwlikia [Cilicia], which, because of the disappearance of the holy right hand of our Lusaworičʻ, had been suspended for twenty-five years; but he later discovered it and restored our holy see.[70] He then journeyed to Erusałēm [Jerusalem] and worshiped in the holy dominical places of Christ. While there, he witnessed the penury of the Armenian monastery of Surb Yakob [St. James], for at that time the Armenian church had incurred financial indebtedness, and the crucifixes, gospels, and chasubles had been mortgaged to the Muslims [*aylazgi*]. And then the Lord Catholicos Karapet journeyed to Egiptos [Egypt] to see Sultan Tahir [Al-Malik al-Ẓāhir Sayf al-Dīn,

[68] This elegy was composed by Mkrtičʻ Nałaš in 1469 under the impact of the plague which occurred in Mesopotamia in the same year. The work concentrates on the effects of the holocaust upon the victims at Mārdīn. The complete text of the elegy can be found in Ē. Xondkaryan, *Mkrtičʻ Nałaš* (Erevan, 1965), pp. 150–164.

[69] This colophon does not give a date; however, on the basis of internal evidence, it is certain that it was written sometime between 1467 and 1469. Xačʻikyan has chosen to place it under 1469. See *XV Dari*, II, p. 285, n. 1.

[70] The reference is to the transfer of the Armenian pontifical see from Sis to Ējmiacin in 1441, at which time the relic of the right hand of St. Gregory the Illuminator, which was a symbol of the pontifical authority, also disappeared, under mysterious circumstances. The see at Sis was restored by Catholicos Karapet Ewdokiacʻi, and has since remained as a regional hierarchy of the Armenian church. For the details concerning these developments see Ōrmanean, *Azgapatum*, cols. 1449, 1456, 1462–1464, 1477, 1478–1480.

Čaḳmaḳ], and he was bestowed with honors by him.[71] He received a precious *xilay* and expensive gifts, as is the custom for kings to give appropriate gifts to high-ranking individuals. He then returned to Erusałēm [Jerusalem] and delivered the church from its debts and [recovered] the sacred vessels from the infidels.

And he arrived from there and occupied the holy see of the Cilicians [Kiwlikec'woc'] . . .

7. Place: monastery of Biwrakan; scribe and author of col.: Mkrtič'; MS. title: Song Book [*Tałaran*].
Source: Xač'ikyan, *XV Dari*, II, no. 370b, p. 290

. . . This was copied in the year 918 of the Armenian Era [A.D. 1469], during the catholicosate of the Lord Ṙstakēs of the Armenians, [and] during the khanate of Hasan Bēk [Uzun Ḥasan Beg] . . .

8. Place: city of Xarberd; scribe and author of col.: Yakob; MS. title: Gospel.
Source: Xač'ikyan, *XV Dari*, II, no. 374a, p. 292

. . . This holy Gospel was copied in the year 918 [of the Armenian Era = A.D. 1469] . . . during the pontificate of the Lord Aristakēs . . . [and] during the reign of Hasan Pēk [Uzun Ḥasan Beg] of the nation of archers [azgin netołac'] . . .

1470

1. Place: city of Xarberd; scribe and author of col.: Yakob; MS. title: Gospel.
Source: Xač'ikyan, *XV Dari*, II, no. 380, p. 297

. . . [copied] During the reign of Hasan Pēk [Uzun Ḥasan Beg], of the nation of archers [azgin netołac'], who rules over the territories extending from Babelon [Babylon = Baghdad] to the city of Širaz [Shīrāz] and Trapizon [Trebizond], who scored numerous victories in numerous places, and who vanquished and slew three *łans* [khans] in one year, namely, Čihanšay [Djihānshāh] and his sons, and

[71] Karapet made his journey to Egypt to secure the Mamlūk Sultan's recognition of his new position as spiritual leader of the Armenians under the Sultan's jurisdiction, which also included Syria and Cilicia. See Sanjian, *Armenian Communities in Syria*, p. 227.

Pusayit Łan [Tīmūrid Abū Sa'īd Khān], and he captured their domains and fortresses.[72] In the year 919 of the Armenian Era [A.D. 1470] . . .

2. Place: monastery of Veri-Noravank'; scribe and author of col.: Ohannēs; MS. title: Ritual Book [*Maštoc'*].
Source: Xač'ikyan, *XV Dari*, II, no. 382, p. 299

. . . In these days the Tačiks collected tributes; and Uzun Hasan arrived and slew J̌hanša [Djihānshāh], son of Łara Usuf [Ḳara Yūsuf], as well as his sons, and occupied the *t'axt* in his place. And there was intense *t'asup* against and persecution of the Christians; and they forbade the ringing of the bells, and the Christians walked about wearing symbols . . .

3. Place: city of Ostan; purchaser of MS. and author of col.: Awetis; MS. title: Gospel.
Source: Xač'ikyan, *XV Dari*, II, no. 383, p. 299

. . . This colophon was written in bitter and anxious times, when the entire country was quivering and shaking at the hands of the wicked nation of archers [azgin netołac']. Moreover, this is the second year that the rising costs and the scarcity of all kinds of goods, and the plague have lingered on in our country. And all of this came to pass on account of our multitudinous sins.

May the Lord God, through your holy prayers and the intercession of all the saints, remove from us all of these grievous calamities, namely, the plague and famine, the slaying by the sword, and general enslavement; and may He increase the glory of the holy church in the four corners of the earth, like a shining sun, amen! This last colophon was written in the year 919 of our Haykazean Era [A.D. 1470], during the pontificate of the Lord Step'annos [IV of Aghtamar], and the khanate of Hasan Bēk [Uzun Ḥasan Beg], son of Ōt'man Bēk [Ḳara Yoluḳ 'Uthmān Beg], who slew J̌hanšay *mirza* [Djihānshāh Mīrzā], and also put all of his horsemen to flight, and captured the impregnable fortresses, and dominated all the lands . . .

[72] The author of this colophon fails to mention the third ruler slain by Uzun Ḥasan; cf. colophon no. 1 under 1469, which mentions the third as Ḥasan 'Alī, son of Djihānshāh.

4. Place: Ałt'amar; scribe and author of col.: Hayrapet; MS. title: Gospel.
   Source: Xač'ikyan, *XV Dari*, II, no. 386, p. 303

... [copied in A.D. 1470] during the pontificate of the Lord Step'anos [IV of Aghtamar], in bitter and anxious times, when the entire country was quivering and shaking at the hands of the wicked nation of archers [azgin netołac']. Moreover, for two years, now, God's intense wrath, namely the plague and the high cost of all goods, [has befallen us] on account of our multitudinous sins. May the Lord God, through your holy prayers and the intercession of all the saints, remove all of these grievous calamities from our country, amen! ...

5. Place: Ałt'amar; scribe and author of col.: Grigor; MS. title: Gospel.
   Source: Xač'ikyan, *XV Dari*, II, no. 387, p. 304

... [completed in A.D. 1470] during the pontificate of the Lord Step'anos [IV of Aghtamar] ... in bitter and grievous times, when we were subjected to levies by the infidels ...

1471

1. Place: Ałt'amar; scribe and author of col.: Hayrapet; MS. title: Grand Ritual Book [*Mayr Maštoc'*].
   Source: Xač'ikyan, *XV Dari*, II, 393a, p. 312

... [copied in A.D. 1470] during the pontificate of the Lord Step'anos [IV of Aghtamar], and during the reign of Hasan Bek [Uzun Ḥasan Beg], in bitter and anxious times, when the entire country was quivering and shaking at the hands of the infidels. Moreover, this is the third year that God's acute wrath, namely the plague, has not vanished from our country. And all of this [came to pass] on account of my multitudinous sins. May the Lord God, through your holy prayers and the intercession of all the saints, remove all afflictions from amongst you, namely, the plague and famine, the slaughter and general enslavement, from among all of us creatures, amen! ...

2. MS. title: Collection of Sermons [*Čarəntir*].
   Source: Xač'ikyan, *XV Dari*, II, no. 394, p. 313

. . . [copied] during the reign of the baron Hasan [Uzun Ḥasan], in the year 920 of our [Armenian] Era [A.D. 1471]. This is the third year that Hasan Bēk [Uzun Ḥasan Beg] has reigned in Pars [Fārs], Arewels [the east], and Miǰaget [Mesopotamia], in the north and in the south, peacefully [and] by the will of God.

3. Place: monastery of Hayocʻ-Tʻaṙ; MS. title: Gospel.
Source: Xačʻikyan, *XV Dari*, II, no. 395, p. 314

. . . [copied] in the year 920 of the Haykazean Era [A.D. 1471], in most grievous times, when we lived in anguish at the hands of the infidels and unjust tax-collectors, who persecuted and plundered our Armenian nation.

. . . And in /// Uzun Hasan /// son of As . . . /// Bēk [Beg] /// he arrived and captured /// the land and the *tʻaxtʻ* of Tʻawriz [Tabrīz] and the [office of] *pʻatʻšah* [padishah], and he slew Ian and J̌ahašē [Djihānshāh], son of Usupʻ [Ḳara Yūsuf] ///.

4. Place: monastery of Hayocʻ-Tʻaṙ; scribe and author of col.: Step'annos; MS. title: Gospel.
Source: Xačʻikyan, *XV Dari*, II, no. 396a, p. 315

. . . [completed] in the year 920 of the Armenian Era [A.D. 1471], and in most grievous times, during the khanate of Uzun Hasan, and the pontificate of the Lord Catholicos Ṙəstakēs at the holy see of Ēǰmiacin . . .

5. Place: monastery of Ałǰocʻ in Kʻełoy-Jor in canton of Ararat; scribe and author of col.: Vardan; MS. title: Gospel.
Source: Xačʻikyan, *XV Dari*, II, no. 397, pp. 315–316

. . . [copied] in the year 920 of the Haykazean Era [A.D. 1471], during the pontificate of the Lord Aristakēs at the holy see of Ēǰmiacin, and during the reign of King Bagrat [VI] of the Georgians [Vracʻ], and the khanate of Hasan Bēk [Uzun Ḥasan Beg], in bitter and evil and most grievous times, when the Christians were quivering and shaking at the hands of the Muslims [*aylazgi*] and unjust tax-collectors . . .

6. Place: village of Arewyis in province of Siwnikʻ; scribe and author of col.: Grigor; MS. title: Gospel.

Source: Xač'ikyan, *XV Dari*, II, no. 398, p. 316

... [copied] at a time when Hasan Pēk [Uzun Ḥasan Beg] slew Sultan Pusayit' [Tīmūrid Sulṭān Abū Sa'īd].

7. Place: village of Kuk'i in Šhapuneac'-Jor; MS. title: Menology [*Yaysmawurk'*].
Source: Xač'ikyan, *XV Dari*, II, no. 403, p. 319

... [copied in A.D. 1471] during the pontificate of the Lord Ṙstakēs, and the imperial conquest of Hasan Bak [Uzun Ḥasan Beg], who vanquished J̌hanšay [Djihānshāh], and, arriving in the plain of Xōy [Khoi], put Hasan Ali [Ḥasan 'Alī] to flight; and then proceeding to Łarapał [Karabagh], there too he [slew] the Sultan [Abū Sa'īd], the tyrant of Persia [Parskac'].

8. Place: village of Sawkut'lu in Šarvan; scribe and author of col.: Yakob; MS. title: Miscellany [*Žołovacu*].
Source: Xač'ikyan, *XV Dari*, II, no. 404a, p. 319

... [completed] in the year 920 of the Armenian Era [A.D. 1471] ... during the pontificate in Ałuank' [Caucasian Albania] of the Lord T'umay, and during the khanate of Šēranšah [Shīrwānshāh Farrukh Yasār], son of Xalil Pēk [Khalīl Allāh Beg] ...

9. Scribe and author of col.: Vardan; MS. title: Gospel.
Source: Xač'ikyan, *XV Dari*, II, no. 405, p. 321

... [completed in A.D. 1471] during the reign of Hasan Bek [Uzun Ḥasan Beg], who slew J̌hanša [Djihānshāh] and dominated our entire country ...

10. Scribe and author of col.: Yovanēs; MS. title: Gospel.
Source: Xač'ikyan, *XV Dari*, II, 406a, p. 321

... the accursed and wicked people attacked the village of Šatwan; and they waged *łazay* and killed seven individuals. Oh, Oh, pitiful death! All of this came to pass because of our sins ...

11. Place: begun in village of Aṙest and completed at monastery of Xaṙabastay; scribe and author of col.: Mēlk'isēd; MS. title: Gospel.

Source: Xač'ikyan, *XV Dari*, II, no. 407a, p. 322

. . . [copied] during the pontificate of the Lord Ṙəstakēs . . . and during the tyrannical rule of Uzun Hasan, in the year 920 of the Great [Armenian] Era [A.D. 1471] . . .

12. Scribe and author of col.: Mkrtič'; MS. title: Gospel.
Source: Xač'ikyan, *XV Dari*, II, no. 417, p. 328

. . . this holy Gospel was completed . . . during the khanate of Hasan Bēk [Uzun Ḥasan Beg], who dominated numerous cantons and lands . . . in the year 920 of the Armenian Era [A.D. 1471] . . .

1472

1. Place: city of Arckē; scribe and author of col.: Movsēs Arckec'i; MS. title: Hymnal [*Ganjaran*].
Source: Xač'ikyan, *XV Dari*, II, no. 424b, pp. 333–337; Hakobyan, *Manr Žam.*, II, 218–221

In the year 900 of the Armenian Era,
Plus sixteen years more [A.D. 1467],
The great king in the east,
The peace-loving J̌əhanšay [Djihānshāh],
Issued orders all around,
And assembled numerous troops.
With them he invaded Asorestan [Assyria]
To crush the *mir* Hasan [Mīr Uzun Ḥasan].
But Hasan Bēk [Uzun Ḥasan Beg], the brave *p'ahlawan*,
With the troops that he recruited
Found J̌əhanšay [Djihānshāh] when he was asleep,
Isolated from his troops and unguarded;
And he slew him then and there,
As well as his son, Muhamat [Muḥammad Mīrzā].
And the evil horsemen, who came back,
Took much booty and *t'ałt'an*.
Hasan Ali [Ḥasan 'Alī], the wicked beast,
Who was imprisoned at Maku [Mākū],
Escaped and went toward Łap'an [Ghapan];
He broke open the *hazinay*,

And distributed so many gifts
That many flocked to his side;
Two hundred thousand and even more
Assembled there by his side.
In the following year [A.D. 1468],
The Ał-łoyluc‘ik‘ [Aḳ-Ḳoyunlu] grew stronger;
They invaded Hayastan [Armenia]
And reached the shores of the Erasx [Araxes].
Hasan Ali [Ḥasan ‘Alī], that wretched fool,
Briefly encamped in the forest,
Where his troops rebelled
And came and joined his enemies.
Hasan Ali's [Ḥasan ‘Alī] men were terror-struck,
And leaving the army took to flight;
And when Sultan Hasan [Uzun Ḥasan] arrived,
Countless of the remainder submitted to him.
Occupying the *t‘ałt‘* in the *šahastan*,
He brought the land under his sway,
All countries were pacified,
Like the child on its mother's bosom.
Hasan Ali [Ḥasan ‘Alī] and all his men
Took to flight and arrived in Č‘ałat‘ay [Čaghatai].
They took Busayit [Tīmūrid Abū Sa‘īd] and came back,
Together with all of his forty sons.
They assembled their forces
To wage war and vent their ire;
Hasan Ali's [Ḥasan ‘Alī] troops and his [Abū Sa‘īd] men
Joined together and became as one.
When the hour of evening arrived,
And when their lamps were lit,
They came out and joined in battle,
And some were slain and others fled.
But Hasan Bēk [Uzun Ḥasan Beg], the valiant king,
Because of whom all this came to pass,
Arrived there with peaceful intent
And their army he plundered.
He slew Busayit [Abū Sa‘īd] there,
Also his captured sons,
Also Hasan Ali [Ḥasan ‘Alī], the unfortunate one,
His son and many others.
This *andōlvat‘* Hasan Ali [Ḥasan ‘Alī]
Built a church at Maku [Mākū],

Which was named St. Vardan;[73]
Yet he could not help himself,
By the will of the Father in heaven.
The Ał-łoyluk' [Aḳ-Ḳoyunlu] grew stronger;
They captured and held Babelon [Babylon = Baghdad];
They reached as far as Amṙsan,
Which truly is Xorasan [Khurāsān].
Three years later [A.D. 1470],
From the time he seized the *t'alt'*,
The great Sultan Hasan *p'atšah* [Uzun Ḥasan Pādishāh]
Dispatched troops to K'rtastan [Kurdistān].
The great general Sulēyman [Sulaymān b. Bižan]
Stealthily arrived with troops,
And so intensely besieged them
And took us all by great surprise.
But Sulēyman Bēk [Sulaymān b. Bižan Beg] remained there
No more than two months;
For the K'ərd [Kurds] grew stronger
And sought to crush them.
Fearful of this they withdrew
And wintered in the city of Van.
But the K'urd [Kurds] made *daxiray*,
And much matériel they prepared.
Again, in the following year,
In the Armenian year 920 [A.D. 1471],
They came back here from yonder.
The prince Xalil [Ṣūfī Khalīl] went to Muš [Mush],
The brave Sulēyman [Sulaymān b. Bižan] to Bałēš [Bitlīs],
And Bayanduṙ Łōc' *imirzay* [Bayandur Łoč Mīrzā]
Captured the entire *t'uman* of Xlat' [Khilāṭ].
In the following year [A.D. 1472],
During the period of Lent,
When it was the Tačik's' Ramadan,
The K'rd [Kurds] of the citadel of Kalahok' [Galhuk],
Came to Muš [Mush] with an evil design,
To vanquish the prince Xalil [Ṣūfī Khalīl],
And to torture all the Christians
With atrocities of many kinds.

[73] Some Muslim rulers, in their efforts to obtain the support of the native populations, on occasion sought to win the favor of influential clergy by extending the privileges of the church, by offering gifts, and sometimes even by constructing churches. In this instance, Ḥasan 'Alī either built the church himself or, more probably, permitted the local clergy to construct it.

But the king [St. Karapet] of Tarōn [Ṭarūn]
And the protector of all men,
The great Forerunner [*Karapet*], the voice of the Word,
Who baptized the Lord in the Yordanan [Jordan River],[74]
Smote and expelled K'arim Ała [Karīm Agha],
As well as all his troops.
Many froze in the snow,
And others perished by the sword.
And the *amiray* Bayanduṙ Łoc' [Amīr Bayandur Łoč],
Having laid siege to the citadel of Xlat' [Khilāṭ],
At the conclusion of six months
Captured Xlat' [Khilāṭ] and Bličayn [Blejan],
Demolished the citadel of Xlat' [Khilāṭ];
He took the citadel's defenders
Into his own army,
And then marched toward J̌əziray [Djazīra].
For the K'rd [Kurds] of the land of Buxtan [Bohtān]
Had withdrawn to J̌əziray [Djazīra],
And slaying all the T'urk' [Turks] therein
Entrenched themselves in the citadel.
When they heard the voice of Bayanduṙ [Bayandur Łoč],
For battle they prepared;
And when their forces they marshaled,
They were smitten and expelled;
Some died by the sword
And others drowned in the river;
Bayanduṙ [Bayandur] captured the J̌əziray [Djazīra],
Also seven citadels in Buxtan [Bohtān].
He came to the canton of Bznunik',
Which is known as Arckē;
He brought water from Cəṙget
To the village of Pēšnagomer alone.
On the fifteenth of the month of July,
He brought water from Zambełk,
Three days later they cut it off,
But on [the feast of] the Holy Cross it flowed again.[75]
And the valiant king Hasan Bēk [Uzun Ḥasan Beg]
Entrusted the *t'alt'* of Širaz [Shīrāz]
To his son Sultan Xalil [Sulṭān Khalīl],

[74] This passage refers to the monastery of St. Karapet (that is, St. John the Baptist) at Mush which was regarded by the Armenians of the region as their protector.
[75] This corresponds to September 13, 1472.

To defend his eastern domain.
And he returned to Asorestan [Assyria],
Arrived in the canton of Tarōn [Ṭarūn],
Demolished the citadel from its foundation,
And offered gifts to the monastery of Glak.[76]
He sent troops to the land of Rūm [Hṙomac' tun];
They reached the great city of T'ołat' [Tokat],
They took gold and silver as *t'ałt'an*,
All the *kumaš* they burned by fire.
And the *p'atšah* [Pādishāh Uzun Ḥasan] left for Syria
[Šamay tun],
But the citizens of the *šahastan* of Halap [Aleppo]
Refused to submit to him.
Bałēš [Bitlīs], built by Alexander [the Great],
Was besieged by Sulēyman [Sulaymān b. Bižan],
For a year and five months,
And in the year nine hundred and twelve [A.D. 1473]
The K'urd [Kurds] surrendered its citadel to the T'urk'man
[Turkmens];
They were punished by the Lord,
For one thousand men went into the citadel,
And six hundred of them rotted therein,
Only eight men and the *Amiray* [amir] remained alive.

2. Place: monastery of Arjəroy; scribe and author of col.: Melk'isēt'; MS. title: Ritual Book [*Maštoc'*].
Source: Xač'ikyan, *XV Dari*, II, no. 425, p. 337

... [copied] in the year 921 of our [Armenian] Era [A.D. 1472] ... during the catholicosate of the Lord Յṙəstakēs at Ējmiacin, and during the barony of Hasan Bek [Uzun Ḥasan Beg] ...

1473

1. Place: village of Sori in region of Hizan; scribe and author of col.: Yovsēp'; MS. title: Gospel.
Source: Xač'ikyan, *XV Dari*, II, no. 433, p. 342

... This holy Gospel was copied in the year 922 of the Armenian Era [A.D. 1473], in bitter and anxious times, during the khanate of Uzun

[76] See note 73 above.

Hasan, who in this year marauded K'rdstan [Kurdistān], and captured Bałēš [Bitlīs], Xlat' [Khilāṭ], Muš [Mush], and Bohtank' [Bohtān], and he shed much blood, and he plundered the Tačiks. He then marched into the land of Rūm [Hoṙomoc' erkir]; and the Sultan of Msr [Egypt] and the *Łan* [Khan] and Xondk'ar of Ṙum [Rūm; that is, Sultan Mehmet II, Fatih], with seven hundred thousand horsemen, prepared to do battle against him. They fought from sunrise until sunset, and 20,000 men were killed from both sides, and both sides took to flight. And Hasan Łan [Uzun Ḥasan Khān] sojourned in Davrēž [Tabrīz]. May the Lord God save us the Christians from the nation of archers [azgn netołac'], amen! And I took to flight and sojourned in the village of Sori in the region of Hizan where, living in anguish, I copied this holy Gospel . . .

2. Place: city of Akisi; MS. title: Gospel.
Source: Xač'ikyan, *XV Dari*, II, no. 434, p. 343

. . . I copied this holy Gospel . . . during the imperial conquest of Hasan [Uzun Ḥasan], of the nation of archers [netołac' azg] . . .

In this year [A.D. 1473], the wicked *xovandk'ar*, who is called Č't'ax [Mehmet II, Fatih], came with numerous and countless troops from Rūm [Hoṙomoc' ašxarh] to our country. He first came to Eznkay [Erzindjān] and set the city on fire / / / and only a small number of troops came out to resist Č't'ax. But Č't'ax was unaware of the ambuscades of our troops, and they [Č't'ax and his men] came forward and began to battle against the few troops who faced them. But then those who were in hiding came out from the rear and encircled the troops of Č't'ax; and there ensued a fierce battle from the morning until evening. At first our troops were defeated; but [later], by God's command, Č't'ax's forces were defeated, for there came a violent wind which blew off the dust of the earth upon Č't'ax, and the dust was so intense that the one could not see the other. And our troops went in pursuit and committed a fierce slaughter of the forces of Č't'ax. They also captured [Khāṣṣ Murād Pasha, commander of the Ottoman army] and, after bringing him before Hasan [Uzun Ḥasan], they slew him. Thus, thanks to the mercy of God, our country [was saved] from the forces of Č't'ax / / / and their leader, who was called *xovandk'ar*, took to flight and entrenched himself in the fortress, together with his despicable troops who numbered some sixty thousand. For this fortress . . . was as large as a city, and it was locked with enormous *znǰils* and planks / / / And the baron was left with only a few troops; and the troops of Č'tʻax left the fortress and began to repair to their own land; but the troops who were with the baron abandoned him and took to flight, and Č'tʻax escaped and fled. And Hasan [Uzun Ḥasan] mobilized troops and / / /

3. Place: canton of Xačʻenajor; scribe and author of col.: Sargis; MS. title: Gospel.
Source: Xačʻikyan, *XV Dari*, II, no. 435, p. 344

In these times when, on account of our multitudinous sins, the Christians were threatened by the nation of infidels . . . during the khanate of Hasan Bēk [Uzun Ḥasan Beg], who invaded the land of Rūm [Hoṙomocʻ ašxarh] and committed manifold acts of wickedness against the Tačiks; and during the catholicosate of the Lord Ṙastakēs of the Armenians . . .

4. Place: village of Aṙest or Bandumahi and monastery of Suxaray; scribe and author of col.: Melkʻisētʻ; MS. title: Grand Ritual Book [*Mayr Maštocʻ*].
Source: Xačʻikyan, *XV Dari*, II, no. 436, p. 344

. . . [copied in A.D. 1473] During the pontificate of the Lord Sargis [II, Ajatar], and the reign of Uzun Hasan, who in this year was crushed by Čʻatʻał [Mehmet II, Fatih] . . .

5. Place: village of Srkłunkʻ in Vayi-Jor; scribe and author of col.: Dawitʻ; MS. title: Gospel.
Source: Xačʻikyan, *XV Dari*, II, no. 438, p. 346

. . . [copied] in the year 922 of the Armenian Era [A.D. 1473], during the khanate of Hasan Bēk [Uzun Ḥasan Beg], grandson of Payəntur [Ḳara Yoluḳ ʻUthmān], who dominated numerous lands and cities; [and] during the catholicosate of the Lord Ǝṙəstakēs at Vałaršapat, and the barony in our province of the Baron Jum . . .

6. Place: village of Urc in canton of Ararat; scribe and author of col.: Xačʻatur; MS. title: Missal [*Čašocʻ*].
Source: Xačʻikyan, *XV Dari*, II, no. 439, p. 347

. . . [copied] in the year 922 of the Haykazean Era [A.D. 1473], during the pontificate of the Armenians of the Lord Aristakēs at the holy see of Ējmiacin, and during the reign of the great King [Bagrat VI] of Georgia [Vrac‘], and the khanate of Hasan Bēk [Uzun Ḥasan Beg], grandson of Awt‘man [Ḳara Yoluḳ ‘Uthmān] . . .

7. Place: city of Xlat‘; scribe and author of col.: Yovanēs; MS. title: Grand Ritual Book [*Mayr Maštoc‘*].
Source: Xač‘ikyan, *XV Dari*, II, no. 442, p. 348

. . . [copied in A.D. 1473] during the catholicosate of the Lord Ǝṙəstakēs, and during the reign of Hasan Bēk [Uzun Ḥasan Beg] . . .

8. Place: region of Samc‘xē; scribe and author of col.: Yakob; MS. title: Medical Book [*Bžškaran*].
Source: Xač‘ikyan, *XV Dari*, II, no. 443b, p. 350

. . . [copied] during the pontificate of the Lord Ǝṙəstak‘ēs, [and] during the reign of the baron Ławrławrē [Qwarqwaré] . . .

9. Place: city of Van; scribe and author of col.: Karapet; MS. title: Missal [*Čašoc‘*].
Source: Xač‘ikyan, *XV Dari*, II, nos. 445a, b, p. 351

. . . [completed] in the year 922 of the Armenian Era [A.D. 1473], during the pontificate of the Lord and *rabunapet* Sargis [II, Ajatar] . . . and during the reign of Sōlt‘an Xasan Bēk [Sulṭān Uzun Ḥasan Beg] . . .

. . . In the year 922 [of the Armenian Era = A.D. 1473]. Xasan [Uzun Ḥasan] was defeated by Č‘it‘ał [Mehmet II, Fatih], and we know not what will befall us.

10. Place: city of Erznkay; scribe and author of col.: Manuēl; MS. title: Gospel.
Source: Xač‘ikyan, *XV Dari*, II, no. 448, p. 354

. . . Copied in the year 922 of the Armenian Era [A.D. 1473] . . . during the reign of the baron Hasan [Uzun Ḥasan], and the pontificate of the Lord Sargis [II, Ajatar]; in bitter and evil times . . .

1474

1. Place: Vayoc'-Jor; scribe and author of col.: Zak'ēos; MS. title: Menology [*Yaysmawurk'*].
Source: Xač'ikyan, *XV Dari*, II, no. 454m, p. 360

I reached this point [in copying this manuscript] ... it was reported that Hasan Bēk [Uzun Ḥasan Beg] was crushed ...

2. Place: city of Tp'xis; scribe and author of col.: Astuacatur; MS. title: Gospel.
Source: Xač'ikyan, *XV Dari*, II, no. 455, p. 362

... [copied in A.D. 1474] during the reign of King Bakrat [Bagrat VI] in Georgia [Vrac'] ...

3. Place: monastery of Cłak'; scribe and author of col.: Pawłos; MS. title: Gospel.
Source: Xač'ikyan, *XV Dari*, II, no. 461, p. 365

... [copied] in the year 923 of the Armenian Era [A.D. 1474], during the reign of Hasan Bēk [Uzun Ḥasan Beg] and of his sons ... In this year, Hasan Bak [Uzun Ḥasan Beg] laid siege [*xsar*] to Bałēš [Bitlīs] and slaughtered many Kurds [Marac' azg]; [but] he is most beneficent toward our Armenian nation, for he is not taking captives; and this must be attributed to the providence of God ...

4. Place: city of Van; scribe and author of col.: Vardan; MS. title: Gospel.
Source: Xač'ikyan, *XV Dari*, II, no. 462, p. 366

... [copied] in the year 923 of the Armenian Era [A.D. 1474], during the reign of Hasan Bēk [Uzun Ḥasan Beg], and the pontificate of the newly anointed Catholicos, the Lord Sargis [II, Aǰatar] ...

5. Place: city of Xizan; scribe and author of col.: Yovanēs; MS. title: Gospel.
Source: Xač'ikyan, *XV Dari*, II, no. 463a, p. 366

... [copied] in the year 923 of the Great Armenian Era [A.D. 1474], during the catholicosate of the Haykazean nation of the Lord Sargis

[II, Aǰatar] and of our catholicosate at Ałt'amar of the Lord Step'annos [IV], and during the khanate of Hasan Bēk [Uzun Ḥasan Beg] . . .

6. Place: village of Sori in region of Hizan; scribe and author of col.: Yovsēp'; MS. title: Gospel.
Source: Xač'ikyan, *XV Dari*, II, no. 464a, p. 368

. . . [copied] during the pontificate of the Lord Catholicos Step'anos [IV] at Axt'amar, and during the khanate of the Tačik tyrant Uzun Hasan, and in the year 923 of the Armenian Era [A.D. 1474] . . .

1475

1. Place: village of Srkłunk' in Vayijor; scribe and author of col.: Dawit'; MS. title: Gospel.
Source: Xač'ikyan, *XV Dari*, II, no. 475, pp. 377–378

. . . [copied] in the year 924 of the Armenian era [A.D. 1475], during the khanate of Hasan Bēk [Uzun Ḥasan Beg], grandson of Payəntur [Ḳara Yoluḳ 'Uthmān] . . .

2. Place: canton of Tarberuni or Berkri; scribe and author of col.: Grigor Berkrc'i; MS. title: Gospel.
Source: Xač'ikyan, *XV Dari*, II, no. 478, p. 382

. . . In this year [A.D. 1475], the King at T'awrēz [Tabrīz] was Hasan Bēk [Uzun Ḥasan Beg], who had come from Miǰaget [Mesopotamia] and now dominates the eastern lands; and we are suffering manifold anguish . . .

3. Place: city of Van; scribe and author of col.: Azariay; MS. title: Gospel.
Source: Xač'ikyan, *XV Dari*, II, no. 480, p. 383

. . . [copied] In the year 924 of our [Armenian] Era [A.D. 1475]. And during the catholicosate at Ēǰmiacin of [the Lord] Sargis [II, Aǰatar], and the catholicosate at Ałt'amar of [the Lord] Step'anos [IV], and during the reign of Hasan Bēk [Uzun Ḥasan Beg] . . .

4. Place: city of Van; scribe and author of col.: Karapet; MS. title: Gospel.
Source: Xač'ikyan, *XV Dari*, II, no. 481a, p. 384

... [copied] in the year 924 of our [Armenian] Era [A.D. 1475], during the pontificate of the Lord Yohanēs [VII, Ajakir], and during the reign of Xasan Bēk [Uzun Ḥasan Beg] ...

5. Place: city of Van; scribe and author of col.: Karapet; MS. title: Gospel.
Source: Xač'ikyan, *XV Dari*, II, no. 482, p. 385

... [completed in A.D. 1475] during the reign of Hasan Bēk [Uzun Ḥasan Beg] ...

6. Place: Ałt'amar; scribe and author of col.: Nersēs; MS. title: Gospel.
Source: Xač'ikyan, *XV Dari*, II, no. 483a, p. 385

... [copied] in the year 924 of our [Armenian] Era [A.D. 1475], during the pontificate of my brother, the Lord Catholicos Step'anos [IV of Aghtamar], and during the imperial conquest of Hasan Bēk [Uzun Ḥasan Beg] ...

7. Place: monastery of Bazenc'; scribe and author of col.: Əřəstakēs; MS. title: Gospel.
Source: Xač'ikyan, *XV Dari*, II, no. 484, p. 386

... [copied] in the year 924 of the Armenian Era [A.D. 1475], in bitter and anxious times, when we know not what will befall our Armenian nation amongst the wolves.

8. Place: Əstəmpawl; purchaser of MS. and author of col.: Awetik'; MS. title: Gospel.
Source: Xač'ikyan, *XV Dari*, II, no. 490, p. 389

On the sixth of the month of June, in the year 924 of our Armenian Era [A.D. 1475], the Ismaelites [Ismayēlac'ik'] captured Kafay [Kafa].[77] And this holy Gospel was captured and brought to Əstəm-

[77] The reference is to the conquest of Kafa by the Ottomans.

pawl [Istanbul]; and I, Awetik', purchased it and offered it to the church of St. Sargis . . .

Remember the baron Awetik', the last recipient of this holy Gospel, as well as his parents, who acquired this holy Gospel from the Muslims [*aylazgi*], who captured it in Kafay [Kafa] and brought it to Əstəmpawl [Istanbul] . . .

9. Place: Erusałēm [Jerusalem]; scribe and author of col.: Sołomon; MS. title: Gospel.
Source: Xač'ikyan, *XV Dari*, II, no. 491, p. 390

. . . In the year 924 of our Armenian Era [A.D. 1475], when this holy Gospel was copied, the Tačiks [the Ottomans] captured Kafa. They carried off many captives and committed much destruction; and there was intense grief and mourning among the Christians. And all of this came to pass on account of our sins . . .

1476

1. Scribes and authors of col.: Grigor and Yovsēp'; MS. title: Menology [*Yaysmawurk'*].
Source: Xač'ikyan, *XV Dari*, II, no. 495, p. 392

. . . in this year [A.D. 1476], there arrived the bloodthristy *beklarbek* [and] lord of the *t'ałt'*, the human-faced wild beast, the barbarous and brutal Hasan [Uzun Ḥasan], son of the baron Awt'man [Ḳara Yoluḳ 'Uthmān]. He went to Georgia [Virs] with numerous troops, and enveloped us with a dark mist and fog on account of our manifold sins. And they carried off 36,000 into captivity, excepting those whom they massacred and slew with the sword. He committed much destruction and decimated the Christians, so much so that we asked the mountains to fall on us and the hills to cover us up [cf. Luke 23:30; Revelation 6:16; Hosea 10:8]. And not only this; they also banished numerous people to the east and to the west. They separated the father from his son, the daughter from her mother, the brother from his brother, and the dear ones from their beloved. And all of this came to pass on account of our multitudinous sins . . .

2. Scribe and author of col.: [Step'anos Č'mškacagc'i?]; MS. title: Song Book [*Tałaran*].

Source: Xač'ikyan, *XV Dari*, II, no. 496, pp. 393–396

Woe unto us a thousand times,
For by the Muslims [*aylazgi*] we were trampled;
For our fathers ate sour grapes,
Snatched [food] from their children's teeth.
They committed countless sins,
And brought to us darkness and gloom;
They committed sins like beasts,
They were destroyed in the abyss.
Because of their haughtiness
And of their devious and crooked ways,
They anathematized the clerical leaders,
The scions of the Lusaworič' [St. Gregory the
Illuminator].
For the pontiff Aristakēs,
The corporeal angel on earth,
Was slain by King / / /
And they bitterly persecute.
The divinely borne holy pontiff,
Descended from the Part'ew [Parthians],
The Lord forthwith removed from our midst,
For we, master-haters, were unworthy.
He [God] delivered us into the hands of the Muslims
[*aylazgi*],
The Hagar Tačik nation,
Who persecute us on all sides
And keep us in tears all the time.
Our priests they deprecate,
The Christians they persecute,
/ / / the churches they blaspheme,
They spit on the Cross.
Despite all these calamities,
We cease not to sin,
But walk with evil
Without fearing the Lord on high.
Because of this the Lord is wrathful
And wills to punish us
Through the impure Hagar nation [azgn Hagaray],
And causes bitterness to our nation of Aram [azgs
Aramay];
For He changed into bitterness

The goodwill of the *p'atšah* [padishah]
Hasan Bēk [Uzun Ḥasan Beg] the Ał-Łōlu
[Aḳ-Ḳoyunlu].
Tax-collectors everywhere
Drag us off and beat up our nation of Aram
[Aramay azg];
Silver and pure gold they demand,
And copper coins from those who have them not.
A blue symbol on the Christians he put,
To distinguish them from the infidels.
He said the dead should be carried low,
And to measure the necks of children with a cord.
He transgressed the command of their master [the
Prophet Muhammad],
Whom they allege to be a *p'ēłambar*;
They collected the *xarač* from the priests
And also from the young deacons.
Moreover, the ringing of the [church] bells,
The symbol of [Archangel] Gabriel's trumpet,
He prohibited everywhere,
In villages, monasteries, and cities.
And because of my sins
The Lord God is angry with us;
He changes the heart of the tyrants
To deprive us of our lives.
Such came to pass in this year,
In the year nine hundred and twenty-five
Of the Armenian Era [A.D. 1476],
Which is called the year of the scorpion.
P'adšah Hasan [Pādishāh Uzun Ḥasan], the great
sultan,
Issued orders everywhere,
And mobilized numerous troops,
To destroy Vrac'tan [Georgia].
They were in all a hundred thousand,
Both horsemen and foot soldiers;
They entered Tp'xis [Tiflis] very boldly,
Captured it and laid it in ruins.
King Bagrat [VI] of Vrac'tan [Georgia]
Had gone to Lakzstan [Daghestan]
To wage war and vent his ire,
Leaving the country without its master.

And this was by the will of God,
Because of the Georgians' [Vrac' azg] sins,
For they seduced the sultan with bribes,
And wrested Gołgot'ay [Golgotha] from us.[78]
When they heard the voice of the T'urk'man
[Turkmens],
They all left and took to flight,
And hid themselves in the woods and among bushes,
And others took refuge in fortresses.
They captured and remained in Tp'xis [Tiflis],
And the rest submitted voluntarily.
A regiment of horsemen they formed,
And dispatched it to Gōri.
They arrived and captured the citadel,
Slew the men with the sword,
Three hundred who were there,
Carried off the women and children.
They then went into the woods,
They searched for fifteen days,
They captured them one and all,
They brought them out in fetters;
They slew the men with the sword,
As well as the aged women;
They slew the priests,
And drank their blood.
Who can relate in writing?
Or count the number of the dead?
Who can listen to the whining
Of those who were smeared with blood?
Newly wed brides and grooms / / /
They took the women and children and went away . . .
And when they separated
The children from their mothers,
Some their mothers / / /

3. Place: city of Tp'xis; scribe and author of col.: Mkrtič'; MS. title: Hymnal [*Šaraknoc'*].
Source: Xač'ikyan, *XV Dari*, II, no. 497, p. 396

. . . [copied] in bitter and evil times, when we were suffering from the

[78] For a discussion of the Armeno-Georgian struggles for control of Golgotha in the Holy Sepulcher at Jerusalem, see Sanjian, *Armenian Communities in Syria*, pp. 172–173.

tyranny of the infidels; during the khanate of Hasan Bēk [Uzun Ḥasan Beg], who carried off captives from Vrac'tun [Georgia] and destroyed the city of P'aytakaran; and during the pontificate of the Lord Sargis [II, Ajatar].

4. MS. title: Ritual Book [*Maštoc'*].
Source: Xač'ikyan, *XV Dari*, II, no. 498a, p. 397

... [copied in A.D. 1476], in bitter and evil times, for on all sides the Tačiks harass and persecute the Christians. We are suffering, on account of our multitudinous sins, from the tributes, captivity, famine, slaughter, and other multifarious griefs and anguish. May the Lord God deliver us all who believe in Him from their hands, amen! ...

5. Place: monastery of Ayrivank'; scribe and author of col.: Step'annos; MS. title: Gospel.
Source: Xač'ikyan, *XV Dari*, II, no. 499a, b, pp. 397–398

... [copied] during the pontificate of the Lord Sargis [II, Ajatar] at the holy see of Ējmiacin ... and during the khanate of Hasan Bēk [Uzun Ḥasan Beg], son of Awt'man [Ḳara Yoluḳ 'Uthmān], in bitter and grievous times, when we were suffering at the hands of the infidels and unjust tax-collectors ...

This holy Gospel was illuminated ... in bitter and anxious times, for Hasan Bēk [Uzun Ḥasan Beg] invaded Vrastan [Georgia] and carried off captives; in the year 926 [of the Armenian Era = A.D. 1477].

6. Place: monastery of Veri-Noravank' in canton of Vayoc'-Jor; scribe and author of col.: Pawłos; MS. title: Gospel.
Source: Xač'ikyan, *XV Dari*, II, no. 500a, p. 398

... This was completed on the nineteenth of the month of Nawasard, in the year 925 of the Armenian Era [A.D. 1476], during the khanate of Hasan Pēk [Uzun Ḥasan Beg], and during the pontificate of the Lord Sargis [II, Ajatar] ...

7. Place: monastery of Bolorajor in Vayoc'-Jor; restorer of MS. and author of col.: Zak'ariay; MS. title: Missal [*Čašoc'*].

Source: Xač'ikyan, *XV Dari*, II, no. 501, p. 400

... This [manuscript] was restored in the year 925 of the Great Armenian Era [A.D. 1476], during the khanate of Payandur Hasan Bēk [Bayandur Uzan Ḥasan Beg], son of Awt'man Bēk [Ḳara Yoluḳ 'Uthmān Beg]; during the catholicosate of the Lord Sargis [II, Aǰatar] ... and the rule of the baron J̌um ...

8. Place: canton of Vardijor or Vayijor; MS. title: Hymnal [*Šaraknoc'*].
Source: Xač'ikyan, *XV Dari*, II, no. 502, p. 400

... [copied] during the khanate of Hasan Bēk [Uzun Ḥasan Beg], grandson of Payəndur [Ḳara Yoluḳ 'Uthmān], who occupied the *t'axt'* of Hulawu[79] [Hūlāgū Khān]; in the year 925 of the Haykazean Era [A.D. 1476], during the incumbency of [the Lord] Yovhanēs [VII, Aǰakir] at [the holy see of] Vałaršapat ...

9. Place: monastery of Ankuneac'; scribe and author of col.: Zak'ar; MS. title: Nersēs Šnorhali's Encyclical Letter.
Source: Xač'ikyan, *XV Dari*, II, no. 503, p. 401

... Written on the twentieth of December, in the year 925 of the Armenian Era [A.D. 1476] ... during the khanate of Hasan Pēk [Uzun Ḥasan Beg], and the barony of Husēn Pēk [Ḥusayn Beg], [who] in the year 925 [of the Armenian Era = A.D. 1476] marched against the king ...

10. Place: city of Arckē in canton of Bznunik'; scribe and author of col.: Yovanēs; MS. title: Gospel.
Source: Xač'ikyan, *XV Dari*, II, no. 504, p. 402

... [copied] during the pontificate of the Lord Yohanēs [VII, Aǰakir], Catholicos of All Armenians, and during the reign of Amir Hasan Bahaduṙ [Amīr Uzun Ḥasan Bahadur]; in the year 925 of our [Armenian] Era [A.D. 1476] ...

11. Place: Ałt'amar; scribe and author of col.: Abełay; MS. title: Menology [*Yaysmawurk'*].

[79] The "t'axt' of Hulawu" is the Armenian expression for the "fief of Hūlāgū."

Source: Xač'ikyan, *XV Dari*, II, no. 505, p. 402

... [completed] during the pontificate of the Lord Step'anos [IV of Aghtamar], in the year 925 of the Armenian Era [A.D. 1476], in bitter and most grievous times, when we were subjected to levies and were in the servitude of the nation of archers [azgin netołac'] ...

12. Place: Ałt'amar; scribe and author of col.: Hayrapet; MS. title: Collection of Sermons [*Čaṙəntir*].
Source: Xač'ikyan, *XV Dari*, II, no. 508, p. 407

... [completed] during the pontificate of the Lord Step'annos [IV of Aghtamar], and in the year 925 of the Armenian Era [A.D. 1476], in bitter and most grievous times, when we were subjected to levies and when we were in the servitude of the nation of archers [azgin netołac'] ...

1477

1. Place: village of Ēgēpat in canton of Basen; scribe and author of col.: Melk'isēt'; MS. title: Gospel.
Source: Xač'ikyan, *XV Dari*, II, no. 522, p. 415

... [copied in A.D. 1477] in bitter and evil times, when justice had given way and injustice and confusion had intensified everywhere ... on account of my multitudinous sins; when the infidels had increased and the Christians had decreased in number; during the reign in Georgia [Vrac'] of King Bagrat [VI], and when the *at'abēk* [atabeg] was Ławrławrē [Qwarqwaré]; and during the khanate of the Tačik Uzun Hasan, grandson of Awt'man [Ḳara Yoluḳ 'Uthmān].

In the year 925 of the Armenian Era [A.D. 1476], in the month of September, countless Tačik troops assembled and marched forth to wage *łaza* against Vrac'tun [Georgia]. He [Uzun Ḥasan] camped on the bank of the river K'uṙ [Kura], in the city of P'aytakaran, which is now called Tp'xis [Tiflis]. He spread his troops throughout Georgia [Vrac' ašxarh]; and he reached as far as the borders of Ap'xaz [Abkhazia]. And, ascending the summit of the Kovkas [Caucasus] mountain, they assembled in one place the enormous booty and the captives, and he [Uzun Ḥasan] committed many atrocities. Thirty-two thousand individuals were carried off into captivity, and forty-eight thousand men were put to the sword. We were horrified when we heard of and witnessed all this, for the merciful God subjected the

Christians to the cruel sword because of my sins; for the merciful God permitted Satan to enter the merciless heart of the Tačiks and to carry out his wishes. May the Lord God deliver all of us Christians from the infidels and the temptations of Satan, amen! . . .

2. MS. title: Gospel.
Source: Xač'ikyan, *XV Dari*, II, no. 523, p. 416

. . . [copied in A.D. 1477], in bitter and evil times, for in this year Hasan Bēk [Uzun Ḥasan Beg], grandson of Awt'man [Ḳara Yoluḳ 'Uthmān], attacked the city of P'aytakaran, which now is called Təp'xis [Tiflis]. He plundered and carried off captives, and he conducted a terrible slaughter in the country; and who can / / /

3. Place: monastery of Yovhannavank' in canton of Ararat; scribe and author of col.: Gabriēl; MS. title: Grand Ritual Book [*Mayr Maštoc'*].
Source: Xač'ikyan, *XV Dari*, II, no. 524b, c, pp. 417–418

. . . In the year 925 [of the Armenian Era = A.D. 1476] Hasan Bēk [Uzun Ḥasan Beg] carried off captives from Vrastan [Georgia].

. . . Vrastun [Georgia], whence Hasan Bēk [Uzun Ḥasan Beg] carried off 32,000 captives; in the year 925 [of the Armenian Era = A.D. 1476].

4. Place: monastery of Yankiwneac' in Ašota-Jor; scribe and author of col.: Zak'aria; MS. title: Gospel.
Source: Xač'ikyan, *XV Dari*, II, no. 525, p. 418

. . . [copied in A.D. 1477] during the reign of the baron Hasan [Uzun Ḥasan], who plundered the region of Tp'xis [Tiflis] and captured 60,000 men. They slew 30,000 with the sword, and carried off 30,000 as captives. Woe unto me a thousand times . . .

5. Place: monastery of Yankuneac' in Ašota-Jor; scribe and author of col.: Zak'aria; MS. title: Gospel.
Source: Xač'ikyan, *XV Dari*, II, no. 526, p. 419

. . . [copied in A.D. 1477] during the khanate of Hasan Pēk [Uzun Ḥasan Beg] . . .

6. Author of col.: Step'anos; MS. title: Gospel.
Source: Xač'ikyan, *XV Dari*, II, no. 529, p. 420

... [illuminated] in bitter and anxious times, for Hasan Bēk [Uzun Ḥasan Beg] invaded and carried off captives from Vnastun [Georgia]; in the year 926 [of the Armenian Era = A.D. 1477].

7. Place: city of Bałēš; scribe and author of col.: Karapet Abełay; MS. title: Hymnal [*Šaraknoc'*].
Source: Xač'ikyan, *XV Dari*, II, no. 531, p. 421

... [copied] during the sultanate of Hasan Bēk [Uzun Ḥasan Beg], and the catholicosate of Yovhannēs [VII, Aǰakir].

8. Place: village of Šatwan in province of Ṙštunik'; scribe and author of col.: Melk'isēt'; MS. title: Hymnal [*Ganjaran*].
Source: Xač'ikyan, *XV Dari*, II, no. 533, p. 423

... [copied] in the year 926 of the Haykazean Era [A.D. 1477] ... and during the imperial conquest of Ałup Łan [Ya'ḳūb Bayandur Khān] ...[80]

1478

1. Recipient of MS. and author of col.: Amir; MS. title: Menology [*Yaysmawurk'*].
Source: Xač'ikyan, *XV Dari*, II, no. 538, p. 425

... In the year 927 of the Armenian Era [A.D. 1478], on the twenty-eighth of [the month of] *Aranc'*. In this time, the baron Hasan [Uzun Ḥasan] invaded Vrac'tun [Georgia] and devastated it. He slew numerous people with the sword, he committed destruction, and he carried off 40,000 individuals into captivity. Who can describe in writing the suffering of these people? They demolished numerous churches, they destroyed crucifixes and books, as well as ecclesiastical vessels. And he [Uzun Ḥasan] died a cruel death, like the accursed child slayer Herovt'ēs [Herod the Great] ...

[80] Ya'ḳūb Bayandur Khān assumed the throne at Tabrīz on July 16, 1478; hence, the date of the colophon is erroneous. The error was made by either the scribe or a later copyist.

2. Place: monastery of Argelan near Berkri, in canton of Tarberuni; scribe and author of col.: Grigor Berkrecʻi; MS. title: Hymnal [*Šaraknocʻ*].
Source: Xačʻikyan, *XV Dari*, II, no. 539, pp. 425–426

... [completed in A.D. 1478] during the pontificate of the Lord Yovhannēs [VII, Aǰakir] and of the Lord Archbishop Sargis Eznkacʻi [Catholicos Sargis II, Aǰatar?] ... who performed a deed of great valor by delivering [some of the] captives carried off by Hasan Pēk [Uzun Ḥasan Beg] from Vracʻtan [Georgia], which took place in this year. Moreover, in these days, Ōłurlu [Oghurlu Muḥammad], son of Hasan Bēk [Uzun Ḥasan Beg], from his father's troops, but without his consent / / / ...

3. Place: village of Srkłunkʻ in Vayi-Jor; scribe and author of col.: Dawitʻ; MS. title: Collection of Sermons [*Čaṙəntir*].
Source: Xačʻikyan, *XV Dari*, II, no. 541a, c, pp. 427, 428

... This Holy Testament was begun and completed in bitter and anxious times, when we were quivering at the hands of the infidels, for charity and mercy among men have disappeared, and fathers tend to annihilate their children, children their fathers, and brothers their brothers. May the divine care and His paternal mercy protect us believers from these murderous times, amen!

... This book was completed in the year 927 of the Armenian Era [A.D. 1478], during the khanate of Yayłup Pēk [Yaʻḳūb Bayandur Beg], son of Hasan Bēk [Uzun Ḥasan Beg] and grandson of Awtʻman [Ḳara Yoluḳ ʻUthmān]. In this year, he [Yaʻḳūb] killed his brother Sultan Xalil [Sulṭān Khalīl] and seized the sultanate ...

> ... During the khanate of the new *pʻatʻšah* [padishah],
> Xalil Sultan [Sulṭān Khalīl], who now reigns,[81]
> Who was alarmed by the Georgians [Vracʻ].

4. Place: village of Kukʻi; scribe and author of col.: Manwēl; MS. title: Hymnal [*Ganjaran*].
Source: Xačʻikyan, *XV Dari*, II, no. 544, p. 430

[81] It is obvious that this was written some time before the major colophon, that is, the one immediately before this. The latter mentions Yaʻḳūb Bayandur, who slew his brother Sulṭān Khalīl, as the ruler.

. . . [completed] in bitter and anxious times, when we were being persecuted by the infidels who impose levies and cause manifold anguish. And they are keeping the Christians in terror and in Tartarus [*tartaros*]; and we rest our hopes in God's mercy, that He may deliver us from the infidels and from all temptations, amen! . . .

5. Place: Ałt'amar; scribe and author of col.: Hayrapet; MS. title: Gospel.
Source: Xač'ikyan, *XV Dari*, II, no. 545, p. 431

. . . [copied in A.D. 1478] during the pontificate of the Lord Catholicos Step'anos [IV of Aghtamar], in bitter and anxious times, when the entire country was quivering and shaking at the hands of the wicked nation of archers [azgin netołac'], on account of our multitudinous sins . . .

6. Place: Erusałēm and Pawntos; scribe and author of col.: Nikołayos; MS. title: Hymnal [*Šaraknoc'*].
Source: Xač'ikyan, *XV Dari*, II, no. 548, p. 433

I began [to copy this manuscript] at Holy Erusałēm [Jerusalem] in the year 927 [of the Armenian Era = A.D. 1478]; and then I came to the famous monastery called Awag, and I copied there for a little while. And from there, fearful of the wicked Č'it'ax [Mehmet II, Fatih], I came to our city of Pawntos [Pontus = Trebizond] . . . And while I was there I suffered much grief . . .

1479

1. Place: village of Ařest (or Bantumahi) in canton of Tarberunik' and Ǝncani?; scribe and author of col.: Melk'isēt'; MS. title: Hymnal [*Šaraknoc'*].
Source: Xač'ikyan, *XV Dari*, II, no. 553, p. 436

This was copied in the year 928 [of the Armenian Era = A.D. 1479] . . . in the canton of Tarberuni, in the village of Ařest, which is also called Bantumahi . . . And half of it was copied at Ǝncani (?) . . . for we fled away from the infidels, because Hasan Bēg [Uzun Ḥasan Beg] died and he was succeeded on the throne by his son Sōlt'an Xalil [Sulṭān Khalīl]. But the other son, Ałubēk [Ya'ḳūb Beg], with numerous troops rose in rebellion against his brother and killed him, and he reigned in his entire domain. At the present time he has left for the east with numerous troops to fight against the Č'ałat' [Čaghatai]; and may God's will be done!

2. Place: city of Arčēš in K'ajberunik'; scribe and author of col.: Yovhannēs [Mangasarenc']; MS. title: Gospel.
Source: Xač'ikyan, *XV Dari*, II, no. 554, p. 437

... [copied in A.D. 1479] during the pontificate of the Lord Catholicos Yovanēs [VII, Ajakir], and when the *p'at'šah* [padishah] of our land was Eałup Bēk [Ya'ḳūb Beg] ...

3. Place: city of Muš; scribe and author of col.: Pawłos; MS. title: Gospel.
Source: Xač'ikyan, *XV Dari*, II, no. 556a, p. 438

... [copied] in the year 928 of the Armenian Era [A.D. 1479], and during the reign of Eałup Xan Bayandur [Ya'ḳūb Bayandur Khān] of the nation of archers [azgin netołac'] ...

4. Place: fortress of Sinamut in city of Xarberd; scribe and author of col.: Yohannēs; MS. title: Menology [*Yaysmawurk'*].
Source: Xač'ikyan, *XV Dari*, II, no. 557, p. 438

... [copied] in the year 928 of the Haykazean Era [A.D. 1479], during the amirate of Melik' Aslan Tułłatarc'i [Malik Arslan, the Dhu'l-Ḳadrid], of the nation of archers [azgin netołac'] ...

1480

1. Place: city of Əstampawl; scribe and author of col.: Martiros; MS. title: Psalms.
Source: Xač'ikyan, *XV Dari*, II, no. 563a, p. 441

... [copied] when the great *xōndk'ar*, Sultan Muhamat [Mehmet II, Fatih], marched against Uzun Hasan and vanquishing him put him to flight. Escaping his [Mehmet's] fury, he fled to T'avrēž [Tabrīz]. But he [Mehmet] turned back and marched into the canton of

Xaxt'ik', and set on fire the city called Babert' [Bayburt] and demolished it. He also captured an excellent and choice Psalm Book and brought it to Ǝstəmpōl [Istanbul]; and the medical doctor Amirtovlat' found and delivered this holy book from captivity. This occurred in the year 922 [of the Armenian Era = A.D. 1473].

Moreover, in the year 928 [of the Armenian Era = A.D. 1479], the *xōntk'ar* [Mehmet II] deported [*surkun*] the Armenians from the land of Łaraman [Ḳaramān]. They also brought me, this worthless dust Martiros, with them to Kostandnupōlis [Constantinople], and put me under the care of our holy vardapet Lord Mat'ēos Sebastac'i and the vardapet Abraham Trapizonec'i. They both had been brought here by the *xondk'ar*, who also offered them the [Armenian] patriarchal office; but they both declined, for they preferred hermitical life to honors offered by man . . .

2. Place: Biwzandia-Kostandinupawlis; scribe and author of col.: Nersēs; MS. title: The Chronicles of Michael the Syrian and Samuēl Anec'i.
Source: Xač'ikyan, *XV Dari*, II, no. 564, p. 443

. . . [copied in A.D. 1480] during the reign of Sultan Mahmat [Mehmet II, Fatih], in times of anguish and anxiety, for he raised an intense storm upon the Christians and also upon his own people, by transplanting them from place to place, by imposing levies, and by causing other anguish.

. . . I copied this in times of bitterness, for they brought us from Amasia [Amasya] to Kostandinupawlis [Constantinople] by force and against our will; and I copied this tearfully and with much lamentation . . .

3. Place: monastery of Varag; scribe and author of col.: Karapet; MS. title: Miscellany [*Žołovacu*].
Source: Xač'ikyan, *XV Dari*, II, no. 566, p. 444

. . . [copied] in the year 929 of our [Armenian] Era [A.D. 1480], during the catholicosate of the Lord Sargis [II, Ajatar] . . . and during the imperial conquest of the nation of archers [netołakan azg], in bitter and grievous times . . .

4. Place: Ałt'amar; scribe and author of col.: Hayrapet; MS. title: Ritual Book [*Maštoc'*].

Source: Xač'ikyan, *XV Dari*, II, no. 567, p. 446

. . . [completed] during the pontificate of the Lord Catholicos Step'an [Step'annos IV of Aghtamar], [and] during the reign of Ałup Bēk [Ya'ḳūb Beg], in the year 929 of our [Armenian] Era [A.D. 1480], in bitter and anxious times. Because of our multitudinous sins, we were subjected to levies by the infidels . . .

Bibliography, Appendixes

Bibliography

Note: In alphabetizing entries, simple letters are placed before those with diacritical marks. Thus, for example, the sequence for the C's goes: C, C', Č, Č'.

Abgaryan, G. V. *Matenadaran* (Library of Manuscripts). Erevan, 1962.

Abrahamyan, A. G. *Hovhannes Imastaseri Matenagrut'yunə* (The Works of John the Philosopher). Erevan, 1956.

——— *Hay Gri ev Grč'utyan Patmut'yun* (History of the Armenian Alphabet and Paleography). Erevan, 1959.

Ačaṙean, H. *Hayoc' Grerə* (The Armenian Alphabet). Vienna, 1928.

——— *Hayerēn Armatakan Baṙaran* (Etymological Dictionary of Armenian). 7 vols. Erevan, 1926–1935.

Ačaṙyan, H. *Hayoc' Lezvi Patmut'yun* (History of the Armenian Language). 2 vols. Erevan, 1940–1951.

——— *Hayoc' Anjnanunneri Baṙaran* (Dictionary of Armenian Personal Names). 5 vols. Erevan, 1942–1962.

Agat'angełay Patmut'iwn Hayoc' (History of Armenia by Agathangelos), publ. by G. Tēr-Mkrtč'ean and S. Kanayeanc'. Tiflis, 1909.

Akinean, N. *Gawazanagirk' Kat'ołikosac' Ałt'amaray* (Chronicle of the Catholicoses of Ałt'amar). Vienna, 1920.

Albornez, A. de. *Juan Chrisostomo y su influencia social en el imperio bizantino.* Madrid, 1934.

Ališan, Łewond M. *Yušikk' Hayreneac' Hayoc'* (Memories of the Armenian Fatherland). 2 vols. Venice, 1869–1870.

——— *Šnorhali ew Paragay Iwr* (Šnorhali and His Times). Venice, 1873.

——— *Sisuan, Hamagrut'iwn Haykakan Kilikioy ew Lewon Mecagorc* (Sisuan; Documentary Study of Armenian Cilicia and Leon the Great). Venice, 1885.

——— *Ayrarat.* Venice, 1890.

——— *Sisakan, Tełagrut'iwn Siwneac' Ašxarhi* (Sisakan; The Topography of the Province of Siwnik'). Venice, 1893.

——— *Hayapatum; Patmič'k' ew Patmut'iwnk'* (Armenian History; Historians and Histories of Armenia). 2 vols. Venice, 1901–1902.

Ali-zade, A. Social, Economic, and Political History of Azerbaijan, Thirteenth and Fourteenth Centuries (in Russian). Baku, 1956.

Allen, W. E. D. *A History of the Georgian People.* London, 1932.

Anasyan, H. S. *Haykakan Ałbyurnerə Byuzandiayi Ankman Masin* (The Armenian Sources on the Fall of Byzantium). Erevan, 1957.

Anasyan, H. S. *Haykakan Matenagitut'yun, V–XVIII DD.* (Armenian Bibliology, Fifth to Eighteenth Centuries). Vol. I. Erevan, 1959.

Arevshatian, S. S. "Abraam Ankirskii: Plach na vzatie Konstantinopolia," *Vizantiiskii Vremmenik* (Moscow), 7 (1953): 452–460.

Aṙak'el Dawriżec'i. *Patmut'iwn Hayoc'* (History of Armenia). Vagharshapat, 1896.

Attwater, S. *St. John Chrysostom.* Milwaukee, 1939.

Avtaliantz, John. "Memoir of the Life and Writings of St. Nerses Clajensis, Surnamed the Graceful, Pontiff of Armenia," *Asiatic Society of Bengal, Journal* (Calcutta), 5 (1836): 129–157.

Awgerean, Mkrtič', ed. *Liakatar Vark' Srboc'* (Complete Lives of the Saints). 12 vols. Venice, 1810–1814.

Bailey, H. W. "Irano-Indica II," *BSOAS*, vol. 13 (1949).

Barthold, W. *12 Vorlesungen über die Geschichte der Türken Mittelasiens.* Berlin, 1935.

Barxudaryan, S. G., ed. *Divan Hay Vimagrut'yan* (Corpus of Armenian Inscriptions). Vol. II. Erevan, 1960.

Barxutareanc', M. *Arc'ax.* Baku, 1895.

Baṙgirk' Nor Haykazean Lezui (New Dictionary of the Armenian Language), compiled by G. Awetik'ean, X. Siwrmēlean and M. Awgerean. 2 vols. Venice, 1836–1837.

Basmadjian, K. J. *Léon VI of Lusignan.* Paris, 1908.

——— "Publications des oeuvres d'Amirdovlat," in *Bulletin de la Société Française d'Histoire de la Médecine* (Paris), vol. 19 (1925), nos. 3–4.

Bauer, P. Chrysostomus. *Der heilige Johannes Chrysostomus und seine Zeit.* Munich, 1929–1930.

Bedrossian, Matthias. *New Dictionary Armenian-English.* Venice, 1875–1879.

Benveniste, E. "Emprunts Iraniens en Arménien," in *Transactions of the Philological Society* (London), 1945.

Bertel's, E. E. History of Persian-Tačik Literature (in Russian). Moscow, 1960.

Blake, Robert P., and Richard N. Frye, eds. and trans. "History of the Nation of the Archers (the Mongols) by Grigor of Akanc'," *Harvard Journal of Asiatic Studies*, 12. 3–4 (Dec. 1949): 269–443. Also published as a separate volume: Cambridge, Mass., 1954.

Blochet, E. *Introduction à l'histoire des Mongols par Fadl Allah Rashid ed-Din* (Gibb Memorial Series, XII). Leyden, 1910.

Boré, E. "Touchante élégie sur la prise de Constantinople, arrivée l'an 902 de notre ère, époque fatale et douloureuse, où le Seigneur fit encore éclater violemment sa colère contre la nation des Latins et des Grecs," *Nouveau Journal Asiatique* (Paris), 15 (1835): 271–298.

Bouvat, Lucien. *L'Empire mongol.* Second period. Paris, 1927.

Brockelmann, C. *Mitteltürkischer Wortschatz* (*Mahmud al Kāšgarī*). Budapest-Leipzig, 1928.

Brosset, M., trans. from the Armenian. "Mélodie élégiaque sur la prise de Stamboul," in C. Lebeau, *Histoire du Bas-Empire* (ed. J. Saint-Martin), XXI (Paris, 1836), 307–314.

Brosset, M., trans. from the Armenian. *Histoire de la Siounie par Stéphannos Orbélian.* 2 vols. St. Petersburg, 1864.

——— ed. "Description des monastères arméniens d'Haghbat et de Sanahin, par l'archimandrite Jean de Crimée," *Imperatorskaya Akademiya Nauk. Mémoires.* (St. Petersburg), series 7, vol. 6, no. 6 (1863). Armenian and Russian texts.

Browne, E. G. *A Literary History of Persia.* Vol. III. Cambridge, England, 1928.

Carleton, James G. "Calendar: Christian," *Encyclopaedia of Religion and Ethics*, III (New York, 1932), 84–91.

Charmoy, François Bernard, trans. from the Persian. *Chèref-Nâmeh ou fastes de la nation Kourde par Chèref-ou'dinne.* 2 vols., with 2 parts each. St. Petersburg, 1868–1875.

Cleaves, Francis W. "The Mongolian Names and Terms in the *History of the Nation of the Archers by Grigor of Akanc'*," *Harvard Journal of Asiatic Studies*, 12 (1949): 400–443.

——— "The Mongolian Documents in the Musée de Téhéran," *Harvard Journal of Asiatic Studies*, 16. 1–2 (June 1953): 1–107.

Conybeare, F. C. *A Catalogue of the Armenian Manuscripts in the British Museum.* London, 1913.

Covakan, N. V. "Tat'ew," *Sion* (Jerusalem), June–July 1950, pp. 197–202.

Č'amč'ean, Mik'ayēl. *Patmut'iwn Hayoc'* (History of the Armenians). 3 vols. Venice, 1781–1786.

Demetrakou, D. *Mega Lexikon Tes Ellenikes Glosses.* Athens, 1938.

Deny, Jean. "La Légende de 'l'eau des sauterelles' et de l'oiseau qui détruit ces insectes," *Journal Asiatique*, 222 (1933): 323–340.

Der Nersessian, Sirarpie. *Aght'amar: Church of the Holy Cross.* Cambridge, Mass., 1965.

Dethier, A. "Abraham prêtre arménien. Mélodie élégiaque sur la prise de Stamboul," *Monumenta Hungariae Historica*, vol. XXII, pt. 2 (Buda-Pest, 1872), pp. 225–248.

Doerfer, Gerhard. *Türkische und Mongolische Elemente im Neupersischen*, vol. II: *Türkische Elemente im Neupersischen.* Wiesbaden, 1965.

Dulaurier, Edouard. *Recherches sur la chronologie arménienne.* Vol. I. Paris, 1859.

Eganyan, Ō., et al. *C'uc'ak Jeřagrac' Maštoc'i Anvan Matenadarani* (Catalogue of Manuscripts in the Maštoc' Library). Vol. I. Erevan, 1965.

"Élégie sur la prise d'Édesse," in Edouard Dulaurier, *Recueil des historiens des croisades, Documents arméniens* (Paris, 1869), vol. I, 223–268.

Encyclopaedia of Islam. 4 vols, Leyden-London, 1913–1934. *New Edition*, 2 vols, Leiden-London, 1960——(in progress).

Eremyan, S. T. *Hayastanə əst "Ašxarhac'oyc'i"* (Armenia According to the "Ašxarhac'oyc'"). Erevan, 1963.

Ēp'rikean, H. S. *Bnašxarhik Bařaran* (Dictionary of Natural Geography). 2 vols. Venice, 1900–1905.

Flemming, Barbara. *Landschaftsgeschichte von Pamphylien, Pisidien und Lykien im Spätmittelalter*. Wiesbaden, 1964.

Géographie D'Aboulféda, Texte arabe, publ. by J. T. Reinaud and William Mac Guckin de Slane. Paris, 1840.

Gershevitch, Ilya. *A Grammar of Manichean Sogdian*. 2nd ed., Oxford, 1961.

Ginzel, F. K. *Handbuch der mathematischen und technischen Chronologie*. Leipzig, 1914.

Gordlevskii, V. A. Selected Writings (in Russian). Vol. I. Moscow, 1960.

Grégoire de Narek. Le livre de prières. Introduction, ed. and trans. by Isaac Kéchichian (*Sources chrétiennes*, no. 78). Paris, 1961.

Grekov, B. D., and A. Yu. Yakubovsky. *Zolotaya Orda i ee padenie*. Moscow-Leningrad, 1950.

Grønbech, Kaare. *Komanisches Wörterbuch, Turkischer Wortindex zu Codex Cumanicus*. Copenhagen, 1942.

Grousset, René. *Histoire de l'Arménie des origines à 1071*. Paris, 1947.

Grundriss der Iranischer Philologie. Strassbourg, 1898–1901.

Haïm, S. *New Persian-English Dictionary*. 2 vols. Teheran, 1934–1936.

Hakobyan, V. A., ed. *Manr Žamanakagrut'yunner, XIII–XVIII DD*. (Short Chronicles, Thirteenth to Eighteenth Centuries). 2 vols. Erevan, 1951–1956.

Hastings, James, ed. *Dictionary of the Bible*. Rev. ed. by Frederick C. Grant and H. H. Rowley. New York, 1963.

Herzfeld, Ernst. *Zoroaster and His World*. Vol. II. Princeton, 1947.

Hinz, Walther. *Irans Aufstieg zum nationalstaat im funfzehnten Jahrhundert*. Berlin-Leipzig, 1936.

History of the Caucasian Albanians by Movsēs Dasxuranci, trans. by C. J. F. Dowsett. Oxford University Press, 1961.

Hitti, Philip K. *History of the Arabs*. 4th ed. London, 1949.

Hony, H. C. *A Turkish-English Dictionary*. 2nd ed. Oxford, 1957.

Hrushevsky, Mykhailo. *Istoriya Ukrayiny-Rusy*. Vol. IV. Kiev-Lvov, 1907.

Hübschmann, Heinrich. *Armenische Grammatik: Erster Teil, Armenische Etymologie*. 2nd ed. Darmstadt, 1962.

——— "Die altarmenische Ortsnamen," in *Indogermanische Forschungen*. Strassbourg, 1904, vol. 16, pp. 197–490.

Ḥudūd al-'Ālam, "*The Regions of the World*," A *Persian Geography*, trans. and explained by V. Minorsky. Oxford, 1937.

Ibn Baṭṭūṭā. *Voyages d'Ibn Batouta*, ed. and trans. by C. Defrémery and B. R. Sanguinetti. 4 vols. Paris, 1853–1858.

Inčičean, Łukas. *Ašxarhagrut'iwn Č'oric' Masanc' Ašxarhi, Masn Ařajin: Asia* (Geography of the Four Continents of the World, Part I: Asia). Vol. I. Venice, 1806.

——— *Storagrut'iwn Hin Hayastaneayc': Mec Hayk'* (Description of Ancient Armenia: Armenia Major). Venice, 1822.

Islâm Ansiklopedisi. Istanbul.

Justi. *Iranisches Namenbuch*. Marburg, 1895.

J̌alalean, Sargis. *Čanaparhordut'iwn i Mecn Hayastan* (Travels in Armenia Major). 2 parts. Tiflis, 1858.

J̌uharyan, K. *Sovetakan Hayastani Patmakan Hušarjannerə* (The Historical Monuments in Soviet Armenia). Erevan, 1961.

Kahane, H. and R., and A. Tietze. *The Lingua Franca in the Levant.* Urbana, Illinois, 1958.

Karst, J. "Geschichte der armenischen Philologie," *Schriften der Elsass-Lothringischen Wiss. Gesellschaft zu Strassburg*, Series C, 2. Heidelberg, 1930.

Kiwlēsērean, Babgēn. *C'uc'ak Hayerēn J̌eṙagrac' Karmir Vanuc'n Ankiwrioy* (Catalogue of the Armenian Manuscripts in the Monastery of Karmir in Ankara). Antilias, Lebanon, 1957.

Kostaneanc', Karapet. *Vimakan Taregir: C'uc'ak Ẓołovacoy Arjanagrut'eanc' Hayoc'* (Annal of Inscriptions: Collection of Armenian Inscriptions). St. Petersburg, 1913.

Köprülü, M. F. *Les Origines de l'empire ottoman.* Paris, 1935.

Lalayean, E. *C'uc'ak Hayerēn J̌eṙagrac' Vaspurakani* (Catalogue of the Armenian Manuscripts in Vaspurakan). Vol. I. Tiflis, 1915.

Lane-Poole, Stanley. *The Mohammedan Dynasties.* Paris, 1925.

Langlois, Victor. *Collection des historiens anciens et modernes de l'Arménie.* 2 vols. Paris, 1867–1869.

——— "Voyage à Sis, capitale de l'Arménie au moyen âge," in *Journal Asiatique* (Paris), series 5, 5 (1855): 257–300.

——— "Les Ruines de Lampron en Cilicie," in *Revue de l'Orient, de l'Algérie et des colonies* (Paris), new series, 12 (1860): 119–122.

Lettera dell'Amicitia e dell'Vnione di Costantino gran Cesare. Venice, 1683.

Łafadaryan, K. *Hovhannavank'ə ev Nra Arjanagrut'yunnerə* (Hovhannavank' and Its Inscriptions). Erevan, 1948.

——— *Sanahni Vank'ə ev Nra Arjanagrut'yunnerə* (The Monastery of Sanahin and Its Inscriptions). Erevan, 1957.

Łazaray P'arpec'woy Patmut'iwn Hayoc' ew T'ułt' aṙ Vahan Mamikonean (History of Armenia by Łazar P'arpec'i and the Epistle to Vahan Mamikonean). Tiflis, 1904.

Macler, Frédéric. "Calendar: Armenian," *Encyclopaedia of Religion and Ethics*, vol. III (New York, 1932), pp. 70–73.

Malxaseanc', S. *Hayerēn Bac'atrakan Baṙaran* (Descriptive Dictionary of Armenian). 4 vols. Erevan, 1944–1945.

Manandean, Y., and H. Ačaṙean. *Hayoc' Nor Vkanerə* (Modern Armenian Martyrs). 2 vols. Vagharshapat, 1902.

Mansuroğlu, Mecdut. "On Some Titles and Names in Old Anatolian Turkish," *Ural-Altaische Jahrbücher*, 27. 1–2 (1955): 94–97.

Manvelichvili, Alexandre. *Histoire de Géorgie.* Paris, 1951.

Markwart, J. "Die Entstehung der armenischer Bistümer," *Orientalia Christiana*, 27 (1932): 153.

Mesrob Erēc'. *Patmut'iwn S. Nersisi Hayoc' Hayrapeti* (History of Catholicos St. Nersēs of the Armenians) (*Sop'erk' Haykakank'*, vol. VI). Venice, 1853.

Meyer, L. S. *Jean Chrysostome, maître de perfection chrétienne*. Paris, 1933.

Mik'ayelyan, V. A. *Łrimi Haykakan Gałut'i Patmut'yun* (History of the Armenian Colony of the Crimea). Erevan, 1964.

Miller, William. *Trebizond, the Last Greek Empire*. London, 1926.

Minorsky, V. "Some Early Documents in Persian," *Journal of the Royal Asiatic Society*, 1942.

Molitor, J. *Glossarium Ibericum* (Corpus Scriptorum Christianorum Orientalium, Subsidia 20). Vol. I. Louvain, 1962.

Mostaert, Antoine, and F. W. Cleaves. "Trois documents mongols des Archives secrètes vaticanes," *Harvard Journal of Asiatic Studies*, 15: 419–506 (1952).

——— *Les Lettres de 1289 et 1305 des ilkhan Aryun et Öljeitü à Philippe le Bel* (Harvard-Yenching Institute, Scripta Mongolica Monograph Series 1, Cambridge, Mass., 1962).

Muhammad, Mirza, ed. *Ta'rikhi Jahan-gusha of Juwayni, Composed 1260* (Gibb Memorial Series, vol. II). London, 1916.

Murad, Friedrich. *Ararat und Masis*. Heidelberg, 1901.

Nève, Félix. "Étude sur Thomas de Medzoph, et sur son histoire de l'Arménie au XVe siècle," *Journal Asiatique* (Paris), series 5, 6 (1855): 221–281.

——— "Exposé des guerres de Tamerlan et de Schah-Rokh dans l'Asie occidentale, d'après la chronique arménienne inédite de Thomas de Medzoph," *Académie royale des sciences, des lettres et des beaux-arts de Belgique. Mémoires couronnés* (Brussels), vol. 11 (1861), no. 4.

d'Ohsson, C. M. *Histoire des Mongols*. La Haye and Amsterdam, 4 vols., 1834–1835.

Oskean, Hamazasp. *Vaspurakan-Vani Vank'erə* (The Monasteries of Vaspurakan-Van). 3 vols. Vienna, 1940–1947.

Ōrbelean, Step'anos. *Patmut'iwn Nahangin Sisakan* (History of the Province of Siwnik'). Tiflis, 1910.

Ōrmanean, Małak'ia. *Azgapatum* (National History). 3 vols. Constantinople-Jerusalem, 1913–1927.

The Oxford Universal Dictionary. 3rd ed. Oxford, 1955.

Pachymeres, Georgius. *De Michaele et Andronico Palaeologis, libri tredecim*. 2 vols. Bonn, 1835.

Patmut'iwn Varuc' S. Nersisi Šnorhalwoy (History of the Life of Saint Nersēs the Graceful) (*Sop'erk' Haykakank'*, vol. XIV). Venice, 1854.

Pelliot, Paul. *Notes on Marco Polo, I, Ouvrage posthume*. Paris, 1959.

——— *Notes sur l'histoire de la Horde d'or suivies de quelques noms turcs d'hommes et de peuples finissant en "ar"*. Paris, 1949.

Połarean, Norayr. *Mayr C'uc'ak Jeřagrac' Srboc' Yakobeanc'* (Grand Catalogue of the Manuscripts in the Monastery of St. James). Vols. II–V. Jerusalem, 1953–1960.

Pōłosean, Yovhannēs. *Hayastani Ašxarhagrut'iwn: Patmakan, Tełagrakan, K'ałak'akan ew Tntesakan* (Geography of Armenia: Historical, Topographical, Political and Economic). Paris, 1952.

Pratt, Ida A. *Armenia and the Armenians; A List of References in the New York Public Library*. New York, 1919.

P'ap'azean, M. *Hnut'iwnk' Vanōrēic' Siwneac' Ašxarhi* (The Antiquities of the Monasteries in the Province of Siwnik'). Vagharshapat, 1895.

P'irłalēmean, Łewond. *Nōtark' Hayoc'*. Constantinople, 1888.

Radloff, Wilhelm. *Versuch Eines Wörterbuches der Türk-Dialecte*. Vol. I. The Hague, 1960.

Ramsay, W. M. *The Historical Geography of Asia Minor* (Royal Geographical Society, Supplementary Papers, vol. IV, London, 1890).

Recueil des Historiens des Croisades, Documents Arméniens. 2 vols. Paris, 1859–1906.

Redhouse, James W. *A Turkish and English Lexicon*. Constantinople, 1921.

Runciman, Steven. *The Fall of Constantinople*. Cambridge, Eng., 1965.

Rüdt-Collenberg, W. H. *The Rupenides, Hethumides and Lusignans; The Structure of the Armeno-Cilician Dynasties*. Paris, 1963.

Saint-Martin, J. A. *Mémoires historiques et géographiques sur l'Arménie*. 2 vols. Paris, 1818–1819.

Samuēl K'ahanayi Anec'woy Hawak'munk' i Groc' Patmagrac' (The Priest Samuēl Anec'i's Collection of Historical Works), publ. by Aršak Tēr-Mik'ēlean. Vagharshapat, 1893.

Sanjian, Avedis K. *The Armenian Communities in Syria under Ottoman Dominion*. Cambridge, Mass., 1965.

——— "*Crazatik* 'Erroneous Easter'—A Source of Greco-Armenian Religious Controversy," *Studia Caucasica* (The Hague), 2 (1966): 26–47.

Sarafian, Kevork A. *History of Education in Armenia*. Los Angeles, 1930.

Sargisean, Barseł. *Mayr C'uc'ak Hayerēn Jeṙagrac' Matenadaranin Mxit'areanc' i Venetik* (Grand Catalogue of the Armenian Manuscripts in the Mekhitarian Library at Venice). 2 vols. Venice, 1914–1924.

Sargisean, Barseł, and Grigor Sargsean. *Mayr C'uc'ak Hayerēn Jeṙagrac' Matenadaranin Mxit'areanc' i Venetik* (Grand Catalogue of the Armenian Manuscripts in the Mekhitarian Library at Venice). Vol. III. Venice, 1966.

Schlumberger, G. *Le Siège, la prise et le sac de Constantinople en 1453*. Paris, 1926.

Siwrmēean, Artawazd. *Mayr C'uc'ak Hayerēn Jeṙagrac' Erusałēmi Srboc' Yakobeanc' Vank'i* (Grand Catalogue of the Armenian Manuscripts in the Monastery of St. James at Jerusalem). Vol. I. Jerusalem, 1948.

Smbatean, Artak. "Hamaṙōt Patmut'iwn Tat'ewi Vank'i" (Brief History of the Monastery of Tat'ew), *Tat'ew Tarec'oyc'*, 1930, pp. 276–351.

Smbateanc', Mesrovb. *Tełagir Gełark'uni Covazard Gawaṙi* (Topography of the Canton of Gełark'uni). Vagharshapat, 1896.

——— *Nkaragir Surb Karapeti Vanic' Ernǰakoy ew Šrǰakayic' Nora* (Description of the Monastery of Saint Karapet in Ernǰak and Its Environs). Tiflis, 1904.

Smirnov, V. D. *Krymskoe Khantsvo pod verkhovenstvom Otomanskoi Porty do nachala XVIII veka*. St. Petersburg, 1887.

Söz Derleme Dergisi. Vol. I. Istanbul, 1939.

Spuler, Bertold. *Die Mongolen in Iran: Politik, Verwaltung und Kultur der Ilchanzeit 1220–1350*. 2nd ed. Berlin, 1955.

——— *Die Goldene Horde: Die Mongolen in Russland, 1223–1502*. Wiesbaden, 1965.

Sruanjteanc', Garegin. *T'oros Ałbar, Hayastani Čambord* (T'oros Ałbar; Traveler in Armenia). 2 vols. Constantinople, 1879.

Steingass, F. *Persian-English Dictionary*. 3rd ed. London, 1947.

Šahnazareanc', Karapet. *Dašanc' T'łt'oy K'nnut'iwnn u Herk'umə* (Examination and Refutation of the Letter of Concord). Paris, 1862.

Šahxat'unean, Yovhannēs. *Storagrut'iwn Kat'ołikē Ējmiacni, ew Hing Gawaṙac'n Araratay* (Description of the Cathedral of Etchmiadzin and of the Five Cantons of Ararat). 2 vols. Etchmiadzin, 1842.

Tašean, Yakovbos. *C'uc'ak Hayerēn Jeṙagrac' Kayserakan Matenadaranin i Vienna* (Catalog der armenischen Handschriften in der K. K. Hofbibliothek zu Wien). Vienna, 1891.

——— *C'uc'ak Hayerēn Jeṙagrac' Matenadaranin Mxit'areanc' i Vienna* (Catalog der armenischen Handschriften in der Mechitharisten-Bibliothek zu Wien). Vienna, 1895.

——— *Aknark Mə Hay Hnagrut'ean Vray; Usumnasirut'iwn Hayoc' Grč'ut'ean Aruestin* (A Cursory View on Armenian Paleography; A Study of the Art of Armenian Calligraphy). Vienna, 1898.

Tchobanian, A. "Lamentation sur la prise de Constantinople," *La Roseraie d'Arménie*, vol. III, Paris, 1929.

Tēr-Minasyan, E., ed. *Ełišēi Vasn Vardanay ew Hayoc' Paterazmin* (Ełišē on Vardan and the Armenian War). Erevan, 1957.

Tēr Movsisean, M. *Haykakan Erek' Mec Vank'eri Tat'ewi, Hałarcni ew Dadi Ekełec'inerə ew Vanakan Šinut'iwnnerə* (The Churches of the Three Great Armenian Monasteries of Tat'ew, Hałarcin, and Dad, and Their Monastic Buildings). Jerusalem, 1938.

Thomson, R. "*Vardapet* in the Early Armenian Church," *Le Muséon*, 75. 3–4 (1962): 367–384.

Torkomian, V. *Amirdolvathe d'Amassie, médecin arménien du XVe siècle; sa vie et ses ouvrages*. Paris, 1914.

Tournebize, François. "Léon V de Lusignan dernier roi de l'Arméno-Cilicie," *Études publiées par des pères de la Compagnie de Jésus* (Paris), 122 (1910): 60–79, 196–203.

Vasiliev, A. A. *History of the Byzantine Empire, 324–1453*. 2 vols. Madison, Wisconsin, 1961.

Vladimirtsov, B. *Le Régime social des mongols; Le féodalisme nomade*. Paris, 1948.

Von Gabain, A. *Alttürkische Grammatik*. Leipzig, 1950.

Vullers. *Lexicon Persico-Latinum Etymologicum*. 2nd ed. Graz, 1962.

Waley, Arthur. *The Secret History of the Mongols*. New York, 1964.

Wehr, Hans. *A Dictionary of Modern Written Arabic*. Ithaca, N.Y., 1961.

Xač'eryan, L. G. *Grč'ut'yan Arvesti Lezvakan-K'erakanakan Tesut'yunə*

Mijnadaryan Hayastanum (The Linguistic-Grammatical Theories of the Art of Manuscript Production in Medieval Armenia). Erevan, 1962.

Xač'ikyan, L. S., ed. *XIV Dari Hayeren Jeṙagreri Hišatakaranner* (Colophons of Armenian Manuscripts of the Fourteenth Century). Erevan, 1950.

——— *XV Dari Hayeren Jeṙagreri Hišatakaranner* (Colophons of Armenian Manuscripts of the Fifteenth Century). *Masn Aṙajin, 1401–1450* (Part I, 1401–1450), Erevan, 1955. *Masn Erkrord, 1451–1480* (Part II, 1451–1480), Erevan, 1958.

——— "XIV–XV Dareri Haykakan Gyułakan Hamaynk'i Masin" (On the Armenian Village Community in the Fourteenth and Fifteenth Centuries), *Patma-Banasirakan Handes*, 1 (1958): 110–133.

Xalat'eanc', Grigor. *Yišatakaran Ałētic' Grigori Xlat'ec'woy* (Memorial of Tragedies by Grigor Xlat'ec'i). Vagharshapat, 1897.

Xondkaryan, Ē. *Mkrtič' Nałaš*. Erevan, 1965.

Yeghisheh. New York, 1952. (English and modern Armenian translations.)

Yovsēp'ean, Garegin. *Grč'ut'ean Aruestə Hin Hayoc' Mēj* (The Art of Manuscript Production among the Ancient Armenians). Vagharshapat, 1913.

——— *Xałbakeank' kam Pṙōšeank'* (The Xałbakeans or Pṙōšeans). Vol. I. Vagharshapat, 1913.

——— *Hawuc' T'aṙi Amenap'rkič'ə ew Noynanun Yušarjanner Hay Aruesti Mēj* (The All Savior Church of Hawuc' T'aṙ and Eponymous Monuments in Armenian Art). Jerusalem, 1937.

——— *Niwt'er ew Usumnasirut'iwnner Hay Aruesti ew Mšakoyt'i Patmut'ean* (Materials and Studies for the History of Armenian Art and Culture). Vol. II. New York, 1943.

[Yovsēp'ean], Garegin I Kat'ołikos. *Yišatakarank' Jeṙagrac'* (The Colophons of Manuscripts). Vol. I. Antilias, Lebanon, 1951.

Zambaur, E. de. *Manuel de Généalogie et de Chronologie pour l'histoire de l'Islam*. Hanover, 1927.

Zenker, Jules Theodore. *Dictionnaire Turc-Arabe-Persan*. Leipzig, 1866–1876.

Appendix A. Personal Names

Note: In alphabetizing entries, simple letters are placed before those with diacritical marks. Thus, for example, the sequence for the C's goes: C, C‘, Č, Č‘.

Abdal (variant: Abtal): 1403 (no. 7). Mentioned as the amir of the village of Mokunk‘ or Mgunk‘ (see App. C); otherwise unidentified.

Abel: 1458 (no. 1). Abel, the second son of Adam, slain by his older brother Cain. (See *Dictionary of Bible*, p. 3.)

Abgar: 1449 (no. 1). Brother of Mkrtič‘ Nałaš [q.v.]. He was probably the *tanutēr* (householder) of the village of Poṙ in the district of Bitlīs. (See Ačaṙyan, *HAB*, I, 9, no. 5; III, 408–410, no. 168.)

Abraham: 1422 (no. 1). Abraham; the first Jewish patriarch. (See *Dictionary of Bible*, pp. 5–6.)

Abraham Ankiwrac‘i: 1453 (no. 3). Author of a contemporary elegy on the fall of Constantinople; a number of hymns and a chronicle of Armenian history are also attributed to him. (See Anasyan, *Matenagitut‘yun*, I, cols. 81–88, including a bibliography.)

Abraham Trapizonec‘i: 1480 (no. 1). An Armenian clergyman from Trebizond; he is said to have been brought to Istanbul by Sultan Mehmet II Fatih to assume the office of Patriarch, which he declined.

Abtal: 1433 (no. 3). *See* Abdal.

Abu-Bak‘r: 1407 (nos. 2, 4). The Tīmūrid Abū Bakr, son of Mīrānshāh and grandson of Tīmūr Lang. (See Bouvat, *L'Empire mongol*, pp. 34, 35, 54, 59; "Tīmūrids," *EI*, OE, IV, 779–782.)

Abusait (variants: Abusayit, Bawsait, Busaid, Busait, Busayid, Busayit, Busayit‘, Pawsayit): 1318 (no. 2). Ilkhan Abū Sa‘īd Bahādur (1316–1335) of Persia. (See Spuler, *Mongolen in Iran*, p. 117–127, and Index, p. 504; Spuler, *Goldene Horde*, pp. 93–96; W. Barthold, "Abū Sa‘īd," *EI*, OE, I, 103–104; Cleaves, *Mongolian Documents*, p. 55, n. 2; *Chèref-Nâmeh*, II. 1, 376–393 *passim*.)

Abusayit: 1331 (no. 3). *See* Abusait.

Adibek: 1457 (no. 2). An amir (probably Kurdish), who ruled in the region of Khilāṭ.

Ahmat: 1386 (no. 2), 1400 (no. 1), 1417 (no. 1), 1422 (no. 1). Sulṭān (or Khān) Aḥmad Djalā'ir, son of the Djalā'irid Uwais and grandson of Ḥasan Buzurg. He was captured and executed in 1410 by the Ḳara-Ḳoyunlu Ḳara Yūsuf. (See Bouvat, *L'Empire mongol*, pp. 33–35, 45,

49–58 *passim*, 88, 89, 106–114; "Tīmūr Lang," *EI*, OE, IV, 778; J. M. Smith, Jr., "Djalāyir, Djalāyirid," *EI*, NE, II, 401–402.)

Ahmat: 1425 (nos. 1, 4), 1428 (no. 1). Sulṭān Aḥmad, chief of the Kurds in the districts of Van and Ostan [Wusṭān]; he was defeated and slain in 1426 by the Ḳara-Ḳoyunlu Amīr Iskandar. (See C. Huart, "Ḳara-Ḳoyunlu," *EI*, OE, II, 741.)

Aladin: 1398 (no. 1). Probably 'Alā' al-Dīn. It can perhaps be assumed that, since the colophon was written in the canton of Ałbak (see App. C), which was part of the Kurdish territory of Hakkārī, he was the amir of this district.

Alek'sandr (variants: Alēk'sandr, Alēk'sianos, Ałek'sandr, Ałēk'sandr, Ałēk'sandrē): 1420 (no. 3), 1437 (no. 1), 1438 (no. 2), 1459 (no. 5). King Alexander I the Great (1412–1443), son of Constantine I of Imereti (Western Georgia) and the last member of the Bagrationi (Bagratuni) dynasty to enjoy a long reign as king of united Georgia. (See Allen, *History*, pp. 126–127; Manvelichvili, *Histoire*, pp. 254–255.)

Alēk'sandr: 1424 (no. 3), 1436 (no. 1), 1462 (no. 2). *See* Alek'sandr.

Alēk'sianos: 1458 (no. 1). *See* Alek'sandr.

Ali: 1435 (no. 5), 1436 (no. 6). 'Alī Bayandur Beg (A.H. 832-842; A.D. 1428–1438), son and successor of the Aḳ-Ḳoyunlu Ḳara Yoluḳ 'Uthmān and father of Uzun Ḥasan. (See V. Minorsky, "Aḳ-Ḳoyunlu," *EI*, NE, I, 311–312; "Mārdīn," *EI*, OE, III, 273–277; "Uzun Ḥasan," *EI*, OE, IV, 1065.)

Ali Mirzay: 1452 (no. 5). 'Alī Mirzā, son of 'Alī Sheker. (See *Chèref-Nâmeh*, I. 2, p. 66.)

Ali P'ašax: 1336 (no. 1). 'Alī Pādshāh, Ilkhanid governor of Baghdad. (See "Ḥasan Buzurg," *EI*, OE, III, 279–280; *Chèref-Nâmeh*, II. 1, 391–393; Spuler, *Mongolen in Iran*, pp. 126–130, 223, 288.)

Alibēk: 1442 (no. 1). An Armenian baron of the village of Serkewili (see App. C). (See Xač'ikyan, *XV Dari*, I, p. 668.)

Alinax: 1308 (no. 1), 1310 (no. 1). Armenian lord of Lambron and Tarsus, and brother of King Het'um II of Cilicia. (See W. H. Rüdt-Collenberg, *The Rupenides, Hethumides and Lusignans*, Paris, 1963, p. 72.)

Ališak'ar: 1452 (no. 5). 'Alī Sheker, ruler of Shehrezul or Shahrizur. (See *Chèref-Nâmeh*, I. 2, 66.)

Alitaš or Alibaš: 1338 (no. 2). The reading of this name is uncertain (see Xač'ikyan, *XIV Dari*, p. 307, n. 1); it could be either 'Alī Taš or 'Alī Baš. He appears to have been a relative or an ally of Damurtaš [q.v.].

Alt'un Pułay: 1337 (no. 2). Altūn Bugha, *nā'ib* (governor) of the Mamluk province of Aleppo; he invaded Cilicia in 1337.

Ałbuła: 1419 (no. 2). Aghbugha (Arabic Aḳ-bughā), also known as Béka Jaqeli; atabeg of the Georgian district of Samtzkhé and father of the atabeg Ioanné. (See Allen, *History*, p. 124.)

Ałēk'sandr: 1419 (no. 2), 1437 (no. 6), 1443 (no. 4). *See* Alek'sandr.

Ałek'sandr: 1438 (no. 6). *See* Alek'sandr.

Ałek'sandrē: 1438 (no. 5). *See* Alek'sandr.

Ałlału: 1318 (no. 1). Alaghu or Alughu? Mentioned as a Mongol tax-collector; otherwise unidentified.

Ałubēk: 1479 (no. 1). *See* Ałup.

Ałup (variants: Ałubēk, Eałup, Yayłup): 1477 (no. 8), 1480 (no. 4). Ya'ḳūb Bayundur Beg or Khān, son of the Aḳ-Ḳoyunlu ruler Uzun Ḥasan, whom he succeeded on the throne at Tabrīz after slaying his brother Sulṭān Khalīl on July 16, 1478; he reigned until his death in A.H. 896 (A.D. 1490/1). (See V. Minorsky, "Aḳ-Ḳoyunlu," *EI*, NE, I, 311–312; "Tabrīz," *EI*, OE, IV, 583–593; *Chèref-Nâmeh*, II. 1, 492–493.)

Amir Hasan: 1321 (no. 1). Armenian prince of the region of Vayoc'-Jor (see App. C). (See Ačaṙyan, *HAB*, I, 132, no. 3.)

Amir Melek': 1468 (no. 5). Amīr Malik, Kurdish ruler of the principality of Khizān. (See *Chèref-Nâmeh*, II. 1, 57.)

Amirtovlat': 1480 (no. 1). Well-known Armenian physician and author of many medical works. (See V. Torkomian, *Amirdolvathe d'Amassie, médecin arménien du XVe siècle; sa vie et ses ouvrages*, Paris, 1914; K. J. Basmadjian, "Publications des oeuvres d'Amirdovlat," in *Bulletin de la Société Française d'Histoire de la Médecine*, Paris, 1925, vol. XIX, nos. 3.4.)

Anania: 1401 (no. 1). Ananias; a devout Christian at Damascus and a disciple who instructed and baptized Paul after his conversion, and restored his sight. (*Dictionary of Bible*, p. 30.)

Anawarzec'i: 1302 (no. 1), 1306 (no. 3). *See* Grigor (Anawarzec'i).

Aram: 1393 (no. 1). Aram. (See *Dictionary of Bible*, p. 48.) The reference is to either the Aramaeans or the land of the Arameans. (Cf. Isaiah, 7:2, which renders Aram—the form in the Armenian text—as Syria.)

Arapšah: 1452 (no. 5), 1459 (no. 2). 'Arab-Shāh, an influential Aḳ-Ḳoyunlu Turkmen amir and general in the service of Uzun Ḥasan. (See *Chèref-Nâmeh*, I. 2, 118; V. Minorsky, "Uzun Ḥasan," *EI*, OE, IV, 1065; "Kurds," *ibid.*, II, 1142.)

Argatios: 1453 (no. 3). Emperor Arcadius (395–408). (See Vasiliev, *History*, I, 90f.)

Aristakēs (variants: Ǝṙəstakēs, Ǝṙətak'ēs, Ṙastakēs, Ṙəstakēs, Ṙstakēs): Catholicos of the Armenian church at Etchmiadzin (1465–1469). (See Ōrmanean, *Azgapatum*, cols. 1482, 1495, 1500, 1503.)

Arławn: 1304 (no. 6). *See* Arłun.

Arłun (variant: Arławn): 1302 (no. 2), 1304 (no. 3), 1307 (no. 1). Ilkhān Arghūn Khān (1284–1291) of Persia. (See Spuler, *Mongolen in Iran*, esp. pp. 79–86, 257–259; W. Barthold, "Arghūn," *EI*, OE, I, 430; Cleaves, "Mongolian Names and Terms," pp. 406–407.)

Arłut'ay: 1417 (no. 1). A member of the Pṙošean Armenian princely family, and a prince of the region of Vayoc'-Jor (see App. C) in Siwnik' province. (See Ačaṙyan, *HAB*, I, 285, no. 4.)

Arp'ay: 1336 (no. 1). Ilkhan Arpa Khān (1335–1336) of Persia. (See Spuler, *Mongolen in Iran*, pp. 128, 129, 131, 145, 186, 197, 223, 251, 260;

"Čingizids," *EI*, NE, II, 44–47; J. M. Smith, Jr., "Djalāyir, Djalāyirid," *ibid.*, II, 401–402.)

Ařak'el, Priest: 1449 (no. 1). Father of Mkrtič' Nałaš [q.v.]. (See Ačaṙyan, *HAB*, I, 210, no. 45.)

Ařak'el Bałišec'i: 1453 (no. 2). The author of a contemporary elegy on the fall of Constantinople, as well as of historical, panegyrical, narrative, and spiritual poems, and martyrological and religious works in prose. (See Anasyan, *Matenagitut'yun*, I, cols. 1106–1143, and bibliography.)

Asad: 1386 (no. 3). Asad al-Dīn Zarrīn Čang; Kurdish malik or amir of Ostan [Wusṭān]. (See V. Minorsky, "Kurds," *EI*, OE, II, 1145.)

Askandar: 1437 (no. 1). *See* Sk'andar.

Askantar: 1436 (no. 5). *See* Sk'andar.

Astuacatur: 1451 (no. 3). Brother of Mahdasi Pōłos, who commissioned a Gospel MS.; he was slain by the Muslims.

Astuacatur Sat'əlmiš: 1453 (no. 3). One of the Armenians whom Sultan Mehmet II Fatih brought from Ankara to Istanbul in 1453. (See Ačaṙyan, *HAB*, I, 243, no. 121.)

Asur: 1389 (no. 1). Ashurbanipal (668–626 B.C.), son and successor of Esarhaddon on the throne of Assyria. (See *Dictionary of Bible*, p. 64.)

Ašraf (variants: Ašrap', Ašraw): 1351 (no. 2), 1357 (no. 1), 1436 (no. 3). Čūbānid Malik Ashraf, son of Tīmūrtash and grandson of Amīr Čūbān. He was noted for his cruelty and exactions, which provoked an intervention by Djānībeg Khān of the Golden Horde, who defeated and executed him in 1355. (See Spuler, *Mongolen in Iran*, pp. 133–137; Fr. Taeschner, "Akhīdjūḳ," *EI*, NE, I, 325; J. M. Smith, Jr., "Djalāyir, Djalāyirid," *ibid.*, II, 401–402; "Ḥasan Küčük," *EI*, OE, III, 280; V. Minorsky, "Tabrīz," *ibid.*, IV, 583–593; *Chèref-Nâmeh*, II. 1, 396, 398, 400, 401, 402.)

Ašrap': 1349 (no. 1), 1425 (no. 6). *See* Ašraf.

Ašraw: 1358 (no. 1). *See* Ašraf.

Aštar(?): 1349 (no. 1). The reading of this name is uncertain; he is mentioned as a Turkmen tyrant.

Atom, Ustay: 1452 (no. 4). An Armenian craftsman who recovered a MS.

Awdal: 1437 (no. 8). Mentioned as a ruler of Khizān; otherwise unidentified.

Awdul: 1425 (no. 6). Probably 'Abdullāh; mentioned as the grandson of Sahat' [q.v.]; otherwise unidentified.

Awetik': 1409 (no. 2). An Armenian priest, who was martyred on December 11, 1409.

Awetik': 1475 (no. 8). An Armenian, probably a merchant, who recovered a MS. brought to Istanbul from Kafa in 1475.

Awljat'u: 1306 (no. 4). Ilkhan Öldjaytü or Uldjāytu. *See* Xarbanda.

Awšəntr: 1341 (no. 3). *See* Awšin, King.

Awšin: 1308 (no. 1). Oshin; Armenian baron in Cilicia.

Awšin: 1307 (no. 6). Oshin; constable or commander-in-chief of the army in the Armenian kingdom of Cilicia. (See Ačaṙyan, *HAB*, V, 238–239, no. 24.)

Awšin, Baron: 1325 (no. 2). Oshin; grand baron in the Armenian kingdom of Cilicia, and one of three regents during the childhood of King Leon IV.

Awšin, King (variants: Awšəntr, Ošin): 1310 (no. 2), 1313 (nos. 1, 3), 1314 (no. 1), 1315 (no. 2), 1325 (no. 2), 1327 (no. 2), 1332 (no. 1), 1336 (no. 3), 1338 (no. 1). King Oshin (1308–1320) of the Armenian kingdom of Cilicia. (See Rüdt-Collenberg, *Rupenides*, pp. 16, 22.)

Awt'man (variants: Łara Ōt'man, Łaray Ōt'man, Ōt'man): 1422 (no. 2), 1425 (no. 1), 1429 (no. 2), 1431 (no. 1), 1435 (nos. 1, 5), 1445 (no. 6), 1449 (no. 1), 1473 (no. 6), 1476 (nos. 1, 5, 7), 1477 (nos. 1, 2), 1478 (no. 3). Ḳara Yoluḳ (Yülük) 'Uthmān Bayundur, founder of the Aḳ-Ḳoyunlu federation of Turkmen tribes in the region of Diyarbakir. (See V. Minorsky, "Aḳ-Ḳoyunlu," *EI*, NE, I, 311–312; "Mārdīn," *EI*, OE, III, 273–277.) Some colophons erroneously refer to him as the father of Uzun Ḥasan; in actual fact, the latter was his grandson.

Awzpēk (variant: Ōzpēk): 1341 (no. 3). Özbek Khān (1313–1341), ruler of the Golden Horde. (See Spuler, *Goldene Horde*, index, p. 535; "Batu'ids," *EI*, NE, I, 1106–1108; Pelliot, *Notes sur l'histoire*, pp. 92–94.)

Ayvat: 1453 (no. 3). One of the Armenians brought by Sultan Mehmet II Fatih from Ankara to Istanbul. (See Ačaṙyan, *HAB*, I, 144, no. 1.)

Ayxanənlu: 1439 (no. 1). The reading of the first *n* in this name is uncertain (see Xač'ikyan, *XV Dari*, I, p. 496, n. 1). He appears to have been an Aḳ-Ḳoyunlu Turkmen, who invaded the canton of Ekełeac' (see App. C) in 1439.

Azap: 1452 (no. 5). An unidentified Turkoman at Mārdīn, whose head was cut off by Rustam Turkhān-oghlu.

Bagrat: 1399 (no. 1), 1419 (no. 2), 1422 (no. 1). King Bagrat V (1360–1395) of Georgia. (See Allen, *History*, pp. 122–124; Manvelichvili, *Histoire*, pp. 243–244.)

Bagrat (VI) (variants: Bakrat, Bak'rat): 1465 (no. 1), 1471 (no. 5), 1473 (no. 6), 1476 (no. 2), 1477 (no. 1). King Bagrat VI (1466–1478) of Karthlo-Imereti in Georgia. (See Allen, *History*, pp. 135–138; Manvelichvili, *Histoire*, pp. 264–265.)

Bakrat: 1474 (no. 2). *See* Bagrat (VI).

Bak'rat: 1466 (no. 2). *See* Bagrat (VI).

Bawsait: 1334 (no. 1). *See* Abusait.

Bayanduṙ Łōč': 1472 (no. 1). Bayandur Beg, an Aḳ-Ḳoyunlu general who played an important role in the military campaigns of Uzun Ḥasan and Ya'ḳūb. (See Xač'ikyan, *XV Dari*, II, p. 472; *Chèref-Nâmeh*, II. 1, 493.)

Bazun, Baron: 1367 (no. 1). Armenian constable in Cilicia, son of Lewon Bazunenc'. (See Ačaṙyan, *HAB*, I, 361–362, no. 3.)

Bešk'en (variant: Bēšk'ēn): 1349 (no. 1). An Armenian prince of the Ōrbelean family, son of Burt'el and Vaxax; prince in the province of

Siwnik'. (See Garegin Yovsēp'ean, *Xałbakeank' Kam Přōšeank'*, vol. I, Vagharshapat 1913, p. 202; Brosset, *Siounie*, II, 182.)

Bēkum-Xat'un: 1462 (no. 3). Begum-Khāṭūn, wife of the Ḳara-Ḳoyunlu Djihānshāh, son of Ḳara Yūsuf. (See C. Huart, "Ḳara-Ḳoyunlu," *EI*, OE, II, 741.)

Bēlēk Bēk: 1415 (no. 1). An unidentified Kurdish ruler in the district of Hakkārī.

Bēšk'en (variant: Bēšk'ēn): 1412 (no. 1), 1428 (no. 6), 1437 (no. 1), 1438 (no. 2). Armenian prince in the province of Siwnik', of the Ōrbelean family; he is also mentioned as the lord of Lori. (See Ališan, *Sisakan*, p. 96; *Hayapatum*, p. 558; Brosset, *Siounie*, II, 182.)

Bēšk'en: 1348 (no. 2). *See* Bešk'en.

Bēšk'ēn: 1419 (no. 2). *See* Bēšk'en.

Birt'ēl: 1348 (no. 2). *See* Burt'el.

Biwrdel: 1349 (no. 1). *See* Burt'el.

Biwrt'ēl: 1401 (no. 2). *See* Burt'el.

Biwrt'ēl (variant: Burt'el): 1401 (no. 2), 1438 (no. 2). Son of Ivanē Ōrbelean; mentioned, together with his brother Smbat, as prince in the province of Siwnik'. (See Ališan, *Sisakan*, p. 96; Č'amč'ean, *Patmut'iwn*, III, 443; Brosset, *Siounie*, II, 182.)

Blēl: 1456 (no. 2). One of the purchasers of a Gospel MS.

Boyrt'el: 1321 (no. 2). *See* Burt'el.

Bułda (variant: Pułtay): 1306 (no. 3). A prince of the Ōrbelean family in province of Siwnik'. (See Ačaŕyan, *HAB*, I, 420–421, no. 2.)

Burdel: 1386 (no. 1). *See* Burt'el.

Burt'el (variants: Birt'ēl, Biwrdel, Biwrt'ēl, Boyrt'el, Burdel, Burt'ēl): 1310 (no. 2), 1321 (no. 1), 1331 (no. 3), 1419 (no. 2). Ōrbelean prince in province of Siwnik'; son of Ēlikum, and father of Beškēn and Ivanē. (See Yovsēp'ean, *Xałbakeank'*, pp. 21, 199, 202, 204; Brosset, *Siounie*, II, 182.)

Burt'ēl: 1306 (no. 3). *See* Burt'el.

Busaid: 1321 (no. 2). *See* Abusait.

Busait: 1320 (no. 2), 1322 (no. 1), 1330 (no. 2), 1331 (no. 1), 1335 (no. 2). *See* Abusait.

Busait: 1440 (no. 3). Abū Sa'īd, son of the Ḳara-Ḳoyunlu Ḳara Yūsuf and brother of Amīr Iskandar and Djihānshāh. (See C. Huart, "Ḳara-Ḳoyunlu," *EI*, OE, II, 741.)

Busait (variants: Busayit, Pusayit, Pusayit'): 1469 (no. 1). The Tīmūrid Sultan Abū Sa'īd b. Muḥammad b. Mīrānshāh b. Tīmūr (1458–1468). (See Bouvat, *L'Empire mongol*, pp. 136–146; J. Aubin, "Abū Sa'īd," *EI*, NE, I, 147–148.)

Busayid: 1329 (no. 1), 1335 (no. 3). *See* Abusait.

Busayit: 1318 (no. 4), 1319 (nos. 2, 3), 1329 (no. 2), 1331 (no. 2), 1333 (no. 3). *See* Abusait.

Busayit: 1472 (no. 1). *See* Busait.

Busayit': 1335 (no. 1). *See* Abusait.

Catur: 1432 (no. 2). Mentioned as the "master, prefect and overseer" of the city of Bǰni (see App. C).

Čanipek: 1354 (no. 3). *See* Čanipēk.

Čanipēk (variants: Čanipek, J̌anibēk, J̌anipēk): 1346 (nos. 2, 3), 1356 (no. 1). Djānībeg Khān (1342–1357), son of Özbeg Khān, of the Golden Horde. (See Spuler, *Goldene Horde*, esp. pp. 99–109; Pelliot, *Notes sur l'histoire*, pp. 98–101.)

Čawar Bēk: 1449 (no. 8). Mentioned as the ruler of canton of Daranałeac' (see App. C); otherwise unidentified.

Čhangir: 1452 (no. 5). *See* J̌hangir.

Čhankir: 1452 (no. 5). *See* J̌hangir.

Čhanša: 1452 (no. 5). *See* J̌ihanšah.

Čhanšah: 1452 (no. 5), 1468 (no. 2). *See* J̌ihanšah.

Čhanšay: 1452 (no. 5). *See* J̌ihanšah.

Čihankir: 1446 (no. 5). Djihāngīr, a Turkoman who ransacked the canton of Ekełeac' (see App. C) in 1446.

Čihanšah: 1450 (no. 3), 1462 (no. 9). *See* J̌ihanšah.

Čihanšay: 1441 (no. 4), 1470 (no. 1). *See* J̌ihanšah.

Č'agam (variant: Č'ak'am): 1468 (no. 4). An unidentified Muslim ruler in Cilicia.

Č'ak'am: 1464 (no. 16). *See* Č'agam.

Č'alibēg: 1365 (no. 2). Apparently a khan of the Golden Horde, known only from his coins of A.H. 767/768 (A.D. 1366/1367), and mentioned in Spuler as Ğānībeg II. (See Spuler, *Goldene Horde*, pp. 120–121.)

Č'at'ał: 1473 (no. 4). *See* Č'it'ax.

Č'axmax: 1441 (nos. 6, 10). Al-Malik al-Ẓāhir Sayf al-Dīn, Čaḳmaḳ (1438–1453), Mamluk sultan of Egypt of the Burji dynasty. (See Sobernheim, "Čaḳmaḳ," *EI*, NE, II, 6; Hitti, *Arabs*, pp. 694–695.) *See also* Melik' Tahar.

Č'aysar: 1310 (no. 2). A prince of the Ōrbelean family in the province of Siwnik'. (See Ačaṙyan, *HAB*, IV, 212, no. 1.)

Č'ekir: 1403 (no. 6). The Turkoman Bistām Djāgīr. (See V. Minorsky, "Tabrīz," *EI*, OE, IV, 583–593.)

Č'it'ał: 1473 (no. 9). *See* Č'it'ax.

Č'it'ax (variants: Č'at'ał, Č'it'ał, Č't'ax): 1455 (no. 8), 1473 (no. 2), 1478 (no. 6). The term *çitak* is attested in Central Anatolian and Rumelian Turkish dialects, and also as a Turkish loan word in modern Bulgarian, as meaning boor, ruffian, quarrelsome individual (see *Söz Derleme Dergisi*, vol. I, Istanbul, 1939, pp. 342–343). It appears to have been used as a nickname of Sultan Mehmet II Fatih.

Č'opan (variant: Č'ōpan): 1321 (no. 2). Amīr Čoban (or Čūbān), a member of the Čūbānid family of Mongol amirs, who served with distinction under the Ilkhans Arghūn, Gaykhātū, Ghāzān, and Uldjāytū. (See Spuler, *Mongolen in Iran*, esp. pp. 120–128; Cleaves, *Mongolian Documents*, pp. 92–93, n. 8; R. M. Savory, "Čūbānids (Čobanids)," *EI*, NE, II, 67–68.)

Č'ōpan: 1319 (no. 2). *See* Č'opan.

Č't'ax: 1473 (no. 2). *See* Č'it'ax.

Dadan: 1335 (no. 4). Dathan, a Reubenite, who conspired with his brother Abiram against Moses, and was consumed by fire from heaven. (See *Dictionary of Bible*, p. 201.)

Damurtaš: 1338 (no. 2). The false Tīmūrtash. *See* T'amurt'aš.

Daniel: 1411 (no. 1), 1422 (no. 1), 1462 (no. 3). The Jewish Prophet Daniel, who spent his career at the court of Mesopotamian rulers. (See *Dictionary of Bible*, pp. 199–200.)

Daniēl: 1349 (no. 2). An Armenian householder, who received a MS. in 1349.

Dareh: 1462 (no. 2). Darius I the Great, King of Persia (522–486 B.C.).

David: 1435 (no. 3). The second and greatest of the kings of Israel. (See *Dictionary of Bible*, pp. 201–203.)

Dawit': 1304 (no. 6). King David VII (1292–1311) of Georgia. (See Allen, *History*, p. 120; Manvelichvili, *Histoire*, pp. 238–239.)

Dawit': 1395 (no. 1), 1397 (no. 2), 1400 (nos. 1, 2), 1401 (nos. 4, 5, 7), 1402 (no. 1), 1404 (no. 2), 1405 (no. 4), 1407 (no. 1), 1413 (nos. 1, 2), 1414 (no. 5), 1415 (nos. 1, 2), 1417 (nos. 4, 5), 1419 (nos. 3, 4), 1420 (nos. 1, 4, 5), 1421 (nos. 11, 13), 1423 (no. 2), 1425 (nos. 1, 8), 1428 (nos. 1, 5), 1431 (no. 3), 1445 (no. 1). Catholicos Dawit' III (1393–1433) of the Armenian See of Aghtamar (see App. C). (See Ōrmanean, *Azgapatum*, cols. 1393, 1396–1400, 1424; Akinean, *Gawazanagirk' Kat'olikosac' Alt'amaray*, pp. 70–85.)

Dawit', Baron: 1425 (no. 11). Armenian prince of Hamšēn (see App. C).

Dawut (variants: Dayud, Dayut, Dayut'): 1427 (no. 3). Amīr Davud, ruler of the Kurdish principality of Khizān. (See *Chèref-Nâmeh*, II. 1, 57.)

Dayud: 1442 (no. 4). *See* Dawut.

Dayut: 1421 (no. 12), 1431 (no. 3). *See* Dawut.

Dayut': 1417 (no. 2). *See* Dawut.

Diatin: 1362 (no. 1). Diādīn (a Kurdicized form of Ḍiyā' al-Dīn), a Kurdish amir of the Rūzagī tribe who ruled at Bitlīs. (See *Chèref-Nâmeh*, II. 1, 244; V. Minorsky, "Kurds," *EI*, OE, II, 1144.)

Dinipēk: 1341 (no. 3). Tinibeg or Tini Bäg Khān (1341–1342), son of Özbeg Khān, of the Golden Horde. He was murdered by his brother, Djānībeg Khān, in 1340, after a reign of only a few months. (See Spuler, *Goldene Horde*, pp. 99, 238, 239; Pelliot, *Notes sur l'histoire*, pp. 96–98.)

Eałup: 1479 (nos. 2, 3). *See* Ałup.

Eli: 1428 (no. 4). An Armenian who gave refuge to a scribe at Arckē (see App. C).

Ep'rem: 1393 (no. 1). Ephraim; refers to either the land or the tribe. (See *Dictionary of Bible*, p. 263; Isaiah, 7:2.)

Eremia Ełkesac'i: 1442 (no. 1). Lit., "Jeremiah the Elkoshite." The author of the colophon erroneously refers to the Prophet Jeremiah as the

Elkoshite, instead of K'ełkeay, the son of Hilkiah (see Jeremiah 1:1); the Elkoshite was the prophet Nahum (see Nahum 1:1).

Eremiay: 1346 (no. 1). The Prophet Jeremiah. (See *Dictionary of Bible*, pp. 465–470.)

Esayi: 1304 (no. 3). The Prophet Isaiah. (See *Dictionary of Bible*, pp. 423–427.)

Esayi (variant: Yesayi): 1313 (no. 1). Known in Armenian sources as Esayi Nč'ec'i. In 1284 he assumed the abbotcy of the monastery of Glajor (see App. C) in the province of Siwnik'; he trained numerous scholars and was the author of many well-known works. (See Ališan, *Hayapatum*, pp. 525–526, 546; *Sisakan*, pp. 131–137.)

Ezdin: 1414 (no. 5), 1445 (no. 1). *See* Ēzdin.

Ezdinšēr: 1415 (no. 2). *See* Ēzdin.

Ēač'i: 1313 (no. 1). A prince of the Pṙōšean or Xałbakean family, in the canton of Vayoc'-Jor in Siwnik'. (See Yovsēp'an, *Xałbakeank'*, I, 181–189.)

Ēdil Šrwan: 1349 (no. 1). Nūshīrwān al-'Ādil. (See Spuler, *Mongolen in Iran*, pp. 135–136, 197.)

Ēlēgan: 1417 (no. 1). Brother of Zazay [q.v.]; an Armenian prince in Xač'en (see App. C).

Ēlēgum: 1417 (no. 1). Brother of Zazay [q.v.]; an Armenian prince in Xač'en (see App. C).

Ēlikum: 1306 (no. 3). Son of the Ōrbelean Tarsayič, and brother of the historian Step'anos Ōrbelean; mentioned as "prince of princes" in Siwnik'; he died in 1300. (See Ališan, *Sisakan*, pp. 144, 192, 193, 205, 525; Č'amč'ean, *Patmut'iwn*, III, 263, 284, 291; Brosset, *Siounie*, II, 182.)

Ēstinšēr: 1469 (no. 3). *See* Ēztinšēr.

Ēzdanbaxš: 1465 (no. 6). An Armenian merchant from Ardjīsh who, upon his return from the countries in the east, died at Tabrīz.

Ēzdin (variants: Ezdin, Ēztin, Ezdinšēr, Ēzdinšer, Zendin): 1392 (no. 1), 1401 (no. 5), 1418 (no. 3), 1419 (nos. 3, 4), 1428 (no. 1), 1440 (no. 2), 1444 (no. 2). Amīr 'Izz al-Dīn Shīr (probably an arabicization of the Kurdish name Yozdan-Shīr), Kurdish ruler of the Shambo tribe in Hakkārī. (See V. Minorsky, "Kurds," *EI*, OE, II, 1145; "Wān," *ibid.*, IV, 1119–1121; *Chèref-Nâmeh*, I. 2, 115–117.)

Ēzdinšer: 1405 (no. 4), 1421 (no. 10). *See* Ēzdin.

Ēztin: 1410 (no. 3). *See* Ēzdin.

Ēztinšēr (variant: Ēstinšēr): 1452 (no. 4). 'Izz al-Dīn Shīr, Kurdish amir of Hakkārī, son of Asad al-Dīn Zarrīn Čang. (See *Chèref-Nâmeh*, I. 2, 118, 120, 444 n. 417.)

Ǝṙəstakēs: 1464 (no. 5), 1472 (no. 2), 1473 (nos. 5, 7). *See* Aristakēs.

Ǝṙəstam: 1437 (no. 1). Ṙustam; an Ōrbelean prince, son of Bēšk'en; after the defeat of the Ḳara-Ḳoyunlu Iskandar, Bēšk'en, Ṙustam, and their relatives migrated to Lori. (See Xač'ikyan, *XV Dari*, I, p. 700.)

Ǝṙəstak'ēs: 1473 (no. 8). *See* Aristakēs.

Ǝsk'andar: 1426 (no. 4), 1428 (no. 7). *See* Sk'andar.
Fařuxšah: 1451 (no. 5). Brother of P'ašay [q.v.].
Gabriel: 1476 (no. 2). The Archangel Gabriel. (See *Dictionary of Bible*, p. 309.)
Gagik: 1462 (nos. 3, 6). King Gagik Arcruni (908–937) of Vaspurakan; he is known in Arabic sources as Djādjīḳ or Ibn al-Dayrānī. (See Ačaṙyan, *HAB*, I, 431–432, no. 16.)
Gawrgē: 1331 (no. 1). *See* Gawrgi.
Gawrgē: 1447 (no. 2). *See* Gawrki.
Gawrgi (variants: Gawrgē, Gēorg, Gorgēn): 1323 (no. 1). King Giorgi V Brtsqinwalé (the Brilliant, or Splendid), 1316–1346, of Georgia. (See Manvelichvili, *Histoire*, pp. 241–243; Allen, *History*, pp. 120–122; Spuler, *Mongolen in Iran*, pp. 98, 100, 125, 126, 234.)
Gawrki (variants: Gawrgē, Gēorgi, Giawrgi, Gorgi, Kawrki): 1459 (no. 5), 1466 (no. 3). King Giorgi VIII (1446–1466) of Georgia. (See Manvelichvili, *Histoire*, pp. 255–263.)
Gēorg: 1330 (no. 1). *See* Gawrgi.
Gēorg: 1425 (no. 9). The vardapet Gēorg Erznkac'i; well-known medieval Armenian pedagogue and author of a number of commentaries and other works; he died in 1416. (See Ačaṙyan, *HAB*, I, 467–468, no. 102.)
Gēorg, Surb: 1459 (no. 4). St. George; the legendary Cappadocian Christian prince martyred during the reign of Emperor Diocletian.
Gēorgi (variant: Gōrgi): 1396 (no. 1), 1399 (no. 1). King Giorgi VII (1395–1407). (See Manvelichvili, *Histoire*, p. 245; Allen, *History*, pp. 124–126.)
Gēorgi: 1452 (no. 2). *See* Gawrki.
Giawrgi: 1462 (no. 1). *See* Gawrki.
Gołiat': 1389 (no. 1). Goliath, the giant slain by David in single combat. (See *Dictionary of Bible*, p. 339.)
Gorg, Baron: 1453 (no. 3). One of the Armenians brought by Ottoman Sultan Mehmet II Fatih from Ankara to Istanbul.
Gorgēn: 1321 (no. 1). *See* Gawrgi.
Gorgi: 1463 (no. 4), 1465 (no. 1). *See* Gawrki.
Gōrgi: 1400 (no. 1). *See* Gēorgi.
Gratianos: 1453 (no. 2). Emperor Gratian (375–383), who ruled in the west. (See Vasiliev, *History*, I, 66, 79.)
Grigor: 1417 (no. 4), 1420 (no. 5). Catholicos Grigor VIII Xanjołat (1411–1418). (See Ōrmanean, *Azgapatum*, cols. 1408–1412.)
Grigor: 1441 (nos. 6, 9), 1443 (no. 5), 1444 (nos. 1, 3, 4), 1445 (no. 2), 1447 (nos. 1, 2), 1449 (nos. 3, 4, 6, 7, 8), 1450 (nos. 1, 5), 1451 (nos. 1, 2, 4, 5), 1452 (nos. 2, 3), 1453 (nos. 4, 5, 6, 8), 1454 (nos. 1, 2, 4, 5, 6), 1455 (nos. 1, 2, 3), 1456 (nos. 3, 4, 5, 6), 1457 (nos. 3, 4, 5), 1458 (nos. 3, 4), 1459 (nos. 1, 5), 1460 (nos. 1, 2, 3, 5), 1461 (nos. 2, 4, 8), 1462 (nos. 2, 11), 1463 (nos. 9, 13), 1464 (no. 15), 1465 (no. 2), 1466 (no. 1), 1468 (no. 2). Catholicos Grigor X J̌alalbēkeanc' or Makuec'i

(1443–1465) at Etchmiadzin. (See Ōrmanean, *Azgapatum*, cols. 1470–1499; Ačaṙyan, *HAB*, I, 615, no. 637.)

Grigor: 1441 (no. 10), 1444 (no. 8). Catholicos Grigor IX Musabēgeanc' (1439–1441). During his reign the seat of the Armenian catholicosate was transferred from Sis to Etchmiadzin in 1441, but he continued as regional catholicos in Cilicia until his death in 1451. (See Ōrmanean, *Azgapatum*, cols. 1444–1456.)

Grigor: 1451 (no. 3). Father of Guhar [q.v.].

Grigor: 1465 (no. 6). An Armenian who journeyed to Iṣfahān in search of his son, but on his return died at Sulṭānīya.

Grigor (Anawarzec'i) (variants: Grigorios, Grigoris): 1302 (no. 2), 1304 (no. 6), 1305 (no. 1), 1306 (no. 3). Catholicos Grigor VII Anawarzec'i (1293–1307), known for his pro-Latin tendencies; he is also the author of a number of literary works. (See Ōrmanean, *Azgapatum*, cols. 1196–1244.)

Grigor, Ṙayēs: 1371 (no. 3). A layman who accompanied the priest Simēon at the monastery of Tēr Yuskan Ordi.

Grigor Lusaworič', Surb (variants: Grigor, Surb; Lusaworič'): 1307 (no. 5), 1315 (no. 1), 1325 (no. 1), 1454 (no. 1), 1458 (no. 1), 1462 (no. 3). St. Gregory the Illuminator; the first catholicos of the Armenian church. (See Ōrmanean, *Azgapatum*, cols. 44–81; Langlois, *Collection*, I, 97–200.)

Grigor, Surb (Lusaworič'): 1310 (no. 3), 1453 (no. 2). *See* Grigor Lusaworič', Surb.

Grigor Xlat'ec'i (Cerenc'): 1425 (no. 5), 1446 (no. 1), 1453 (no. 2). Author of a historical chronicle; editor of a number of ecclesiastical books; and copyist of a large number of MSS. He was murdered in 1426 by the Rūzagī Kurds. (See Ačaṙyan, *HAB*, I, 608–610, no. 568; V, 310, no. 80.)

Grigorios: 1303 (no. 5). *See* Grigor (Anawarzec'i).

Grigoris: 1302 (no. 1). *See* Grigor (Anawarzec'i).

Gugun: 1419 (no. 2). Armenian prince of Ełegis (see App. C); son of Inanik and father of Tarsayič. (See Xač'ikyan, *XV Dari*, I, p. 686.)

Guhar: 1451 (no. 3). Daughter of Grigor; she was hurled down by the Muslims from the fortress of Zṙayl (see App. C).

Hači-Kire: 1456 (no. 7). Ḥadjdjī Girāy b. Ghiyāth al-Dīn b. Tāsh-Tīmūr, founder of an independent Tatar kingdom, known under the dynastic name Girāy, which ruled the Crimean Peninsula for three centuries (fifteenth to eighteenth). (See W. Barthold, "Ḥadjdjī Girāi," *EI*, OE, III, 204; "Giray," *ibid.*, II, 171; Halil Inalcik, "Girāy," *EI*, NE, II, 1112–1114; B. Spuler, "Čingizids," *ibid.*, II, 44–47; Spuler, *Goldene Horde*, pp. 157, 168, 170–176, 345.)

Hagar: 1393 (no. 1), 1449 (no. 1). Hagar, the handmaid of Abraham's wife, Sarah, and mother of his eldest son, Ishmael or Ismael. (See *Dictionary of Bible*, p. 358.)

Hamza, Sultan: 1449 (no. 1). *See* Hamzay, Sultan.

Hamzay, Sultan (variant: Hamza): 1437 (no. 7), 1444 (nos. 7, 8). Sulṭān Ḥamza Bayundur, son of Ḳara Yoluḳ (Yülük) ʿUthmān. (See V. Minorsky, "Aḳ-Ḳoyunlu," *EI*, NE, I, 311–312; "Mārdīn," *EI*, OE, III, 273–277; "Uzun Ḥasan," *EI*, OE, IV, p. 1065.)

Hamzay, Sultan: 1452 (no. 5). Sulṭān Ḥamza, son of the Aḳ-Ḳoyunlu Djihāngīr.

Hasan: 1452 (no. 5), 1457 (no. 1), 1460 (no. 12), 1464 (no. 10), 1467 (nos. 5, 6), 1468 (no. 3), 1469 (nos. 2, 4, 7, 8), 1470 (nos. 1, 3), 1471 (nos. 1, 2, 5, 6, 7, 9, 12), 1472 (nos. 1, 2), 1473 (nos. 1, 2, 3, 5, 6, 7, 10), 1474 (nos. 1, 3, 4, 5), 1475 (nos. 1, 2, 3, 5, 6), 1476 (nos. 1, 2, 3, 5, 6, 7, 8, 9, 10), 1477 (nos. 2, 3, 4, 5, 6, 7), 1478 (nos. 1, 2, 3), 1479 (no. 1). *See* Uzun Hasan.

Hasan: 1466 (no. 8). Ḥasan Khān; mentioned as the amir of Kharpūt, otherwise unidentified.

Hasan Ali: 1458 (no. 5), 1462 (no. 3), 1463 (no. 7), 1467 (no. 7), 1468 (nos. 1, 5), 1469 (nos. 1, 4), 1471 (no. 7), 1472 (no. 1). Ḥasan ʿAlī, son of the Ḳara-Ḳoyunlu Djihānshāh. After a rebellion against his father, he was imprisoned for twenty-five years as a result of which his mind was affected. He escaped from prison, and was welcomed by the Aḳ-Ḳoyunlu Uzun Ḥasan. In 1467, Ḥasan ʿAlī ascended the throne at Tabrīz; but a year later he was captured and put to death by the forces of Uzun Ḥasan. With his death, the main branch of the Ḳara-Ḳoyunlu dynasty came to an end. (See C. Huart, "Ḳara-Ḳoyunlu," *EI*, OE, II, 741; V. Minorsky, "Uzun Ḥasan," *ibid.*, IV, 1066.)

Hasan Carecʿi: 1422 (no. 1). Armenian prince of Bǰni (see App. C); he was killed, together with his three sons, by the forces of Tīmūr Lang. (See Ačaṙyan, *HAB*, III, 60, no. 65.)

Hasantʿamur: 1318 (no. 1). Ḥasan Tīmūr or Esen Temür; mentioned as a Mongol tax-collector.

Hawkitʿ Atom: 1451 (no. 5). An Armenian householder, and husband of Pʿašay [q.v.].

Hayrapet: 1431 (no. 3). An Armenian who purchased a MS., probably at Khizān.

Herovtʿēs: 1478 (no. 1). Herod the Great. (See *Dictionary of Bible*, p. 379.)

Hetʿum: 1302 (no. 1), 1303 (no. 5), 1304 (nos. 2, 6), 1305 (no. 1), 1306 (nos. 1, 3). King Hetʿum II (1294–1307) of the Armenian kingdom of Cilicia, who was slain by Būlārgī in 1307. (See Rüdt-Collenberg, *Rupenides*, pp. 16, 22, 71.)

Hetʿum: 1307 (no. 6), 1308 (no. 1). Grand Baron in the Armenian kingdom of Cilicia; he was slain in 1307 by Būlārgī. (See Ačaṙyan, *HAB*, III, 73, no. 21.)

Hetʿum Nłrcʿi: 1325 (no. 2), 1327 (no. 2), 1367 (no. 1). An Armenian nobleman in Cilicia; one of three regents during the childhood of King Leon IV. (See Rüdt-Collenberg, *Rupenides*, pp. 68–69.)

Hṙipʿsimē, St.: 1462 (no. 3). One of the Christian virgins put to death by

King Tiridates III of Armenia. (See Ōrmanean, *Azgapatum*, cols. 51–52.) *See also* Gayianeanc'; Hṙip'simeanc' (App. D).

Hulawu (variant: Hulayun): 1476 (no. 8). Hūlāgū Khān (d. 1265), grandson of Čingiz Khān and founder of the Ilkhanid Mongol kingdom in Persia. (See Spuler, *Mongolen in Iran*; W. Barthold, "Hūlāgū," *EI*, OE, III, 332–333; "Il-Khāns," *ibid.*, II, 469; B. Spuler, "Čingizids," *EI*, NE, II, 44–47. For the variant forms of the name, see Cleaves, "Mongolian Names and Terms," p. 422.)

Hulayun: 1307 (no. 1). *See* Hulawu.

Husēn Pēk: 1476 (no. 9). Ḥusayn Beg; unidentified ruler.

Iału Bak: 1439 (no. 1). Probably Ya'ḳūb b. 'Uthmān Ḳara Yoluḳ. (See Walther Hinz, *Irans Aufstieg zum nationalstaat im funfzehnten Jahrhundert*, Berlin-Leipzig, 1936, p. 143; *Islam Ansiklopedisi*, I, "Ak-Koyunlu," pp. 264–265.)

Ian: 1471 (no. 3). Unidentified.

Ibrahim Ała: 1371 (no. 3). Ibrāhīm Agha; an unidentified Kurdish chief in the canton of K'aǰberunik'; his son allegedly recovered his eyesight thanks to an Armenian Gospel.

Iktiš: 1428 (no. 4). An Armenian woman who gave refuge to the scribe Karapet, who had fled from the atrocities of the Kurds.

Ildrum: 1400 (no. 4), 1401 (no. 6), 1402 (no. 1), 1422 (no. 1). Yîldîrîm (the Thunderbolt), surname of Ottoman Sultan Bāyezīd I (1389–1403). He earned the surname after he distinguished himself as an impetuous soldier in the battle of Efrenk-yazîsî against the Ḳaramānids in 1386. (See Halil Inalcik, "Bāyazīd I," *EI*, NE, I, 1117–1119; L. Bouvat, "Tīmūr Lang," *EI*, OE, IV, 778–779; Fr. Taeschner, "Anḳara," *EI*, NE, I, 509–511.)

Inanik: 1419 (no. 2). *See* Iwanē.

Isahak, St.: 1307 (no. 5), 1315 (no. 1). *See* Sahak, St.

Isaz: 1456 (no. 2). One of the purchasers of a Gospel MS.

Iskandar: 1425 (no. 2). *See* Sk'andar (son of Ḳara Yūsuf).

Isk'andar: 1425 (no. 4), 1427 (no. 2), 1428 (no. 4), 1435 (no. 4). *See* Sk'andar (son of Ḳara Yūsuf).

Isk'antar: 1423 (no. 2), 1428 (no. 3). *See* Sk'andar.

Ivanē: 1348 (no. 2). *See* Iwanē.

Ivanē (variant: Iwanē): 1419 (no. 2). Ioanné or Iwané, atabeg of Samtzkhé in Georgia, son of Aghbugha or Aḳ-bughā. (See Allen, *History*, pp. 124–126.)

Iwanē (variants: Inanik, Ivanē): 1349 (no. 1), 1401 (no. 2). Ōrbelean prince, son of Burt'el and father of Gugun and Smbat. (See Ališan, *Sisakan*, pp. 47, 115, 148, 181, 202, 525; Yovsēp'ean, *Xałbakeank'*, p. 202; Brosset, *Siounie*, II, 182.)

Iwanē: 1396 (no. 1). *See* Ivanē.

Iwsuf: 1420 (no. 2). *See* Łara Yusuf.

J̌ahanša: 1441 (no. 2), 1459 (no. 4), 1461 (no. 2), 1462 (nos. 2, 11). *See* J̌ihanšah.

J̌ahanšah: 1442 (no. 1), 1443 (nos. 4, 5, 6), 1447 (nos. 1, 2), 1451 (no. 4), 1452 (no. 3), 1459 (no. 5), 1460 (nos. 2, 3), 1461 (no. 1), 1463 (no. 13), 1464 (nos. 2, 5), 1466 (no. 3). *See* J̌ihanšah.

J̌ahanšay: 1441 (no. 1), 1461 (no. 8), 1464 (no. 15). *See* J̌ihanšah.

J̌ahašē: 1471 (no. 3). *See* J̌ihanšah.

J̌ahaynšay: 1462 (no. 2). *See* J̌ihanšah.

J̌aǰuṙ: 1443 (no. 4). An unidentified prince.

J̌alal: 1417 (no. 1). An Armenian prince of Xač'en (see App. C), related to Zazay [q.v.].

J̌alaladawli: 1417 (no. 1). Son of Zazay.

J̌anhanša: 1467 (no. 1). *See* J̌ihanšah.

J̌anhanšay: 1440 (no. 3). *See* J̌ihanšah.

J̌anibēk: 1358 (no. 1). *See* Čanipēk.

J̌anibēk: 1451 (no. 5). Son of P'ašay [q.v.]; he was slain by the Muslims at Khizān. (See Ačaṙyan, *HAB*, IV, 291, no. 1.)

J̌anipēk: 1350 (no. 1). *See* Čanipēk.

J̌anšay: 1469 (no. 2). *See* J̌ihanšah.

J̌əhanša: 1441 (no. 9), 1446 (nos. 1, 2), 1450 (nos. 1, 5), 1464 (no. 11). *See* J̌ihanšah.

J̌əhanšah: 1453 (no. 5), 1462 (no. 3). *See* J̌ihanšah.

J̌əhanšay: 1444 (no. 2), 1452 (no. 4), 1456 (no. 3), 1462 (no. 6), 1472 (no. 1). *See* J̌ihanšah.

J̌ənxanšah: 1445 (no. 4). *See* J̌ihanšah.

J̌əxanšay: 1455 (no. 5), 1457 (no. 2). *See* J̌ihanšah.

J̌hangir (variants: Čhangir, Čhankir): 1445 (no. 6), 1449 (no. 1). Djihāngīr Bayundur, son of 'Alī, brother of Uzun Ḥasan, and grandson of the Aḳ-Ḳoyunlu Ḳara Yoluḳ (Yülük) 'Uthmān. He died in 1469. (See V. Minorsky, "Uzun Ḥasan," *EI*, OE, IV, 1065; "Aḳ-Ḳoyunlu," *EI*, NE, I, 311–312.)

J̌hanša: 1437 (no. 9), 1438 (no. 3), 1449 (no. 6), 1450 (no. 1), 1454 (no. 5), 1456 (no. 5), 1457 (no. 1), 1458 (nos. 1, 6, 7), 1459 (nos. 2, 3, 6), 1460 (nos. 5, 7, 9, 11, 13), 1461 (no. 4), 1462 (no. 5), 1463 (no. 7), 1465 (nos. 3, 4), 1466 (nos. 6, 7), 1467 (no. 7), 1468 (no. 1), 1469 (no. 4), 1470 (no. 2), 1471 (no. 9). *See* J̌ihanšah.

J̌hanšah: 1438 (nos. 1, 3), 1442 (nos. 2, 3), 1443 (nos. 1, 3), 1444 (nos. 1, 3), 1445 (no. 3), 1447 (no. 3), 1453 (no. 4), 1454 (no. 6), 1455 (nos. 2, 3), 1458 (nos. 1, 3), 1460 (nos. 1, 8, 12), 1461 (no. 3), 1462 (no. 3), 1463 (nos. 5, 8, 10), 1465 (no. 6), 1469 (no. 1). *See* J̌ihanšah.

J̌hanšay: 1438 (no. 4), 1441 (no. 3), 1443 (no. 2), 1445 (nos. 1, 2, 5), 1446 (no. 4), 1449 (nos. 3, 4), 1451 (no. 3), 1453 (nos. 6, 8), 1454 (nos. 2, 3), 1456 (nos. 1, 4, 6), 1457 (nos. 3, 5), 1458 (nos. 1, 4, 5), 1459 (nos. 7, 8), 1460 (nos. 4, 6), 1462 (nos. 3, 8), 1463 (nos. 3, 6, 9, 14), 1464 (nos. 4, 6, 7, 9), 1465 (nos. 2, 5), 1466 (nos. 1, 4, 5), 1467 (nos. 2, 4, 6, 7), 1468 (no. 1), 1469 (no. 3), 1470 (no. 3), 1471 (no. 7). *See* J̌ihanšah.

J̌ianšay: 1458 (no. 2). *See* J̌ihanšah.

J̌ihanša: 1441 (no. 5), 1451 (no. 1), 1455 (no. 6), 1457 (no. 3). *See* J̌ihanšah.

J̌ihanšah (variants: Čhanša, Čhanšah, Čhanšay, Čihanšah, Čihanšay, J̌ahanša, J̌ahanšah, J̌ahanšay, J̌ahašē, J̌ahaynšay, J̌anhanša, J̌anhanšay, J̌anšay, J̌əhanša, J̌əhanšah, J̌əhanšay, J̌ənxanšah, J̌əxanšay, J̌hanša, J̌hanšah, J̌hanšay, J̌ianšay, J̌ihanša, J̌ihanšay, J̌xanša, J̌xanšay): 1451 (no. 2), 1453 (no. 1), 1455 (no. 1), 1462 (no. 10). Djihānshāh or Djahānshāh; Ḳara-Ḳoyunlu ruler, son of Ḳara Yūsuf. After submitting to Shāhrukh in 1434, he was installed as governor-general of Ādharbaydjān. He subsequently added new provinces to his domain, including 'Irāḳ 'Adjamī, Iṣfahān, Fārs, Kirmān, and Khurāsān, and established his capital at Herāt. His death occurred on November 11, 1467; the sources are not agreed on its circumstances. (See L. Bouvat, "Shāhrukh Mīrzā," *EI*, OE, IV, 265–266; V. Minorsky, "Tabrīz," *ibid.*, 583–593; C. Huart, "Ḳara-Ḳoyunlu," *ibid.*, II, 741; *Chèref-Nâmeh*, II. 1, 458–459, 460, 477, 480, 482, 483, 483–485; Bouvat, *L'Empire mongol*, pp. 89, 108, 115, 140–141, 143.)

J̌ihanšay: 1440 (no. 1), 1461 (no. 5). *See* J̌ihanšah.

J̌uhar: 1451 (no. 3). Mother of Mahdasi Pōłos, who commissioned a Gospel MS. (See Ačaṙyan, *HAB*, IV, 303, no. 8.)

J̌um: 1473 (no. 5), 1476 (no. 7). A member of the Pṙōšean family; prince of Vayoc'-Jor in Siwnik'. (See Ačaṙyan, *HAB*, IV, 308, no. 2; Xač'ikyan, *XV Dari*, II, pp. 565–566.)

J̌xanša: 1444 (no. 4). *See* J̌ihanšah.

J̌xanšay: 1435 (no. 4), 1437 (nos. 3, 5), 1451 (no. 5), 1453 (no. 7), 1454 (no. 4), 1457 (no. 1). *See* J̌ihanšah.

Karapet: 1395 (no. 1), 1396 (no. 1), 1397 (no. 2), 1400 (no. 2), 1401 (nos. 4, 8). Catholicos Karapet I, Kełec'i or Bokik (1392–1404). (See Ōrmanean, *Azgapatum*, cols. 1374–1394.)

Karapet: 1417 (no. 1). Catholicos of the Caucasian Albanian church. (See Ačaṙyan, *HAB*, II, 593, no. 119; p. 596, no. 156.)

Karapet: 1446 (no. 6), 1464 (no. 16), 1469 (no. 6). Catholicos Karapet Ewdokiac'i (1446–1477) of the Armenian see at Sis. (See Ōrmanean, *Azgapatum*, cols. 1478–1479, 1489.)

Karapet: 1465 (no. 6). An Armenian merchant from Ardjīsh who was slain on his return from Sulṭānīya.

Karapet, Priest: 1463 (no. 9). An Armenian clergyman who was slain at Ardjīsh.

Karaypet, Ṙayēs: 1371 (no. 3). An Armenian layman.

Kawrki: 1466 (no. 2), 1468 (no. 2). *See* Gawrki.

Kir Luka (variant: Kiwṙlikē): 1453 (no. 3). Lucas Notaras; the Byzantine Megadux. (See Runciman, *Fall of Constantinople.*)

Kirakos [Virapec'i]: 1442 (nos. 3, 4), 1443 (no. 6), 1444 (no. 8). He was elected catholicos after the transfer of the Armenian see from Sis to Etchmiadzin in 1441; but two years later he was removed from office. (See Ōrmanean, *Azgapatum*, cols. 1457–1469.)

Kiwr̃likē: 1453 (no. 1). *See* Kir Luka.

Korx: 1335 (no. 4). Korah, who rebelled against Moses. (See *Dictionary of Bible*, p. 560.)

Kostandianos: 1350 (no. 1), 1356 (no. 1). *See* Kostandin (IV).

Kostandianos: 1365 (no. 2). *See* Kostandin, King.

Kostandianos: 1419 (no. 2). *See* Kostandin I.

Kostandianos: 1453 (nos. 2, 3). Emperor Constantine I the Great (306–337). (See Vasiliev, *History*, I.)

Kostandil: 1412 (no. 1). *See* Kostandin I.

Kostandin: 1308 (no. 1), 1310 (no. 2), 1313 (nos. 1, 3), 1315 (no. 2), 1319 (no. 2), 1321 (nos. 1, 2), 1322 (no. 2), 1323 (no. 2). Catholicos Constantine III (1307–1322) Kesarac'i, also called Katukec'i. (See Ōrmanean, *Azgapatum*, cols. 1245–1268.)

Kostandin: 1325 (nos. 2, 3). Catholicos Constantine IV, Lambronac'i or Drazarkc'i (1323–1326). (See Ōrmanean, *Azgapatum*, cols. 1269–1271.)

Kostandin (variants: Kostandianos, Kostandil): 1411 (no. 1), 1417 (no. 1). King Constantine I of Georgia. (See Allen, *History*, p. 126.)

Kostandin: 1431 (nos. 1, 3), 1432 (nos. 1, 3, 4, 5), 1433 (no. 3), 1435 (nos. 1, 2, 4, 5), 1436 (nos. 1, 3, 5, 6), 1437 (nos. 3, 5, 7), 1438 (nos. 1, 4, 5), 1449 (no. 1). Catholicos Constantine VI Vahkac'i or Vahkec'i (1430–1439). (See Ōrmanean, *Azgapatum*, cols. 1427–1443.)

Kostandin: 1453 (no. 3). Emperor Constantine XI Palaeologus (1449–1453), the last of the Byzantine emperors. (See Vasiliev, *History*, II.)

Kostandin: 1465 (no. 1). King Constantine II of Kartli-Imereti (1466–1478) in Georgia. (See Manvelichvili, *Histoire*, pp. 265–266.)

Kostandin (IV): 1346 (no. 1). King Constantine III (1344–1362) of the Armenian kingdom of Cilicia. (See Rüdt-Collenberg, *Rupenides*, pp. 16, 22.)

Kostandin, Baron: 1325 (no. 2). Constantine; constable or commander-in-chief in the Armenian kingdom of Cilicia, and one of the regents during the childhood of King Leon IV. (See Ačar̃yan, *HAB*, II, 669, no. 127.)

Kostandin, King (variant: Kostandianos): 1367 (no. 1), 1371 (no. 1). King Constantine IV (1364–1373) of the Armenian kingdom of Cilicia. (See Rüdt-Collengerg, *Rupenides*, pp. 16, 22.)

K'arim Ała: 1472 (no. 1). Karīm Agha; leader of the Thanezy Kurds in the fortress of Galhuk, located in the region of the Djazīra.

K'urd: 1310 (no. 1). An Armenian prince, of the Vač'utean family, of the fortress of Anberd (see App. C), and father of prince Tayir [q.v.].

K'urd: 1310 (no. 1), 1335 (no. 4). Vač'utean prince of the fortress of Anberd (see App. C), and son of prince Tayir [q.v.].

Lang-T'amur: 1429 (no. 1). *See* Lank-T'amur.

Lank-T'amur (variants: Lang-T'amur, Lanka-T'amur, T'amur, T'amur-Lang, T'amur-Lank, T'ēmur-Lank). Tīmūr Lang (Tamerlane) (1336–1405), the notorious Mongol conqueror of Asia, who claimed to be a descendant of Chingiz Khan. He died shortly after he began his campaign against China, at the age of seventy-one, having reigned thirty-six years. His reputation is that of a cruel conqueror, as evidenced by the fact that, after capturing certain cities, he slaughtered thousands of defenders and built pyramids of their skulls. He worked with all his might for the spread of Islam. (See Bouvat, *L'Empire mongol*, pp. 5–8, 17–76; Spuler, *Goldene Horde*; J. H. Saunders, trans., *Tamerlane*—English trans. of late fourteenth-century Arabic work by Aḥmad ibn 'Arabshāh—1936; L. Bouvat, "Tīmūr Lang," *EI*, OE, IV, 777–779.)

Lanka-T'amur: 1400 (no. 1). *See* Lank-T'amur.

Levon: 1341 (no. 3). *See* Lewon (IV).

Lewon: 1302 (no. 1). King Leon II (1270–1288/9) of the Armenian kingdom of Cilicia. (See Rüdt-Collenberg, *Rupenides*, pp. 16, 22, 67.)

Lewon: 1361 (no. 3). King Leon V (1374–1375); the last sovereign of the Armenian kingdom of Cilicia; he died in 1393. (See François Tournebize, "Léon V de Lusignan dernier roi de l'Arméno-Cilicie," in *Etudes publiées par des pères de la Compagnie de Jésus*, Paris, 1910, 122: 60–79, 196–203; K. J. Basmadjian, *Léon VI of Lusignan*, Paris, 1908; Rüdt-Collenberg, *Rupenides*, pp. 16, 22, 76.)

Lewon (III) (variant: Lēon): 1308 (no. 1). King Leon III (1301–1307) of Cilicia; he was slain by Būlārgī. (See Rüdt-Collenberg, *Rupenides*, pp. 16, 22, 74.)

Lewon (IV) (variants: Levon, Lēovn, Łewon): 1321 (no. 1), 1322 (no. 2), 1323 (no. 2), 1325 (nos. 2, 3), 1327 (nos. 1, 2), 1329 (no. 2), 1330 (no. 1), 1331 (nos. 1, 2, 3), 1332 (nos. 1, 2), 1333 (no. 3), 1334 (no. 1), 1335 (no. 2), 1336 (no. 3), 1337 (nos. 2, 3), 1338 (no. 1). King Leon IV (1320–1341) of the Armenian kingdom of Cilicia. (See Rüdt-Collenberg, *Rupenides*, pp. 16, 22, 75.)

Lewon Bazunenc': 1367 (no. 1). Father of the constable Bazun in the Armenian kingdom of Cilicia. (See Ačaṙyan, *HAB*, II, 425, no. 38.)

Lēon: 1307 (no. 6). *See* Lewon (III).

Lēovn: 1336 (no. 5). *See* Lewon (IV).

Liparit: 1367 (no. 1). Grand marshal in the Armenian kingdom of Cilicia; he was killed in combat in 1370. (See Ališan, *Sisuan*, pp. 227, 538, 542; Ališan, *Yušikk' Hayreneac' Hayoc'*, I, 265, II, 509–512; Rüdt-Collenberg, *Rupenides*, p. 73.)

Lusaworič': 1453 (no. 2), 1462 (nos. 3, 6, 7), 1469 (no. 6), 1476 (no. 2). *See* Grigor Lusaworič', Surb.

Łan: 1458 (no. 1). Probably Khān; the reference is to Shāh-Ḳubād, who killed his father, the Ḳara-Ḳoyunlu Iskandar, in the castle of Alindjak. (See C. Huart, "Ḳara-Ḳoyunlu," *EI*, OE, II, 741; Bouvat, *L'Empire mongol*, p. 115.)

Łara Eusuf: 1413 (no. 1), 1447 (no. 3), 1455 (no. 3). *See* Łara Yusuf.

Łara-Łati: 1453 (no. 3). Probably Ḳara Ḳāḍī; he is said to have been appointed by Ottoman Sultan Mehmet II Fatih as judge of Istanbul after its conquest in 1453.

Łara Mahmat (variant: Łaray Mahmat): 1386 (no. 2), 1441 (no. 1). Ḳara Muḥammad Tūrmush; a dynast of the Ḳara-Ḳoyunlu Turkoman dynasty which reigned in Persia and Mesopotamia. (See C. Huart, "Ḳara-Ḳoyunlu," *EI*, OE, II, 741.)

Łara Ōt'man: 1435 (no. 4). *See* Awt'man.

Łara Usuf: 1407 (no. 2), 1408 (no. 3), 1411 (no. 5), 1422 (no. 1), 1426 (no. 4), 1435 (no. 4), 1454 (no. 3), 1457 (no. 1), 1459 (no. 5), 1460 (no. 8), 1462 (no. 8), 1470 (no. 2). *See* Łara Yusuf.

Łara Yusuf (variants: Iwsuf, Łara Eusuf, Łara Usuf, Łaray Iwsiwf, Łaray Iwsuf, Łaray Usuf, Łaray Yusuf, Usep', Usf, Usuf, Usup', Xara Usuf, Yusov, Yusuf, Yusup'): 1392 (no. 2), 1407 (no. 1), 1408 (no. 1), 1417 (nos. 2, 3), 1419 (no. 3), 1421 (no. 3), 1444 (no. 2). Ḳara Yūsuf, son of the Ḳara-Ḳoyunlu Ḳara Muḥammad Tūrmush, whom he succeeded as ruler of Persia and Mesopotamia in 1390, with Tabrīz as his capital. He died in the town of Udjān on November 12, 1420, at the age of sixty-five after reigning fourteen years. (See C. Huart, "Ḳara-Ḳoyunlu," *EI*, OE, II, 741; L. Bouvat, "Shāhrukh Mīrzā," *ibid.*, IV, 265–266; V. Minorsky, "Tabrīz," *ibid.*, 583–593; Bouvat, *L'Empire mongol*, esp. 88–89.)

Łarapand: 1335 (no. 4). *See* Xarbanda.

Łaray Hasan: 1343 (no. 2). Ḳara Ḥasan, who sacked Khilāṭ in 1343; otherwise unidentified.

Łaray Iwsiwf: 1387 (no. 2). *See* Łara Yusuf.

Łaray Iwsuf: 1443 (no. 3). *See* Łara Yusuf.

Łaray Mahmat: 1386 (no. 2). *See* Łara Mahmat.

Łaray Ōt'man: 1457 (no. 1). *See* Awt'man.

Łaray Usuf: 1393 (no. 2), 1415 (no. 2), 1418 (no. 2), 1419 (no. 1), 1421 (no. 7), 1422 (no. 1), 1428 (no. 1), 1436 (no. 3), 1459 (no. 7), 1460 (no. 6), 1464 (no. 4), 1465 (no. 2), 1466 (no. 5). *See* Łara Yusuf.

Łaray Yusuf: 1410 (no. 3), 1417 (no. 5), 1420 (no. 5), 1445 (no. 1). *See* Łara Yusuf.

Łarbandałul: 1318 (no. 1). *See* Xarbanda.

Łarpanta: 1310 (no. 1). *See* Xarbanda.

Łasəm: 1455 (no. 6). Amīr Ḳāsim, Kurdish ruler of the principality of Khizān.

Ławrławrē: 1465 (no. 1), 1466 (no. 2), 1473 (no. 8), 1477 (no. 1). The first two texts refer to Qwarqwaré (Qvarqvaré, Ḳwarḳwaré) II, the atabeg of Samtzkhé in Georgia, who died in 1466. (See Allen, *History*, pp. 136–138; Manvelichvili, *Histoire*, pp. 256, 258, 260–266.) The exact identity of the last two references is uncertain, for the chronology of the rulers of Samtzkhé following the death of Qwarqwaré II is rather confused. (See Allen, *History*, pp. 138–139; Manvelichvili, *Histoire*, p. 265.)

Łazan (variant: Xazan): 1301 (no. 1), 1302 (nos. 1, 2), 1303 (nos. 1, 5), 1304 (nos. 2, 3, 5, 6), 1335 (no. 4). The Ilkhanid Ghāzān Khān (1295–1304), eldest son of Arghūn Khān. His reign was marked by a period of prosperity in war and administration. A man of great ability, he established a permanent staff to deal with legal, financial, and military affairs, put on a firm basis the monetary system and the system of weights and measures, and perfected the mounted postal service. He was the first Mongol ruler who definitely adopted Islam, with a large number of his subjects. (See Spuler, *Mongolen in Iran*; "Ghāzān, Maḥmūd," *EI*, NE, II, 1043. For the name Łazan, see Paul Pelliot, *Notes on Marco Polo*, *I*, *Ouvrage Posthume*, Paris, 1959, pp. 119–121.)

Łazar: 1318 (no. 1). An Armenian monk; mentioned as the gatekeeper of the monastery of Varag (see App. C).

Łazar: 1456 (no. 2). One of the purchasers of a Gospel MS.

Łewon: 1323 (no. 1), 1327 (no. 1). *See* Lewon (IV).

Łəlič-Aslan: 1444 (no. 2). *See* Łlič-Aslan.

Łlič-Aslan (variant: Łəlič-Aslan): 1445 (no. 1), 1459 (no. 2). Kïlïdj Arslan b. Pīr ʻAlī, governor of Erzindjān and uncle of the Aḳ-Ḳoyunlu Djihāngīr. (See V. Minorsky, "Uzun Ḥasan," *EI*, OE, IV, 1065.) He is mentioned in the texts as *kołmnapet* (see App. F) of the regions of Van and Ostan [Wusṭān], that is Hakkārī.

Łut'lumelik': 1453 (no. 2). Mother of Aṙak'el Bałišec'i [q.v.].

Mahamat: 1453 (no. 3). *See* Muhamat, Sultan.

Mahmat: 1480 (no. 2). *See* Muhamat, Sultan.

Mahmed: 1306 (no. 1). *See* Mahmet.

Mahmet (variant: Mahmed): 1307 (no. 5), 1315 (no. 1), 1422 (no. 1), 1458 (no. 1). The Prophet Muhammad of Islam.

Mahmut: 1446 (no. 5). Maḥmūd; mentioned as the brother of the amir of the fortress of Kemakh, otherwise unidentified.

Mahmut Bēk: 1462 (no. 3). Maḥmūd Beg; mentioned as the foster-brother of J̌ihanšah [q.v.].

Mahmut Łan: 1337 (no. 3). Probably the Ilkhanid Muḥammad Khān (1336–1338). (See Spuler, *Mongolen in Iran*, p. 533.)

Mahmut'ag, Sultan: 1456 (no. 7). Maḥmūdek (in Russian sources, Makhmutek), who about 1445, together with his father Ulu-Muḥammad, founded a powerful Tatar kingdom in Ḳazān after having been banished from the Golden Horde. (See Spuler, *Goldene Horde*, p. 165; W. Barthold, "Ḳazān," *EI*, OE, II, 837–838.)

Mamay: 1365 (no. 1), 1371 (no. 1), 1377 (no. 1). Mamay, a Tatar general of the Golden Horde. (See Spuler, *Goldene Horde*, pp. 112, 120, 121, 126–128.)

Martiros: 1371 (no. 3). An Armenian layman, whose crippled son was allegedly healed by a Gospel MS.

Martiros: 1459 (no. 1). Mentioned as the prelate of the Armenian bishopric of Constantinople. (See Ačaṙyan, *HAB*, III, 282, no. 125.)

Martiros: 1480 (no. 1). An Armenian scribe who was deported to Constantinople from Ḳaramān.

Martiros, Vardapet: 1371 (no. 3). A member of the monastic order of Tēr Yuskan Ordi.

Mat'ēos Sebastac'i: 1480 (no. 1). An Armenian clergyman from Sebastia;

he is said to have been brought to Istanbul by Mehmet II Fatih to assume the office of patriarch, an offer which he declined. (See Ačaṙyan, *HAB*, III, 228, no. 86.)

Melek': 1421 (no. 10). *See* Melik' Mahmad.

Melik': 1415 (no. 2), 1419 (no. 4), 1445 (no. 1). *See* Melik' Mahmad.

Melik' Aslan: 1479 (no. 4). Malik Arslān (1454–1465), a member of the Dhu'l-Ḳadrid Turkoman dynasty which ruled for nearly two centuries (1337–1522) the region of Marash-Malatya, with Elbistan as their center, as clients first of the Mamluk and later of the Ottoman sultans. (See J. H. Mordtmann-[V. L. Ménage], "Dhu'l-Ḳadr," *EI*, NE, II, 239–240; V. Minorsky, "Uzun Ḥasan," *EI*, OE, IV, 1068; J. H. Kramers, "Kharput," *ibid.*, pp. 914–916.)

Melik' Mahmad (variants: Melek', Melik', Melik' Mahmat, Mēlēk', Mēlik' Mahmad, Mēlik' Mahamad): 1418 (no. 3). Malik Muḥammad, son of 'Izz al-Dīn Shīr; a Kurdish ruler of the Shambo tribe in Hakkārī. (See *Chèref-Nâmeh*, I. 2, 117; V. Minorsky, "Kurds," *EI*, OE, II, 1142; "Wān," *ibid.*, IV, 1119–1121.)

Melik' Mahmat: 1417 (no. 5). *See* Melik' Mahmad.

Melik' Tahar: 1441 (no. 6). Al-Malik al-Ẓāhir Sayf al-Dīn, Čaḳmaḳ (1438–1453), Mamluk sultan of Egypt. (See Hitti, *Arabs*, pp. 694–695.) *See also* Č'axmax.

Mesrop (variants: Mesrovb, Mesrovp): 1367 (no. 1). Catholicos Mesrop I Artazec'i (1359–1372). (See Ōrmanean, *Azgapatum*, cols. 1321–1328.)

Mesrovb: 1371 (no. 1). *See* Mesrop.

Mesrovp: 1365 (no. 2). *See* Mesrop.

Mēlēk': 1420 (no. 4). *See* Melik' Mahmad.

Mēlik' Mahamad: 1444 (no. 2). *See* Melik' Mahmad.

Mēlik' Mahmad: 1428 (no. 1), 1444 (no. 2). *See* Melik' Mahmad.

Mhamat: 1452 (no. 5). *See* Muhamat Mirza.

Minč'ak': 1367 (no. 1). Mentioned as the amir of Tarsus. In Armenian sources he is also referred to as Manč'ak and Mič'ak' Shahar-oghlu. (See Ališan, *Sisuan*, p. 542a.)

Miranša (variant: Miranšay): 1400 (no. 4), 1401 (no. 6), 1405 (no. 1). Mīrānshāh (less commonly known as Djalāl al-Dīn Gurgha), one of the sons of Tīmūr Lang. He was killed in battle with Ḳara Yūsuf in 1408. (See Spuler, *Mongolen in Iran*, p. 248; L. Bouvat, "Tīmūrids," *EI*, OE, IV, 779–780; V. Minorsky, "Tabrīz," *ibid.*, pp. 583–593; L. Bouvat, "Shāhrukh Mīrzā," *ibid.*, pp. 265–266; *Chèref-Nâmeh*, II. 1, 438–439, 440; Bouvat, *L'Empire mongol.*)

Miranšay: 1422 (no. 1). *See* Miranša.

Mkrtič' Nałas: 1449 (no. 1). Prelate of the Armenians of Mesopotamia; also a well-known poet and painter. (See Ē. Xondkaryan, *Mkrtič' Nałaš*, Erevan, 1965; Ačaṙyan, *HAB*, III, 408–410, no. 168.)

Muhamat, Sultan (variants: Mahamat, Mahmat): 1459 (no. 1), 1480 (no. 1). Muḥammad (Mehmet, Mehemmed) II, Fatih (1451–1481),

Ottoman sultan and conqueror of Constantinople. (See J. H. Kramers, "Muḥammad II," *EI*, OE, III, 658–660.)

Muhamat Mirza (variant: Mhamat): 1472 (no. 1). Muḥammad Mīrzā, son of the Ḳara-Ḳoyunlu Djihānshāh. (See C. Huart, "Ḳara-Ḳoyunlu," *EI*, OE, II, 741; *Chèref-Nâmeh*, II. 1, 485.)

Murat: 1453 (no. 3), 1457 (no. 2). Murād II (1421–1451), Ottoman sultan, son and successor of Muḥammad (Mehmet) I. He is especially noted for his organization of the Ottoman army. (See J. H. Kramers, "Murād II," *EI*, OE, II, 728–730.)

Murat Bēk: 1452 (no. 5). Murād Beg, son of the Aḳ-Ḳoyunlu Djihāngīr and great-grandson of Ḳara Yoluḳ 'Uthmān.

Murvat': 1468 (no. 6). A Muslim from the village of Č'uk'i, near the town of Gankřay (see App. C); he sold an Armenian MS. at Ankara.

Mxit'ar: 1341 (no. 3), 1346 (no. 1), 1350 (no. 1), 1354 (no. 2), 1356 (no. 1). Catholicos Mxit'ar I Gřnerc'i (1341–1355). (See Ōrmanean, *Azgapatum*, cols. 1287–1315.)

Nabugotonosor: 1386 (no. 2). Nebuchadnezzar, son and successor of Nabopolassar, founder of the Neo-Babylonian empire (604–561 B.C.). (See *Dictionary of Bible*, p. 693.)

Nabupałsar: 1389 (no. 1). Nabopolassar, founder of the Chaldean kingdom in 625 B.C. (See *Dictionary of Bible*, pp. 130, 693.)

Nałaš: 1469 (no. 5). *See* Mkrtič' Nałaš.

Nanik: 1386 (no. 1). Mother of Prince Smbat of Orotan in Siwnik' province. (See Ačaṙyan, *HAB*, IV, 21.)

Narekac'i: 1425 (no. 3). St. Grigor Narekac'i (of Narek); well-known medieval Armenian mystic poet. The text refers to his best-known work, *The Book of Lamentations*, which has been published in numerous editions. (See *Grégoire de Narek. Le Livre de prières*, trans. and ed. by Isaac Kéchichian, *Sources chrétiennes*, no. 78, Paris, 1961.)

Nasr: 1426 (no. 5). Probably Amīr Nāṣir al-Dīn Muḥammad of the Dhu'l-Ḳadrid Turkoman dynasty, who ruled from 1399 to 1442. (See J. H. Mordtmann—[V. L. Ménage], "Dhu'l-Ḳadr," *EI*, NE, II, 239–240.) He is mentioned in the text as the amir of Mārdīn, but the roster of the rulers of this town does not include anyone by that name.

Nasr, Sultan: 1337 (no. 2). Al-Malik al-Nāṣir Muḥammad (1293–1294, 1298–1308, 1309–1340), Mamluk sultan of Egypt of the Baḥri dynasty. (See Hitti, *Arabs*, p. 673.)

Nek'amat: 1449 (no. 1). Builder of the Armenian cathedral of Āmid. (See Ačaṙyan, *HAB*, IV, 71, no. 2; Ališan, *Hayapatum*, p. 574.)

Nersēs: 1303 (no. 5). Armenian prelate of the bishopric of Erzindjān. (See Ačaṙyan, *HAB*, IV, 53, no. 81.)

Nersēs: 1307 (no. 5), 1315 (no. 1), 1325 (no. 1), 1365 (no. 2), 1441 (no. 8), 1461 (no. 7). Catholicos Nersēs I Part'ew, the Great (353–373). During his incumbency, the Council of Aštišat, held in A.D. 354, adopted new regulations for reform of the administration of the Armenian church. He is also noted for the large number of religious, educational, and social institutions which he founded throughout Armenia. He met his death by poisoning at the instigation of King Pap who endeavored to bring the Armenian ecclesiastical institution under the control of the political authority. (See Ōrmanean, *Azgapatum*, cols. 116–154; Grousset, *Histoire de l'Arménie*, pp. 134–137.) The colophons refer to his vision. (See above, 1307, no. 5, n. 5.)

Nersēs: 1405 (no. 4). Catholicos Nersēs IV Šnorhali or Klayec'i (1166–1173). He is noted for the negotiations which he conducted for the union of the Armenian and Greek Orthodox churches. He is also the author of numerous literary works, including an elegy written on the occasion of the fall of Edessa to the Muslims in 1144. (See Awgerean, *Liakatar Vark' Srboc'*, V, 330–343; Ōrmanean, *Azgapatum*, cols. 961–992; *Patmut'iwn Varuc' S. Nersisi Šnorhalwoy—Sop'erk' Haykakank'*, no. XIV—Venice, 1854; Ł. Ališan, *Šnorhali ew Paragay Iwr*, Venice, 1873. Consult also John Avtaliantz, "Memoir of the Life and Writings of St. Nerses Clajensis, surnamed the Graceful, Pontiff of Armenia," in *Asiatic Society of Bengal, Journal*, Calcutta, 1836, 5: 129–157; "Elégie sur la prise d'Edesse," in Edouard Dulaurier, *Recueil des historiens des croisades, Documents arméniens*, Paris, 1869, vol. I, 223–268.)

Nersēs: 1453 (no. 2). Father of Aṙak'el Bałišec'i [q.v.].

Nersēs: 1464 (no. 3). Prelate of the Armenian bishopric of Ankara.

Nur-Alwand: 1450 (no. 2). This should probably read Nūr al-Ward (see Stanley Lane-Poole, *The Mohammedan Dynasties*, Paris, 1925, p. 175). According to the text, he attacked and plundered Ardjīsh; he is otherwise unidentified.

Nuradin: 1406 (no. 2). Armenian prince of Mākū; he belonged to the Catholic faith. His rule came to end in 1426, when he was removed from the fortress of Mākū by the Ḳara-Ḳoyunlu Iskandar. (See V. Minorsky, "Mākū," *EI*, OE, III, 180–182; Ačaṙyan, *HAB*, IV, 93, no. 5.)

Ohanēs: 1464 (no. 8). *See* Yohanēs (Alb.).

Ois: 1371 (no. 2). *See* Oyis.

Onorios: 1453 (nos. 2, 3). Emperor Honorius, son of Theodosius, who ruled in the west. (See Vasiliev, *History*, I, 66.)

Ošin: 1319 (no. 2). *See* Awšin, King.

Oyis (variants: Ois, Yois): 1362 (no. 1), 1422 (no. 1). Sulṭān Uwais, son of the Djalā'ir or Ilakān Shaykh Ḥasan Buzurg, whom he succeeded at Baghdad in 1356. He died on October 10, 1374. (See Spuler, *Mongolen in Iran*, p. 136; V. Minorsky, "Uwais I," *EI*, OE, IV, 1061–1062; J. M. Smith, Jr., "Djalāyir, Djalāyirid," *EI*, NE, II, 401–402; Bouvat, *L'Empire mongol*, p. 33.)

Ōłurlu: 1478 (no. 2). Oghurlu (Ughurlu) Muḥammad, eldest son of the Aḳ-Ḳoyunlu Uzun Ḥasan. (See V. Minorsky, "Uzun Ḥasan," *EI*, OE, IV, 1067, 1068; "Aḳ-Ḳoyunlu," *EI*, NE, I, 311–312; *Chèref-Nâmeh*, II. 1, 488–491; Bouvat, *L'Empire mongol*, p. 144.)

Ōt'man: 1425 (nos. 5, 10), 1432 (no. 5), 1435 (nos. 2, 3), 1470 (no. 3). *See* Awt'man.

Ōt'man: 1453 (no. 3). 'Uthman I, founder of the Ottoman dynasty. In the text, Aṙak'el Ankiwrac'i refers to Mehmet II Fatih as the *t'oṙn* of 'Uthmān. The term *t'oṙn* means grandson, granddaughter, grandchild; in the context, however, it is used in the sense of descendant. Mehmet II was actually the son of Murād II and the grandson of Muḥammad (Mehmet) I.

Ōzpēk: 1354 (no. 3). *See* Awzpēk.

Pak'il or Pak'iš: 1361 (no. 2). The reading of this name is uncertain (see Xač'ikyan, *XIV Dari*, p. 451, n. 1); I cannot identify him.

Pałtin: 1337 (no. 2). Armenian form of Baldwin; marshal in the Armenian kingdom of Cilicia and father of King Kostandin IV; he died in 1336. (See Ališan, *Sisuan*, pp. 149, 154, 412–413; *Hayapatum*, p. 112; Ačaṙyan, *HAB*, IV, 219–220, no. 6.)

Papa: 1453 (no. 3). Father of Ayvat [q.v.].

Papak': 1313 (no. 1). Brother of Ēač'i [q.v.]; prince of Vayoc'-Jor in Siwnik'. (See Ačaṙyan, *HAB*, IV, 225, no. 4.)

Pawłos: 1418 (no. 2), 1419 (nos. 1, 2), 1428 (no. 5). *See* Pōłos.

Pawsayit: 1330 (no. 1). *See* Abusait.

Payəndur (variant: Payəntur): 1476 (no. 8). Bayundur, the name of one of the Oghuz (Turkmen) tribes in the region of Diyarbakir in post-Mongol times which constituted the Aḳ-Ḳoyunlu federation, whose rulers belonged to the Bayundur tribe. (See Faruk Sümer, "Bayindir," *EI*, NE, I, 1133; V. Minorsky, "Aḳ-Ḳoyunlu," *ibid.* pp. 311–312.) The texts refer to Ḳara Yoluḳ (Yülük) 'Uthmān, the real founder of the Aḳ-Ḳoyunlu power, who is identified by his tribal name.

Payəntur: 1473 (no. 5), 1475 (no. 1). *See* Payəndur.

Paytamur: 1361 (no. 3). Mentioned as the amir of Aleppo.

Pelarłoy: 1307 (no. 6). *See* Pularłu.

Petros Xpaeanc': 1337 (no. 2). Baron and prince in the Armenian kingdom of Cilicia; he was dispatched by King Leon IV as an emissary to the amir of Aleppo. (See Ališan, *Sisuan*, p. 559; Ačaṙyan, *HAB*, IV, 251, no. 82.)

Pōłos (variant: Pawłos): 1419 (no. 5), 1421 (nos. 11, 12), 1425 (no. 11), 1426 (no. 5), 1427 (no. 2), 1428 (no. 3). Catholicos Pōłos II Gaṙnec'i (1418–1430). (See Ōrmanean, *Azgapatum*, cols. 1413–1426.)

Pōłos, Mahdasi: 1451 (no. 3). The commissioner of a Gospel MS. (See Ačaṙyan, *HAB*, IV, 281, no. 83.)

Pṙoš: 1332 (no. 2). An Armenian prince of the Xałbakean family; a great prince, who participated in the conquests of Hūlāgū Khān. His family was named after him Pṙōšean; he died in 1284. (See Yovsēp'ean, *Xałbakeank'*, pp. 85–136; Ališan, *Sisakan*, pp. 119–121, 137, 139, 140, 156, 174–176; *Hayapatum*, p. 529; Ačaṙyan, *HAB*, IV, 268–269, no. 2.)

Pularłu (variant: Pelarłoy): 1308 (no. 1). Būlārgī. (See Spuler, *Mongolen in Iran*, pp. 106–111.)

Pułtay: 1310 (no. 2). *See* Bułda.

Pusait: 1323 (no. 1), 1325 (no. 3), 1332 (nos. 1, 2), 1335 (no. 5). *See* Abusait.

Pusayid: 1335 (no. 4). *See* Abusait.

Pusayit: 1323 (no. 2), 1327 (no. 1). *See* Abusait.

Pusayit: 1470 (no. 1). *See* Busait.

Pusayit‘: 1471 (no. 6). *See* Busait.

P‘anos, Ṙayēs: 1371 (no. 3). An Armenian layman.

P‘ašay: 1451 (no. 5). A pious lady who commissioned a Gospel MS. at Van. (See Ačaṙyan, *HAB*, V, 186, no. 10.)

P‘awlat Łan: 1383 (no. 1). Probably Bulad Temür Khān of the Golden Horde. (See Spuler, *Goldene Horde*, p. 115; cf. Grekov and Yakubovsky, *Zolotaya Orda i ee padenie*, pp. 392–395.)

P‘ir Ali: 1438 (no. 1). Pīr ‘Alī, one of the amirs under vassalage of the Ḳara-Ḳoyunlu Djihānshāh; he held the fortress of Amuk, whence he raided the regions of Ardjīsh and Arckē. (See Xač‘ikyan, *XV Dari*, I, p. 797.)

P‘ir Bak (variant: P‘iri Pak): 1452 (no. 5). Pīr Beg; a general whom the Ḳara-Ḳoyunlu Djihānshāh sent to Āmid to help Djihāngīr against his brother Uzun Ḥasan.

P‘ir Bēk: 1445 (no. 1). *See* P‘iri Bēk.

P‘ir Hiwsēn: 1412 (no. 1). *See* P‘ir Husen.

P‘ir Husen (variants: P‘ir Hiwsēn, P‘iwr Husin): 1411 (no. 3). Pīr Ḥusayn; mentioned as the son of Sahat‘ [q.v.].

P‘ir Łaip: 1425 (no. 6). Probably Pīr Ghā’ib; mentioned as the grandson of Sahat‘ [q.v.].

P‘ir Putax: 1465 (nos. 5, 6). Pīr Budaḳ, son of the Ḳara-Ḳoyunlu Djihānshāh. In 1465 he rebelled against his father at Baghdad; after a year's siege Djihānshāh obtained by a ruse the submission of his son and put him to death. (See C. Huart, "Ḳara-Ḳoyunlu," *EI*, OE, II, 741; *Chèref-Nâmeh*, II. 1, 482, 483, 483–484.)

P‘iri Bēk (variant: P‘ir Bēk): 1433 (no. 1), 1436 (no. 2), 1440 (no. 2). Pīr Beg, grandson of ‘Izz al-Dīn Shīr of Hakkārī; he captured and plundered the island of Aghtamar in Lake Van.

P‘iri Pak: 1452 (no. 5). *See* P‘ir Bak.

P‘irumar: 1417 (no. 1). Pīr ‘Umar, one of the generals of the Ḳara-Ḳoyunlu Ḳara Yūsuf; he was killed by his kinsman Iskandar. (See L. Bouvat, "Shāhrukh Mīrzā," *EI*, OE, IV, 265–266; Xač‘ikyan, *XV Dari*, I, p. 797.)

P‘iwr Husin: 1414 (no. 1). *See* P‘ir Husen.

Ṙamatan: 1346 (no. 3), 1350 (no. 1). Ramaḍān, mentioned as governor and judge of Solghat (Solkhad) in the Crimea, during the reign of Djānībeg Khān of the Golden Horde.

Ṙap‘sak: 1337 (no. 2), 1468 (no. 3). Rab-shakeh, the title of an Assyrian officer who was sent by Sennacherib to Hezekiah to demand the surrender of Jerusalem. (See *Dictionary of Bible*, p. 830.)

Ṙastakēs: 1473 (no. 3). *See* Aristakēs.

Ṙəstakēs: 1471 (nos. 4, 11). *See* Aristakēs.
Ṙstakēs: 1465 (no. 4), 1468 (no. 3), 1469 (no. 7), 1471 (no. 7). *See* Aristakēs.
Ṙustam: 1452 (no. 5). *See* Ṙustam T'rxan- Awłli.
Ṙustam T'rxan-Awłli (variants: Ṙustam, Ṙust'am, T'arxan-Awłli, T'rxan-Awłli): 1452 (no. 5). Rustam Turkhān-oghlu, a general in the army of the Ḳara-Ḳoyunlu Djihānshāh, who participated in the struggles for power between the Aḳ-Ḳoyunlu brothers Uzun Ḥasan and Djihāngīr. He was seized and put to death by Uzun Ḥasan. (See Hakobyan, *Manr Žam.*, I, 168; II, 152.)
Ṙust'am: 1452 (no. 5). *See* Ṙustam T'rxan-Awłli.
Sahak, St. (variant: Isahak): 1325 (no. 1), 1410 (no. 1), 1411 (no. 4), 1441 (no. 1). Catholicos Sahak I Part'ew (387–436); during his incumbency, the Armenian alphabet was invented and the Bible was translated into Armenian. (See Ōrmanean, *Azgapatum*, cols. 179–225.) *See above*, 1307 (no. 5), note 6.
Sahat': 1414 (no. 1), 1425 (no. 6). An unidentified Muslim ruler, probably of the province of Ayrarat; mentioned as the father of Pīr Ḥusayn, and the grandfather of Pīr Ghā'ib and Awdul.
Sargis: 1473 (nos. 4, 9, 10), 1474 (nos. 4, 5), 1475 (no. 3), 1476 (nos. 3, 5, 6, 7), 1480 (no. 3). Catholicos Sargis II Ajatar (1469–1474). (See Ōrmanean, *Azgapatum*, cols. 1504–1505.)
Sargis Eznkac'i: 1478 (no. 2). Probably Catholicos Sargis II Ajatar. (See Ačaṙyan, *HAB*, IV, 451, no. 439.)
Sargis, St.: 1446 (no. 5). The legendary St. Sergius. (For the various traditions, see Ačaṙyan, *HAB*, IV, 402–404, no. 1.)
Sargis, Vardapet: 1464 (no. 3). A well-known pedagogue and prelate of the Armenians in the Crimea. (See Xač'ikyan, *XV Dari*, II, p. 570, no. 52; cf. Ačaṙyan, *HAB*, IV, 445–446, no. 377.)
Saribēk: 1432 (no. 1). The wife of Catur [q.v.].
Sawalan: 1452 (no. 5). Son of 'Alī Sheker (*see* Ališak'ar); one of the generals of the Ḳara-Ḳoyunlu Djihānshāh. In 1457 he was sent to Āmid to help Djihāngīr in the struggle against his brother Uzun Ḥasan; but, when Djihāngīr lost the battle, Sawalan was captured by Uzun Ḥasan.
Sełbestros: 1453 (no. 3). Pope Sylvester I (314–335), who was contemporary with Emperor Constantine I the Great. The spurious Donation of Constantine was supposedly given to Sylvester.
Sētali: 1459 (no. 2). Probably Sayyid 'Alī; an unidentified chief of the Rūzagī Kurdish tribe in Hakkārī.
Simēon: 1453 (no. 2). Simeon, the righteous and devout man who took the infant Jesus in his arms and blessed Him when He was presented in the Temple. (See Luke 2:25–35.)
Simēon Barip'aš: 1453 (no. 3). One of the Armenians brought by Sultan Mehmet II Fatih from Ankara to Istanbul. (See Ačaṙyan, *HAB*, IV, 511, no. 166.)
Sint'amur: 1318 (no. 1). Probably Sin Temür; mentioned as a Mongol tax-collector, otherwise unidentified.

Skandar: 1424 (no. 2). *See* Sk'andar.

Sk'andar (variants: Askandar, Askantar, Ǝsk'andar, Iskandar, Isk'andar, Isk'antar, Skandar, Sk'andar, Sk'antar): 1422 (no. 1), 1423 (no. 1), 1424 (nos. 1, 3), 1425 (nos. 1, 3, 6, 8), 1426 (nos. 2, 3), 1428 (nos. 1, 2, 5, 6), 1432 (no. 1), 1435 (no. 3), 1436 (nos. 3, 4), 1437 (no. 3), 1438 (nos. 1, 3, 4), 1440 (no. 3), 1445 (no. 1), 1458 (no. 1). Amīr Iskandar, eldest son and successor of the Ḳara-Ḳoyunlu Ḳara Yūsuf. He was murdered by his son Shāh-Ḳubād in the castle of Alindjak in 1437. (See C. Huart, "Ḳara-Ḳoyunlu," *EI*, OE, II, 741; V. Minorsky, "Tabrīz," *ibid.*, IV, 583–593; *Chèref-Nâmeh*, II. 1, 456, 458–459, 460; II. 2, 252, n. 985.)

Sk'antar: 1421 (no. 11), 1425 (no. 11), 1426 (no. 5), 1427 (no. 3), 1431 (no. 3), 1432 (nos. 3, 4), 1449 (no. 4). *See* Sk'andar.

Sk'antar, Baron: 1464 (no. 14). Iskandar; mentioned as the ruler of Kełi (see App. C), otherwise unidentified.

Smbat: 1386 (no. 1), 1401 (no. 2), 1406 (no. 1), 1412 (no. 1), 1417 (no. 1), 1419 (no. 2). Ōrbelean prince in Siwnik' province and son of Ivanē; mentioned as lord of Orotan (see App. C) and Tat'ew (see App. C), as well as of Uplistzikhé in Georgia. He died in 1421. (See Ališan, *Sisakan*, p. 96; Č'amč'ean, *Patmut'iwn*, III, 443; Ačaṙyan, *HAB*, IV, 562, no. 141.)

Sōlt'an Xalil: 1479 (no. 1). *See* Sultan Xalil.

Spandiar: 1422 (no. 1). Ispend or Espān; one of the sons of the Ḳara-Ḳoyunlu Ḳara Yūsuf, who deprived his brother, Shāh Muḥammad, of the governorship of the province of Baghdad and reigned in his place until his death in 1444. (See Faruk Sümer, "Kara-Koyunlular," *Islâm Ansiklopedisi*, VI, 299; C. Huart, "Ḳara-Ḳoyunlu," *EI*, OE, II, 741.)

Step'an: 1480 (no. 4). *See* Stap'annos, Cath.

Step'anos: 1313 (no. 3). Prelate of the Armenian bishopric of Sebastia [Sivas]. (See Ačaṙyan, *HAB*, IV, 638, no. 266.)

Step'anos: 1321 (no. 1). Son of J̌alal [q.v.]; a member of the Ōrbelean family and metropolitan bishop of Siwnik'. (See Xač'ikyan, *XIV Dari*, p. 746.)

Step'anos: 1361 (no. 1). This appears to be an abbot or bishop, and not a catholicos.

Step'anos: 1435 (no. 3). Prelate of the Armenian bishopric of Bitlīs; he gave refuge to the clergy and people whose towns were attacked by the Kurds. (See Ačaṙyan, *HAB*, IV, 658–659, no. 498.)

Step'anos: 1437 (no. 8). Mentioned as catholicos of the see of Aghtamar, but his identity is uncertain. (See Ačaṙyan, *HAB*, IV, 642, no. 312; p. 657, no. 481.) Catholicos Step'anos IV held the office during the years 1464–1489, while Step'anos III held it in the years 1336–1346.

Step'anos: 1464 (nos. 13, 14), 1465 (no. 7), 1470 (nos. 4, 5), 1471 (no. 1), 1474 (no. 6), 1475 (nos. 3, 6), 1476 (no. 11), 1478 (no. 5). *See* Step'annos, Cath.

Step'anos, Mahdasi: 1457 (no. 1). Recipient of a MS; he is said to have expended a large sum of money to rescue Armenian captives.

Step'anos, Vardapet: 1371 (no. 3). A member of the monastic order of Tēr Yuskan Ordi.

Step'anos Iwanē: 1419 (no. 2). Metropolitan bishop of Siwnik', son of Smbat [q.v.] and grandson of Ivanē. (See Ališan, *Sisakan*, p. 241; Č'amč'ean, *Patmut'iwn*, III, 471; Ačaṙyan, *HAB*, IV, 657, no. 483.)

Step'annos: 1340 (no. 1). Catholicos Step'annos III (1336–1346) of the Armenian see of Aghtamar. (See Akinean, *Gawazanagirk'*, pp. 58–63; Ačaṙyan, *HAB*, IV, 643, no. 320.)

Step'annos: 1451 (no. 3). Father of Mahdasi Pōłos, who commissioned a Gospel MS.; he was slain by the Muslims.

Step'annos P'ir: 1445 (no. 1). An Armenian churchman who spent many years as missionary in Asia Minor; he is known for his restoration of churches. (See Ačaṙyan, *HAB*, IV, 651, no. 408.)

Step'annos Vardapet: 1462 (no. 3). Son of the priest Yusik [q.v.]; he led a saintly life and died in 1251. He was buried in the monastery of Argelan [q.v.]. (See Ačaṙyan, *HAB*, IV, 620–621, no. 136.)

Step'annos, Cath. (variants: Step'an, Step'anos): 1466 (no. 6), 1468 (no. 1), 1469 (no. 2), 1470 (no. 3), 1474 (no. 5), 1476 (no. 12). Catholicos Step'annos IV (1464–1489) of the Armenian see of Aghtamar. (See Ōrmanean, *Azgapatum*, col. 1501; Akinean, *Gawazanagirk'*, pp. 109–119; Ačaṙyan, *HAB*, IV, 670, no. 635.)

Sulayiman Bahadur Xan: 1342 (no. 1). Sulaymān Bahādur Khān (1339–?); an Ilkhanid who figured in the struggle for succession after the death of Abū Sa'īd Khān. (See V. Minorsky, "Tabrīz," *EI*, OE, IV, 583–593; and "Ḥasan Küčük," *ibid.*, III, 280; Spuler, *Mongolen in Iran*, pp. 133–136.)

Sulayiman Xan: 1343 (no. 1). *See* Sulayiman Bahadur Xan.

Sulēyman: 1453 (no. 3). Sulaymān; an Ottoman official who is said to have been appointed by Sultan Mehmet II Fatih as governor of Istanbul in 1453.

Sulēyman: 1472 (no. 1). Sulaymān b. Bižan; a prominent general of the Aḳ-Ḳoyunlu ruler Uzun Ḥasan. (See *Chèref-Nâmeh*, II. 1, 262–265; Xač'ikyan, *XV Dari*, II, p. 573.)

Sulēyman, Amir: 1456 (no. 5), 1459 (no. 3). Amīr Sulaymān, a Kurdish ruler in the principality of Khizān. (See *Chèref-Nâmeh*, II. 1, 57.)

Sulēyman Pak: 1453 (no. 1). Sulaymān Beg, son of the Dhu'l-Ḳadrid Nāṣir al-Dīn Muḥammad, who succeeded him in 1442 as ruler of the regions of Marash-Malatya, Kayseri, and Kharput. He died in 1465. (See J. H. Mordtmann—[V. L. Ménage], "Dhu'l-Ḳadr," *EI*, NE, II, 239–240.) Xač'ikyan (see *XV Dari*, II, p. 573) refers to him erroneously as the sultan of Egypt.

Sultan Xalil (variants: Sōlt'an Xalil, Xalil Sultan): 1472 (no. 1), 1478 (no. 3). Sulṭān Khalīl, son of the Aḳ-Ḳoyunlu ruler Uzun Ḥasan, born of the latter's principal wife, Saldjūḳ-Shāh-Begum. In 1472 he was appointed governor of Shīrāz, and in 1478 he succeeded to his father's throne, but was soon killed and succeeded by his brother Ya'ḳūb. (See V. Minorsky, "Uzun Ḥasan," *EI*, OE, IV, 1065, 1066, 1068, 1069; *Chèref-Nâmeh*, II. 1, 489, 492.)

Sultanšay: 1451 (no. 5). Brother of P'ašay [q.v.]. (See Ačaṙyan, *HAB*, IV, 584, no. 5.)

Šahəṙux: 1430 (no. 2), 1437 (no. 1). *See* Šahṙux.

Šahruh: 1435 (no. 3). *See* Šahṙux.

Šahṙuh: 1432 (no. 1), 1438 (no. 3), 1445 (no. 1). *See* Šahṙux.

Šahṙuł: 1430 (no. 1). *See* Šahṙux.

Šahṙux (variants: Šahəṙux, Šahruh, Šahṙuh, Šahṙuł, Šałṙux, Šaxruh, Šaxṙuh, Šaxṙux): 1421 (nos. 1, 8), 1429 (no. 1), 1437 (no. 2), 1438 (nos. 1, 2), 1440 (no. 3), 1441 (no. 7), 1458 (no. 1). Shāhrukh Mīrzā (1404–1447), the fourth son of Tīmūr Lang and the first of the Tīmūrid sovereigns. (See Bouvat, *L'Empire mongol*, pp. 96–122; L. Bouvat, "Shāhrukh Mīrzā," *EI*, OE, IV, 265–266; "Tīmūrids," *ibid.*, pp. 779–780.)

Šah-Suar: 1468 (no. 4). Shāhsuwār (A.H. 872–77; A.D. 1467/8–1472/3), a member of the Dhu'l-Ḳadrid family. He was executed by the Mamluks at Cairo in 1472. (See J. H. Mordtmann—[V. L. Ménage], "Dhu'l-Ḳadr," *EI*, NE, II, 239–240; R. Anhegger, "Adana," *ibid.*, I, 182–183; M. Canard, "Cilicia," *ibid.*, II, 34–39.)

Šałṙux: 1421 (no. 9), 1428 (no. 1), 1436 (no. 1). *See* Šahṙux.

Šaməzdin (variants: Šəməzdin, Šmzdin): 1422 (no. 1). Shams al-Dīn, son of Ḥadjdjī Sharaf; Kurdish amir of the principality of Bitlīs. He was slain by the Ḳara-Ḳoyunlu Iskandar in 1424. (See *Chèref-Nâmeh*, II. 1, 249–253; II. 2, 252 n. 985.)

Šamsadin (variants: Šamšadin, Šməzdin): 1454 (no. 5). Shams al-Dīn, surnamed Dushevār (the Inflexible), a Kurdish ruler of the principality of Bitlīs. According to the texts, he was chosen by the amirs to replace his insane uncle Shaykh Maḥmūd in 1445 or 1446. But Sharaf al-Dīn (see *Chèref-Nâmeh*, II. 1, 256–262) claims that after the death of Amīr Sharaf anarchy prevailed in the principality, and that eventually his son Shams al-Dīn triumphed (hence the name Dushevār) and reigned as undisputed ruler.

Šamšadin: 1445 (no. 3), 1455 (no. 2). *See* Šamsadin.

Šapan: 1428 (no. 6). Mentioned as the householder in the village of Ankełakut' (see App. C); otherwise unidentified.

Šaraf: 1458 (no. 5), 1459 (no. 8), 1460 (no. 12), 1462 (no. 3), 1463 (nos. 2, 3), 1467 (no. 2). Amīr or Malik Sharaf, mentioned in the texts as Kurdish ruler of the principality of Bitlīs. Cf. *Chèref-Nâmeh*, II. 1, 262–265, which asserts that Amīr Ibrāhīm, son of Amīr Ḥadjdjī Muḥammad, was the ruler of the same principality during the period in question.

Šaxruh: 1421 (no. 5). *See* Šahṙux.

Šaxṙuh: 1422 (no. 1). *See* Šahṙux.

Šaxṙux: 1435 (no. 4). *See* Šahṙux.

Šex: 1419 (no. 5). Al-Mu'ayyad Shaykh (1412–1421), Mamluk Sultan of Egypt of the Burji dynasty. (See Hitti, *Arabs*, pp. 694–695.)

Šex Bayazit': 1426 (no. 4). Shaykh Bāyazīd, one of the sons of the Djalā'irid Sultan Uwais I. In A.H. 784–785 (A.D. 1382/3–1383/4) he carved a fief for himself out of Persian Kurdistan and 'Irāḳ 'Adjamī. (See J. M. Smith, Jr., "Djalāyir, Djalāyirid," *EI*, NE, II, 401–402; V. Minorsky, "Uwais I," *EI*, OE, IV, 1061–1062; "Kurds," *ibid.*, II, 1141.)

Šex Hasan: 1331 (no. 1), 1354 (no. 2). Shaykh Ḥasan Buzurg, son of Ḥasayn Gurgān. He was appointed by the Ilkhan Abū Sa'īd as governor of Asia Minor. Subsequent to Abū Sa'īd's death in 1335, Buzurg played an important role in the struggle for the throne and was instrumental in the breakdown of the Ilkhanid empire. He finally established himself at Baghdad in 1339–40, where he founded the Djalā'irid dynasty; and he reigned there until his death in 1356. (See "Ḥasan Buzurg," *EI*, OE, III, 279–280; J. M. Smith, Jr., "Djalāyir, Djalāyirid," *EI*, NE, II, 401–402; R. M. Savory, "Čūbānids (Čobanids)," *ibid.*, II, 67–68; *Chèref-Nâmeh*, II. 1, 389, 396, 401, 405; Bouvat, *L'Empire mongol*, pp. 29, 33.)

Šex Hasan: 1341 (no. 2), 1342 (no. 1), 1354 (no. 2). Shaykh Ḥasan Küčük (Little Ḥasan), so-called to distinguish him from his contemporary and rival Shaykh Ḥasan Buzurg. He was the son of the Čūbānid Tīmūrtash and grandson of Amīr Čūbān. He was murdered, on December 15, 1343, by his wife, 'Izzat Malik. (See "Ḥasan Küčük," *EI*, OE, III, 280; R. M. Savory, "Čūbānids (Čobanids)," *EI*, NE, II, 67–68; *Chèref-Nâmeh*, II. 1, 392–393, 396, 398; Spuler, *Mongolen in Iran*, pp. 131–135, 145, 196, 347, 355.)

Šex Hasan: 1446 (no. 5). Shaykh Ḥasan; mentioned in the text as the ruler of the fortress of Kemakh, otherwise unidentified.

Šex Mahmat: 1438 (no. 4), 1446 (no. 1). *See* Šex Mahmud.

Šex Mahmud (variants: Šex Mahmat, Šex Mahmut, Šix Mahmat): 1445 (no. 3). Shaykh Maḥmūd, a Kurdish amir of the principality of Bitlīs. The texts assert that he was deposed in 1445 or 1446 by the Kurdish chiefs on the grounds of insanity, and that he was replaced by his nephew, Shams al-Dīn. In contrast, Sharaf al-Dīn claims that the insane ruler was Amīr Sharaf who died in office, and that his only son, Shams al-Dīn, was too young to succeed him immediately after his death. (See *Chèref-Nâmeh*, II. 1, 256–257.)

Šex Mahmut: 1436 (no. 3). *See* Šex Mahmud.

Šəməzdin: 1428 (no. 1). *See* Šaməzdin.

Šēranšah: 1471 (no. 8). Shīrwānshāh Farrukh Yasār (1462–1501), son and successor of Sultan Khalīl Allāh, both of whom ruled in Shīrwān. (See W. Barthold, "Shīrwānshāh," *EI*, OE, IV, 385; *Chèref-Nâmeh*, II. 2, 409–410, n. 299.)

Šix Mahmat: 1443 (no. 2). *See* Šex Mahmud.

Šməzdin: 1446 (no. 1). *See* Šamsadin.

Šmzdin: 1428 (no. 1). *See* Šaməzdin.

Tahir: 1400 (no. 1), 1422 (no. 1). Sulṭān Tāhir Djalā'ir, son of the Djalā'irid Sulṭān Aḥmad of Baghdād. (See J. M. Smith, Jr., "Djalāyir, Djalāyirid," *EI*, NE, II, 401–402; V. Minorsky, "Tiflis," *EI*, OE, IV, 752–763.)

Tahir: 1446 (no. 6), 1469 (no. 6). Al-Malik al-Ẓāhir Sayf al-Dīn, Čaḳmaḳ (1438–1453), Mamluk sultan of Egypt of the Burji dynasty. (See M. Sobernheim, "Čaḳmaḳ," *EI*, NE, II, 6.) *See also* Č'axmax.

Tamurtaš: 1338 (no. 1). The false Tīmūrtash. *See* T'amurt'aš.

Tarsaič: 1306 (no. 3). Ōrbelean prince in Siwnik', mentioned as great atabeg of Armenia and Georgia; father of the historian Step'anos Ōrbelean. He died in 1290. (See Brosset, *Siounie*, II, 182.)

Tarsayič: 1419 (no. 2). Son of Gugun [q.v.].

Tayir: 1310 (no. 1), 1335 (no. 4). Son of the Armenian prince K'urd [q.v.] of the fortress of Anberd.

Trdat: 1453 (no. 2), 1462 (no. 3). King Tiridates III of Armenia who, after his conversion at the hands of St. Gregory the Illuminator, proclaimed Christianity as the official religion of Armenia. (See Ōrmanean, *Azgapatum*, cols. 44–81; Langlois, *Collection*, I, 97–200.)

T'adēos, Priest: 1409 (no. 3). Recipient of a Gospel MS. (See Ačaṙyan, *HAB*, II, 251–252, no. 56.)

T'amar: 1462 (no. 2). Queen Tamara, wife of King Alexander I (1412–1443) of Georgia.

T'amur: 1336 (no. 4). This appears to be Tugha (Togha) Tīmūr, the Mongol governor of Khurāsān, who figured in the struggle for the throne after the death of the Ilkhān Abū Sa'īd in 1335. (See articles "Ḥasan Buzurg" and "Ḥasan Küčük," *EI*, OE, III, 279–280.)

T'amur: 1388 (no. 2), 1391 (no. 1), 1395 (no. 2), 1397 (no. 1), 1400 (nos. 2, 4, 5), 1401 (nos. 1, 4, 6, 7), 1403 (nos. 1, 2, 3, 4), 1404 (nos. 1, 2), 1405 (nos. 2, 3, 4), 1407 (nos. 2, 4), 1410 (no. 2), 1411 (no. 1), 1417 (no. 1), 1422 (no. 1), 1435 (no. 4), 1437 (no. 1), 1438 (no. 2). *See* Lank-T'amur.

T'amur-Lang: 1397 (no. 2), 1400 (no. 2). *See* Lank-T'amur.

T'amur-Lank: 1388 (nos. 1, 3), 1400 (no. 1), 1401 (nos. 2, 5), 1402 (no. 1). *See* Lank-T'amur.

T'amurt'aš (variants: Damurtaš, Tamurtaš): 1342 (no. 1). This text refers to Tīmūrtash or Demirtash, the second son of Amīr Čūbān, who during the reign of the Ilkhān Abū Sa'īd was appointed governor of Anatolia (1316). After Abū Sa'īd put his brother Dimashḳ Khwādja to death (August 1327), Tīmūrtash fled to Egypt, where the Mamluk Sultan al-Nāṣir Muḥammad put him to death on August 21, 1328. (See Spuler, *Mongolen in Iran*, pp. 121–126; see also I. H. Uzunçarşili, "Ashraf Oghullarî," *EI*, NE, I, 702–704; V. F. Büchner, "Sīs," *EI*, OE, IV, 453–455; R. M. Savory, "Čūbānids (Čobanids)," *EI*, NE, II, 67–68; *Chèref-Nâmeh*, II. 1, 385; II. 2, 373, n. 178.) On the other hand, the texts of 1338 (nos. 1, 2) refer to the false or impostor Tīmūrtash.

After the death of the Ilkhan Abū Sa'īd (1335), the Čūbānid Ḥasan Küčük, who had remained in hiding in Asia Minor, pretended that his father Tīmūrtash had not been slain in Egypt; rather, he had escaped from prison and had arrived in Asia Minor. He made a Turkish slave play the part of his father. He almost fell a victim to his guile, for his pretended father tried to dispose of him by assassination. In the end, Ḥasan succeeded in disposing of the false Tīmūrtash. (See Spuler, *Mongolen in Iran*, p. 131; "Ḥasan Küčük," *EI*, OE, III, 280.)

T'arxan-Awłli: 1452 (no. 5). *See* Ṙustam T'rxan-Awłli.

T'awak'al: 1400 (no. 5). A well-to-do Armenian householder in Aleppo who recovered a Gospel MS. at Antep. (See Xač'ikyan, *XV Dari*, I, p. 703, no. 1.)

T'awxt'amiš (variant: T'uxt'amiš): 1384 (no. 1). Toḳtamîsh or Tokhtamîsh Khān (1377–1395) of the White Horde. (See Grekov and Yakubovsky, *Zolotaya Orda i ee padenie*, pp. 336–373; W. Barthold, "Toḳtamîsh," *EI*, OE, IV, 807–809; B. Spuler, "Batu'ids," *EI*, NE, I, 1106–1108; Pelliot, *Notes sur l'histoire*, pp. 70 and 71; *Chèref-Nâmeh*, II. 1, 422, 423, 427; Spuler, *Goldene Horde*.)

T'ēmur-Lank: 1405 (no. 1). *See* Lank-T'amur.

T'ēodoros (variant: T'oros): 1386 (no. 2), 1392 (no. 3), 1393 (no. 1). Catholicos T'ēodoros II Kilikec'i (1382–1392), who was treacherously slain by Malik 'Umar. (See Ōrmanean, *Azgapatum*, cols. 1354–1373.)

T'ēodos: 1453 (nos. 2, 3.) Emperor Theodosius I. (See Vasiliev, *History*, I, 43, 66, 67, 79–83, 87, 88.)

T'ēodos P'ok'r: 1453 (no. 3). Emperor Theodosius II the Younger (408–450). (See Vasiliev, *History*, I, esp. 96–104.)

T'orgoma Meci: 1333 (no. 1). Torgoma or Togarmah the Great, one of the legendary ancestors of the Armenian people.

T'oros: 1307 (no. 6). King Toros III (1293–1298) of the Armenian kingdom of Cilicia. (See Rüdt-Collenberg, *Rupenides*, pp. 16, 22.)

T'oros: 1367 (no. 1). Grand marshal in the Armenian kingdom of Cilicia, and father of Liparit [q.v.]. (See Rüdt-Collenberg, *Rupenides*, p. 73.)

T'oros: 1393 (no. 1). *See* T'ēodoros.

T'ovma Mecop'ec'i: 1438 (no. 1). A well-known medieval Armenian churchman; abbot of the monastery of Mecop' and pedagogue in its school. He is the editor of a number of philosophical works, and the author of a history of Tīmūr Lang and of a work describing the circumstances which led to the transfer of the Armenian pontificate from Sis to Etchmiadzin in 1441, in which he played a leading role. (See Félix Nève, "Etude sur Thomas de Medzoph, et sur son histoire de l'Arménie au XVe siècle," *Journal Asiatique*, Paris, 1855, series 5, 6: 221–281; Nève, "Exposé des guerres de Tamerlan et de Schah-Rokh dans l'Asie occidentale, d'après la chronique arménienne inédite de Thomas de Medzoph," in *Académie royale des sciences, des lettres et des beaux-arts de Belgique. Mémoires couronnés*, Brussels, 1861, vol. 11, no. 4.)

T'rxan-Awłli: 1452 (no. 5). *See* Ṙustam T'rxan-Awłli.

T'umay: 1471 (no. 8). Catholicos of the Caucasian Albanian church.

T'umay, Priest: 1371 (no. 3). An Armenian priest.

T'umay K'ahanay: 1451 (no. 3). Brother of Mahdasi Pōłos, who commissioned a Gospel MS. (See Ačaṙyan, *HAB*, II, 333, no. 157.)

T'uxt'amiš: 1422 (no. 1). *See* T'awxt'amiš.

Uayis (variant: Uyanis): 1452 (no. 5). Uwais of Ruhā, brother of the Aḳ-Ḳoyunlu rulers Uzun Ḥasan and Djihāngīr. He was slain in A.H. 880 (A.D. 1475/6) by the troops of Uzun Ḥasan. (See V. Minorsky, "Uzun Ḥasan," *EI*, OE, IV, 1065, 1067.)

Usep': 1436 (no. 5). *See* Łara Yusuf.

Usf: 1409 (no. 1). *See* Łara Yusuf.

Usuf: 1414 (no. 3), 1417 (nos. 1, 4), 1418 (no. 4), 1419 (no. 2), 1422 (no. 1), 1425 (no. 6), 1426 (no. 3), 1427 (no. 2), 1441 (no. 1), 1443 (nos. 1, 4), 1449 (nos. 3, 4), 1452 (no. 3), 1457 (no. 3), 1458 (no. 1), 1460 (nos. 1, 2), 1464 (no. 2), 1465 (no. 3). *See* Łara Yusuf.

Usup': 1411 (no. 3), 1414 (no. 1), 1447 (no. 2), 1451 (no. 4), 1471 (no. 3). *See* Łara Yusuf.

Uyanis: 1452 (no. 5). *See* Uayis.

Uzun Hasan (variants: Hasan, Xasan): 1454 (no. 2), 1467 (nos. 4, 7), 1469 (no. 1), 1470 (no. 2), 1471 (nos. 3, 4, 11), 1473 (nos. 1, 4), 1474 (no. 6), 1477 (no. 1), 1480 (no. 1). Uzun Ḥasan Bayundur (1453–1478), a ruler of the Aḳ-Ḳoyunlu Turkoman dynasty, son of 'Alī and grandson of Ḳara Yūsuf. He began his career as prince of Diyarbakir and eventually became sovereign of a powerful state comprising Armenia, Mesopotamia, and Persia. (See Bouvat, *L'Empire mongol*, pp. 89, 90, 143–145, 185–191; V. Minorsky, "Uzun Ḥasan," *EI*, OE, IV, 1065–1069; "Aḳ-Ḳoyunlu," *EI*, NE, I, 311–312; C. Huart, "Ḳara-Ḳoyunlu," *EI*, OE, II, 741; V. Minorsky, "Tiflis," *ibid.*, IV, 752–763; *Chèref-Nâmeh*, II. 1, 484–485, 488–489, 490–492.)

Vač'ē: 1335 (no. 4). This appears to be the founder of the Vač'utean Armenian princely family. (See Ačaṙyan, *HAB*, V, 40–41, no. 12.)

Vahram: 1376 (no. 1). Husband of Fimi, who purchased a Gospel MS. at Ayas. (See Ačaṙyan, *HAB*, V, 28, no. 84.)

Vałt'ank: 1443 (nos. 5, 6). *See* Vaxtang.

Vasak: 1307 (no. 6). An Armenian prince in Cilicia who was slain by Būlārgī in 1307.

Vasak: 1332 (no. 2). Grandson of Pṙoš [q.v.].

Vasak: 1453 (no. 1). Armenian prince of the province of Siwnik', known in Armenian history as a traitor, since he sided with the Persians in the Armeno-Persian war of A.D. 451. (See "Élisée Vartabed; Histoire de Vartan et de la guerre des arméniens," in Langlois, *Collection*, II, 177–251; *Yeghisheh*, New York, 1952, English and Armenian texts.)

Vasil: 1337 (no. 2). Clerk or secretary of King Leon IV of Cilicia. He was dispatched as an emissary to Egypt to negotiate a peace with the Mamluk sultan. (See Ališan, *Hayapatum*, pp. 537, 539; *Sisuan*, pp. 149, 260, 412; Ačaṙyan, *HAB*, V, 60, no. 59.)

Vaxax: 1349 (no. 1). Wife of Ōrbelean Burt‘el, and mother of Bešk‘en [q.v.] and Iwanē [q.v.].

Vaxtang (variants: Vałt‘ank, Vaxt‘ank): 1443 (no. 4). King Wakhtang IV (1443–1446) of Georgia, son and successor of Alexander I. (See Manvelichvili, *Histoire*, p. 255.)

Vaxt‘ank: 1442 (no. 1). *See* Vaxtang.

Višel: 1465 (no. 3). Mentioned as the overseer of the region of Ełivard (see App. C). (See Ačaṙyan, *HAB*, V, 122.)

Xač‘atur, Priest: 1371 (no. 3). An Armenian priest.

Xalil: 1472 (no. 1). Ṣufī Khalīl, one of the principal generals of the Aḳ-Ḳoyunlu Uzun Ḥasan. (See V. Minorsky, "Tiflis," *EI*, OE, IV, 752–763; "Kurds," *ibid.*, II, 1142; "Uzun Ḥasan," *ibid.*, IV, 1066; *Chèref-Nâmeh*, I. 2, 118; II. 1, 493.)

Xalil Pēk: 1471 (no. 8). Khalīl Allāh (1417–1462), sultan of Shīrwān, of the Shīrwānshāh family. (See V. Minorsky, "Shīrwānshāh," *EI*, OE, IV, 385; C. Huart, "Ḥaidar (Shaikh Ḥaidar)," *ibid.*, III, 218; *Chèref-Nâmeh*, II. 1, 456–457; II. 2, 409–410, n. 299.)

Xalil Sultan: 1478 (no. 3). *See* Sultan Xalil.

Xalim-Xat‘un: 1465 (no. 6). The wife of an Armenian merchant from Ardjīsh.

Xamuš: 1456 (no. 2). One of the purchasers of a Gospel MS.

Xara Usuf: 1416 (no. 2). *See* Łara Yusuf.

Xarband: 1313 (no. 1), 1325 (no. 3). *See* Xarbanda.

Xarbanda (variants: Łarapand, Łarbandałul, Łarpanta, Xarband, Xarbanday, Xarpand, Xarpanda, Xarpandawłəl, Xarpandawłul, Xarpanday, Xarpant, Xarvand): 1307 (no. 1). Ilkhān Olčaitu (Uldjāytu, Öldjaytü) Khudābanda (1304–1316) of Persia, son of Arghūn Khān and a great-grandson of Hūlāgū Khān. The surname of Kharbanda, which was given to him in his youth, has given rise to various explanations (see the poem by Rashīd al-Dīn reproduced in Browne, *A Literary History of Persia*, III, 46 sq.; Ibn Baṭṭūṭā, *Voyages d'Ibn Batouta*, II, 115; Blochet, *Introduction à l'histoire des Mongols*, XII, 51; Pachymeres, *De Michaele et Andronico Palaeologis*, II, 459, who calls him Karmpantes; d'Ohsson, *Histoire des Mongols*, IV, 481). After embracing Islam, Olčaitu adopted the name Muḥammad, and at the same time changed his surname to Khudābanda (a form which does not appear in any of the colophons). (See Spuler, *Mongolen in Iran*; *Goldene Horde*, pp. 81–84; J. H. Kramers, "Olčaitu Khudābanda," *EI*, OE, III, 974–975; *Chèref-Nâmeh*, II. 1, 371–372, 376, 378; also Mostaert and Cleaves, *Les Lettres des ilkhan Aryun et Öljeitü à Philippe le Bel.*) *See also* Awlǰat‘u.

Xarbanday: 1312 (no. 1). *See* Xarbanda.

Xarpand: 1304 (no. 6). *See* Xarbanda.

Xarpanda: 1314 (no. 1). *See* Xarbanda.

Xarpandawłəl: 1304 (no. 5), 1308 (no. 2). *See* Xarbanda.

Xarpandawłul: 1316 (no. 1). *See* Xarbanda.

Xarpanday: 1304 (no. 4), 1307 (no. 4). *See* Xarbanda.
Xarpant: 1306 (no. 3). *See* Xarbanda.
Xarvand: 1310 (no. 2). *See* Xarbanda.
Xasan: 1473 (no. 9), 1475 (no. 4). *See* Uzun Hasan.
Xazan: 1303 (nos. 3, 4, 6). *See* Łazan.
Xočay Yali: 1355 (no. 1). Probably Khoja 'Alī; an unidentified ruler who is said to have besieged Erzindjān.
Xošładam: 1435 (no. 2). Mentioned as a *nā'ib*, probably of Çemişkezek; it appears that he was an Armenian.
Xoyan Xat'un: 1335 (no. 4). Wife of the prince K'urd [q.v.].
Xul: 1439 (no. 1). A general who is said to have invaded the canton of Ekełeac' (see App. C) in 1439 with 100,000 troops; otherwise unidentified.
Xut'lupak: 1450 (no. 3). Ḳuṭlu Beg, mentioned as the master of Erzindjān; otherwise unidentified.
Yakob: 1330 (no. 1), 1333 (no. 3), 1335 (no. 2), 1337 (no. 3). *See* Yakovb.
Yakob: 1392 (no. 1). He brought a MS. to Van from Aghtamar; he was slain by Turkish horsemen at Narek (see App. C).
Yakob: 1414 (nos. 3, 4). Catholicos Yakob II Ssec'i. According to the chronology of Ōrmanean (see *Azgapatum*, cols. 1395, 1405) he reigned from 1404 to 1411, but the texts refer to him as late as the year 1414.
Yakob: 1453 (no. 2). The Vardapet Yakob Łrimec'i, known as the author of calendrical, grammatical, and other literary works. He also served as a scribe to Aṙak'el Bałišec'i [q.v.].
Yakovb (variant: Yakob): 1327 (nos. 1, 2), 1329 (no. 2), 1331 (no. 2), 1332 (no. 2), 1336 (nos. 3, 5), 1338 (no. 1). Catholicos Yakob II Tarsonac'i or Anawarzec'i (1327–41, 1355–59). (See Ōrmanean, *Azgapatum*, cols. 1272–1286, 1316–1320.)
Yarat'in (variant: Yorat'nay): 1343 (no. 1). Eretna, an Uyghur chief whom the Ilkhan Abū Sa'īd appointed governor in Asia Minor under the general suzerainty of Shaykh Ḥasan Buzurg. He later appears (after 1340) as an independent sovereign over all those territories of central Asia Minor which the Turkoman principalities that arose after the breakdown of the Seljuk-Mongol regime had not divided among themselves, with his capital first at Sīwās [Sivas] and then at Kayseri. He died in 1352, leaving his principality to his son Ghiyāth al-Dīn Muḥammad. (See C. Cahen, "Eretna," *EI*, OE, II, 705–707; Fr. Taeschner, "Amasya," *ibid.*, I, 431–432, and "Anḳara," *ibid.*, I, 509–511; J. M. Smith, Jr., "Djalāyir, Djalāyirid," *ibid.*, II, 401–402; R. Hartmann—[Fr. Taeschner], "Erzindjan," *ibid.*, II, 711–712; Spuler, *Mongolen in Iran*, pp. 134, 355.)
Yašēx T'amur: 1375 (no. 2). Ašiq Temür al-Māridānī, Mamluk governor of Aleppo, 1363–1365, 1371–1376. (See E. de Zambaur, *Manuel de Généalogie et de Chronologie pour l'histoire de l'Islam*, Hanover, 1927, p. 35.)
Yaxiayna: 1355 (no. 1). Mentioned as the ruler of Erzindjān; otherwise unidentified.

Yayłup: 1478 (no. 3). *See* Ałup.
Yesayi: 1332 (no. 2). *See* Esayi (Nč'ec'i).
Yohan Orotnec'i Kaxik: 1445 (no. 1). *See* Yovhannēs Orotnec'i.
Yohanēs: 1428 (no. 4). An Armenian at Arckē (see App. C) who gave shelter to the scribe Karapet.
Yohanēs: 1428 (no. 7). Probably a catholicos of the Caucasian Albanian church. (See Ačaṙyan, *HAB*, III, 647, no. 861.)
Yohanēs: 1437 (no. 9). An Armenian bishop who sold a MS.
Yohanēs: 1475 (no. 4), 1476 (no. 10). *See* Yovhannēs, Cath.
Yohanēs (Alb.) (variant: Ohanēs): 1466 (no. 3). Catholicos of the Caucasian Albanian church. (See Ačaṙyan, *HAB*, III, 675–676, no. 1148.)
Yohannēs: 1421 (no. 7). Brother of Karapet, the author of col. 1421 (no. 7).
Yohannēs: 1463 (no. 1). Bishop and abbot of the Armenian monastery of St. Karapet at Muš [Mush]; he was slain by the Muslims in 1463. (See Xač'ikyan, *XV Dari*, II, p. 194, note, and p. 545, no. 170; *Hayoc' Nor Vkanerə*, pp. 299–304.)
Yois: 1361 (no. 1). *See* Ois.
Yorat'nay: 1346 (no. 1). *See* Yarat'in.
Yovanēs: 1425 (no. 2). An Armenian householder who recovered a MS.
Yovanēs: 1464 (no. 12). He recovered a Gospel MS.
Yovanēs: 1479 (no. 2). *See* Yovhannēs, Cath.
Yovanēs Urpel (variant: Yovhanēs): 1310 (no. 2). A member of the Ōrbelean family, son of Liparit and metropolitan bishop of Siwnik'. (See Yovsēp'ean, *Xałbakeank'*, pp. 187–188; Ališan, *Sisakan*, pp. 181, 194, 198; Ačaṙyan, *HAB*, III, 609–610, no. 477.)
Yovannēs K'ahanay: 1449 (no. 1). Brother of Mkrtič' Nałaš [q.v.]. (See Ačaṙyan, *HAB*, III, 676, no. 1157.)
Yovhanēs: 1321 (no. 1). *See* Yovanēs Urpel.
Yovhanēs: 1476 (no. 8). *See* Yovhannēs, Cath.
Yovhannēs: 1453 (no. 2). Son of Aṙak'el Bałišec'i [q.v.].
Yovhannēs, Cath. (variants: Yohanēs, Yovanēs, Yovhanēs): 1477 (no. 7), 1478 (no. 2). Catholicos Yovhannēs VII Ajakir (1474–1484) of Etchmiadzin. (See Ōrmanean, *Azgapatum*, cols. 1507, 1511, 1513–1514.)
Yovhannēs Orotnec'i (variant: Yohan Orotnec'i Kaxik): 1386 (no. 1). A well-known medieval Armenian pedagogue, and author of many religious, theological, and philosophical works; he was a staunch opponent of the Fratres Unitores Catholic missionaries in Armenia. (See Ačaṙyan, *HAB*, III, 628–629, no. 652.)
Yovhannēs Oskeberan: 1453 (no. 2). John Chrysostom, Patriarch of Constantinople (398–404). (See P. Chrysostomus Baur, *Der heilige Johannes Chrysostomus und seine Zeit*, Munich, 1929–1930; L. S. Meyer, *Jean Chrysostome, maître de perfection chrétienne*, Paris, 1933; S. Attwater, *St. John Chrysostom*, Milwaukee, 1939; A. de Albornez, *Juan Chrisostomo y su influencia social en el imperio bizantino*, Madrid, 1934; Vasiliev, *History*, I, 94–96.)

Yōhanēs, Xoǰay: 1465 (no. 6). An Armenian merchant at Ardjīsh; he was slain by bandits at Iṣfahān.

Yōvsēp', Priest: 1371 (no. 3). An Armenian priest.

Yusik, Priest: 1462 (no. 3). Father of Step'annos Vardapet [q.v.].

Yusov: 1420 (no. 3). *See* Łara Yusuf.

Yustinianos (variant: Ustianos): 1453 (no. 3). Emperor Justinian I, the Great. (See Vasiliev, *History*, I.)

Yusuf: 1411 (no. 2), 1418 (no. 3), 1421 (nos. 3, 5), 1437 (no. 1), 1444 (no. 1). *See* Łara Yusuf.

Yusup': 1407 (no. 4), 1443 (nos. 5, 6). *See* Łara Yusuf.

Zak'ar: 1437 (no. 3). *See* Zak'aria, III.

Zak'arē: 1304 (no. 5), 1308 (no. 2). *See* Zak'aria, I.

Zak'aria: 1386 (no. 2), 1387 (no. 2), 1392 (nos. 2, 3), 1393 (no. 1), 1400 (no. 2), 1401 (no. 5), 1402 (no. 1), 1421 (no. 13). Catholicos Zak'aria II (1369–1393) of the Armenian see of Aghtamar. (See Akinean, *Gawazanagirk'*, pp. 67–70; Ačaṙyan, *HAB*, II, 188, no. 46; Ōrmanean, *Azgapatum*, col. 1376.)

Zak'aria, I (variant: Zak'arē): 1301 (no. 1), 1304 (no. 2), 1306 (nos. 1, 2, 4), 1307 (no. 3), 1310 (no. 3), 1316 (no. 1), 1318 (nos. 1, 2, 4), 1319 (no. 3), 1320 (no. 2), 1327 (no. 1), 1330 (no. 2), 1331 (no. 3), 1333 (no. 4), 1335 (no. 3), 1337 (no. 3). Catholicos Zak'aria I Sefedinean (1296–1336) of the Armenian see of Aghtamar, younger brother and successor of Catholicos Step'annos III Tłay. (See Akinean, *Gawazanagirk'*, pp. 45–58; Ōrmanean, *Azgapatum*, cols. 1203, 1281; Ačaṙyan, *HAB*, II, 185–186, no. 29.)

Zak'aria, III (variant: Zak'ar): 1419 (no. 3), 1436 (no. 2), 1444 (nos. 2, 4, 5, 6), 1445 (no. 1), 1449 (no. 2), 1451 (nos. 3, 5), 1452 (no. 4), 1454 (nos. 1, 3, 6), 1455 (nos. 3, 4, 5), 1456 (no. 5), 1458 (no. 6), 1459 (nos. 2, 9), 1460 (nos. 9, 13), 1461 (nos. 3, 5), 1462 (nos. 3, 4, 5, 6, 7, 8), 1463 (nos. 1, 3, 4, 5, 6, 8, 10, 12), 1464 (nos. 4, 6, 7, 11, 12, 13). Catholicos Zak'aria III (1434–1464) of the Armenian see of Aghtamar. Before 1434 he is mentioned in the texts as coadjutor catholicos. In 1460, Djihānshāh offered him the office of catholicos at Etchmiadzin, as well, but he was eventually poisoned by his adversaries. (See Akinean, *Gawazanagirk'*, pp. 85–108; Ačaṙyan, *HAB*, II, 193–194, no. 81; Ōrmanean, *Azgapatum*, cols. 1424, 1490–1497.)

Zazay: 1417 (no. 1). Armenian prince in Xač'en (see App. C).

Zēndin: 1398 (no. 1). *See* Ēzdin.

Zōrababēl: 1462 (no. 3). Zerubbabel or Zorababel. (See *Dictionary of Bible*, pp. 1056–1057, 1058.)

Appendix B. Scribes and Authors of Colophons

Abdəl-Aziz: 1459 (no. 2)
Abełay: 1476 (no. 11)
Abraham: 1306 (no. 2), 1310 (no. 3), 1315 (no. 1)
Abraham Ankiwrac'i: 1453 (no. 3). *See also* App. A
Alek'san, Son of: 1388 (no. 1)
Alēk'sanos: 1449 (no. 5)
Amir: 1478 (no. 1)
Amirdovlat' Amasiac'i: 1459 (no. 1)
Amir-P'ašay: 1441 (no. 7)
Amir-Sargis: 1396 (no. 1)
Anania: 1464 (no. 16)
Andrēas: 1362 (no. 1)
Anton: 1464 (no. 8)
Arłun: 1386 (no. 3)
Aṙak'el Bałišec'i: 1453 (no. 2). *See also* App. A
Aṙak'el [Orotnec'i]: 1404 (no. 1)
Aṙak'el Siwnec'i: 1403 (nos. 3, 4)
Astuacatur: 1417 (no. 5)
Astuacatur: 1418 (no. 3)
Astuacatur: 1437 (no. 3), 1445 (no. 4)
Astuacatur: 1438 (no. 2)
Astuacatur: 1449 (no. 1)
Astuacatur: 1474 (no. 2)
Astuacatur, Xōjay: 1425 (no. 3)
Atom: 1460 (no. 7), 1466 (no. 5)
Atom: 1464 (no. 13)
Awag: 1337 (no. 1)
Awetik': 1425 (no. 9)
Awetik': 1437 (no. 7)
Awetik': 1444 (no. 7)
Awetik': 1456 (no. 7)
Awetik': 1475 (no. 8)
Awetis: 1401 (no. 3)
Awetis: 1470 (no. 3)
Awetis (son of Nater): 1365 (no. 1)
Azaria: 1351 (no. 3)
Azaria: 1464 (no. 7)
Azariay: 1463 (no. 9), 1475 (no. 3)

Azariay: 1466 (no. 2), 1468 (no. 2)
Barseł: 1336 (no. 4)
Barseł: 1368 (no. 2)
Barseł: 1441 (no. 2)
Barseł Vardapet: 1325 (no. 2)
Catur: 1432 (no. 2)
Cerun: 1401 (no. 4)
Daniēl: 1303 (no. 1), 1306 (no. 1), 1307 (no. 2)
Daniēl: 1409 (no. 4), 1436 (no. 2)
Daniēl: 1451 (no. 4)
Daniēl: 1460 (no. 8)
Dawit‘: 1432 (no. 1)
Dawit‘: 1459 (no. 6), 1473 (no. 5), 1475 (no. 1), 1478 (no. 3)
Dawit‘: 1462 (no. 1)
Dawit‘ Episkopos: 1453 (no. 1)
Dawit‘ [Merdinc‘i]: 1452 (no. 5)
Dawit‘ Mšec‘i: 1368 (no. 1)
Dawit‘ Mšec‘i: 1408 (no. 2)
Ełia: 1407 (no. 2)
Ep‘rem: 1354 (no. 2)
Eremia: 1449 (no. 8)
Eremia: 1464 (no. 14)
Esayi Nč‘ec‘i: 1303 (no. 2), 1323 (no. 1). *See also* App. A
Ǝŕəstakēs: 1475 (no. 7)
Fimi: 1376 (no. 1)
Gabriēl: 1477 (no. 3)
Galust: 1442 (no. 3), 1443 (nos. 5, 6), 1447 (no. 2), 1452 (no. 3)
Gaspar Hamt‘ec‘i: 1426 (no. 6)
Gēorg: 1387 (no. 3)
Gorg, Xoǰa: 1424 (no. 1)
Grigor: 1308 (no. 1)
Grigor: 1329 (no. 2)
Grigor: 1351 (no. 1)
Grigor: 1354 (no. 1), 1355 (no. 2)
Grigor: 1403 (no. 6)
Grigor: 1407 (no. 2)
Grigor: 1416 (no. 2)
Grigor: 1419 (no. 1)
Grigor: 1421 (no. 6)
Grigor: 1426 (no. 4)
Grigor: 1429 (no. 1)
Grigor: 1431 (no. 1), 1445 (no. 6)
Grigor: 1435 (no. 1)
Grigor: 1441 (no. 2)
Grigor: 1444 (no. 8)
Grigor: 1444 (nos. 5, 6), 1449 (no. 2)

Karapet: 1443 (no. 4)
Karapet: 1445 (no. 2)
Karapet: 1451 (no. 5), 1454 (no. 4), 1458 (no. 2), 1461 (no. 6), 1462 (no. 8), 1467 (nos. 5, 6, 8), 1473 (no. 9), 1475 (nos. 4, 5)
Karapet: 1461 (no. 7)
Karapet: 1480 (no. 3)
Karapet Abełay: 1477 (no. 7)
Kirakos: 1351 (no. 2)
Kirakos: 1405 (no. 3)
Kirakos: 1424 (no. 2)
Kirakos: 1426 (no. 5)
Kirakos: 1438 (no. 4)
Kirakos Agrkc'i: 1334 (no. 1)
Kirakos Eznkayec'i: 1330 (no. 1)
Kirakos [J̌ōškanc']: 1454 (no. 5), 1463 (no. 3), 1467 (no. 2)
Kiwrion: 1321 (no. 1), 1333 (no. 3)
Kozma: 1400 (no. 5)
Łazar: 1414 (no. 5)
Łazar: 1415 (no. 2)
Łazar: 1424 (no. 3)
Łazar: 1431 (no. 2)
Łazar: 1450 (no. 3)
Łazar: 1457 (no. 1)
Łazar: 1468 (no. 5)
Małagiay: 1463 (no. 13), 1464 (no. 15).
Manawēl: 1428 (nos. 7, 8)
Manuēl: 1405 (no. 1)
Manuēl: 1419 (no. 5)
Manuēl: 1473 (no. 10)
Manwēl: 1478 (no. 4)
Margarē: 1468 (no. 3)
Markos: 1384 (no. 1), 1401 (no. 8)
Martiros: 1303 (no. 4), 1304 (no. 1)
Martiros: 1420 (no. 3)
Martiros: 1450 (no. 4)
Martiros: 1480 (no. 1)
Matt'ē: 1321 (no. 2)
Matt'ēos: 1395 (no. 2), 1407 (no. 2), 1411 (no. 1)
Matt'ēos: 1425 (no. 7)
Matt'ēos: 1437 (no. 4)
Mat'ēos: 1447 (no. 1), 1452 (no. 1), 1459 (no. 5)
Mat'ēos: 1460 (no. 5)
Matt'ēos: 1465 (no. 3), 1469 (no. 4)
Matt'ēos Monozon: 1417 (no. 1)
Mat'ēos Šrvanec'i: 1464 (no. 9)
Melk'isedek: 1332 (no. 3)

Melk'isedek: 1412 (no. 1)
Melk'iset': 1453 (no. 4)
Melk'isēdek: 1338 (no. 2)
Melk'isēt': 1462 (no. 11)
Melk'isēt': 1472 (no. 2)
Melk'isēt' (variant: Mēlk'isēd): 1473 (no. 4), 1479 (no. 1)
Melk'isēt': 1477 (no. 1)
Melk'isēt': 1477 (no. 8)
Melk'isēt' Bałišec'i: 1428 (no. 2)
Mēlk'isēd: 1471 (no. 11). *See also* Melk'isēt'
Minas: 1322 (no. 2)
Minas: 1435 (no. 2)
Minas: 1444 (no. 8)
Minas: 1446 (no. 6)
Minas Derǰanec'i: 1354 (no. 3)
Mkrtič': 1302 (no. 1)
Mkrtič: 1304 (no. 4)
Mkrtič': 1307 (no. 4)
Mkrtič': 1331 (no. 1)
Mkrtič': 1344 (no. 1)
Mkrtič': 1371 (no. 2)
Mkrtič': 1405 (no. 3)
Mkrtič': 1414 (no. 3)
Mkrtič': 1432 (no. 4)
Mkrtič': 1436 (no. 6)
Mkrtič': 1443 (no. 1)
Mkrtič': 1450 (no. 2)
Mkrtič': 1456 (nos. 5, 6)
Mkrtič': 1459 (no. 3), 1468 (no. 1)
Mkrtič': 1463 (no. 4)
Mkrtič': 1469 (no. 7)
Mkrtič: 1471 (no. 12)
Mkrtič': 1476 (no. 3)
Mkrtič' Ełegec'i: 1421 (no. 5)
Mkrtič' [Nałaš]: 1418 (no. 1), 1469 (no. 5). *See also* App. A
Movsēs Ankełakut'ec'i: 1428 (no. 6)
Movsēs Arckec'i: 1472 (no. 1)
Mxit'ar: 1318 (no. 3)
Mxit'ar: 1430 (no. 1)
Mxit'ar: 1437 (no. 2)
Mxit'ar: 1440 (no. 1)
Mxit'ar Anec'i: 1321 (no. 3)
Mxit'ar Eznkayec'i: 1314 (no. 2)
Mxit'ar (Mecop'ec'i): 1313 (no. 2)
Mxit'arič': 1406 (no. 2)
Nahapet: 1374 (no. 1)

Nater: 1339 (no. 1), 1341 (no. 1), 1346 (nos. 2, 3)
Nersēs: 1323 (no. 2)
Nersēs: 1343 (no. 1)
Nersēs: 1348 (no. 3)
Nersēs: 1375 (no. 2)
Nersēs: 1397 (no. 2)
Nersēs: 1431 (no. 3)
Nersēs: 1457 (no. 6), 1460 (no. 10), 1461 (no. 5), 1475 (no. 6)
Nersēs: 1480 (no. 2)
Nersēs Krakc'i: 1335 (no. 6)
Nersēs Taronac'i: 1332 (no. 1)
Nikolayos: 1463 (no. 10)
Nikołayos: 1478 (no. 6)
Ohannē T'mok'uec'i: 1442 (no. 1)
Ohannēs: 1470 (no. 2)
Ovannēs: 1319 (no. 3). *See also* Yovannēs (1318)
Pawłos: 1310 (no. 2).
Pawłos: 1313 (no. 1)
Pawłos: 1398 (no. 2)
Pawłos: 1466 (no. 8)
Pawłos: 1474 (no. 3)
Pawłos: 1476 (no. 6)
Pawłos: 1479 (no. 3)
Petros: 1363 (no. 1)
Petros: 1387 (no. 2), 1392 (no. 2)
Petros: 1398 (no. 1)
Petros: 1426 (no. 3)
Ṙstakēs: 1315 (no. 2)
Ṙstakēs: 1397 (no. 1)
Sałat'ēl: 1421 (no. 10)
Sargis: 1306 (no. 3)
Sargis: 1314 (no. 1)
Sargis: 1320 (no. 2)
Sargis: 1325 (no. 1)
Sargis: 1335 (no. 5)
Sargis: 1336 (no. 3)
Sargis: 1340 (no. 1)
Sargis: 1342 (no. 1)
Sargis: 1367 (no. 1)
Sargis: 1375 (no. 1)
Sargis: 1383 (no. 1)
Sargis: 1401 (no. 2), 1409 (no. 1)
Sargis: 1418 (no. 4)
Sargis: 1421 (no. 9)
Sargis: 1438 (no. 3)
Sargis: 1441 (no. 8)

Sargis: 1446 (no. 5)
Sargis: 1449 (no. 7)
Sargis: 1455 (no. 7), 1463 (no. 14)
Sargis: 1473 (no. 3)
Sargis T'mok'ec'i: 1414 (no. 1)
Sarkawag: 1310 (no. 1)
Sařačenc': 1456 (no. 2)
Serob: 1302 (no. 2)
Sēt': 1403 (no. 5)
Simēon: 1335 (no. 7)
Simēon: 1351 (no. 3)
Simēon: 1371 (no. 3)
Simēon: 1392 (no. 1)
Simēon: 1400 (no. 3)
Simēon: 1421 (no. 11)
Simēon: 1422 (no. 2)
Simēon: 1439 (no. 1)
Simēon: 1460 (no. 1)
Sion: 1348 (no. 2), 1351 (no. 1)
Sołomon: 1475 (no. 9)
Step'annos: 1313 (no. 3)
Step'annos: 1337 (no. 2)
Step'annos: 1354 (no. 3), 1371 (no. 1)
Step'annos: 1355 (no. 1)
Step'annos: 1369 (no. 1)
Step'annos: 1388 (no. 3)
Step'annos: 1404 (no. 2), 1410 (no. 3)
Step'annos: 1415 (no. 1)
Step'annos: 1419 (no. 3)
Step'annos: 1419 (no. 4)
Step'annos: 1420 (no. 5)
Step'annos: 1451 (no. 3)
Step'annos: 1463 (no. 1), 1466 (no. 7)
Step'annos: 1466 (no. 3)
Step'annos: 1471 (no. 4)
Step'annos: 1476 (no. 5), 1477 (no. 6)
Step'anos: 1348 (no. 1)
Step'anos: 1388 (no. 2)
Step'anos: 1395 (no. 1)
Step'anos: 1425 (no. 6)
Step'anos: 1426 (no. 2)
Step'anos: 1428 (no. 5)
Step'anos: 1430 (no. 2)
Step'anos: 1436 (no. 3), 1446 (no. 1), 1454 (no. 6)
Step'anos: 1456 (nos. 3, 4), 1460 (no. 9)
Step'anos: 1460 (no. 13)

Step'anos: 1461 (no. 1)
Step'anos: 1461 (no. 8)
Step'anos: 1464 (no. 1), 1476 (no. 2)
Step'anos: 1464 (no. 2)
Step'anos: 1464 (no. 11)
Step'anos (son of Nater): 1363 (no. 3), 1368 (no. 3)
Šmawon: 1437 (no. 1)
Tērtēr Erewanc'i: 1341 (no. 3)
Tirac'u: 1305 (no. 1)
Tirac'u: 1388 (no. 2)
Tiratur: 1462 (no. 2)
T'adēos: 1303 (no. 3)
T'awak'al: 1400 (no. 5)
T'oros: 1329 (no. 1)
T'oros: 1336 (no. 5)
T'oros: 1361 (no. 3)
T'ovma: 1456 (no. 1)
T'ovma Mecep'c'i: 1441 (no. 9). *See also* T'ovmay Mecop'ec'i
T'ovma Mecop'ec'i: 1427 (no. 1), 1435 (no. 3). *See also* T'ovmay Mecop'ec'i
T'ovma Siwnec'i: 1411 (no. 2)
T'ovmay Mecop'ec'i (variants: T'ovma Mecep'c'i, T'ovma Mecop'ec'i): 1407 (no. 3), 1410 (no. 1)
T'uma: 1336 (no. 2)
T'uma: 1391 (no. 1)
T'uma: 1410 (no. 2)
T'uma: 1444 (no. 3)
T'uma: 1449 (no. 4)
T'uma Minasenc': 1428 (no. 1). *See also* T'umay Minasenc'
T'umas: 1405 (no. 3)
T'umašay: 1462 (no. 3)
T'umay: 1421 (nos. 2, 10)
T'umay: 1423 (no. 3)
T'umay: 1432 (no. 3)
T'umay: 1433 (no. 1)
T'umay: 1463 (no. 12)
T'umay Arčišec'i: 1336 (no. 1)
T'umay Mecop'ac'i: 1449 (no. 3)
T'umay Minasenc' (variant: T'uma Minasenc'): 1420 (no. 1), 1425 (no. 1), 1440 (no. 2), 1444 (no. 2), 1445 (no. 1), 1446 (no. 2)
T'umay T'avrizec'i: 1403 (no. 1)
Umid: 1467 (no. 1)
Vahan: 1349 (no. 1)
Vardan: 1303 (no. 6)
Vardan: 1319 (no. 1)
Vardan: 1416 (no. 1)
Vardan: 1421 (no. 13)

Vardan: 1441 (no. 3), 1446 (no. 4)
Vardan: 1453 (nos. 6, 8), 1465 (no. 5), 1467 (no. 4), 1471 (no. 9), 1474 (no. 4)
Vardan: 1460 (no. 2), 1471 (no. 5)
Vardan: 1461 (no. 4)
Vardan Łrimec'i: 1366 (no. 1)
Vasil: 1337 (no. 2)
Vrt'anēs: 1456 (no. 1)
Xač'atur: 1304 (no. 6)
Xač'atur: 1325 (no. 3)
Xač'atur: 1330 (no. 2)
Xač'atur: 1386 (no. 2)
Xač'atur: 1455 (no. 8)
Xač'atur: 1457 (no. 3), 1460 (no. 3), 1461 (no. 2), 1473 (no. 6)
Xač'atur: 1462 (no. 6), 1463 (no. 8)
Xač'er: 1307 (no. 3)
Xosrov: 1356 (no. 1)
Yakob: 1318 (no. 1)
Yakob: 1318 (no. 2)
Yakob: 1322 (no. 1)
Yakob: 1386 (no. 1)
Yakob: 1425 (no. 5)
Yakob: 1426 (no. 1)
Yakob: 1457 (no. 4)
Yakob: 1458 (no. 7)
Yakob: 1464 (no. 4)
Yakob: 1466 (no. 8), 1469 (no. 8), 1470 (no. 1)
Yakob: 1467 (no. 7)
Yakob: 1471 (no. 8)
Yakob: 1473 (no. 8)
Yakob Aspisənkc'i: 1408 (no. 1)
Yakovb: 1304 (no. 3)
Yohanēs: 1392 (no. 3)
Yohanēs: 1407 (no. 4)
Yohanēs: 1409 (no. 3)
Yohanēs: 1421 (no. 8), 1424 (no. 3)
Yohanēs: 1436 (no. 1)
Yohanēs: 1438 (no. 2)
Yohanēs: 1449 (no. 6)
Yohanēs: 1457 (no. 2)
Yohanēs: 1458 (no. 3)
Yohanēs Aparanerec'i: 1400 (no. 4), 1401 (no. 6)
Yohanēs Ezənkec'i: 1419 (no. 5)
Yohannēs: 1327 (no. 2)
Yohannēs: 1425 (no. 8), 1450 (no. 5)
Yohannēs: 1427 (no. 3)

Yohannēs: 1428 (no. 3)
Yohannēs: 1438 (no. 6)
Yohannēs: 1442 (no. 4)
Yohannēs: 1455 (no. 6)
Yohannēs: 1464 (no. 6). *See also* Yovanēs (Arckec'i)
Yohannēs: 1479 (no. 4)
Yohannēs Mangasarenc': 1445 (no. 5). *See also* Yovhannēs Mangasarenc'
Yohannēs Sebastac'i: 1411 (no. 3)
Yovan: 1338 (no. 3)
Yovan: 1462 (no. 5)
Yovanēs: 1308 (no. 2)
Yovanēs: 1319 (no. 2)
Yovanēs: 1331 (no. 2)
Yovanēs: 1358 (no. 1)
Yovanēs: 1378 (no. 1)
Yovanēs: 1400 (no. 2)
Yovanēs: 1402 (no. 1), 1407 (no. 1), 1417 (no. 3)
Yovanēs: 1405 (no. 3)
Yovanēs: 1411 (no. 4), 1421 (no. 3)
Yovanēs: 1443 (no. 2)
Yovanēs: 1450 (no. 1)
Yovanēs: 1452 (no. 2)
Yovanēs: 1453 (no. 7)
Yovanēs: 1454 (no. 3)
Yovanēs: 1460 (no. 11)
Yovanēs: 1464 (no. 12)
Yovanēs: 1468 (no. 6)
Yovanēs: 1471 (no. 10)
Yovanēs: 1473 (no. 7)
Yovanēs: 1474 (no. 5)
Yovanēs (Arckec'i) (variants: Yohannēs, Yovhannēs): 1459 (no. 8), 1460 (no. 6), 1463 (no. 6), 1465 (no. 2), 1476 (no. 10)
Yovanēs Mangasarenc': 1465 (no. 6). *See also* Yovhannēs Mangasarenc'
Yovanēs Mankasarenc': 1454 (no. 2), 1457 (no. 5). *See also* Yovhannēs Mangasarenc'
Yovanēs Selaenc'i: 1425 (no. 10)
Yovannēs: 1304 (no. 5)
Yovannēs (variant: Ovannēs): 1318 (no. 4)
Yovannēs: 1320 (no. 1)
Yovannēs: 1327 (no. 1)
Yovannēs: 1331 (no. 3)
Yovannēs: 1333 (no. 1)
Yovannēs: 1338 (no. 1)
Yovannēs: 1377 (no. 1)
Yovannēs: 1399 (no. 1)
Yovannēs: 1458 (no. 6)

Yovannēs-Alinax: 1370 (no. 1)
Yovhannēs: 1301 (no. 1)
Yovhannēs (?): 1305 (no. 2)
Yovhannēs (variants: Yovanēs, Yovannēs): 1337 (no. 3), 1349 (no. 2)
Yovhannēs: 1363 (no. 2)
Yovhannēs: 1384 (no. 1)
Yov[hannēs]: 1402 (no. 2)
Yovhannēs: 1421 (no. 4)
Yovhannēs: 1423 (no. 1)
Yovhannēs: 1436 (no. 5)
Yovhannēs: 1438 (no. 1), 1443 (no. 7)
Yovhannēs: 1441 (no. 4)
Yovhannēs: 1455 (no. 2). *See also* Yovhannēs Mangasarenc‘
Yovhannēs: 1459 (no. 7), 1461 (no. 3). *See also* Yovanēs (Arckec‘i)
Yovhannēs Mangasarenc‘ (variants: Yohannēs Mangasarenc‘, Yovanēs Mangasarenc‘, Yovanēs Mankasarenc‘, Yovhannēs): 1463 (no. 7), 1469 (no. 1), 1479 (no. 2)
Yovhannēs Nałaš: 1346 (no. 1)
Yovsēp‘: 1414 (no. 2)
Yovsēp‘: 1414 (no. 4)
Yovsēp‘: 1446 (no. 3)
Yovsēp‘: 1453 (no. 5), 1466 (no. 4)
Yovsēp‘: 1463 (no. 2)
Yovsēp‘: 1473 (no. 1), 1474 (no. 6)
Yovsēp‘: 1476 (no. 1)
Yovsian: 1306 (no. 4), 1316 (no. 1)
Yōsēp‘: 1437 (no. 9)
Yōvasab Aparanec‘i: 1421 (no. 14)
Yusēp‘: 1437 (no. 8)
Zak‘ar: 1458 (no. 7)
Zak‘ar: 1460 (no. 4)
Zak‘ar (I) (variant: Zak‘aria): 1476 (no. 9), 1477 (no. 5)
Zak‘aray: 1417 (no. 2). *See also* Zak‘aria (I)
Zak‘arē: 1361 (no. 1)
Zak‘arē: 1375 (no. 1)
Zak‘aria: 1462 (no. 10)
Zak‘aria: 1477 (no. 4). *See also* Zak‘ar (I)
Zak‘aria (I) (variant: Zak‘aray): 1401 (no. 5), 1413 (no. 1)
Zak‘ariay: 1304 (no. 2)
Zak‘ariay: 1476 (no. 7)
Zak‘ēos: 1474 (no. 1)
Zawrvar Erēc‘: 1462 (no. 9)

Appendix C. Geographical Terms

Note: Map follows page 459.

Aflisc'ixē: 1412 (no. 1). Uplistziké (lit., the castle of Uplos); fortress-city on the middle course of the Kura river in Iberia, and capital of the Kartlian Bagratids. (See Allen, *History*, p. 427; cf. Eremyan, *Ašx.*, p. 60.)

Aguleac': 1436 (no. 5). Monastery (also called Surb T'ovma = St. Thomas) in Agulis [q.v.]. (See Ēp'rikean, *Baṙaran*, I, 13–15.)

Agulis: 1425 (no. 7), 1432 (no. 3). Village or town in canton of Gołt'n [q.v.] in Siwnik' province. (See Ēp'rikean, *Baṙaran*, I, 10–18; Hübschmann, *AO*, p. 400; Oskean, *Vank'er*, II, 676–725.)

Ahar: 1456 (no. 2). Administrative center of Kara-dagh district in Ādharbaydjān. (See Ēp'rikean, *Baṙaran*, I, 93; Xač'ikyan, *XV Dari*, II, p. 589.)

Akanc': 1453 (no. 5), 1466 (no. 4). Town; N of Arčēš (Ardjīsh) in canton of K'ajberunik' in Vaspurakan province. (See Ēp'rikean, *Baṙaran*, I, 77–78.)

Akisi: 1473 (no. 2). The exact location of this city is unknown.

Akner: 1303 (no. 6), 1322 (no. 2). Monastery, in village of the same name, in canton of C'axut in Cilicia Tracheia. (See Ēp'rikean, *Baṙaran*, I, 78; Ališan, *Sisuan*, pp. 153–156, 535.)

Alənja (variant: Alənjay): 1425 (no. 1). *See* Ernjak.

Alənjay: 1437 (no. 3). *See* Alənja.

Ałał: 1422 (no. 1). Village: W shore of Lake Van, in canton of Bznunik' in Turuberan province. (See Ēp'rikean, *Baṙaran*, I, 97.)

Ałat'amar: 1454 (no. 6). *See* Ałt'amar.

Aławnic': 1340 (no. 1). Monastery; location unknown.

Ałbak (variant: Axbak): 1425 (no. 1). Arabic: Albāq; canton (also called Barmn) in province of Vaspurakan. (See Saint-Martin, *Mémoires*, I, 177; Hübschmann, *AO*, p. 344.)

Ałčałalay: 1411 (no. 3). Also known as Tigrana-Berd [q.v.]; the fortress of Akçakale, on right bank of Akhurian river, near ancient city of Bagaran or Bagran [q.v.] in vilayet of Kars in E Turkey. (See Xač'ikyan, *XV Dari*, I, p. 802.)

Ałek'sandr: 1336 (no. 1). Rare variant of Armenian Ałek'sandria, that is, the city of Alexandria in Egypt.

Ałestew: 1436 (no. 1). Georgian: Akstafa; an affluent of the Kura river in region of Kazakh in Georgia. (See Ēp'rikean, *Baṙaran*, I, 114.)

Ałēt‘: 1327 (no. 1), 1331 (no. 2), 1337 (no. 3), 1349 (no. 2), 1421 (no. 1), 1422 (no. 1). Village, formerly inhabited by Armenians, in region of Xlat‘ (Khilāṭ), now in ruins. (See Ēp‘rikean, *Bararan*, I, 100.)

Ałjn: 1443 (no. 1). Canton, now in province of Diyarbakir in Turkey; known in Roman times as Arzanene, it is also called in Armenian sources Ałjnik‘ and Arzn. It was the administrative center of the Ałjnean, an ancient Armenian feudal family. (See Hübschmann, *AO*, pp. 248–251, 305–308, 310–312; *Arm. Gram.*, p. 403; R. N. Frye, "Arzan," *EI*, NE, I, 679; Saint-Martin, *Mémoires*, I, 65, 156–157; II, 361.)

Ałǰoc‘: 1442 (no. 3), 1443 (nos. 5, 6), 1447 (no. 2), 1452 (no. 3), 1460 (no. 2), 1471 (no. 5). Monastery, near village of the same name, in region of K‘ełoy-Jor [q.v.] in Ayrarat province. (See Ēp‘rikean, *Bararan*, I, 113–114.)

Ałt‘amar (variants: Ałat‘amar, Axt‘amar): 1303 (no. 1), 1304 (no. 5), 1306 (no. 1), 1307 (no. 2), 1308 (no. 2), 1327 (no. 1), 1333 (no. 4), 1354 (no. 1), 1355 (no. 2), 1392 (no. 1), 1395 (no. 1), 1397 (no. 2), 1400 (no. 2), 1401 (no. 4), 1409 (no. 4), 1417 (no. 4), 1420 (nos. 1, 5), 1421 (nos. 2, 10, 11), 1425 (no. 1), 1428 (nos. 1, 5), 1431 (no. 3), 1433 (no. 1), 1436 (no. 2), 1437 (no. 8), 1440 (no. 2), 1444 (nos. 2, 4, 5), 1445 (no. 1), 1446 (no. 2), 1449 (no. 2), 1452 (no. 4), 1455 (nos. 3, 4), 1459 (nos. 2, 9), 1460 (no. 10), 1461 (no. 5), 1462 (nos. 3, 5, 7), 1463 (nos. 11, 12), 1465 (no. 7), 1466 (no. 6), 1467 (nos. 2, 3), 1470 (nos. 4, 5), 1471 (no. 1), 1474 (no. 5), 1475 (nos. 3, 6), 1476 (nos. 10, 11), 1478 (no. 5), 1480 (no. 4). Island of Aghtamar (Arabic-Persian-Turkish: Akhtamār), now deserted, near S shore of Lake Van. In the tenth century, King Gagik fortified the island, built a magnificent church (see Sirarpie Der Nersessian, *Aght'amar: Church of the Holy Cross*, Cambridge, Mass., 1965), and made the island the center of the Arcruni Armenian kingdom of Vaspurakan. In 1113 Aghtamar became the seat of a regional catholicosate of the Armenian church, which retained its existence until World War I. (For an extensive bibliography on Aghtamar, see Avedis K. Sanjian, *The Armenian Communities in Syria under Ottoman Dominion*, Cambridge, Mass., 1965, p. 327, n. 122. See also Saint-Martin, *Mémoires*, I, 55, 140, 141, 252; II, 429.) The colophons refer to the island, the village or town, or the catholicosal see; only one text refers to the *nahang*, province, of Aghtamar, which actually applies to the jurisdictional scope of the see.

Ałuank‘ (variants: Ałvank‘, Ałwan, Tunn Ałuanic‘): 1420 (no. 2), 1428 (no. 7), 1456 (no. 1), 1471 (no. 8). The country of Caucasian Albania (Greek: Albanoi; Persian: Aran; Arabic: Arrān, al-Rān; Georgian: Rani). Until A.D. 387 it comprised the territories between the Kura and Araxes rivers in the Trans-Caucasus. Under the Umayyads and Abbasids it was a semi-independent country ruled by local Armenian and Albanian dynasties subject to the Arabs; under the Mongols it was joined to Ādharbaydjān and was named Ḳara-bāgh. (See R. N. Frye,

"Arrān," *EI*, OE, I, 660.) Albania now is part of the Azerbaijan SSR and the Daghestan ASSR. Besides the country, the colophons refer to the Caucasian Albanian church and its catholicosate, which lasted until the end of the nineteenth century. The country was Christianized from Armenia in the fourth century, and its church maintained close contacts with the Armenian church, whose catholicoses as a rule ordained the Albanian catholicoses. *See also* Ałuanic', App. D.

Ałunay: 1459 (no. 2). Village, on S shore of Lake Van, in proximity of island of Ałt'amar.

Ałuvank: 1422 (no. 1). Village in region of Xlat' (Khilāṭ). (See Xač'ikyan, *XV Dari*, I, p. 802; cf. Ēp'rikean, *Bararan*, I, 297–298.

Ałvank': 1464 (no. 8). *See* Ałuank'.

Ałwan: 1422 (no. 1). *See* Ałuank'.

Amarasay: 1428 (nos. 7, 8). Monastery; some 45 km. from Shushi in plain of Mūghān. It was, first, the seat of an Albanian bishopric, and then the seat of the catholicoses of the Albanian church. (See *The History of the Caucasian Albanians by Movsēs Dasxuranci*, trans. C. J. F. Dowsett, London, 1961.) There is at present a village named Amaras in mountainous Ḳara-bāgh. (See Eremyan, *Ašx.*, p. 34.)

Amasia: 1480 (no. 2). Town of Amasya (ancient Amaseia) in N Anatolia and capital of a province in Turkey; the Hellenistic fortress is now in ruins. (See Fr. Taeschner, "Amasya," *EI*, NE, I, 431–432.)

Amid: 1469 (no. 3). *See* Amit'.

Amit' (variants: Amid, Hamit', Yamit'): 1397 (no. 1), 1422 (no. 1), 1425 (nos. 1, 9), 1431 (no. 1), 1432 (no. 5), 1435 (nos. 3, 5), 1449 (no. 1), 1452 (no. 5), 1453 (no. 1), 1464 (no. 10), 1468 (no. 1). Town of Āmid; capital of Diyarbakir (Turkish: Diyarbakîr) province in Mesopotamia. (See "Diyār Bakr," *EI*, NE, II, 343–344; Spuler, *Mongolen in Iran*, pp. 34, 45, 99, 102, 129–136 *passim.*)

Amṙsan: 1472 (no. 1). The author of the colophon claims that this was another name for Khurāsān.

Amu: 1335 (no. 1). The river Āmū-daryā (Latin: Oxus; Arabic: Djīḥun), northernmost boundary of Khurāsān. (See B. Spuler, "Āmū Daryā," *EI*, NE, I, 454–457.)

Amuk: 1428 (no. 1), 1438 (no. 1), 1454 (no. 1). Fortress, on a promontory situated on S shore of Lake Van. In the valley below the promontory was also the village of Amuk, now called Hamok or Amik. (See Ēp'rikean, *Bararan*, I, 138; Eremyan, *Ašx.*, p. 35; Xač'ikyan, *XV Dari*, II, p. 589.)

Anapatik: 1361 (no. 1). Village in a valley in district of Hakkārī in province of Van.

Anarzab: 1307 (no. 6). *See* Anarzaba.

Anarzaba (variant: Anarzab): 1468 (no. 4). Town, now called Anavarza (Arabic: 'Ayn Zarba), S of Sis and N of Miṣṣīṣa. Under the Armenian kingdom, it was the capital of Cilicia Pedias and the second most important city in Cilicia. The city and its fortress were destroyed by the

Mamluks in 1374, after which it lost all importance; today the place is in ruins. (See "'Ayn Zarba," *EI*, NE, I, 789–790; Ramsay, *Historical Geography*.)

Anberd: 1310 (no. 1). Region in canton of Aragacotn in Ayrarat province; also a fortress in Mt. Aragac NW of village of Biwrakan in Armenian SSR. (See Hübschmann, *AO*, p. 399.)

Ancłnapat: 1405 (no. 4). Monastery, S of Lake Van, in canton of Ṙštunik' [q.v.] in Vaspurakan province. (See Oskean, *Vank'er*, I, 141–143; Xač'ikyan, *XV Dari*, I, p. 803; cf. Ēp'rikean, "Ancłnapar," in *Bararan*, I, 212.)

Anc'mnc'ik: 1367 (no. 1). Name of a small valley and brook in Cilicia Pedias, near city of Sis. (See Ēp'rikean, *Bararan*, I, 251.)

Ani: 1398 (no. 1), 1422 (no. 1). In medieval times there were several towns in Asia Minor called Ani. These two texts seem to refer to the town (or fortress) of Kemakh, which in Armenian sources was also known as Ani. (See Ēp'rikean, *Bararan*, I, 182–186.) *See also* Kamax.

Ankełakut': 1428 (no. 6). Large village in canton of Cłak (or Cłuk) in Siwnik' province. (See Hübschmann, *AO*, p. 400.)

Ankiwria (variants: Ankuria, Ankuṙia): 1453 (no. 3). The town of Ankara in central Anatolia, now capital of Turkey. (See Fr. Taeschner, "Anḳara," *EI*, NE, I, 509–511.)

Ankuneac' (variants: Yankuneac', Yankiwneac'): 1476 (no. 9). Monastery in region of Ašota-Jor [q.v.].

Ankuria: 1464 (no. 3). *See* Ankiwria.

Ankuṙia: 1468 (no. 6). *See* Ankiwria.

Ant'ap (variant: Ant'ap'): 1468 (no. 4). City of Antep (now Gaziantep; Arabic: 'Ayntāb), SE of Anatolia. (See M. Canard, "'Ayntāb," *EI*, NE, I, 791.)

Ant'ap': 1400 (no. 5). *See* Ant'ap.

Apahunik': 1323 (no. 2). Canton (Arabic: Badjunays), formerly the domain of the Apahuni, an Armenian feudal family; its boundaries correspond to the present Turkish sanjak of Malazkirt. (See Hübschmann, *AO*, pp. 329–330.)

Ap'xaz: 1441 (no. 1), 1477 (no. 1). Country of Abkhāz or Abkhazia, now NW Georgian SSR, between the Black Sea and the Greater Caucasus. (See W. Barthold–[V. Minorsky], "Abkhāz," *EI*, NE, I, 100–102.)

Ara, Mt.: 1469 (no. 4). Mountain in E range of Mt. Aragac, in canton of Aragacotn in Ayrarat province; known in Turkish as Karni-Yarîk. (See Ēp'rikean, *Bararan*, I, 288–289; Eremyan, *Ašx.*, p. 38.)

Arabstan: 1442 (no. 1). Lit., land of the Arabs; a geographical term used to denote the Persian province of Khuzistān. (See "'Arabistān," *EI*, NE, I, 561.)

Arapkir: 1446 (no. 6). Town of Eskishehir, about 70 km. N of Malatya, in E Anatolia. It should not be confused with the modern Turkish town of Arapkir, capital of a ḳāḍā in Malatya province, S of Eskishehir. (See M. Streck–[Fr. Taeschner], "'Arabkīr," *EI*, NE, I, 603.)

Ararat (variants: Ayrarad, Ayrarat): 1432 (no. 2), 1442 (nos. 1, 3), 1443 (nos. 5, 6), 1447 (no. 2), 1452 (no. 3), 1457 (no. 3), 1460 (no. 3), 1462 (no. 3), 1465 (nos. 3, 4), 1469 (no. 4), 1471 (no. 5), 1473 (no. 6), 1477 (no. 3). The central, largest, and most important province of Armenia Major. (See Hübschmann, *AO*, pp. 278–283, 361–368, 398; Friedrich Murad, *Ararat und Masis*, Heidelberg, 1901.)

Arckē (variants: Arckoy, Arjkēoy): 1421 (no. 3), 1422 (no. 1), 1425 (no. 1), 1428 (no. 4), 1438 (no. 1), 1441 (no. 5), 1443 (no. 3), 1447 (no. 3), 1459 (no. 7), 1460 (nos. 6, 7, 8), 1463 (no. 6), 1464 (nos. 4, 5, 6), 1466 (no. 5), 1467 (no. 7), 1472 (no. 1), 1476 (no. 10). (1) Canton, NE of Lake Van in Turuberan province. (See Ēp'rikean, *Bararan*, I, 303–304.) (2) Town, now called Adilcevaz, N of Lake Van; it had two fortresses, one at the foot and the other on the peak of the mountain. (See Hübschmann, *AO*, pp. 328–329.) (3) Monastery, also called in Armenian sources St. Step'anos, Dastak, and C'ipna, on a small island NW of Lake Van, opposite town of Arckē. (See Ēp'rikean, *Bararan*, I, 304.)

Arckoy: 1338 (no. 3). *See* Arckē (3).

Arcnunik': 1371 (no. 3). *See* Arcruni.

Arcruni (variants: Arcnunik', Arcrunis): 1386 (no. 2). Canton, known also as Arzanene, W of Lake Van, bounded on S by the Tigris; the original domain of the Arcruni Armenian feudal family.

Arcrunis: 1386 (no. 2). Town; it should probably be identified with the town of Arzan in Arcrunis province. *See* Arcruni.

Arčes: 1457 (no. 5). *See* Arčēš.

Arčēš (variants: Arčes, Arǰēš): 1307 (no. 4), 1422 (no. 1), 1425 (no. 1), 1428 (no. 2), 1432 (no. 4), 1438 (no. 1), 1441 (no. 4), 1444 (no. 3), 1445 (no. 5), 1450 (no. 2), 1454 (no. 2), 1455 (no. 2), 1461 (no. 3), 1462 (nos. 3, 5), 1463 (nos. 7, 9), 1465 (no. 6), 1469 (no. 1), 1479 (no. 2). (1) Canton, which corresponded to ancient K'aǰberunik' [q.v.]. (2) Town (Arabic: Ardjīsh; Turkish: Erçiş) NE bank of Lake Van. As a result of the northward movement of the lake's waters the town's last inhabitants left about the middle of the nineteeenth century; today the ruins of the city are mainly under water. (See C. Cahen, "Ardjīsh," *EI*, NE, I, 627.)

Arc'ax: 1417 (no. 1). One of the provinces of Armenia Major, corresponding roughly to the present region of mountainous Ḳara-bāgh. Armenian sources also refer to it as Gargar, P'ok'r Siwnik', Xač'enk', and Seaw Aygi. (See Hübschmann, *AO*, pp. 349–351.)

Arewmtakan Cov: 1315 (no. 2). Lit., Western Sea; this is one of the names by which the Armenians referred to the Mediterranean Sea.

Arewyis: 1471 (no. 6). Small canton (also called Arewik') in canton of Gołt'n; it now corresponds to the district of Mełri in Armenian SSR. (Ēp'rikean, *Bararan*, I, 297–299; Eremyan, *Ašx.*, p. 39.)

Argelan (variant: Argilan): 1331 (no. 3), 1449 (no. 6), 1457 (no. 1), 1464 (no. 7), 1478 (no. 2). Monastery, also called Tēr Yuskan Ordi, in city of Berkri [q.v.] in Aṙberuni canton. (See Hübschmann, *AO*, p. 404; Oskean *Vank'er*, I, 357–378.)

Argilan: 1462 (no. 3). *See* Argelan.

Arjkēoy: 1319 (no. 1). *See* Arckē (3).

Arǰēš: 1422 (no. 1). *See* Arčēš.

Arǰəroy: 1472 (no. 2). Village and monastery in region of Arčēš (Ardjīsh) in K'aǰberunik' province. (See Xač'ikyan, *XIV Dari*, p. 667; cf. Ēp'rikean, *Baṙaran*, I, 324.)

Arǰonic': 1449 (no. 3). Monastery W. of Armizonk' village, between Mt. Sip'an and monastery of Mecop' in K'aǰberunik'. (See Oskean, *Vank'er*, II, 412–416.)

Arłni: 1444 (no. 7), 1445 (no. 6), 1449 (no. 1), 1453 (no. 1). Known also in Armenian sources as Arłana and Arkni; Arabic: Arghanī; Turkish: Ergani. (1) Fortress, NW of Diyarbakir. (2) Town, on highroad from Diyarbakir to Kharput (Turkish: Harput). (See *Chèref-Nâmeh*, I.1, pp. 140, 148, 468–469; Besim Darkot, "Ergani," *EI*, NE, II, 707.)

Armizawnk': 1463 (no. 14). Village in region of Arčēš (Ardjīsh). (See Ēp'rikean, *Baṙaran*, I, 320.)

Artamēt: 1369 (no. 1). Village or town, E bank of Lake Van and SW of city of Van, in canton of Tosp in Vaspurakan province. (See Ēp'rikean, *Baṙaran*, I, 326–329.)

Artaz: 1315 (no. 2), 1406 (no. 2), 1426 (no. 4). Known also in Armenian sources as Artawaz and Artazakē; a canton in Vaspurakan province. It was the domain of the Amatuni, an Armenian feudal family, with the fortress-city of Mākū as its center. (See Hübschmann, *AO*, p. 344.)

Arzəṙum: 1419 (no. 1). *See* Arzrum.

Arzn: 1435 (no. 2). A variant name by which Armenian sources referred to Ałjn [q.v.].

Arzrum (variants: Arzəṙum, Aṙzəṙum): 1387 (no. 3). City of Erzerum, situated between the valleys of the Karasu and Araxes rivers. In ancient times the Armenians called it Karin or Karnoy K'ałak' (cf. Arabic Ḳālīḳalā); after A.D. 415 it was called Theodosiopolis by the Romans. (See Halil Inalcik, "Erzerum," *EI*, NE, II, 712; Hübschmann, *AO*, pp. 287–290; Saint-Martin, *Mémoires*, I, 69.)

Aṙak'eloc': 1320 (no. 1). Monastery in region of Muš (Mush); also known in Armenian sources as Surb Łazaru Vank'.

Aṙberd: 1466 (no. 6). Monastery, S of Lake Van, in P'asavank' village in Mokk' province. (See Oskean, *Vank'er*, I, 144–145.)

Aṙest: 1471 (no. 11), 1473 (no. 4), 1479 (no. 1). Village or town, also called Bandumahi, NE bank of Lake Van. (See Ēp'rikean, *Baṙaran*, I, 246; Eremyan, *Ašx.*, p. 37.)

Aṙēn: 1371 (no. 3). Village, N bank of Lake Van, in Arckē canton. (See Ēp'rikean, *Baṙaran*, I, 246.)

Aṙənǰik: 1400 (no. 1). Village in region of Arckē. (See Xač'ikyan, *XIV Dari*, p. 667; *XV Dari*, I, p. 803.)

Aṙzəṙum: 1422 (no. 1). *See* Arzrum.

Asia: 1302 (no. 1). The continent of Asia.

Asorestan: 1335 (no. 1), 1400 (no. 1), 1472 (no. 1). Assyria; the name by which the Armenians referred to Mesopotamia under Sasanid rule, in particular its middle and lower regions. (See Hübschmann, *Arm. Gram.*, p. 22, no. 17, and p. 341, no. 38.)

Asorik' (variant: Asoris): 1437 (no. 5), 1449 (nos. 3, 4). The term by which the Armenians referred to classical Syria. (See Hübschmann, *Arm. Gram.*, p. 22, no. 17, and p. 341, no. 38.) In the colophons the references are generally to the region of modern northern Syria.

Asoris: 1307 (no. 5), 1315 (no. 1), 1325 (no. 1). *See* Asorik'.

Aspahan (variant: Ispahan): 1453 (no. 7), 1457 (nos. 1, 5), 1462 (nos. 3, 6). Ancient city of Aspadana, now Iṣfahān, in central Iran, midway between Teheran and Shīrāz. (See C. Huart, "Iṣfahān," *EI*, OE, II, 528–530; Hübschmann, *Arm. Gram.*, pp. 21–22; Spuler, *Mongolen in Iran.*)

Ašota-Jor: 1477 (nos. 4, 5). Presumably a valley, whose exact location is uncertain; it was either in province of Ayrarat or province of Siwnik'. (See Xač'ikyan, *XV Dari*, II, p. 589.)

Ašxarhn Honakan: 1422 (no. 1). Lit., the Hunnic land. *See* Honac' Ašxarh.

Ašxarhn Vrac': 1442 (no. 3). Lit., the land of the Georgions. *See* Vrac'tun.

Atana (variant: Atanay): 1468 (no. 4). The city of Adana in S Anatolia; situated in N part of the plain of Cilicia, on W bank of the Seyḥan river. Except for brief intervals, it was held by the Armenian Kingdom of Cilicia from 1132 until 1359. (See R. Anhegger, "Adana," *EI*, NE, I, 182–183.)

Atanay: 1337 (no. 2), 1361 (no. 3). *See* Atana.

Atrana: 1453 (no. 3). City of Edirne (Adrianople), now capital of Edirne province in European Turkey. (See M. Tayyib Gökbilgin, "Edirne (Adrianople)," in *EI*, NE, II, 683–684.)

Atrpaičan: 1408 (no. 1). *See* Atrpatakan.

Atrpatakan (variant: Atrpaičan): 1407 (no. 2), 1422 (no. 1). Persian province of Ādharbaydjān (Azerbaijan), extending from the Caspian Sea to the W of Lake Urmia. (See V. Minorsky, "Ādharbaydjān (Azarbāydjān)," *EI*, NE, I, 188; Hübschmann, *Arm. Gram.*, pp. 23–24, no. 20.)

Avan: 1453 (no. 4). Town in canton of Kotayk' in Ayrarat province, situated W of Duin. (See Hübschmann, *AO*, p. 410.)

Avrel: 1428 (no. 1). *See* Ōrēl.

Awag (variant: Awak'): 1336 (no. 5), 1478 (no. 6). Monastery in canton of Ekełeac' [q.v.] or Daranałeac' [q.v.]; also called in Armenian sources T'adēos Aṙak'eloy Vank'. (See Ēp'rikean, *Baṙaran*, II, 3.)

Awak': 1439 (no. 1), 1464 (no. 1). *See* Awag.

Awans: 1304 (no. 5), 1308 (no. 2). Village, N of city of Van, near shore of Lake Van; now called Iskele-Köyü. (See Ēp'rikean, *Baṙaran*, I, 346.)

Awənka: 1397 (no. 1). Probably Awnik [q.v.].

Awnik: 1422 (no. 1). Village and fortress, now called Civan-Kale, in Hawnuneac' canton of Ayrarat province. (See Ēp'rikean, Baŕaran, I, 348; Chèref-Nâmeh, II. 2, 247.)

Awrēl: 1452 (no. 5). See Ōrēl.

Awšakan: 1414 (no. 1). Village in canton of Aragacotn; 15 km. N of Etchmiadzin. It is usually spelled Ōšakan. (See Hübschmann, AO, pp. 410, 479.)

Awt'mna: 1348 (no. 3). Monastery, near city of Tiwrik [q.v.]. (See Ēp'rikean, Baŕaran, I, 347–348.)

Axalc'ixē: 1396 (no. 1). See Axalc'xay.

Axalc'xay (variants: Axalc'ixē, Axəlcəxē, Axəlc'xay, Axlc'xay, Yałlcxa): 1438 (no. 3). Town of Akhal Tsikhe (Persian and Arabic: Akhiskha; Turkish: Ahiska; Arabic: Akhsīkhath), on the Poskhov river, and center of Georgian province of Samtskhé (later Saatabago). (See V. Minorsky, "Akhsikha," EI, NE, I, 325.) The colophons refer to the town, its fortress, and to the district of Akhal Tsikhe.

Axavanc': 1459 (no. 2). Village on S shore of Lake Van, across from island of Aghtamar, where the catholicos of this see had a second official residence. The village was also known in Armenian sources as Axavanac', Axavans, and Axavank'. (See Ēp'rikean, Baŕaran, I, 71.)

Axbak: 1351 (no. 2), 1398 (no. 1). See Ałbak.

Axəlcəxē: 1422 (no. 1). See Axalc'xay.

Axəlc'xay: 1441 (no. 7). See Axalc'xay.

Axlc'xay: 1445 (no. 2). See Axalc'xay.

Axt'amar: 1386 (no. 2), 1389 (no. 1), 1392 (no. 3), 1398 (no. 1), 1400 (no. 1), 1457 (no. 6), 1474 (no. 6). See Ałt'amar.

Ayan: 1322 (no. 1). A variant of Ayas [q.v.].

Ayas (variants: Ayan, Yayas): 1335 (no. 6), 1337 (no. 2), 1376 (no. 1). Port-city, now known as Ayas/Yumurtalīk, W shore of the Gulf of Alexandretta (Iskenderun), to the E of the mouth of the Djayḥān (Pyramus) river. During the Armenian kingdom of Cilicia it served as an important center of international trade; it was known to European traders as Ajazzo or Lajazzo. (See Fr. Taeschner, "Āyās," EI, NE, I, 778–779; Ramsay, Historical Geography, pp. 385–386.)

Aylax: 1464 (no. 9). Region in canton of Cłuk in Siwnik' province. (See Ēp'rikean, Baŕaran, I, 143; Xač'ikyan, XV Dari, II, p. 589.)

Ayrarad: 1447 (no. 1). See Ararat.

Ayrarat: 1302 (no. 1), 1303 (no. 3), 1304 (no. 4), 1308 (no. 1), 1422 (no. 1), 1436 (no. 4), 1453 (no. 2). See Ararat.

Ayrivank': 1429 (no. 1), 1444 (no. 1), 1447 (no. 1), 1452 (no. 1), 1459 (no. 5), 1476 (no. 5). Monastery, also known as Gełarday Vank', in valley of Gaŕni in Ayrarat province. (See Hübschmann, AO, p. 398.)

Azax: 1341 (no. 3). City of Azov (Arabic: Azak), at the mouth of the Don river in the Crimea. (See H. Inalcik, "Azaḳ," EI, NE, I, 808; Spuler, Goldene Horde, pp. 113, 115, 199.)

Babel Ašxarhn: 1335 (no. 1). Lit., the land of Babel; Babylonia, that is, Iraq.

Babelac'woc' Ašxarh (variants: Babel ašxarhn, Babilac'woc' ašxarh): 1303 (no. 4), 1315 (no. 1), 1325 (no. 1). Lit., the land of the Babylonians; Babylonia, that is, Iraq.

Babelon: 1318 (no. 1), 1395 (no. 1), 1397 (no. 1), 1400 (no. 1), 1417 (no. 1), 1422 (no. 1), 1446 (no. 2), 1464 (no. 7), 1466 (no. 4), 1470 (no. 1), 1472 (no. 1). Babylon; used synonymously with Bałdat [q.v.], that is, the city of Baghdad.

Baberd (variant: Babert'): 1341 (no. 1), 1346 (no. 1), 1453 (no. 1). (1) Fortress-city of Bayburt (Arabic: Bāybūrd, Bayburt) in Erzerum province, on left bank of the Čorox (Turkish: Çoruh) river, about 100 km. NW of city of Erzerum. (2) District, with the fortress-city as its center. (See V. J. Parry, "Bāybūrd (Bayburt)," *EI*, NE, I, 1128; Saint-Martin, *Mémoires*, I, 70; Hübschmann, *AO*, p. 413.)

Babert': 1480 (no. 1). *See* Baberd.

Babilac'woc' ašxarh: 1307 (no. 5). *See* Babelac'woc' ašxarh.

Bagaran (variant: Bagran): 1411 (no. 3). (1) Fortress-city, on right bank of Akhurian (Turkish: Arpa-çay) river, in canton of Aršarunik' in Ayrarat province. (2) Name of a canton, with the fortress-city as its center. (See Hübschmann, *AO*, pp. 410–411; *Arm. Gram.*, p. 113, no. 85.)

Bagran: 1422 (no. 1). *See* Bagaran.

Baguan (variant: Bagwan): 1462 (no. 3). Town, on left bank of the Euphrates river, in canton of Bagrewand in Ayrarat province; known also in Armenian sources as Dic'awan, Bagnac' Awan, Bagawan, Bagarwan, and Atši-Bagwan (cf. Arabic and Persian: Bagarvan, Badjarvan). (See Hübschmann, *AO*, p. 411; *Arm. Gram.*, p. 113, no. 85.)

Bagwan: 1421 (no. 1). *See* Baguan.

Balu: 1437 (no. 7). The canton of Palu, situated E of Kharput in E Turkey. (See Saint-Martin, *Mémoires*, I, 94, 165; II, 435.)

Bałdat (variants: Bałtat, Pałdat): 1401 (no. 4), 1422 (no. 1), 1428 (no. 4), 1446 (nos. 2, 3, 4), 1450 (no. 1), 1457 (no. 2), 1464 (no. 5), 1465 (nos. 5, 6). The city of Baghdad. *See also* Babelon.

Bałēš: 1410 (no. 2), 1418 (no. 1), 1422 (no. 1), 1425 (no. 1), 1428 (nos. 1, 2), 1435 (no. 3), 1436 (no. 3), 1438 (no. 4), 1443 (nos. 1, 2), 1445 (no. 3), 1446 (no. 1), 1449 (no. 1), 1450 (no. 1), 1454 (nos. 5, 6), 1456 (nos. 3, 4), 1457 (no. 2), 1458 (no. 5), 1459 (no. 8), 1460 (no. 9), 1462 (no. 3), 1463 (nos. 1, 2, 3), 1467 (no. 2), 1472 (no. 1), 1473 (no. 1), 1474 (no. 3), 1477 (no. 7). (1) Fortress-city of Bitlis (Arabic: Badlīs, Bitlīs), now in province of Van. (2) Canton, bounded on N and W by canton of Muš (Mush), on E by province of Van, and on S by canton of Słerd (Si'irt). (See Hübschmann, *AO*, p. 324; Saint-Martin, *Mémoires*, I, 103; G. L. Lewis, "Bidlīs (Bitlis)," *EI*, NE, I, 1206–1207; *Chèref-Nâmeh*, I. 1, 510–512; II. 2, 162–163.)

Bałtat: 1354 (no. 2), 1422 (no. 1). *See* Bałdat.
Bandumahi (variant: Bantumahi): 1371 (no. 3), 1473 (no. 4). *See* Aṙest.
Bantumahi: 1479 (no. 1). *See* Bandumahi.
Bari-K'aruk: 1361 (no. 3). It is not certain whether this was a village, fortress, or town. It was probably located in the vicinity of the seaport of Ayas in Cilicia.
Barjraberd: 1468 (no. 4). *See* Barjr-Berd.
Barjr-Berd (variants: Barjraberd, Barjr-Bert): 1303 (no. 4). Arabic: Barsbard; fortress, NW of Sis in Cilicia Tracheia. (See Ēp'rikean, *Baṙaran*, I, 407–409.)
Barjr-Bert: 1304 (no. 1). *See* Barjr-Berd.
Barmn: 1398 (no. 1). *See* Ałbak.
Basen: 1336 (no. 4), 1422 (no. 1), 1477 (no. 1). Canton, also known in Armenian sources as Baseank' (Greek: Phasiane), in Ayrarat province; E of Erzerum, near source of Araxes river. (See Hübschmann, *AO*, pp. 362–363; Saint-Martin, *Mémoires*, I, 107, 253.)
Bawlłi: 1410 (no. 2). Location unknown.
Baxvanic': 1445 (no. 1). Village in canton of Ṙštunik' in Vaspurakan province. (See Ēp'rikean, *Baṙaran*, I, 376.)
Bayazit: 1462 (no. 3). The fortress of the city of Bāyazīd, S of Mount Ararat, close to the Turkish frontier with Iran. (See V. J. Parry, "Bāyazīd," *EI*, NE, I, 1117.)
Bazenc': 1475 (no. 7). *See* Bazenic'.
Bazenic' (variant: Bazenc'): 1454 (no. 3), 1455 (no. 3). Monastery and village in Sparkert canton in the region of Mokk'. (See Oskean, *Vank'er*, III, 839.)
Berdak: 1306 (no. 4). Village in region of city of Van in Vaspurakan province. (See Oskean, *Vank'er*, I, 231.)
Berkri: 1301 (no. 1), 1307 (no. 3), 1318 (no. 2), 1371 (no. 3), 1421 (no. 6), 1426 (no. 3), 1475 (no. 2), 1478 (no. 2). (1) Canton, corresponding to the ancient Armenian canton of Aṙberani, in Vaspurakan province. (2) City, NE of Lake Van and E of city of Arčēš (Ardjīsh). (See Saint-Martin, *Mémoires*, I, 137; II, 427; *Chèref-Nâmeh*, I. 1, 503–504, 519.)
Betłahem: 1437 (no. 6). Monastery, in city of Tiflis, Georgia.
Biwrakan: 1469 (no. 7). Village and fortress, on left bank of Anberd river, in Aragacotn canton of Ayrarat province. (See Hübschmann, *AO*, p. 414.)
Biwzandia: 1453 (nos. 2, 3), 1480 (no. 2). The city of Byzantium. (See Vasiliev, *History*, I, 57, 58, 84.)
Bǰni: 1422 (no. 1), 1432 (no. 2), 1460 (no. 1). Village in E part of canton of Nig in Ayrarat province. (See Ēp'rikean, *Baṙaran*, I, 433–436.)
Bličayn: 1472 (no. 1). Fortress of Bleǰan, N of Xlat' (Khilāṭ). (See Ēp'rikean, *Baṙaran*, I, 425.)
Bohtank' (variant: Buxtan): 1473 (no. 1). The Kurdish district of Bohtān or Buhtān, S of Lake Van, the area between the Tigris and the Bohtān-su and the Little Khābūr. (See M. Streck, "Bohtān (Buhtān)," *EI*, OE, I, 739–740.)

Bolorajor: 1476 (no. 7). Monastery in Vayoc'-Jor in Siwnik' province. (See Ēp'rikean, *Bařaran*, I, 428.)

Bstoy: 1336 (no. 1). Village in canton of Gołt'n in Siwnik' province. (See Ēp'rikean, *Bařaran*, I, 438.)

Bt'ni, Mt.: 1351 (no. 3). Mountain in Ekełeac' (Erzindjān) canton. (See Ēp'rikean, *Bařaran*, I, 411.)

Buxtan: 1472 (no. 1). *See* Bohtank'.

Bznunik': 1327 (no. 1), 1331 (no. 2), 1337 (no. 3), 1349 (no. 2), 1472 (no. 1), 1476 (no. 10). Canton, which included the cities of Arčēš (Ardjīsh), Arckē, and Xizan (Hizan); it was the domain of the Bznuni Armenian feudal family. (See Hübschmann, *AO*, pp. 328–329.)

Car: 1411 (no. 2). Canton, also known in Armenian sources as Sisakan, and Sisakan Ostan, in Siwnik' province; its principal center was the town of Car. (See Ēp'rikean, *Bařaran*, II, 238–240; Eremyan, *Ašx.*, p. 82.)

Cařutijor: 1331 (no. 1). Canton in Ayrarat province.

Cəřget: 1472 (no. 1). Village, E of city of Muš (Mush) in E Anatolia. (See Ēp'rikean, *Bařaran*, II, 255.)

Cłak: 1422 (no. 1), 1474 (no. 3). Village on W shore of Lake Van, in canton of Bznunik'. (See Oskean, *Vank'er*, III, 938–939.)

Cnanařič: 1439 (no. 2). Monastery in canton of Daranałeac' [q.v.].

Cpat: 1413 (no. 2), 1421 (no. 13), 1423 (no. 2). Monastery in region of Mokk' [q.v.]. (See Oskean, *Vank'er*, III, 815–821.)

Člimon: 1338 (no. 1). Monastery in canton of Ekełeac' [q.v.] in E Anatolia.

Čziray (variant: J̌əziray): 1452 (no. 5). Town of Djazīrat b. 'Omar, on the right (west) bank of the central course of the Tigris. (See R. Hartmann, "Djazīrat b. 'Omar," *EI*, OE, I, 1030–1031; Saint-Martin, *Mémoires*, I, 162; *Chèref-Nâmeh*, I. 1, 474–476.)

C'ałman: 1432 (no. 5). A Kurdish canton in the region of Çemişkezek. (See Xač'ikyan, *XV Dari*, I, p. 809.)

C'awłac'k'ar (variant: C'awłeac'-K'ar): 1437 (no. 4). Village and monastery in Vayoc'-Jor in Siwnik' province. (See Hübschmann, *AO*, p. 476.)

C'ipna: 1425 (no. 5), 1450 (no. 1). *See* C'ipnay.

C'ipnay (variant: C'ipna): 1393 (nos. 1, 2), 1408 (no. 3), 1417 (no. 4), 1419 (no. 1), 1446 (no. 1), 1457 (no. 2). Monastery, on island of C'ipan in Lake Van, near promontory now called Adabaghi. (See Oskean, *Vank'er*, I, 135–138.)

C'łnay: 1467 (no. 1). Monastery in canton of Gołt'n in Siwnik' province.

Č'ałat'ay: 1452 (no. 5), 1472 (no. 1). Čaghatai or Čaghatay, the Central Asian khanate. (See W. Barthold–[J. A. Boyle], "Čaghatay Khānate," *EI*, NE, II, 2–4.)

Č'mškacag: 1435 (nos. 1, 2). *See* Č'mškacak.

Č'mškacak (variant: Č'mškacag): 1432 (no. 5), 1436 (no. 6). Canton of Çemişkezek in E Anatolia, SW of Erzindjān. (See Saint-Martin, *Mémoires*, I, 94, 95, 165; II, 431; Hübschmann, *AO*, p. 463.)

Č'uk'i: 1468 (no. 6). Village in the region of Gankṙay [q.v.].

Dahavrēž: 1304 (no. 3). *See* T'avrēz.

Dałman: 1457 (no. 5). Town of Dāmghān, on main highway between Teheran and Mashad, some 344 km. E of Teheran. (See D. N. Wilber, "Dāmghān," *EI*, NE, II, 107.)

Damaskos: 1401 (no. 1), 1422 (no. 1), 1468 (no. 1). City of Damascus in Syria. (See N. Elisséeff, "Dimashḳ," *EI*, NE, II, 277–291.) *See also* Dəməšx.

Daranałeac': 1425 (no. 9), 1439 (nos. 1, 2), 1449 (no. 8), 1450 (no. 4), 1464 (no. 1). Daranissa of the ancient Greeks; canton, later known as Kamax (Kemakh), in Armenia Major. (See Hübschmann, *AO*, pp. 283–284; Eremyan, *Ašx.*, p. 49.)

Darband: 1436 (no. 3). Town of Derbend in Daghistan, called Bāb al-Abwāb by the Arabs in the Middle Ages; also designation of a pass and fortress at E end of the Caucasus. (See D. M. Dunlop, "Bāb al-Abwāb," *EI*, NE, I, 835–836; Hübschmann, *Arm. Gram.*, p. 36, no. 53; Spuler, *Mongolen in Iran*, and *Goldene Horde*.)

Davrēž: 1426 (no. 4), 1473 (no. 1). *See* T'avrēz.

Dawrēz: 1453 (no. 2). *See* T'avrez.

Dawrēž: 1425 (no. 4), 1429 (no. 1), 1432 (no. 1). *See* T'avrēz.

Dayvrēž: 1441 (no. 1). *See* T'avrēz.

Derǰan: 1446 (no. 5). Canton, known in ancient times as Derxene, Derzene, or Xerxene; now called Tercan, in Turkish province of Erzincan, in the valley of the Euphrates W of Erzerum. The colophons also refer to the canton's two subdivisions: Nerk'in-Derǰan (Inner or Interior Derǰan) and Verin-Derǰan (Upper Derǰan). (See Hübschmann, *AO*, p. 287; Saint-Martin, *Mémoires*, I, 44, 45.)

Dəməšx (variants: Dməšx, Dmšx): 1405 (no. 4). Cf. Arabic Dimashḳ; Damascus. (See N. Elisséeff, "Dimashḳ," *EI*, NE, II, 277–291; Steingass, p. 535b.)

Diarbak: 1435 (no. 3). Town of Diyār Bakr or Diyarbakïr (Diyarbakir) in E Anatolia. (See "Diyār Bakr," *EI*, NE, II, 343–344.)

Diza Jor: 1398 (no. 1). Lit., Valley of Diza; probably situated S. of Lake Van, in vicinity of Çölemerik and Gawaṙ. (See *Chèref-Nâmeh*, I. 1, 177–178.)

[D]klat: 1397 (no. 1). The river Didjla (modernized and arabicized form of Diglat in cuneiform inscriptions; cf. modern Turkish Dicle Nehri), that is, the Tigris river. (See Hübschmann, *AO*, p. 421; *Arm. Gram.*, p. 292, no. 13; R. Hartmann–[S. H. Longrigg], "Didjla," *EI*, NE, II, 249–251; *Dictionary of Bible*, p. 382). Eremyan (*Ašx.*, p. 86) claims that the term referred to that part of the Tigris which extends beyond the point where the eastern and western branches of the river merge.

Dməšx: 1436 (no. 1). *See* Dəməšx.

D[mšx]: 1401 (no. 4). *See* Dəməšx.

Duṙn Alanac': 1400 (nos. 1, 2). Lit., Gate of the Alans; the pass of Darial (Arabic: Bāb al-Lān or Bāb Allān) in the middle Caucasus, E of Mt. Kazbek and S of Vladikavkas. (See D. M. Dunlop, "Bāb al-Lān (Bāb

Allān)," *EI*, NE, I, 837; *Ḥudūd al-ʿĀlam*, "*The Regions of the World*," *A Persian Geography*, trans. and ed. by V. Minorsky, Oxford, 1937, pp. 401, 446.)

Edem: 1453 (no. 2). Eden; the reference is to the Garden of Eden. (See *Dictionary of Bible*, p. 229; Hübschmann, *Arm. Gram.*, p. 300, no. 4; Baṙgirkʿ, I, 646; Malxaseancʿ, *HBB*, I, 549.)

Edesia: 1397 (no. 1). The ancient city of Edessa in Mesopotamia, at the site of present-day Urfa (Arabic: al-Ruhā) in E Anatolia.

Egeay: 1322 (no. 2). The ancient name of the port-city of Ayas [q.v.]; cf. ancient Greek names Aigai, or Aegae. (See Eremyan, *Ašx.*, p. 52.)

Egiptos: 1305 (no. 1), 1327 (no. 2), 1337 (no. 2), 1446 (no. 6), 1449 (no. 1), 1453 (no. 1), 1469 (no. 6). The common Armenian term for Egypt (cf. Greek Aigyptos). (See *Dictionary of Bible*, p. 231.)

Ekełeacʿ (variant: Ekełecʿ): 1340 (no. 2), 1351 (no. 3), 1370 (no. 1), 1416 (no. 2), 1422 (no. 2), 1425 (no. 9), 1429 (no. 2), 1432 (no. 1), 1439 (no. 1), 1446 (no. 5). Canton (Greek: Achilisēnē; Latin: Acilisinae), now corresponding to the region of Erzincan in E Anatolia. (See Hübschmann, *AO*, p. 286; *Arm. Gram.*, p. 403.)

Ekełecʿ: 1338 (no. 1). *See* Ekełeacʿ.

Ełegeacʿ: 1419 (no. 2), 1426 (no. 1), 1437 (no. 4), 1449 (no. 5), 1460 (no. 5). Another term used synonymously for Vayocʿ-Jor [q.v.] in Siwnikʿ province. (See Hübschmann, *AO*, p. 423.)

Ełegis: 1306 (no. 3). Town, now known as Alageaz (formerly also Ełegikʿ or Ełegeacʿ Awan) in canton of Vayocʿ-Jor in Siwnikʿ province. (See Ēpʿrikean, *Baṙaran*, I, 673–676.)

Ełivard: 1465 (nos. 3, 4), 1466 (no. 1), 1468 (no. 2), 1469 (no. 4). Town (now a village) in the region of Etchmiadzin in the district of Erevan, between the Kʿasał and Hrazdan rivers. (See Ēpʿrikean, *Baṙaran*, I, 682–685.)

Ełrdot (variant: Ełrdut): 1463 (no. 1), 1466 (no. 7). Monastery, W of Muš (Mush) on Mt. Sim, in Tarōn canton. (See Ēpʿrikean, *Baṙaran*, I, 686.)

Ełrdut: 1460 (no. 12). *See* Ełrdot.

Ełujor: 1460 (no. 5). Village in Vayocʿ-Jor canton of Siwnikʿ province.

Epʿrat: 1312 (no. 1), 1337 (no. 2), 1388 (no. 3), 1395 (no. 1). The Euphrates river. (For its etymology, see Hübschmann, *AO*, pp. 426–427; also consult *Dictionary of Bible*, p. 276.)

Erapōlis: 1436 (no. 6). Hierapolis, the ancient name of Čʿmškacak [q.v.].

Erasx: 1422 (no. 1), 1472 (no. 1). Variant of Arakʿs (cf. Greek: Araxes; Georgian: Rakhsi or Arazi; Arabic: al-Rass), the largest and best known river in historic Armenia. (See Hübschmann, *AO*, p. 424.)

Ereran (variant: Ēreran): 1349 (no. 1), 1432 (no. 1). 1463 (no. 13). Monastery, N of Van, near village of Ererin in canton of Aṙberani. (See Oskean, *Vankʿer*, I, 346–348.)

Erewan (variant: Ērewan): 1422 (no. 1). Erevan. Town in Kotaykʿ canton of Ayrarat province; now capital of Armenian SSR. (See Hübschmann, *AO*, p. 425.)

Erənčak: 1441 (no. 7). *See* Ernǰak.

Erənǰak: 1400 (no. 1), 1422 (no. 1). *See* Ernǰak.

Erinǰak: 1422 (no. 1). *See* Ernǰak.

Erkayn-Ənkuzeac' (variant: Erkēn-Ənkuzec'): 1435 (no. 2). Village in canton of C'ałman [q.v.] in the region of Çarsancak. (See Ēp'rikean, *Bařaran*, I, 713.)

Erkēn-Ənkuzec': 1432 (no. 5). *See* Erkayn-Ənkuzeac'.

Erkir Lewonoy: 1351 (no. 2). Lit., the land of Leon; that is, Cilicia.

Erkirn Xaramni: 1335 (no. 6). Lit., the land of the Ḳaramān; that is, Ḳaramān or Ḳaramān-ili (ancient Caramania), whose boundaries generally included the lands of Lycaonia, the Cilician Taurus, and the whole southern Anatolian coast territory as far as Adalia. (See J. H. Kramers, "Ḳaramān," *EI*, OE, II, 744–745.)

Ernčak: 1458 (no. 1). *See* Ernǰak.

Ernǰak (variants: Erənčak, Erənǰak, Erinǰak, Ernčak): 1386 (no. 1), 1422 (no. 1), 1435 (no. 3), 1438 (no. 3). (1) Canton (Arabic: Alindjaḳ or Ālindja) in Siwnik' province. (2) City and fortress (also called Alənǰay; Arabic: Alindjaḳ), SE of Naxiǰewan, on left bank of Ernǰak river. The ruins of the fortress are now called Alinca-kale. (See V. Minorsky, "Alindjaḳ or Ālindja," *EI*, NE, I, 404; Hübschmann, *AO*, p. 426; Saint-Martin, *Mémoires*, I, 143, 146, 173; II, 125, 139.)

Erusałēm: 1335 (no. 6), 1366 (no. 1), 1368 (no. 1), 1386 (no. 2), 1392 (no. 3), 1400 (no. 5), 1419 (no. 5), 1421 (no. 7), 1436 (no. 1), 1441 (nos. 7, 10), 1445 (no. 1), 1453 (no. 2), 1469 (no. 6), 1475 (no. 9), 1478 (no. 6). The city of Jerusalem.

Erznkay: 1431 (no. 2), 1473 (no. 10). *See* Eznkay.

Ewstat'ē: 1395 (no. 2), 1400 (no. 3), 1401 (no. 2), 1406 (no. 1), 1407 (no. 2), 1437 (no. 1). *See* Tat'ew.

Ezənkay: 1450 (no. 3), 1464 (no. 1). *See* Eznkay.

Eznka: 1422 (no. 2), 1446 (no. 5), 1453 (no. 1). *See* Eznkay.

Eznkay (variants: Erznkay, Ezənkay, Eznka): 1303 (no. 5), 1334 (no. 1), 1338 (no. 1), 1340 (no. 2), 1355 (no. 1), 1387 (no. 3), 1403 (no. 5), 1425 (nos. 9, 10), 1428 (no. 4), 1446 (no. 5), 1449 (no. 7), 1450 (no. 1), 1451 (no. 1), 1452 (no. 5), 1453 (no. 1), 1473 (no. 2). (1) Canton, with city of the same name as its center. (2) Town and fortress, now called Erzincan (Arabic: Erzindjān), in E Anatolia, on N bank of the Karasu (northern tributary of the Euphrates). (See R. Hartmann–[Fr. Taeschner], "Erzindjan," *EI*, NE, II, 711–712; Saint-Martin, *Mémoires*, I, 71, 72.)

Ēgēpat: 1477 (no. 1). Village in canton of Verin Basen in Ayrarat province. (See Ēp'rikean, *Bařaran*, I, 802.)

Ēǰmiacin (variant: Ēǰmiaycin): 1441 (no. 9), 1444 (nos. 1, 3, 4), 1447 (no. 1), 1449 (nos. 3, 4), 1450 (no. 1), 1453 (no. 2), 1454 (no. 2), 1456 (nos. 3, 5), 1457 (no. 5), 1458 (no. 4), 1459 (no. 5), 1460 (no. 2), 1461 (no. 1), 1462 (nos. 3, 5, 11), 1464 (no. 12), 1465 (nos. 2, 4), 1468 (no. 3), 1471 (nos. 4, 5), 1472 (no. 2), 1473 (no. 6), 1475 (no. 3), 1476 (no. 5). Etchmiadzin. Monastery and cathedral in canton of Aragacotn in Ayrarat province, situated S of ancient Armenian capital of Vagharshapat; original seat of the Armenian catholicosate which, after many peregrinations, was transferred again to Etchmiadzin in 1441, where it has since remained. (See Ēp'rikean, *Bařaran*, I, 809–831; Hübschmann, *AO*, p. 428; Ōrmanean, *Azgapatum*.)

Ējmiaycin: 1451 (no. 4). *See* Ējmiacin.

Ēreran: 1464 (no. 15). *See* Ereran.

Ērewan: 1405 (no. 1). *See* Erewan.

Ēzd: 1457 (no. 5). City of Yazd or Yezd in central Iran. (See C. Huart, "Yazd," *EI*, OE, IV, 1161; Spuler, *Mongolen in Iran*, esp. pp. 143–145.)

Ɛncani (?): 1479 (no. 1). A village; probably in the region of Berkri [q.v.].

Ɛřštōneac' Cov: 1401 (no. 1). Lit., the Sea of the Rshtunis; one of the names by which the Armenians referred to Lake Van.

Ɛstambul: 1453 (no. 1). *See* Stambul.

Ɛstampawl: 1480 (no. 1). *See* Stambul.

Ɛstəmpawl: 1475 (no. 8). *See* Stambul.

Ɛstəmpōl: 1464 (no. 3), 1480 (no. 1). *See* Stambul.

Ɛstənbawl: 1457 (no. 2). *See* Stambul.

Gamałiēl: 1363 (no. 2), 1374 (no. 1), 1397 (no. 2), 1427 (no. 3), 1442 (no. 4), 1455 (no. 6), 1468 (no. 5). Monastery in canton of Xizan [q.v.]. (See Oskean, *Vank'er*, III, 843–851.)

Gamirk' (variant: Tunn Gamrac'): 1422 (no. 1). Variant name for the Anatolian region of Cappadocia. (See Ēp'rikean, *Bařaran*, II, 277.)

Ganjak: 1428 (no. 4). The town of Gandja in Persian Ādharbaydjān, situated S of Tabrīz and Maragha and SE of Lake Urmia. (See Hübschmann, *Arm. Gram.*, pp. 33–34, no. 47.)

Ganjak: 1436 (no. 1), 1466 (nos. 2, 3), 1468 (no. 2). (1) The province of Gandja in the Trans-Caucasus; now part of Azerbaijan SSR. (2) Town of Gandja (now called Kirovabad) in province of the same name. (See W. Barthold–[J. A. Boyle], "Gandja," *EI*, NE, II, 975–976; Saint-Martin, *Mémoires*, I, 150, 151, 220, 365; II, 103, 415, 455; Hübschmann, *AO*, pp. 416–417; *Arm. Gram.*, pp. 33–34, no. 47.)

Ganjasar: 1417 (no. 1). Monastery in canton of Xač'en in Arc'ax province. (See Hübschmann, *AO*, p. 417; Ēp'rikean, *Bařaran*, I, 462–464.)

Ganjē: 1335 (no. 7). Fortress in Cilicia, situated at the foot of the Taurus mountains. (See Ēp'rikean, *Bařaran*, I, 465.)

Gankřay: 1468 (no. 6). Capital of ancient Paphlagonia; situated between the rivers Şirin-su and Aci-su, which flow into the Halys. (See *Chèref-Nâmeh*, II. 2, 428–429.)

Gařnaker: 1466 (no. 2), 1468 (no. 2). Monastery, near village of the same name, in canton of P'arisos in Arc'ax province. (See Hübschmann, *AO*, p. 417; Ēp'rikean, *Bařaran*, I, 466.)

Gařni: 1429 (no. 1). Canton in Siwnik' province, with fortress-city of the same name as its center; the ruins of the fortress are located 35 km.

E of Erevan. (See Hübschmann, *AO*, p. 342; Saint-Martin, *Mémoires*, I, 145, 242; II, 101, 115, 259, 421.)

Gavazan: 1436 (no. 1). Fortress in canton of Ałestew, now the district of Noyemberyan in Armenian SSR. (See Xač'ikyan, *XV Dari*, I, p. 804; Ēp'rikean, *Baŕaran*, I, 500.)

Gawaṙ: 1398 (no. 1). Kawār or Kēwar, near Djūlāmerg, in district of Hakkārī. (See V. Minorsky, "Kurds," *EI*, OE, II, 1141.)

Gawaṙuc': 1362 (no. 1). This appears to be the plain of Diza in district of Hakkārī, S of Lake Van. (See Ēp'rikean, *Baŕaran*, I, 499–500.)

Gawaš: 1418 (no. 3), 1459 (no. 2). (1) Canton, W of Ostan [Wusṭān], corresponding to Ṙštunik' [q.v.] of the Armenian sources. (2) Village, now called Gevaş, near S shore of Lake Van. (See V. Minorsky, "Kurds," *EI*, OE, II, 1145.)

Gayl Get: 1453 (no. 1). Town, now called Kelkit, S of Trabzon (Trebizond) and Gümüşane. (See Ēp'rikean, *Baŕaran*, I, 453–454.)

Gelan: 1457 (no. 1). Region of Gīlān or Ghilan in NW Iran, between the Elburz mountains and Caspian Sea. (See Cleaves, *Mongolian Documents*, p. 57, n. 2; Spuler, *Mongolen in Iran*.)

Gełam: 1451 (no. 4). Region named after mountains called Geł or Gełam and the lake called Gełamay Covak (cf. Turkish: Gök-çay; Persian: Deriay-i Shirin), now called Sevan. The region was also known in Armenian sources as Gełark'uni or Gełark'unik'. (See Ēp'rikean, *Baŕaran*, I, 501–505.)

Gełark'uni: 1319 (no. 2). Monastery in village of Xorvaget. The province of Arc'ax had a canton called Xoruaget, and it is probable, but not certain, that the village was located in this canton. (Cf. Ališan, *Sisakan*, p. 532.)

Gełark'unik': 1465 (no. 2). Canton in Siwnik' province, now corresponding to the regions of Kamo and Martuni in Armenian SSR. (See Hübschmann, *AO*, p. 348.)

Getamēj: 1411 (no. 2), 1456 (no. 1). Monastery in canton of Car in Arc'ax province. (See Xač'ikyan, *XV Dari*, I, p. 804; *XV Dari*, II, p. 590.)

Gēorg Zawrawar, St.: 1437 (no. 7). Monastery in canton of Balu [q.v.].

Gēorgay Zoravar, St.: 1441 (no. 9). Monastery in K'ajberunik' [q.v.].

Glajor: 1302 (no. 1), 1303 (no. 2), 1313 (no. 1), 1314 (no. 2), 1321 (no. 1), 1323 (no. 1), 1332 (no. 1), 1335 (no. 5). Monastery in canton of Vayoc'-Jor in Siwnik' province. (See Hübschmann, *AO*, p. 416.)

Glak: 1472 (no. 1). Monastery, also known in Armenian sources as Innaknean and Surb Karapet, in canton of Tarōn [q.v.].

Gołgot'ay: 1476 (no. 2). Golgotha, the traditional site of the crucifixion of Christ, in the Church of the Holy Sepulcher at Jerusalem. (See *Dictionary of Bible*, p. 339.)

Gołt'an: 1336 (no. 1), 1467 (no. 1). *See* Gołt'n.

Gołt'n (variant: Gołt'an): 1432 (no. 3). Canton (Greek: Coltini; Latin: Coltene) in Siwnik' province, now corresponding to the regions of

Aprakunis and Ordubad in Armenian SSR. (See Ēp'rikean, *Baṙaran*, I, 542–547; Eremyan, *Ašx.*, p. 48.)

Gori (variant: Gōri): 1438 (no. 6). Town in district of Kartli in Georgia, at the junction of the Liakhvi with the Kura. (See Allen, *History*, pp. 60 n. 5, 407; Spuler, *Mongolen in Iran*, p. 108.)

Gōri: 1476 (no. 2). *See* Gori.

Gṙner: 1303 (no. 4). Monastery, near fortress of Barjr-Berd, in Cilicia Tracheia. (See Ēp'rikean, *Baṙaran*, I, 563.)

Gugark': 1420 (no. 3). The province of Gogarene; now corresponding to the Georgian province of Samtzkhé. (See Allen, *History*, p. 413; Ēp'rikean, *Baṙaran*, I, 555–557; Eremyan, *Ašx.*, p. 48.)

Gumbayt': 1323 (no. 2). Village in canton of Menckert [q.v.].

Halap: 1337 (no. 2), 1361 (no. 3), 1400 (no. 5), 1401 (nos. 1, 4), 1468 (no. 4), 1469 (no. 2), 1472 (no. 1). The city of Aleppo in northern Syria.

Hałbat (variant: Haxbat): 1438 (no. 2), 1455 (no. 1). Monastery in canton of Jorop'or in Gugark' (Samtzkhé) province. (See Brosset, "Description des monastères arméniens d'Haghbat et de Sanahin.")

Hamadan: 1457 (nos. 1, 5). The city of Hamadhān (Old Persian: Hagmatāna; classical: Ecbatana), in the plain at the foot of Mt. Elwend. (See "Hamadhān," *EI*, OE, III, 241–242; Spuler, *Mongolen in Iran*.)

Hamit': 1437 (no. 2). *See* Amit'.

Hamšen: 1425 (no. 11). Canton, formerly known in Armenian sources as Hamamašēn, E of Trebizond, in province of Xałtik'. (See Hübschmann, *AO*, p. 442; Inčičean, *Ašx.*, pp. 395–396.)

Harhoc': 1450 (no. 5). *See* Xarhoc'.

Hawčalay: 1462 (no. 1). Georgian Avčala; a suburb of the city of Tiflis. (See Xač'ikyan, *XV Dari*, II, p. 593.)

Haxbat: 1441 (no. 1), 1458 (no. 3). *See* Hałbat.

Hayastan: The Armenian term for Armenia.

Hayk': 1422 (no. 1), 1437 (no. 5). One of the terms by which the Armenians, in the Middle Ages, referred to their own country. In the two colophons, however, the reference seems to be to the province of Vaspurakan.

Hayk': 1337 (no. 2), 1361 (no. 3). These references are to Cilicia under the Armenian kingdom.

Hayk'ar (variant: Hek'ar): 1363 (no. 1), 1398 (no. 1). The Kurdish principality of Hakkārī or Hakkarīyā in the province of Van on the Persian frontier. (See "Hakkārī," *EI*, OE, III, 226–227.)

Hayk'aray Jor: 1361 (no. 1). The valley of Hakkārī. *See* Hayk'ar.

Hayoc' Mecac' (variant: Mecac' Hayoc'): 1321 (no. 1). Armenia Major.

Hayoc'-T'aṙ: 1464 (no. 2), 1471 (nos. 3, 4). Monastery (better known in Armenian sources as Hawuc' T'aṙ), in canton of Gaṙni in Siwnik' province. (See Garegin Yovsēp'eanc', *Hawuc' T'aṙi Amenap'rkič'ə ew Noynanun Yušarjanner Hay Aruesdi Mēǰ*, Jerusalem, 1937; Hübschmann, *AO*, p. 444.)

Hazarakn: 1316 (no. 1). Lit., Thousand Springs; village whose exact location is unknown.

Hek'ar: 1425 (no. 8). *See* Hayk'ar.

Hermon: 1348 (no. 2), 1351 (no. 1), 1419 (no. 2), 1423 (no. 1), 1426 (no. 1), 1449 (no. 5), 1457 (no. 3), 1460 (no. 4). Monastery in canton of Vayoc'-Jor in Siwnik' province.

Hēšat: 1405 (no. 4), 1428 (no. 1). This term is not attested in any of the Armenian geographers. It is probably a corruption of Hašteank', one of the ancient cantons of Armenia, situated W of the region of Tarōn. (See Hübschmann, *AO*, pp. 291–293.)

Hizan: 1397 (no. 1), 1400 (no. 2), 1401 (no. 5), 1402 (no. 1), 1417 (no. 3), 1425 (no. 4), 1427 (no. 3), 1431 (no. 3), 1451 (no. 5), 1456 (no. 6), 1459 (no. 3), 1468 (no. 1), 1473 (no. 1), 1474 (no. 6). *See* Xizan.

Hndustan: 1400 (no. 1). Hindustan, that is, Afghanistan.

Honac' Ašxarh (variant: Ašxarhn Honakan): 1371 (no. 1), 1384 (no. 1). Lit., land of the Huns; this is one of the designations by which the Armenians referred to the Crimea.

Hoṙmac' Ašxarh (variants: Hoṙmastan, Hoṙmoc' Ašxarh, Hoṙmoc' tun, Hoṙomac' tun, Hoṙomk', Hoṙomoc' ašxarh, Hoṙomoc' erkir, Hṙomac' erkir, Hṙomac' tun, Hṙomanc' erkir, Hṙomoc', Tunn Hoṙomoc'): 1346 (no. 1). The land of Rūm, that is, the territories of the Greeks in Asia Minor. (See Franz Babinger, "Rūm," *EI*, OE, III, 1174–1175.)

Hoṙmastan: 1442 (no. 1). *See* Hoṙmac' Ašxarh.

Hoṙmoc' Ašxarh: 1453 (no. 2). *See* Hoṙmac' Ašxarh.

Hoṙmoc' Tun: 1453 (no. 3). *See* Hoṙmac' Ašxarh.

Hoṙomac' Tun: 1449 (no. 1). *See* Hoṙmac' Ašxarh.

Hoṙomk': 1335 (no. 1), 1422 (no. 1). *See* Hoṙmac' Ašxarh.

Hoṙomoc' Ašxarh: 1473 (nos. 2, 3). *See* Hoṙmac' Ašxarh.

Hoṙomoc' Erkir: 1473 (no. 1). *See* Hoṙmac' Ašxarh.

Hṙē: 1449 (no. 6), 1457 (no. 1), 1458 (no. 2), 1460 (no. 2), 1462 (nos. 3, 6), 1468 (no. 1). The city of Herāt or Harāt in NW Afghanistan; the city also gave its name to a province. (See M. Longworth Dames, "Herāt," *EI*, OE, III, 299; Spuler, *Mongolen in Iran*, esp. pp. 155–160.)

Hṙomac' Erkir: 1387 (no. 2). *See* Hoṙmac' Ašxarh.

Hṙomac' Tun: 1472 (no. 1). *See* Hoṙmac' Ašxarh.

Hṙomanc' Erkir: 1464 (no. 3). *See* Hoṙmac' Ašxarh.

Hṙomoc': 1445 (no. 1). *See* Hoṙmac' Ašxarh.

Hṙovm: 1453 (no. 1). *See* Hṙom.

Hṙovmklay: 1464 (no. 16). Fortress (Latin: Arx Romanorum; Arabic: Rūm Ḳal'a or Ḳal'at al-Rūm), on the right bank of the Euphrates, SE of Samosata and NE of Aleppo. It was the seat of the Armenian pontificate from 1147 until 1292. (See Saint-Martin, *Mémoires*, I, 196–197, 442, 443; E. Honigmann, "Rūm Ḳal'a," *EI*, OE, III, 1175–1177.)

Iloyvank': 1415 (no. 2). Monastery in village of Ili, situated in valley of Ostan (Wusṭān) in Vaspurakan province. (See Oskean, *Vank'er*, I, 158–161.)

Irał: 1457 (no. 5), 1462 (nos. 3, 5), 1463 (no. 7). Medieval Armenian term for the country of Iraq. (See M. Hartmann, "Al-'Irāḳ," *EI*, OE, II, 513–519). The texts do not distinguish between al-'Irāḳ al-'Arabī (Arab Iraq) and al-'Irāḳ al-'Adjamī (Persian Iraq).

Islampol: 1453 (no. 3). Islāmbol; in Turkish, literally Islamfull. A variant form of Istanbul, describing the new character of Constantinople after its capture by the Ottomans. (See J. H. Mordtmann, "Constantinople," *EI*, OE, I, 867–876.) Mordtmann suggests that the form Islāmbol appeared in the sixteenth century; the present text indicates that the form was used as early as the year 1453. (See Anasyan, *Haykakan Ałbyurnerə*, pp. 58–59.)

Ispahan: 1454 (no. 2), 1465 (no. 6). *See* Aspahan.

Israēl: 1318 (no. 2), 1442 (no. 1). *See* Israyēl.

Israēł: 1302 (no. 1), 1442 (no. 1). *See* Israyēl.

Israyel: 1400 (no. 2). *See* Israyēl.

Israyēl (variants: Israēl, Israēł, Israyel): 1416 (no. 1), 1438 (no. 2). Israel. (See *Dictionary of Bible*, pp. 429–449.)

Jagavank': 1425 (no. 6). Monastery, near village of Jag, in canton of Kotayk' in Ayrarat province. (See Hübschmann, *AO*, p. 446.)

Joroc': 1420 (no. 3). Canton in province of Gugark' [q.v.]; it now corresponds to the region of Alaverdi in Armenian SSR. (See Hübschmann, *AO*, p. 447; Xač'ikyan, *XV Dari*, I, p. 807.)

Joroyvank': 1449 (no. 4). Monastery in canton of Tosp or K'ajberunik'. (See Hübschmann, *AO*, p. 447; Oskean, *Vank'er*, I, 251–254.)

J̌ahan: 1304 (no. 1), 1337 (no. 2). *See* J̌ahun.

J̌ahun: 1329 (no. 1), 1331 (no. 2), 1337 (no. 3). The river Djayḥān (ancient Pyramus; modern Turkish: Ceyhan), one of the two rivers which cross Cilicia and flow into the Mediterranean. (See "Djayḥān," *EI*, NE, II, 502–503.)

J̌ermajor: 1451 (no. 3). Canton, now called Pervari, in the valley of the Bohtan-su, S of Lake Van. (See Hübschmann, *AO*, p. 464; Eremyan, *Ašx.*, p. 78.)

J̌ermuk: 1452 (no. 5). Town of Çermik (Arabic: Ḥiṣn al-Ḥamma), NW of Diyarbakir and N of Siverek. (See Hübschmann, *AO*, p. 464; Eremyan, *Ašx.*, p. 59.)

J̌əziray: 1472 (no. 1). *See* Čziray.

J̌ławna: 1330 (no. 1). Monastery; its exact location is unknown.

J̌orehangist: 1429 (no. 2). Monastery in the region of Erzindjān (Erzincan) in E Anatolia.

J̌ulamerk: 1398 (no. 1), 1442 (no. 2). Fortress-city in the extreme SE region of Turkey; now a small town called Çölemerik (Arabic: Djulamerk), about 3 km. from the Great Zab, a tributary of the Tigris. (See Fr. Taeschner, "Čölemerik," *EI*, NE, II, 57; Saint-Martin, *Mémoires*, I, 141; *Chèref-Nâmeh*, I. 1, 176, 536.)

J̌ułay: 1325 (no. 3). The ancient and once important town of Djulfa (usually referred to as Eski or Old Djulfa to distinguish it from Djulfa in Iṣfahān) in Armenia, on the N bank of the Araxes. (S. M. Streck, "Djulfa," *EI*, OE, I, 1061.)

Kac: 1465 (no. 2). Village in canton of Gełarkʻuni in Siwnikʻ province. (See Ēpʻrikean, *Baṙaran*, II, 263.)

Kafa: 1365 (no. 2), 1383 (no. 1), 1475 (no. 9). *See* Kafay.

Kafay (variant: Kafa): 1344 (no. 1), 1384 (no. 1), 1421 (no. 14), 1449 (no. 1), 1455 (no. 8), 1456 (no. 7), 1475 (no. 8). Town of Kafa or Kaffa (in ancient times as well as now called Theodosia), on S shore of the Crimean Peninsula. (See Hrushevsky, *Istoriya*, IV, 298–299; W. Barthold, "Kafa," *EI*, OE, II, 617–618; Spuler, *Goldene Horde*, pp. 234–236, 392–397.)

Kagtʻancʻ: 1409 (no. 3). Village in canton of Mokkʻ [q.v.]. (See Ēpʻrikean, *Baṙaran*, II, 275.)

Kalahokʻ: 1472 (no. 1). Fortress of Galhuk in the region of the Djazīra. (See *Chèref-Nâmeh*, I. 1, 151; Ēpʻrikean, *Baṙaran*, II, 262.)

Kamax: 1446 (no. 5), 1450 (no. 3), 1453 (no. 1), 1462 (no. 9), 1464 (no. 1). Town and fortress of Kemakh or Kemah (Arabic: Kemākh) in province of Erzerum, SW of Erzincan on S bank of the Euphrates. (See "Kemākh," *EI*, OE, II, 846–847; Saint-Martin, *Mémoires*, I, 72, 73; II, 433, 435.)

Kan: 1341 (no. 1). Village in Taykʻ, situated in a plain NW of Erzerum. (See Ēpʻrikean, *Baṙaran*, II, 275–276.)

Kapadovk: 1422 (no. 1). The country of Cappadocia in central Asia Minor; the more common Armenian form is Kapadovkia. (See Ēpʻrikean, *Baṙaran*, II, 277; *Dictionary of Bible*, p. 127.)

Kapan: 1322 (no. 1). *See* Łapʻan.

Kapos (variant: Kapʻos): 1425 (no. 9). Monastery, situated W of Erzincan. (See Xačʻikyan, *XIV Dari*, p. 669; *XV Dari*, I, p. 806.)

Kapʻos: 1416 (no. 2). *See* Kapos.

Kaputicʻ: 1422 (no. 1). Fortress in canton of Aršarunikʻ in Ayrarat province.

Karapet, St.: 1368 (no. 1), 1408 (no. 2), 1463 (no. 1). Monastery in canton of Tarōn; also known in Armenian sources as Glak and Innaknean. (See Ēpʻrikean, *Baṙaran*, II, 284–290.) *See also* Glak.

Karatash: 1462 (no. 3). The text reads kʻaradašt, lit., rocky field. The transcription of this term seems to be erroneous, as evidenced by the fact that the fortress of Manačihr [q.v.] was known in Turkish as Karatash, meaning "black rock."

Karin: 1335 (no. 2), 1422 (no. 1). The ancient Armenian name of Erzerum. (See Minorsky, "Some Early Documents in Persian," p. 188, n. 2; Herzfeld, *Zoroaster and His World*, II, 767, n. 23.) *See also* Arzrum.

Karmir: 1435 (no. 1), 1436 (no. 6). Monastery near village of Agarak in region of Çemişkezek in E Anatolia. (See Hübschmann, *AO*, pp. 439–440; Oskean, *Vankʻer*, II, 506–527.)

Karpʻi: 1304 (no. 4). Village in canton of Aragacotn in Ayrarat province; NW of Erevan. (See Ēpʻrikean, *Baṙaran*, II, 293–297.)

Kars (variant: Karuc'): 1422 (no. 1). Fortress-city, now capital of province of the same name in NE Turkey, on the bank of the Akhurian river. (See W. Barthold, "Kars," *EI*, OE, II, 774–775; Saint-Martin, *Mémoires*, I, 107, 111, 375.)

Karuc': 1412 (no. 2). Ancient Armenian name of Kars [q.v.].

Kasbic' Cov (variants: Kaspic' Cov, Kazbic' Cov): 1307 (no. 5), 1315 (no. 1), 1325 (no. 1), 1329 (no. 1), 1331 (no. 2). The Caspian Sea.

Kaspic' Cov: 1312 (no. 1). *See* Kasbic' Cov.

Kazaria: 1368 (no. 3). Gazaria or Gazzaria, the colony founded by the Genoese in the Cirmea with Kafa as its capital. (See W. Barthold, "Kafa," *EI*, OE, II, 617–618; Hrushevsky, *Istoriya*, IV, 299–300.)

Kazbic' Cov: 1337 (no. 3). *See* Kasbic' Cov.

Kec'anay-Jor: 1458 (no. 6). Canton, SW of Mokk' [q.v.] and contiguous with district of Bitlīs. (See Ep'rikean, *Bařaran*, II, 385.)

Keč': 1365 (no. 1). Town and fortress of Kerč (also Kerch or Kertch), in E Crimea, on the Kerč Strait of the Black Sea and at the E end of the Kerč Peninsula. (See W. Barthold, "Kerč (Kertch)," *EI*, OE, II, 856–857; Spuler, *Goldene Horde*, pp. 237, 314, 398.)

Kełi: 1452 (no. 5), 1453 (no. 1), 1464 (no. 14). Town and fortress, now called Kĭğĭ, SW of Erzerum and E of Erzincan. (See Ēp'rikean, *Bařaran*, II, 355–363; Eremyan, *Ašx.*, p. 60.)

Kesaria: 1464 (no. 10). The region of Caesarea in Cappadocia (ancient Caesarea Mazaca; Turkish: Kayseri, Arabic: Ḳaiṣarīya). (See Ramsay, *Historical Geography*, pp. 303–304; M. Streck, "Ḳaiṣarīya," *EI*, OE, II, 662–663.)

Kiket': 1459 (no. 4). Village situated SW of Tiflis in Georgia. (See Xač'ikyan, *XV Dari*, II, p. 592.)

Kilikec'woc' Ašxarh: 1336 (no. 3). Lit., land of the Cilicians. *See* Kilikia.

Kilikē: 1305 (no. 1), 1335 (no. 6). *See* Kilikia.

Kilikia (variants: Kilikec'woc' ašxarh, Kilikē, Kiłikē, Kiwlikeay, Kiwlikia, Kulikeay): 1302 (no. 1), 1304 (no. 1), 1306 (no. 1), 1335 (nos. 1, 7), 1337 (no. 2), 1375 (no. 2), 1432 (no. 5), 1437 (no. 7). Cilicia; region in SE Asia Minor, between the Mediterranean Sea and the Taurus range, and bounded on NW by the Anatolian plateau and on E by the Amanus mountains. Cilicia is divided naturally into three geographical regions: (1) Cilicia Tracheia, the mountainous region to the west; (2) Cilicia Pedias, a product of the alluvial deposits of the Sayḥān (ancient Saros) and Djayḥān (ancient Pyramus) rivers; and (3) the Cilician Taurus. In 1080 the Armenians founded a barony in Cilicia, which later became a kingdom. It maintained its independence until 1375, when the Armeno-Cilician Kingdom was incorporated into the Mamluk empire. (See M. Canard, "Cilicia," *EI*, NE, II, 34–39; Ēp'rikean, *Bařaran*, II, 394–400; *Dictionary of Bible*, p. 163.) The texts refer to the kingdom, as well as to the catholicosate of the Armenian church. After the transfer of this see to Etchmiadzin in 1441, the texts refer to the regional catholicosate of Cilicia at Sis.

Kiłikē: 1305 (no. 1). *See* Kilikia.

Kipros: 1426 (no. 6). The island of Cyprus in the E Mediterranean.

Kirakos, St.: 1351 (no. 3). Monastery in canton of Ekełeac‘, near the foot of Mt. Bt‘ni [q.v.].

Kiwlikeay: 1315 (no. 1). *See* Kilikia.

Kiwlikia: 1325 (no. 1), 1469 (no. 6). *See* Kilikia.

Kočak: 1453 (no. 1). Canton, now located in region of Dersim in Anatolia. (See Xač‘ikyan, *XV Dari*, II, p. 592.)

Kołmann Vrac‘: 1399 (no. 1). Lit., land of the Georgians. *See* Vrac‘tun.

Kołuc‘: 1428 (no. 4), 1461 (no. 4). Monastery, near town of Arckē, N of Lake Van. (See Oskean, *Vank‘er*, II, 417–418.)

Konkṙay: 1464 (no. 10). Village in region of Kayseri in central Anatolia. (See Xač‘ikyan, *XV Dari*, II, p. 592.)

Kopatap‘: 1336 (no. 1). Monastery in canton of Gołt‘n in Siwnik‘ province. (See Ēp‘rikean, *Baṙaran*, I, 438.)

Kopitaṙ: 1468 (no. 4). Fortress of Gubidara in Cilicia, situated between Barjr-Berd and Molewon. (See Ališan, *Sisuan*, pp. 157–158.)

Kostandinupawlis (variants: Kostandinupolis, Kostandnupawlis, Kostand-nupōlis, Kostantinoypawl): The city of Constantinople, capital of the Byzantine empire. (See Vasiliev, *History*, II.)

Kostandinupolis: 1453 (no. 3). *See* Kostandinupawlis.

Kostandnupawlis: 1449 (no. 1), 1457 (no. 2). *See* Kostandinupawlis.

Kostandnupōlis: 1480 (no. 1). *See* Kostandinupawlis.

Kostantinoypawl: 1459 (no. 1). *See* Kostandinupawlis.

Kovaṙa: 1468 (no. 4). The fortress of Kawarrā in Cilicia Pedias, on the river Djayḥān. (See Ališan, *Sisuan*, pp. 64, 210, 392, 538.)

Kovkas: 1312 (no. 1), 1477 (no. 1). The Caucasus. In both texts the reference is to the Caucasus mountains.

Krcanis: 1436 (no. 1). The village of Krtsanisi, SW of Tiflis, in Georgia. (See Allen, *History*, p. 413.)

Krtunaki K‘arkit‘: 1367 (no. 1). This is an unidentified landmark in the vicinity of Sis. (See Ališan, *Sisuan*, p. 541.)

Ktuc‘: 1414 (no. 2), 1462 (no. 6), 1463 (no. 8). Monastery on the island of Č‘k‘atan in Lake Van. (See Oskean, *Vank‘er*, I, 51–86; Eremyan, *Ašx.*, p. 76.)

Kuk‘i: 1332 (no. 2), 1471 (no. 7), 1478 (no. 4). Village and monastery in Šapuneac‘-Jor [q.v.].

Kulikeay: 1307 (no. 5). *See* Kilikia.

Kur (variant: K‘uṙ): 1417 (no. 1). The Kur (Russian: Kura; Arabic: Kurr; Georgian: Kura and Mtkvari); largest river in the Caucasus and chief river of the Georgian SSR and the Azerbaijan SSR. (See W. Barthold, "Kur," *EI*, OE, II, 1119.)

K‘ajberunik‘: 1307 (no. 4), 1325 (no. 1), 1371 (no. 3), 1387 (no. 2), 1392 (no. 2), 1400 (no. 1), 1410 (no. 1), 1411 (no. 4), 1421 (nos. 3, 7), 1428 (no. 2), 1432 (nos. 1, 4), 1435 (no. 3), 1441 (nos. 4, 9), 1444 (no. 3), 1445 (no. 5), 1449 (nos. 3, 4), 1453 (no. 5), 1454 (no. 1), 1455 (no. 2),

1457 (no. 5), 1458 (no. 4), 1461 (no. 3), 1462 (nos. 3, 5), 1463 (no. 7), 1466 (no. 4), 1479 (no. 2). The region of Arčēš (Ardjīsh), NE of Lake Van, formerly known as the canton of Ałiovit. (See Hübschmann, *AO*, pp. 329, 478.)

K'ałdēac'oc' Ašxarhn: 1422 (no. 1). Lit., the land of the Chaldaeans; that is Chaldaea, the district in the SE of Babylonia. (See *Dictionary of Bible*, p. 130.)

K'arpah: 1425 (no. 1). Canton in province of Vaspurakan. (See Ēp'rikean, *Bararan*, I, 219; Xač'ikyan, *XV Dari*, I, p. 810.)

K'ašan: 1457 (no. 1). Town of Kāshān in central Iran, situated N of Iṣfahān. (See Spuler, *Mongolen in Iran*, pp. 31, 437.)

K'ełoy-Jor (variant: Kełoyjor): 1442 (no. 3), 1443 (nos. 5, 6), 1471 (no. 5). Valley near Gaṙni in Siwnik' province. (See Hübschmann, *AO*, p. 479.)

K'ełoyjor: 1452 (no. 3). *See* K'ełoy-Jor.

K'oštenc': 1425 (no. 11). Monastery in canton of Hamšen [q.v.]. (See Inčičean, *Ašx.*, p. 397.)

K'rdastan (variants: K'rdstan, K'rtastan): 1428 (no. 3). Lit., land of the Kurds; that is Kurdistan. (See V. Minorsky, "Kurdistān," *EI*, OE, II, 1130–1132.)

K'rdstan: 1445 (no. 1), 1473 (no. 1). *See* K'rdastan.

K'rman: 1457 (nos. 1, 5), 1458 (no. 2), 1462 (nos. 3, 6). City of Kermān or Kirmān (ancient Carmana) in SE central Iran; capital of Persian province of the same name SW of the great central Iranian desert. (See J. H. Kramers, "Kirmān," *EI*, OE, II, 1028–1033; Hübschmann, *Arm. Gram.*, p. 47, no. 93; Spuler, *Mongolen in Iran*, esp. pp. 31–33, 147–149, 152–155.)

K'rtastan: 1472 (no. 1). *See* K'rdastan.

K'ṙnay: 1332 (no. 1). Village in canton of Ernǰak.

K't'isoy: 1428 (no. 8). Monastery in canton of Dizak in Caucasian Albania. (See Ēp'rikean, *Bararan*, I, 563–564; Eremyan, *Ašx.*, p. 89.)

K'uṙ: 1428 (no. 4), 1477 (no. 1). *See* Kur.

Lakstan (variant: Lakzstan): 1442 (no. 1). The older name of Daghestan, bounded by the Caspian Sea on the E and by Azerbaijan SSR on the S; now constituting an autonomous SSR. (See W. Barthold—[A. Bennigsen], "Dāghistān," *EI*, NE, II, 85–89.)

Lakzstan: 1476 (no. 2). *See* Lakstan.

Lambron: 1376 (no. 1). Town and fortress, now called Namrun Yayla, NE of Tarsus in Cilicia. (See Victor Langlois, "Les Ruines de Lampron en Cilicie," in *Revue de l'Orient, de l'Algérie et des colonies*, Paris, 1860, new series, 12: 119–122.)

Lawčin: 1462 (no. 1). Valley of Lochinis Khevi, near the town of Rustavi in Georgia. (See Xač'ikyan, *XV Dari*, II, p. 591.)

Lawṙi: 1424 (no. 3), 1458 (no. 3). *See* Loṙi.

Łełan: 1466 (no. 3). Village and monastery, near the town of Xotrǰur, in canton of Ganjak [q.v.]. (See Ēp'rikean, *Bararan*, II, 92.)

Lewon Berd: 1468 (no. 4). Fortress (lit., fortress of Leon), near Sis in Cilicia. (See Ēpʻrikean, Baṙaran, II, 97.)

Likeacʻ: 1422 (no. 1). Genitive plural of "Likia," Lycia. The reference is to the Lycian Sea (ancient Mare Lycium); but the author errs in locating Smyrna on the Lycian rather than on the Lydian coast.

Lim: 1306 (no. 2), 1310 (no. 3), 1315 (no. 1), 1394 (no. 1), 1421 (no. 3), 1454 (nos. 1, 2), 1457 (no. 1). Island, located NE part of Lake Van; also famous Armenian monastery named Lim or Limn. (See Oskean, Vankʻer, I, 3–51.)

Lori: 1332 (no. 3). See Loṙi.

Loṙi (variants: Lawri, Lori): 1438 (no. 2), 1441 (no. 2). (1) Town and fortress in district of Tashiri in Gugarkʻ, N of Débéda. (See Allen, History, p. 414.) (2) Region which was part of Tashiri, with fortress of Lori as its capital. (See Ēpʻrikean, Baṙaran, II, 116–121.)

Lōngšēn: 1330 (no. 2). Village; location unknown.

Lusaworičʻ, St.: 1449 (no. 8). Monastery on Mt. Sepuh in region of Kemakh in province of Erzerum.

Łalatʻan: 1398 (no. 2), 1464 (no. 3). See Łalatʻia.

Łalatʻia (variants: Łalatʻan, Xalatan): 1453 (no. 3). The suburb of Galata in Constantinople. (See Vasiliev, History, II, 459, 593, 616, 625, 685.)

Łapʻan (variant: Kapan): 1457 (no. 2), 1472 (no. 1). (1) Canton in Siwnikʻ province; now district of Ghapan in Armenian SSR. (2) Town and fortress in district of the same name. (See Hübschmann, AO, p. 348; Ališan, Sisakan, pp. 290–291, 294–296; Barxudaryan, Divan, p. 5.)

Łaraman: 1480 (no. 1). The district of Ḳaramān (also Ḳaramān-ili; ancient Caramania) in Asia Minor, comprising Lycaonia, the Cilician Taurus, and the whole S Anatolian coast territory as far as Adalia. (See J. H. Kramers, "Ḳaramān," EI, OE, II, 744–745.)

Łarapał: 1471 (no. 7). The mountainous part of Caucasian Albania formerly known as Arcʻax, and called Ḳara-Bāgh (also Karabagh, Karabakh) since the thirteenth century. It now constitutes SW Azerbaijan SSR on E slopes of the Lesser Caucasus; its population is mostly Armenian. (See C. Huart, "Ḳara-Bāgh," EI, OE, II, 727.)

Łarasu: 1365 (no. 1). Town of Ḳarasubazar (now called Belogorsk), on the Ḳarasu river, in the Crimea. (See V. Mikʻayelyan, Łrim, pp. 79, 98, 107–108, 135–136.)

Łazar, St.: 1378 (no. 1), 1388 (no. 2), 1468 (no. 1). Monastery, near Muš (Mush), in canton of Tarōn; also called Aṙakʻeloc̣ [q.v.].

Łazwin (variant: Łzuin): 1457 (no. 1). Town of Ḳazwīn in Iran, 100 miles from Teheran at the foot of Mt. Elburz. (See C. Huart, "Ḳazwīn," EI, OE, II, 840; Spuler, Mongolen in Iran.)

Łəlatʻ: 1450 (no. 1). See Xlatʻ.

Łlatʻ: 1457 (no. 2). See Xlatʻ.

Łrim (variant: Xrim): 1346 (no. 3), 1356 (no. 1), 1357 (no. 2), 1365 (no. 1), 1377 (no. 1), 1401 (no. 8), 1403 (no. 6), 1464 (no. 3). (1) Old name of the town of Solghat or Solkhad (now called Stariy Ḳrim), situated SW of Kafa and NE of Sudak in the Crimea. (2) The Crimean Peninsula. (See "Ḳrim (the Crimea)," *EI*, OE, II, 1084–1085.)

Łzuin: 1391 (no. 1). *See* Łazwin.

Majar: 1371 (no. 3). Village in canton of K'ajberunik' [q.v.].

Maku: 1406 (no. 2), 1426 (no. 4), 1428 (no. 1), 1458 (nos. 2, 5), 1459 (no. 2), 1472 (no. 1). (1) Town and fortress of Mākū in S part of Artaz province in Persian Armenia. (2) District or khanate of Mākū, now comprising NW extremity of Iran. (See V. Minorsky, "Mākū," *EI*, OE, III, 180–182; Saint-Martin, *Mémoires*, I, 135, 136.)

Malēzker: 1464 (no. 8). Monastery in Caucasian Albania. (See Xač'ikyan, *XV Dari*, II, p. 593.) Its exact location is unknown.

Małard (variant: Małardē): 1427 (no. 2), 1430 (no. 1). Monastery in canton of Šambi-Jor, SW of Old Djulfa, at the junction of Araxes and Karmir rivers. (See Ališan, *Sisakan*, pp. 514–522; Xač'ikyan, *XV Dari*, I, p. 807; Oskean, *Vank'er*, II, 527–570.)

Małardē: 1440 (no. 1). *See* Małard.

Manačihr: 1462 (no. 3). Ancient fortress of Menuahinili, situated on S shore of Lake Van and opposite island of Aghtamar; built on a promontory now called Karatash. The fortress and promontory are also known in Armenian sources as K'arn Manakert and Barjr-K'ar. (See Hübschmann, *AO*, pp. 339, 450; *Arm. Gram.*, p. 50, no. 105; Ēp'rikean, *Bařaran*, I, 104; Eremyan, *Ašx.*, p. 89.) *See also* Karatash.

Manuēli: 1429 (no. 1). Monastery in canton of Gařni [q.v.].

Marmet: 1421 (no. 11). Village, NW of Van, in Vaspurakan province. (See Hübschmann, *AO*, pp. 408, 452.)

Maškuor: 1325 (no. 2). Monastery in the Amanus mountains.

Matnevan: 1402 (no. 3). Monastery, near the city of Xlat' (Khilāṭ) in canton of Bznunik'.

Matrasay: 1403 (no. 1). Village in province of Shīrwān.

Mawřkay: 1441 (no. 8). Canton, location unknown.

Mawšrēfi: 1335 (no. 7). Village in Cilicia Tracheia, at the foot of Taurus mountains; probably in vicinity of fortress of Ganjē. (See Ališan, *Sisuan*, pp. 118–119.)

Maxt'lša: 1367 (no. 1). A tributary of the river Djayḥān, in vicinity of Sis, in Cilicia. (See Ališan, *Sisuan*, pp. 531, 541, 542.)

Mecac' Hayoc': 1323 (no. 1). *See* Hayoc' Mecac'.

Mecop': 1313 (no. 2), 1407 (no. 3), 1409 (no. 1), 1410 (no. 1), 1411 (no. 4), 1427 (no. 1), 1428 (no. 3), 1435 (no. 3), 1444 (no. 3). Monastery, situated N of Arčēš (Ardjīsh). (See Oskean, *Vank'er*, II, 419–442.)

Menckert: 1468 (no. 3). (1) Town of Malāzgerd (Turkish: Malazgird; Arabic: Malāzdjird), N of Lake Van. (2) District, which now constitutes part of Van province in Turkey. (See V. F. Büchner, "Malāzgerd," *EI*, OE, III, 201–202; Hübschmann, *AO*, pp. 449–450.)

Merdin (variants: Mertin, Mērdin, Mērtin): 1397 (no. 1), 1417 (no. 3), 1428 (no. 4), 1452 (no. 5). (1) Town of Mārdīn in province of

Diyarbakir. (2) Fortress, 300 ft. above town of Mārdīn. (See V. Minorsky, "Mārdīn," *EI*, OE, III, 273–277; Saint-Martin, *Mémoires*, I, 160–161; *Chèref-Nâmeh*, I. 1, 444–446; Spuler, *Mongolen in Iran*.)

Mertin: 1426 (no. 5), 1452 (no. 5). *See* Merdin.

Mējerkray: 1307 (no. 5). *See* Mijerkreay.

Mējerkreay: 1422 (no. 1). *See* Mijerkreay.

Mērdin: 1401 (no. 1), 1407 (no. 1), 1422 (no. 1). *See* Merdin.

Mērtin: 1428 (no. 3), 1453 (no. 1), 1469 (no. 5). *See* Merdin.

Mənžənkert: 1336 (no. 4). Town and fortress in Erzerum province, N of Malāzgerd and E of Ani, medieval capital of Armenia. (See Hübschmann, *AO*, p. 453; Saint-Martin, *Mémoires*, I, 109; II, 101; *Chèref-Nâmeh*, I. 1, 190–191, 471, 555; II. 2, 14–15, 74.)

Məsər: 1422 (no. 1), 1453 (no. 2). *See* Msr.

Mgunk' (variant: Mokunk'): 1403 (no. 7). Village in canton of Tarōn, situated E of Muš (Mush). (See Hübschmann, *AO*, p. 326; Inčičean, *Ašx.*, p. 188.)

Mijaget: 1335 (no. 1), 1422 (no. 1), 1431 (no. 1), 1437 (no. 7), 1449 (no. 1), 1452 (no. 5), 1471 (no. 2), 1475 (no. 2). The common Armenian term for Mesopotamia, generally referring to Syrian Mesopotamia, the alluvial plain between the Euphrates and Tigris rivers. (See Eremyan, *Ašx.*, p. 71.)

Mijaget Asoroc': 1395 (no. 1). Syrian Mesopotamia.

Mijagetac' Asorwoc': 1428 (no. 4). Genitive plural of Mijaget Asoroc' [q.v.].

Mijerkray: 1315 (no. 1), 1325 (no. 1). *See* Mijerkreay.

Mijerkreay (variants: Mējerkray, Mējerkreay, Mijerkray): 1355 (no. 2). A term used for Asia Minor. (See Eremyan, *Ašx.*, p. 13.)

Mlun: 1337 (no. 2). *See* Mulewon.

Mokk': 1413 (no. 2), 1423 (no. 2), 1433 (no. 2), 1455 (no. 5), 1466 (no. 6), 1469 (no. 2). The smallest province of Armenia Major, located S of Lake Van in the valley of the eastern Tigris; known in Latin sources as Moxoene, and Byzantine sources as Mōeks. (See Hübschmann, *AO*, pp. 254–255, 331–333; *Arm. Gram.*, p. 404; Saint-Martin, *Mémoires*, I, 175.)

Moks: 1409 (no. 3). Town in province of Mokk', on the river Khabūr.

Mokunk': 1433 (no. 3). *See* Mgunk'.

Mōl: 1365 (no. 1). Apparently a place in the Crimea; its exact location is unknown.

Msər: 1335 (no. 6). *See* Msr.

Msr (variants: Məsər, Msər): 1304 (no. 3), 1325 (no. 2), 1361 (no. 3), 1422 (no. 1), 1426 (no. 6), 1458 (no. 1), 1468 (no. 4), 1473 (no. 1). Cf. Arabic Miṣr, Egypt.

Mulewon (variant: Mlun): 1337 (no. 2). Fortress, located between Lambron and Barjr-Berd, in Cilicia. Known in Arabic sources as Ḥiṣn al-Mlūn; in Latin, Mons Livonis or Montis Livonis; in Ottoman, Molen or Molvane. (See Ališan, *Sisuan*, pp. 141–143.)

Mułan: 1422 (no. 1). The steppe region of Mūghān or Muḳan, located between the Caspian Sea and the Andarab-Karasu. (See V. Minorsky, "Mūḳān (Mūghān)," *EI*, OE, III, 710–711; Cleaves, *Mongolian Documents*, p. 59, n. 7.)

Muš: 1368 (no. 1), 1408 (no. 2), 1457 (nos. 1, 2), 1460 (no. 12), 1462 (no. 3), 1463 (no. 1), 1466 (no. 7), 1468 (no. 1), 1472 (no. 1), 1473 (no. 1), 1479 (no. 3). (1) Town of Muš or Mush (Turkish Muş), near S bank of the Murat Nehri, some 70 km. W of Xlat' (Khilāṭ). In Islamic times the name Ṭarūn was sometimes used for the town of Muš. (2) Fortress; now in ruins. (3) District, which corresponds to the ancient Moxoene. (4) The large fertile plain. (See J. H. Kramers, "Mūsh," *EI*, OE, III, 746–747; Saint-Martin, *Mémoires*, I, 102.)

Narek: 1392 (no. 1), 1415 (no. 1), 1417 (no. 5), 1419 (no. 4), 1420 (no. 4). Monastery in village of the same name, situated SW of Aghtamar and NE of Bitlīs. (See Oskean, *Vank'er*, I, 189–200.)

Naxč'əwan: 1422 (no. 1). *See* Naxiǰewan.

Naxiǰawan: 1304 (no. 3). *See* Naxiǰewan.

Naxiǰewan (variants: Naxč'əwan, Naxiǰawan, Naxǰawan): 1384 (no. 2). (1) Town (ancient Naxuana; Arabic: Nashawā), on left bank of the Araxes river. (2) District, now corresponding to the Nakhichevan Autonomous SSR, bordering on Iran and Turkey in the south, and separated from the Azerbaijan SSR by a strip of Soviet Armenia and from Iran and Turkey by the Araxes river. (See V. Minorsky, "Nakhčuwān (Nakhičewān)," *EI*, OE, III, 839–840; Hübschmann, *AO*, pp. 346, 455; Saint-Martin, *Mémoires*, I, 131, 132.)

Nayipenc': 1468 (no. 4). Location unknown; probably somewhere between Antep and Lewon-Berd in Cilicia.

Nerk'in-Derǰan: 1453 (no. 1). *See* Derǰan.

Nəsebin: 1422 (no. 1). The town of Naṣībīn or Nusaybīn (modern Turkish: Nizip) in Diyarbakir province in Mesopotamia. (See E. Honigmann, "Naṣībīn," *EI*, OE, III, 858–860.)

Nəwan: 1428 (no. 1). Location unknown; probably somewhere in the vicinity of Lake Van.

Nkar: 1401 (no. 7). Monastery in canton of Ṙštunik' [q.v.]. (See Hübschmann, *AO*, p. 455; Oskean, *Vank'er*, I, 200–204.)

Nłir: 1336 (no. 3), 1337 (no. 2). Fortress, known in Latin sources as Nigrinum and in Arabic as Ḳal'at Nughayr or Nuḳayr, in the Amanus mountains. (See Ališan, *Sisuan*, pp. 411–413.)

Nṙnawnic': 1303 (no. 3). Monastery in Ayrarat province; its exact location is unknown.

Nvəndi: 1392 (no. 2). Village in canton of K'aǰberunik' [q.v.].

Orotan (variant: Orotayn): 1386 (no. 1). Fortress on left bank of river of the same name in canton of Orotn in Siwnik' province. (See Pōłosean, *Hayastani Ašx.*, p. 192; Barxudaryan, *Divan*, p. 99; cf. Hübschmann, *AO*, p. 462.)

Orotayn: 1422 (no. 1). *See* Orotan.

Ostan: 1386 (no. 3), 1392 (no. 1), 1393 (no. 1), 1400 (no. 2), 1401 (nos. 1, 4), 1402 (no. 1), 1411 (no. 5), 1425 (no. 1), 1426 (no. 3), 1428 (nos. 1, 5), 1444 (no. 2), 1445 (no. 1), 1452 (no. 4), 1459 (no. 2), 1461 (no. 6), 1462 (no. 3), 1467 (no. 8), 1470 (no. 3). (1) Town, known in Islamic sources as Wusṭān or Wasṭān (modern Turkish Vostan), in Van province, situated on S shore of Lake Van. (2) District, with town of the same name as its center. (See Hübschmann, *AO*, pp. 460–461; Saint-Martin, *Mémoires*, I, 141; II, 427.)

Ōrēl (variant: Avrel, Awrēl): 1452 (no. 5). The exact location of this town is unknown; it was probably in the vicinity of Sulṭānīya. (See Hakobyan, *Manr Žam.*, II, 214, n. 23.)

Ōrtubazar: 1329 (no. 2). Xač'ikyan (*XIV Dari*, p. 672) suggests that this might be the city of Sulṭānīya in Persian Iraq.

Ōšin: 1452 (no. 5). Probably the region of the town of Ushnuh, situated SW of Lake Urmia. (See Hakobyan, *Manr Žam.*, II, 215, n. 25.)

Pahakn Honac': 1400 (no. 1). Lit., Gate of the Huns; a designation by which the Armenians referred to the Gate of the Alans. (See Ēp'rikean, *Bararan*, I, 594.)

Palaxoru: 1461 (no. 7). Monastery in canton of Xałtik'. *See* Xaxt'ik'.

Palhawean Ašxarh: 1335 (no. 1). Lit., Palhaw land. Palhaw is a variant of Pahlaw, which was used synonymously with Part'ew, that is, Parthian, or Parthia. In the text it is used as a geographical term meaning Parthia. (See Hübschmann, *Arm. Gram.*, pp. 63–65, no. 140.)

Pałdat: 1466 (no. 7). *See* Bałdat.

Pałras: 1468 (no. 4). Fortress, known in Greek sources as Págrai, and Latin Pagrius, situated S of Iskenderun and Beylan, on a tributary of the Orontes river. (See Ališan, *Sisuan*, pp. 425–427.)

Pars: 1453 (no. 6), 1458 (no. 6), 1471 (no. 2). The province of Pārs (ancient Greek: Parsa and Persis; Arabic: Fārs), in S Iran, on the Persian Gulf. (See L. Lockhart, "Fārs," *EI*, NE, II, 811–812; Spuler, *Mongolen in Iran.*)

Parsic': 1387 (no. 2), 1428 (no. 4), 1449 (no. 1). Genitive plural of Pars, lit. of the Pars. The term is also used in a geographical sense, that is, Persia.

Parsic' Ašxarh: 1387 (no. 1), 1400 (no. 1), 1468 (no. 1). Lit., land of the Persians. *See* Parskastan.

Parskac' Tun: 1458 (no. 2). Lit., land of the Persians. *See* Parskastan.

Parskac'tan: 1422 (no. 1). Variant of Parskastan.

Parskastan (variants: Parsic' ašxarh, Parskac' tun, Parskac'tan, Tunn Parskac'): 1400 (no. 1), 1422 (no. 1), 1454 (no. 4), 1462 (no. 6). Lit., land of the Persians; that is, Persia. (See Hübschmann, *Arm. Gram.*, p. 67, no. 145.)

Paŕuagrak: 1455 (no. 7). Monastery, location unknown.

Pawntos: 1478 (no. 6). *See* Pontos.

Pēšnagomer: 1472 (no. 1). Village in the region of Arckē [q.v.]. (See Hakobyan, *Manr Žam.*, II, 223, n. 23.)

Połaz Ałek'sandri: 1453 (no. 3). Lit., the Strait of Alexander; the reference is to that part of the Bosphorus which the Turks now call Boğaz-Içi. (See Anasyan, *Haykakan Ałbyurnerə*, p. 56.) For the etymology of połaz, see Doerfer, II, 344–345, no. 792.)

Pondosi Cov: 1325 (no. 1). *See* Pontosi Cov.

Pontac'woc' Ašxarh: 1307 (no. 5), 1315 (no. 1), 1325 (no. 1). Lit., land of the Ponteans. The references are to the region of Trebizond. *See* Trapizon.

Pontos (variant: Pawntos): 1464 (no. 1). The city of Trebizond on the Black Sea. *See* Trapizon.

Pontosi Cov (variant: Pondosi Cov): 1307 (no. 5), 1312 (no. 1), 1315 (no. 1), 1329 (no. 1), 1331 (no. 2), 1337 (no. 3), 1449 (no. 1). Lit., Sea of Pontus; that is, the Black Sea. (See D. M. Dunlop, "Baḥr Bunṭus," *EI*, NE, I, 927.)

Poṙ: 1418 (no. 1), 1449 (no. 1). Village, SE of Bitlīs.

Pslenc'acvuk' (?): The reading is uncertain; it appears to be a landmark in the vicinity of Sis in Cilicia. (See Ališan, *Sisuan*, p. 541.)

Pursa: 1453 (no. 3). The town of Bursa (ancient Prusa or Prusia) in the N foothills of Mysian Olympus; capital of the Ottoman state from 1326 until 1402. (See H. Inalcik, "Bursa," *EI*, NE, I, 1333–1336.)

P'asavank' (variant: P'asayvank'): 1466 (no. 6), 1469 (no. 2). Village, S of Lake Van in district of Mokk'. (See Oskean, *Vank'er*, III, 883–884.)

P'asayvank': 1455 (no. 5). *See* P'asavank'.

P'aytakaran: 1452 (no. 2), 1476 (no. 3), 1477 (nos. 1, 2). The texts state that this was a name by which Tiflis or Tbilisi, the present capital of Georgia, was formerly known, but this identification has been disputed. (See Hübschmann, *AO*, p. 270; Inčičean, *Storagrut'iwn Hin Hayastaneayc'*, pp. 327f.)

P'ok'r Akoṙ: 1451 (no. 3). Monastery in region of J̌ermajor [q.v.). (See Oskean, *Vank'er*, III, 814.)

P'ok'r Siwnik': 1312 (no. 1). Lit., Siwnik' Minor; another designation for the province of Arc'ax [q.v.]. (See Ēp'rikean, *Baṙaran*, I, 340.)

P'rkič': 1446 (no. 6). Monastery in Arapkir [q.v.].

Ṙa[. . .]lēn: 1397 (no. 1). This should probably read Ṙasəlen. *See* Ṙasəlēn.

Ṙasəlēn: 1452 (no. 5). The town of Ra's al-'Ayn in Turkish province of Rakka, midway between Urfa and Nizip.

Ṙē: 1457 (no. 1). Town of Raiy, Rai, Ray, or Rey (in classical sources Rages, Rhagae) in Media (Persia). Its ruins can be seen about 5 miles SSE of Teheran. (See V. Minorsky, "Raiy," *EI*, OE, III, 1105–1108; Spuler, *Mongolen in Iran*; Hübschmann, *Arm. Gram.*, p. 70, no. 158.) The reference seems to be to the district of Raiy.

Ṙštunik': 1400 (no. 2), 1401 (no. 7), 1418 (no. 3), 1419 (no. 3), 1424 (no. 1), 1425 (no. 4), 1445 (no. 1), 1462 (no. 4), 1464 (no. 13), 1469 (no. 3), 1477 (no. 8). Canton in Vaspurakan province, situated S of Lake Van. (See Hübschmann, *AO*, pp. 339–340.)

Ṙum: 1473 (no. 1). Rūm; the Islamic name for the former Greek territories in Asia Minor. (See Franz Babinger, "Rūm," *EI*, OE, III, 1174–1175; Hübschmann, *Arm. Gram.*, p. 362, no. 244.)

Salmast: 1419 (no. 1), 1456 (no. 2). Town of Salmās, situated NW of Lake Urmia, in Persian Azerbaijan. (See V. Minorsky, "Salmās," *EI*, OE, IV, 117–118.)

Sałmosavank': 1436 (no. 4). Monastery in canton of Aragacotn in Ayrarat province. (See Hübschmann, *AO*, p. 465.)

Samarłand (variants: Samərłand, Səmərłand, Səmərłant, Səmərłənd, Səmrłand, Smərłan, Smərłənd, Smrłand): 1400 (no. 1), 1422 (no. 1), 1429 (no. 1). The city of Samarkand in Transoxiana. (See H. H. Schaeder, "Samarḳand," *EI*, OE, IV, 129–131; Spuler, *Mongolen in Iran*.)

Samc'xē: 1473 (no. 8). The province of Samtzkhé (also called Meskhia, Zemo Kartli, and Saatabago), now the region of Akhaltzikhé in the Georgian SSR. It is bounded on the N by the Black Sea, on the E by Trialeti and Somkheti, on the S by Armenia, and on the W by the Pontic Alps. (See Allen, *History*, p. 421.)

Samərłand: 1432 (no. 1). See Samarłand.

Samison: 1421 (no. 14). The port city of Samsun (ancient Amisus, Amisos; Arabic: Ṣāmṣūn), on N coast of Asia Minor, now in province of Sivas. (See J. H. Mordtmann, "Ṣāmṣūn," *EI*, OE, IV, 140–141.)

Samšuildē: 1442 (no. 1). *See* Šamšuldē.

Samšultē: 1441 (no. 1). *See* Šamšuldē.

Sanahin: 1399 (no. 1), 1420 (no. 3), 1421 (no. 8), 1424 (no. 3), 1437 (no. 1). Monastery in village of the same name, now located near the copper mines of Alaverti in district of Kirovakan in Armenian SSR. (See Karo Łafadaryan, *Sanahni Vank'ə ev nra Arjanagrut'yunnerə*, Erevan, 1957; Brosset, "Description des monastères arméniens d'Haghbat et de Sanahin.")

Sargis, St.: 1475 (no. 8). Monastery in Istanbul.

Saruk'arman: 1365 (no. 1). The town of Sarî-kerman in the Crimea. (See *Géographie d'Aboulféda, Texte arabe*, publ. by J. T. Reinaud and William Mac Guckin de Slane, Paris, 1840, pp. 32, 33, 200, 214; V. D. Smirnov, *Krymskoe Khantsvo pod verkhovenstvom Otomanskoi Porty do nachala XVIII veka*, St. Petersburg, 1887, p. 56.)

Sasunk': 1462 (no. 3). (1) The town of Sasun in E Anatolia, situated S of Muš (Mush) and W of Bitlīs. (2) Canton in Armenian province of Ałjnik'; known in ancient Armenian sources as Sanasunk'. (See Hübschmann, *AO*, pp. 315–316; Saint-Martin, *Mémoires*, I, 163, 164, and II, 361, 431.)

Satał: 1453 (no. 1). Town, known in Greek sources as Sátala and in Latin as Satala, near the source of the river Kelkit in E Anatolia. (See Eremyan, *Ašx.*, p. 80.)

Saway: 1457 (no. 1). Town in central Iran, located between Teheran and Hamadhān. (See *Chèref-Nâmeh*, I. 1, p. 415.)

Sawkut'lu: 1471 (no. 8). Town in district of Shīrwān on W shore of the Caspian Sea.

Sawlt'aniay: 1428 (no. 4). *See* Sultaniay.

Sawray: 1452 (no. 5). *See* Sori.

Sebastia (variant: Sewast): 1313 (no. 3), 1333 (no. 2), 1343 (no. 1), 1422 (no. 1). (1) City of Sebastia or Sebaste, now called Sivas (cf. Arabic Sīwās) in central Turkey. (2) District, which corresponds to part of ancient Cappadocia. (See E. Rossi, "Sīwās," *EI*, OE, IV, 465–466.)

Sepuh, Mt.: 1449 (no. 8). Mt. Ḳara-Dāgh in E Anatolia. (See Hübschmann, *AO*, pp. 466–467.)

Serkewili: 1442 (no. 1). Village near Mułni in canton of Aragacotn in Ayrarat province. (See Hübschmann, *AO*, p. 467.)

Sevan: 1451 (no. 4). Island in lake of the same name in Armenian SSR. (See W. Barthold, "Gökčai," *EI*, OE, II, 173.)

Sewast: 1401 (no. 1), 1436 (no. 3), 1438 (no. 3). *See* Sebastia.

Sewerak': 1437 (no. 2). Town of Siverek in Turkish province of Diyarbakir. (See Saint-Martin, *Mémoires*, I, 160, 165; *Chèref-Nâmeh*, I. 1, 141, 143, 469, and II. 2, 33.)

Səmərłand: 1422 (no. 1). *See* Samarłand.

Səmərłant: 1403 (no. 3). *See* Samarłand.

Səmərłənd: 1395 (no. 1), 1400 (no. 2), 1422 (no. 1). *See* Samarłand.

Səmrłand: 1469 (no. 2). *See* Samarłand.

Sinamut: 1444 (no. 8), 1479 (no. 4). Fortress in the town of Kharput in Asia Minor.

Sirunk'ar: 1468 (no. 3). Monastery in canton of Menckert [q.v.].

Sis: 1308 (no. 1), 1335 (no. 6), 1336 (no. 3), 1361 (no. 3), 1367 (no. 1), 1375 (nos. 1, 2), 1393 (no. 1), 1417 (no. 4), 1421 (no. 11), 1468 (no. 4). The capital city of the Armenian Kingdom of Cilicia, now called Kozan, 65 km. NE of Adana. (See V. F. Büchner, "Sīs," *EI*, OE, IV, 453–455; Ramsay, *Historical Geography*, p. 385; Victor Langlois, "Voyage à Sis.") Sis was also the seat of the Armenian catholicosate; and after 1441 the seat of the regional catholicosate of Cilicia.

Siwnik': 1310 (no. 2), 1321 (no. 1), 1323 (no. 1), 1335 (no. 5), 1348 (no. 2), 1401 (no. 2), 1407 (no. 4), 1408 (no. 1), 1441 (no. 7), 1453 (no. 1), 1469 (no. 6), 1471 (no. 6). Province in Armenia Major, also called Sisakan (in classical sources Sakasene; Old Persian: Sīsagān; Middle Persian: Sīsakān; Arabic: Sīsadjān); it was the domain of the Siwni Armenian feudal family. (See Hübschmann, *AO*, pp. 263–266.)

Siwnis Mecn: 1422 (no. 1). Lit., Siwnik' Major. Variant of Siwnik' [q.v.].

Słerd: 1424 (no. 1). Town of Siirt, situated in a valley about 30 miles SW of Bitlīs and about 18 miles N of the Tigris, in Turkish province of Diyarbakir. (See J. H. Kramers, "Se'erd, Si'ird or Saïrd," *EI*, OE, IV, 202–203; Saint-Martin, *Mémoires*, I, 165, 170; *Chèref-Nâmeh*, I. 1, 140, 147, and II. 2, 271.)

Smərłan: 1405 (no. 1). *See* Samarłand.

Smərłənd: 1389 (no. 1). *See* Samarłand.

Smrłand: 1388 (no. 3). *See* Samarłand.
Sop'ia: 1453 (no. 3). The cathedral of Aya Sofya in Constantinople. (See K. Süssheim–[Fr. Taeschner], "Aya Sofya," *EI*, NE, I, 774–777; Vasiliev, *History*, I, 187–192.)
Soranc' Orc'eanc': 1362 (no. 1). Village in the plain of Gawaṙuc' [q.v.].
Soravank': 1458 (no. 6). Village in Kec'anay-Jor [q.v.] in Mokk' province.
Sori (variants: Sawray, Suray): 1473 (no. 1), 1474 (no. 6). Village in the canton of Xizan (Khizān). (See Xač'ikyan, *XV Dari*, II, p. 368; Oskean, *Vank'er*, III, 878–880; cf. Hakobyan, *Manr Žam.*, II, 214, n. 22.)
Sōlt'ania: 1465 (no. 6). *See* Sultaniay.
Sōlt'aniay: 1428 (no. 3). *See* Sultaniay.
Spatkert: 1388 (no. 1). Also known in Armenian sources as Sparkert; canton in Mokk' province, near the region of Xizan (Khizān). (See Xač'ikyan, *XV Dari*, I, p. 809.)
Srkłunk': 1459 (no. 6), 1473 (no. 5), 1475 (no. 1), 1478 (no. 3). Village in canton of Vayoc'-Jor [q.v.], in Siwnik' province.
Stambawl: 1453 (no. 1). *See* Stambul.
Stambul (variants: Ǝstambul, Ǝstampawl, Ǝstəmpawl, Ǝstəmpōl, Ǝstənbawl, Stambawl, Stampol, Stampōl, Stəmbawl, Stəmpawl, Stəmpol): 1453 (no. 1). The city of Istanbul. (See "Istanbul," *Islâm Ansiklopedisi*, vol. V, pt. 2, Istanbul, 1959, pp. 1135–1214.)
Stampol: 1453 (no. 3). *See* Stambul.
Stampōl: 1449 (no. 1). *See* Stambul.
Stat'ew: 1408 (no. 1). *See* Tat'ew.
Stəmbawl: 1398 (no. 2). *See* Stambul.
Stəmpawl: 1464 (no. 1). *See* Stambul.
Stəmpol: 1453 (no. 2). *See* Stambul.
Suhara: 1325 (no. 1). *See* Suxaray.
Suharay: 1393 (no. 1). *See* Suxaray.
Sultaniay (variants: Sawlt'aniay, Sōlt'ania, Sōlt'aniay, Sult'ania, Sult'aniay): 1341 (no. 2), 1354 (no. 2), 1368 (no. 2). The town of Sulṭānīya in Persian Iraq; now in northern Iraq, on the watershed between the rivers Zanjan and Abhar. (See V. Minorsky, "Sulṭānīya," *EI*, OE, IV, 548–549; Spuler, *Mongolen in Iran*; Cleaves, *Mongolian Documents*, pp. 102–103, n. 59.)
Sult'ania: 1465 (no. 6). *See* Sultaniay.
Sult'aniay: 1337 (no. 1). *See* Sultaniay.
Sulxat': 1354 (no. 3), 1363 (no. 3). *See* Surxat'.
Sułda: 1365 (no. 2). The seaport of Sughdāḳ (Latin and Italian: Soldaia, Soldachia; Old Russian: Surož), in the Crimea. (See W. Barthold, "Sughdāḳ," *EI*, OE, IV, 502–503; Spuler, *Goldene Horde*, esp. pp. 397–399.)
Suray: 1452 (no. 5). *See* Sori.
Surbkanc': 1433 (no. 2). Village in Mokk' province.
Surłat': 1356 (no. 1). *See* Surxat'.

Surxat' (variants: Sulxat', Surłat'): 1346 (nos. 2, 3), 1350 (no. 1), 1354 (no. 3), 1371 (no. 1). The town of Solghat or Solkhad (now called Starîy Ḳrîm, Old Ḳrîm; Turkish: Eski Ḳrim), in the Crimea, situated SW of Kafa and NE of Sudak. (See Mykhailo Hrushevsky, *Istoriya Ukrayiny-Rusy*, IV, Kiev and Lvov, 1907, p. 297; W. Barthold, "Ḳrîm," *EI*, OE, II, 1084–1085.)

Suxaray (variants: Suhara, Suharay): 1400 (no. 1), 1421 (no. 7), 1454 (no. 1), 1457 (no. 1), 1473 (no. 4). Monastery, also called Xaṙabastay [q.v.], in village of Xaṙabast in canton of K'aǰberunik'. (See Ēp'rikean, *Baṙaran*, II, 150–151; Oskean, *Vank'er*, II, 396–412.)

Sxgay: 1425 (no. 2). Village, near monastery of Varag [q.v.], in the vicinity of Van. (See Oskean, *Vank'er*, I, 265–268.)

Šahapōnk': 1387 (no. 1). Fortress in the district of Naxiǰewan. (See Hübschmann, *AO*, pp. 457–458; Eremyan, *Ašx.*, p. 73.)

Šam (variants: Šamatun, Šamay Tun, Šamb, Šambn): 1400 (nos. 4, 5), 1401 (no. 6), 1468 (no. 4). Arabic: Shām or al-Shām; that is, Syria in its historic sense. (See H. Lammens, "al-Shām," *EI*, OE, IV, 292–302.)

Šamatun: 1422 (no. 1). *See* Šam.

Šamay Duṙn: 1469 (no. 1). Lit., the Gate of Shām; the reference is to the Syrian or Amanus Gates. (See Ališan, *Sisuan*, pp. 5, 404, 414, 416.)

Šamay Tun: 1472 (no. 1). *See* Šam.

Šamb: 1303 (no. 6), 1304 (no. 1), 1367 (no. 1), 1401 (no. 1). *See* Šam.

Šambi-Jor: 1427 (no. 2). (1) The region around the junction of the Araxes and Karmir rivers. (2) Village or town (also known in Armenian sources as Darašamb or Šamb; and in Turkish, Dereyi-Şamb), on E bank of the Araxes, near Old Djulfa and Naxiǰewan. (See Hübschmann, *AO*, p. 458; Ališan, *Sisakan*, pp. 514–515.)

Šambn: 1303 (no. 4). *See* Šam.

Šamiram: 1438 (no. 1), 1462 (no. 3). Semiramis; one of the names by which the Armenians referred to the fortress of Van. (See Ḥübschmann, *AO*, p. 458; *Arm. Gram.*, p. 296, no. 41.)

Šamšuldē (variants: Samšuildē, Samšultē, Šamšultay, Šamšultē): 1440 (no. 3), 1442 (no. 3), 1443 (no. 2). The town and fortress of Shamshwildé, situated SW of Tiflis in Georgia. (See Allen, *History*, p. 421; Hübschmann, *AO*, pp. 465–466.)

Šamšultay: 1441 (no. 3). *See* Šamšuldē.

Šamšultē: 1458 (no. 1). *See* Šamšuldē.

Šaplxeroy K'ar: 1367 (no. 1). This seems to be a landmark in the vicinity of Sis in Cilicia. (See Ališan, *Sisuan*, p. 541.)

Šarvan: 1471 (no. 8). *See* Šrvan.

Šatwan: 1464 (no. 13), 1471 (no. 10), 1477 (no. 8). Village, situated NW of monastery of Narek, in canton of Ṙštunik'. (See Hakobyan, *Manr Žam.*, I, 123, n. 34.)

Šhapuneac'-Jor: 1471 (no. 7). Valley in the district of Šahapunik', which corresponds to present-day valley of the river Shahbuz. (See Eremyan, *Ašx.*, pp. 64, 73.)

Šik'ar: 1361 (no. 2). This appears to be a region in the vicinity of Kharput in E Turkey; its exact location is unknown.

Šinamēj: 1307 (no. 4). Village in canton of K'ajberunik' [q.v.].

Širaz: 1453 (no. 7), 1454 (no. 2), 1457 (nos. 1, 5), 1458 (no. 2), 1462 (nos. 3, 6), 1470 (no. 1), 1472 (no. 1). The town of Shīrāz in SW Iran; also the name of a province. (See C. Huart, "Shīrāz," *EI*, OE, IV, 376–377; Spuler, *Mongolen in Iran*, esp. pp. 143–145.)

Šiṙean: 1453 (no. 1). The canton of Sharian (modern Turkish: Şiran), situated S of Trabzon (Trebizond) in E Anatolia.

Šłrkay: 1304 (no. 1). River, near the fortress of Barjr-Berd [q.v.] in Cilicia.

Šōš: 1462 (no. 3). The author identifies this with the city of Iṣfahān; actually, however, the term corresponds to Susa (modern Shush), the ancient capital of Elam and later one of the capitals of the Persian empire. (See *Dictionary of Bible*, p. 943; Hübschmann, *Arm. Gram.*, p. 298, no. 48.)

Šruan: 1417 (no. 1). *See* Šrvan.

Šrvan (variants: Šarvan, Šruan): 1403 (no. 1), 1417 (no. 1). The district of Shīrwān, Shīrwan, or Sharwān, on W shore of the Caspian Sea. Under the Shīrwānshāh and during the Mongol period, its territory included the lands from the Kura to Derbend, with its capital at Shamākhī. (See W. Barthold, "Shīrwān," *EI*, OE, IV, 382–383; Spuler, *Mongolen in Iran*.)

Šušu: 1428 (no. 7). The village of Shushu in district of Amarasay in Caucasian Albania.

Tačkastan: 1458 (no. 1). Lit., land of the Tačiks. (See Tačik, App. D.) This term, which basically means Arabia, is used here as a generic Persian term meaning the lands inhabited by the Muslims. (See Hübschmann, *Arm. Gram.*, pp. 87–88, no. 205.)

Tann Vrac': 1323 (no. 1). Lit., in the land of the Georgians; that is, Georgia.

Tarawn: 1468 (no. 1). *See* Tarōn.

Tarberuni: 1306 (no. 4), 1414 (no. 3), 1475 (no. 2), 1478 (no. 2). *See* Tarberunik'.

Tarberunik' (variant: Tarberuni): 1462 (no. 3), 1464 (no. 7), 1479 (no. 1). Canton, also known as Turuberan, which corresponds to the region of Berkri [q.v.]. (See Hübschmann, *AO*, pp. 251–254; Eremyan, *Ašx.*, p. 85.)

Tarōn (variant: Tarawn): 1320 (no. 1), 1329 (no. 1), 1368 (no. 1), 1378 (no. 1), 1388 (nos. 2, 3), 1408 (no. 2), 1463 (no. 1), 1472 (no. 1). Canton, now corresponding to the region of Muš (Mush), situated W of Lake Van. Known in Latin sources as Taraunitium; in Greek, Tárauna, Tarán; in Arabic, Ṭarūn. Until the ninth century it was the domain of the Mamikonean Armenian feudal family, with its center at Muš. (See Hübschmann, *AO*, pp. 322–327; *Arm. Gram.*, p. 404.)

Tarson (variants: Tarsoy, Tarsus): 1361 (no. 3), 1468 (no. 4). The town of Ṭarsūs (modern Turkish: Tarsus) in SE Turkey, in the plain of Cilicia. (See Fr. Buhl, "Ṭarsūs," *EI*, OE, IV, 679.)

Tarsoy: 1367 (no. 1). *See* Tarson.

Tarsus: 1337 (no. 2). *See* Tarson.

Tašk'awbru: 1401 (no. 8). Cf. Turkic Taš-Köprü; fortress in the Crimea; its exact location is unknown.

Tat'ew (variants: Ewstat'ē, Stat'ew): 1321 (no. 2), 1407 (no. 3). Monastery in SE part of canton of Cłuk in Siwnik' province; now in district of Goris in Armenian SSR. (See Ališan, *Sisakan*, pp. 222–247; Artak Smbatean, "Hamaṙōt Patmut'iwn Tat'ewi Vank'i," in *Tat'ew Tarec'oyc'*, 1930, pp. 276–351; M. Tēr Movsēsean, *Haykakan Erek' Mec Vank'er*, 1938, pp. 4–72; N. V. Covakan, "Tat'ew," *Sion*, June–July 1950, pp. 197–202; Hübschmann, *AO*, p. 472; Brosset, *Siounie*, II, 112–120.)

Tayk': 1341 (no. 1). Tao; a district of Samtzkhé in Georgia, between the rivers Tortomi and Olti. (See Hübschmann, *AO*, pp. 357–361; Eremyan, *Ašx.*, p. 84; Allen, *History*, p. 425.)

Tayšoł: 1419 (no. 3), 1469 (no. 3). *See* Tšoł.

Tepur: 1462 (no. 2). Village in district of Somkheti in Georgian SSR. (See Xač'ikyan, *XV Dari*, II, p. 595.)

Teṙewanc', Mt.: 1341 (no. 1). Mountain in Tayk' (Georgian: Tao) in the district of Samtzkhé.

Tērpet: 1462 (no. 4). Monastery in Vaspurakan province. (See Oskean, *Vank'er*, I, 378–379.)

Təp'xis: 1422 (no. 1), 1438 (no. 5), 1458 (no. 1), 1477 (no. 2). *See* Tp'xis.

Tikrana-Berd: 1411 (no. 3). *See* Ałčałalay.

Tip'xis: 1437 (no. 6). *See* Tp'xis.

Tivrik: 1348 (no. 3). *See* Tiwrik.

Tiwrik (variant: Tivrik): 1450 (nos. 2, 3), 1462 (nos. 9, 10). The town of Divriği, Diwrīgi, or Difrīgī (in Byzantine sources, Tephrikè; Arabic, al-Abrīk or al-Abrūk), in Turkish province of Sivas. (See J. Sourdel-Thomine, "Diwrīgī," *EI*, NE, II, 340.)

Tnisay: 1452 (no. 5). Apparently a place in the vicinity of Mārdīn.

Tosp: 1462 (no. 3). A canton, called Thospitis in classical sources, in the province of Vaspurakan. (See Hübschmann, *AO*, pp. 340–341, 347, 476.)

Tp'xis (variants: Təp'xis, Tip'xis, Tup'xis): 1304 (no. 6), 1436 (no. 1), 1452 (no. 2), 1463 (no. 4), 1474 (no. 2), 1476 (nos. 2, 3), 1477 (nos. 1, 4). The city of Tiflis or Tbilisi, capital of Georgia. (See V. Minorsky, "Tiflis," *EI*, OE, IV, 752–763.)

Trapizon: 1383 (no. 1), 1449 (no. 1), 1464 (no. 1), 1470 (no. 1). The seaport of Trebizond (modern Turkish: Trabzon), in NE Turkey on the Black Sea. (See William Miller, *Trebizond, the Last Greek Empire*, 1926; J. H. Kramers, "Ṭarabzun," *EI*, OE, IV, 660–662.)

Tšoł (variant: Tayšoł): 1404 (no. 2), 1410 (no. 3). Village in canton of Ṙštunik' [q.v.].

Tun Vrac': 1346 (no. 1), 1407 (no. 1). Lit., land of the Georgians; that is, Georgia. *See* Vrac'tun.

Tunn Ałuanic‘: 1417 (no. 1). Lit., the land of the Albanians; that is, Caucasian Albania. *See* Ałuank‘.

Tunn Gamrac‘: 1400 (no. 1). *See* Gamirk‘.

Tunn Hoṙomoc‘: 1402 (no. 1). Lit., the land of the Rūm. *See* Hoṙmac‘ Ašxarh.

Tunn Parskac‘: 1405 (no. 1). Lit., the land of the Persians; that is, Persia. *See* Parskastan.

Tunn Šamay: 1304 (no. 3). Lit., the land of Šam. *See* Šamatun.

Tunn Vrac‘: 1416 (no. 2), 1417 (no. 1). Lit., the land of the Georgians; that is, Georgia. *See* Vrac‘tun.

Tunn Yudayanc‘: 1393 (no. 1). Lit., the land of the Judaeans; that is, Judaea.

Tunn Yunac‘: 1422 (no. 1). Lit., the land of the Greeks; the reference is to Rūm or Asia Minor.

Tup‘xis: 1462 (no. 1). *See* Tp‘xis.

T‘ac‘u: 1437 (no. 8). Village in the region of Xizan [q.v.]. (See Ēp‘rikean, *Baṙaran*, II, 20.)

T‘adēos, St.: 1315 (no. 2). Monastery, situated S of the fortress of Mākū, in Vaspurakan province. (See Ēp‘rikean, *Baṙaran*, II, 1–3.)

T‘arvēz: 1422 (no. 1), 1456 (no. 2). *See* T‘avrēz.

T‘avrēz (variants: Dahavrēž, Davrēž, Dawrēz, Dawrēž, Dayvrēž, T‘arvēz, T‘avrēž, T‘awrēz, T‘awrēž, T‘awriz, T‘awvrēz): 1408 (no. 1), 1422 (no. 1), 1425 (nos. 1, 8), 1428 (no. 1), 1438 (no. 2), 1445 (no. 5), 1450 (no. 5), 1452 (no. 5), 1458 (nos. 1, 2, 5), 1465 (no. 6), 1468 (no. 3). The city of Tabrīz in NW Iran and capital of the province of Ādharbaydjān. (See V. Minorsky, "Tabrīz," *EI*, OE, IV, 583–593.)

T‘avrēž: 1336 (no. 2), 1337 (no. 1), 1342 (no. 1), 1407 (no. 1), 1417 (no. 3), 1441 (no. 1), 1480 (no. 1). *See* T‘avrēz.

T‘awrēz: 1357 (no. 2), 1417 (no. 1), 1422 (no. 1), 1423 (no. 1), 1428 (no. 4), 1435 (no. 4), 1450 (nos. 1, 3), 1453 (no. 1), 1462 (nos. 3, 6), 1475 (no. 2). *See* T‘avrēz.

T‘awrēž: 1410 (no. 2). *See* T‘avrēz.

T‘awriz: 1471 (no. 3). *See* T‘avrēz.

T‘awvrēz: 1468 (no. 1). *See* T‘avrēz.

T‘ełeneac‘: 1302 (no. 1). Monastery in canton of Nig in Ayrarat province. (See Hübschmann, *AO*, p. 430.)

T‘ēawdoypawlis: 1314 (no. 1). *See* T‘ēodupawlis.

T‘ēodupawlis (variant: T‘ēawdoypawlis): 1346 (no. 1). The city of Theodosiopolis. *See* Arzrum.

T‘il: 1304 (no. 1). Town and fortress in Cilicia Pedias, situated E of Anarzaba [q.v.].

T‘ilguran (variant: T‘ilkuran): 1452 (no. 5). Town, situated W of Āmid. (See Ēp‘rikean, *Baṙaran*, II, 41; Hakobyan, *Manr Žam.*, II, 213, n. 3.)

T‘ilkuran: 1388 (no. 3). *See* T‘ilguran.

T‘lak: 1370 (no. 1). Town in canton of Ekełeac‘ [q.v.].

T'ołat': 1472 (no. 1). *See* T'ōxat'.

T'ort'anay: 1450 (no. 4). Monastery, probably located in the town of T'ordan situated E of Mt. Sepuh [q.v.], in canton of Kemakh. (See Ēp'rikean, *Bar̄aran*, II, 47–48.)

T'ōxat' (variant: T'ołat'): 1469 (no. 6). The town of Tokat, situated S of the middle course of the river Tozanli-Su, in province of Sivas. (See J. H. Kramers, "Toḳat," *EI*, OE, IV, 806–807; Saint-Martin, *Mémoires*, I, 188.)

T'raka: 1409 (no. 3). The author of the text mentions this as another name for the province of Mokk' [q.v.].

T'urk'əstan: 1407 (no. 1). *See* T'urk'stan.

T'urk'stan (variant: T'urk'əstan): 1417 (no. 3). Turkistan or Turkestan, land of the Turks. (See W. Barthold, "Turkistān," *EI*, OE, IV, 895–896). In the texts the term is used for the lands held by the Ḳara-Ḳoyunlu Turkmens under Ḳara Yūsuf.

Uranc': 1433 (no. 1), 1436 (no. 2). Village in canton of Kec'an in Vaspurakan province. (See Xač'ikyan, *XV Dari*, I, p. 808.)

Urc: 1457 (no. 3), 1460 (no. 3), 1461 (no. 2), 1473 (no. 6). Village in canton of the same name in Ayrarat province. (See Ēp'rikean, *Bar̄aran*, I, 323; Eremyan, *Ašx.*, p. 76.)

Urha (variant: Urxa): 1422 (no. 1). Town of Urfa (Syriac: Orhāi; Arabic: al-Ruhā'), the former Edessa; in E Turkey, N of the present-day Syrian border. (See E. Honigmann, "Orfa," *EI*, OE, III, 993–998; Hübschmann, *Arm. Gram.*, p. 298, no. 50; Saint-Martin, *Mémoires*, I, 158.)

Urtab, Mt.: 1435 (no. 3). Mountain in the vicinity of Bitlīs.

Urxa: 1395 (no. 1). *See* Urha.

Ur̄nkar: 1318 (no. 4), 1319 (no. 3), 1335 (no. 3). Monastery in village of Gayt'is in canton of K'ajberunik'. (See Xač'ikyan, *XV Dari*, II, p. 72, no. 99; Oskean, *Vank'er*, II, 443–444.)

Uxtn Tēr Yuskan Ordin (variant: Yuskay Ordi): 1371 (no. 3). Lit., monastery of the son of the Lord Yusik; this is another name for the monastery of Argelan [q.v.] in canton of Berkri.

Vahkay: 1468 (no. 4). The town and fortress of Vahka (Greek: Baxa; modern Turkish: Feke) in Cilicia, situated N of Sis. (See Ališan, *Sisuan*, pp. 161–163.)

Vahraway: 1322 (no. 1). Village in canton of Arewik' in Siwnik' province. (See Ališan, *Sisakan*, pp. 299, 302; Inčičean, *Ašx.*, p. 272.)

Vałaršakert (variant: Vałaškert): 1421 (no. 5). The town of Aleşkirt (Arabic: Walāškird) in E Turkey, midway between city of Kars and Lake Van. (See Hübschmann, *AO*, pp. 468–469; Saint-Martin, *Mémoires*, I, 124.)

Vałaršapat (variant: Vałaršaypat): 1444 (nos. 3, 8), 1447 (no. 1), 1449 (no. 8), 1450 (no. 1), 1452 (nos. 1, 3), 1453 (no. 2), 1456 (no. 3), 1458 (nos. 3, 4), 1460 (no. 1), 1462 (no. 7), 1464 (no. 7), 1465 (no. 2), 1468 (no. 3), 1473 (no. 5), 1476 (no. 8). Vagharshapat. Ancient capital of

Armenia in canton of Aragacotn in Ayrarat province; now the town of Etchmiadzin, situated W of Erevan. (See Hübschmann, *AO*, p. 469; *Arm. Gram.*, p. 79, no. 178; Eremyan, *Ašx.*, p. 82.)

Vałaršaypat: 1464 (no. 5). *See* Vałaršapat.

Vałaškert: 1421 (no. 1). *See* Vałaršakert.

Van: 1304 (no. 5), 1308 (no. 2), 1391 (no. 1), 1392 (no. 1), 1413 (no. 1), 1418 (no. 2), 1422 (no. 1), 1424 (nos. 1, 2), 1425 (nos. 2, 3, 4), 1426 (no. 3), 1428 (no. 1), 1435 (no. 1), 1437 (no. 5), 1438 (no. 1), 1441 (no. 3), 1442 (no. 2), 1445 (nos. 1, 2), 1446 (no. 4), 1451 (no. 5), 1453 (nos. 6, 8), 1454 (no. 4), 1458 (no. 2), 1459 (no. 2), 1462 (nos. 3, 8), 1463 (nos. 9, 10), 1465 (no. 5), 1467 (nos. 4, 5, 6), 1472 (no. 1), 1473 (no. 9), 1474 (no. 4), 1475 (nos. 3, 4, 5). (1) The town and fortress of Van in SE Turkey on E shore of lake of the same name. (2) Canton or district in Vaspurakan province. (See V. Minorsky, "Wān," *EI*, OE, IV, 1119–1121; Hübschmann, *AO*, pp. 340, 469; Saint-Martin, *Mémoires*, I, 137–140.)

Varag: 1318 (no. 1), 1369 (no. 1), 1401 (no. 3), 1421 (nos. 5, 10), 1444 (no. 4), 1453 (no. 7), 1467 (no. 6), 1480 (no. 3). Monastery, situated E of city of Van. (See Oskean, *Vank'er*, I, 268–339.)

Vardan, St.: 1418 (no. 3). Monastery near the village of Gawaš in canton of Ṙštunik' [q.v.].

Vardan, St.: 1472 (no. 1). Church in the town of Maku [q.v.].

Vardijor: 1476 (no. 8). Apparently the older name of the canton of Vayoc' Jor [q.v.] in Siwnik' province.

Vardnšēn: 1341 (no. 1). Village in the district of Tayk' [q.v.]. (See Eremyan, *Ašx.*, p. 79.)

Vardpatrik: 1405 (no. 3). Monastery in the canton of Kotayk' in Ayrarat province.

Vaspurakan: 1304 (no. 2), 1391 (no. 1), 1421 (no. 11), 1432 (no. 1), 1441 (no. 3), 1445 (no. 2), 1462 (nos. 4, 6), 1463 (no. 8). One of the provinces of historic Armenia, known in Pahlevi as Vāspuhrakān and in Arabic as Basfurradjān; now corresponding to the regions E and S of Lake Van. (See Hübschmann, *AO*, pp. 261–263, 339–347; *Arm. Gram.*, pp. 80–81, no. 182, and p. 87, no. 205.)

Vaspurakan: 1388 (no. 1). Mentioned as the name of a city, which cannot be identified; the reference is probably to the city of Van in Vaspurakan province.

Vatneac': 1417 (no. 1). *See* Vatniar.

Vatniar (variant: Vatneac'): 1411 (no. 1). The plain of Čalaghan, near the town of Derbend. (See Ēp'rikean, *Bařaran*, I, 109, 593; Eremyan, *Ašx.*, pp. 82–83.)

Vayijor: 1476 (no. 8). *See* Vayoc'-Jor.

Vayi-Jor: 1473 (no. 5), 1475 (no. 1), 1478 (no. 3). *See* Vayoc'-Jor.

Vayoc'-Jor (variants: Vayijor, Vayi-Jor, Vayoc'jor, Vayojor, Vayoyjor, Vayujor): 1348 (no. 2), 1351 (no. 1), 1463 (no. 5), 1474 (no. 1), 1476 (nos. 6, 7). Canton in Siwnik' province; now corresponding to the regions of Ełegnajor and Azizbekov in Armenian SSR. (See Hübschmann, *AO*, pp. 348, 469; Eremyan, *Ašx.*, p. 82.)

Vayoc'jor: 1333 (no. 3). *See* Vayoc'-Jor.

Vayojor: 1313 (no. 1). *See* Vayoc'-Jor.

Vayoyjor: 1302 (no. 1), 1335 (no. 5). *See* Vayoc'-Jor.

Vayujor: 1314 (no. 2). *See* Vayoc'-Jor.

Verastun: 1441 (no. 1). *See* Vrac'tun.

Veri Noravank': 1333 (no. 3), 1470 (no. 2), 1476 (no. 6). Monastery, better known as Noravank', in canton of Vayoc'-Jor [q.v.] in Siwnik' province. (See Hübschmann, *AO*, p. 456.)

Veri Varag: 1425 (no. 3). Monastery, situated E of city of Van on Mt. Verin Varag. It should not be confused with monastery of Varag [q.v.].

Verin-Derǰan: 1453 (no. 1). *See* Derǰan.

Virs: 1476 (no. 1). Variant of Virk', the Armenian term for Iberia. (See Eremyan, *Ašx.*, pp. 83–84.) It is used here for Georgia. *See* Vrac'tun.

Vnastun: 1477 (no. 6). The author seems to have used this form deliberately, as a pun, in place of Vrastun or Vrastan. Literally, it means land of wrong, injury, loss, etc., with an obvious reference to the atrocities committed by Uzun Ḥasan in Georgia. (See Xač'ikyan, *XV Dari*, II, p. 420.)

Vrac' Ašxarh: 1307 (no. 1), 1321 (no. 1), 1387 (no. 1), 1400 (no. 1), 1401 (no. 2), 1412 (no. 1), 1437 (no. 1), 1438 (no. 2), 1477 (no. 1). Lit., land of the Georgians. *See* Vrac'tun.

Vrac'akan Gawaṙn: 1335 (no. 1). Lit., the Georgian canton. *See* Vrac'tun.

Vrac'tan: 1436 (no. 1), 1476 (no. 2), 1478 (no. 2). *See* Vrac'tun.

Vrac'tun (variants: Ašxarhn Vrac', Kołmann Vrac', Tun Vrac', Tunn Vrac', Verastun, Virs, Vrac' Ašxarh, Vrac'akan Gawaṙn, Vrac'tan, Vrastan, Vrastun): 1417 (no. 1), 1422 (no. 1), 1436 (no. 1), 1440 (no. 1), 1441 (nos. 1, 3), 1443 (no. 2), 1444 (no. 4), 1450 (no. 1), 1458 (no. 1), 1464 (no. 1), 1476 (no. 3), 1477 (no. 1), 1478 (no. 1). The country of Georgia. (See W. E. D. Allen, *A History of the Georgian People*, London, 1932; A Manvelichvili, *Histoire de Géorgie*, Paris, 1951; A. Dirr, "Georgia," *EI*, OE, II, 131–132; V. Minorsky, "Tiflis," *ibid.*, IV, 752–763; Eremyan, *Ašx.*, pp. 83–84.)

Vrastan: 1400 (no. 2), 1476 (no. 5), 1477 (no. 3). *See* Vrac'tun.

Vrastun: 1477 (no. 3). *See* Vrac'tun.

Vtvak, Mt.: 1341 (no. 1). Mountain in the district of Tayk' [q.v.].

Xač'atur: 1304 (no. 1). Monastery in Cilicia, near fortress-city of Barjr-Berd [q.v.]. (See Ēp'rikean, *Baṙaran*, II, 138.)

Xač'en: 1417 (no. 1). Canton, known in Arabic sources as Khādjīn or Khāshīn, in Arc'ax province. (See Hübschmann, *AO*, p. 349.)

Xač'enajor: 1473 (no. 3). Valley in the canton of Xač'en [q.v.] in Arc'ax province. (See Ēp'rikean, *Baṙaran*, II, 139.)

Xalatan: 1398 (no. 2). *See* Łalat'ia.

Xalifi: 1464 (no. 16). Village near Hṙovmklay [q.v.].

Xałteac': 1346 (no. 1), 1461 (no. 7). *See* Xaxt'ik'.

Xałteac' Jor: 1332 (no. 3). Valley around the middle course of Çoruh Nehri in NE Anatolia. *See* Xaxt'ik'.

Xarberd (variant: Xardberd): 1400 (no. 5), 1444 (no. 8), 1453 (no. 1), 1466 (no. 8), 1469 (no. 8), 1470 (no. 1), 1479 (no. 4). The town of Kharput or Harput (now called Elaziğ), situated N of a great plain in the area bounded on W and S by the Euphrates, in the N by the Murad-Su, and in the E by the chain of the Armenian Taurus. (See J. H. Kramers, "Kharput," *EI*, OE, II, 914–916; Hübschmann, *AO*, pp. 432–433; Saint-Martin, *Mémoires*, I, 95, 96.)

Xardberd: 1361 (no. 2). *See* Xarberd.

Xarhoc' (variant: Harhoc'): 1425 (no. 8). Village in the region of Xizan [q.v.]. (See Ēp'rikean, *Bararan*, II, 166.)

Xaṙabasta: 1325 (no. 1), 1425 (no. 5). *See* Xaṙabastay.

Xaṙabastay (variant: Xaṙabasta): 1393 (no. 1), 1400 (no. 1), 1421 (no. 7), 1454 (no. 1). 1458 (no. 4), 1471 (no. 11). *See* Suxaray.

Xaṙan: 1449 (no. 1). The town of Harran (Arabic: Ḥarrān), situated SE of Urfa, in Turkish province of Rakka. (See Eremyan, *Ašx.*, p. 55; *Chèref-Nâmeh*, I. 1, 235; *Dictionary of Bible*, p. 364.)

Xaxt'ik' (variant: Xałteac'): 1480 (no. 1). Variant of regular form Xałtik'; the region situated E of the district of Trebizond which was known as Chaneti; it has also been called Lazistan after its native inhabitants, the Lazgis. (See Hübschmann, *AO*, p. 432.)

Xayik': 1403 (no. 5). Village in E Anatolia, near Erzincan. (See Xač'ikyan, *XV Dari*, I, p. 805; cf. Ēp'rikean, *Bararan*, II, 130.)

Xizan (variants: Hizan, Xzan): 1363 (no. 2), 1395 (no. 1), 1407 (no. 1), 1417 (no. 2), 1421 (no. 12), 1422 (no. 1), 1442 (no. 4), 1456 (no. 5), 1460 (no. 11), 1468 (no. 5), 1474 (no. 5). (1) Town and fortress, now called Hizan, situated S of Lake Van and SE of Bitlīs. (2) The district of Hizan, with town of the same name as its center. (See Saint-Martin, *Mémoires*, I, 175–176; *Chèref-Nâmeh*, I. 1, 180–181; II. 2, 40–41.)

Xlat' (variants: Łəlat', Łlat', Xłat'): 1343 (no. 2), 1402 (no. 3), 1421 (no. 1), 1422 (nos. 1, 3), 1428 (no. 1), 1435 (no. 3), 1437 (no. 3), 1445 (no. 4), 1462 (no. 3), 1472 (no. 1), 1473 (nos. 1, 7). The town and fortress of Khilāṭ or Akhlāṭ (in classical sources: Chaleat or Chaliat; Syriac: Kelath), situated NW corner of Lake Van. It was largely destroyed by an earthquake in 1246 and is now in ruins and uninhabited; the new town, called Ahlat, lies E of the ruins on the lake shore. (See Fr. Taeschner, "Akhlāṭ or Khilāṭ," *EI*, NE, I, 329–330; Saint-Martin, *Mémoires*, I, 103, 104; C. d'Ohsson, *Histoire des Mongols*, III, 20, 21, 35–45; *Chèref-Nâmeh*, I. 1, 506–507; Hübschmann, *AO*, p. 328.)

Xłat': 1437 (no. 3). *See* Xlat'.

Xorasan: 1307 (no. 1), 1335 (no. 1), 1391 (no. 1), 1422 (no. 1), 1435 (no. 4), 1442 (no. 1), 1449 (no. 6), 1453 (nos. 2, 6), 1457 (no. 1), 1458 (nos. 1, 2, 4, 7), 1460 (no. 3), 1461 (no. 2), 1462 (nos. 3, 6), 1464 (no. 2), 1468 (no. 1), 1469 (no. 1), 1472 (no. 1). The country of Khurāsān, comprising the lands situated S of the river Āmū-daryā and N of the Hindū-kush; politically, it also embraced Transoxiana and Sidjistān. (See C. Huart, "Khorāsān," *EI*, OE, II, 966–967; Hübschmann, *Arm. Gram.*, p. 45, no. 85; Spuler, *Mongolen in Iran*; and *Goldene Horde*.)

Xorin: 1305 (no. 1). Monastery in Cilicia, in the vicinity of the fortress-city of Barjr-Berd. (See Ēpʻrikean, *Baṙaran*, II, 203.)

Xorttʻancʻ: 1464 (no. 9). Village in the region of Aylax, which constituted a part of the canton of Cluk in Siwnikʻ province. (See Xačʻikyan, *XV Dari*, II, p. 592.)

Xorvaget: 1319 (no. 2). Village; its exact location is uncertain. The province of Arcʻax had a canton called Xoruaget; it seems probable that the village in question was located in the same canton. (See Ališan, *Sisakan*, p. 532.)

Xōy: 1459 (no. 2), 1471 (no. 7). (1) The town of Khoi (Arabic: Khuwayy), in the Persian province of Ādharbaydjān, situated on a plateau 70 miles NW of Tabrīz. (2) The plain of Khoi. (See C. Huart, "Khoi," *EI*, OE, II, 963.)

Xrim: 1346 (no. 2), 1371 (no. 1), 1384 (no. 1). *See* Łrim.

Xumitʻ: 1331 (no. 1). Monastery in the canton of Caṙutijor in Ayrarat province. (See Xačʻikyan, *XIV Dari*, p. 669.)

Xutʻ: 1462 (no. 3). Fortress in canton of the same name in Tarōn, situated NW of Bitlīs. (See Ēpʻrikean, *Baṙaran*, II, 191–193; Eremyan, *Ašx.*, p. 55.)

Xzan: 1420 (no. 5). *See* Xizan.

Yakob, Surb: 1469 (no. 6). The cathedral and monastery of the apostles SS. James in Jerusalem, and seat of the Armenian patriarchate in the Holy City. (See Sanjian, *The Armenian Communities in Syria*, pp. 95–225.)

Yałlcxa: 1416 (no. 2). *See* Axalcʻxay.

Yamitʻ: 1452 (no. 5). *See* Amitʻ.

Yankiwneacʻ: 1477 (no. 4). *See* Ankuneacʻ.

Yankuneacʻ: 1477 (no. 5). *See* Ankuneacʻ.

Yarates: 1310 (no. 2). Monastery in the village of Aratēs, in the canton of Vayocʻ-Jor in Siwnikʻ province. (See Ēpʻrikean, *Baṙaran*, I, 289–290.)

Yayas: 1468 (no. 4). *See* Ayas.

Yełevankʻ: 1426 (no. 3). Monastery in the canton of Berkri. (See Oskean, *Vankʻer*, I, 348–349.)

Yohanavankʻ: 1310 (no. 1), 1477 (no. 3). Monastery in the canton of Aragacotn in Ayrarat province. (See Karo Łafadaryan, *Hovhannavankʻə ev Nra Arjanagrutʻyunnerə*, Erevan, 1948.)

Yordanan: 1472 (no. 1). The river Jordan in the Holy Land. (See *Dictionary of Bible*, pp. 526–527; Hübschmann, *Arm. Gram.*, p. 295, no. 32.)

Yuskay Ordi: 1414 (no. 3). *See* Uxtn Tēr Yuskan Ordin.

Zambełk: 1472 (no. 1). This appears to be the name of a spring N of Lake Van. (See Hakobyan, *Manr Žam.*, II, 223, n. 24; cf. Ēpʻrikean, *Baṙaran*, I, 757.)

Zəṙel (variant: Zṙayl): 1442 (no. 2). Fortress in the region of Šatax (modern Turkish: Şatak), situated S of Lake Van and W of Çölemerik. (See *Chèref-Nâmeh*, I. 1, 177; Ēp'rikean, *Baṙaran*, I, 801; Eremyan, *Ašx.*, p. 52.)

Zion, New: 1318 (no. 2), 1407 (no. 1). The name Zion is frequently used in the Psalms and the Prophets as a synonym for Jerusalem. (See *Dictionary of Bible*, p. 1058.) In Armenian usage it is also symbolic of heaven.

Zmiwṙ: 1422 (no. 1). The seaport of Izmir (Smyrna) in W Turkey, on the Bay of Izmir in the Aegean Sea. (See J. H. Mordtmann, "Izmīr (Smyrna)," *EI*, OE, II, 567–569.)

Zṙayl: 1451 (no. 3). *See* Zəṙel.

Appendix D. Peoples, Nations, and Tribes

Abet'akan: 1446 (no. 5). Japhetic; composed of Abet', "Japheth," plus adjectival suffix -akan. This is one of several designations by which the Armenians referred to themselves; it originated in the tradition that Hayk, the legendary ancestor of the Armenians, was a descendant of Japheth. (See Malxaseanc', *HBB*, III, 382; "Japheth," *Dictionary of Bible*, p. 459.)

Ał-Łoyluc'ik': 1472 (no. 1). The Aḳ-Ḳoyunlu. *See* Ał-Łōlu.

Ał-Łoyluk': 1472 (no. 1). The Aḳ-Ḳoyunlu. *See* Ał-Łōlu.

Ał-Łōlu (variants: Ał-Łoyluc'ik', Ał-Łoyluk'): 1476 (no. 2). Aḳ-Ḳoyunlu; lit., those of the White Sheep. The name of the federation of Turkmen tribes, which rose in the region of Diyarbakir in post-Mongol times (in the fourteenth century) and lasted until ca. 1502. (See V. Minorsky, "Aḳ-Ḳoyunlu," *EI*, NE, I, 311–312.)

Aluanic': 1303 (no. 3), 1331 (no. 1). Genitive plural of Ałuank', the Armenian term for the (Caucasian) Albanians. (See *The History of the Caucasian Albanians by Movsēs Dasxuranci*, trans. C. J. F. Dowsett; R. N. Frye, "Arrān," *EI*, NE, I, 660.) The first reference is to the country of the Albanians in the Trans-Caucasus, and the second to the catholicosate of the Albanian church. (For a bibliography of works on the Albanians and their church, consult Anasyan, *Matenagitut'yun*, I, cols. 613–622.) *See also* Ałuank' (App. C).

Apaneri: 1468 (no. 4). Mentioned as a Turkmen tribe; otherwise unidentified.

Apu: 1384 (no. 1). Mentioned as the tribe to which Tokhtamîsh Khān of the White Horde belonged.

Arap: 1449 (no. 1). Variant spelling of Armenian Arab, "Arab" (see Malxaseanc', *HBB*, I, 251.)

Aršakuneac': 1453 (no. 2). Genitive plural of Aršakuni; lit., of the Aršakunis or Arsacids. *See* Aršakuni.

Aršakuni: 1307 (no. 5), 1315 (no. 1), 1325 (no. 1). The name of the Parthian Arsacid dynasty, a branch of which ruled in Armenia (A.D. 54–428). (For its etymology, see Hübschmann, *Arm. Gram.*, p. 27, no. 24.) The references are to the Armenian Arsacids.

Asorik': 1449 (no. 1). The Syrian Christians; composed of Asori, "Syrian," plus the Armenian plural suffix -k'. *See also* Asorik' (App. C).

Asoroc': 1303 (no. 3), 1444 (no. 3). Genitive plural of Asori; lit., of or belonging to the Syrians. In both texts the reference is to the land of the Syrians, that is, northern Syria. *See* Asorik'.

Aylazgac‘: 1400 (no. 3). Genitive plural of *aylazgi* [q.v.].

Aylazgeac‘: 1441 (no. 7). Genitive plural of *aylazgi* [q.v.].

Aylazgi: 1335 (no. 2), 1351 (no. 2), 1420 (no. 2), 1422 (no. 1), 1426 (no. 4), 1438 (no. 2), 1445 (no. 6), 1453 (no. 3), 1456 (no. 2), 1458 (no. 4), 1460 (no. 2), 1463 (no. 3), 1467 (no. 8), 1469 (no. 6), 1471 (no. 5), 1475 (no. 8), 1476 (no. 2). Lit., belonging to a different nation, race, people, tribe, and so forth. In Armenian sources it was originally applied to non-Jews; later it was used generally for non-Christians; and in the period in question the term was applied to the Muslims. (See *Bar̄girk*‘, I, 85; Małxaseanc‘, *HBB*, I, 76.)

Aylazgik‘: 1368 (no. 1), 1386 (no. 2), 1406 (no. 1), 1407 (no. 3), 1408 (no. 1), 1423 (no. 3), 1453 (no. 2). Plural of *aylazgi* [q.v.].

Azgi netawłi*:* 1304 (no. 5). *See* azgn netołac‘.

Azgi netołac‘*:* 1331 (no. 5). *See* azgn netołac‘.

Azgin Marac‘*:* 1405 (no. 4). *See* Azgn Marac‘.

Azgin netołac‘*:* 1312 (no. 1), 1333 (no. 3), 1408 (no. 3), 1411 (no. 3), 1420 (no. 1), 1421 (no. 8), 1425 (no. 1), 1426 (no. 5), 1428 (no. 1), 1441 (no. 4), 1443 (no. 1), 1444 (no. 5), 1449 (no. 2), 1454 (no. 6), 1455 (no. 4), 1459 (no. 9), 1462 (no. 3), 1463 (no. 11), 1464 (no. 13), 1465 (no. 7), 1467 (no. 3), 1469 (no. 8), 1470 (nos. 1, 3, 4), 1476 (nos. 11, 12), 1478 (no. 5), 1479 (nos. 3, 4). *See* azgn netołac.

Azgin T‘orgomean: 1411 (no. 1). Lit., of the Torgomian nation. The reference is to the Ḳara-Ḳoyunlu Turkmens. *See* Azgn T‘orgoma.

Azgn Hagaray: 1476 (no. 2). Lit., the nation of Hagar. The reference is to the Turkmens. *See* Azgn Hagaru.

Azgn Hagarean: 1335 (no. 1). Lit., the Hagarian nation. The reference is to the Ismaelites. *See* Azgn Hagaru.

Azgn Hagaru (variants: azgn Hagaray, azgn Hagarean, Hagar, Hagarac‘ik‘, Hagarac‘oc‘): 1346 (no. 1), 1426 (no. 1). Lit., the nation of Hagar, referring to the descendants of Hagar, the handmaid of Abraham's wife, Sarah, and mother of his eldest son, Ishmael or Ismael. (See *Dictionary of Bible*, p. 358.) In Armenian sources generally the term is applied to the Arabs (see Malxaseanc‘, *HBB*, III, 8); the references in the colophons, however, are to the Muslims, such as the Turkmens, Tačiks. The above two texts refer to the Turkmens.

Azgn Ismaelac‘oc‘: 1314 (no. 1). Lit., the nation of the Ismaelites. The reference is to Xarbanda (see App. A). *See* Azgn Ismayēli.

Azgn Ismaēlean: 1416 (no. 1). Lit., the Ismaelite nation. The reference is to the Turkmens. *See* Azgn Ismayēli.

Azgn Ismayelay: 1407 (no. 1). Lit., the nation of Ismael. The reference is to the Turkmens. *See* Azgn Ismayēli.

Azgn Ismayeli: 1305 (no. 1). Lit., the nation of Ismael. The reference is to the Mamluks. *See* Azgn Ismayēli.

Azgn Ismayēlac‘: 1336 (no. 3). Lit., the nation of the Ismaelites. The reference is to the Mamluks. *See* Azgn Ismayēli.

Azgn Ismayēlean: 1409 (no. 4). Lit., the Ismaelite nation. The reference is to the Turkmens. *See* Azgn Ismayēli.

Azgn Ismayēli (variants: azgn Ismaelac'oc', azgn Ismaēlean, azgn Ismayelay, azgn Ismayeli, azgn Ismayēlac', azgn Ismayēlean, azgn Ismayili, Ismaeli, Ismaēlac'oc'n, Ismayelac'oc' azg, Ismayelac'oc'n, Ismayelac'woc', Ismayēlac'ik', Ismayēlakan azgac', Ismayēlean, Ismayēlean azg, Ismayēleank'): 1306 (no. 3), 1307 (no. 2), 1315 (no. 2), 1335 (no. 6), 1336 (no. 4), 1349 (no. 2), 1370 (no. 1), 1460 (no. 9), 1463 (no. 3). Lit., the nation of Ismael, referring to Ismael or Ishmael, eldest son of Abraham by his concubine Hagar. (See "Ishmael," *Dictionary of Bible*, p. 428.) According to Muslim tradition the Arabs are said to be the descendants of Ishmael. In the colophons the term is used synonymously with Azgn Hagaru [q.v.] and is applied to the Islamized Mongols, Turkmens, Mamluks, and so forth.

Azgn Ismayili: 1304 (no. 3). Lit., the nation of Ismael. The reference is to the Mamluks. *See* Azgn Ismayēli.

Azgn K'rdstanac': 1329 (no. 1). Lit., the nation of Kurdistan, that is, the Kurds of Kurdistan. (For a summary discussion of this people, see V. Minorsky, "Kurds," *EI*, OE, II, 1132–1155.) *See also* Azgn Marac'.

Azgn Marac' (variants: azgin Marac', Marac', Marac' azg): 1393 (no. 1), 1425 (no. 5). Lit., the nation of the Mars, one of the Armenian designations for the Kurds. (See *Bargirk'*, II, 216–217.) *See also* Azgn K'rdstanac'.

Azgn netołac' (variants: azgi netawłi, azgi netołac', azgin netołac', azgn netołakan, azinn netołac', netołac', netołac' azg, netołakan, netołakan azg, netołakank'): 1302 (no. 1), 1303 (no. 3), 1305 (no. 2), 1307 (nos. 1, 2, 3, 5), 1308 (nos. 1, 2), 1310 (nos. 1, 3), 1315 (nos. 1, 2), 1321 (no. 1), 1327 (no. 1), 1335 (no. 5), 1337 (no. 1), 1340 (no. 2), 1348 (no. 1), 1355 (no. 1), 1386 (no. 2), 1388 (no. 2), 1393 (nos. 1, 2), 1397 (no. 1), 1407 (no. 2), 1421 (no. 6), 1444 (no. 2), 1462 (no. 4), 1473 (no. 1). Lit., the nation of archers. This seems to have been a generic term used for the nomads of Central Asia. It was applied not only to the Mongols, but before them to the Seljuks and later to the Turkmen tribes, as well. (See J. Markwart, "Die Entstehung der armenischer Bistümer," *Orientalia Christiana*, vol. 27, 1932, p. 153.)

Azgn netołakan: 1413 (no. 2). *See* Azgn netołac'.

Azgn Parsic': 1371 (no. 3). Lit., the nation of the Pars. *See* Parsic'.

Azgn T'at'arac': 1417 (no. 1). Lit., the nation of Tartars. *See* T'at'ar.

Azgn T'orgoma (variant: azgin T'orgomean): 1437 (no. 1). Lit., the nation of T'orgom. This is a generic term used in Armenian sources for the nomads from Central Asia. In the text the term is applied in reference to Ḳara Yūsuf. (For the principal usage of the term see zarms T'ork'omean.)

Azgn T'urk'ac': 1336 (no. 5), 1453 (no. 2). Lit., the nation of the Turks. *See* T'urk'.

Azgn Vrac': 1441 (no. 1). Lit., the nation of the Georgians. *See* Vrac'.

Azgs Aramay (variant: azgs Arameni): 1476 (no. 2). Lit., our nation of Aram. This is another designation by which the Armenians referred to themselves. (See Malxaseanc', *HBB*, I, 253.) It is based on the ancient tradition that the Armenians were the descendants of Aram. (For Aram, see *Dictionary of Bible*, p. 48.)

Azgs Arameni: 1315 (no. 2). *See* Azgs Aramay.

Azinn netołac': 1307 (no. 5), 1315 (no. 1). *See* Azgn netołac'.

Bagratuni: 1452 (no. 2). The Bagratids; the name of one of the ancient and medieval feudal Armenian families and ruling dynasties. (See René Grousset, *Histoire de l'Arménie des origines à 1071*, Paris, 1947, pp. 341–584.)

Bayandur (variants: Payandur, Payəntur): 1479 (no. 3). Bayandur, Bayundur, or Bayîndîr; the name of one of the Oghuz (Turkmen) tribes. To this clan belonged the rulers of the Aḳ-Ḳoyunlu federation of Turkmen tribes. (See Faruk Sümer, "Bayîndîr," *EI*, NE, I, 1133; V. Minorsky, "Aḳ-Ḳoyunlu," *ibid.*, pp. 311–312.)

Biwrt'elean: 1417 (no. 1). Belonging to the princely family of Biwrt'el. The members of this family were better known as the Ōrbēlean [q.v.]. *See also* App. A, Biwrt'ēl, Burt'el.

Čałat': 1407 (no. 4), 1453 (no. 7). *See* Č'ałat'ay.

Č'ałat': 1421 (nos. 1, 5), 1422 (no. 1), 1449 (no. 6), 1479 (no. 1). *See* Č'ałat'ay.

Č'ałat'ay (variants: Čałat', Č'ałat', J̌ałat', J̌ałat'ay, J̌ładayk'): 1421 (no. 1), 1429 (no. 1), 1432 (no. 1), 1438 (no. 1), 1454 (no. 2), 1462 (no. 6). Čaghatai, the name of the nomad population and warrior caste of Mā warā' al-Nahr (Transoxiana). (For the various usages of the term, see W. Barthold, *12 Vorlesungen über die Geschichte der Türken Mittelasiens*, Berlin, 1935. Also consult Cleaves, "Mongolian Names and Terms," pp. 417–418; W. Barthold–[J. A. Boyle], "Čaghatay Khān" and "Čaghatay Khānate," *EI*, NE, II, 2–4.

Dulłarac'i: 1453 (no. 1). *See* Dulłatarc'i.

Dulłatarc'i (variants: Dulłarac'i, Tulłarac'i): 1453 (no. 1). Dhu'l-Ḳadrid; that is, belonging to the Dhu'l-Ḳadr Turkmen dynasty, which ruled over the region of Marash and Malatya (as clients first of the Mamluk and later of the Ottoman sultans), from 1337 until 1522. (See J. H. Mordtmann–[V. L. Ménage], "Dhu'l-Ḳadr," *EI*, NE, II, 239–240.)

Ebrayec'ik': 1365 (no. 2). Lit., the Hebrews; that is, the Jews. The term is derived from Eber, the eponymous ancestor of the Hebrews. (See "Eber" and "Hebrew," *Dictionary of Bible*, pp. 227, 370.)

Egiptac'woc': 1441 (nos. 6, 10), 1453 (no. 1). Genitive plural of Egiptac'i, "Egyptian." The references are to the Mamluks of Egypt.

Ǝřōškan: 1425 (no. 5), 1446 (no. 1), 1459 (no. 2). Rūzagī or Rōzagī; the name of a Kurdish tribe which inhabited the regions of Diyarbakir, Van, and Shehrezul. (See *Chèref-Nâmeh*, I. 1, 57–58, 62; V. Minorsky, "Kurds," *EI*, OE, II, 1144.)

Farsah: 1468 (no. 4). Varsaq, the name of a division of the Turkmen tribe in the service of the Mamluks. (See Barbara Flemming, *Landschaftsgeschichte von Pamphylien, Pisidien und Lykien im Spätmittelalter* Wiesbaden, 1964, p. 88.)

Frank (variants: Frankac' azgn, Frankac', Fṙang azgn, P'ṙankac', P'ṙankn, Yazgac'ən Fərankin): 1453 (nos. 2, 3), 1464 (no. 3). This is a general term applied to the Christians of Europe or the Latin West. (For the various uses of the term see Malxaseanc', *HBB*, IV, 629; see also *Baṙgirk'*, II, 963, 1037.)

Frank azgn: 1453 (no. 3). Lit., the Frank nation. *See* Frank.

Frankac': 1453 (no. 3). Lit., of the Franks. *See* Frank.

Frankac' azgn: 1453 (no. 2). Lit., the nation of the Franks. *See* Frank.

Fṙang azgn: 1335 (no. 6). Lit., the Frank nation. *See* Frank.

Fṙang-ut'iwn: 1453 (no. 1). Abstract noun form of Frank; lit., Frankishness; the reference is to the religion of the Franks, Roman Catholicism.

Fṙankac': 1453 (no. 1). Lit., of the Franks. *See* Frank.

Gayianeanc': 1453 (no. 3). Genitive plural of Gayianeank'; lit., of or belonging to the group of Gayianē. According to Armenian tradition, Gayianē was the leader of a group of virgins who, having been persecuted by the Roman Emperor Diocletian because of their Christian faith, left Rome and finally arrived in Armenia. In A.D. 301 Gayianē and her followers were put to death by King Tiridates III of Armenia. (See Ōrmanean, *Azgapatum*, cols. 51–52.)

Hagar: 1476 (no. 2). The reference is to the Tačiks. *See* Azgn Hagaru.

Hagarac'ik': 1431 (no. 2). Lit., the descendants of Hagar. The reference is to the Turkmens. *See* Azgn Hagaru.

Hagarac'oc': 1303 (no. 3). Genitive plural of Hagarac'i, lit., descendant of Hagar. *See* Azgn Hagaru.

Haykan azgi: 1333 (no. 1). *See* Haykean azg.

Haykazean, Haykaznean: Composed of Hayk, "Hayk," plus azn, "race, tribe," plus genitive singular case ending *-ean*; that is, "belonging to the race of Hayk," the legendary ancestor of the Armenians. It is used in the colophons as an adjective, referring to the ancient Armenian calendar. (See *Baṙgirk'*, II, 31–32; Malxaseanc', *HBB*, III, 38.)

Haykean azg (variants: Haykan azgi, seṙs Haykay): 1335 (no. 1). Lit., nation of Hayk, that is, the Armenian nation or the Armenians. (See *Baṙgirk'*, II, 32; Malxaseanc', *HBB*, III, 38.)

Honac': 1400 (no. 1), 1422 (no. 1). Genitive plural of Hon, "Hun"; lit., of the Huns. In the colophons the term is applied to the Golden Horde.

Hoṙmac': 1403 (no. 2). Genitive plural of Hoṙom [q.v.]; the reference is to the Ottomans.

Hoṙom (variants: azgin Hṙomoc', Hoṙmac', Hoṙmoc', Hoṙomoc', Hṙomayakan, Hṙomayec'ik'): 1335 (no. 6), 1453 (nos. 1, 3), 1464 (no. 3). Basically, the term means "Roman." In the colophons its use corresponds to Rūm in Islamic sources, that is, the Greeks of Asia Minor. (See *Baṙgirk'*, II, 120; Malxaseanc', *HBB*, III, 131. Regarding the change from Greek *rh* to ancient Armenian *hṙ*, see Hübschmann, *Arm. Gram.*, p. 328.)

Hoṙmocʻ: 1453 (no. 3). Genitive plural of Hoṙom [q.v.].

Hoṙomocʻ: 1310 (no. 2), 1453 (no. 1). Genitive plural of Hoṙom [q.v.]. The two references are to the Byzantine Greeks.

Hṙipʻsimeancʻ: 1453 (no. 3). Genitive plural of Hṙipʻsimean, "follower of Hṙipʻsimē," one of the virgins put to death by King Tiridates III of Armenia. *See* Gayianeancʻ.

Hṙomayakan: 1365 (no. 2). Adjectival form of Hoṙom [q.v.]. In the colophon the term is applied to the Genoese in the Crimea.

Hṙomayecʻikʻ: 1365 (no. 2). Nominative plural of Hṙomayecʻi, "Roman." *See* Hoṙom. In the colophon the term is applied to the Genoese in the Crimea.

Hṙomayecʻwocʻ: 1303 (no. 4). Genitive plural of Hṙomayecʻi, "Roman"; lit., of the Romans. The reference is to the Roman calendar.

Ismaeli: 1450 (no. 4). Lit., of Ismael. The reference is to the Turkmens. *See* Azgn Ismayēli.

Ismaēlacʻocʻn: 1307 (no. 4), 1441 (no. 1). Genitive plural of Ismaēlacʻi, with definite article -n; lit., of the Ismaelites. The first reference is to the Muslims in general, and the second to the Turkmens. *See* Azgn Ismayēli.

Ismayelacʻocʻ azg: 1314 (no. 1). Lit., nation of the Ismaelites. The reference is to Xarbanda (see App. A). *See* Azgn Ismayēli.

Ismayelacʻocʻn: 1303 (no. 6), 1341 (no. 1), 1346 (no. 1). Genitive plural of Ismayelacʻi, with definite article -n; lit., of the Ismaelites. The reference is to the Muslims. *See* Azgn Ismayēli.

Ismayelacʻwocʻ: 1411 (no. 4). Genitive plural of Ismayelacʻi; lit., of the Ismaelites. *See* Azgn Ismayēli.

Ismayēlacʻikʻ: 1475 (no. 8). Nominative plural of Ismayēlacʻi; lit., the Ismaelites. The reference is to the Ottomans. *See* Azgn Ismayēli.

Ismayēlakan azgacʻ: 1443 (no. 4). Lit., of the Ismaelite nations. The reference is to the Turkmens. *See* Azgn Ismayēli.

Ismayēlean: 1365 (no. 2). Genitive singular of Ismayēl; lit., of or belonging to Ismael, Ismaelite. *See* Azgn Ismayēli.

Ismayēlean azg: 1365 (no. 2). Lit., Ismaelite nation. *See* Azgn Ismayēli.

Ismayēleankʻ: 1335 (no. 1). Lit., the Ismaelites. The reference is to the Muslims. *See* Azgn Ismayēli.

Israyeleancʻn: 1422 (no. 1). Genitive plural of Israyelean, "Israelite," with definite article -n. One of the terms used in Armenian for the Israelites or the Jews.

J̌ałatʻ: 1436 (no. 1), 1465 (no. 6). *See* Čʻałatʻay.

J̌ałatʻay: 1421 (no. 4), 1428 (no. 1). *See* Čʻałatʻay.

J̌hut: 1449 (no. 1). Cf. Persian juhūd, "the Jews." (See Malxaseancʻ, *HBB*, IV, 141; Hübschmann, *AO*, p. 465.) The usual Armenian terms for the Jews are Hreaykʻ, Ebrayecʻikʻ, and Israyelacʻikʻ.

J̌ładay-kʻ: 1400 (no. 3). Plural of J̌ładay. *See* Čʻałatʻay.

Kilikec'oc': 1323 (no. 1), 1325 (no. 3), 1397 (no. 2), 1401 (no. 4), 1444 (no. 8). Genitive plural of Kilikec'i, "Cilician." *See* Kilikec'woc'.

Kilikec'woc' (variants: Kilikec'oc', Kiwlikec'woc'): 1327 (no. 1), 1331 (no. 2), 1337 (no. 3), 1386 (no. 2), 1395 (no. 1), 1400 (no. 2), 1427 (no. 2), 1436 (no. 6), 1441 (no. 10). Genitive plural of Kilikec'i, "Cilician"; lit., of or belonging to the Cilicians. The references are to the Armenians of Cilicia, as well as to their kingdom or catholicosate in the same region. These terms are also used to designate the country of Cilicia.

Kiwlikec'woc': 1446 (no. 6), 1469 (no. 6). Genitive plural of Kiwlikec'i, a variant of Kilikec'i. *See* Kilikec'woc'.

K'ərd: 1472 (no. 1). *See* K'urd.

K'rd: 1472 (no. 1). *See* K'urd.

K'urd (variants: K'ərd, K'rd, K'urt'): 1371 (no. 3), 1393 (no. 1), 1417 (no. 3), 1425 (no. 3), 1427 (no. 3), 1428 (no. 4), 1440 (no. 2), 1442 (no. 4), 1455 (nos. 2, 6), 1462 (no. 3), 1468 (no. 5), 1472 (no. 1). The Kurds. Although the forms of these terms are singular, in a number of colophons, they are used in a plural sense.

K'urt': 1338 (no. 1), 1414 (no. 2), 1425 (no. 5), 1449 (no. 1), 1452 (no. 5). *See* K'urd.

Ladinac'woc': 1384 (no. 1). Genitive plural of Ladin, "Latin"; lit., of or belonging to the Latins. In the context the reference is to the Genoese.

Łara-Łoyunlu: 1452 (no. 5). The Ḳara-Ḳoyunlu, lit., those of the Black Sheep; the name of the Turkmen dynasty which reigned in Persia and Mesopotamia (1375–1468). (See C. Huart, "Ḳara-Ḳoyunlu," *EI*, OE, II, 741.)

Łaray-T'at'ar: 1422 (no. 1). Ḳara Tatar. (See W. Barthold, "Tatar," *EI*, OE, IV, 700–702.)

Mahmedakan: 1446 (no. 6). *See* Mahmetakan.

Mahmetakan (variant: Mahmedakan): 1304 (no. 1), 1387 (no. 2), 1441 (no.1). A Muhammadan, a follower of the Prophet Muhammad of Islam; a Muslim.

Mahmetakank': 1449 (no. 1). Plural of Mahmetakan [q.v.].

Makabayeanc'n: 1422 (no. 1). Genitive plural of Makabayec'i, plus definite article -n; lit., of the Maccabees, the name of the Jewish family otherwise known as Hasmonaeans, who led the revolt against Syria and also furnished the dynasty of rulers in the state which was subsequently formed. (See "Maccabees," *Dictionary of Bible*, pp. 603–606.)

Marac': 1303 (no. 3), 1435 (no. 3). Genitive plural of Mar. *See* Azgn Marac'.

Marac' azg: 1474 (no. 3). Lit., nation of the Mars. *See* Azgn Marac'.

Məsəlman, Məsəlman-k': 1453 (no. 3). Cf. Persian musulmān, derived from Muslimān, the Persian plural of Arabic *Muslim*, a follower of the religion of Islam. (See Zenker, p. 848a.) The -k' of the second form is the Armenian plural suffix.

Mogakank': 1335 (no. 1). Lit., those who professed the religion of the magi, that is, Zoroastrianism. In the colophon the reference seems to be to the heathen Mongols before they adopted the religion of Islam.

Mułal: 1303 (no. 4). Borrowed from the older variant of the Persian designation *Mughal* for the Mongols. (Concerning the usage of the term, see *Ta'rikhi Jahan-gusha of Juwayni*, composed in 1260, ed. by Mirza Muhammad, in E. J. W. Gibb Memorial Series, London, 1916, II, 134; see also Cleaves, "Mongolian Names and Terms," p. 424.)

Nestorakank': 1449 (no. 1). Nestorians; composed of Nestor, "Nestorius," plus adjectival suffix -akan, plus plural suffix -k'.

Netołac': 1325 (no. 1), 1387 (no. 1), 1457 (no. 1). Genitive plural of netoł, "archer." *See* Azgn netołac'.

Netołac' azg: 1363 (no. 1), 1402 (no. 3), 1421 (no. 9), 1445 (no. 4), 1473 (no. 2). Genitive plural of netoł, "archer," and azg, "nation"; lit., "nation of archers." *See* Azgn netołac'.

Netołakan: 1437 (no. 2). Composed of netoł, "archer," plus adjectival suffix -akan. *See* Azgn netołac'.

Netołakan azg: 1306 (no. 1), 1307 (no. 4), 1318 (no. 1), 1333 (no. 4), 1342 (no. 1), 1480 (no. 3). *See* Azgn netołac'.

Netołakank': 1336 (no. 2). Plural of netołakan [q.v.].

Ninuec'ik': 1335 (no. 6). The Ninevans; composed of Ninuē, "Nineveh," plus the Armenian suffix of attribution -c'i, plus plural suffix -k'. (For the etymology of the Armenian form Ninuē, see Hübschmann, *Arm. Gram.*, p. 295, no. 35.)

Ōrbelean: 1437 (no. 1). *See* Ōrbēlean.

Ōrbēlean (variants: Ōrbelean, Ōrpelean): 1438 (no. 2). The name of the feudal Armenian dynasty which held extensive domains in the Armenian province of Siwnik' under the hegemony of the Mongols. (See Brosset, *Siounie*, I, 209–241; II, 182.)

Ōrpelean: 1401 (no. 2). *See* Ōrbēlean.

Pahlawuni: 1453 (no. 2). Parthian (see Hübschmann, *Arm. Gram.*, pp. 63–65, no. 140). The term is used here to indicate the Parthian origin of the Armenian Aršakuni or Arsacid dynasty. *See also* Aršakuni; Part'ewac'.

Parsic' (variants: azgn Parsic', Parsiks, Parskac'): 1303 (no. 3), 1400 (no. 5), 1421 (no. 8), 1422 (no. 1), 1432 (no. 1), 1437 (no. 1), 1451 (no. 2). Lit., of or belonging to the Pars; that is, of the Persians. (See Hübschmann, *Arm. Gram.*, p. 67, no. 145.) It is also used in a geographic sense meaning "Persia."

Parsiks: 1417 (no. 3). Accusative plural of Parsik, "Persian"; that is, the Persians. *See* Parsic'.

Parskac': 1471 (no. 7). Genitive plural of Parsik, "Persian"; that is, of the Persians. *See* Parsic'. This term is also used in the sense of Persia.

Part'ewac': 1476 (no. 2). Genitive plural of Part'ew, "Parthian." (See Hübschmann, *Arm. Gram.*, pp. 63–65, no. 140, and p. 508.) *See also* Pahlawuni.

Payandur: 1476 (no. 7). The reference is to Uzun Ḥasan. *See* Bayandur.

Payəntur: 1453 (no. 1). The reference is to Djihānshāh. *See* Bayandur.

P'r̊angac': 1310 (no. 2). Genitive plural of P'r̊ang, the older Armenian form of Frank, "Frank"; lit., of the Franks. The reference is to the Latins. *See* Frank.

P'r̊ank'n: 1366 (no. 1). Composed of P'r̊ank, variant of P'r̊ang, "Frank," with definite article -n; that is, the Frank; in the context it is used in a plural sense. *See* Frank.

Ser̊s Haykay: 1315 (no. 2). Lit., of our race or nation of Hayk; that is, the Armenians. *See* Haykean azg.

Skiwt'ac'woc': 1442 (no. 1). Genitive plural of Skiwt'ac'i, "Scythian." The reference is to the Turkmens.

Šamc'ik': 1468 (no. 4). Composed of Šam, "Syria," plus the Armenian suffix of attribution -c'i, plus plural suffix -k': lit., the inhabitants of Syria. The reference is to the Mamluks of Syria.

Šamōan: 1445 (no. 1). The Kurdish tribe of Shambo, to which belonged the amirs of the principality of Hakkārī. (See *Chèref-Nâmeh*, I. 2, 115–121; II. 2, 118, n. 517; V. Minorsky, "Kurds," *EI*, OE, II, 1145.)

Tačik: 1318 (no. 1), 1335 (no. 6), 1349 (no. 1), 1371 (no. 1), 1384 (no. 1), 1387 (no. 2), 1391 (no. 1), 1401 (nos. 1, 4), 1422 (no. 1), 1441 (no. 1), 1442 (no. 1), 1453 (nos. 1, 2, 3, 4), 1455 (no. 1), 1462 (no. 3), 1464 (nos. 1, 3), 1465 (no. 6), 1468 (no. 4), 1470 (no. 2), 1472 (no. 1), 1473 (nos. 1, 3), 1474 (no. 6), 1475 (no. 9), 1476 (nos. 2, 3), 1477 (no. 1). Cf. Pahlevi tāčik, "Arab." (See Hübschmann, *Arm. Gram.*, pp. 86–87, no. 205.) It is used as a generic term for the Muslims, for it is applied to the Tatars, Turkmens, Ottomans, Mamluks, and so forth.

Tułarc'i: 1468 (no. 4). *See* Dułłatarc'i.

T'amurc'ik': 1401 (no. 1). Composed of T'amur, "Tīmūr (Lang)," plus suffix of attribution -c'i, plus plural suffix -k'; lit., the followers of Tīmūr. In the context the reference is to the troops of Tīmūr Lang.

T'at': 1449 (no. 1). Tāt or Tat, a Turkic designation for non-Turks, mainly people of Iranian origin. (See V. Minorsky, "Tāt or Tat," *EI*, OE, IV, 697–700.)

T'at'ar: 1303 (no. 3), 1310 (no. 2), 1338 (no. 1), 1365 (no. 1), 1393 (no. 1), 1394 (no. 1), 1414 (no. 2), 1422 (no. 1), 1426 (no. 2), 1449 (no. 1), 1462 (no. 3). The Tatars. (See W. Barthold, "Tatar," *EI*, OE, IV, 700–702; Cleaves, "Mongolian Names and Terms," p. 428.)

T'iwrk'mēn: 1423 (no. 2). *See* T'urk'man.

T'orgoma: 1436 (no. 5). Adjectival form of T'orgom. The reference is to the Ḳara-Ḳoyunlu Turkmen ruler Iskandar. *See* azgn T'orgoma.

T'orgomacin: 1407 (no. 2), 1428 (no. 7). Compound construction: T'orgom, plus liaison vowel a, plus cin, "birth"; lit., born of T'orgom. The first reference is to Ḳara Yūsuf and the second to his son, Iskandar. *See* azgn T'orgoma.

T'orgomac'i: 1428 (no. 8), 1446 (no. 3). Composed of T'orgom, plus the Armenian suffix of attribution -c'i; lit., descendant of T'orgom. The references are to the Turkmens. *See* azgn T'orgoma.

T'orgomean: 1425 (no. 6). Genitive singular of T'orgom; lit., of or belonging to T'orgom. The reference is to the Ḳara-Ḳoyunlu Turkmen ruler Iskandar. *See* azgn T'orgoma.

T'orgomeank': 1393 (no. 1). Nominative plural of T'orgomean [q.v.]. The reference is to the Turkmens.

T'urk' (variants: azgn T'urk'ac', T'urk'ac', T'urk'n): 1366 (no. 1), 1371 (no. 3), 1392 (no. 1), 1393 (no. 1), 1398 (no. 2), 1407 (no. 1), 1417 (no. 2), 1421 (no. 4), 1422 (no. 1), 1425 (no. 1), 1428 (no. 1), 1444 (no. 2), 1445 (no. 1), 1449 (no. 1), 1451 (no. 5), 1453 (no. 3), 1454 (no. 3), 1455 (no. 2), 1459 (no. 3), 1462 (no. 1), 1468 (no. 4). The Turks. (See W. Barthold, "Turks," *EI*, OE, IV, 900–908; Doerfer, II, 483–495, no. 888.)

T'urk'ac': 1303 (no. 3). Genitive plural of T'urk' [q.v.].

T'urk'iman: 1431 (no. 2). *See* T'urk'man.

T'urk'man (variants: T'iwrk'mēn, T'urk'iman, T'urk'men): 1367 (no. 1), 1407 (no. 4), 1417 (no. 1), 1419 (no. 2), 1421 (nos. 1, 5, 8), 1422 (no. 1), 1424 (no. 3), 1425 (no. 3), 1426 (no. 1), 1427 (no. 1), 1429 (no. 1), 1435 (no. 3), 1437 (no. 4), 1441 (no. 1), 1445 (no. 4), 1453 (no. 1), 1458 (nos. 3, 6), 1462 (no. 3), 1464 (no. 10), 1468 (no. 4), 1472 (no. 1), 1476 (no. 2). The Turkmens or Turkomans. (See W. Barthold, "Turkomans," *EI*, OE, IV, 896–898; Doerfer, II, 498–499, no. 892.)

T'urk'men: 1417 (no. 1). *See* T'urk'man.

T'urk'n: 1421 (no. 14). Composed of T'urk', plus definite article -n. *See* T'urk'.

Vardananc': 1453 (no. 1). This is the common designation for the Armenians who, under the leadership of Vardan Mamikonean, the commander-in-chief of the Armenian army, participated in the battle of Awarayr in A.D. 451 against the superior Persian forces. This is considered to be the first war ever waged in defense of the Christian faith. (See Langlois, *Collection*, II, 177–251; *Yeghisheh*, New York, 1952.)

Vrac': 1303 (no. 3), 1304 (no. 6), 1321 (no. 1), 1330 (no. 1), 1331 (no. 1), 1391 (no. 1), 1400 (no. 1), 1401 (no. 2), 1411 (no. 1), 1417 (no. 1), 1419 (no. 2), 1420 (no. 3), 1422 (no. 1), 1424 (no. 3), 1432 (no. 2), 1436 (no. 1), 1437 (nos. 1, 6), 1438 (nos. 2, 5, 6), 1441 (no. 1), 1442 (no. 1), 1443 (nos. 5, 6), 1447 (no. 2), 1452 (no. 2), 1458 (no. 1), 1459 (no. 5), 1462 (no. 1), 1465 (no. 1), 1466 (nos. 2, 3), 1468 (no. 2), 1471 (no. 5), 1473 (no. 6), 1474 (no. 2), 1477 (no. 1), 1478 (no. 3). Lit., of or belonging to the Georgians. In the colophons the term is also used in a geographical sense, that is, Georgia.

Vrac' azg: 1476 (no. 2). Lit., nation of the Georgians. *See also* Vrac'.

Xaraman: 1335 (no. 7). The Ḳaramān-oghlu or Ḳaramānids, who inhabited the district of Ḳaramān (Ḳaramān-ili, Caramania). (See J. H. Kramers, "Ḳaramān," *EI*, OE, II, 744–745.) *See also* Łaraman (App. C).

Xaramnc'ik': 1367 (no. 1). Lit., inhabitants of Xaraman, "Ḳaramān"; that is, the Ḳaramān-oghlu or Ḳaramānids. *See* Xaraman.

Xorazm: 1387 (no. 1), 1393 (no. 1), 1401 (no. 2), 1421 (no. 8), 1422 (no. 1), 1438 (no. 2). The Khwārizmī; that is, the inhabitants of the country of Khwārizm in Central Asia. During the Mongol period, the term was applied to Islamic Central Asia in general, which explains why Tīmūr Lang and Shāhrukh are referred to as Khwārizmīs. (See W. Barthold, "Khwārizm or Khīwa," *EI*, OE, II, 908–912.)

Yazgac'ən Fərankin: 1453 (no. 3). Lit., the Frankish nations. *See* Frank.

Yunac': 1453 (no. 3). Genitive plural of Yoyn, "Greek"; lit., of or belonging to the Greeks. The reference is to the Byzantine Greeks. (See Hübschmann, *Arm. Gram.*, p. 56, no. 122.)

Yunakan: 1453 (no. 3). Composed of Yoyn, "Greek," plus adjectival suffix -akan; that is, belonging or pertaining to the Greeks.

Zarms T'ork'omean: 1315 (no. 2). Lit., our nation of T'orgom or Togarmah. This is another designation by which the Armenians referred to themselves. It is based on the ancient tradition that the Armenians were the descendants of Togarmah. (See J. Karst, "Geschichte der armenischen Philologie," *Schriften der Elsass-Lothringischen Wiss. Gesellschaft zu Strassburg*, Series C, 2, Heidelberg, 1930, pp. 169–184; *Recueil des Historiens des Croisades, Documents Arméniens*, I, 231, 526, 805; *Bar̃girk'*, I, 819; Malxaseanc', *HBB*, II, 120.) For another use of the term T'orgomean *see* azgn T'orgoma.

Appendix E. Biblical Quotations or References

The Books of the Old Testament

Nehemiah 12:44. 1453 (no. 2)
Psalms 7:15. 1446 (no. 5)
Psalms 72:1. 1304 (no. 3)
Psalms 78:63–64. 1453 (no. 3)
Psalms 78:65–66. 1453 (no. 3)
Psalms 78:69. 1453 (no. 3)
Psalms 79:1. 1453 (nos. 2, 3)
Psalms 79:2. 1453 (no. 3)
Psalms 79:3. 1442 (no. 3), 1453 (no. 3)
Psalms 79:4. 1453 (nos. 2, 3)
Psalms 99:4. 1304 (no. 3)
Psalms 106:40–41. 1453 (no. 3)
Isaiah 5:24. 1453 (no. 2).
Isaiah 11:6. 1304 (no. 3)
Lamentations of Jeremiah 1:12. 1442 (no. 1)
Daniel 7:7. 1417 (no. 1).
Daniel 7:19. 1417 (no. 1)
Daniel 7:23. 1417 (no. 1)
Hosea 10:8. 1307 (no. 1), 1386 (no. 1), 1400 (no. 1), 1411 (no. 3), 1441 (no. 8), 1456 (no. 3), 1461 (no. 7), 1476 (no. 1)

The Books of the New Testament

Matthew 5:44. 1449 (no. 1)
Matthew 10:8. 1464 (no. 3)
Matthew 21:41. 1417 (no. 1), 1426 (no. 4)
Matthew 24:20. 1450 (no. 3), 1469 (no. 3)
Matthew 26:52. 1446 (no. 3)
Mark 2:17. 1453 (no. 2)
Mark 3:24. 1363 (no. 3)
Mark 13:8. 1416 (no. 2)
Mark 14:38. 1469 (no. 3)
Luke 11:17. 1363 (no. 3)
Luke 23:29. 1401 (no. 2)
Luke 23:30. 1307 (no. 1), 1386 (no. 1), 1400 (no. 1), 1411 (no. 3), 1441 (no. 8), 1456 (no. 3), 1461 (no. 7), 1476 (no. 1)

John 10:11. 1462 (no. 3)
John 10:16. 1462 (no. 3)
John 11:52. 1462 (no. 3)
Romans 11:25. 1453 (no. 2)
St. John's Revelation 6:16. 1307 (no. 1), 1386 (no. 1), 1400 (no. 1), 1411 (no. 3), 1441 (no. 8), 1456 (no. 3), 1461 (no. 7), 1476 (no. 1)

Appendix F. Glossary of Foreign Terminology

Abełay: 1366 (no. 1), 1387 (no. 2), 1441 (no. 2). Cf. Syriac *aβīlā*, monk, friar (see Hübschmann, *Arm. Gram.*, p. 299, no. 1; Ačaṙyan, *HLP*, I, 336). It corresponds to Greek *monachós,* and Latin *monachus*, *religiosis* (see *Baṙgirk'*, I, 2). In Armenian usage it applies to a celibate priest ranking one step lower than the vardapet [q.v.].

Ała: 1371 (no. 3), 1472 (no. 1). Cf. Turkic *agha* (<*aqa*, older brother). It is used here in the Ottoman Turkish meaning of chief, master, or landowner. (See Doerfer, I, 131–133, no. 21; H. Bowen, "Agha," *EI*, NE, I, 245–246.)

Amanat': 1337 (no. 2). Cf. Persian *amānat* (Arabic *amāna*), security, surety, warranty, guaranty (see Wehr, p. 29; Ačaṙyan, *HLP*, II, 189; Malxaseanc', *HBB*, I, 55).

Amir (variants: *amiray, ēmir*): 1386 (no. 3), 1392 (no. 1), 1398 (no. 1), 1401 (no. 4), 1403 (no. 7), 1410 (no. 3), 1414 (no. 5), 1417 (no. 2), 1418 (no. 3), 1419 (nos. 3, 4), 1421 (no. 12), 1426 (no. 5), 1427 (no. 3), 1431 (no. 3), 1433 (no. 3), 1442 (no. 4), 4443 (no. 2), 1446 (no. 1), 1454 (no. 6), 1455 (no. 2), 1459 (no. 8), 1476 (no. 10). Cf. Arabic *amīr* (related to Syriac, according to Ačaṙyan, *HLP*, I, 336, and II, 190; *Baṙgirk'*, I, 71), commander, governor, prince. (For its various uses in Islamic history, see A. A. Duri, "Amīr," *EI*, NE, I, 438–439.) In the Middle Ages, Muslim rulers of Armenia were generally referred to as *amiray* (see Ačaṙyan, *HAB*, I, 120). Until the mid-nineteenth century, the title *amira* or *amiray* was also given to high-ranking and wealthy Armenians in Istanbul under the Ottoman government.

Amirapet: 1393 (no. 1), 1402 (no. 1), 1425 (no. 1). A hybrid form (Arabic *amīr*, plus Armenian *pet*, chief) for the Arabic *amīr al-umarā'*, chief amir, commander-in-chief of the army (see K. V. Zettersteén, "Amīr al-Umarā'," *EI*, NE, I, 446). In Armenian sources *amirapet* refers to a chief Muslim ruler (cf. *Baṙgirk'*, I, 71).

Amiray: 1337 (no. 2), 1361 (no. 3), 1367 (no. 1), 1393 (no. 1), 1401 (no. 5), 1402 (no. 1), 1417 (no. 1), 1422 (no. 1), 1425 (no. 4), 1436 (no. 3), 1453 (no. 1), 1459 (no. 3), 1462 (no. 3), 1472 (no. 1). *See* amir.

Amirza: 1425 (nos. 1, 3), 1426 (no. 3), 1428 (no. 1), 1437 (nos. 3, 5), 1443 (no. 2), 1444 (no. 2), 1445 (nos. 3, 4), 1446 (nos. 1, 2), 1456 (no. 4), 1458 (no. 5), 1460 (no. 9). See *mirza.*

Amirzay: 1410 (no. 2), 1425 (no. 2), 1426 (no. 5), 1445 (nos. 1, 6), 1450 (no. 1), 1452 (no. 5), 1455 (no. 6), 1456 (no. 3), 1462 (no. 3). See *mirza.*

Amirzē: 1443 (no. 2). See *mirza.*

Amovsacin: 1304 (no. 3). Lit., born of Amoz; it refers to the Prophet Isaiah. (See Isaiah 1:1; *Dictionary of Bible,* p. 29.)

Anasax: 1422 (no. 1). Cf. Middle Turkic *yasaḳ,* law, with Armenian negative prefix *an-*; used here in the sense of lawless. See also *asax.*

Andōlvatʿ: 1472 (no. 1). Cf. Persian *dovlat* (Arabic *dawla*), luck, prosperity, fortune, with Armenian negative prefix *an-*; used here in the sense of unfortunate, luckless.

Anmərwatʿ: 1422 (no. 1). Cf. Ottoman Turkish *mürvet,* dialectal form of *mürüvvet* (Arabic *murūwa*), the ideal of manhood, comprising all knightly virtues; especially manliness, valor, chivalry, generosity, sense of honor (see Hony, *Turkish-English Dictionary,* p. 257; Wehr, p. 902), with Armenian negative prefix *an-*. It is used here in the sense of unchivalrous.

Ansleh: 1462 (no. 1). Cf. Arabic *silāḥ,* arms, weapon, armament, with Armenian negative prefix *an-*; used here in the sense of unarmed. See also *sələx.*

Anšaḷawatʿ: 1422 (no. 1). Cf. Persian *id.* (Arabic *shaqāwa*), compassion, pity, sympathy (see Zenker, p. 547a), with Armenian negative prefix *an-*. It is used here in the sense of merciless, pitiless, cruel.

Anxalatʿ: 1336 (no. 1). Cf. Arabic *ghalaṭ,* error, mistake, blunder; incorrect, wrong, with Armenian negative prefix *an-*. It is used here in the sense of unerring. (See Hübschmann, *Arm. Gram.,* p. 267, no. 62.)

Aparas: 1339 (no. 1). Variant form of *aparasan* or *aperasan,* unbridled, unrestrained, licentious, insolent, impudent (see *Baṙgirkʿ,* I, 274). It is apparently borrowed from Pahlevi *apērasan* (see Malxaseancʿ, *HBB,* I, 208). It is used here in the sense of unbridled, unrestrained.

Arancʿ: 1478 (no. 1). Variant form of *Aracʿ*; the sixth month of the ancient Armenian calendar (see *Baṙgirkʿ,* I, 341).

Areg: 1420 (no. 1), 1464 (no. 9). The eighth month of the ancient Armenian calendar (see *Baṙgirkʿ,* I, 351).

Arłučʿi: 1304 (no. 3). Cf. Middle Turkic *yarghuči,* judge, who issues a verdict according to the Turkic or Mongolian common law (*yasa*). (See *Codex Cum.,* p. 115.)

Aṙlex (the text reads *aṙlṙex*): 1318 (no. 1). Cf. Middle Turkic (*y*)*arligh,* order, official decree (see Brockelmann, *Mitteltürkischer Wortschatz,* p. 79). This was an imperial decree given by the Mongol khans. (See Blake and Frye, "Archers," p. 387, n. 34.)

Asax: 1422 (no. 1). Cf. Middle Turkic *yasaḳ,* law (see Ačaṙyan, *HLP,* II, 275; Blake and Frye, "Archers," p. 384, n. 6). See also *anasax.*

Asparapet: 1307 (no. 6). A word that goes back (via Middle Persian) to Old Persian **spādapati-* (see Ačaṙyan, *HLP,* I, 285). It is used here in the sense of generalissimo, general-in-chief, corresponding to Greek *archistrátēgos,* and Latin *princeps militiae, imperator exercitus* (see *Baṙgirkʿ,* II, 738). For the history of this word and for later Armenian borrowings, see Hübschmann, *Arm. Gram.,* p. 240, no. 588.

At'abag: 1419 (no. 2). See *At'abēk.*

At'abēk (variants: *at'abag, at'apak*): 1477 (no. 1). Cf. Turkic *atabeg* or *atabak.* Originally, the term meant tutor of the successor to the throne (see Gordlevskii, "Selected Writings," I, 71). Under the Seljuks and their successors, it was the title of a high dignitary; and under the Ottomans it was applied to military chiefs. (See Doerfer, II, 7–8, no. 415; C. Cahen, "Atabak (Atabeg)," *EI*, NE, I, 731; for additional bibliography also consult Blake and Frye, "Archers," p. 385, n. 14). The term does not occur in Armenian sources before the arrival of the Mongols in Armenia (see *Bařgirk'*, I, 11).

At'apak: 1396 (no. 1). See *at'abēk.*

Axt'armay: 1426 (no. 4). Cf. Ottoman Turkish *aktarma*, to move from one receptacle to another; to transship; to turn topsy-turvy (see Hony, *Turkish-English Dictionary*, p. 10; cf. Doerfer, II, 16–17, no. 433; Radloff, col. 119). It was used figuratively and as a derisive epithet by members of the Armenian church to describe their fellow countrymen who had adhered to Roman Catholicism. (See Ačaṙyan, *HLP*, II, 275; Malxaseanc', *HBB*, I, 44.)

Azat: 1313 (no. 1), 1401 (no. 2). Cf. Persian *āzād*, free (see Haïm, I, 12), and Pahlevi *āzāt* (see Ačaṙyan, *HLP*, I, 240). It appears in Armenian sources from the earliest times and was used, within the context of the feudal system, for the members of the nobility (see *Bařgirk'*, I, 4; Malxaseanc', *HBB*, I, 6).

Azex: 1422 (no. 2). Cf. Middle Turkic (Kipčak) *azyx*, food, provisions (see *Codex Cum.*, p. 46).

Bahadur: 1342 (no. 1). See *Bahaduř.*

Bahaduř (variants: *bahadur, bahatur, pahatur*): 1422 (no. 1), 1445 (no. 6), 1458 (no. 1), 1476 (no. 10). Cf. Persian *bahādur*, hero, champion (see Doerfer, II, 366–377, no. 817; Cleaves, *Mongolian Documents*, pp. 56–57). It was used as a surname and an honorific title among Muslim dynasties. (See D. Sinor, "Bahadūr," *EI*, NE, I, 913; cf. Blake and Frye, "Archers," p. 389, n. 53, and pp. 435–436.)

Bahatur: 1329 (no. 2). See *bahaduř.*

Bak: See *Bēk.*

Baron: Cf. Old French *baron* (French *baron*; Italian *barone*; Latin *baro*), baron, prince, sovereign, master, lord (see Hübschmann, *Arm. Gram.*, p. 390, no. 8).

Beklarbek: 1476 (no. 1). Cf. Turkic *beglerbegi*, a title meaning beg of begs, going back to the Iranian idea of a ruler. Under the Ottomans the title was originally applied to the commander-in-chief of the army; it subsequently meant provincial governor, and finally it was no more than an honorary rank. (See V. L. Ménage, "Beglerbegi, Baylerbeyi," *EI*, NE, I, 1159–1160; Doerfer, II, 406–410, no. 829.)

Beř: 1428 (no. 5). See *beřn.*

Beřn (variant: *beř*): 1446 (no. 1), 1457 (no. 2). It is the same word as in Persian *bar*, a load (see Haïm, I, 198). In Armenian usage it meant not only a heavy load or cargo borne by man, animal, carriage or ship, but also goods for sale (see *Bařgirk‘*, I, 481; Malxaseanc‘, *HBB*, I, 360).

Bēhēšt: 1441 (no. 1). Cf. Persian *bihišt*, paradise (see *Grundriss*, vol. I, pt. 2, p. 25).

Bēk (variants: *bak, pak, pēk*)*:* Cf. Turkic *beg*, lord (see Doerfer, pp. 389–406, no. 828; H. Bowen, "Beg or Bey," *EI*, NE, I, 1159). In Armenian sources it is generally used in the sense of prince (see Ačaṙyan, *HLP*, II, 275; *HAB*, I, 409; *Bařgirk‘*, I, 487).

Biwr: 1422 (no. 1). The older Armenian spelling of this word is *bewr*, probably borrowed from an east Iranian dialect (cf. Sogdian *brywr* and Ossetian *bēwrä*), meaning ten thousand (see *Grundriss*, I, pt. 2, p. 35; Gershevitch, *Grammar of Manichean Sogdian*, p. 198, para. 1316). In Armenian the word also means myriad, large quantity, countless (see Ačaṙyan, *HLP*, I, 248).

Blgihon: 1389 (no. 1). This appears to be a weapon or an instrument of war; I do not know its exact meaning and etymology.

Buxtank‘: 1349 (no. 2). Cf. Arabic *buhtān*, calumny, slander, false accusation; lie, untruth (see Steingass, p. 210; Wehr, p. 78; Haïm, I, 293). The Armenian form has the plural suffix *-k‘*.

Č‘arx: 1389 (no. 1). Cf. Persian *charkh*, wheel (see Steingass, p. 390; Haïm, I, 589).

Č‘awl: 1422 (no. 1). Cf. Turkic *çöl*, desert, wilderness (see Radloff, III, col. 2043; Malxaseanc‘, *HBB*, IV, 34).

Dahekan (variant: *dekan*)*:* 1349 (no. 2). Cf. Persian *dahgān*, name of a gold coin, corresponding to Greek *drakhmē* (see Hübschmann, *Arm. Gram.*, p. 133, no. 158).

Daman: 1462 (no. 3). Cf. Arabic *ḍamān*, which had a variety of meanings: civil liability in the widest meaning of the term; suretyship or guarantee; and tax-farming. (See "Ḍamān," *EI*, NE, II, 105; R. Le Tourneau, "Bayt al-Māl," *ibid.*, pp. 1141–1149.) The Armenians generally used it in the sense of tax (see Ačaṙyan, *HLP*, II, 191). In the text the verbal expression *daman aṙnul* means to seek justice.

Damdam: 1389 (no. 1). This onomatopoeic word seems to be connected with Arabic *damdama*, rumbling noise, rumble (see Wehr, p. 292). The form in the text, *dmdmēin*, is the third person plural imperfect of the infinitive *dmdmem*, to make a rumbling noise.

Danušman: 1335 (no. 6), 1446 (no. 5). Cf. Persian *dānishūmand*, learned, wise (see Steingass, p. 501). In Armenian, however, it referred specifically to a Muslim learned man or *mulla* (see Ačaṙyan, *HLP*, I, 252).

Daran: 1452 (no. 5), 1462 (no. 3). Cf. Pahlevi *dāran*, container (see Hübschmann, *Arm. Gram.*, pp. 136–137, no. 174; Ačaṙyan, *HLP*, I, 253). In the first text it means cupboard, closet; in the second it is used in the sense of subterranean dwelling or hiding place. (See Ačaṙyan, *ibid.*)

Darpas: 1453 (no. 3). Cf. Persian *darvās* or *darvāza*, gate, large door (see Hübschmann, *Arm. Gram.*, p. 137, no. 175; Haïm, I, 811). In Armenian usage it came to mean royal or princely palace (see Ačaṙyan, *HLP*, I, 253; *Baṙgirk'*, I, 603–604), corresponding to the Turkish *kapu* or *seray*.

Dawlat': 1426 (no. 4). See *andōlvat'*.

Daxiray: 1472 (no. 1). Cf. Arabic *dhakhīra*, treasure, supplies; provisions, food; (military) ammunition (see Wehr, p. 308).

Dekan: 1368 (no. 1), 1408 (no. 2), 1441 (no. 2), 1449 (no. 1). A variant form of *dahekan* (>*dekan*). See *dahekan*.

Despak: 1304 (no. 3). Seems to be related to Pahlevi **dēspak*, an ancient covered carriage, without wheels, drawn by men or animals. (See Hübschmann, *Arm. Gram.*, p. 140, no. 190; cf. Ačaṙyan, *HLP*, I, 254; *Baṙgirk'*, I, 610.)

Dēp'al: 1462 (no. 2). Cf. Georgian *dedopali*, queen (see J. Molitor, *Glossarium Ibericum*, Louvain, 1962, I, 109; cf. Ačaṙyan, *HLP*, II, 222).

Dhawl: 1389 (no. 1). Cf. Ottoman Turkish *daūl* (Arabic *ṭabl*), drum (see Radloff, III, 1646; cf. Malxaseanc', *HBB*, I, 531).

Dimosakan: 1449 (no. 1). Adjectival form, composed of *dimos* (from Greek *dēmos*, people, nation, tribe), plus adjectival suffix *-akan*. This term was used in the sense of public, government, or municipal (see Hübschmann, *Arm. Gram.*, p. 346, no. 96; cf. Ačaṙyan, *HLP*, II, 15). In the text the reference is to the tax which the Armenian bishops collected from their communities in behalf of the state treasury.

Ditapet: 1462 (no. 3). A compound noun: *dēt* plus liaison vowel *a* plus *pet*. The first component may be compared with Pahlevi *dīt*, sight; Pahlevi *dītan* (Old Persian *didiy*) meant to watch, inspect, examine (see Hübschmann, *Arm. Gram.*, p. 141, no. 194; cf. Ačaṙyan, *HLP*, I, 254). The second component, *pet* (from Middle Persian *pat*), means chief, leader, master (see Hübschmann, *Arm. Gram.*, p. 299, no. 538). The word *ditapet* was used in the sense of chief overseer, superintendent, and more specifically denoted high-ranking clergymen, such as a bishop, patriarch, or catholicos (see *Baṙgirk'*, I, 626).

Dram: 1337 (no. 2), 1375 (no. 2), 1401 (nos. 5, 8), 1417 (no. 2), 1422 (nos. 1, 2), 1428 (no. 5). Cf. Pahlevi *dram* (Greek *drakhmē*), the name of a weight and a coin (see Hübschmann, *Arm. Gram.*, pp. 145–146, no. 208; cf. H. W. Bailey, "Irano-Indica II," *BSOAS*, 13:129, 1949).

Dšxoy: 1462 (no. 3). An old Armenian word meaning queen (see *Bargirk'*, I, 637; Malxaseanc', *HBB*, I, 534; for its suggested etymology, see Ačaṙean, *Armatakan Baṙaran*, II, 577–578).

Elč'i: 1304 (no. 3). Cf. Middle Turkic *elči*, envoy, messenger, usually in a diplomatic sense (see Doerfer, II, 203–207, no. 656; *Codex Cum.*, p. 87; B. Lewis, "Elči," *EI*, NE, II, 694; Cleaves, *Mongolian Documents*, p. 81, n. 17; Mostaert and Cleaves, "Trois documents mongols des Archives secrètes vaticanes," p. 461; Mostaert and Cleaves, *Les Lettres des ilkhan Aryun et Öljeitü à Philippe le Bel*, p. 26).

Ēmir: 1445 (no. 1). *See* amir.

Ēmirza: 1453 (no. 5). See *Mirza.*

Ēmnut'iwn: 1422 (no. 1). Abstract noun form; composed of *ēmin* (Arabic *amn*), safety, peace, security, protection (see Zenker, p. 97b), plus Armenian abstract suffix *-ut'iwn.* It is used here in the sense of security.

Ǝṙayis (variant: *ṙayēs*)*:* 1366 (no. 1). Cf. Arabic *ra'īs,* one at the head, or in charge of; head; chieftain; leader; chief (see Wehr, p. 318; Zenker, p. 474c). It is used in the texts to denote an influential representative of a village or town (see Xač'ikyan, *XIV Dari,* p. 665).

Ǝṙzak: 1422 (no. 1), 1453 (no. 3), 1468 (no. 4). Cf. Arabic *arzāḳ* (sing. *rizḳ*), livelihood, subsistence; property, possessions, wealth, fortune (see Wehr, pp. 336–337; Ačaṙyan, *HLP,* II, 192).

Flori: 1464 (no. 1). Derived from Italian *florino,* a silver coin, used in the Black Sea colonies, either directly or via Ottoman *flori* (see Radloff, IV, col. 1954).

Fṙuč: 1367 (no. 1). Cf. Arabic *furdj,* onlooking, watching, inspection, viewing (see Wehr, p. 702).

Gałjn: 1393 (no. 1). A botanical term; a harmful weed, corresponding to Latin *cuscuta* (see Malxaseanc', *HBB,* I, 407). Other sources claim that it is the hop, or *cuscuta lupuliformis* (see *Baṙgirk',* I, 524), or monk's rhubarb (see Bedrossian, *Dictionary,* p. 109).

Ganjalaws: 1365 (no. 2). Cf. Ottoman Turkish *qonsolos* (see Radloff, II, 548), a consul, or representative of the interests of foreign states in Islamic countries (see B. Spuler, "Consul," *EI,* NE, II, 60).

Gawazan: 1449 (no. 1). Cf. Pahlevi **gavāzan,* staff, register (see Hübschmann, *Arm. Gram.,* p. 126, no. 130). In Armenian sources the word is used as the order, table, or register, especially of kings, princes, patriarchs, and so forth. (See Ačaṙyan, *HLP,* I, 250.) In the text the reference is to Armenian parish communities.

Gundustapl: 1325 (no. 2). Borrowed from Italian *contestabile* (cf. Old French *conestable*). (See Hübschmann, *Arm. Gram.,* p. 389, no. 2.) It is used in Armenian sources in the sense of commander-in-chief.

Guntustapl-ut'iwn: 1367 (no. 1). Abstract noun form of *gundustapl* [q.v.].

Halal: 1368 (no. 1), 1408 (no. 2), 1421 (no. 7), 1425 (no. 3), 1441 (no. 7), 1459 (no. 2). Cf Arabic *ḥalāl,* lawful, legal, licit, legitimate; lawful possession (see Wehr, p. 199). In the texts it is used in the sense of honestly earned.

Haram: 1337 (no. 2). Cf. Arabic *ḥarām,* canonically prohibited, unlawful (see Wehr, p. 171; Malxaseanc', *HBB,* III, 65).

Haramiks: 1465 (no. 6). Cf. Arabic *ḥarāmī,* thief, dishonest man, bandit. To this is added the Armenian plural suffix *-k'* and English plural *-s.* (See Malxaseanc', *HBB,* III, 65.)

Hasay: 1401 (no. 1). See *xas.*

Hasrat'amah (variant: *xasrat'amah*)*:* 1465 (no. 6). A hybrid composite: *hasrat'* borrowed from Arabic *ḥasrat,* grief, sorrow, pain, distress, affliction (see Wehr, p. 177), plus liaison vowel *a,* plus Armenian *mah,* death. It is used in the sense of death from grief.

Hayrapetut'iwn: 1301 (no. 1). This term corresponds to Latin *patriarchatus.* In Armenian usage it means patriarchate, catholicosate, chief episcopacy (see *Bařgirk'*, II, 53). In this and in subsequent colophons, the term *hayrapet* (corresponding to Greek *patriárchēs*, Latin *patriarcha*) is rendered as pontiff, and the term *hayrapetut'iwn* as pontificate whenever they refer to the catholicoses of the Armenian church or to their office. This is to distinguish them from the terms *patriark'* or *patriarg* (patriarch) and *patriark'ut'iwn* (patriarchate).

Hazinay: 1472 (no. 1). Cf. Arabic *khazīna*, treasure house, exchequer, riches, coffer (see Zenker, p. 407b).

Hesar: 1441 (no. 2). See *xsar.*

Hēšim hači: 1453 (no. 3). I cannot identify the first term. The second is borrowed from Arabic *ḥadjdjī*, an epithet used for individuals who have performed the pilgrimage to Mecca. The text refers to an Armenian, Baron Gorg, from Ankara, and in Armenian usage the applicable epithet would be *mahtesi* (see *mahdasi*), referring of course to the pilgrimage to Jerusalem.

Hiwk'm: 1451 (no. 2.) See *Huk'm.*

Hsar: 1400 (no. 1), 1422 (no. 1). See *xsar.*

Huk'm (variant: *hiwk'm*)*:* 1417 (no. 2), 1422 (no. 1). Cf. Arabic *ḥukm*, judgment, valuation, opinion; decision; (legal) judgment, verdict, sentence; condemnation, conviction; administration of justice; jurisdiction; regulation, rule, provision, order, ordinance, decree; command, authority, control, dominion, power; government, regime (see Wehr, p. 196). In both texts the term is used in the sense of order or command.

Illar: 1436 (no. 1). Borrowed from Čaghatai Turkic *ilghār*, flying column, advance cavalry unit which is dispatched into enemy territory, light cavalry (see Radloff, I, 1489; Doerfer, I, 193–194, no. 70).

Imirza: 1428 (no. 4), 1441 (no. 1), 1444 (no. 1), 1453 (nos. 6, 8), 1458 (no. 4), 1460 (no. 7), 1463 (no. 10), 1465 (no. 2), 1467 (nos. 4, 7). See *mirza.*

Imirzay: 1440 (no. 1), 1449 (no. 1), 1472 (no. 1). See *mirza.*

Imirzē: 1437 (no. 2). See *mirza.*

J̌abřən: 1368 (no. 2). Cf. Persian *gabr* (Arabic *djabr*), a Zoroastrian, infidel (see Vullers, *Lexicon Persico-Latinum Etymologicum*, II, 950; E. E. Bertel's *History of Persian-Tačik Literature*, p. 51). The Armenian form has the final definite article *-n*; the *ə* is written to add a syllable to the poetic line.

J̌alat': 1391 (no. 1), 1465 (no. 6). Cf. Arabic *djallād*, executioner, hangman (see Wehr, p. 130).

J̌ambl: 1367 (no. 1). Cf. Old Franch *chambrelan*, chamberlain (see Ačaŕyan, *HLP*, II, 301).

Kalogerosk': 1453 (no. 3). Cf. vernacular Greek *kalógeros*, monk (see Demetrakou, *Mega Lexikon*, IV, 3576–3577); to this is added the Armenian plural suffix *-k'*.

Kalokriayk‘: 1453 (no. 3). Cf. vernacular Greek *kalógria*, nun (see Demetrakou, *Mega Lexikon*, IV, 3577); to this is added the Armenian plural suffix -*k‘*.

Kapič: 1401 (nos. 5, 8), 1468 (no. 1). Cf. Pahlevi *kapīč*, a measure for grain, used as equivalent to Greek *khoiniks* (see Hübschmann, *Arm. Gram.*, p. 165, no. 303; cf. Ačaṙyan, *HLP*, I, 265; *Baṙgirk‘*, I, 1055; Xač‘ikyan, *XV Dari*, I, p. xv, n. 3; *XV Dari*, II, p. cxxv).

Karapet: 1307 (no. 5), 1315 (no. 1), 1355 (no. 2), 1358 (no. 1), 1400 (no. 1), 1403 (no. 1), 1437 (no. 1), 1458 (no. 1), 1472 (no. 1). Lit., forerunner, precursor (see Hübschmann, *Arm. Gram.*, p. 166, no. 306), used in reference to St. John the Baptist. (See *Dictionary of Bible*, pp. 303–304.) In the texts the term is used in conjunction with *Neṙn* [q.v.].

Kat‘ołikos (variant: *kat‘ułikos*): Borrowed from Greek *catholicós*, catholicos (see Hübschmann, *Arm. Gram.*, p. 353, no. 166). This title was originally applied to the supreme hierarch of the Armenian church; after the establishment of the regional sees of Aghtamar and Cilicia it was used for the hierarchs of these sees as well.

Kat‘ułikos: 1302 (no. 2). See *kat‘ołikos*.

Klay: 1387 (no. 1), 1445 (no. 6). Cf. Arabic *ḳal‘a*, fortress, stronghold, fort, citadel (see Wehr, p. 787; Hübschmann, *Arm. Gram.*, p. 269, no. 85).

Kołmnapet: 1444 (no. 2), 1445 (no. 1). This Armenian word is used synonymously with the terms *kołmnakal* and *kołmnapah*; they correspond to Greek *stratēgòs*, and Latin *dux*, *praepositus* (see *Baṙgirk‘*, I, 112).

Krknoy Zatik: 1387 (no. 1). A variant of the Armenian term *Krknazatik*, the Sunday following Easter. This feast is also referred to in Armenian as *Erkrord Zatik*, Second Easter, or *Nor Kiraki*, lit. New Sunday. (See Malxaseanc‘, *HBB*, II, 505; *Baṙgirk‘*, I, 1135.)

Kumaš: 1472 (no. 1). Cf. Arabic *ḳumāsh*, cloth, fabric, material (see Wehr, p. 790; Ačaṙyan, *HLP*, II, 195). In Armenian it is generally used in the sense of precious cloth (see Malxaseanc‘, *HBB*, II, 482).

K‘ałoc‘: 1463 (no. 1). The name of the fifth month of the ancient Armenian calendar (see *Baṙgirk‘*, II, 922).

K‘awsa: 1400 (no. 5). Cf. Ottoman Turkish *köse*, beardless (see Radloff, II, 1293).

K‘ēmiay: 1449 (no. 1). Cf. Arabic *kīmya*, the elixir, or philosopher's stone, alchemy (see Wehr, p. 850; Haïm, II, 686; Ačaṙyan, *HLP*, I, 271; II, 189).

Laš: 1338 (no. 2), 1452 (no. 5). Cf. Persian *lāš*, carrion, corpse, carcase (see Steingass, p. 1111). In Armenian it is also used as an adjective meaning evil, impure (see Malxaseanc‘, *HBB*, II, 184, 433).

Lotos: 1453 (no. 3). Cf. Turkish *lodos*, southwind (Greek *nótos*). (See Kahane-Tietze, *Lingua Franca*, pp. 547–548, no. 818; Anasyan, *Haykakan Ałbyurnerə*, p. 57.)

Lułak: 1337 (no. 2). Variant form of *lołak*, the Armenian name for the sea animal which corresponds to Greek *nēchtòs*, and Latin *natans*, *natatile* (see *Bařgirk'*, I, 892). In the text it is probably used in the sense of fish or seafood in general.

Łabal: 1462 (no. 6). Cf. Arabic *ḳabāla*, contract, agreement; bail, guaranty, suretyship, liability, responsibility (see Wehr, p. 471; Malxaseanc', *HBB*, II, 389). It is used in the text in the sense of contract.

Ładi (variant: *xati*)*:* 1393 (no. 1). Cf. Arabic *ḳāḍī*, Muslim judge, who adjudicates and issues verdicts on the basis of the *sharī'a*. (See T. W. Juynboll, "Ḳāḍī," *EI*, OE, II, 606–607.)

Łan: see *xan*.

Łap'utan: 1453 (no. 3). Cf. Ottoman Turkish *kapudan* (itself derived from Italian *capitano*), captain (see Kahane-Tietze, *Lingua Franca*, pp. 139–145, no. 152).

Łarip-ni: 1384 (no. 2). The word *łarip* is borrowed from Arabic *gharīb*, stranger, foreigner, alien; those living abroad, those away from home, emigrés (see Wehr, p. 668). The *-ni* is a plural suffix.

Łatēstan: 1449 (no. 1). Xač'ikyan suggests that this word is the plural of *ładi* [q.v.]. (See *XV Dari*, I, p. 814.)

Łatərla: 1453 (no. 3). Cf. Ottoman Turkish *qadirga*, in the eastern Mediterranean a common designation of the galley. (See Kahane-Tietze, *Lingua Franca*, pp. 523–526, no. 785.)

Ławl: 1417 (no. 2). Cf. Arabic *ḳawl*, word, utterance, statement, report, testimony (see Wehr, p. 797). In Armenian it meant stipulation, vow (see Ačařyan, *HLP*, II, 197).

Łaza (variant: *łazay*)*:* 1453 (nos. 2, 3), 1477 (no. 1). Cf. Arabic *ghazāh*, the raids made by the Ghāzis against the infidels. (For a discussion of the raids by the Ghāzīs of Rūm, see M. F. Köprülü, *Les origines de l'empire ottoman*, Paris, 1935, pp. 101–107.) In Armenian the term was used in the sense of holy war (see Xač'ikyan, *XV Dari*, I, p. 814).

Łazay: 1422 (no. 1), 1471 (no. 10). See *łaza*.

Łupay: 1449 (no. 1). Cf. Arabic *ḳubba*, cupola, dome; cupolaed structure, dome-shaped edifice, domed shrine (see Wehr, p. 337; Ačařyan, *HLP*, II, 195).

Mahdasi (variant: *małt'asi*)*:* 1441 (no. 7), 1451 (no. 3), 1457 (no. 1). Derived from Arabic *maḳdisī* or *muḳaddasī*, holy, sacred, sanctified (see Ačařyan, *HLP*, II, 198). The term was used by Armenians as an epithet for individuals who performed the pilgrimage to the Holy Places in Jerusalem.

Mal: 1337 (no. 2), 1457 (no. 2). Cf. Arabic *māl*, property, possessions, chattels, goods; wealth, affluence; fortune, estate; money, assets (see Wehr, pp. 931–932). This was a rent paid to the divan, in cash or in produce, by peasants and city-dwellers for the privilege of using the soil. (See A. Ali-zade, "Social, Economic, and Political History of Azerbaijan," p. 240; cf. Xač'ikyan, *XV Dari*, II, p. lxiv; Cleaves, "Mongolian Names and Terms," p. 438.)

Małt'asi: 1464 (no. 12). See *mahdasi*.

Marajaxt: 1337 (no. 2), 1367 (no. 1). Derived from Old French *mareschal* (cf. modern French *maréchal*), marshal (see Ačaṙyan, *HLP*, II, 300; Hübschmann, *Arm. Gram.*, p. 390, no. 4).

Marajaxt-ut'iwn: 1367 (no. 1). The abstract noun form of *marajaxt* [q.v.].

Mareri: 1407 (no. 4). The name of the tenth month of the ancient Armenian calendar (see *Baṙgirk'*, II, 224).

Mažaṙostun: 1367 (no. 1). The reading and meaning of this word is uncertain.

Mehek: 1453 (no. 3). See *mehekan.*

Mehekan (variant: *Mehek*)*:* 1389 (no. 1), 1393 (no. 1). The name of the seventh month of the ancient Armenian calendar (see *Baṙgirk'*, II, 245).

Melik' (variants: *mēlēk'*, *mēlik'*)*:* 1349 (no. 1), 1419 (no. 4), 1458 (no. 5). Cf. Arabic *malik*, king, sovereign, monarch (see Ačaṙyan, *HLP*, II, 199; see also M. Plessner, "Malik," *EI*, OE, III, 204).

Mertin (*dram*)*:* 1424 (no. 1). Apparently the currency named after the town of Mārdīn in the province of Diyarbakir.

Mēlēk': 1463 (no. 3). See *melik'*.

Mēlik': 1386 (no. 3), 1467 (no. 2). See *melik'*.

Mənara: 1422 (no. 1). See *mnira.*

Məzkit': 1453 (no. 3). See *mzkit'*.

Mir: 1398 (no. 1), 1402 (no. 3), 1422 (no. 1), 1454 (no. 5), 1472 (no. 1). Cf. Persian *mīr* (from the Arabic *amīr*), a title, applied generally to princes, approximating in meaning to the Persian title *mīrzā*. (See R. Levy, "Mīr," *EI*, OE, III, 505.)

Mirza: (variants: *amirza, amirzay, amirzē, ēmirza, imirza, imirzay, imirzē, mirzay, mirzē, mrzay*)*:* 1428 (no. 6), 1438 (no. 4), 1444 (no. 4), 1452 (no. 5), 1463 (no. 3), 1467 (no. 1), 1469 (no. 2), 1470 (no. 3). Borrowed from Persian *Mīrzā* or *Mirzā*, a hybrid composite meaning son of a prince. In addition to its original meaning, the title was also given to noblemen and others of good birth. (See R. Levy, "Mīrzā or Mirzā," *EI*, OE, III, 516.)

Mirzay: 1405 (no. 1), 1452 (no. 5). See *mirza.*

Mirzē: 1442 (no. 1). See *mirza.*

Mnaray: 1449 (no. 1). See *mnira.*

Mnira (variants: *mənara, mnaray, mniray*)*:* 1401 (no. 1), 1442 (no. 1). Cf. Arabic *manāra*, minaret (see Wehr, p. 1009; Ačaṙyan, *HLP*, II, 199).

Mniray: 1401 (no. 1), 1422 (no. 1). See *mnira.*

Molnay (variant: *mōlnay*)*:* 1393 (no. 1). A vulgar form for *mawlā*, Muslim clergyman, learned man in theology, reader; attested in Arabic and other Near Eastern Islamic languages as *molla* and *molna* (see Zenker, p. 894a).

Mot': 1422 (no. 2). Borrowed from Latin *modius*, a measure, muid (see Hübschmann, *Arm. Gram.*, p. 366, no. 276; Xač'ikyan, *XV Dari*, II, p. cxxvi).

Mōlnay: 1446 (no. 5). See *molnay.*

Mrzay: 1459 (no. 2). See *mirza.*

Msk'it': 1401 (no. 1). See *mzkit'*.

Mulk': 1428 (no. 1). Borrowed from Arabic *mulk*, property, possessions, goods and chattels, fortune, wealth; estate; landed property, real estate (see Zenker, p. 878a; Xač'ikyan, *XV Dari*, II, pp. cxx–cxxi). It is used in the text in the sense of property or estate.

Mułrik': 1453 (no. 2). Cf. Arabic *mukrī*, reciter of the Qur'ān (see Wehr, p. 753; Ačaṙyan, *HLP*, II, 199). The Armenian form has the plural suffix *-k'*.

Murtaṙ: 1389 (no. 1). Cf. Persian *murdār*, carrion, corpse; (fig.) impure, dirty, polluted, obscene (see Steingass, p. 1212). In the text it is used in the sense of corpse.

Musx: 1449 (no. 1). Cf. Arabic *musk* or *misk*, musk (see Steingass, p. 1238; Zenker, p. 847a).

Muxanat': 1391 (no. 1). Cf. Ottoman Turkish *muhanat* (Arabic *mahānat*), being despicable, contemptible, abject; baseness, meanness (see Hony, *Turkish-English Dictionary*, p. 246; Steingass, p. 1351). It is used in Armenian in the sense of treacherous, perfidious (see Malxaseanc', *HBB*, III, 450).

Mzkit' (variants: *məzkit'*, *msk'it'*)*:* 1401 (no. 1), 1452 (no. 5). Cf. Persian *mazgit* or *mizgit*, small mosque (see Steingass, p. 1223; cf. Hübschmann, *Arm. Gram.*, p. 271, no. 96).

Nafałay: 1449 (no. 1). Cf. Arabic *nafaḳa*, expenditure, fortune, money (see Zenker, p. 916a). It is used here in the sense of means of livelihood.

Nałaray: 1389 (no. 1). Cf. Persian *naqāra*, a kettledrum (Steingass, p. 1418; Ačaṙyan, *HLP*, II, 200).

Namaz: 1453 (no. 2). Cf. Persian *namāz*, prayers, those especially prescribed by law (see Steingass, p. 1425). It is used in Armenian exclusively for Muslim worship or prayers (see Malxaseanc', *HBB*, III, 440).

Nawasard: 1315 (no. 2), 1392 (no. 1), 1419 (no. 3), 1452 (no. 5), 1462 (no. 3), 1476 (no. 6). The name of the first month of the ancient Armenian calendar (see *Baṙgirk'*, II, 408; Hübschmann, *Arm. Gram.*, p. 202, no. 435).

Naxavkay: 1393 (no. 1), 1452 (no. 4). Lit., the first martyr, or protomartyr; an epithet used specifically for Stephen, the first Christian martyr. (See *Dictionary of Bible*, p. 938.) The Armenian church celebrates the feast of St. Stephen between December 24 and 26. (See Malxaseanc', *HBB*, III, 434.)

Nayip: 1337 (no. 2), 1435 (no. 2). Cf. Arabic *nā'ib*, literally substitute, delegate; it was used to designate the deputy or lieutenant of the sultan or the governors of the chief provinces. (See H. A. R. Gibb and C. Collin Davies, "Nā'ib," *EI*, OE, III, 837–838; cf. Cleaves, *Mongolian Documents*, p. 60, n. 11.)

Neṙn: 1307 (nos. 1, 5), 1315 (no. 1), 1355 (no. 2), 1358 (no. 1), 1365 (no. 2), 1388 (no. 2), 1400 (no. 1), 1403 (no. 1), 1407 (no. 1), 1422 (no. 1), 1435 (no. 3), 1437 (no. 1), 1458 (no. 1). The etymology of this term, which in Armenian usage means Antichrist, is uncertain; the prevailing view is that it is derived from the name of the Roman Emperor Nero. (See *Baṙgirkʻ*, II, 413; Malxaseancʻ, *HBB*, III, 451.) In the colophons, as well as in other Armenian sources, the term is applied to the enemies of the Christian faith, notably the Muslim conquerors or rulers. (For a discussion of the subject see "Antichrist," *Dictionary of Bible*, pp. 35–36.)

Nlmuns: 1422 (no. 1). Cf. Persian *naghm* (derived from Arabic *naḳb*) making a hole, digging out, making hollow; excavation; a mine, a trench (see Steingass, p. 1418). The Armenian form is the plural accusative; and it is used in the text in the sense of subterranean dwelling or hiding place (see Malxaseancʻ, *HBB*, III, 466).

Noyin: 1335 (no. 4), 1342 (no. 1). Borrowed from Mongolian *nōyān*, a general term for military officer. (For its various forms and meanings, consult Doerfer, I, 526–529, no. 389; Cleaves, "Mongolian Names and Terms," pp. 405–406; Pelliot, *Notes sur l'histoire de la Horde d'Or*, p. 17, 195 n. 1).

Pahatur: 1431 (no. 1). See *bahaduṙ*.

Pak: see *bēk*.

Pap: 1453 (no. 1). Derived from Latin *papa*, pope (see Hübschmann, *Arm. Gram.*, p. 370, no. 318).

Pēk: 1436 (no. 6). See *bēk*.

Polis: 1453 (no. 2). Borrowed from Greek *polis*, city.

Purč: 1453 (no. 3). Cf. Arabic *burdj*, tower, castle (see Wehr, p. 50; Ačaṙyan, *HLP*, II, 202).

Pʻadšah: 1476 (no. 2). See *pʻatʻšah*.

Pʻahlawan: 1472 (no. 1). Cf. Persian *pahlavān* (Turkish *pehlivan*), wrestler, hero, champion (see Haïm, I, 375). It is used in Armenian as an adjective meaning strong, stout (see Malxaseancʻ, *HBB*, IV, 497).

Pʻašah: 1304 (no. 4). Cf. Persian *pādshāh*, the name for Muslim rulers. (For its etymology, see Mecdut Mansuroğlu, "On Some Titles and Names in Old Anatolian Turkish," *Ural-Altaische Jahrbücher*, vol. XXVII, nos. 1–2 [1955], pp. 94–97. See also Doerfer, II, 420–424, no. 838; J. Deny, "Pasha," *EI*, OE, III, 1030–1033.

Pʻatšah: 1462 (no. 3), 1465 (no. 6), 1472 (no. 1), 1476 (no. 2). See *pʻatʻšah*.

Pʻatʻšah (variants: *pʻadšah, pʻatšah*): 1421 (no. 8), 1452 (no. 4), 1461 (nos. 1, 3), 1462 (nos. 3, 5, 11), 1463 (nos. 7, 8), 1467 (no. 6), 1469 (no. 1), 1471 (no. 3), 1478 (no. 3), 1479 (no. 2). Cf. Persian *pādshāh*, the name for Muslim rulers, king, sovereign (see Franz Babinger, "Pādishāh," *EI*, OE, III, 1017; Ačaṙyan, *HLP*, I, 289).

Pʻēlambar: 1476 (no. 2). Cf. Persian *peyghāmbar*, prophet, messenger (see Haïm, I, 387; Cleaves, *Mongolian Documents*, p. 42, n. 3). It is used in Armenian exclusively in reference to the Prophet Muhammad. (See Ačaṙyan, *HLP*, I, 290.)

Pʻilon: 1449 (no. 1). Borrowed from Greek *phelōnes*, mantle, cloak, overcoat (see Hübschmann, *Arm. Gram.*, p. 386, no. 481). In Armenian usage it means a coat worn by ecclesiastics during liturgical services.

P'ošiman: 1453 (no. 2). Cf. Persian *pashīmān*, remorseful, rueful, sorry, regretful, penitent (see Haïm, I, 365).

Rabunapet: 1332 (no. 2), 1425 (nos. 5, 9), 1473 (no. 9). Hybrid composite term: *rabuni*, rabbi, master, doctor, instructor, plus *pet*, chief; used in the sense of chief master or doctor, pontiff (see Hübschmann, *Arm. Gram.*, p. 376, no. 367).

Rabuni: 1438 (no. 1), 1453 (no. 2). See *rabunapet.*

Ṙaƚiat': 1452 (no. 5). Cf. Arabic *ra'iat*, subject people, herd, non-Muslim subjects of the Ottomans (see Zenker, p. 466a; cf. Cleaves, *Mongolian Documents*, p. 63, n. 11; cf. also *ṙaya, ṙayat'*, in Malxaseanc', *HBB*, IV, 157).

Ṙamadan: 1472 (no. 1). Borrowed from Arabic *Ramaḍān*; the name of the ninth month of the Muhammadan calendar; it is also the name of the Muslim fast observed in the same month. (See M. Plessner, "Ramaḍān," *EI*, OE, III, 1111.)

Ṙayēs: 1371 (no. 3). Scc *Əṙayis.*

Sahat': 1453 (no. 3). Cf. Arabic *sā'at*, clock, with substitution of glottal stop by *h*, as in Kipčak (see *Codex Cum.*, p. 210).

Sahmi: 1420 (no. 1). The name of the third month of the ancient Armenian calendar (see *Baṙgirk'*, II, 688).

Santalun: 1453 (no. 3). Derived from Greek *sandálion*, boat (see Kahane-Tietze, *Lingua Franca*, pp. 564–567, no. 839), with Armenian plural suffix *-un.*

Səlex: 1422 (no. 1). Cf. Arabic *silāḥ*, arms, weapon, armament (see Ačaṙyan, *HLP*, II, 204). See also *ansleh.*

Sōlt'an: 1473 (no. 9). See *Sultan.*

Sultan (variant: *sōlt'an*)*:* 1306 (no. 3). Derived from Arabic *sulṭān*, a ruler, monarch, sovereign; a potentate, emperor, king (see Steingass, p. 693b; and for its various usages consult J. H. Kramers, "Sulṭān," *EI*, OE, IV, 543–545).

Surat': 1422 (no. 1). Cf. Arabic *ṣūrat*, face, countenance, look (see Steingass, p. 795; Wehr, p. 530).

Surkun: 1480 (no. 1). Cf. Ottoman Turkish *sürgün*, banishment, place of exile (see Hony, *Turkish-English Dictionary*, p. 328).

Šah: 1428 (no. 3), 1431 (no. 1), 1443 (no. 2), 1449 (no. 1), 1458 (no. 7), 1468 (no. 3). Borrowed from Persian *shāh*, king (see V. F. Büchner, "Shāh," *EI*, OE, IV, 256–257; Steingass, p. 726a).

Šahastan: 1421 (no. 1), 1422 (no. 1), 1428 (no. 4), 1449 (no. 1), 1453 (no. 2), 1462 (no. 3), 1468 (no. 1), 1472 (no. 1). Borrowed from Persian *šahristān*, large fortified city (see Steingass, p. 770; Ačaṙyan, *HLP*, I, 276; Ačaṙean, *Hayerēn Armatakan Baṙaran*, V, 230–231). In text 1453 (no. 2) it appears to have been used in the sense of the land of the shah, that is Persia. (See Anasyan, *Haykakan Aƚbyurnerə*, p. 79.)

Šk'rik-k': 1304 (no. 3). Cf. Georgian *šikriki*, messenger, courier (see

Ačaṙyan, *HLP*, II, 223; Xačʻikyan, *XIV Dari*, p. 665), with Armenian plural suffix *-kʻ*.

Tahiri (dram): 1375 (no. 2). Mentioned as the name of a currency.

Tanutēr: 1400 (no. 5), 1422 (no. 1), 1425 (no. 2), 1426 (no. 3), 1428 (no. 6), 1438 (no. 1), 1451 (no. 5), 1459 (no. 2). Lit., master of a house, head of a family, householder; chief of a tribe or race. In the colophons the term is applied to well-to-do and influential village chiefs, elected by the local community, who administered the economic affairs of the village in behalf of the feudal lords. (See L. Xačʻikyan, "XIV-XV Dareri Haykakan Gyułakan Hamaynkʻi Masin," *Patma-Banasirakan Handes*, 1958, no. 1, pp. 110–133; Xačʻikyan, *XV Dari*, II, pp. lxxxix–xciii.)

Tartaros: 1303 (no. 4), 1307 (no. 2), 1348 (no. 1), 1401 (no. 3), 1478 (no. 4). Borrowed from Greek *tártaros*, tartarus, hell (see Hübschmann, *Arm. Gram.*, p. 383, no. 447).

Tawlpand: 1336 (no. 2). Cf. Persian *dolband* or *dūlbānd*, turban (see Haïm, I, 844, 875).

Teaṙnəndaṙaǰ: 1459 (no. 2). The Armenian term for Candlemas Day.

Trē: 1425 (no. 1). The fourth month of the ancient Armenian calendar (see *Baṙgirkʻ*, II, 897).

Tukat: 1318 (no. 1). The reading of this word is uncertain. If *tukat*, cf. French *ducat*, a gold (or silver) coin of varying value (see *The Oxford Universal Dictionary*, 3rd ed., Oxford, 1955, p. 569; Ačaṙyan, *HLP*, II, 301).

Tʻałtʻ: see *tʻaxtʻ*.

Tʻałtʻan: 1472 (no. 1). See *tʻaxtʻan.*

Tʻaman: 1438 (no. 1). Cf. Turkic *taman* (* < *tanma(n)*), which is also attested in Mongolian of the thirteenth and fourteenth centuries, for example, the *Secret History* (para. 274). During the period in question, it was the designation for the largest military-administrative unit made up of conquered territories. The tenant of a *taman* was called in Mongolian *ta(n)mači(n)* (see, for example, *Secret History*, paras. 274, 281). Another name for *taman* was *tümän*, of Tokharian origin (*tümän* meaning 10,000). (I am indebted for this information to Professor Omeljan Pritsak.) See also *tʻuman.*

Tʻamuri (tʻankay): 1449 (no. 6), 1457 (no. 2). In the first text it is mentioned in conjunction with *tʻankay* [q.v.], and in the second it is mentioned alone. It appears to be a particular denomination of the Mongolian coin *tanga*, and presumably named after Tīmūr Lang.

Tʻankay: 1392 (no. 1), 1437 (no. 9), 1446 (no. 1), 1449 (nos. 1, 6), 1468 (no. 1). Cf. Mongolian *tanga*, the name of the silver coin which formed the main currency of the Mongol world from the end of the fourteenth to the beginning of the sixteenth century. (See Doerfer, II, 587–592, no. 946; J. Allan, "Tanga or Tangča," *EI*, OE, IV, 650; Hübschmann, *Arm. Gram.*, p. 266, no. 47; Xačʻikyan, *XV Dari*, II, p. cxxii; *XIV Dari*, p. xxxviii, n. 1.)

T'arxan: 1425 (no. 7). Cf. Turkic *tarxan* (>Mongolian *darxan*), and Persian *tarxān*, which during the Mongol period meant exempt from taxation. (See B. Vladimirtsov, *Le régime social des mongols; Le féodalisme nomade*, Paris, 1948, pp. 119, 218; Hübschmann, *Arm. Gram.*, p. 266, no. 50.) It is used here in the sense of tax exempt.

T'asup (variant: *t'axsup*)*:* 1426 (no. 4), 1470 (no. 2). Cf. Ottoman Turkish *taassub* (Arabic *ta'aṣṣub*), bigotry; religious persecution; fanaticism; superstition (see Hony, *Turkish-English Dictionary*, p. 338; Steingass, p. 309). In both texts it is used in the sense of religious persecution.

T'axsup: 1336 (no. 2). See *t'asup*.

T'axt: 1428 (no. 4). See *t'axt'*.

T'axtan: 1453 (no. 3). See *t'axt'an*.

T'axt' (variants: *t'ałt'*, *t'axt*)*:* Compare Persian *taxt*, throne (see Ačaṙyan, *HLP*, I, 258).

T'axt'an (variants: *t'ałt'an*, *t'axtan*)*:* 1422 (no. 1). Cf. Persian *takht*, spoil, plunder, prey; assault, invasion (see Steingass, p. 273; cf. Ačaṙyan, *HLP*, I, 258). It is used here in the sense of plunder.

T'axt'aneac': 1344 (no. 1). Third person singular aorist form of *t'axt'an* [q.v.].

T'op': 1453 (no. 3). Cf. Turkic *top*, gun, cannon; artillery (see Doerfer, II, 596–601, no. 948; Zenker, p. 604a).

T'uman: 1472 (no. 1). Cf. Turkic-Mongolian *tümän* (<Tokharian *tumane*), ten thousand; the largest military and administrative unit within the Mongolian army. (See A. von Gabain, *Alttürkische Grammatik*, Leipzig, 1950, p. 345. For its use under the Mongols, see Vladimirtsov, *Le Régime social*, pp. 134–135, 171f. For additional bibliographical information, consult Blake and Frye, "Archers," pp. 388, n. 42; Cleaves, "Mongolian Names and Terms," p. 436.)

Ust'ay: 1452 (no. 4). Cf. the colloquial form *ustā* of Persian *ustād*, master, teacher, one who is skilled in an art or profession, artisan (see Steingass, p. 49; Haïm, I, 75–76). In the text it is used in the sense of master craftsman or builder.

Vardapet: 1313 (no. 1), 1325 (no. 2), 1336 (no. 3), 1371 (no. 3), 1386 (no. 1), 1392 (no. 1), 1426 (no. 3), 1437 (no. 9), 1438 (no. 1), 1445 (no. 1), 1446 (no. 1), 1453 (no. 2), 1462 (nos. 3, 6), 1464 (no. 3), 1480 (no. 1). This Armenian term means doctor; lecturer; master, preceptor; archimandrite. (See E. Benveniste, "Emprunts Iraniens en Arménien; Etudes Iraniennes," *Transactions of the Philological Society*, 1945, London, 1946, p. 69; see also R. Thomson, "*Vardapet* in the Early Armenian Church," *Le Muséon*, vol. LXXV, nos. 3–4 [1962], pp. 367–384.)

Vardavaṙ: 1426 (no. 6). The Armenian term for the feast of the Transfiguration of our Lord. (See *Baṙgirk'*, II, 792–793.)

Vełar: 1449 (no. 1). Borrowed from Latin *velarium*, curtain, awning (see Hübschmann, *Arm. Gram.*, p. 383, no. 441). In Armenian usage it means the hood worn by an ecclesiastic.

Veraditoł: 1302 (no. 2), 1454 (no. 1), 1463 (no. 12). A compound noun used synonymously with *ditapet* [q.v.] and *hayrapet* (see *Hayrapetut'iwn*).

Xač'alam: 1462 (no. 3). Hybrid word: *xač'*, from Persian *khāj*, cross (see Steingass, p. 437), and Arabic *'alam*, standard, sign, flag (see *ibid.*, p. 864). This is an ecclesiastical standard used in ceremonies of the Armenian church. (See Malxaseanc', *HBB*, II, 244.)

Xalič'ay: 1449 (no. 1). Cf. Ottoman Turkish *qaliča* (cf. modern Turkish *kaliçe*), a small rug, a small costly carpet (see Zenker, p. 684b).

Xan (variant: *łan*)*:* A Turkic title for a ruler. (For details regarding its history and usage, see W. Barthold, "Khān," *EI*, OE, II, 897–898; also Cleaves, "Mongolian Names and Terms," p. 421).

Xandak (variant: *xantak*)*:* 1422 (no. 1). Cf. Arabic *khandaḳ*, ditch, fosse, moat (see Steingass, p. 477; Hübschmann, *Arm. Gram.*, p. 267, no. 64).

Xanǰal: 1465 (no. 6). Cf. Arabic *khandjar*, a dagger, sword, poniard (see Steingass, p. 476).

Xantak: 1453 (no. 3). See *Xandak.*

Xapr: 1335 (no. 6). Cf. Arabic *khabar*, news, information, intelligence, report, rumor, story (see Wehr, p. 225).

Xarač: 1464 (no. 1), 1476 (no. 2). Cf. Arabic *kharādj*, land tax imposed by Muslim rulers. (For its history, consult T. W. Juynboll, "Kharādj," *EI*, OE, II, 902–903; see also Hübschmann, *Arm. Gram.*, p. 268, no. 68.)

Xas (variant: *hasay*)*:* 1425 (no. 7). Cf. Arabic *khaṣṣ*, intended for the exclusive use of (the sovereign), belonging to the sovereign or state (see Zenker, p. 400a; see also Cleaves, *Mongolian Documents*, pp. 69–71, n. 12).

Xasat: 1337 (no. 2). Cf. Arabic and Persian *qisṭ*, a portion, share; an installment; a measure (see Steingass, p. 969; Redhouse *Turkish and English Lexicon*, p. 1453). The form in which this word is attested in Armenian lexicons is *xast* (see Malxaseanc', *HBB*, II, 247). In the present text it seems to have been used in the sense of a measure.

Xasrat'amah: 1451 (no. 5). See *hasrat'amah.*

Xati: 1335 (no. 6). See *ładi.*

Xilat': 1453 (no. 2). See *xilay.*

Xilay (variants: *xilat'*, *xlay*)*:* 1335 (no. 4), 1469 (no. 6). Cf. Arabic *khil'a*, a robe which the sovereign bestows, as a gift, on the person whom he wishes to honor. (See C. Huart, "Khil'a," *EI*, OE, II, 955.)

Xlay: 1449 (no. 1), 1462 (no. 3). See *xilay.*

Xočay: 1355 (no. 1). See *xoǰa.*

Xoǰa (variants: *xočay, xoǰay, xōǰay*)*:* 1424 (no. 1), 1451 (no. 5), 1462 (no. 3). Borrowed from Persian *khoja*, a man of distinction, a master or owner, a wealthy man, a teacher; a venerable, old man (see Steingass, p. 479a–b; Haïm, I, 745; see also C. Huart, "Khʷādja," *EI*, OE, II, 865). In Armenian usage the term was also applied as an epithet for a wealthy merchant (see Malxaseanc', *HBB*, II, 312).

Xoǰay: 1465 (no. 6). See *xoǰa.*

Xondk'ar (variants: *xovandk'ar, xōndk'ar, xōntk'ar*): 1453 (no. 1), 1453 (no. 3), 1473 (no. 1), 1480 (no. 1). Cf. *khunkiār* (apparently an abbreviation for *khudāwendigiār*), a title given to all the Ottoman sultans, at least until the seventeenth century, along with that of *pādishāh.* (See J. H. Kramers, "Khudāwendigiār," *EI*, OE, II, 971.)

Xostak: 1421 (no. 3). Cf. Pahlevi *x*^{v}*āstak,* property, estate (see Hübschmann, *Arm. Gram.*, p. 161, no. 284; Ačaṙyan, *HLP*, I, 263).

Xovandk'ar: 1473 (no. 2). See *xondk'ar.*

Xōǰay: 1425 (no. 3), 1459 (no. 2). See *xoǰa.*

Xōndk'ar: 1480 (no. 1). See *xondk'ar.*

Xōntk'ar: 1480 (no. 1). See *xondk'ar.*

Xsar (variants: *hesar, hsar*): 1398 (no. 2), 1422 (nos. 1, 2), 1424 (no. 1), 1425 (nos. 4, 9), 1428 (no. 1), 1437 (no. 3), 1446 (no. 5), 1452 (no. 5), 1453 (no. 3), 1465 (no. 5), 1466 (no. 7), 1474 (no. 3). Cf. Arabic *ḥiṣār,* besieging, encompassing; a fortified town, a fort, castle (see Hübschmann, *Arm. Gram.*, p. 269, no. 85; Steingass, p. 421). In Armenian usage the verb *xsarel* meant to lay siege.

Yinanc': 1463 (no. 1). Also known in Armenian as *Yinunk'*, the period of fifty days from Easter to Pentecost (see *Baṙgirk'*, II, 359).

Znǰil: 1473 (no. 2). Cf. Persian *zanjīr* or *zinjīr* (Turkish *zincir*), chain, fetters (see Hübschmann, *Arm. Gram.*, p. 265, no. 40; Haïm, I, 1022). Ačaṙyan suggests that the word was borrowed from Turkish (see *HLP*, II, 276).

Žłul: 1452 (no. 5). Cf. Arabic *shughl* or *shughul,* work, occupation, employment; business; diversion, amusement, pastime (see Steingass, p. 748). It is used here in the sense of occupation, diversion.

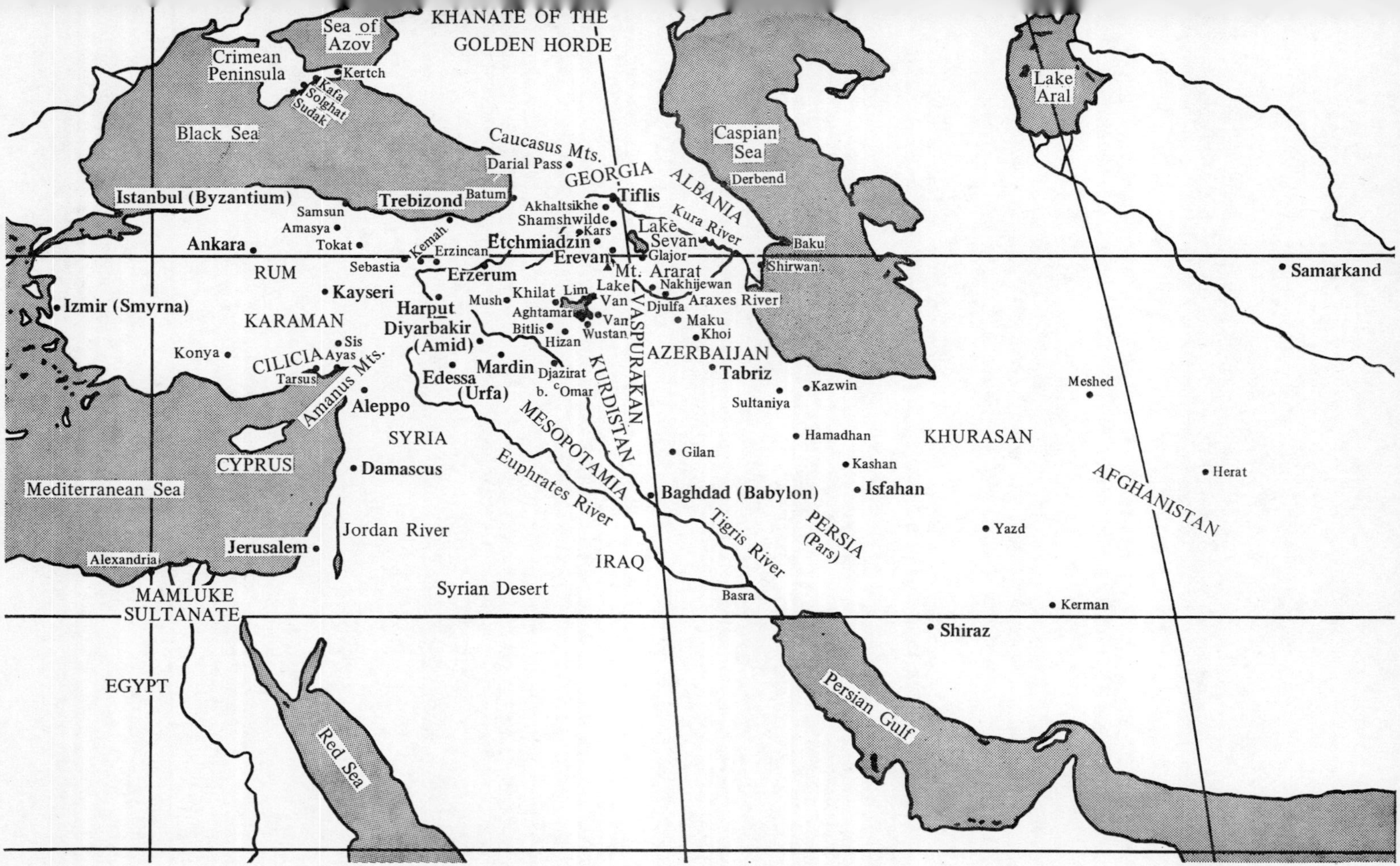
KHANATE OF THE
GOLDEN HORDE
Sea of Azov
Crimean Peninsula
Kertch
Kafa
Solghat
Sudak
Black Sea
Caucasus Mts.
Darial Pass
GEORGIA
ALBANIA
Caspian Sea
Derbend
Lake Aral
Istanbul (Byzantium)
Trebizond
Batum
Samsun
Amasya
Tokat
Tiflis
Akhaltsikhe
Shamshwilde
Kars
Kura River
Lake Sevan
Baku
Ankara
Kemah
Erzincan
Etchmiadzin
Erevan
Glajor
Shirwan
Sebastia
Mt. Ararat
Samarkand
RUM
Erzerum
Lake Van
Nakhijewan
Kayseri
Mush
Khilat
Lim
Araxes River
Izmir (Smyrna)
Harput
Aghtamar
Van
Djulfa
KARAMAN
Diyarbakir
Bitlis
Wustan
Maku
Khoi
VASPURAKAN
(Amid)
Hizan
Sis
Konya
Ayas
AZERBAIJAN
CILICIA
Amanus Mts.
Mardin
Djazirat
Tabriz
Tarsus
Edessa
(Urfa)
b. cOmar
KURDISTAN
Kazwin
Meshed
Aleppo
Sultaniya
MESOPOTAMIA
SYRIA
Hamadhan
KHURASAN
Gilan
CYPRUS
Damascus
Kashan
Herat
Mediterranean Sea
Euphrates River
Baghdad (Babylon)
Isfahan
AFGHANISTAN
Jordan River
Tigris River
PERSIA
(Pars)
Yazd
Jerusalem
IRAQ
Alexandria
Syrian Desert
Basra
Kerman
MAMLUKE
SULTANATE
Shiraz
EGYPT
Persian Gulf
Red Sea